British Choral Singing

British Choral Singing

A History from Medieval Times to the Present Day

Peter Ward Jones

THE BOYDELL PRESS

© Peter Ward Jones 2026

All Rights Reserved. Except as permitted under current legislation
no part of this work may be photocopied, stored in a retrieval system,
published, performed in public, adapted, broadcast,
transmitted, recorded or reproduced in any form or by any means,
without the prior permission of the copyright owner

The right of Peter Ward Jones to be identified as the author of this work has been
asserted in accordance with sections 77 and 78 of the
Copyright, Designs and Patents Act 1988

First published 2026
The Boydell Press, Woodbridge

ISBN 978 1 83765 294 5 (hardback)
ISBN 978 1 83765 319 5 (paperback)

The Boydell Press is an imprint of Boydell & Brewer Ltd
and of Boydell & Brewer Inc.
website: www.boydellandbrewer.com

Our Authorised Representative for product safety in the EU is Easy Access System
Europe – Mustamäe tee 50, 10621 Tallinn, Estonia, gpsr.requests@easproject.com

A CIP catalogue record for this book is available
from the British Library

The publisher has no responsibility for the continued existence or accuracy
of URLs for external or third-party internet websites referred to in this book,
and does not guarantee that any content on such websites is,
or will remain, accurate or appropriate

Figures 1–4 and 6–9 are reproduced with permission of the Bodleian Libraries, University of Oxford (2025). The author and publisher are grateful to all the institutions and individuals listed for permission to reproduce the materials in which they hold copyright. Every effort has been made to trace the copyright holders; apologies are offered for any omission, and the publisher will be pleased to add any necessary acknowledgement in subsequent editions.

For Michael and Sarah

Contents

	List of Illustrations	viii
	Preface	ix
	Acknowledgements	x
	Notes to the Reader	xi
	Introduction	1
1	The Medieval Choir	5
2	From Reformation to Civil War	35
3	From the Restoration to Georgian Enlightenment	67
4	The Musical Festival and Choral Society in the Victorian Era	120
5	Church and Cathedral Choirs in the Nineteenth Century	171
6	World War to World War, 1914–1945	216
7	Into the Second Elizabethan Era	262
8	Enter the New Millennium	303
	Further Reading	317
	Notes	321
	Bibliography	390
	Index	420

Illustrations

1. Motet 'Alma iam ad gaudia / Alme matris Dei / Alleluia. Per te' from the Worcester Fragments; Oxford, Bodleian Library, MS lat. liturg. d. 20, fols 15v–16. — 14

2. John Taverner: Mass *Gloria tibi Trinitas*, contratenor part; Oxford, Bodleian Library, MS Mus. Sch. E. 378, fol. 4. — 33

3. William Boyce: *Cathedral Music*, vol. 3 (London, 1773), p. 136. — 97

4. Three Winchester lay clerks in 1820; Hampshire Record Office: DC/D8/2/3/3/1; reproduced with permission of the Dean and Chapter of Winchester Cathedral. — 103

5. Charles Burney, *Account of the Musical Performances in Westminster Abbey, and the Pantheon, May 26th, 27th, 29th; and June the 3d, and 5th, 1784. in Commemoration of Handel* (London, 1785); Oxford, Bodleian Library, Douce B subt. 272, Pl. VII. — 115

6. Birmingham Musical Festival, 1846: programme for the première of *Elijah*; Oxford, Bodleian Library, Deneke 301. — 124

7. Edward Elgar: *The Dream of Gerontius*, vocal score (London, Novello, 1900). — 141

8. Sight-reading tests for the Sheffield 1896 Festival; J.A. Rodgers, *Dr. Henry Coward* (London, 1911), p. 29. — 152

9. Choir of Child Okeford, Dorset in 1930; *English Church Music*, vol. 1, no. 1 (1931). — 237

10. Girl choristers of Salisbury Cathedral in 1991; reproduced with kind permission of Salisbury Museum ©. — 272

Preface

The present work is intended as a history of choral singing in Britain, in both sacred and secular spheres, rather than a study of its choral music. There have been several general surveys of the latter over the past century, from Edmund Fellowes's *English Cathedral Music* (1941) to John Caldwell's *The Oxford History of English Music* (1991–9), and most recently, Andrew Gant's *O Sing unto the Lord* (2015). Although the music will naturally come into discussion of choir repertoire, there will be no detailed analysis of compositions or musical style.

Its origins date back to the last exhibition I organized at the Bodleian Library, Oxford in the winter of 2008/9, *Hallelujah! The British Choral Tradition*, which partly commemorated the 2009 anniversaries of Purcell, Handel, Haydn and Mendelssohn, all of whom had close connexions with British choral life. Its exhibits ranged from a 10th-century Winchester troper to the manuscript of Howard Goodall's theme music for *The Vicar of Dibley*, taking in the Eton Choirbook, Tallis's 40-part motet, Handel's conducting score of *Messiah*, Elgar's *The Kingdom*, and Britten's *War Requiem*, among the highlights. I had hoped to produce something for publication to coincide with the exhibition, but time constraints prevented it, and the ability to proceed with it at a more leisurely pace in my retirement has hopefully resulted in a better volume than would otherwise have been the case.

There has been much published material to draw on, including studies of the music at individual cathedrals, histories of choral societies and festivals, and musicians' biographies, as well as such fundamental works as Frank Harrison's *Music in Medieval Britain*, or, more recently, Timothy Day's investigation of changes in English singing style over the past century or so, *I Saw Eternity the Other Night*. No less important has been the musical periodical literature of the past two hundred years which has naturally furnished a rich harvest of information, none more so than *The Musical Times*, itself born out of the rise of the mass sight-singing movement of the 1840s and then chronicling the nation's choral life in all its diversity for well over a century. Choirs of various types have always been part of my life and I hope that this exploration of the multi-stranded tapestry of their history will prove informative and perhaps occasionally entertaining to present-day choralists.

Acknowledgements

My first thanks go to David Clover, Edward Higginbottom, Harry Diack Johnstone, Diarmaid MacCulloch and David Smith, who have read drafts of the text in part or in full, and offered invaluable comments, as have three readers for Boydell & Brewer. A particular debt is owed to Martin Holmes and the music staff of the Bodleian Library, who have efficiently tracked down sometimes elusive material from remote storage. The British Library and the Music Faculty Library, Oxford have also been of great assistance. In addition, the following individuals have most kindly and promptly supplied information: Alan Clarke, Robin Darwall-Smith, Tom Davies (King's College, Cambridge), Joseph Fort, Stephen Moore, Emily Naish (Salisbury Cathedral Archives), Richard Newsholme, David Rydill (Hampshire Record Office), Michael Stansfield, Eleanor Swire (Winchester Cathedral), Kate Taylor (RSCM) and Lucy Williams (Salisbury Museum). Finally, my warmest thanks to Michael Middeke, Henry Lafferty and colleagues at Boydell & Brewer, not forgetting my copyeditor, Anna Davies, for all their efforts in bringing this book to fruition.

Notes to the Reader

As the term 'choir' can be applied to both a group of singers and the area of a cathedral or monastery in which they sing, in order to avoid ambiguity, I have throughout used the form 'quire' to denote the latter (though naturally retaining the original in quotations).

Full references to sources are provided in the Notes at the end, together with general overviews of the literature pertinent to individual chapters. Although the millennium is the nominal dividing line between the last two chapters, it has proved logical to allow some freedom as to where certain matters are discussed, while the coronation of King Charles III provided a suitable point of closure. Since online website resources are most easily found these days by keyword searching, I have not provided individual URLs for YouTube citations, and those for other websites generally lead only to the home page, from which the appropriate section can be traced. All website references, including Wikipedia and YouTube, were last accessed and checked on 8 Feb. 2025.

Pitch: c'-b' is the octave from middle C upwards; c-b the octave below, and C-B the octave below that.

Introduction

Two fundamental questions arise when considering the topic of British choral life: what exactly constitutes a choir and where do the boundaries of choral music lie? How many people do you need before you call a group of singers a choir rather than a vocal ensemble? Asked to define a 'choir' and a 'choral sound', many would say that its essence lay in the doubling of voices on the individual parts, so that eight voices might be considered a minimum for a group singing in four parts. That said, church choirs may be found with fewer numbers, either from the lack of recruits, or as a deliberate choice by those churches who perhaps employ a professional quartet of singers – such a group may fulfil the functions of a choir, even though the resulting sound is not one which would necessarily be described as 'choral'. The doubling of parts, however, is not always a pre-requisite for a 'choral sound'; it is also partly a question of texture. Although a four-part work sung by single voices may not sound 'choral', an eight-part one sung this way comes much closer. And all would agree that Tallis's forty-part motet, 'Spem in alium', originally conceived for, and still usually sung by single voices, is certainly a choral work. Nevertheless, however undefined the borderline, there is a generally recognized distinction between what are called vocal ensembles and choirs. While no-one would call the six voices of The King's Singers a choir, by the time you get to the eponymously named The Sixteen, that is undoubtedly one, even if of 'chamber' size. The one thing that perhaps defines any sort of choir, as opposed to the singing of a church congregation or a football crowd, is that is pre-supposes a degree of rehearsal, or at least the exercising of already acquired skills.

The same grey area applies when defining choral music. For most of the medieval period, polyphony in the choirs of cathedrals and monasteries was performed by solo voices only, yet we would count it as choral music, since these soloists were operating within a larger choral body. And although we may view choral music as that essentially written to be sung by doubled voices, it is common nowadays for sacred music of the Renaissance period in particular to be sung one to a part by vocal ensembles, as indeed it frequently was originally. On the other hand, music originally conceived for individual voices, such as Tudor/Jacobean madrigals or the eighteenth-century glee, has often in the course of history come to be sung by full choirs. Taking all these ambiguities into consideration, however, this book focuses mainly on the performance of music written for what are generally considered 'choirs' rather than solo-voice ensembles.

It is misleading to think in terms of a single British choral tradition, for in reality a series of different traditions has emerged over the centuries. The oldest is naturally that of the cathedral choir, whose history can be traced back for the best part of a thousand years. Yet, as will become evident, its nature and many of its functions have changed radically over time. Choirs in parish and other churches had their own varied development from the eighteenth century onwards, not necessarily influenced by cathedral practices. From the same time came the gradual evolution of the secular choral society, and within that sphere are found offspring such as the male voice choir, born of the Industrial Revolution, and with its own distinctive traditions.

The adjective 'glorious' is sometimes invoked in association with the idea of the nation's choral traditions, but it is not one that can be rightly applied for most of its history. The present-day excellence of both sacred and secular choirs is a very recent phenomenon, and rose-tinted glimpses into the past are deceptive. But for their legal incorporation into the statutes of the ancient cathedrals, there have been many occasions on which their choirs could have found themselves considered more trouble than they were worth. When it comes to assessing standards of singing, relativism plays an important role. If we were able to hear even praised pre-twentieth-century choirs, we would probably be shocked at some of the sounds. Matters like refinement of tuning, precision of ensemble, and vocal blend, which we value so highly today, were often simply less important to our forebears. This is not to say that they were incapable of criticizing what they heard, but rather that they were able to find satisfaction in performances that would have lacked the finesse that we now expect. It was not so long ago that it was almost normal to expect a choir singing unaccompanied to have let pitch sink a little by the time they got to the end. Above all, there was not the opportunity for ready comparison now open to us. Even today, we can probably all recall performances (especially perhaps the first time we heard a work) which seemed magnificent at the time, but which with hindsight we might consider distinctly sub-standard. That was certainly true of my first acquaintance with the B minor Mass as a seventeen-year-old playing timpani for a local choral society in Chester Cathedral – it was almost certainly a performance of no great distinction, yet it made an indelible impression on my teenage self, which no subsequent one has quite captured.

It is only since the early twentieth century that it has been possible to listen to the sounds of choirs of the past through recordings – facilitated considerably of late through the medium of the internet. One resource in particular, the Archive of Recorded Church Music (www.recordedchurchmusic.org), created by Colin Brownlee, with its vast collection of commercial, BBC and private recordings, together with associated documentation, of which a generous selection is made available on YouTube, has opened up numerous avenues of investigation. What is immediately apparent is not only how much change has taken place in matters like tempi, vibrato and blend over the decades, but also how diverse can be the sound of choirs of the same era. If that is true of the recent past, and within a restricted liturgical tradition, it only emphasizes how little we can know of how choirs sounded in earlier centuries. Whereas in the last century we discovered much about historical instruments and instrumental practice, which has enabled us to some extent to reproduce their sounds, that is untrue of voices. Historical descriptions of singing techniques before the nineteenth century are too vague to offer any real insights as to how choirs might have sounded – and, even if we did know, there is no guarantee that we would want to emulate it. Modern choirs singing music of the past aim at a sound in keeping with present-day concepts of fine tone, varied as that can be. If there is a criticism to be made, it is that professional ensembles can at times sound almost too perfect and over-manicured when they present earlier music – all very beautiful but in danger of being somewhat removed from the spirit of the original. But choirs are living organisms, ever changing, and as subject to the ups and downs of fortune as any football team – a change of director can be as dramatic in its consequences as that of any football manager.

Choral singing is above all a social activity – something emphasized more than ever by its disruption during the recent pandemic. It has also inevitably involved matters of social class. Although, for example, in Tudor times a gentleman (or even a lady) may have indulged in a madrigal or two in the privacy of their own home, any organized singing in public at a professional or serious amateur level was very much the province of the artisan/shopkeeper/clerk class until the latter part of the nineteenth century. Only then do we see the gradual entry of the professional middle classes into choral society life, while many personnel of cathedral choirs would remain towards the lower end of the social scale until well into the twentieth century. The current view of choirs as being a largely middle-class phenomenon is quite a recent development, though it is now modified somewhat through the broader social spectrum offered by the growing popularity of 'community choirs'. There is now certainly a huge variety of choirs to participate in, and people are still prepared to make considerable effort to be transported into the world of choral music with all its potential health-enhancing properties, physical and mental.

This work certainly does not aim at beating any nationalist drum in focussing on British choral history. Indeed, readers may very well emerge from it with any idealized image they may have received rather diminished. And while British choral traditions have in the course of history penetrated many parts of the world, there has also been much cross-fertilization of late, as we have increasingly become acquainted with the rich choral cultures of other nations in Europe and beyond. As exchanges between choirs here and abroad testify, few human activities can bring nations together more than when they join together in sharing a love of singing.

Chapter 1
The Medieval Choir

The story of British choral music up to around the time of the Black Death (1348) is essentially that of activity in its monasteries and cathedrals, after which, up to the Reformation in the middle of the sixteenth century, other institutions also begin to play a significant part. The liturgies of the early church started to take systematic shape in the fourth to sixth centuries, although it was not until the era of Charlemagne in the eighth and ninth centuries that standard forms emerged from many diverse local practices. With references to psalms and hymns being sung in Christian worship from the earliest days, music in one form or another has always played an important role, and the 150 psalms of the Hebrew Bible were eventually to form a backbone of worship throughout the Western church.[1] Chanting – at its simplest, essentially the use of heightened speech – is a natural feature of many religions, serving principally as a means of elevating words from the realm of the everyday. Sung liturgy also came to have the practical benefits of aiding clarity in large buildings, and of preventing the words being rushed – you cannot easily gabble when chanting! For the whole of the Middle Ages, communal services (as opposed to private Masses) appear to have been more or less sung throughout, except for any sermon – certainly in monasteries and cathedrals.[2] In the twenty-first century we are accustomed to much of the liturgy (and especially the lessons) being spoken, even in the most musical of establishments. The continuous singing still found in the Orthodox churches perhaps offers the closest impression of the atmosphere of Western medieval practice, as does the fact that their liturgy is celebrated in an area closed off from the laity, as was the case both in the quire of a cathedral or monastic church, and (to a lesser extent) the chancel of a parish church.

The Institutions and Their Personnel

As a result of the Celtic monasticism of St Patrick and St Columba, and the mission from Rome led by St Augustine in 597, by the end of the seventh century the whole of Anglo-Saxon Britain was Christianized, with the country divided into dioceses under a bishop, alongside numerous monasteries outside the diocesan system. The Viking invasions of the following two centuries saw much disruption, especially to monastic life, but a revival in the tenth century and changes following the Norman Conquest created a pattern of church organization which was to last until the Reformation. This resulted in nineteen cathedrals in England, four in Wales and a varying number in the twelve medieval Scottish dioceses, while the number of monasteries and nunneries eventually ran into many hundreds – up to 800–1,000 in the fourteenth century has been estimated – split between the various orders, of which the Benedictines were the most numerous and wealthy.[3] The great majority were very small, but the larger Benedictine houses delighted in liturgical splendour, and it was they who fostered the greatest musical developments in the early medieval period.

Compared with the continent, Britain had few cathedrals, and these came to be of two types. All were initially staffed by ordinary priests, but from the tenth century several were reorganized as cathedral monasteries, headed by a prior, with the monks constituting the worshipping community – the diocesan bishop being the titular abbot, but normally residing elsewhere. Early examples included Canterbury, Ely, Winchester and Worcester. Others followed after the Norman Conquest, but attempts to have all so designated failed, and the remaining nine English cathedrals followed the usual continental model, with a dean heading a group of canons – men in the holy orders of priest, deacon or sub-deacon – who constituted the governing body or 'chapter'.[4] These were the 'secular' cathedrals – i.e. the canons were not living under a monastic rule – and included places like Exeter, Lincoln, Salisbury and York. The number of canons ranged from about twenty-five to over fifty, and each derived their income from an estate linked to the canonry, which could be quite lucrative.[5] Both the crown and the papacy soon found themselves unable to resist profiting from this situation, so that many administrative and other posts at court and elsewhere came to be paid for by granting the office holder a canonry, with the result that many canons were non-resident. A small group of resident canons, who lived in separate houses in the cathedral close, rather than a monastic dormitory, provided the day-to-day governance of the cathedral. In order, however, to provide sufficient personnel to sustain worship in the cathedral, by the thirteenth century it became a general rule for all the canons, both resident and non-resident, to have a 'vicar' (literally a 'deputy'), resulting in a total of some 350 in the nine secular cathedrals.[6] This development of a body of vicars appears to have been a specifically English one, and was not copied from continental models.[7] Since their principal duty was to sing the cathedral services, they eventually became known as 'vicars choral', though this term does not occur until the sixteenth century. Like the canons, the vicars had to be in holy orders, the younger ones in the minor orders of deacon and sub-deacon, whereas the older ones tended to be full priests.[8] After being first examined in singing, they served for a year on probation before their appointment was made permanent. They were usually at least partly paid by the particular canon who appointed them (with all the potential problems of nepotism and other favouritism), and in the early days, those of the resident ones often lived with them, and may have provided them with domestic help.[9] In some cathedrals all vicars received equal pay, the canons having paid into a common fund; elsewhere it could be related to an individual canon's income, so making some vicarages more desirable than others.[10]

Although the origins of the modern cathedral choir, and indeed the idea of the 'choir' as a separate singing group, can be discerned in the establishment of vicars choral, it would be quite wrong to see them as such in the earlier Middle Ages. From the outset, the secular cathedrals followed the same pattern of services as the monastic establishments. In theory, canons and vicars choral all joined in the singing, and the duties of the vicars extended to assistance with the lessons and ceremonial. In a large cathedral establishment, between the resident canons and the vicars there might be sixty or more officiating in the quire at major services, although full attendance was not expected at all the daily Offices. But by the thirteenth century at the latest, it was clear that the vicars were not mere deputies for their canons. As the complexity of the liturgy increased, a body of men was needed specifically devoted to its execution, since it was beyond the capability of many of the resident canons, who often had other interests and duties, and whose residency itself was frequently subject to much absence.[11]

Boys also had their place in monasteries and cathedrals in the early medieval period. In the case of the monasteries (including the monastic cathedrals), since at least the time of St Benedict in the sixth century, boys had been taken in as oblates – that is, their parents gave a son, typically about eight years old, to a monastery, together with perhaps a gift of land; it entailed a commitment for them to eventually become adult members of the monastic community.[12] Although the boys would have sung with the monks, this was merely part of their devotional life; they were in no sense present because of their singing abilities, and so cannot be viewed as 'choristers' in any modern sense. The practice of child oblation, however, died out by the mid-twelfth century in monasteries (though it continued for girls in nunneries), and from then on boys did not appear in the monastic quire, although, as we shall see, they were later to form part of newly created Lady Chapel choirs.

By way of contrast, the secular cathedrals had boys singing in the quire throughout the medieval period. Unlike the oblates, they were not committed to the cathedral for life, though they were probably initially introduced mainly with a view to producing future priests and vicars rather than for their singing. Although Lincoln and York had twelve boys, and Exeter and Salisbury fourteen, the typical number in the thirteenth and fourteenth centuries was between six and ten.[13] Their joining in the plainsong (an octave above the men) would have made little impact against several dozen adults. But they also performed other functions, such as serving as thurifers and candle bearers, as well as being called upon to read lessons; at major feasts the liturgy occasionally assigned special singing and non-singing roles to them alone.[14] As their voices changed, some would have remained in the stalls, fulfilling other ceremonial roles as 'altarists', perhaps en route to becoming a vicar choral. Suitable ex-choristers were often able to continue their education at the local grammar school, so furthering their prospects of decent employment. The boys did not live together in the early days; some lived at home, others with canons, also performing domestic duties for them. In many cases parents would have been happy to see their sons become choristers, since it was a means of ensuring they received some education; in addition to musical instruction, Latin grammar was the other essential element in their tuition. At Exeter, and doubtless elsewhere, they were excused attendance at some lesser services to allow for schooling.[15] For those residing with canons, it also meant that parents had one less mouth to feed. At Exeter, each chorister, including those living at home, was assigned to a resident canon, who fed them – a system which, rather exceptionally, lasted until the Reformation.[16] A post of 'Master of the Choristers', responsible for the boys' musical tuition, emerged, usually held by one of the vicars choral, and in the early days was not considered of great importance. In later times the boys sometimes lived with the Master, as was the case at Wells in the fifteenth century, a tradition which prevailed in some places until the nineteenth century. Overall responsibility for the music lay (as it still does today) with the precentor (originally called the cantor), a senior member of the chapter, who in practice delegated much of the work to his deputy, the succentor. Between them they would have selected the appropriate chants, allotted solo parts, and directed all aspects of the ceremonial. It was the precentor too who would normally have selected the choristers.[17] Nor did his authority just lie within the cathedral, for he generally supervised the teaching of singing in all the town's churches, and sometimes throughout the diocese – all, no doubt, in an attempt to secure uniformity of practice.[18]

Forms of Worship

The idea of a virtually continuous stream of worship, day and night, in which recitation of the psalms was a major element, was a feature of some early monastic communities in the Middle East. The sixth-century Rule promulgated by St Benedict saw its transformation in Western monasticism into a pattern of eight services or 'Offices' spread through the day, consisting of psalms, lessons and prayers. These were Matins, Lauds, Prime, Terce, Sext, None, Vespers and Compline. Of these Matins (originally held at midnight, later transferred to dawn) and Vespers (at mid-afternoon) were the most important and were to become the most intricate musically, while some of the minor Offices were run together – Lauds, for example, became tacked onto the end of Matins. Alongside the Offices was a daily communal celebration of the Mass (Morrow Mass), and High Mass, both of which took place in the morning. Other Masses were celebrated privately in side chapels in memory of particular individuals who (or whose relatives) had paid for them. Antiphonal singing, particularly of the psalms, was an early custom in both monasteries and secular cathedrals, the participants facing each other on either side of the quire, which was furnished with two stepped rows of stalls on each side. In the secular cathedrals the boys formed a third row of singers, and stood below the lower set of stalls without any desks in front of them – they were expected to stand most of the time, though evidently a bench was provided, since at Wells, for example, they were allowed to sit during certain items, such as the many lessons at Matins.[19] The adults had an easier time, since their hinged seats not only allowed for normal sitting at appropriate times, but a projecting ledge on the underside (the 'misericord') enabled them to partly squat while supposedly standing. In the secular cathedrals the two sides of the quire were identified as 'decani' and 'cantoris' after the seats allotted to the dean and cantor (precentor) respectively, a tradition which continues to the present day.[20] The singing was directed by 'rulers' (*rectores chori*), usually two in number, from a lectern placed between the stalls.

The early medieval period was marked by an enormous increase in the complexity of worship. Within the basic repetitive routine, numerous variations in detail were found, depending on the liturgical season, while the many feast days (including saints' days) were graded, with the most important receiving the greatest degree of ritual and musical enrichment. The liturgy was also embellished through the interpolation of extra texts and/or music, called tropes, into standard items such as the Kyrie of the Mass. This growth reached its zenith in the eleventh century, at which point it had become so obviously over-elaborate that the following period saw some degree of retreat, though by any modern standards it remained extremely intricate, and the medieval era as a whole saw great attention paid to the detail of liturgical celebration. A distinction in Britain, however, was to be found between the forms of monastic worship and that of the secular cathedrals. While the monasteries followed the pattern of liturgy laid down by Rome, the secular cathedrals developed their own forms – not major diversions, but significant variants in matters such as prayers and the ranking of feasts. Salisbury, Hereford and York each had their own forms, of which the Salisbury one, known as the Sarum Use (from the site of the old cathedral) became that generally adopted throughout the kingdom, including the Chapel Royal and parish churches. But only those well acquainted with their liturgy on a daily basis would have noticed the differences between the Roman and native uses; to an outsider they would have appeared identical.[21]

Unadorned monophonic plainsong was the main, and indeed often the only music of most services right up to the Reformation. It varied from the simple tones used for the psalms, which were basically recited on a single note with inflections at the ends of each half of the verse, to elaborate melodies with extended melismas on individual syllables. By no means all of it, however, was intended to be sung 'chorally'; the more intricate melodies, such as those for the Gradual and Alleluia of the Mass, were usually meant for performance by a soloist.

It is important to note that in the medieval period generally, the chant was essentially transmitted orally and sung from memory. The texts were naturally available in written form, but only the principal participants would have had a copy in front of them. It was one of the stipulations for novice monks and vicars choral that they should be able to recite the whole of the psalms by heart within a year of admission. This was perhaps not as difficult a task as might be imagined. All 150 psalms were normally sung through each week during the daily Offices, so they would rapidly become familiar. After the Reformation, cathedrals sang through the whole psalter once a month at Matins and Evensong, so that up to the general discontinuation of daily sung Matins in the early twentieth century, many an experienced chorister and lay clerk could probably have performed equal feats of memory, and even today the Evensong psalms will be firmly entrenched in the memory of many choristers, young and old. Nowadays we wonder at memorizing abilities of, for example, concert pianists, or those who can recite the whole of Shakespeare's sonnets, but in the essentially oral culture of the Middle Ages, memorization of large amounts of liturgical language would have been second nature. There is also the practical consideration that much would have been sung in at least semi-darkness, especially in the winter months, and only the lecterns would have been lit by candles except on the more important feast days.[22] Imperfections in an individual's memory were of no consequence, since the collective memory of the worshipping community would ensure general continuity. Unanimity in both pitch and timing must often have been rather approximate – perhaps more like the hymn singing of a modern congregation than the polished sound of plainsong heard, for example, on the recordings of the monks of Solesmes. But the liturgy was not performed for the sake of listeners. Pilgrims visiting cathedral and monastic shrines, as they did in great numbers throughout the Middle Ages, may have overheard parts of services from outside the quire, but in no sense did they constitute a congregation – the parish church was the place for them to gather for regular worship.

While definitive texts could be established in written form at an early date, the same was not true of the music, which took several centuries to evolve a notation that enabled at least certain elements of the chant to be permanently recorded. The process of oral transmission of the music is clear from the way notation developed. The earliest known notation, from the ninth century, is essentially an aide-memoire in the form of signs, called 'neumes', which, as far as the pitch is concerned, merely indicated the general direction of pitch movement, as well as showing the distribution of notes to syllables. The oldest British manuscripts with notation, the so-called Winchester Tropers (housed in Oxford and Cambridge, and preserving the plainsong of Winchester's Anglo-Saxon Old Minster) date from the tenth and eleventh centuries, and show a move towards defining pitch more exactly by placing the neumes at higher or lower levels.[23] Greater precision was soon achieved with the addition of a guiding ruled line or lines, which then evolved by the thirteenth century into the modern stave – generally a four-line one proved sufficient for plainsong. Behind the development of exact notation of pitch lay a concern for creating uniformity across the Church, for inevitably, with purely oral transmission, considerable local variation tended to occur. But the development of precise notation did not mean that copies were provided for all. Only the precentor/cantor and other rulers of the choir would have had a book in front of them. It has been suggested that they used hand-signs to indicate the direction of pitch to the rest of the singers, but evidence for it remains disputed.[24] Having sung the opening phrase of a chant alone, as was customary, the rulers probably relied on 'follow my leader' practice for those chants which were unfamiliar to the majority, as must have often been the case with the many chants peculiar to individual feasts. It has been estimated that the whole annual repertory could reach 5,000 melodies,[25] though the process of becoming acquainted with so many chants was perhaps not as formidable as might be imagined, since they move mostly stepwise and are constructed from a limited number of stock patterns. It would therefore have been much easier to 'sing along' with an unfamiliar chant than it is to master the far more unpredictable course of some modern hymn tunes.

If pitch was only approximately represented in early neumatic notation, that notation did also offer indications of other features of the chant – including phrasing, rhythm, and ornamentation, though we still do not understand the exact significance of some of the signs.[26] As with so many aspects of medieval music, we also know virtually nothing of how medieval chant sounded, although it would have seldom resembled the smooth even flow of most modern chant performances, which derives from the style established by the monks of Solesmes in the late nineteenth century – very beautiful it may be, but its historical authenticity is certainly dubious. It is now widely accepted that certain types of chant were sung, not in even notes, but with some rhythmic fluidity, at least in the earlier medieval period, even if again we are not sure exactly how.[27] As for the vocal quality, it has been suggested that, compared with the style of Solesmes, it may have had an open throated sound, projected from the front of the mouth, with pulsating notes, and sliding between pitches being used. Analogies to the style of singing heard today in the Eastern Mediterranean and India have been suggested.[28] Being sung day in, day out, performance matters were simply handed on orally, without any need to write anything down for the benefit of future historians.

Feast days (of varying degrees of importance) could be distinguished by, amongst other things, special vestments, incense and processions. And from the tenth century onwards, such days began to be singled out musically by the introduction of polyphonic treatment of certain items. In many ways the whole impulse for the development of music and liturgy through the medieval period can be seen to stem from a desire to give variety and enrichment to what were basically very repetitive ceremonies. In its simplest form this could consist of merely duplicating the plainsong melody at the interval of a fourth or fifth above – so-called 'parallel organum' – but it rapidly became more sophisticated and creative in both improvised and written-down forms. Two- and three-part writing developed in both a note-against-note style (known as 'conductus') and in a more melismatic manner, where the plainsong might appear in slow-moving notes (the 'tenor' – i.e. 'holding' – part) with one or two florid parts above it, each normally having different words, which were sung simultaneously – comprehension of the text by listeners being of no consideration. This was the medieval 'motet' (from the French *mot*), a term which later, for music of the fifteenth century onwards, came to be applied more loosely to most sacred polyphonic compositions not part of the Ordinary of the Mass. The essential feature, however, is that polyphonic performance was the preserve of soloists, and was to remain so until the second half of the fifteenth century. The only true 'choral' sound at the time was that of unison plainsong sung by the whole worshipping community, and even here, as we have seen, much of the more elaborate chant was entrusted to a soloist. Although the simplest type of parallel organum might conceivably have been sung by a whole body of singers, there is no evidence to suggest this happened in practice. But as polyphony moved beyond simple types that could be improvised within strict rules, it needed musical notation (known as 'mensural') which defined both pitch and rhythm, and had to be performed from a book rather than from memory.

The development of polyphonic music in England up to the fourteenth century appears to have taken place mostly in the greater Benedictine monasteries.[29] This, however, may just reflect the fact that the few surviving sources come mainly from monastic establishments. It is hard to believe that musicians in the secular cathedrals would not also have been keen to exploit its possibilities. It is easy to see how small groups of enthusiasts among the monks and vicars choral could have wanted to enhance festal celebrations musically. Early polyphony was confined to music for major feasts, and to items which in plainsong were already the preserve of soloists, such as Responsories of the Office, or Graduals and Alleluias, which belonged to the Proper of the Mass – those texts which varied with the season or feast day. Some individual parts of the Ordinary – the Kyrie, Gloria, Credo, Sanctus, Benedictus and Agnus Dei – which remained textually fixed in every Mass, also began to receive polyphonic settings, although until the fifteenth century there was no concept in England of the Ordinary being set to music as a unified whole, such as we nowadays think of as a musical setting of the Mass. Three-part writing was the norm by the thirteenth century, initially within a total compass of nine to eleven notes, which tended to expand to two octaves in the fourteenth century, and all was performed by adult male voices – just what types of voices will be discussed later. Some of the earliest English polyphony from the thirteenth century survives in the so-called Worcester Fragments – now isolated leaves remaining from manuscripts originating at the monastic cathedral of Worcester, and preserved in Worcester Cathedral Library, the Bodleian Library, Oxford and the British Library.[30] As seen in Figure 1, the motet fills two pages of an opening, and is not laid out in score form, but with the parts written out separately, the two upper ones (with florid writing) on opposing pages while the slowly moving plainsong 'tenor' is notated concisely at the foot of both. From the size of the pages (11 x 7¾ inches), it is obvious

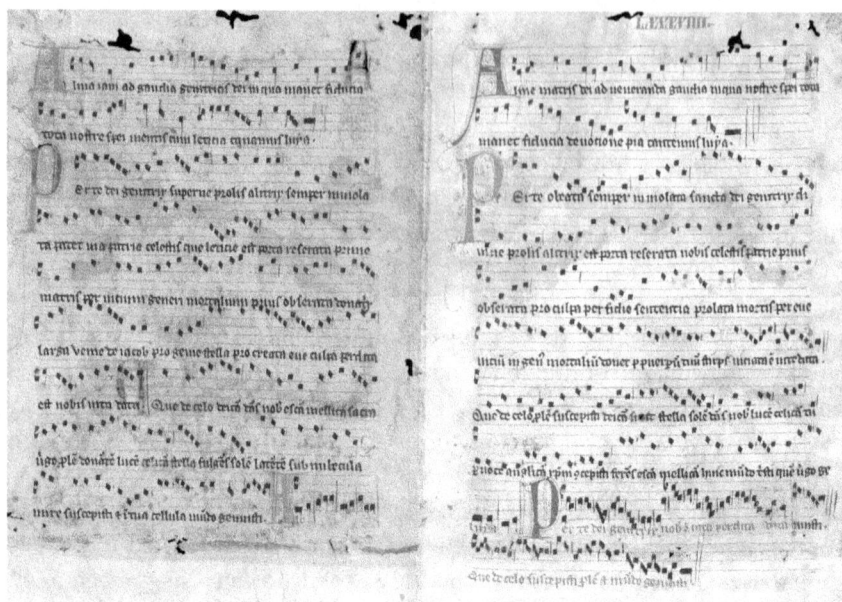

Figure 1   Motet 'Alma iam ad gaudia / Alme matris Dei / Alleluia. Per te' from the Worcester Fragments; Oxford, Bodleian Library, MS lat. liturg. d. 20, fols 15v–16.

that this could only be performed by three solo singers, who would have gathered round a lectern placed between the stalls. Other music, however, might be written with all the parts moving together, note-against-note – the so-called 'conductus' style – for which modern score form was employed.

In the secular cathedrals, by the thirteenth century at the latest, the vicars choral were carrying the main burden of the daily services.[31] With the dean and resident canons living separately and having interests and duties beyond the cathedral, their sense of communal organization tended to weaken – a process which had started as early as the eleventh century. By way of contrast, the vicars choral gradually came to live a more communal life. From living with their individual canons or in town outside the cathedral close, from the fourteenth century they came increasingly to live in specially constructed accommodation – the 'vicars close', which combined the privacy of individual dwellings with a communal hall for meals and often their own chapel – very like a small Oxford or Cambridge college. Today, splendid examples of such closes remain at Lichfield, Lincoln, and, above all, Wells. The dean and chapter probably encouraged such developments as a means of trying to exercise more discipline over the vicars, and there was reluctance from some of those accustomed to the freedom of the town to being corralled into more communal living.[32] The vicars heavily outnumbered the resident canons, even if the obligation for every canon (resident and non-resident) to have a vicar was not always observed in practice. From the fourteenth century the vicars sought to increase their security and status by becoming legal corporations, with consequent statutes and rights, including that to acquire property – the town's citizens often knew them as landlords.[33] Once past their probationary year, the vicars had tenure for life, regardless of any decline in singing ability or infirmity, similar to the way in which parish incumbents had freehold of their posts until reforms in the second half of the twentieth century. It was a situation which was to cause problems for those in charge of the music right through to the twentieth century. They could lose their posts only in cases of serious misconduct.[34] The vicars of Wells were the first to incorporate in 1348 and were followed by others over the next century. These corporations survived the Reformation, and, while many subsequently disappeared, those of Lichfield and Wells continued in existence until final abolition following the Cathedral Measures Act of 1931.

The college of vicars had their own rules for regulating life in the close, though the dean and chapter had ultimate disciplinary power over them. However different the medieval religious mindset might have been from our own, the vicars, despite their sacred calling, proved all too human in their weaknesses, which remained remarkably similar through the ages. Generally, each week miscreants were summoned to appear before the chapter for reprimand. We know of their misdeeds because they were faithfully recorded in the chapter acts.[35] Offences included frequenting alehouses, unseemly behaviour in the quire, absenteeism, keeping women in their houses, and brawling. Fines were the most usual punishment, with the threat of dismissal for repeated misbehaviour. It is easy to imagine antagonism developing between the wealthy dean and canons and the ill-paid vicars, as for example we know happened at Lincoln in the early fifteenth century, when quarrels with the unpopular dean, John Macworth, sometimes reduced attendance of the vicars to six or eight.[36] Yet, on the whole the canons often took a fairly lenient view of misconduct, especially in the matter of associating with women, perhaps in part because their own behaviour was not above reproach. It was not uncommon for vicars to co-habit long term in their college accommodation. If being hauled up regularly before the chapter appears to be treating them in the manner of juveniles, it must be remembered that many were young men in their late teens and early twenties, still only in minor orders, and so it is hardly surprising that a celibate life was often unappealing.[37] Unsurprising too were the outbursts of gang warfare with youths of the town, however unthinkable in a present-day context. Absenteeism is readily understandable, given that cathedrals generally had between twenty-five and fifty vicars, and a full attendance was not expected at the more minor Offices of the day. In the early fourteenth century York stipulated that a minimum of twelve vicars per side respectively should be present at every service, while Salisbury stipulated thirteen.[38] With a large cohort of vicars, some were undoubtedly tempted to consider their presence unnecessary. Here again the authorities could be remarkably lenient. Under the 1338 statutes of Wells, only after six months absenteeism without just cause could a vicar be deprived of his office.[39] Sometimes a more general set of warnings was issued, as at Wells in 1298, where it was noted:

> It is the custom of certain of the Vicars to leave the choir during Divine Service and to gossip with lay persons of doubtful reputation in the nave and behind pillars, under colour of buying the goods exposed there for sale.... All buying and selling in the nave of the church is strictly forbidden.... The singing in choir, both of psalms and other pieces of music, must be even and no one must go faster than his neighbour. All should listen carefully at the pauses, both in the middle and at the end of the verses.... No Vicar who has been convicted of keeping a concubine and of having children by her is to allow their mother to visit him, to be present at social functions where she is likely to be present or to speak with her.... If the Vicar have an unmelodious voice or lack knowledge of singing, the Dean and Chapter may confer the Vicariate on another more suitable ....[40]

Problems were still evident forty years later, when it was ordered in 1338 that 'the Vicars must wear suitable clothes, neither too long nor too short, their hair must not cover their ears and must be tonsured in the approved fashion as an indication that they have cast aside things of earth and have instead a share in a "royal priesthood".' There was also a complaint that 'they take part in dances and masques and day and night prowl round the streets and lanes of the city leading a riotous existence, singing and shouting (*cum cantu et tumultu*) and this to the great discredit of the office of the clergy, great insult to the Divine Majesty and great scandal to the people', while 'some of the Vicars are in the habit of frequenting alehouses, playing backgammon and of conducting themselves in a highly unbefitting manner. ... The bearing of arms by the clergy is strictly forbidden both by divine and human law; yet, nevertheless, some of the Vicars and Altarists are so forgetful of their obligations in this matter that they carry swords, inflict grievous bodily harm on others and even commit heinous sacrileges. ... It has come to the ears of the Dean and Chapter that certain Vicars are in the habit of taking part in drinking-bouts in which all oblige themselves to drink the same amount and he who makes the most drunk and drinks the longest cups himself receives the greatest praise.'[41]

At Salisbury in the fifteenth century matters of reproof included bringing pet dogs into the quire.[42] It would be easy to fill pages with anecdotes of such misdeeds, entertaining as they may be, but chapter records necessarily tend mostly to record problems arising in the community, and just as it would be foolish to judge a school's quality solely by reference to its punishment book, so too chapter records should not be considered as portraying a true overall picture of the establishment. No doubt many vicars were conscientious, peace-loving, and morally upright, and were never a cause of concern to the authorities. It may well have been for the off-duty diversion of monks or vicars that the most famous piece of medieval secular music, 'Sumer is icumen in', was composed. This sophisticated piece for six voices (a four-part round with two-part underpinning) is thought to date from around the middle of the thirteenth century and can only have originated amongst skilled church composers of polyphony.[43] It is an isolated example, but one which suggests that there must have been a good deal of such music, which has failed to survive the centuries.

It is interesting to note that some latitude was given with regard to arrival time for services. In the thirteenth century at Wells, you could arrive for the Office services up to the end of the first psalm without penalty of a fine, and likewise up to the first Collect at Mass. This provision was perhaps a reflection of the lack of personal timepieces. The tolling of a bell would have given warning, but not all would necessarily have been within earshot. Processional entry of the choir for a service (as opposed to ritual processions) belongs to a much later age. As for the misbehaviour of choristers, time-honoured chastisement continued to be their lot right through to the twentieth century. Communal living for them was generally slow to develop, though at Lincoln, the bishop, Richard Gravesend, made provision for a choristers' house as early as 1264.[44] Choristers' life, however, had its lighter moments. At many cathedrals, the ceremony of the Boy Bishop was observed annually and dates back to at least the thirteenth century. Traditionally at the feast of St Nicholas (5 December) the choristers elected one of their number as Boy Bishop, who, endowed with suitable episcopal robes, then proceeded to preside over the services on Holy Innocents Day (28 December), stopping short, of course, at celebrating Mass. The duties usually included delivering a sermon which had been written by an adult. An extract from a very long Gloucester specimen of 1558 gives some flavour of what medieval choristers were liable to get up to, despite the ever-present threat of the rod, as the 'bishop' reels off their faults:

> ... I kan not let this passe ontouched how boyyshly thei behave themselves in the church, how rashly thei cum into the quere without any reverence; never knele nor cowntenaunce to say any prayer or Pater noster, but rudely squat down on ther tayles, and justle with ther felows for a place; a non thei startes me owt of the quere agayne, and in agayne and out agayne ... but only to gadd and gas abrode, and so cum in agayne and crosse the quere fro one side to another and never rest, without any order.[45]

The tradition of the Boy Bishop lasted until the Reformation,[46] and was revived at some cathedrals in the late twentieth century.

The Later Middle Ages

The fourteenth and fifteenth centuries saw many significant developments in institutions, liturgy and personnel, as well as in the music itself, which resulted at the end of the period in the emergence of something beginning to resemble the modern cathedral choir. A key catalyst was the practice of devotion to the Virgin Mary, which had begun to gain popularity from the late twelfth century onwards and which in the next century saw the creation of Lady Chapels in both monasteries and cathedrals, usually built on to the east end of the building beyond the quire and high altar. The chapel was principally used for the daily or weekly morning celebration of a Mass in Mary's honour (Lady Mass), and in the afternoon for an act of devotion, to which was added a hymn to the Virgin (usually termed nowadays a 'votive antiphon') such as *Salve regina*, or *Ave regina caelorum*.[47] Unlike services in the quire, those in the Lady Chapel were open to the public, and served to nourish popular devotion. The evolution of the medieval choir and its music was strongly allied to the development of such devotional activity. Initially, in monastic establishments these 'out of quire' services were sung by a small group of three or four monks, evidently often those with some musical ambition, for although plainsong still predominated, polyphonic items began to play an increasing role, and by far the largest quantity of surviving English polyphony of the thirteenth and fourteenth centuries, both of Mass movements and motets (of which the votive antiphon is a sub-species), is associated with Marian devotion. In the secular cathedrals a few vicars choral undertook the Lady Chapel duties, for which they received extra remuneration.[48] At Hereford in 1330, thanks to a substantial bequest, no fewer than ten additional vicars were engaged to help in the Lady Chapel, although they were also required to assist in the quire services, since Hereford's unusual constitution had hitherto provided for fewer vicars than generally found elsewhere.[49] At this time there appears to have been a relaxation of the requirement for wholesale memorization of the chant, at least in secular establishments, which allowed newcomers to assimilate the chant with the aid of books.[50]

A significant fourteenth-century development occurred when the monasteries began to set up their Lady Chapel choirs with outsiders, either three or four laymen, or a small number of boys from the almonry schools (grammar schools attached to many monasteries), or a combination of both.[51] Equally important, the monasteries began to engage a professional lay musician specifically to instruct the boys. The boys themselves would still have only joined in the plainsong, although the master would have taught the more able to improvise descant over the plainsong to prescribed rules.[52] Presumably only one boy at a time would have improvised, but it would have added some variety to the sound of undiluted monophony. Whether such descanting was a daily occurrence, or only practised on festal occasions, is just one of the many things about which we are forced to remain ignorant. Performance of written polyphony, in both the Lady Mass and the votive antiphon, remained at this period in the hands of men, and was still reserved for important feasts. Westminster Abbey's experience provides an interesting example of this development and how it changed over time. In the mid-fourteenth century the Abbey – as its name implies, a monastic church – evidently suffered from the predations of the Black Death and had already in the 1350s engaged a lay musician to help the monks re-establish their music. Then in 1384 another outside singer, Walter Whitby, was appointed, who soon created and taught a group of almonry boys to sing in the Lady Chapel, presumably supplementing the monks. This was followed in 1393 by the employment of four professional adult lay singers, again mainly for Lady Chapel duty, though, exceptionally, they were also required to contribute to the main services in the monks' quire on ten principal feasts of the year. The boys, however, were disposed of about 1400, and they would only reappear in the Lady Chapel choir towards the end of the fifteenth century, by which time most such choirs contained both boys and men.[53] Thus the idea of a choir as a distinct group of specialist musicians, including an experienced 'Master of the Choristers', took root from the late fourteenth century onwards, even in monastic communities. In this way the greater monasteries came more to resemble the secular cathedrals, where the vicars choral and choristers already had a considerable separate identity. Decisions as to the constitution of monastic choirs, however, were purely local, and some establishments continued to set up boys' choirs for their Lady Chapels at the turn of the fourteenth century, including Ely, Winchester and Worcester.

The gradual opening of singers' posts in both monastic and secular institutions to laymen, not obliged to take any degree of holy orders, was in part caused by the general decline in numbers of those taking such orders after the Black Death. But it meant that it became possible for someone to pursue a career as a church musician without committing himself to abandoning his lay status.[54] This went together with the gradual relaxation of the obligation for the number of vicars to equal that of canons; Wells, for example, which had more than fifty canons, had only thirty-four vicars in 1437, and twenty-three in 1500.[55] At the same time, the choristers, who in earlier days might have been looked upon chiefly as potential future ordinands, now also became the 'nursery' for the growing demand for skilled lay clerks. By reducing the requirement to take orders, the Church made it easier for itself to recruit singers of high ability, increasingly necessary for the growing complexity of the musical repertoire.

The fourteenth century also saw another institution come to prominence: the Chapel Royal, which was not a building, but the ecclesiastical staff of the sovereign. Although the King would have had chaplains from early Christian times, it appears to have been the thirteenth century before a body of priests and clerks can be identified, which not only performed the liturgy in the chapels created in his various palaces, but also accompanied the King on his travels through the kingdom or abroad – including visits to France in 1475, 1513 and 1520. By the first half of the fourteenth century its staff consisted of a dean and about sixteen 'Gentlemen', of which typically over half would be in priestly orders (chaplains) and the rest in a minor order or lay members (clerks), together with a small number of boys (perhaps three to five). Its numbers fluctuated over the next century, dependent on the royal finances and the desire of the King for ceremonial display. For the Chapel Royal was an essential part of the whole court establishment. It offered daily worship to the Almighty on behalf of the King, who would typically only be present in person on Sundays and high feasts. It reached perhaps its greatest numerical strength under Henry V, when in 1421 there were thirty-two Gentlemen and sixteen choristers, only for it to shrink after Henry's death in 1423. From this time on an increasing proportion of the men were laymen, as high musical ability took precedence in appointments.[56] The 1420s also saw the formal creation of the post of sub-dean, who did the day-to-day running of the Chapel.[57]

By the end of the fifteenth century it had an average of about 28–32 Gentlemen and 10–12 boys. The posts of Gentlemen became highly sought after – not only were they far better paid than vicars choral at cathedrals, but a rota system was in operation. Although all had to be present on Sundays and important feast days, only half were on duty on other days, and there were periods when the whole choir was stood down; this naturally offered plenty of scope for additional freelance employment. As for the choristers, the Chapel Royal had the royal prerogative to 'impress' boys from most other institutions, and the Master of the Children (a post held by one of the Gentlemen) would tour the country in search of talent. However initially disturbing a boy may have perhaps found it, being uprooted from say Lincoln to the London court, for many it was doubtless ultimately a blessing. For when their voices changed, provision was made for suitable boys to be sent on to the universities, while others might find employment at court or in the household of one of the many magnates in the court circle.[58] A few other choirs came to have the right of impressment – St Paul's, St Stephen's, Westminster, and St George's, Windsor, while Cardinal Wolsey also succeeded in obtaining the right for his own household chapel. Although men could also be pressed into royal service, it is doubtful whether this often happened, given the obvious advantages of royal employment. Not all choirs were open to depredation, since, in order to fend off impressment, it was possible for institutions to purchase letters of immunity from the King, providing the crown with yet another source of income.[59]

The services of the medieval Chapel Royal were essentially private affairs and probably only ever attended by members of the upper echelons of the court.[60] The survival of one major source of polyphonic music from the Chapel Royal, dating from the early fifteenth century, shows how it was by then in the forefront of developments. The Old Hall manuscript, now in the British Library,[61] is thought to have started life in the household chapel of Henry V's brother, Thomas, Duke of Clarence, before being taken over by the Chapel Royal itself on Thomas's death in 1421. It is remarkable amongst other things for being the first English manuscript where compositions are attributed to individual composers – hitherto anonymity had prevailed. So, for the first time the works of composers such as John Dunstable (*c.*1390–1453) and Leonel Power (*d.*1445) are identified, and royal interest and skill in music at the time is clear from a Gloria and a Sanctus attributed to 'Roy Henry' – thought at one time to refer to Henry IV, but now considered to be Henry V.[62] The works of the Old Hall manuscript are still basically composed for solo men's voices in three and four parts, although there are indications that some passages may have been sung with the parts doubled, marking a first move towards true 'choral' polyphony, which was really to emerge later in the century.[63] The music of Dunstable's generation was characterized by its euphonious, rich sound, partly due to the predominance of thirds in the harmony. Designated the *contenance angloise* ('English manner'), it was known and admired on the continent, where its influence can be discerned in the music of the generation of Dufay (1397–1474) and Binchois (*c.*1400–1460).

An interesting sidelight on the development of true choral music is also to be found in the emergence of the polyphonic carol in the early fifteenth century. In origin a dance-song with French roots, the carol, with both sacred and secular texts, had become a form of popular monophonic song in England by the fourteenth century. In contrast to the varied nature of these earlier carols, the polyphonic carols are almost all sacred in essence, with Christmas and the Virgin Mary being the most common themes. Their strophic form was characterized by a refrain (termed a 'burden') alternating with verses. The polyphonic carol was the province of professional singers, and most were probably performed in church as an adjunct to the formal liturgy – use in processions or as a substitution for the liturgical item of the *Benedicamus Domino* in the Offices of the Christmas season have been suggested as possible roles, though definite evidence is lacking.[64] English, Latin, and mixed ('macaronic') texts are found, with the verses for two solo voices, and the burden in two or three parts, 'There is no rose of such virtue', being a well-known and typical example. What is particularly relevant from the choral point of view is that, in a number of carols, the burden is marked 'chorus', which can (but need not be) be interpreted as being meant for the parts to be doubled. Like the indications in the Old Hall manuscript, they hint at early moves towards a larger body taking part in polyphonic performance.[65] Amongst these carols is the most famous, the 'Agincourt Carol', written in the aftermath of the 1415 battle, whose words straddle the sacred/secular divide (which in any case in the Middle Ages had no firm border), combining an account of the event ('Owre kynge went forth to Normandy') with an exhortation to give thanks to God for the victory ('Deo gratias Anglia, redde pro victoria'). Such a carol may well have been sung more in the vicars' hall or at a courtly feast than in church.

Besides the emergence of the Chapel Royal, another major development of the fourteenth century was the creation of institutions commemorating the dead. Although chantry chapels (intended for private Masses to be said for the soul of deceased notables) had begun to appear, either as side chapels or independent buildings, since at least the twelfth century, it was the Black Death of 1348 and subsequent outbreaks of the plague that made death and its commemoration such a dominant feature of life in the later Middle Ages. While chantry chapels continued to be added to cathedrals and other large churches, some magnates, clerical and secular, had more ambitious plans for their perpetual remembrance. Instead of bestowing gifts on monasteries, as was the prevalent custom in earlier times, the wealthy increasingly turned to founding collegiate institutions of various kinds, particularly those in which educational and devotional roles were combined. In 1379 William of Wykeham, Bishop of Winchester and

Chancellor of England, founded New College, Oxford to take 70 scholars together with a chapel establishment of 10 chaplains, 3 clerks and 16 choristers, the latter according to the statutes to be boys 'knowing how to read and sing competently' ('competenter legere et cantare'). The founder's intention was in large part to create an institution for the education of priests, helping make good the ravages of the Black Death.[66] At the same time he also founded Winchester College to act as a feeder institution, which was to educate 70 'poor scholars'; it again had a chapel with 10 priest-fellows, 3 chaplains, 3 clerks and 16 choristers. Sixteen was a comparatively large number of choristers, but this was not out of musical necessity. The boys at this period were still only involved in singing plainsong, not polyphony. The large number was due much more to the founder having an eye to their being encouraged eventually to pursue the priestly road. Some of the sixteen would have been deployed in assisting in other aspects of the ceremonial, and all would have been involved in performing domestic duties such as serving in hall. Wykeham's institutions were to provide the model for Henry VI when he founded Eton College and King's College, Cambridge in 1440 and 1441, for William Waynflete founding Magdalen College, Oxford in 1458, and for Cardinal Wolsey when he founded the last of the great pre-Reformation Oxford colleges, Cardinal College (later Christ Church) in 1525. In each case sixteen choristers were stipulated in the statutes, when most cathedrals averaged only eight to twelve. The term 'choral foundations', commonly applied to these Oxford and Cambridge colleges, means that the constitution of the choir was laid down in the college's statutes, and so it could not be arbitrarily altered or abolished – a change in the statutes would be necessary to do so. In the case of all the above, except for Cardinal College (which took over the old priory of St Frideswide), it was only several decades after their foundation that their present chapels came into use; indeed at King's, although the building of its chapel was begun in 1448, the fabric was not finished until 1515 and it was the 1540s before its fitting-out was completed,[67] services being apparently held in a temporary chapel until then. The pre-Reformation liturgy for which that magnificent building was designed, was thus celebrated in it for a mere handful of years.

Also in the fourteenth century, but without the educational element, two other important religious collegiate institutions came into existence under royal aegis: St Stephen's, in the royal palace of Westminster, and St George's Chapel, Windsor, both established in 1348 with substantial choral resources, quite independent of the Chapel Royal itself.[68] The fifteenth century also reveals new choral activity elsewhere. In Lincolnshire, Tattershall College was founded in 1439 as a chantry college, whose staff of 6 chaplains, 6 clerks and 6 choristers were to maintain daily worship in commemoration of the founder, Baron Ralph de Cromwell and his grandmother. Its musical establishment had increased to 10 clerks and 10 boys by 1500, and John Taverner was a clerk (and probably Master of the Choristers) there in the 1520s before moving to Wolsey's new Cardinal College in Oxford. The households of the greater ecclesiastics and nobles continued to maintain their own chapels, generally on a small scale – about 1517, the Earl of Northumberland's establishment, with a dean, 6 priests, 11 lay clerks and 6 boys, was probably a comparatively large one,[69] though easily outdone by Cardinal Wolsey, whose chapel in the 1520s had a dean, sub-dean, 30 singing men (14 of them priests), 12 boys and a Master of the Choristers.[70] This rivalled Henry VIII's Chapel Royal itself, perhaps unwisely on Wolsey's part; even if it didn't play a direct part in his downfall in 1529, it probably didn't help relations between them.

Also significant were various collegiate parish churches, run either by a dean/provost and canons, rather like a cathedral but without diocesan responsibilities, such as found at Beverley, Ripon, Southwell and Warwick, or by a warden and fellows, as at Manchester. They followed the musical pattern of the secular cathedrals, but with quite small forces of clerical/lay men and a few boys. As for parish churches in general, we know virtually nothing of musical activity in them before the fifteenth century, and have only tantalizingly fragmentary information for that century, mostly gleaned from churchwardens' accounts.[71] For the great majority we assume that, if plainsong was sung at all, it would have been just the priest and parish clerk who took part, although in those parishes which also employed a chantry priest, he was usually obliged also to assist with singing the regular services.[72] However, the various religious guilds, which increasingly flourished in the late medieval devotional atmosphere, could play an important role in patronizing music in some urban parish churches throughout the country as well as in the capital. With membership including prominent citizens of the town (and often admitting women), they typically created or supported a chantry in a principal church, paying for its priests and helping the church with the expenses of a song school and singing clerks. This was the situation in places like St Botolph's, Boston (with the guilds of St Mary and Corpus Christi), St James, Louth (Lady and Trinity guilds) and Ludlow (Palmers guild).[73] Boston in particular maintained a large choir of 10 chaplains, 10–12 lay clerks and 8–10 choristers, and John Taverner served there as a lay clerk (and presumably Master of the Choristers) in the 1530s after his departure from Oxford. Sometimes the guild patronage specifically supported a daily afternoon act of Marian devotion, which could attract substantial attendance from the citizenry after work. An early example is recorded around 1388 with the Mary guild at All Saints, Northampton, when the *Salve regina* and other antiphons were sung in polyphony and the organ was played.[74]

In wealthy Bristol, All Saints was a church which maintained a regular choir, judging by the substantial list of its music books made in 1524.[75] But the great majority of parishes, if they wanted to enhance festivals musically with polyphony, would have borrowed expert singers from a nearby monastery, cathedral or collegiate institution. Once into the sixteenth century, there is certainly evidence that, in the decades preceding the Reformation, a fair number of town churches were engaging small groups of singers for festivals, and some maintained song schools for boys. Although the evidence is very unevenly distributed, traces of such choral activity are widespread, including several churches in Devon and Cornwall, where inventories sometimes included books of polyphony.[76] Naturally enough, activity is most apparent in London parishes, where there was ready availability of singers from off-duty members of the Chapel Royal and other institutions. Many of the Gentlemen of the Chapel Royal were members of the City Fraternity of St Nicholas, a guild of parish clerks.[77] No doubt there was also an element of competition between some of around a hundred churches packed into the City. A few maintained permanent choirs, such as St Mary-at-Hill, where, from having two clerks and two choristers in 1491, it increased its forces to four men in 1522, founded a choir school in 1523 and had at least six regular clerks by 1530. It was here that Thomas Tallis was briefly a member in 1537–8.[78] Other City churches with regular choirs included St Dunstan-in-the-East, St Dunstan-in-the-West and St Michael's, Cornhill, while in Westminster, St Margaret's was able to avail itself of the choral staff of the Chapel Royal, the Lady Chapel choir of the Abbey and Wolsey's chapel.[79] There is the very occasional mention in the early sixteenth century of members of a parish congregation helping out with the singing in the chancel, as at Faversham and Goudhurst in Kent, where they presumably just assisted with the plainsong.[80] Such activity was evidently a result of local enthusiasm; how widespread it may have been remains unknown. The provision of rood lofts in parish churches, which became common from the fifteenth century, may have provided an additional place from which singing could on occasions take place, as well as somewhere to accommodate an organ.[81] The congregation itself played a purely passive role – they went along to 'hear' Mass – a phrase still commonly encountered in Roman Catholic circles up to the mid-twentieth century before the reforms of Vatican II.

It was in the course of the fifteenth century that music was to undergo major changes that brought us nearer to the modern idea of a cathedral choir. In the first half of the century polyphony gradually ceased to be reserved for major festivals, and became a more everyday experience, featuring especially in the Lady Mass and votive antiphon celebrated daily in the Lady Chapel; indeed, most of the surviving polyphony from the fifteenth century (admittedly a tiny fraction of what must have been composed) continued to be Marian in nature. At the same time composers were increasingly treating the Ordinary of the Mass as an artistic whole, basing the separate movements on a single melody (and not necessarily a plainsong one). Up to the middle of the century, the music was still designed for three or four solo adult voices. Such singers also engaged in improvised polyphony, adding an extra one or two lines against a plainsong melody, according to strict rules. One particular form of this, 'faburden' – basically creating a string of three-part first inversion chords – took popular hold in this century.[82] Again we do not know whether this was practised on a daily basis or reserved for special occasions. Likewise with improvising a single line over the plainsong, called 'descant', which was also amongst the skills which boy choristers were taught. It might be thought that only one at a time would have indulged in such improvisation. It would seem, however, that it was not unknown for more than one singer to improvise simultaneously, judging from the late sixteenth-century condemnation by Thomas Morley, when he noted:

> As for singing upon a plainsong, in times past, in England ... it has been the greatest part of the usual music that is sung in any church, which indeed causes me to marvel how men acquainted with music can delight to hear such confusion as of force must be among so many, singing extempore. But some have stood in an opinion, which to me seems not very probable, that men accustomed to descanting will sing together upon a plainsong without singing either false chords or forbidden descant, one to another, which till I see it, I will ever think impossible.[83]

It may well be that lay clerks found it irresistible to break out into descanting regardless of possible inharmonious clashes, and we must remember that, unless they were employed by a parish church, they were not (at least intentionally) singing to a congregation; all present would have notionally have been joining in the plainsong. A possible modern analogy might be congregational hymn singing, in which a few individuals contribute their own improvised harmonies.

From the middle of the fifteenth century two gradual and related developments were to radically transform the sound, and indeed the constitution of choirs. After centuries of participating only in the plainsong, boys began to contribute to the performance of written polyphony. This entailed an increase in the standard number of voice parts from three or four to five – from a typical compass of up to about two octaves for three men's voices alone to one of up to three octaves for both men and boys.[84] The result was a far richer sonority, which went hand in hand with a transition to genuine 'choral' performance, with the individual voice parts being no longer sung by one singer. One reason behind this may have been the increasing proportion of skilled laymen in choirs like the Chapel Royal, who would have been reluctant to leave the performance of polyphony to just three or four of their brethren. Changes in musical style also accompanied this shift; already in the first half of the fifteenth century, the often intricate rhythms of solo polyphony were giving way to simpler, smoother lines, which would prove more suited to, and capable of performance by, a larger body of singers. At the same time, we should not exaggerate the size of the forces employed in the early stages of choral polyphony. In the middle of the fifteenth century most choir members were only accustomed to plainsong, and many would initially probably have lacked the ability or inclination to sing polyphony. But as new appointments came to be made, skill in polyphony was increasingly stipulated as a requirement, as at Ripon Minster in 1503, where the statute declared that 'no vicar or deacon should be admitted thenceforth unless he could sing both plainsong and composed polyphony', and at York by 1507 all the existing vicars were expected to learn to sing polyphony.[85] Nevertheless, 'choral' performance in many cases would have meant no more than two singers to a part, at least as far as the men were concerned, and perhaps even with the boys, considering that, of the average 8–12 in a late fifteenth-century cathedral choir, some would be initially too inexperienced and some had other ceremonial duties to fulfil. Even music conceived as choral would no doubt often in practice have been performed one voice to a part, as indeed it continues to be sung today by some of our professional vocal ensembles.

The most famous surviving source of this new style of writing is the Eton Choirbook, compiled in the first years of the sixteenth century for use in the College chapel at the daily afternoon act of devotion to the Virgin, when the book was placed on a lectern in front of her image in the Ante-Chapel.[86] (As noted above, the college was founded just as much as a chantry as a charitable educational institution.) Its music, probably composed from c.1485 onwards, comprises for the most part settings of the Magnificat (the Song of Mary), and votive antiphons in her honour. It was in the second half of the fifteenth century that the Magnificat in the Vespers service began to become an important focus of polyphonic treatment.[87] The majority of pieces in the Eton book are in 4 to 6 parts, though there is one item in 9 parts, as well as a 13-part canonic setting of the Apostles Creed. Such variety of texture in fact came to characterize the music of the period, while music for men's voices alone also continued to be composed. The Eton book is large (23 x 17 inches), the music being laid out with the individual parts following one another on the two pages of an opening. Despite the generous size of the notation, twelve to fifteen singers at most would have been grouped round it. Although the choirbook indicates that certain sections were designed for single voice performance, what we know of the staffing of the chapel in the way of skilled polyphonic singers suggests that the 'choral' sections probably only involved doubling the number of voices (perhaps slightly more with the boys' parts), so that the sound was that of a 'consort' rather than a 'grand' choir, and this was to remain characteristic of cathedral-type choirs for many centuries to come.[88] Nevertheless, with its florid lines and still comparatively sophisticated rhythms, the Eton Choirbook clearly demonstrates the high degree of proficiency achieved by the choir in these early days of true 'choral' performance. This was evidently mirrored elsewhere, judging by the equally flamboyant music composed by Richard Davy about 1490 for the choir of Magdalen College, Oxford.[89] Similar music is found in another large volume, the Caius Choirbook, thought to have been intended for the collegiate chapel of St Stephen's, Westminster, and although no music book associated with the Chapel Royal has survived from this period, it too must have displayed similar skills.

A significant development that went with the involvement of the choristers in polyphony was the growing importance of the role of the Master of the Choristers. While the boys only sang plainsong, one of the vicars choral in a cathedral would have held the post, with the comparatively straightforward duties of teaching reading, plainsong, and, to the more proficient, improvised descant – and the same would have applied to the specially appointed Master of the Choristers of monastic Lady Chapel choirs. That the post might, nevertheless, be held by a distinguished musician is testified by the figure of the composer Leonel Power, who from 1438 to his death in 1445 was in charge of the boys of the Canterbury Lady Chapel choir, and who actually wrote a treatise on teaching the rudiments of music.[90] As the boys began to have to master new skills, it meant more time devoted to practice, and so potentially less to their general education – a problem which would continue to pose challenges for centuries to come. In the second half of the century, institutions increasingly appointed lay musicians to fulfil the more demanding task of teaching the boys their expanded role, and such musicians, who are often known to us also as composers, were liable to move from one establishment to another in search of better conditions. Lincoln and Salisbury in the 1460s were early examples of such specific appointments.[91] At Magdalen the post was designated *Informator choristarum*, a title which has been retained there to the present day. This role in pre-Reformation times was normally separate from that of organist, which was a minor post, held by one or more of the men of the choir. Although by the fifteenth century, at least one small organ was routinely found in cathedrals, monasteries, and a good number of parish churches, we know little about the use to which they were put. In part they may have served rather like bells, as producers of joyful 'noise' at appropriate moments, or to fill in moments of repose during ceremonial. The organ certainly came to be used *in alternation* with the plainsong or polyphony of the choir, particularly in longer items such as the Te Deum. Such 'versets' would commonly have been improvised (making use of the plainsong melody), but we have written examples from the sixteenth century. What the organ did *not* do was to accompany the choir – that function first appears in post-Reformation times towards the end of the sixteenth century. It is suggested that the organ may sometimes have doubled (or even substituted for) the plainsong, but there is no firm evidence for such a practice.[92]

An important and contentious question concerns the types of voices involved in the performance of polyphony. It has long been assumed that the typical three-part solo polyphony of the fourteenth and early fifteenth centuries, with a range of up to two octaves, was sung by two voices in the tenor/baritone range (sometimes labelled 'tenor' and 'contratenor') and an upper part (sometimes called 'triplex') sung by a falsetto alto. 'Contratenor' literally meant a part sung 'against' the tenor, and similar in range, while 'tenor' did not designate a specific voice range (as we now conceive it) but the part that, at least originally, 'held' the plainsong melody, usually in longer value notes than the added parts. In modern times we have become familiar with performances with an alto on top from recordings of groups such as the Hilliard Ensemble, who, rather exceptionally, did aim at a 'medieval' sound, however imperfect our knowledge of such a sound may be. The clefs on the page at first sight might suggest this voice arrangement, but in the medieval period there was no correlation between what appears to be, say, a 'middle C' and the pitch at which it was sung. In recent years the whole idea of the use of the falsetto alto voice at this period has been challenged, notably by Andrew Parrott, who argues that the falsetto alto did not appear in cathedral choirs until after the Restoration in the middle of the seventeenth century.[93] The detailed argument is too involved to be gone into here, but the outcome suggests that the three-part texture was intended for a high tenor, a low tenor/baritone (on the 'tenor' part) and a bass voice. The idea of the 'tenor' part being sung in the modern baritone range helps explain occasional contemporary references to the tenor voice being the 'usual' man's voice, and the admonition to avoid having too many 'tenors' in your choir. It corresponds very much to the situation today, where most men are by nature baritones, and have to decide whether to develop their upper or lower registers so as to fit into the standard tenor and bass roles of a modern choir. The three-voice polyphony with its compass of no more than two octaves would conveniently fit a modern pitch range from

G to g'. When boys were added in the second half of the fifteenth century, taking the most common five-part texture as an example, they would have supplied not just a top treble part, but the next highest part as well, labelled 'medius', or in English 'meane'. From a two-octave compass, the new sonority often expanded to three octaves – basically extended at the higher end, though the bass part may also have gone a little lower. This division of boys into 'trebles' and 'meanes' – that is into trebles and altos – was to last until the Reformation. The idea of boys with unchanged voices singing alto may not correspond to our usual image of a British cathedral choir, but later examples are to be found from the nineteenth century onwards. Both New College, Oxford and St John's College, Cambridge included boy altos around 1890.[94] Peterborough Cathedral out of necessity after the First World War relied totally on boys for the alto line in the 1920s, while the Roman Catholic choir of Westminster Cathedral, both during the First War and since the days of George Malcolm in the 1950s has used boys, plus sometimes one adult. A few boy altos were also to be found in the lists of nineteenth-century festival choruses. That some boys naturally sing in a lower range than others should not surprise us, and in Germanic lands the boy alto has been standard in all-male choirs since the Reformation, including at the Thomaskirche in Leipzig and the Kreuzkirche in Dresden, as well as in Catholic choirs like the Regensburger Domspatzen and the Vienna Boys Choir. And they naturally continue to flourish in Britain in all-boys' schools with a choral programme. In coming to his conclusions, Parrott believes that 'the very process of accommodating the modern "countertenor" to these repertories may have further distorted our perception of the music itself.'[95] Bound up with the question of voice types is that of the pitch at which the music was sung; a matter which has also generated much argument in the past half-century. Since, however, much of the evidence comes from the seventeenth century, discussion will be left until the next chapter, when the whole question of pitch can be brought into focus.

The Final Decades of the Pre-Reformation Choir

The highest point of development of the medieval choir was reached by the opening of the sixteenth century. It was also the period at which the sheer quantity of liturgical celebration, particularly in cathedrals, was astonishing. In addition to the normal daily Offices and Masses, the late fifteenth century also saw the rise of a special devotion to Jesus, with a Jesus Mass being celebrated in the nave or in a special Jesus Chapel, usually on Fridays. At Lincoln, for example, it has been calculated that there were 38 daily Masses in 1506, and 44 in 1531.[96] Of course, most of the Masses were in no sense choral, but private chantry ones, celebrated by a priest alone or with the assistance of a server (perhaps a boy). They did, however, frequently provide opportunity for vicars choral in full priestly orders to supplement their incomes by also acting as chantry priests – and their Masses were held early in the morning, before the important choral Office of Matins. Collegiate institutions would have seen far less activity, though considerably more than found in any present-day cathedral or church of whatever denomination. It has been estimated that there might have been 200 choirs capable of singing polyphony in secular institutions (cathedrals, colleges, household chapels and parishes), and that over 50 monasteries (including monastic cathedrals) would have had professional musicians singing polyphony by the 1530s.[97]

Choirs clearly must have varied widely in their abilities, and probably only a few were equal to the demands of the sort of music found in the Eton Choirbook. Still, the best choirs were the object of admiration by foreign visitors, as in the case of the reception of Venetian ambassadors at Henry VIII's court in 1515, when it was reported that 'High Mass was sung by the King's choristers, whose voices are more divine than human; they did not sing, they rejoiced [*non cantavano ma giubilavano*]; and as to the counter-bass voices [i.e. low basses], they probably have not their equal in the world'.[98] The greater monasteries were also increasingly emulating the secular cathedrals chorally, even to the extent that, contrary to established custom, some of them allowed boys as well as professional lay singers into the monks' quire on greater feasts, as was the case in Winchester at the end of the fifteenth century.[99] The monks, used to hearing full five-part polyphony of their Lady Chapel choirs, may have felt that festal High Mass was lacking musically by comparison.

Yet the nature of the music did not meet with universal approval. The Dutch humanist scholar Desiderius Erasmus was a strong critic of over-elaborate music, whether plainsong or polyphony, when it prevented the words from being clearly heard. He visited England five times between 1499 and 1517, and was particularly harsh on the English monasteries, where 'they think God is pleased with ornamental neighings and agile throats'.[100] He was certainly not alone in demanding reform of the monasteries; they were becoming generally unpopular through abuse of their wealth and privilege, leading even the profligate Cardinal Wolsey to seek change. Although Erasmus's musical strictures were found within his general condemnation of contemporary monastic culture, he would certainly have extended his objections to the musical activities of other ecclesiastical bodies. His opinions were undoubtedly shared by some within the English church long before Reformation ideas flowed in from the continent, and indeed a trend can be discerned in the music of the 1520s and 1530s towards a less luxuriant manner, influenced in part by the new imitative and more syllabic style which characterized continental music of the Josquin des Prez generation from the 1490s onwards. The Masses composed by John Taverner for Cardinal College in the late 1520s are less florid than the music of the Eton Choirbook of thirty years previously. We may still be a long way from the radically simplified music of the early Reformation, but the direction of travel can already be discerned. The music sung by British choirs at this time appears to have been wholly native in origin, in so far as we can assess from the very few surviving musical sources. Unlike earlier centuries, when sources like the Old Hall manuscript included much music from abroad (especially France), there was apparently no importation of the latest music by composers like Josquin and Binchois into the British choral repertoire.

One practical change that occurred in the early decades of the sixteenth century was a gradual move away from performing from a large choirbook displaying all the parts, to the use of individual partbooks, each containing only the music for a particular voice – separate parts might also be written on parchment scrolls in the case of single items. This meant that instead of moving to sing polyphonic items from a centrally placed lectern, the singers could now remain in the choirstalls. The innovation was not a specifically British one – some of the very earliest printed polyphony issued in Italy by Ottoviano Petrucci in the first years of the century took the form of partbooks. It was to be the way cathedral choirs would sing for at least the next 350 years – only in the middle of the nineteenth century did they routinely start singing from scores. The six so-called Forrest-Heyther partbooks, dating from John Taverner's years at Cardinal College in the 1520s, are one of the earliest sets to survive, and are distinguished by what are evidently caricatures of the composer at the head of his *Missa Gloria tibi Trinitas* (Figure 2).[101] Such early sets as survive (admittedly very few) contain only a single book for each voice (indicated also by contemporary inventories of choir books) and suggest that for at least most of the sixteenth century only one side of the choir was involved in singing from them – sets for both cantoris and decani are first traceable in the early seventeenth century. Well-endowed choirs, like the Chapel Royal, are likely to have been in the vanguard of the whole choir participating when singing from the choirstalls. Having just one side of the choir singing polyphony may mirror the early common practice that the two sides in the quire exchanged on a weekly basis the duties of supplying people to undertake the monotoned parts of services (including the lessons) from one side and singing the more demanding solo chants on the other.[102]

If this chapter has focussed almost entirely on England, this reflects the lack of information we have on choral activity elsewhere. We do know that nine Scottish cathedrals followed England in adopting the Sarum Use,[103] and the copying of an important source of early polyphony at St Andrews

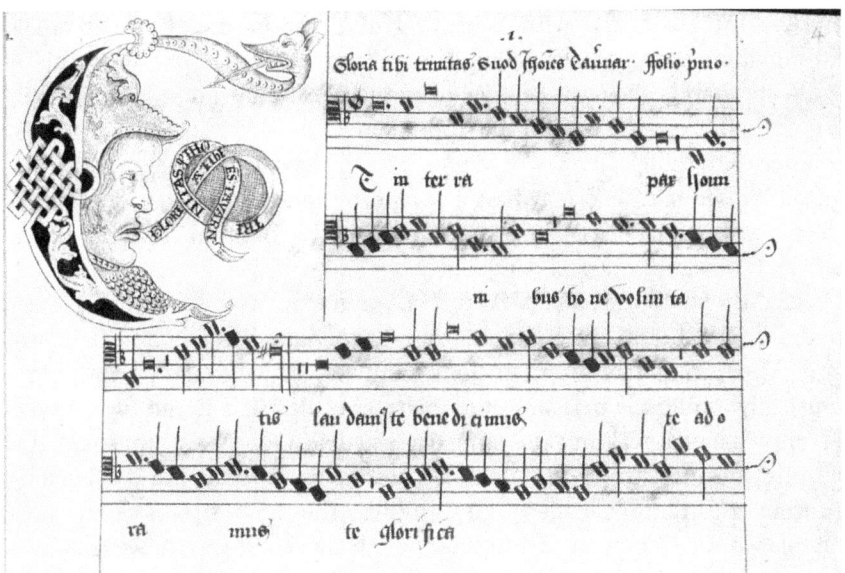

Figure 2   John Taverner: Mass *Gloria tibi Trinitas*, contratenor part, with a caricature of the composer at the head; Oxford, Bodleian Library, MS Mus. Sch. E. 378, fol. 4.

Cathedral Priory, probably in the 1230s, indicates at least an interest in such music there. How much they actually performed of what is mostly French repertoire is an open question, although the manuscript also contains items of apparently more local origin.[104] A Scottish Chapel Royal was only founded at Stirling by James IV in 1501, with sixteen canons and six boys, and was apparently most active in its first two decades of existence.[105] It must, however, have achieved considerable competence if, as generally accepted, the elaborate works of the Scottish composer Robert Carver were written for it. In the mid-sixteenth century too, there was still choral activity at St Andrews, where one of the canons, David Peebles, was well known as a composer. We are even more ignorant about Welsh choralism, and we simply don't have information on how far its cathedrals and abbeys went beyond plainsong.[106] This is also largely also true of Ireland, although we know the monastic cathedral of Christ Church, Dublin introduced four boys to sing in its Lady Chapel in 1480.[107] A similar lack of knowledge applies to music in nunneries, where the few written references come from the fifteenth and sixteenth centuries. The liturgical routine of Office and Mass followed that of the male monasteries, with a cantor directing the plainsong and singing or allotting to others the solo chanting, and all novices were expected to learn to sing competently. Apart from two three-voice Marian antiphons written in a fourteenth-century non-musical manuscript associated with Wherwell nunnery in Hampshire, there is little evidence of nuns enriching their liturgy with polyphony.[108] This is understandable, given the relative paucity of girls' education (despite their largely being recruited from the upper classes) and the small size of most nunneries,[109] though there would undoubtedly have been cases of musically gifted individuals, who may have been permitted to improvise descant on the plainsong. The overall impression is that nuns found spiritual fulfilment without the aid of musical complexity.

Such then was the state of British choral music on the eve of the Reformation. The choirs, estimated at around 250, varied tremendously in size and constitution, from three or four men with or without a few boys in a musically ambitious parish, to the thirty-two men and ten to twelve boys of the Chapel Royal and the similarly-sized St George's, Windsor.[110] But despite the increase in numbers of choirs singing polyphony, plainsong continued to dominate the liturgy, and was the only form of music most people would ever encounter in their parish church. It was, however, also a period which saw the height of popular devotion in the form of pilgrimages to sites of saintly relics, and even in monastic churches, lay attendance was possible at Lady and Jesus Masses, which were held in areas open to the public. There the devout may have heard choral polyphony, as too may have ordinary parishioners whose churches managed to enhance at least major festivals by hiring singers, with the inhabitants of London understandably being most likely to experience such opportunities.

Whatever perturbation was taking place in royal circles from Henry VIII's marital problems and his need for money to finance military campaigns, in the choral world there would have been little premonition in the 1520s of the revolution to come – the decade in which Cardinal Wolsey had the confidence to create two new collegiate institutions at Cardinal College, Oxford and St Mary's College, Ipswich. The singers could scarcely have suspected that their familiar world was about to be dramatically shattered.

Chapter 2
From Reformation to Civil War

When Henry VIII removed the English Church from the authority of the pope in 1534 as a result of the latter's refusal to grant annulment of Henry's marriage to Catherine of Aragon, it was to prove the catalyst for events which were to bring about profound changes for the church's music and musicians. Although the theological repercussions of the Reformation set in motion by Martin Luther in 1517 soon found discussion and support in England, it was firmly repressed and its sympathisers persecuted, until Henry's break from Rome enabled English reformers to embolden themselves. For choirs, the first realization that their traditional life was under threat came with the dissolution of the monasteries between 1536 and 1540. For the most part they were no longer in the vanguard of choral life, but the greater monastic houses were still significant centres of choral activity, with perhaps as many as fifty having choirs involving the employment of boys and lay adults.[1] Although the monks were pensioned off and many monastic buildings were destroyed, not all their musical bodies were disbanded. The eight old monastic cathedrals remained, transformed into secular establishments headed by a dean and chapter – many of the posts being occupied by former monks – with a choir of boys, minor canons and lay clerks, doubtless formed in part from the previous Lady Chapel choirs, but now regularly occupying the stalls of the quire. Such was the transformation effected at Canterbury, Carlisle, Durham, Ely, Norwich, Rochester, Winchester and Worcester. But Henry's reorganisation did not stop there, for, in addition, five former monastic churches which had never been cathedrals, were given that status as mother churches of the newly created dioceses of Bristol, Chester, Gloucester, Oxford and Peterborough. Westminster Abbey was also briefly made London's second cathedral at this time, but, after reverting to an abbey under Mary Tudor, in 1560 it was turned into a 'royal peculiar', which it remains to the present day.

The thirteen old and new monastic cathedrals were collectively known as cathedrals of the New Foundation to distinguish them from the ten Old Foundation secular institutions like Hereford, Lincoln and Salisbury. The size of the choral establishment laid down in the new statutes varied but was fairly modest compared to the numbers of vicars choral in most of the Old Foundation cathedrals, even if the latter commonly fell short of their statutory numbers. Roughly equal numbers of minor canons (i.e. ordained clergy, equivalent to those ordained vicars choral of the Old Foundations) and lay clerks were prescribed; these ranged from small establishments of six of each at Bristol, Chester and Gloucester, or eight minor canons and four lay clerks at Carlisle, to the largest complements at Winchester (twelve of each) and Canterbury (fourteen minor canons and twelve lay clerks); six to ten boys was the norm.[2] Although lay clerks had primary responsibility for the singing, the minor canons were expected to join in the chanting while the traditional liturgy survived.[3] The comparatively large number of clergy reflects the fact that in the early 1540s the full traditional round of daily services (including chantry Masses) with all their ritual was still being observed. That change was set to continue soon became evident, with the Archbishop of Canterbury, Thomas Cranmer, prominent among the reformers. His views on music are largely unknown, but he evidently disliked long-winded melismatic chant, and wished to see 'for every syllable a note'.[4] As early as 1536, copies of the Bible in Latin and English were ordered to be set up in every church, so that the people could read it for themselves. It was one step from this to an order in 1543 that the lessons at Matins and Evensong (already a commonly used term for Vespers before the Reformation) were to be read in English, followed in 1544 by the publication of an English translation of the Litany. The King himself remained quite traditional in liturgical matters, but with his death in 1547 and the accession of the 9-year-old Edward VI (the country being governed by a regency council), dramatic change took place. 1548 saw the abolition of all chantries,[5] along with most collegiate churches (whose chief function was to support them) – prayers for the dead were out, and chantry income was largely sequestered by the crown. Few collegiate churches actually had sizable choirs, but those which did included Beverley, Fotheringhay, Ottery St Mary, Ripon, Tattershall, St Mary's, Warwick and St Stephen's, Westminster, most of which became ordinary parish churches.[6] The collegiate bodies of Oxford and Cambridge, however, were spared, thanks to their primary educational function; so too were their choral establishments, although at Cambridge, the choir of King's was disbanded in 1549, and revived only in 1553 after Mary had come to the throne. More significant for musicians was the loss of chantries in cathedrals, for those vicars choral in priestly orders relied on chantry duties to supplement their income. All this occurred just at the time when priests were allowed to marry, with the additional financial responsibilities that could bring.

In 1548 whole services in English were permitted, after a period which had witnessed them held in odd mixtures of Latin and English.[7] This was followed in 1549 by the publication of Book of Common Prayer, in the compilation of which Cranmer played a leading role, and use of which was made compulsory throughout the country. The Latin Mass disappeared, transformed into English as 'The Supper of the Lord and the Holy Communion, commonly called the Mass', the latter reference being omitted in the ensuing more Protestant 1552 edition. The eight daily Offices were reduced to two, with a new form of Matins constructed from the old Matins, Prime and Lauds, and Evensong, combining elements of Vespers and Compline. In cathedrals, Matins was generally held at 9 or 10 a.m. and Evensong at 3 or 4 p.m. (sometimes varying with the season), times which would remain fundamentally unchanged until the twentieth century.[8] They continued to be constituted of psalms, lessons and prayers, together with hymns like the Te Deum and Magnificat, which came to be termed 'canticles'. That other ingredient of the daily Offices rendered chorally, the anthem, receives no mention in the 1549 Prayer Book or its sixteenth-century successors. Only with the post-Restoration 1662 edition is it granted an official place in the liturgy. Yet it is clear from the earliest surviving set of partbooks with music for the English liturgy, that anthems did find a place in the Offices from the outset. The so-called 'Wanley partbooks', dating from around 1548–50, contain seventeen works actually designated as 'antem', as well as similar items without any appellation.[9] The term derives from the older 'antiphon' (Latin '*antiphona*'), and it seems fairly certain that, just like the pre-Reformation 'votive antiphons', they were added on at the end of Matins and Evensong, or possibly used as introits at the beginning of services. It is in the Wanley manuscripts that we see the birth of the English anthem, including one work still very much in the repertoire today, Thomas Tallis's 'If ye love me'. Music in four parts predominates, although there are some items in three and five parts; most pieces are for men's voices, but a number also involve boys. It is thought the set was probably compiled for a London parish church rather than a cathedral, but in view of the large quantity of music it contains (129 pieces), clearly a parish which had been accustomed to singing polyphony regularly (rather than just at festivals), which had a permanent contingent of singing men, and the ability to call upon boys from time to time – St Mary-at-Hill is a likely candidate. Of course, the presence of 129 pieces in these partbooks does not mean that they were all sung by the choir to which they belonged; most were presumably copied from other sources to provide a substantial repertoire from which to choose appropriate items, just as a modern choir would sing only a selection of items contained in an anthem anthology. In addition to anthems, the Wanley books contain several canticle settings and no fewer than ten complete settings for Holy Communion (i.e. those items which constituted the Ordinary of the Mass). This is unsurprising, since at this stage of the Reformation, the Mass in its English transformation was still the main focus of liturgical life, and theological arguments over its nature produced much controversy among the reformers.

The Wanley books are unfortunately one of the very few surviving sources from the early Reformation years, and by far the largest.[10] But they demonstrate that, in London at least, composers in the late 1540s were quickly beginning to fulfil the need for a new repertoire in English, and taking to heart the insistence that there should be 'a plain and distinct note for every syllable one', as laid down in early injunctions issued to cathedrals.[11] In a few cases, existing Latin works were adapted to English texts, as happened with two Taverner Masses in the Wanley books, but this does not appear to have been a particularly common practice, and much of the Latin repertoire would in any case have been considered too florid to meet the new precept. Today we associate early attempts at providing simple music for the Reformed church primarily with the work of John Marbeck, who in 1550 published *The Booke of Common Praier Noted*, containing note-against-note monophonic settings of the canticles and the Ordinary of the Communion, which was evidently issued with at least semi-official approval. The compilers of the 1549 book still foresaw choral elements being retained in the Communion service in churches where it was usual, for 'The clearkes shall sing' is a direction before all five items of the Ordinary. Marbeck's book can only have seen a brief period of use, since no new edition was produced to bring it into line with the 1552 Prayer Book, and it has been suggested that it may have failed to gain popularity owing to its considerable melodic deviance from the style of traditional plainsong.[12] Marbeck's music, however, was only intended to be sung by choirs – it was not until its revival in the nineteenth century that it began to be considered suitable for congregational participation, and its Communion setting then gained a popularity which lasted until the liturgical reforms of the late twentieth century, and still finds a place in those churches which retain the traditional language texts.[13]

The Return of Catholicism under Queen Mary

The Edwardian years were brief – Edward VI died as a boy of 15 in 1553, with the country still under a regency council. During this time Thomas Cranmer moved the Reformation in the more radical Protestant direction promoted by the likes of John Calvin and Henry Bullinger rather than that of Martin Luther, a position reflected in the 1552 edition of the Prayer Book.[14]

In the revised Communion service, there is no longer any reference to clerks singing. Edward VI, despite his youth, was firmly behind the reformers. The more radical of them had no love of cathedrals and their liturgical life, and if Edward VI had lived longer, they may well have disappeared as worshipping entities, as they did in Calvin's Geneva, and were to in Scotland, where John Knox's Calvinism eventually won the day. The accession of the Catholic Mary Tudor, following the failure of the scheme to secure the throne for the Protestant Jane Grey, has therefore come to be seen as an important factor in 'saving' the cathedral choral tradition for posterity.[15]

Under Mary, England was returned to the Catholic fold, with Archbishop Cranmer imprisoned and eventually burnt at the stake. For choirs, it meant the restoration of the Latin liturgy and ceremonial. Although the old Latin service books had been ordered to be destroyed in December 1549, the vicars at Canterbury, and no doubt elsewhere, had secreted books away, and were able to bring them out again, while plenty of new copying activity was also needed. Yet in those uncertain times, it is not hard to imagine that cathedral worship was only a pale reflection of that of twenty years earlier. Amongst the problems encountered must have been the fact that only the older boys in the choir would have had any acquaintance with the old Sarum liturgy. Apart from anything else, the Church was in a parlous financial situation, having been stripped of its luxuriant income and so many of its physical assets by the crown under Henry VIII and Edward VI. Mary was in no position to set about reviving chantries, and though favouring monasticism, she succeeded in restoring only Westminster as an abbey in 1556.[16] Enthusiasm for the return of Catholicism would have varied widely; it was evidently warmly welcomed in the more conservative areas such as Lincolnshire and the West Country, which had shown most resistance to the Reformation, while meeting very mixed reaction elsewhere, particularly in urban areas. Although priests refusing to accept the change were dismissed, and many leading reformers sought refuge on the continent, lay choir personnel appear to have been relatively unaffected. This was certainly true of the Chapel Royal, where both Catholic and Protestant adherents among the Gentlemen remained in post, the Protestant priests having been replaced.[17] It is difficult to ascertain just how much new Latin music was composed during Mary's reign, but works by William Mundy, John Sheppard and Thomas Tallis can be assigned to these five brief years, which also naturally saw the return of music in honour of the Virgin Mary, after Lady Mass had been abolished in 1547 and all statues of her ordered to be removed from churches in 1550.

Enter the Elizabethan Era

Mary's reign was to prove even shorter than Edward VI's, and on her death in 1558, her half-sister, Elizabeth, immediately reinstated the Protestant church of Edward VI, but with significant changes of direction, some of which had vital importance for the future of church music. With the Church still very split between radical and the more traditionally minded reformers, Elizabeth sought a careful middle path, helped by her being able to appoint the moderate Matthew Parker as Archbishop of Canterbury. A new edition of the Prayer Book was published in 1559, which closely followed the more radical one of 1552, but Elizabeth issued a series of Injunctions to each cathedral. Here her own preferences were made clear; as if to make up for the lack of any reference to music in the Prayer Book, not only did she demand that existing choirs should be maintained, but she stipulated that a 'modest and distinct song' be permitted, and that 'for the comforting of such that delight in music' there might be 'an hymn or suchlike song, to the praise of Almighty God, in the best sort of melody and music that may be conveniently devised' at the beginning or end of Matins and Evensong.[18] Thus, thanks to Mary's rescuing choirs from the threat of dissolution, Elizabeth was now able to entrench their position within the reformed church. Dissention between the traditionalists and Puritans (as the radical reformers came to be known), however, continued in many cathedrals, and a Puritan bishop or dean could impose severe restrictions on the music of his cathedral, as did Bishop Robert Horne at Winchester in 1571, when he ordered

> that in the quire no note shall be used in song that shall drown any word or syllable, or draw out in length or shorten any word or syllable, otherwise than by the nature of the word it is pronounced in common speech, whereby the sentence cannot be well perceived by the hearers. And also the often reports or repeating of notes with words or sentences whereby the sense may be hindered in the hearer shall not be used.[19]

Doubtless some authorities would have liked to disband their choirs entirely, but this would have required a change of the statutes, to which the Queen would never have agreed, but it did mean that some choirs must have felt that they were only there on sufferance.

How did the adult members of choirs cope with the uncertain and ever-changing situation in which they found themselves over the middle years of the century? We have no first-hand accounts of their experiences, but it is not hard to imagine how they may have reacted. A diversity of theological opinion within them is only to be expected. Some eagerly embraced the reformers' cause, notably John Marbeck, who, when organist at Windsor, was arrested in 1543 for heresy and condemned to death, only to be pardoned by Henry VIII and restored to office. In later life he published a number of virulent anti-papist tracts. Most, however, would seem to have gone along with the prevailing winds – as did most parochial clergy. Christopher Tye, for example, Master of the Choristers at Ely from 1541 and later a member of the Chapel Royal, composed Latin church music during Henry's reign, then evidently showed enthusiasm for the Protestant cause and contributed to the earliest English repertoire, only for him to revert to Latin composition during Marian times, and then finally to become an Anglican priest in the early Elizabethan years. Some, like Byrd, personally remained faithful to Roman Catholicism, while being amenable to serving the needs of the reformed church.

On the matter of routine, the consolidation of the daily Offices to Matins and Evensong along with a drastic reduction in the number of Masses, was probably welcome to many, though it meant that singing in cathedrals became an essentially part-time occupation, and any remnant of the monastic ideal of a virtually continuous cycle of prayer finally disappeared. Even more than previously, lay clerks had to find additional employment to supplement their choir income, a situation which has naturally continued to be the case. Many were tradesmen, and some of these occupations drew disapproval from ecclesiastical authority – innkeeping in particular was forbidden – but recruiting lay clerks was often a problem for cathedrals, and in many cases they had to turn a blind eye. It was exacerbated by the considerable inflation which affected the second half of the sixteenth century, which the authorities, with their reliance on income from land, were unable to relieve by the way of increased remuneration.

Musically, the most obvious change for choirmen must have been the complete disappearance of their traditional elaborate plainsong, much of it firmly ingrained in the minds of the older men. A largely sung liturgy was being replaced by one in which the spoken word came to the fore. It is uncertain just how much of the new services were sung, though intoning of prayers (including the opening General Confession and Lord's Prayer at Matins and Evensong) was certainly general practice judged by later descriptions.[20] But the sound of plainsong did not vanish completely, for it appears that the psalms, in Coverdale's English translation, continued to be chanted in unison to the old plainsong psalm tones, out of which in the course of the seventeenth century would emerge that most distinctive form of the British choral tradition, the harmonised Anglican chant. As for the new English canticles – of which the Te Deum, Benedictus, Magnificat,

Nunc Dimittis were the most important – they too were often chanted to simple tones. With the lack of surviving contemporary musical sources outside London, it is impossible to say how much compositional activity went on in provincial cathedrals at this time, although the music of London musicians would have eventually percolated through to them, especially those in the southern part of the country which had most personal contacts with members of the Chapel Royal.

Developments must have proceeded in a disparate manner at local level, and in the early years especially, a great variety of practice would have been found between cathedrals, both in the quantity and elaborateness of their music, but a distinctive repertoire did gradually evolve. On most days the Preces and Responses ('O Lord, open thou our lips' etc.) tended to be just monotoned, but for festal days composers eventually began to produce harmonised versions, such as those of Tallis and Byrd, to which were often attached special settings of the 'proper' psalms for the feast day – either in simple chanting style or in more anthem-like music.[21] Sundays would probably have had more 'choral' music than weekdays, which in many places would have very 'plain', and perhaps not until the end of the sixteenth century would canticle settings begin to be sung regularly in provincial cathedrals on weekdays,[22] although the idea of composers writing 'paired' settings – Te Deum and Benedictus (or Jubilate), Magnificat (or Cantate Domino) and Nunc Dimttis (or Deus Misereatur) – can be found from the earliest years. The early continuing importance of Holy Communion, as reflected in the ten settings in the Wanley books, was quickly to disappear. From the pre-Reformation Mass being a daily occurrence, it soon became usual for Holy Communion to have only a Sunday weekly celebration, with this declining further over the following decades, when even in cathedrals a full celebration was commonly held only monthly. In its place the standard Sunday morning service came to consist of Matins followed by the Litany and the first part only of the Communion service (including a sermon) – the so-called Ante-Communion. The only choral components of the latter were the Kyrie and the Nicene Creed, to which, however, the Sanctus (properly belonging in the second part of the service) came to be added after the Litany as a sort of introduction to the Ante-Communion. This composite form of Sunday morning service was to remain standard throughout the Church of England until the gradual regular restoration of complete Holy Communion in the aftermath of the Oxford Movement in the nineteenth century. The Litany, perhaps somewhat surprisingly, continued to have a prominent part in weekly worship, for it was sung regularly not only on Sundays, but also after Matins on Wednesdays and Fridays; today it has virtually disappeared from the liturgical round of most cathedrals (at least musically), retained only on occasions like Good Friday.

How did the Chapel Royal fare through the Reformation years? In many aspects it was relatively unchanged. Its choral personnel remained at about twenty-four Gentlemen and twelve boys, and the men were paid four times as much as even the best-paid cathedral lay clerk.[23] With so many previous additional perks continuing, it is hardly surprising that it commanded the cream of the country's musical talent. Posts became so sought after that there developed a category of additional unpaid 'Gentlemen Extraordinary', who paid an admission fee for the privilege, in the hope of eventually obtaining a regular full place. It was a system which at times could lead to abuse, for such extras did not have to undergo the usual formal examination for entry, and unsuitable men occasionally found their way into the ranks.[24] It would be surprising to find such a body leading a music revolution which radically reduced their contribution to worship, but in 1548 at the start of Edward VI's reign, willingly or not, they were among the first to experiment with services in English, and were cited as an example for the universities of Oxford and Cambridge to follow before the publication of the Prayer Book.[25] With many of the leading composers among their number, including Tallis and John Sheppard, there would have been no problem in quickly providing musical settings for the new liturgy. The return to a Catholic Chapel Royal under Queen Mary probably caused little commotion – it may be doubted that the Chapel's old music books really were destroyed as an edict of 1549 had demanded, but even if they had been, enough music would have been privately owned by its members to supply any immediate need. New Masses were composed, but, although devotion to the Virgin Mary was revived, rather than adding substantially to the repertoire of votive antiphons in her honour, the Marian years saw more the cultivation of Latin motets on psalm texts.

For the survival of English choral music at this time, Elizabeth's own enthusiasm for music was to prove of critical importance. Not only did she tolerate the Catholics Thomas Tallis and William Byrd as members of the Chapel Royal, but she actively patronized them when she granted them a monopoly over the printing of music and music paper in 1575, which they duly acknowledged in dedicating to her their joint book of motets, *Cantiones sacrae*, published in the same year.[26] Elizabeth had something of the traditionalist attitude of her father when it came to ceremony in worship, and much to the disapproval of Puritan clerics, richly embroidered eucharistic vestments, a crucifix and candles on the altar continued to feature in the Chapel. Regardless of her personal preferences, it is understandable that Chapel Royal worship should have retained a degree of show. Ceremonial was still all-important at court, of which the Chapel Royal was an essential component. Its services may not have been open to the public, but they were witnessed by distinguished foreign visitors and ambassadors, and therefore, an austerely conducted Chapel was unthinkable, and just as in the early sixteenth century, visitors continued to be impressed by what they heard and saw.[27] Nothing further from a typical English cathedral service of the time can be imagined.

The 1549 Act of Uniformity allowed Latin to continue to be used for Matins, Evensong and the Litany in the two universities, partly to encourage continuing facility in the language, and early in Elizabeth's reign a Latin translation of the Prayer Book was published in 1560, with Winchester and Eton colleges also being permitted to use it.[28] How far use was made of this licence is unknown – probably little in the universities, where theological controversies remained strong. Latin sacred music continued to be composed in Elizabethan times, notably by Tallis, Byrd, Morley and Robert White, but very little of it was for liturgical use. Rather, it would have been intended for private devotional or recreational purposes, particularly amongst those who remained Catholics. In such circumstances it would have been sung, not by a formal choir, but by a small domestic group, probably one to a part, and in which female voices could have been involved. In a few cases English texts were adapted to these Latin works and then found their way into cathedral repertoires, but in general the English and Latin repertoires remained apart, and it would be the twentieth century before Latin was sung again in Anglican cathedrals. The Latin Mass continued to be celebrated clandestinely by important Catholic households – this was the age of priest-holes – and it is for one such, the Petre family of Ingatestone Hall, that Byrd principally composed his three Masses and the motets for the Propers of the Mass, published in his two books of *Gradualia* (1605 and 1607). In such cases the 'choir' is again likely to have been one to a part. Byrd's adherence to the Catholic faith evidently grew stronger in old age, especially after the increased persecution of Catholics following the Jesuit plots of the 1570s, which culminated in the execution of Edmund Campion, a Jesuit convert, in 1581. Byrd himself seemed at times to be sailing close to the wind in his association with Jesuits, and it is a measure of how strongly he was protected by the Queen, that he remained immune from prosecution.

Latin motets may possibly have been heard on occasions in the Chapel Royal,[29] given that it was one of the many languages in which the Queen herself was fluent. But it is a Latin work not composed for the Chapel, but almost certainly first performed by its members, that represents one of the most extraordinary musical monuments of the Elizabethan era. This is Tallis's 40-part motet, 'Spem in alium'. That number of voices had no precedent in English choral music, and its composition was apparently the result of a challenge by the Duke of Norfolk for an English composer to equal the achievement of the Italian Alessandro Striggio, who had visited England in 1567, and astonished people with his 40-part motet, 'Ecce beatam Lucem'. Tallis took up the challenge, not only equalling, but easily surpassing in quality the Italian's offering. 'Spem in alium' was probably first performed around 1569, either (as a 1611 account claims) in the long gallery at Arundel House – the London home of the Duke's father-in-law, the Earl of Arundel – or, as John Milsom has suggested, at the Earl's country residence, Nonesuch Palace. The banqueting hall of the latter was octagonal with first-floor balconies, so the work – for eight five-part choirs – could have been performed in the round, with the audience in the middle.[30] Perhaps it had performances at both venues. It was presumably sung one voice to a part, and although the Earl had his own substantial musical establishment, Tallis's own Chapel Royal must have been heavily involved. For such an occasion we might imagine that Tallis himself perhaps copied out the individual parts to ensure correctness, particularly important as regards the rests in this work! We would love to know other details of how it was performed – what sort of direction was employed to keep the singers together, or how much rehearsal was necessary before they successfully negotiated its complexities and all the singers arrived at the end together. It was a unique experiment, which had no imitators. It was, however, revived twice in the early seventeenth century, when it was sung at the investiture as Prince of Wales of Prince Henry in 1610, and, following his early death in 1612, at that of his brother Charles in 1616. On these occasions the work was given with an appropriate text in English, 'Sing and glorify heaven's high majesty'. It is a score with this text that is the earliest surviving source of the work,[31] and interestingly includes a supporting organ part. Was it performed this way (and might the original performance also have had such support), or was it merely to aid rehearsing individual parts? After 1616 the work disappeared from the repertoire, though it was known by repute in the eighteenth century, including to the music historians Charles Burney and Sir John Hawkins.[32] Its subsequent revival from the nineteenth century onwards will be discussed later.

Outside the Capital

The Elizabethan and early Jacobean period is often characterized as a 'golden age' of English music. Few would dispute this claim as far as musical composition is concerned – not only for its sacred works, but also in the fields of the madrigal, lute song, keyboard music and other genres. But when it came to the general state of church music performance, then, apart from the Chapel Royal, where excellence was only to be expected, in the country at large standards were anything but satisfactory. The combination of substantial inflation, the relegation of lay clerks to part-time work, the difficulty in filling vacancies, and the continuing attacks on cathedral music from Puritans, can only have produced low morale in most establishments. Adverse reports on conditions are readily encountered. At Salisbury, one of the better-endowed cathedrals, about 1602 the Master of the Choristers, John Bartlett, was accused by the dean and chapter:

> That notwithstanding your office and duetie and also your protestacions and promises made at your admission you have not well and sufficiently taught and instructed the sayde choristers for the service and singing in the church neither have they by nor are they at this present able (by reason of their want of knowlege and practise in the Church songes and musicke) to sing suerly and perfectly but doe often misse and faile and are out in their singing to the great shame of the teacher and disgrace and discredit of so eminent a Church to which so many strangers doe repaire.[33]

This indicates, incidentally, that cathedrals attracted congregations from outside, though most people were drawn there not for the music, but to hear sermons, which featured so prominently in the reformed church, and where the cathedrals offered better fare than most parish priests could manage. Salisbury seems to have suffered particularly from conflicts of personnel during this period. It was here that John Farrant the elder was Master of the Choristers from 1571, and later organist. His quarrelsome nature eventually led to his threatening the dean with a knife. On dismissal in 1592, he was promptly appointed Master of the Choristers at Hereford, where, however, his behaviour did not improve, for in February 1593 he was fined by his fellow vicars choral because 'he did abuse Sir Wm. Vicary ... with filthy unhonest and contumelious words which are not to be named,'[34] and he resigned at the end of that year. At Southwell in 1594, John Beeston, Master of the Choristers, was ordered 'that hee do from henceforth keape in better order and teach the instructe the choristers in his charge more diligently then he hath done upon paine to bee removed from the charge of them.'[35]

Thomas Morley, who had been organist at Norwich and St Paul's before becoming a Gentleman of the Chapel Royal, complained in *A Plaine and Easie Introduction to Practicall Musicke* (1597) that all singers cared for was to 'cry louder in the choir than their fellows', instead of studying 'how to vowel and sing clean, expressing their words with devotion and passion', and that 'having obtained the living which they sought for, they have little or no care at all, either of their own credit, or well-discharging that duty whereby they have their maintenance.'³⁶ The Reformation did little to change the various vices for which they had been reprimanded in earlier times. The old habits of drunkenness, absenteeism and adultery were all in evidence throughout the Elizabethan and Jacobean periods, and complaints seem to have been especially numerous over this time. Such was exemplified by Thomas Weelkes, one of the most distinguished musicians working outside London. After four years as organist of Winchester College (1598–1602), he moved to Chichester Cathedral, where his early years were probably fairly blameless and productive, and, assuming his service settings were composed at this time, he had a competent choir, including a good treble line. But from 1609 Weelkes was giving trouble to the authorities, at first mainly through absence. In 1617 the bishop ordered the dean and chapter to dismiss him as organist, but he kept his singing place – it was usual for organists to also hold a lay clerk's post as a means of increasing their income. But in 1619 at the bishop's visitation (a regular inquiry by bishops into the state of their cathedrals), Weelkes's colleagues complained that

> Thomas Weelkes, who divers times and very often comes so disguised either from the tavern or alehouse into the choir as is much to be lamented, for in these humours he will both curse and swear most dreadfully, and so profane the service of God (and especially on the Sabbath days) as is most fearful to hear, and [to] the great amazement of all the people present.³⁷

Nevertheless, Weelkes was still employed at the time of his death in 1623 – a case, perhaps, of extreme forbearance in the face of musical genius? At the same time in Lincoln, the organist, Thomas Kingston, was in trouble for the same reason, and it was reported in 1615 that 'he is very often drunk, and that by means thereof he hath by unorderly playing on the organs put the choir out of tune and disordered them' – he moved on to York Minster the following year!³⁸ We should, however, remember that musicians were by no means alone in causing trouble; from the questions asked at episcopal visitations it is clear that the clergy could be just as susceptible to the same misdemeanours. What is perhaps surprising is that singers were prepared on occasions to denounce the behaviour of their fellows, as happened at the bishop's visitation of St Paul's in 1598, when one senior member complained that 'at the singing of the psalmidie divers sitt talkinge that they maybe herde somtyme from one syd of the queere to the other, never almoste singinge any part of the psalms', and that 'the children of the quire, either they use themselves very unreverently in their seats talking and playing, or else they be running about the quire to gentlemen and other poor men for spur money', while another said that the choirmen 'use not to lighte theyr candels et servyce tyme in the darke evenings, for whereas they have every one a candle they syldom lighte above 3 or 4 on a syde, when there shoulde be 9, to the greate disgrace of the Church and theyr own hinderaunce in theyr service.'[39] Clearly they were allowed to take the remains of candles home. Such complaints at least show concern on the part of some choirmen for the repute of their profession and the church.

All such behaviour provided ammunition for Puritan opposition to cathedrals, such as that expressed by two London clergymen, John Field and Thomas Wilcox, in *An Admonition to the Parliament* (1572), where they detected 'popish abuses' everywhere, cathedrals being

> the dens aforesaid of all loitering lubbers, where master Dean, master Vicedean, master Canons or Prebendaries the greater, master petty Canons or Canons the lesser, master Chancellor of the church, master Treasurer (otherwise called Judas the pursebearer), the chief chanter, singing men (special favours of religion), squeaking choristers, organ players, gospeller, pistolers, pensioners, readers, vergers, etc., live in great idleness, and have their abiding.[40]

The Queen was not amused at this attack, and the authors were imprisoned. A decade later, another pamphlet demanded

> that all cathedral churches may be put down, where the service of God is grievously abused by piping with organs, singing, ringing, and trowling of psalms from one side of the choir to another, with the squeaking of chanting choristers, disguised (as are all the rest) in white surplices; some in corner caps and filthy copes, imitating the fashion and manner of Antichrist, the Pope, that man of sin and child of perdition, with his other rabble of miscreants and shavelings.[41]

A few generations later, John Earle, in his light-hearted work *Micro-cosmographie*, while unsparing of choirmen's faults, displayed a certain acknowledgement of their humanity:

> The Common Singing-men in Cathedral Churches are a bad Society, and yet a Company of good Fellowes, that roare deep in the Quire, deeper in the Taverne.... Their pastime or recreation is prayers, their exercise drinking, yet herein so religiously addicted that they serve God oftest when they are drunke.... Upon worky-dayes they behave themselves at Prayers as at their pots, for they swallow them downe in an instant. Their Gownes are lac'd commonly with steamings of ale,

the superfluities of a cup or throat above measure. Their skill in melody makes them the better companions abroad, and their Anthemes abler to sing Catches. Long liv'd for the most part they are not, especially the base, they overflow their banke so oft to drowne the Organs. Briefly, if they escape arresting, they dye constantly in God's Service; and to take their death with more patience, they have Wine and Cakes at their Funerall: and now they keepe the Church a great deale better, and helpe to fill it with their bones as before with their noise.[42]

Yet not all cathedrals should be tarred with the same brush. Norwich was one place where choral services seem to have been conducted with little complaint, despite (or perhaps owing to) strong Puritan elements in its chapter. The statutes around 1570 laid down that 'It shall suffice to have the service in plain note without any parts on the working days, with a psalm in metre at the beginning and ending of prayer, and also before and after sermons and lectures' – i.e. unison singing, which no doubt suited the Puritans. But the cathedral also has memorials to the lay clerk and composer Osbert Parsley, who died in 1588 after 50 years' service under four monarchs, and to William Inglott, chorister and then twice organist, who died in 1621.[43] Parsley's memorial describes him: 'Who here a Singing-man did spend his Days, Full Fifty Years in our Church Melody, His Memory shines bright whom thus we praise.'[44] At Durham too we see that not all those of a Calvinist theological outlook were necessarily opposed to fine music in church, for William Whittingham, dean 1568–79, who had been in exile in Geneva during Mary's reign, used his own money 'to provide the best songs and anthems that could be out of the Queen's chapell, to furnish the quire with all, himself being skillful in music'.[45] The moderate Puritan position was not so much an objection to church music *per se*, as to the excessive resources dedicated to it. As a result, the Elizabethan era was often a troubling time particularly for provincial choirs. In 1563 the stipulation that 'the use of organs and curious singing be removed' was amongst radical proposals debated in the Convocation of clergy; in the end they restricted their request to the removal of organs, which did happen in many parish churches as well as in some university colleges (including King's, Cambridge), but the cathedrals seem to have escaped.[46] Amusing as the more extreme rants now seem to us, they must have caused real anxiety and depressed morale in choirs.

By the end of the century virtually all memory of the old Latin services with their abundant plainsong would have disappeared from cathedral quires. The almost total lack of the survival of manuscript partbooks used in services from Elizabeth's reign makes it difficult to assess just what was being sung in Britain's cathedrals and colleges in the second half of the sixteenth century.[47] In most places the music would probably have been quite modest, both in quantity and quality, certainly by what a twenty-first century congregation at a weekday choral Evensong can expect to experience. With the exception of Thomas Weelkes at Chichester, Thomas Tomkins at Worcester, and the early years of Byrd at Lincoln in the 1560s, few composers of importance were found outside London. Locally composed works would have accounted for some repertoire, but there were clearly networks in play which enabled music produced in the capital to percolate into the provinces. Only one printed collection of music for the Anglican liturgy was issued in Elizabeth's reign, John Day's *Certaine Notes Set Forth in Foure and Three Parts*, published in 1565, though its contents apparently date from the time of Edward VI.[48] Its unpretentious demands may have been intended as much for the dwindling number of parish choirs as for cathedrals, and it probably soon fell out of whatever use it may initially have enjoyed. Manuscript partbooks continued to be the sole resource to sing from right up to the Civil War. When appointed, Gentlemen of the Chapel Royal commonly retained any cathedral post they may have held, returning to the provinces when not on royal duty, as was the case with Thomas Tomkins. This provided one obvious way for music to be transmitted from London, an intermediate copy presumably being necessary to see the music from partbooks in one place transferred to partbooks in another.[49] For those institutions without Chapel Royal contacts, other channels must have been found, and the evidence of the few surviving partbooks from the first half of the seventeenth century demonstrates that this did occur, enabling nationwide circulation of London repertoire. Even such an ambitious and demanding work as Byrd's 'Great' Service, clearly originating at the Chapel Royal, found its way into partbooks at Durham, York and two Cambridge colleges.[50] But many cathedrals would have had quite small repertoires, especially of service settings, which were either repeated frequently, or replaced by simple unaccompanied chanting, as we have seen happened at Norwich on weekdays.

Changes in Style and Performance

The basic concept of Cranmer's 'for every syllable a note' would continue to be the guiding principle for composers setting English liturgical texts. Apart from 'Alleluia' and 'Amen', which naturally lend themselves to extended treatment, it would be Purcell's time before roulades of notes on one syllable began to become common again, and that chiefly in the solo sections of anthems. A major change in the soundscape, however, concerned the role of the organ. From having been used before the Reformation only in alternation with the choir's plainsong or polyphony, particularly in the Te Deum and Magnificat, in Elizabethan England it began to accompany the choir. This occurred initially in the new form of the 'verse' anthem, where substantial parts of the music were given over to one or more solo voices (the 'verse'), contrasting with sections for the full choir. Passages for groups of solo voices within full choir works were not new, as we have seen in the Eton Choirbook repertoire, but there the voices were self-sufficient in terms of harmony. The Elizabethan verse anthem, however, involved passages requiring organ accompaniment to complete the texture. In this it had a similarity to (and was influenced by) the contemporary rise of the so-called 'consort song' for a single voice accompanied by four viols, such as is particularly associated with Byrd in publications such as his *Psalmes, Sonets and Songs of Sadnes and Pietie* of 1588, works designed for domestic use. In fact, a number of Byrd's works, such as 'Christ rising again', are found with both with viol and organ accompaniments, it not being always clear which version came first.[51] The verse anthem grew rapidly in popularity towards the end of Elizabeth's reign, at the expense of the 'full' anthem, which involved the whole choir throughout; it was eventually joined by the similarly structured 'verse service'. The 'verse' format had practical advantages: for many choirs, provided they had a few competent solo voices, deficiencies in the full choir could be mitigated, and there would be less having to be taught to the boys in addition to perhaps satisfying individual singers' vanity. And contrary to present-day practice, it was customary for such singers to ornament their parts in this repertoire.[52] The text was also more clearly heard when delivered by single voices, and could be more expressively set, which may have pacified the more Puritan-minded clergy. Orlando Gibbons's 'This is the record of John' for solo countertenor, SATB chorus and accompaniment for either organ or viol consort, probably dating from the 1610s, is a classic example of the genre, still very much in the repertoire.

With the introduction of organ accompaniment, special 'organ books' began to be created to complement the set of a choir's partbooks. The earliest surviving such books come from the early seventeenth century, and the most important is the so-called 'Batten Organ Book', most probably compiled in the 1630s by the composer and St Paul's vicar choral Adrian Batten.[53] With over 250 items, it is an improbably bulky book to have been put on an organ desk, and is perhaps best viewed as a reference collection, from which copies of selected items could be transferred into more practical volumes. Importantly for us today, it contains many works only known from this source, some of which can be reconstructed from the skeletal keyboard parts. But it is also of interest in that, in addition to verse anthems and services in which the organ is an essential component, many 'full' works are included, which are generally considered to be for unaccompanied singing. While it is possible that such organ parts (which often contain little more than the outer voices) were used in rehearsing the boys' parts – the men, of course, did not rehearse! – it seems that by the 1630s at the latest the organ was actually being used to accompany such pieces. It should not be seen as a way of compensating for weakness (or indeed, on occasions, missing voices) in the choir, though it may have aided ensemble and confidence; rather it represents a change of the choral soundscape, in which it became the norm to expect a choir to be backed up by an organ, whether or not it was harmonically necessary. It was a practice that was to continue right through to the nineteenth century and beyond – only in the twentieth century did church choirs routinely abandon organ support in what was originally (or was it?) 'unaccompanied' repertoire. Modern choirs who resort to the help of an organ in such works may actually be more 'authentic' in their approach than at first appears.

The organ, however, was not the only instrument to find employment in church. The engagement of cornetts and sackbuts (the former a curved woodwind instrument with a trumpet-type mouthpiece, the latter an early form of the trombone) is recorded by various cathedrals as well as the Chapel Royal, either on an occasional or more regular basis, and their use became particularly common in the decade preceding the Civil War. Two of each instrument formed the standard ensemble. The sixteenth-century references appear to be all for special occasions – the visit of the Queen to Christ Church, Oxford in 1566, when 'the quyer sang and play'd with cornetts, *Te Deum*',[54] or on her visit to Worcester in 1575, when cornetts and sackbuts were employed in the cathedral.[55] But later the instruments were often engaged regularly for Sundays and feast days, and in 1637 Canterbury Cathedral went so far as to include the four players in its statutes.[56] It is, however, difficult to establish just what their function was. It might be imagined that they provided instrumental music for processions of civic dignitaries, or the transition from Matins to Ante-Communion. That they actually doubled the choir's parts at first seems unlikely to our modern ears, yet there is evidence that certainly on occasions it is what they did. At the baptism of James I's daughter, Mary, in 1605 at Greenwich, the Chapel Royal sang a verse anthem, 'the chorus whereof was filled with the help of musicall instrumentes',[57] and at Christ Church, Dublin, there is a reference in 1594/5 to musicians playing 'in the quire and helping our vicars'.[58] Notwithstanding the latter situation, their introduction seems to have been caused not so much by a desire to remedy basic deficiencies in the choral sound, as to provide a more impressive sonic experience, bearing in mind that most organs of the period were still very small. The sackbut in particular, could have usefully strengthened the bass notes of the organ, which are often liable to be weak in tone. The only proof of separate partbooks for them is a reference in 1625 at Canterbury to a 'sackbut book' being repaired.[59] With Sundays frequently attracting large congregations at cathedrals to hear the sermon, wind instruments may possibly have also been found useful in accompanying the metrical psalms sung at the beginning and end of services. At Durham, where they were in use from the mid-1620s, the players were also expected to attend on weekdays, though this may have been a rather exceptional example.[60] We are quite used to the sound of such instruments in the continental music of Giovanni Gabrieli, Monteverdi, Praetorius and Schütz; that it was also encountered in Britain should perhaps not surprise us, however foreign to our received ideas of the sound of English church music of the time.

A More Settled Interlude for the Cathedrals

Queen Elizabeth died in 1603, and under her successors James I (and VI of Scotland) and Charles I, what later would be called a 'high church' element in the Church came to prominence, especially in the cathedral world, with a renewed emphasis on the 'beauty of holiness' in worship and the importance of the sacraments – symbolised by the return of the stone altar in place of the wooden communion table ordered to replace it in the early days of the Reformation. At the beginning of the century Westminster Abbey led the way in imitating the Chapel Royal's more ceremonial style, refurbishing its quire and providing gold cloths for the altar,[61] while the Chapel Royal itself appears to have been reinvigorated by James I,[62] and flourished particularly under the more Catholic-minded Charles I, who had married a Catholic, Henrietta Maria of France – she maintained her own Chapel at Somerset House, staffed with French musicians. A larger and extravagantly appointed chapel was inaugurated there in 1636; it attracted large crowds of worshippers, and the proselytising of the Roman Catholic cause by the Queen and her clergy was to become an important ingredient in fanning the flames of the Civil War.[63] Durham in the 1620s became a leading provincial example of this trend, which saw amongst other things an increased amount of more elaborate music in weekday services. It was promoted there chiefly by one of the canons, John Cosin (later Bishop of Durham), even though he was fiercely opposed by another member of the chapter, the Calvinist Peter Smart. In a notorious sermon in 1628, Smart denounced all the ceremonial innovations of Cosin, including low bowing to the altar ('altar-ducking'), copes and the proliferation of candles. On the musical side, he reviled against the displacement of metrical psalms by anthems, excessive organ-playing and the use of 'Shackbuts and Cornets which yield an hydeous noyse'.[64] For his extremism Smart ended up deprived of his positions and imprisoned for eleven years, only to be reprieved and reinstated in 1641.

The appointment in 1633 of the high church William Laud as Archbishop of Canterbury saw him urging cathedrals throughout the land to improve the propriety of their worship. Already, as President of St John's College, Oxford (1611–21), he had seen the re-establishment around 1620 of a small choir (settled in 1637 as having six boys and four men), for which he commissioned Orlando Gibbons's anthem 'This is the record of John'.[65] In Cambridge, Latin was at least occasionally heard at Peterhouse in the 1630s, judging from a Litany and canticle settings composed for the college by William Child and Robert Ramsey.[66] For choirs it meant a period of comparative stability, and a great deal of music copying is in evidence in the 1630s, as witnessed particularly in the large number of pre-Civil War books at Durham, which fortunately survived the conflict.[67] They testify to a perhaps exceptionally large repertoire for a provincial cathedral, and to the spread of repertoire from London, as well as cultivation of their local composers, amongst whom was the William Smith whose set of Preces and Responses is still very much in every cathedral's repertoire.[68] Cosin's reforms, however, were not uniformly welcomed by the choir; in particular the moving of sung Matins from 10 a.m. to 6 a.m. (replacing an existing said Matins held at that hour for the benefit of those heading off for work) was understandably unpopular with the organist, Richard Hutchinson, and at least one lay clerk.[69] It is hard to think of anyone who likes singing at that hour in the morning.

The general extension of repertoire in the 1630s led John Barnard, a minor canon at St Paul's, to assemble a large collection of cathedral music, and to publish a selection of it in 1641 in a set of ten partbooks (five each for the cantoris and decani sides of the choir), under the title *The First Book of Selected Church Musicke*.[70] It was the first publication of English liturgical music since John Day's *Certaine Notes* in 1565, and contained fifty-eight items (canticles, anthems, responses and a Litany), none of which were by living composers – Barnard's preface promised a second volume including more recent works, if the first proved successful. It marked the beginning of the emergence of the idea of a 'canon' of older works, considered to merit a permanent place in a choir's repertoire alongside more contemporary music, so creating a tradition that has endured to the present day. One intention behind Barnard's publication was a desire to provide more accurate versions of works, which in all too many cases became corrupted when at the mercy of manuscript copyists – something that Morley had already commented on, when he remarked '... for [in] copies passing from hand to hand, a small oversight committed by the first writer, by the second will be made worse, which will give occasion to the third to alter much, both in the words and notes, according as shall seeme best to his owne judgement'.[71] It is a sentiment which would be echoed a century later when William Boyce came to edit his *Cathedral Music* anthology. Alas for Barnard, he could not have chosen a more unpropitious time to issue his work. If many cathedral musicians were enjoying a richer musical diet in these decades – though their financial position remained lamentable – it was to prove a short-lived experience.

Parish Church Music

When we come to the effect of the Reformation on parish church choirs, we find a very different situation from that in the cathedrals. With the dissolution of the religious guilds and most collegiate churches, the permanent, if small, parish choirs that they frequently supported also fell away, although at St Mary's, Warwick the town council stepped in to keep its choir in existence.[72] Since the new liturgies of the Book of Common Prayer provided no indication of the role of music, it is no wonder that, at parish level, choral activity rapidly declined, especially in those (the great majority) which had only drafted in singers for major feasts. Most of the London churches which had maintained choirs allowed them to dwindle, until by the 1570s they had virtually all disappeared. There were exceptions – St Dunstan-in-the-West paid six singing men until 1588, while Christ Church, Newgate, had the money spent on singing men diverted for preachers in the early 1580s against the will of many parishioners, only for the singers to be restored in 1595, and a 'singing school' at nearby Christ's Hospital was endowed in about 1609 to provide about twelve choristers for the church, whose choir exceptionally was to be modelled on cathedral lines.[73]

Ludlow was another parish church which maintained comparatively elaborate choral services throughout the Elizabethan era; its choir of six boys and six men, previously patronised by the Palmers Guild, was now provided for partly by the parish and partly by the town corporation. But Ludlow was in a special position, since it was the seat of the Lord President of the Welsh Marches, who, as representative of the sovereign, favoured a certain amount of ceremony. An agreement made in 1581 between the Lord President and the Bishop of Hereford gives details of the way music was to feature in services – perhaps the resolution of a dispute as to its role.[74] In the West Country, too, where traditionalists retained much sway (though

Exeter itself was a Puritan centre), churchwardens' accounts showed support for singers in quite a number of places, such as Chudleigh, Hartland and Launceston, some of which survived until the beginning of the seventeenth century.[75] In a few other places a local music-loving patron may have been keen to support a choir, though such arrangements were always liable to be relatively short-lived. The Queen herself allowed the re-endowment of a few choirs of previous collegiate churches, which had lost them at the general collegiate dissolution of 1548, such as St Mary's, Warwick, Manchester and Newark, but beyond this, she did nothing to promote music at parish church level. Wimborne Minster, having for centuries had the status of a 'royal peculiar' (independent of diocesan control) still had a small choir maintained by the town corporation, which in 1602 consisted of four boys and six men. In 1610 William Emes moved from Winchester Cathedral to Wimborne as organist, remaining there for ten years before returning to Winchester. In his agreement it is noted that the parish follows the order of service 'as is usuallye observed in Cathedrall Churches'.[76] This may not have involved elaborate music – after all, in many provincial cathedrals it was far from ambitious – but the choral establishment remained up to the Civil War. At least one Anglican private chapel of the gentry flourished musically in the early part of the seventeenth century, that of Sir Thomas Middleton Jr at Chirk Castle near Wrexham in North Wales. A surviving set of four partbooks and an accompanying organ book, compiled in the 1630s, contains a repertoire of sixty-five pieces (including service settings), with West Country composers well represented in addition to those from the capital. As the chapel measures only 48 x 20 feet, the choir is likely to have been little more than one to a part. The Chirk organist, William Deane, who features as one of the composers, was also organist at St Giles', Wrexham, which had a notable organ, and may have supported similar musical activity.[77]

Although Puritan sentiment certainly contributed to the decline of parish choirs, there was an equally important factor involved – the rise of the metrical psalm. The idea of producing versions of the psalms in English verse had begun to emerge in the 1530s, but they played no part in public worship until Elizabeth's accession, when the return of hundreds of Protestants who had gone into exile on the continent during Mary's reign, brought with them the custom of singing metrical psalms which they had encountered abroad, particularly under the influence of John Calvin in Geneva. The complete collection of 150 psalms (plus a few other hymns and metrical versions of canticles), as compiled by Thomas Sternhold and John Hopkins, was first issued in 1562 and rapidly went through innumerable printings; it included unaccompanied melodies. Although no provision for such singing was made in the Prayer Book, it was allowed by royal injunction before and after the official liturgy,[78] and (by custom) before and after sermons. Sung to easily learnt tunes, they were eagerly taken up by congregations, who at last were allowed to sing in church. What need had they now for choirs when they could now contribute musically themselves? And for churchwardens it meant one fewer expense to consider. In some places, boys at the local grammar school were taught the new tunes in order to be able to lead the singing in their parish churches,[79] and a few small pre-Reformation song schools also survived, now with the same restricted purpose in view. By the early seventeenth century, however, the need for such assistance declined as the number of different psalm tunes in use was reduced to a mere handful. The practice of 'lining out', whereby the parish clerk read out each line of the psalm before it was sung – clearly prolonging the psalm – is sometimes said to have been introduced during the Commonwealth, but evidence suggests that it may have had far earlier beginnings, especially considering that few members of congregations, even if literate, would have initially possessed their own books.[80] It was to be the early eighteenth century before parish churches began again to enlist the assistance of rehearsed singers in order to improve congregational singing.

Metrical psalm singing was not confined to parish churches. Elizabeth's injunctions also allowed them also in cathedrals, where they would have been popular with the congregations which typically came on Sundays, after attending Matins in their parish church, in order to hear the sermon preached in the second part of the morning service. The Queen had initially been rather lukewarm towards metrical psalms – the poor quality of the verse can hardly have appealed to her aesthetic sense – but she came to see their value in the church at large, and they were even introduced into the Chapel Royal, perhaps to the dismay of the Gentlemen, who in 1630 had to be warned that they were expected to join in singing them.[81] Harmonized versions were published from time to time (for example, by John Day in 1563, Thomas East in 1592 and Thomas Ravenscroft in 1621), chiefly with a view to domestic performance. But the preface to eight four-part tunes by Tallis (including 'Tallis's Canon') which formed an appendix to Archbishop Matthew Parker's version of the Psalter, published in 1567, noted that, 'The Tenor of these partes be for the people when they will syng alone, the other parts, put for greater queers, or to suche as will syng or play them pryvatelye.'[82] It is likely that use was made of such harmonized versions at the Chapel Royal.

Music Outside the Liturgy

The Elizabethan and Jacobean period naturally saw the performance of much ensemble music for voices, both sacred and secular, outside the province of formal choirs. Following in the footsteps of Italian models, the English madrigal and related forms like the ballett, composed by Morley, Weelkes, Wilbye and others, were intended for domestic performance – it was literally 'chamber music' – rarely, if ever, sung by more than one voice to a part. When revived later, from the nineteenth century onwards, it was to be transformed into 'choral music', especially with the rise of 'madrigal societies'. In contrast to church music, there was a sufficient market for madrigals for them to be printed, and the repertoire is overwhelmingly known from printed rather than manuscript sources. Alongside these came also printed collections of devotional music, likewise intended for the 'chamber', such as Byrd's *Psalmes, Sonets, and Songs of Sadnes and Pietie* (1588). It is in the famous preface to this work that Byrd lays out the reasons 'to perswade everyone to learne to sing', listing the physical and mental benefits, which remain more or less equally valid today:

> First, it is a knowledge easily taught, and quickly learned, wher[e] there is a good Master and an apt Skolar.
>
> 2. The exercise of singing is delightfull to Nature, & good to preserve the health of Man.
>
> 3. It doth strengthen all parts of the brest, & doth open the pipes.
>
> 4. It is a singular good remedie for a stutting & stamering in the speech.
>
> 5. It is the best meanes to procure a good pronunciation, & to make a perfect Orator.
>
> 6. It is the onely way to know where Nature hath bestowed the benefit of a good voyce: which guifte is so rare, as there is not one among a thousand, that hath it: and in many, that excellent guift is lost, because they want Art to expresse Nature.
>
> 7. There is not any Musicke or Instruments whatsoever, comparable to that which is made of the voyces of Men, where the voyces are good, and the same well sorted and ordered.
>
> 8. The better the voyce is, the meeter it is to honour and serve God there-with: and the voyce of man is chiefly to be imployed to that ende.[83]

Byrd's conclusion: 'Since singing is so good a thing, I wish all men would learne to sing', leaves uncertain whether his 'men' also included women. We know that at least one Catholic member of the gentry in the 1580s had 'choristers, male and female, members of his household'.[84] But one suspects that it was more normal to find boys on the top line in both sacred and secular domestic contexts. Until at least the end of the eighteenth century, choral activity was overwhelmingly a male preserve.

It is clear from a few surviving Elizabethan partbooks of non-liturgical origin, containing Latin sacred music, both old and new, that it continued to be admired and sung informally in domestic surroundings for its own sake, and not just by Catholics.[85] Although a few of the 34 motets of Tallis and Byrd's *Cantiones sacrae* (1575) may have been heard in Latin at the Chapel Royal (and a handful were adapted to English texts, indicating performance in cathedrals), they were most likely to have been sung outside the liturgy. As for Byrd's three Masses of the 1590s and the motets of the two books of *Gradualia* (1605 and 1607), these could only have been sung liturgically at clandestine celebrations of the Mass in Catholic households, presumably by single voices, even if Byrd might have imagined them echoing in the vaults of a vast cathedral – something that would not occur until the twentieth century. The fact that, daringly, Byrd had these explicitly Catholic works printed, is perhaps a sign that he also wanted them to be appreciated more widely for their intrinsic musical worth. Nevertheless, with the Masses, he took the precaution of ensuring that the word 'Mass' nowhere appears in the editions, which were issued without title-pages. Even if print runs were quite small (as they were generally for music publications of the time), they would certainly have exceeded the quantity needed for secretive worship.[86]

The Pitch Question

As mentioned in the preceding chapter, one of the continuing questions concerning the performance of sixteenth- and early seventeenth-century music is that of the pitch at which it was sung. Since the twentieth century, editions of Tudor church music have most commonly presented the music a minor third higher than the original written pitch. Thus, Gibbons's anthem 'Almighty and everlasting God', which appears in the key of F in its sources, is usually found in A flat in modern editions. This is chiefly owing to the work of Edmund Fellowes, a minor canon of Windsor, who, in the first half of the twentieth century, was the leading editor of church music of this period (as well as of its madrigals and lute songs), and whose numerous editions were issued by Oxford University Press in their *Tudor Church Music* series, making the vast treasury of Tudor music widely available. Fellowes based his editorial decisions about pitch on a nineteenth-century observation of Sir Frederick Gore Ouseley, Professor of Music at Oxford and founder of St Michael's College, Tenbury. Ouseley discovered in his own copy of Thomas Tomkins's *Musica Deo Sacra* (posthumously published in 1668) a printed note in the organ part to the effect that an organ pipe five feet in length produced the note F. From this he concluded that the pitch of organs was almost a minor third higher than those of his own day, and therefore the choir's music should be performed correspondingly higher than written.[87] Recent research, however, has shown 'minor third' transposition to be mistaken. More sophisticated interpretation of the whole question of organ pipe lengths, combined with analysis of a few surviving pipes from the seventeenth century, suggests that, in so far as there was a common pitch standard, it appears to have been rather less than a tone above the present-day standard of $a'=440$.[88] The 'high pitch' transposition, however, continues to find general favour in cathedral and collegiate choirs, since it creates fewer low-register problems for falsetto altos, even though, as we have seen, the whole idea that early countertenor parts were intended for falsetto voices is now highly disputed. High pitch was also the most prominent feature of The Clerkes of Oxenford, a choir created and directed by David Wulstan in 1961, which specialized in Tudor music. It used female sopranos rather than boys and applied upward minor third transposition to pre- as well as post-Reformation music, including that of the Eton Choirbook. It resulted in performances with high soaring top lines, at times strikingly beautiful and 'transporting', if now regarded as historically dubious. Nevertheless, their sound has influenced other groups, notably Peter Phillips's Tallis Scholars, who, while not as extreme as the Clerkes, favour high pitch, based round a falsetto countertenor line. Recent years have, however, seen a much greater variety in choice of pitches for this repertoire by the many different ensembles which have sprung up, very much dependent on the particular vocal makeup of their personnel. With competing musicological ideas about pitch and timbre, most groups, while perhaps taking note of the arguments, opt, as Peter Phillips freely admits, for a sound they basically like.[89] Andrew Parrott's Taverner Choir (and Consort) probably comes closest to a historical approach to pitch, but regardless of their approach to the countertenor part, these present-day professional groups use female sopranos rather than boys, for obvious practical reasons. But even if certainty could be reached on pitch and countertenors, there are many matters such as tempo, dynamics, vibrato and other aspects of vocal quality where we are condemned to perpetual ignorance. In the end, when performing early music, especially that from before the eighteenth century, we go for something which satisfies our current aesthetic tastes, even though these may change quite rapidly and be subject to convincing challenges from new ideas.

Choristers' Lives

How did boy choristers fare in the wake of the Reformation? Their numbers in cathedral-type choirs remained very much the same – six to eight in most places, ten in the richer establishments of Canterbury, Durham, Winchester, Worcester and Westminster Abbey, and twelve at the Chapel Royal, while those university college choirs with statutes stipulating sixteen, retained that number.[90] But with the Reformation came a considerable reduction in their time spent in choral activity, most notably with the disappearance of the daily celebration of High Mass. Moreover, the various non-singing ceremonial duties they had previously performed also disappeared – henceforth they were present purely for their singing. Musically too, from having been accustomed to often singing the two highest parts in works of five or more parts – the 'treble' and 'mean', they found that the immediate post-Reformation period saw the composition of largely four-part music, lacking the higher range treble notes, with the single boys' line coming to be termed the 'mean' part. When there was a gradual return to five-part composition in Elizabethan times, it was an extra countertenor or tenor part which tended to provide the additional voice. There was a brief return to the cultivation of a 'high treble' line around 1600, particularly in a few works of Thomas Weelkes (one of whose services was headed 'Service for Trebles'), but it was a short-lived revival, which did not survive far into the century. Although it is sometimes claimed that boys' unbroken voices often lasted until around seventeen at this time, evidence suggests that this is far from the case, and that a change around fourteen was the norm.[91] At Lichfield, according to Injunctions of 1547 and 1559, each chorister was to be awarded an annual pension of £3 6s 8d for a period of five years after his voice had broken so that he could attend the local grammar school, and similar arrangements were in place at Canterbury, Durham, Exeter, Lincoln, Peterborough and Winchester.[92] Such provision does not suggest a late change of voice. As is the case today, individuals must have varied considerably as to how long their treble voices lasted.

The Reformation years must have caused much confusion musically for boys, with their elaborate Latin music suddenly replaced with the simplest of music in a language they had hitherto never sung in church. No longer were they expected to memorize large quantities of plainsong. With a much reduced singing commitment, there was in theory more time available for their general education, and at Lincoln, for example, they were ordered to attend the Close Grammar School.[93] Henry VIII's creation of new grammar schools (later called 'King's Schools') in places like Canterbury, Chester and Worcester after the dissolution of their monasteries, also provided new opportunities for choristers' education. In practice, however, although suitable ex-choristers were well placed to take advantage of this, the twice-daily cathedral commitment of singing boys commonly often proved an obstacle to satisfactory attendance at such schools. The most common solution was for the choristers to be taught on their own in the cathedral precincts, often by one of the lay clerks. Chorister education was to prove a persistent problem over the centuries, and it was to be the twentieth century with its changes in daily service patterns, before satisfactory solutions could be found. Alongside their education, with the reduction in the choristers' duties, there came a gradual tendency to abandon housing them together, leaving them to either reside at home or with individual members of the cathedral community.[94]

The role of Master of the Choristers, which after the Reformation tended to be combined with that of organist, was critical in establishing the musical competence of the boys, and cases of neglect were reported. At a visitation of New College, Oxford in 1566 it was stated that all but three of the sixteen boys 'could not and had never been instructed to sing'. Their master apparently then fled the college before he could be called to account.[95] On the other hand, the youthful William Byrd, when organist and Master of the Choristers at Lincoln (1563–70) was evidently highly conscientious and travelled to recruit new boys from as far away as Lancashire as well as more locally in Newark and Louth – most of his English service music appears to date from this time, and is testimony to the standards he sought.[96] Unfortunately, less competent holders of the office from the mid-1580s led to a decline in Lincoln's music until the 1620s.[97]

The power structure in cathedrals did not fundamentally alter with the Reformation; the Master of the Choristers continued to have no authority over the choirmen, and overall responsibility for the music remained with the precentor, whose own status in the New Foundation cathedrals was only that of a minor canon, not one of the principal office holders, as was the case historically in those of the Old Foundation.[98] Responsibility for keeping the choir together evidently devolved on one of the senior lay clerks, who beat time with simple movements of the hands, perhaps aided by movements of the shoulders, as continued to be the case in cathedrals until the quite recent custom of having all of the service conducted from between the stalls. In Salisbury, and perhaps elsewhere, this was considered a formal duty, since in 1586 John Farrant the elder, Master of the Choristers since 1571, was made 'moderator temporum et tonarum' ('controller of the times and pitches') with the choir being instructed to obey him – the precentor, however, was still in overall charge of the music, and in the following year Farrant took over the better remunerated post of organist.[99] If the boys had less singing to do in the wake of the Reformation, it became more common for them to learn to play instruments, especially the viol, which would enhance their future employability as much as providing off-duty recreation. Lay clerks too cultivated viol playing, and Canterbury and Lincoln were among cathedrals who maintained sets of viols. Apart, however, from the Chapel Royal, where there is evidence of viols occasionally being used to accompany verse anthems at the end of the sixteenth century, viols rarely appear to have been played in services – keeping them in tune being one reason suggested for not employing them.[100]

London choristers at St Paul's and the Chapel Royal also enjoyed periods when they were formed into acting troupes, appearing both at court and in theatres, performing 'choirboy plays' written by their Masters. This happened chiefly in the years 1560–90 and again briefly in the first decade of the next century. They were, however, not operating 'chorally' in these situations. Such music as was included would have been solo songs or duets for individual boys, with perhaps others accompanying on viols. No doubt the choristers found the experience provided welcome relief from their daily routine, and they would have enjoyed the approbation of their audiences, even if they were subject to financial exploitation by their Masters. For some it probably provided a gateway into professional acting.[101]

Scotland, Wales and Ireland

The Reformation took rather longer to come to fruition in Scotland; closure of monasteries first took place in 1559, and only in 1560 did a decisive breach with Catholicism occur, when Scottish Protestantism began its course towards a distinctive and severe Calvinist identity, which permitted only the unaccompanied congregational singing of metrical psalms. Our knowledge of the extent of the cultivation of music in Scotland's pre-Reformation abbeys, cathedrals and collegiate churches is too scanty to assess how much choral culture disappeared. Although at the Reformation the song schools associated with these institutions were closed, some were continued or later re-opened under the civic authorities, and an act of the Scottish Parliament in 1579 ordered all towns to establish such schools. This was primarily with the intention of providing music instruction to enable a lead to be given in congregational singing – rather as happened in places in England, though on a larger scale. There is evidence that in places singing of metrical psalms in four-part harmony occurred, but this died out by the end of the 1630s along with the song schools, and Scottish psalm singing gradually evolved into the tradition of extremely slow performance with freely improvised ornamentation, becoming a sort of true folk music. Although gradually abandoned in towns from the mid-eighteenth century in favour of more conventional performance, it has survived to the present day in some of the Gaelic Free Presbyterian congregations of the Western Isles.[102] It is a style quite unlike any other western musical tradition, but which has something in common with the ecstatic utterances of those Pentecostal churches indulging in 'speaking in tongues'.

After its brief flourishing in the early sixteenth century, the Scottish Chapel Royal virtually ceased to exist in the wake of the Reformation, at least as a musical body. Although James VI had a new chapel built in 1594 ready for the baptism of his son, Henry, the music on the occasion appears to have consisted of little more than a harmonized version of Psalm 21.[103] Following the union of the English and Scottish thrones, James on a state visit to Scotland in 1617 had the chapel at Holyrood restored, and choral worship was celebrated, with the King wanting them to continue singing daily services, in the hope that it would provide a model for Scottish churches.[104] But the absence of necessary finance meant that regular attendance by the singers quickly became a problem.[105] A further, final revival came under Charles I, when in 1630, Edward Kellie, Master of the Choristers, was sent to London to study the setup at the English Chapel Royal, and to recruit singers, an organist and two men to play cornetts and sackbuts, as well as having music copied – a sure sign of the lack of suitable musicians north of the border.[106] The Scottish Chapel then had a strength of six boys, sixteen men and an organist, and took part in Charles's Scottish coronation in 1633, together with some of the English Chapel. The revival, however, was short-lived, again partly for financial reasons, and the choir ceased to exist in 1638.[107] All in all, the desire of both James and Charles to see the Scottish Chapel Royal maintained, was probably largely due to concern to keep the flag of ceremonial court life flying in Scotland despite their personal absence. But with the collapse of the Chapel, Scottish choralism more or less vanished for over a century.

Our knowledge of music in the four Welsh cathedrals which emerged from the Reformation is virtually non-existent, though given the poverty of the country, in all probability very little music-making went on. The country's main cathedral, St David's, certainly had a small choral establishment, of four boys and eight men, for Thomas Tomkins was there in 1572, when his father, also Thomas, was a vicar choral and later organist, and young Thomas presumably gained his first musical education in the choir.[108] By 1642, however, there were just the four boys, their Master and an organist.[109]

Dublin, on the other hand, continued to have two cathedrals with choral establishments after the Reformation, when in addition to the pre-Reformation secular cathedral of St Patrick's, the former monastic cathedral of Christ Church became a New Foundation institution in 1539 with four boys and eight vicars choral. Numbers fluctuated over the next century (with a shortage of basses being a recurrent note), but in 1635 there were ten men, and two more boys were added that year, with pairs of cornetts and sackbuts also being engaged.[110] All this in a country where the great majority of the population remained Roman Catholic in their allegiance. We know little of musical conditions in the other Irish cathedrals of the time, at Armagh, Cork, Kilkenny and Waterford.

Disaster Strikes

From the 1630s onwards the combination of Charles I's autocratic behaviour in politics and Laud's high-handedness in church matters provoked the Puritan factions into outright revolution. Triggered by Charles's attempt to impose a new Prayer Book on the Scottish church in 1637, ensuing armed conflict in Scotland reached down to the north of England in 1640, when Durham Cathedral was attacked by the Scots. The outbreak of the English Civil War in 1642 witnessed the beginning of the parliamentary forces ransacking cathedrals, although the cessation of choral services was a gradual process. The degree of spoliation varied through the country, but most choirs had been disbanded by 1644, when Parliament abolished the episcopate and the use of the Book of Common Prayer. Down in the more conservative West Country, Exeter managed to continue singing until 1647,[111] while across the Irish Sea, St Patrick's, Dublin did not abandon its choir until 1650.[112] Some organs were certainly destroyed – those which stood prominently on the screen at the entrance to the quire perhaps being particularly vulnerable, as being objects of ostentatious display to the Puritan-minded – but in other places they appear to have been merely put out of commission, or moved elsewhere, as happened with the organ of Magdalen College, Oxford, which ended up in Oliver Cromwell's residence at Hampton Court Palace.[113] In some places where organs remained, they may possibly have helped the congregation in singing the metrical psalms, which would have been the only form of music which continued to echo round those few cathedrals, where any kind of worship (centred on a sermon) continued. The attitude of the more extreme Puritans was summed up by the fervent Calvinist, John Vicars, when he describes the state of Westminster Abbey in 1643, noting

> that whereas there was wont to be heard, nothing almost but roaring boyes, tooting and squeaking of organ-pipes, and the cathedrall catches of Morley, and I know not what trash, now the Popish altar is quite taken away, the bellowing organs are demolisht, and pull'd downe, the treble, or rather, trouble and base singers, chanters, or inchanters, driven out.[114]

In 1645 the use of the Book of Common Prayer was replaced by a *Directory for the Public Worship of God*, in the main laying down general instructions rather than set forms of worship. The widespread ransacking of cathedrals often extended to the destruction of the choir's music books, although in at least two places, Durham and Ely, these were secreted away in good time and survived.[115] Most Puritans did not object to music in itself, even if they viewed anything but congregational singing in church as an unwelcome distraction from the exposition of the biblical message. Cromwell himself maintained a small domestic musical establishment, including two boys, and their music-making extended to the singing of the Latin motets of Richard Dering.[116]

Least affected musically by the changes were the nation's parish churches. Most of the few parish choirs which had continued to exist in Elizabethan times had fallen away by the early seventeenth century, leaving only the choirs of a handful of collegiate parish churches, like Southwell, to be swept away in the 1640s. Parochial congregations, though having to accustom themselves to whatever form of service replaced the Prayer Book, merely carried on singing unaccompanied metrical psalms, as they had been doing for the best part of a century.

How did the revolution affect former choir personnel? For the lay clerks, their cathedral employment had long been only an ill-paid part-time occupation, so many were probably able to devote more time to their other interests, be it innkeeping, carpentry or barbering. Those vicars choral who were ordained and also had a parochial living, could have turned more to their parish work, assuming they could reconcile themselves to the Puritan regime. Hardest hit financially may have been the Gentlemen of the Chapel Royal, which had certainly ceased to exist by the time of Charles I's execution in 1649. They were by far the best rewarded in the country, but compared to the provinces, London would have offered plenty of scope for other employment, musical or otherwise, and the resourceful Gentlemen would have found suitable niches. Perhaps the main casualties were the nation's choristers. Although provision for their education was often highly unsatisfactory, it was probably more than many of them would otherwise have received, and their modest pay (typically £3 6s 8d a year)[117] was often paid at the end of their choir service and could provide money for an apprenticeship. In addition, the opportunity to learn to play instruments would have disappeared, depriving them of further useful skills for later life. The thread of chorister life was to be broken for a whole generation.

Chapter 3
From the Restoration to Georgian Enlightenment

Choral Music Resumes

With the Restoration of the monarchy following Charles II's return to England in May 1660, it is surprising how quickly choral establishments began to be revived. The former structure of the church was reinstated with its bishops, deans and cathedral chapters, together with the reintroduction of the Book of Common Prayer. A definitive, revised edition appeared in 1662, in which for the first time the rubric appears after the collects at Matins and Evensong, 'in quires and places where they sing, here followeth the anthem'. This of course was merely giving official sanction to what had actually been happening ever since the early days of the Reformation. 'Quires' here refers to the area of the cathedral, and other 'places where they sing' would have mainly applied to collegiate chapels. In practice, the anthem could be placed elsewhere; according to Samuel Pepys's diary entries, it came after the sermon at the Chapel Royal, while at St Paul's, on sermon days there were anthems both after the collects and after the sermon, when a metrical psalm would have been the norm.[1]

At court, the Chapel Royal was certainly functioning again by the summer of 1660, and was to attain a post-Restoration establishment of 12 boys and around 20–26 Gentlemen (posts were sometimes left vacant).[2] Although not many of the pre-war Gentlemen returned, competent new voices were not hard to find, given the financial rewards and conditions of service; they included three who had been organists before the war at Winchester, Windsor and Christ Church, Oxford. Far more problematic was the boys' treble line. As anyone who has been involved in running a choir dependent on children's voices knows, much of the learning occurs by a process of osmosis, as newcomers absorb technique and knowledge from their seniors, and in turn pass it on to the next generation. This continuity had been completely lost with the break of over fifteen years since choral services were abandoned, so choirs throughout the country were faced with the considerable task of recruiting and training treble lines from scratch. Since there had been a long tradition of some choristers being sons of lay clerks, a minority might possibly have benefitted from some parental instruction beforehand. The Chapel Royal had the good fortune to appoint Henry Cooke as Master of the Children in September 1660. Known as 'Captain Cooke' from his service in the Royalist cause during the Civil War, he had himself grown up in the Chapel, and as an adult became a noted singer in the Italian manner – meaning he had mastered the art of ornamentation. He set about the task of rebuilding the Chapel Royal treble line, and from the outset was able to find some first-class recruits, who in adult life would become leading musicians themselves, including John Blow, Pelham Humfrey, Michael Wise, and later, Henry Purcell. Cooke was evidently a charismatic figure, rather over-fond of his own singing, but determined to produce a fine set of boys, for which purpose he roamed the country, recruiting from places as far as Worcester, Lichfield and Lincoln.[3] But even at the Chapel Royal it took time to develop a proficient treble line, for the composer Matthew Locke noted that for more than a year after the resumption, it was necessary 'to supply the superiour parts of their musick with cornets and mens feigned voices, there being not one lad, for all that time, capable of singing his part readily'.[4] 'Feigned voices' means they were singing falsetto, and is the first unambiguous reference to this practice in England; it should be noted that they were singing the boys' treble line, not the alto part with which they later came to be associated.[5] Pepys reported on 8 July 1660 that at the Whitehall Palace chapel he heard 'very good musique, the first time I remember ever to have heard the organs and singing-men in surplices in my life', but no boys, apparently, were as yet involved.[6] In contrast, on 14 October 1660 he heard 'an indifferent sermon and after it an anthemne, ill sung, which made the King laugh'.[7] But a competent choir was evidently in being by the time of Charles II's coronation in April 1661, when the Chapel Royal joined forces with the choir of Westminster Abbey.[8] Two years later, Pepys offers an impression of the results of Cooke's training when he reported on his visit to the Whitehall chapel on 22 November 1663:

> ... the anthemne was good after sermon, being the 51. psalme – made for five voices by one of Captain Cookes boys, a pretty boy – and they say there are four or five of them that can do as much. And here I first perceived that the King is a little musicall, and kept good time with his hand all along the anthem.[9]

The style of some of the Chapel Royal's music was about to change radically. Charles's stay in France during the Interregnum had given him a taste for the Italian-flavoured music of the French court. The pre-war court 'violin band' (i.e. a string orchestra) was revived, enlarged, and renamed the 'Twenty-four Violins' in imitation of the French court's 'Vingt-quatre Violons';[10] in addition to their secular duties, from the autumn of 1662 at the latest they began to participate in the choral music of the Chapel, where, however, it seems only a few would have been performing at a time, playing one to a part in the modest-sized Whitehall building.[11] A new type of verse anthem, the so-called 'symphony anthem' developed, with instrumental interludes ('symphonies') before and between the vocal sections, both of which exploited the up-to-date Italian idioms, with lively rhythms and a basically homophonic texture. Such anthems were only performed on Sundays and festival days when the King himself was present, and it seems that the soloists, choir and instruments were placed in separate parts of the chapel, so imitating to a certain extent the Italian polychoral tradition of Gabrieli and Monteverdi's time. One Chapel Royal anthem, Matthew Locke's 'Be thou exalted, Lord', written to commemorate a 1666 naval victory over the Dutch, features three four-part choirs and two groups of instruments, and must have produced a striking impression on its performance in 1667, when it made use of the chapel's various spaces; it appears, however, to have been an exceptional example.[12] The new style had its critics: the diarist John Evelyn as early as 1662 regretted the loss of 'the ancient grave and solemn wind musique accompanying the organ', and characterized the innovation as being 'after the French fantastical light way, better suiting a tavern or play-house than a church'.[13] Cornetts and sackbuts in fact continued to be used in the Chapel Royal until about 1670, though their role remains obscure.[14]

In comparison with the pre-war verse anthem, the Restoration type gave free rein to singers' vocal display, nowhere more evident than in some of Purcell's bass solos, as in 'O sing unto the Lord', written for the pre-eminent deep bass of his time, John Gostling, an especial favourite of Charles II. In addition to his Chapel Royal post, Gostling, who was ordained, held numerous other posts in plurality, including being a minor canon at Canterbury and St Paul's. It was the men of the Chapel Royal who enjoyed the great majority of the 'verse' writing, most typically in ATB trio sections, familiar from Purcell's 'Rejoice in the Lord alway'. Notwithstanding Henry Cooke's establishment of a fine treble line, the boys were seldom given substantial solos in the later Restoration period; where they did contribute to verse sections, it was mostly as part of a solo voice ensemble. The participation of strings did not last beyond the reign of Charles's successor,

James II (1685–8), for with the accession of William and Mary in 1688, such extravagance was abandoned, and the former 'symphony anthems' were henceforth accompanied by the organ alone, with their symphonies shortened.[15] In contrast to the anthem, the style of Restoration canticle settings remained quite conservative in nature, and, except on ceremonial occasions, involved only the organ.

When we turn attention to cathedrals round the country, it is apparent that they too were eager re-establish their choirs quickly. The obstacles they faced were many – physical damage to the buildings (Lichfield in particular was badly affected), organs requiring re-installation, repair or a completely new acquisition, vestments and books all demanding time and money. Nevertheless, Winchester had its full complement of six boys and ten lay clerks boys by September 1660;[16] Ely also started to reassemble its choir that year,[17] while Durham appointed eleven boys and nine lay clerks in March 1661,[18] and St Paul's was at full strength including the boys by November 1661.[19] By 1662 most places in England had choirs back in the stalls, even if there were substantial musical challenges to be confronted. Edward Lowe, who had been organist at Christ Church, Oxford before the war, and resumed his post in 1660, was well aware of the problems, and in 1661 published a little guide entitled:

> A short direction for the performance of cathedrall service: published for the information of such persons as are ignorant of it, and shall be call'd to officiate in cathedrall, or collegiate churches, where it hath formerly been in use.

This provided examples of very simple music for the responses, psalms, canticles and the Litany (adapted from Tallis), designed as a stopgap 'to serve only so long, till the quires are more learnedly musicall, and thereby a greater variety used'.[20] The psalms and canticles were set to plainsong-like tones, with the option of four-part chant-like settings for Sundays and festivals. Knowing that choirs did not necessarily yet have competent boys, Lowe provided versions for men only (AATB) as well as for SATB. Although he was aiming to cater for the precarious current situation, his examples probably reflect what was common pre-war practice in many lesser establishments, particularly on weekdays. It apparently met a need, for the 1661 edition sold out, and Lowe issued a new edition in 1664, with a larger selection of tunes, and brought into line with the texts of the 1662 Prayer Book.

Although the cathedrals appear to have recruited new sets of boys quite quickly, getting them trained up to a satisfactory standard was a far more challenging task. There was no-one in the country at large with the same sort of talents as Henry Cooke. Reports over the following decades testify to the problems that cathedrals were experiencing. At York in 1665 the Chapter ordered that 'the quire be monished that for the future they attempt not to singe any anthem untill they were perfect before by practice under paine of forfeitinge 5s a man and the boyes for every neglect to be whipped by there master'.[21] If the stick ruled at York, then the carrot was tried at Hereford, where in 1661 the chapter made a special payment of 2s 6d each to the boys 'when they began to sing alone in ye chore, for their incouragement'.[22] At his visitation of Gloucester in 1669, the bishop ordered that a couple of the choristers' places be kept vacant 'till a boy be found who hath a good voice and aptness for musick. And that for the first yeare choristers be admitted as probationers onely, that soe, if they fitt not themselves to doe the quire service by the end of the yeare, they may be removed'.[23] In London, St Paul's clearly had early difficulties, judging by Pepys's verdict in 1664, when he was 'most impatiently troubled at the quire, the worst that I ever heard'.[24] The cathedral itself would fall victim to the Great Fire of London two years later, with the subsequent dispersal of choir personnel – although the men continued to receive their remuneration, for it was provided by endowments. In October 1666 the dean of St Paul's wrote to the dean of Lincoln suggesting Lincoln as a potential home for some of them, which was eagerly welcomed there, for the latter replied, 'Boys we want extremely in our quire, not having above 2 or 3 worth keeping, when we should have 8. Those quire-men we have are passable, and we must keep them: but we have but 8 and should have 12;'[25] in the event, however, only one lay clerk appears to have made the move.[26] At St Paul's some singing was resumed at least on an occasional basis in temporary accommodation in the late 1670s, but many choir places were allowed to lapse until the following decade, when a build-up started in anticipation of the opening of Wren's new cathedral in 1697.[27] Apart from the Chapel Royal, the Windsor choir seems to have been among those who recovered best, understandably so, considering that the men were better paid than anywhere except the Chapel Royal – Pepys in 1665 already found 'a good quire of voices'.[28]

Another sign perhaps, of the difficulties encountered at the Restoration are the number of places known to have employed cornetts and sackbuts, sometimes continuing their use for decades. Whereas before the Civil War they appear to have been mainly used to enhance the worship on Sundays and festivals, after 1660 they seem to have been used, at least in part, to alleviate problems with the choir. Exeter acquired a set of instruments,[29] Gloucester employed a cornett player,[30] York used them from at least 1663 to the mid-1670s,[31] and at Durham, where their employment dated back to the 1620s, sackbuts continued in use until 1680, and cornetts perhaps until about 1698, played by ex-choristers.[32] At Canterbury, where they had been put on the establishment in 1637, they were reinstated at the Restoration, but had disappeared by 1670.[33] The lawyer, writer and amateur musician, Roger North, noted that at York and Durham in the 1670s instruments were used 'to supply the want of voices, very notorious there', adding that, since for the upper parts in choirs 'wee can have none but boys, and those none of the best', the cornett, when well played, imitates the boy's voice so well that 'one might mistake it for a choice eunoch'.[34] He would later speculate 'that if female quiristers were taken into quires instead of boys, it would be a vast improvement of chorall musick, becaus they come to a judgment as well as voice, which the boys doe not arrive at before their voices perish', but acknowledged that 'both text and morallity are against it'.[35] If many English cathedrals were struggling, then the impoverished Welsh ones, with small numbers of personnel, were in a worse position, even causing Llandaff to abandon its choir completely in 1691.[36]

The most lasting musical innovation of the Restoration was the creation of the 'Anglican chant' for the psalms. This development apparently originated at the Chapel Royal, from where is quickly spread throughout the country. Hitherto, as already seen, the psalms had still used the traditional plainsong tones with their simple inflections at the ends of each half verse; these were sung unaccompanied and normally in unison, though at festivals (and perhaps on Sundays) often with improvised harmonies in the old faburden manner.[37] At the Restoration, however, the Chapel Royal musicians began to compose new tunes in four-part harmony, retaining a 'reciting' note for the beginning of each half of the verse, but adding a three-note ending to the first half and a five-note one to the second half, so creating a ten-note chant in total. This pattern was derived from the model provided by the first verse of the Venite (Psalm 95) with its short first half and longer second half. Unlike the plainsong tones, where the same reciting note was found in both halves of the verse, the new chant often used different pitches for each half-verse, offering more scope for harmonic change. For the first time also, the organ began to be used to accompany the psalms. In the seventeenth century the chants were all of the 'single' variety, so the ten-note tune was repeated for every verse. The early eighteenth century saw the emergence of the 'double' chant of twenty notes, enabling two verses to be sung before the chant repeated. This not only relieved the monotony of a frequently repeating single chant, but also gave composers more scope for melodic and harmonic invention. The number of chants used in the seventeenth century was small, and like the earlier plainsong tones, all the psalms of a day were sung to the same chant. Chants also came to be used for the canticles when circumstances prevented the singing of full settings, and in the case of the

Venite, this became standard practice – post-Restoration composers rarely composed it alongside the other canticles; some, like John Blow, specifically wrote a chant for the Venite as part of their service settings.[38]

Chanting the psalms in four-part harmony, however, produced problems of its own – it was more difficult to keep a choir together on the reciting note when singing in harmony than when in unison – a situation still familiar today. This was also complicated by the fact that the moment of change from reciting note to the notes of the ending was determined solely by a rule of thumb, which took no account of the natural accentuation of the words – it would be the 1830s before the appearance of psalters marked ('pointed') to show where the changes of note should occur. The problem of keeping singers in step seems to have been acknowledged early on, for it was the custom in the late seventeenth and early eighteenth centuries to sing the words on the reciting note in unison, breaking into harmony only for the endings, which would have been sung in strict slow rhythm.[39] Moreover, even when full harmony became usual, the chants were commonly sung from memory, with a tendency for the inner alto and tenor parts to be improvised, as noted by John Alcock, organist of Lichfield, when he published the first printed collection of chants in 1752.[40] Complaints about the haphazardness of psalm-singing – in particular the habit of rushing through the words on the reciting note – were commonplace. The Norwich organist John Beckwith (1759–1809) commented that psalm singing

> should be very decent, grave, and uniform; the choir attentive to their several parts; the organ not too loud, the length of the concluding semibreve never exceeded ... no hurrying in the longer verses ... It is possible to hear a chant where the men and children are trying which can sing loudest, which can recite fastest, and which can fairly get to the last note first: but with all this irreverent clatter, the grand object is not gained, as the organ contrives to be either behind or before them all the way.[41]

Alcock's chants (all his own composition) also contain many ornaments in the form of passing notes, appoggiaturas and trills, which doubtless reflected common practice, but were hardly an aid to unanimity. Nothing further from the sophisticated – at times over-sophisticated? – style of present-day psalm singing can be imagined. That evolution will be traced later.

The common picture of the Restoration choral world tends to be very London-centric, focused on the splendours of the Chapel Royal and Westminster Abbey, and its leading composers, John Blow and Henry Purcell. Yet in the country at large, the recovery of choirs was a slow process, and mediocrity at best seems to have been prevalent in most institutions for the rest of the century, particularly in the northern areas. In 1676, Thomas Mace, a lay clerk at Trinity College, Cambridge, admitted in *Musick's Monument* that in many cathedrals the music was 'deficient, low, thin and poor', with choirs sometimes operating with only one man per part owing to sickness and other causes, and blaming poor remuneration for the inability of choirs to attract better musically educated singers.[42] Not all was gloom, however. In Oxford, Henry Aldrich at Christ Church, where he was a canon from 1681 and dean from 1689 to his death in 1710, sang with the choir and held weekly meetings for the choirmen in the deanery, when attendance was compulsory – these were not rehearsals of their cathedral repertoire, but opportunity to perform a variety of other music, which doubtless reaped benefits when they were in the quire.[43] Still, if the satirist Thomas Brown (1662–1704) is to be credited with at least half-truths, when he describes the choirmen of St Paul's and Westminster Abbey, age-old habits were well and truly alive at the end of the seventeenth century. In a supposed correspondence between John Blow and the deceased Henry Purcell, Blow comments:

> I have no novelties to entertain you with relating to either the Abb[e]y or St Pauls, for both the quires continue just as wicked as they were when you left 'em; some of 'em dayly come wreeking hot out of a bawdy-house into the church; and others stagger out of a tavern to afternoon prayers, and hickup over a little of the Litany, and so back again. Old Claret-face beats time still upon his cushion stoutly, and sits growling under his purple canopy, a hearty old-fashion'd base, that deafens all about him. Beau Bushy-whig preserves his voice to a miracle, charms all the ladies over against him with his handsome face, and all over head with his singing. Parson Punch makes a very good shift still, and lyricks over his part in an anthem very handsomly.[44]

A major problem faced by most choirs at the Restoration was the loss of their music books. At Durham and Ely most of the old books had been secreted away, but generally choirs had to start again. Fortunately, one surprising resource became available to help re-establish a repertoire. As we have seen, Barnard's *First Book of Selected Church Musick* had been printed in 1641, just before the outbreak of the Civil War. Very few copies appear to have been sold on publication,[45] but sets of the ten partbooks evidently passed into the hands of Britain's first dedicated music publisher, John Playford, who had started in business around 1650, and was to flourish and dominate the trade for several decades. In 1674, in a petition to the King, Playford also claimed that he had rescued and restored to the Chapel Royal its old music books which 'had been embezzled' in Puritan times.[46] At the Restoration he was able to supply copies of Barnard to several cathedrals, usually bound with sheets of blank music paper to cater for additions. It provided a base of services and anthems, though a distinctly old-fashioned one, since, as noted, Barnard had not included works of living composers. Cathedrals added to their copies works of fairly conservative recent composers like William Child and Benjamin Rogers, as well as new locally composed works – Canterbury, Durham and Worcester were particularly strong in producing such material.[47] The new Chapel Royal style was slow to penetrate the provinces. Even at Windsor, they sang no Purcell in his lifetime,[48] and the style itself continued to meet with disapproval in certain quarters. In 1720 the minor composer and collector of sacred music, Thomas Tudway, lamented the 'corruption of that solemn, & grave style, which was establish'd as only proper to be us'd in divine service', which had given way to 'levity, & wantonnes of style'.[49] In general it was the later, simpler music of Blow and Purcell which became part of cathedral repertoires rather than the big showy verse anthems. A great deal of new music copying took place in the post-Restoration years, and it is only from this period onwards that we really begin to have a substantial survival of choirs' partbooks. The task was mostly undertaken by a lay clerk, and the standard payment was 3d. per page (or 4d. for the more demanding organ books). Books were commonly filled from both ends, with a different type of music in each part – typically divided between services and anthems, or full anthems and verse anthems.

Puritan criticism of church music certainly did not disappear after the Restoration. At Chester, the dean and chapter ordered in 1674 that verse services and anthems should be sung rather than full ones, as the words would be more easily heard by the congregation; they also suggested that the canticles might be sung to chants, which regular members of the congregation could learn to join in.[50] The choir was not allowed to aggregate all the singing to itself. Likewise, congregational participation in the psalms, and even in the responses and chorus sections of verse anthems by those able to do so, was encouraged by Edward Wetenhall, 'chanter' (i.e. precentor) of Christ Church, Dublin, and later a bishop:

> There are few, if any of our people, who are the least used to cathedral service, but can, and do sing with the quire the plain tones of the psalms, in which too very often, we sing our most usual hymns, the Te Deum, Magnificat, and the rest. The same I must say of the responds, when (as most commonly) plainly sung. Nay, even in the very Chorus's of our Anthems, as many as can sing musically may, and in the versicles, or any other part of the service, if any cannot or may not vocally join, it is sufficient, that the consent of their hearts distinctly go along with the voices of those who sing.[51]

This was not as revolutionary an idea as may at first appear. Pepys records going to the Chapel Royal in December 1660 'and there did sing my part along with another before the king – and with much ease', and similarly at Westminster Abbey in 1661, where having met a Mr Hooper 'he took me in among the quire and there I sang with them their service'.[52] A few existing single partbooks with no obvious institutional origin suggest that some gentlemen may even have had books specially copied for them to enable their participation.[53] A century later, Granville Sharp, a leader in the campaign for the abolition of slavery and a keen amateur musician, was accustomed to attend St Paul's and join in the choral services.[54] In a twenty-first century cathedral, despite the desire for active congregational involvement in worship, such behaviour would scarcely be welcome! Concern for congregations to be able to discern the words being sung (and perhaps to appease Puritans) resulted at the Restoration in the publication of 'wordbooks' of anthems, notably that compiled by James Clifford, a minor canon of St Paul's, entitled *The Divine Services and Anthems usually Sung in the Cathedrals and Collegiate Choires in the Church of England*, first issued in 1663, with an enlarged edition the following year. Clifford includes a brief guide to the order of services, and also hints at possible congregational participation, when he states his aim was 'that the people may follow the choire in their devotions without any loss or mistake, and be encouraged to learn to assist and comfort in the same melody'.[55] Enterprising choristers were not slow to exploit the commercial opportunities offered by such provision of wordbooks for the congregation. Denis Granville, archdeacon (and later dean) of Durham about 1680 complained of 'the quiristers carrying anthem books, and sometimes Common Prayer-bookes very impertinently and troublesomely to those that do not desire nor need them' – clearly with the expectation of a tip.[56] The provision of such wordbooks was to continue right into the twentieth century.

The Secular Scene and Joint Ventures

The final decades of the seventeenth century saw the scope of choral activity widen with a number of important developments. The first was the emergence of secular music involving choral forces. The Stuart court masques of Charles I's time sometimes involved short choruses, and in the extravagant masque *The Triumph of Peace*, given at Whitehall Palace in 1634, a chorus of twenty-nine voices was assembled from, amongst others, members of the Private Music and the choirs of the Chapel Royal and Westminster Abbey, including seven boys.[57] But the era really began with the advent after 1660 of regular court odes set to music, celebrating principally the

New Year, the King's birthday, and his return to London after a summer spent out of town. Sung by the Chapel Royal, the earliest were not unlike the new-style verse anthems of the period, with modest choral contributions (often just a simple final chorus); later the chorus could be given a larger role, particularly in Purcell's many contributions, and the tradition of New Year and birthday odes, composed usually by the Master of the King's Music, was to continue into the early nineteenth century.[58] Alongside the court odes came a development in the 1680s, which sowed the seeds for the musical festival movement – that of the celebration of St Cecilia. Although the association of the saint with music had medieval origins, it was only in 1683 that England began formally to commemorate St Cecilia's Day, 22 November. In London this took the form of a concert organized by the 'Musical Society', held from 1684 at Stationers' Hall, and preceded from 1693 by a service, usually at St Bride's Church, including choral music with orchestral accompaniment, and a sermon, often in defence of church music.[59] Henry Purcell's D major Te Deum and Jubilate was composed for the 1694 service, and went on to achieve popularity as a festival work, which continued through much of the eighteenth century. The concerts featured a specially written ode in praise of St Cecilia by John Dryden and others, set by composers such as Blow and Purcell, in which the chorus often played a significant part. The finest of these is undoubtedly Purcell's *Hail, bright Cecilia*, written for the 1692 celebrations, when, in addition to virtuosic solos and imaginative instrumental writing, a largish chorus (of perhaps around thirty singers, drawn principally from the Chapel Royal) was evidently to hand, since at one point Purcell asks for it to be reduced to four trebles and two each of the men's voices.[60] The London St Cecilia celebrations continued regularly until 1703, and were imitated elsewhere, including at Oxford, Salisbury and Winchester, enjoying sporadic revivals in the provinces later in the eighteenth century.[61] At Oxford University too, specially composed odes (usually in Latin) featured in the annual summer festivities known as the 'Act', held in Wren's new Sheldonian Theatre from 1669 onwards, and these could include modest choruses, with the singers presumably drawn from the choral foundations.[62]

We are sadly underinformed as to how theatre choruses were constituted in the Restoration period. Although wholly sung-through opera was a rarity (exceptions being the small-scale works of John Blow's *Venus and Adonis* and Purcell's *Dido and Aeneas*), there was plenty of demand for individual theatre singers of both sexes, who contributed to the incidental and entreacte music of largely spoken drama. When the occasional chorus was called for, it would probably mean just the solo singers combining together. But towards the end of the century, Purcell in particular spearheaded a short-lived fashion for dramatic works featuring large quantities of music – the so-called 'semi-operas', including amongst others *Dioclesian*, *The Fairy Queen* and *King Arthur*, in which a substantial number of choruses featured. In London there were almost certainly free-lance singers available outside the ecclesiastical choirs – in many cases probably ex-choristers – who could be called upon when the theatres needed them. Even so, it appears to have been customary for the regular theatre solo singers to have also sung in the choruses.[63] There is evidence, however, that on at least one occasion the boys and men of the Chapel Royal participated in London theatrical productions. In 1674 a royal command was given that those who were to 'sing in ye Tempest at His Royal Highnesse Theatre doe remain in Towne all the week (during his Ma[ties] absence from Whitehall) to performe that service, only Saturdayes to repair to Windsor and to returne to London on Mundayes if there be occasion for them. And that [they] also performe ye like service in ye Opera in ye said Theatre or any other thing in ye like nature where their helpe may be desired upon notice given them thereof'.[64] The incidental music for this production of the *Tempest* was by Matthew Locke, himself a member of the Chapel Royal. Whether this was an exceptional event remains unknown.

The drawing together of choral resources from various choirs for special occasions probably originated at coronations, when, what was by the seventeenth century a tradition, the choirs of the Chapel Royal and Westminster Abbey were combined.[65] The 1685 coronation of James II was celebrated in a particularly extravagant manner, and employed the largest musical forces yet seen in the Abbey, with 20 boys, 48 men and about 36 instrumentalists, distributed in various galleries;[66] the musical high spot was probably John Blow's large-scale anthem 'God spake sometime in visions'. At the end of the century, such joint choirs became a more regular feature of the London scene, particularly with the activities of the Corporation of the Sons of the Clergy.[67] This charity, literally founded by sons of clergy, originally aimed at assisting impoverished clergy and their dependents during the Commonwealth period, and surprisingly held its first festival service in old St Paul's Cathedral in 1655, when presumably only congregational metrical psalms would have been sung. By the 1690s, however, the annual festival had become a major choral occasion, especially after the opening of the new St Paul's in 1697. The resources of the Chapel Royal, Westminster Abbey and St Paul's came together, combined with orchestral accompaniment. Purcell's Te Deum and Jubilate featured in the 1697 celebration, and soon became a regular item until eventually joined by Handel's Utrecht and Dettingen settings of the Te Deum and Utrecht Jubilate.[68] A taste for the grander sound of many voices and instruments together, hitherto only heard on rare occasions such as coronations, was given a significant stimulus by this and the St Cecilia celebrations.

It was only when large-scale forces were involved that they had the assistance of a 'conductor', functioning just as a time-beater and usually employing a rolled-up sheet of paper, though in the earliest known visual portrayal, at the 1685 coronation, John Blow is shown with a stout stick in his hand.[69] Such time beating was primarily aimed at keeping the orchestra together, for the conductor stood with the players, who were placed behind the singers; the latter therefore could not see him, but were expected to take care of themselves, as they did in normal services. Placing the singers in front helps explain the lack of balance problems with the orchestra, which on average could number up to three times their number.[70] The Sons of the Clergy festival has continued at St Paul's to the present day, although now without orchestral accompaniment and with a variety of choirs taking part;[71] it has occasioned the composition of much special music over the centuries, including notable works such as Stanford's Magnificat and Nunc Dimittis in A in 1880, Elgar's 'Give unto the Lord' in 1914 and Bairstow's 'Lord, Thou hast been our Refuge' in 1917. It was occasionally imitated elsewhere, and the amateur composer John Marsh commended the quality of the singing at such a festival in Durham in 1796.[72] More importantly, the Sons of the Clergy originated the idea of associating musical performance with charitable giving, which was to become such a characteristic feature of the eighteenth century.

The Emergence of the Provincial Music Festival

Taking its cue from the St Cecilia and Sons of the Clergy celebrations in London, the early eighteenth century saw the birth in the provinces of the music festival with choral music at its heart. The exact origins of the Three Choirs Festival remain elusive, despite the researches of historians over the past two hundred years.[73] The three cathedral choirs of Gloucester, Worcester and Hereford – conveniently situated within thirty miles of one another – are now believed to have begun a regular joint meeting around 1715, each city hosting the event in turn. Initially the meetings were two-day affairs, with Matins in the cathedral each day, at which the festive Te Deum and Jubilate settings of Purcell and William Croft featured in the early days. Communal feasting followed, with secular music-making in the evenings, which soon came to be followed by one or more balls. The secular music also involved the musical clubs which existed in each city, whose membership would have included many of the cathedral singers – indeed, the idea of the meetings may have originated more with the clubs than the choirs themselves.[74] Combining to produce a much larger sound than the choirs were individually accustomed to, must have been a welcome experience, and one which would eventually be replicated elsewhere, when singers from various neighbouring cathedrals gathered to form at least the backbone of the chorus. Support was clearly forthcoming from the local communities, and especially from 1724 onwards, when the 'Meeting' (as the festival was called until the nineteenth century) added collections in aid of the widows and children of deceased local clergy, again imitating the Sons of the Clergy. The promotion of charitable causes was to be a mainspring of much of the musical festival movement in the eighteenth century, with the beneficiaries often being the many newly created local hospitals. It was also later to provide the clergy with justification for allowing concerts of sacred music to take place in cathedrals and other churches, where hitherto music had been strictly confined to the liturgy. At the Three Choirs, the meeting expanded at mid-century into a three-day affair, and about the same time race meetings were also planned to coincide with the festival, which came to take place permanently in early September. So, it became a main social focus of the year for the upper classes of the three counties, and relied heavily on the patronage of the gentry, who were content to see their entertainment justified by support for a charitable cause.

The musical ambitions of the festival quickly expanded beyond the use of local talent, and solo singers and instrumentalists were engaged from London, so enabling audiences to hear leading performers of the day. At first, the general organisation of each festival was in the hands of a single 'steward', usually a member of one of the choirs, who was also responsible for the financial viability, being expected to guarantee to cover any deficit. The expansion of the festival made for greater financial risk, and as a result by mid-century control had passed into the hands of two stewards recruited from the gentry and wealthier clergy.[75] It was a system which continued to operate for well over a century, but subject to intermittent crises, when people became reluctant to undertake such duties, a situation usually solved by increasing the number of stewards in order to spread the liabilities. Over the early decades the choral element remained almost entirely confined to the two cathedral services, for which, however, the choirs were gradually augmented by singers from places like Oxford and Salisbury. From the late 1750s, however, the role of the choirs would become greater, but before charting this development it is necessary to consider the work of the towering individual who was to influence the course of British choral history more than any other.

George Frideric Handel

By the time Handel first visited England in 1710, he was already fully accomplished as a choral composer, as evidenced by the *Dixit Dominus* and other Latin psalm settings composed during his Italian years (1706–10). Once in England, he was to become acquainted with the ceremonial style of Purcell's Te Deum and Jubilate and various aspects of the English anthem. Even before the accession of his Hanoverian employer as George I in 1714, he was called upon to compose for special occasions involving the Chapel Royal, including a Te Deum and Jubilate celebrating the Treaty of Utrecht (1713). Handel, however, was first and foremost a man of the theatre, with Italian opera dominating his life up to 1732, after which he gradually turned to English oratorio. This was essentially his own creation, and one which was to prove decisive for the whole development of choral life in the country. The composition of church music was never more than a minor occasional activity; he wrote nothing for 'ordinary' cathedral worship – no Evensong can feature 'Handel in A'. His most intensive production of church music came with the eleven early 'Chandos anthems', which, together with a Te Deum, were composed in 1717–18 while Handel lived in the household of James Brydges, Earl of Carnarvon (later Duke of Chandos) at Cannons, his stately home at Little Stanmore, Middlesex. They were all scored for the earl's small musical establishment, with the choruses being probably sung one to a part. They remained relatively unknown to the wider musical world until publication in the 1780s, and only in Victorian times did some of them begin to enter the general choral repertoire.[76] These apart, Handel's contributions to English church music were almost entirely of a ceremonial nature, marking political victories, a royal wedding and funeral, and, above all, the 1727 coronation of George II, for which he (and not, as might have been expected, the Master of the King's Music, Maurice Greene) composed the four celebrated anthems. But although clearly favoured as the royal composer 'par excellence', nominally holding the post of 'Composer to the Chapel Royal' and being liberally rewarded with royal pensions, Handel was never fully tied into the court establishment – he remained at the court's service, while preserving his independence.

The coronation anthems certainly confirmed Handel's status as the true inheritor of church music in the Purcellian manner. For the 1727 coronation the largest musical forces hitherto known in England were assembled, estimated at about 60 vocalists from the Chapel Royal and Westminster Abbey, plus 14 additional singers, including some from the Italian opera, probably all male, with an orchestra of about 60 or more.[77] No wonder William Boyce would later describe it as the 'first grand musical performance at the Abbey'.[78] It may be doubted that Handel's music was heard to best advantage on the day itself. Quite apart from the fact that it appears that some of the performers began 'The King shall rejoice' instead of 'Let thy hand be strengthened', and that 'Zadok the priest' was sung in the wrong place,[79] the general hubbub that was commonplace during coronations did not make for a proper appreciation of the music's qualities. But there had been at least two crowded public rehearsals beforehand, so many would have had the opportunity to become acquainted with the extraordinary power of the music. The concept of the 'sublime', already applied to Handel's music in his lifetime, owes much to this occasion, and would be used to justify the large forces designed to enhance the 'grandeur' of the music later in the century.[80] After the ceremony the anthems soon began to enjoy performances in festival services and concerts, even though they were not published until 1743 – manuscript copies were available from Handel's assistant and amanuensis, John Christopher Smith senior. Of the four, 'Zadok the priest', with its magical and totally original opening build-up to the choral entry, predictably became a firm favourite, often described simply as *the* Coronation Anthem. Sometimes the final 'God save the King' section was performed on its own, usually as a concluding item in a concert. 'Zadok' has found a place in all subsequent coronations, and today it is used *ad nauseam* in television programmes whenever royal ceremonial of any era is invoked.

It could well be the general approbation that greeted the coronation anthems which influenced Handel in the early 1730s to turn his attention to the creation of the English oratorios, in which the chorus was always to play a major role – in contrast to the contemporary Italian oratorio, which, like the opera, was almost entirely given over to solo voices.[81] The declining fortune of Handel's Italian opera ventures in the face of competition from a rival company and from the English ballad operas ushered in by John Gay's *The Beggar's Opera* of 1728, was perhaps only one factor in his change of direction. Starting with *Esther* in 1732, Handel was to compose more than twenty oratorios during the next two decades. Most took dramatic Old Testament stories as their subject, though in no sense were they church works. A few were first given in concert rooms, but for Handel their natural home was the theatre, performed to the same audiences who came to the opera, though given without acting or scenery. As with operas, the oratorios were given several performances a season, according to demand. Handel did not, as often said, create them as substitutes for opera during Lent, when theatrical performances were allegedly banned – in Handel's lifetime they were not, except on Wednesdays and Fridays. Nevertheless, especially later, many of his oratorios were commonly given at that time, and seasons of Lenten oratorios at Covent Garden continued into the nineteenth century.[82]

Just who made up the choruses for Handel's early oratorio performances remains uncertain, though there is no reason to think that they would have exceeded twenty singers. There is no indication that the Chapel Royal participated as a group, though individual men may have done so, and from the 1740s six to eight Chapel Royal boys were regularly supplied by their master. There would also have been free-lance theatrical chorus singers available. We know from surviving parts that it was usual for the soloists to also sing in the choruses. Alongside the oratorios themselves, between 1732 and 1740 Handel composed four other substantial choral works, two of which in particular were to quickly achieve lasting popularity. First in 1732 came *Acis and Galatea*, a radical reworking of a chamber work from his time at Cannons, now having a substantial role for the chorus. Then in 1736 came *Alexander's Feast*, a setting of a Cecilian ode by John Dryden. Its immediate popularity can be judged from the fact that it was published in full score two years later, and soon reprinted – *Acis* had to wait until 1743 before it too appeared in print. It is therefore no surprise that these works were amongst the first to spread his choral music more widely through the country. The other two works were the *Ode for St Cecilia's Day* (1739, setting another Dryden text) and *L'Allegro, il Penseroso ed il Moderato* (1740, from Milton and Charles Jennens); the latter in particular was also to find considerable public favour.

Only one place in England outside London experienced Handel himself directing his own work, when he went to Oxford in July 1733 to provide music for the university's summer Act festivities. Oxford not only heard *Acis and Galatea, Deborah,* and *Esther,* but also the premiere of his latest oratorio, *Athalia.* On this occasion the composer brought his forces from London,[83] but Oxford was set to become a key centre in performing his choral music, especially after the arrival in 1734 of the ardent Handelian William Hayes as organist of Magdalen College and subsequently Professor of Music.[84]

With the exception of *Messiah*, all Handel's oratorios after *Athalia* were premiered in London theatres, with varying degrees of success. Not a single oratorio, however, was published complete in Handel's lifetime; his publisher, John Walsh, issued only selected arias under titles like *The most celebrated songs in the oratorio call'd Athalia*, a reminder that it was the solo numbers that would initially have had wider circulation and appreciation than the choruses. Those who wanted to perform (or just study) a complete oratorio, had to acquire a manuscript copy from John Christopher Smith senior.[85] While it may in part have been due to a desire on Handel's part to keep some control of major works, equally John Walsh may not have considered full scores commercially viable. Only posthumously did such scores begin to appear, starting with *Messiah* in 1767.

The *Messiah* Revolution

Messiah, the work which above all was to transform the choral history of Britain and beyond, was composed with Handel's customary speed in just over three weeks in the summer of 1741. He had been experiencing declining fortunes with his London seasons of opera and oratorio over the last couple of years – in 1739, although the magnificent *Saul* was greeted with enthusiasm, *Israel in Egypt* failed to find public favour. So, he welcomed an opportunity to go to Ireland, perhaps at the invitation of the Lord Lieutenant (William Cavendish, 3rd Duke of Devonshire), in order to give a series of concerts during the 1741/2 season.[86] Dublin was a flourishing cultural centre, accustomed to receiving notable visiting artists in addition to having good resident musicians. Although no firm decision to go to Dublin seems to have been made before October, *Messiah* appears to have been composed with a premiere there in mind, perhaps reflected in the restricted original orchestration (strings, trumpets, timpani and continuo).[87] Handel's initial series of concerts, starting in December, were well received, and included *L'Allegro, Acis and Galatea, Esther* and *Alexander's Feast* at the new concert room ('Musick Hall') in Fishamble Street, which was to host the première of *Messiah* on 13 April 1742. In contrast to the commercial aims of his other concerts, *Messiah* was given for charitable purposes, namely 'for relief of the prisoners in the several gaols, and for the support of Mercer's Hospital in Stephen's Street, and of the Charitable Infirmary on the Inns Quay'.[88] The association of *Messiah* with good causes (and so employed by Handel himself in the last decade of his life) thus goes back to the very first performance, and over the centuries it must have raised more for charity than any other piece of classical music. Handel was a true Georgian with his combination of entrepreneurship, gluttony and charitable spirit.

It is often assumed that the chorus was provided by the boys and men of Dublin's two cathedral choirs (St Patrick's and Christ Church). While the lay clerks certainly participated,[89] and indeed took some of the solo parts, there is no indication that the choristers did – nor is there any mention of them at earlier concerts in which the men had sung. We know that Handel had trained a group of 'chorus singers' for these concerts, presumably adults of both sexes.[90] It is one of the ironies of *Messiah* that a work which would be tackled by amateur choralists worldwide, should contain some of the most technically demanding choruses in any of the composer's works. It seems most unlikely that the Dublin boys would have been capable of mastering such a work at the time – unlike the highly-trained Chapel Royal trebles which Handel used in London. Given the custom of soloists also contributing to the choruses, it seems probable that the soprano soloist, together with adult Dublin singers, provided the top chorus line. The whole chorus may have numbered no more than about sixteen, especially considering that many of the lay clerks were common to both cathedrals.[91] The performance was enthusiastically greeted by a capacity audience of 700, and Handel conducted a second performance on 3 June as the last concert of his stay. Dublin was to remain in love with Handel's choral works, and more performances were recorded there during the composer's lifetime than anywhere else outside London.[92] Cork, too, had an early experience of *Messiah* in 1744 at St Fin Barre's cathedral, probably organized by a recently created Musical Society, and again in aid of charity.[93]

It remained for Handel to introduce *Messiah* to London, which he did at the Covent Garden theatre on 23 March 1743. Compared with Dublin, its reception was decidedly unenthusiastic. Controversy had arisen beforehand, both over the propriety of composing a work with Christ as its subject, and of performing it in a theatre – the Dublin performances, of course, had been in a concert room. To both episcopal authorities and the evangelical movement of John Wesley, the theatres were generally regarded as dens of iniquity, however well patronized by the gentry. Setting biblical words as an 'entertainment' (which, whatever their theme, is how oratorios were regarded, even by Charles Jennens, the compiler of the *Messiah* text) had already brought criticism at the time of *Israel in Egypt*'s creation in 1739.[94] Handel gave just three performances of *Messiah* in 1743, and it was far outranked in popularity that season by *Samson*, which Handel had composed immediately after *Messiah* in the autumn of 1741. He was not to revive *Messiah* until 1745, when it received two performances, and then four years lapsed until he gave a single performance in 1749. As with other oratorios, Handel made changes to *Messiah*, depending on the singers he had at his disposal, so that it never achieved a definitive form. Such changes, however, affected only the solo numbers; with one exception (the substitution of the chorus 'Their sound is gone out' for one with the words 'Break forth into joy' which had concluded 'How beautiful are the feet') the choruses remained just as they were in Dublin, though oboes and bassoons were added to double the chorus lines. Despite Handel's initial lack of success with it, the work did not lack early admirers in England, and the Academy of Ancient Music performed it at the Crown and Anchor tavern in February 1744, while that devoted Handelian William Hayes gave the first English performance outside London at Oxford in 1749, as part of celebrations marking the opening of the Radcliffe Library there. Oxford was to hear more Handel oratorios during the composer's lifetime than any other English town, especially after the opening of the Holywell Music Room in

1748.[95] By way of contrast, a single performance of *Acis and Galatea* was the only substantial work of Handel to be given in Cambridge in the same period, no doubt partly owing to the professor of music, Maurice Greene, being on bad terms with the composer. It would be left to his successor, John Randall, to introduce Handel's oratorios to Cambridge, and many performances from the 1760s onwards were given to raise funds for the building and continued support of Addenbrooke's Hospital.[96]

The transformation in *Messiah*'s popularity came about in 1750, when Handel gave the first of what became annual performances at the Foundling Hospital, in aid of the charity founded by Thomas Coram to take in unwanted children. Performed to a crowded fashionable audience in the hospital's chapel, it marked the first occasion on which the work was given in a sacred building – indeed, perhaps the first time that a non-liturgical event was permitted in a church or chapel. It provided a precedent which would gradually be extended throughout the country, with Bristol the first cathedral to host a *Messiah* in 1758 – it was first performed at the Three Choirs the previous year, though not given in one of its cathedrals until 1759 at Hereford.[97] The propriety of having an 'entertainment', even of a spiritual nature, in buildings designated for worship was to continue to be a cause of controversy among church authorities for well over a century. For some of the Foundling Hospital performances we also have useful information about the exact size of Handel's choruses, which during his lifetime appear not to have exceeded nineteen, including six Chapel Royal trebles (to which should be added the probable assistance of the soloists). These were pitted against an orchestra of about thirty-three players. For later Foundling performances in the 1770s, we find that, although the orchestral numbers remain the same, the choruses had grown considerably in size, when in addition to 31–37 paid singers, there were 24–30 'volunteers' – though exactly who they were remains unknown.[98]

In addition to Handel's own performances of his larger works, a considerable number were given by others in his lifetime, both in and out of London, mostly small-scale affairs by enthusiasts who were either informally or formally organized into societies.[99] The orchestras for such performances can rarely have been furnished with all the prescribed instruments. An advertisement for performances of *Alexander's Feast* and *Judas Maccabaeus* at the Holywell Music Room in Oxford in 1755 stated that 'the following additional instruments, viz an hautboy, trumpet and bassoon' had been engaged to supplement the presumably usual string and continuo ensemble, though even with these additions the performances would still not reflect Handel's full orchestration.[100]

Contemporaries of Handel, such as Maurice Greene, William Boyce, William Hayes and John Stanley, also tried their hand at oratorios and similar choral works, such as odes for ceremonial occasions, but almost all were doomed to fail with the public; only Boyce's *Solomon*, a 'serenata' first performed and published in 1743, was to find modest continuing success. But before tracing the fate of larger-scale works at festivals and elsewhere in the latter part of the century, we need to trace other choral developments of the period.

Parochial Church Music

After the Restoration, the only music in most parish churches continued to be the unaccompanied metrical psalm, still not allotted an official place in the liturgy, but usually sung at the beginning and end of services, and before and after a sermon.[101] Towards the end of the seventeenth century there was growing dissatisfaction with the state of psalm singing, both in content and execution. The doggerel of much of the old Sternhold and Hopkins version was subjected to competition, especially from the 'New Version' of Nahum Tate and Nicholas Brady, published in 1696, designed to be sung to the old tunes. In the event, the new tended to supplement rather than replace the old; a few new tunes were gradually introduced (such as William Croft's 'St Anne' and 'Hanover'), but the real revolution came with the innovations of eighteenth-century Nonconformist hymn writers like Isaac Watts and Philip Doddridge, which, together with the fervent hymn singing promoted by John Wesley and his hymn-writing brother Charles, brought new tunes in their wake.

Developments in parish church music were to take very different forms in town and country parishes, though both involved the emergence of groups of singers with the aim, at any rate initially, of encouraging the congregation's own singing. This is in contrast with the role of such pre-Reformation choirs as existed at parish level, which did not involve the congregation at all. In town parishes, the late seventeenth century saw the creation by high church minded clergy of religious societies of young men, who were to occupy their free time in private devotional meetings, being a more wholesome activity than patronising the alehouse.[102] Their meetings included the singing of metrical psalms, and in turn they began to lead the singing in regular parochial services, of particular help as new tunes were introduced. Such a group of singers was proposed by an anonymous author as early as 1686:

> It would therefore be a commendable thing, if six, eight, or more, sober young men that have good voices, would associate and form themselves into a quire, seriously and concordantly to sing the praises of their creator: A few such in a congregation (especially if the clark make one to lead) might in a little time bring into the church better singing than is common, and with more variety of good tunes, as I have known done.[103]

At the same time, parish churches (or at least the wealthier ones) began to acquire organs, again with the principal objective of accompanying the psalmody. With the organs came a demand for organists – paid posts which could be sought after and competed for, and which in London especially were often occupied by leading musicians of the day. From the late seventeenth century too, another body of singers began to make their appearance in town churches, unconnected with any high church motivation – the children attending the charity schools newly established in many parishes. Both boys and girls took part – naturally sitting separately – trained by the schoolmaster or organist, who might be the same person.[104] The young men's societies proved to have a fairly short life, and were fading away by the 1730s, particularly as the evangelical movement of the Wesleys (itself born of high church principles) provided a new outlet for the enthusiasm of youth.[105] The charity children, however, were to be the mainstay of urban parish music well into the early nineteenth century. If initially introduced to support congregational singing, under a more enterprising master they could be introduced to singing in parts. John Playford's *Whole Book of Psalms in Three Parts*, first published in 1677 and frequently reprinted, was originally intended for domestic use, but proved a popular resource for charity children to sing from in two parts with organ accompaniment.[106] The introduction of organs and choirs did have the positive result of checking the slow singing of the metrical psalms – unlike the situation in Presbyterian Scotland – though by present-day standard the speeds would still have been very slow, and particularly in the early eighteenth century, the organist was accustomed to insert short interludes between each line of a verse.[107] However, far from encouraging the congregation to sing, there was a tendency for the singing to be more or less left to the choir; this was especially evident among the higher classes, who considered communal singing as beneath them. The question of the respective roles of choir and congregation in parish churches would be a cause of controversy lasting to the present day. Simple anthems and even canticle settings might be taught (and sometimes composed) by more adventurous organists wanting to introduce elements of the cathedral service. But not everyone approved of teaching music to charity children. In 1762 William Riley, a London teacher of psalmody, cited among objections raised: 'That it makes them proud, and sets them above their condition. That it makes them songsters and fond of company, consequently bad apprentices and servants', to which he answered that 'there is nothing in this kind of instruction that may make them prouder than children generally are, whose genius is superior to their schoolfellows ... And in this particular their capacity is the principal thing, for they are not taught to sing by the rules of music, as that would be a superfluous qualification for those who are intended for laborious trades and services, and in all probability might render them incapable of answering the good purposes intended, by setting them above their condition.'[108] The phrase 'not taught to sing by the rules of music' implies that the children sang by ear, and did not learn to read music.

The charity children were mostly supported by voluntary donations, and an annual fund-raising charity sermon was held in parish churches, when the children might demonstrate their skill with something more than their regular weekly fare. From 1704 the London charity children also took part in a spectacular annual service, when they came together to process in their uniforms to a large church (from 1782 St Paul's Cathedral) to attend a charity sermon organized by the recently created Society for the Promotion of Christian Knowledge (SPCK), and where they would sing *en masse* a metrical psalm (and in later years other music as well). They could number several thousand, and the deep effect upon the large congregations which gathered for the occasion can be readily imagined. Haydn on his first visit to London heard them in June 1792 and was immensely moved by their performance of a psalm sung to an Anglican chant.[109] The annual celebration was long-lived, surviving until 1877 – a reminder of the continuing condition of the poor in high Victorian times – although the procession through the streets was abandoned earlier, as being demeaning.

The use of charity children was naturally most common in London with its substantial number of comparatively wealthy parishes, although even in the capital there were many churches which, from choice or lack of resources, did without them and continued with unaccompanied psalmody under the leadership of the parish clerk; many, however, did at least introduce an organ by the end of the century. In provincial towns it is likely to have been only the one or two principal churches which were able to afford an organ, organist and charity children. Publication of music principally intended for such choirs increased as the century progressed, where the term 'psalmody' commonly went beyond metrical psalms to include some of the newly developing hymnody of the Wesleys, Watts and others, much of it more secular and modern in style compared with the traditional tunes;

simple anthems either composed or adapted for these forces were also added. Influential too were some of the books produced for the chapels of the various London charitable institutions associated with the established church, though outside the parochial system. Those of the Magdalen Hospital – a place for 'penitent prostitutes' – with titles such as *The Hymns, Anthems and Tunes with the Ode used at the Magdalen Chapel* of 1762, sold widely and went through several editions.

Towards the end of the eighteenth century changes began to occur in many urban choirs, displayed in two different trends, and symptomatic of dissatisfaction with the status quo. Priests on the evangelical wing, anxious to confront the growing appeal of the Methodists (who had formally separated from the established church in 1795), aimed to encourage congregations to sing, and to sing not only the traditional metrical psalms and hymns, which had been increasingly left to the charity children, but also to chant the canticles – i.e. part of the liturgy proper. To this end they did not necessarily discourage the existence of choirs but sought to reform them by restricting their role to chiefly leading the congregation, so reverting to the original purpose of introducing the charity children. The style of chanting the canticles was far removed from the fluidity of present-day 'speech rhythm', being both more rhythmically fixed and slower, and would have been quickly learnt by a congregation, given the weekly repetition of the texts, probably always to the same chants.[110] From the early nineteenth century a few churches began to extend congregational chanting to the prose psalms, when the assistance of the choir was doubtless more necessary, though this was a development that really took hold later.[111] The evangelicals were also a leading force in seeing the new popular hymnody of the Methodists and others increasingly replace the traditional metrical psalms, which was to spread to all types of churches as the nineteenth century advanced.

At the same time there were non-evangelical churches of various shades of churchmanship which sought to reform their music in the direction of imitating features of the cathedral tradition, aiming to enhance the aesthetic quality of their services by recruiting choirs which did not necessarily make use of charity children. Other children, perhaps recruited from the newly established Sunday schools, and adult singers of both sexes might be involved. Here congregations would leave much of the singing to the choir, who, in addition to anthems, would either chant or sing settings of the canticles, and increasingly the prose psalms, leaving congregations mainly to join in the metrical psalms and hymns. Sometimes these choirs were voluntary, but payment was often introduced.[112] They continued, however, to sing from the west end organ gallery or singing pews in the nave. A move to the chancel would come later. As for the music, an increasing number of publications were issued with such parish choirs in mind, providing easy access to repertoire. There was no need for parish choirs to source their music from manuscripts, although it would be normal for only a single copy of a publication to be acquired, with hand copying continuing to be the means of producing sufficient copies for the singers – it would be the second half of the nineteenth century before it became normal for all the choir to be singing from printed music. The most common type of publication contained a mixture of metrical psalm tunes, anthems, hymns and perhaps chants, though there were also plenty of editions with a single type of composition. Both cathedral and town organists contributed to this output, and many were local publications. Among the most popular were Edward Miller's *Psalms of David* (1790) and William Tattersall's *Improved Psalmody* (1794). But at this time, both types of experiment affected only a small part of the established church, and the great majority of urban churches, if they had any sort of choir, continued with their charity children for several decades.

The most radical developments in parish music in the eighteenth century, however, came not in the urban environment, but in country churches (which might extend to smaller market towns). Usually lacking the ability to install organs and the availability of trained musicians, there still arose towards the end of the seventeenth century a desire to improve the singing of metrical psalms. As in the towns, there was a movement by interested clergy to recruit groups of young village men to practise and lead the singing, again no doubt to distract them from other occupation of their free time. What was unusual was the early emphasis on teaching the reading of music. Instruction might in some places have been initially provided by the clergy or parish clerk, if they possessed the ability to do so, which was unlikely in most cases.[113] But there developed a network of itinerant 'singing masters', who would visit a parish for perhaps a month, giving intensive instruction to would-be singers for a small fee. They themselves appear to have been largely self-taught musically, and for some teaching may have been a part-time occupation, as in the case of Matthew Wilkins of Great Milton, Oxfordshire, who was also a butcher. Some would have operated locally, whereas others travelled more widely, and they certainly remained active up to the middle of the eighteenth century. Several published their own books of psalmody, whose contents all too often reveal their limitations as arrangers and composers; they would have sold them to the choirs they instructed, though perhaps only one or two would have been bought per choir. Such books almost invariably included an introductory section, containing the rudiments of music, derived ultimately from John Playford's *A Breefe Introduction to the Skill of Musick*, first published in 1654, which remained influential for over a century.[114]

The effectiveness of such peripatetic instruction, or at least the enthusiasm it generated, is clear from the way that the choirs continued to flourish after the singing master's departure. Part of the success may be due to the fact that the masters themselves came from much the same class as the singers. It may be doubted that many of the singers ever attempted to read the rudiments, whose explanations are often far from easy to comprehend. Indeed, probably only a minority learnt to read music competently, leaving many to sing by ear. They soon began also to practise simple anthems, which would have been sung after, and perhaps before, the service proper, and in places post-service singing could become an extended session. Although initially male only, women were soon admitted, particularly in the north of England, and both published and manuscript music books are mostly laid out for SATB voices.[115] Until towards the end of the eighteenth century the melody of metrical psalms was still placed in the traditional tenor part, even though in practice it was often duplicated by sopranos in the upper octave.[116] The interest which the movement created is clear both from the number of published volumes designed for their use, and from the appearance of many locally composed tunes and anthems. Written by men without any formal musical training, the music naturally has an emphasis on melody, with accompanying harmonies which pay little attention to the conventional rules of part writing or chordal progression. Stylistically their anthems take their cue from the Purcellian verse anthem, with a series of short sections, some scored for solo voices; they commonly featured some simple form of imitative writing ('fuging'), the whole often concluding with a 'Hallelujah'.[117] The sound, however, is completely at variance from that of contemporary cathedral music, and is now considered best viewed as 'vernacular'[118] rather than a sort of folk music, as it is sometimes characterized.[119] In addition to anthems, the country psalmody movement saw the composition of new tunes to metrical psalm texts in a more florid style than the traditional ones, perhaps incorporating solos and duets and sometimes through composed rather than repeating the music for each verse, thus making them virtually indistinguishable from anthems. Such music was of course unsuited to congregational participation; although this could give rise to complaints, it seems that most people in country churches were content to simply listen to the choir.[120]

A special 'singing pew' in the nave might be assigned to the singers, but more commonly a gallery at the west end was erected for them, hence the modern description of this phenomenon as 'West Gallery Music'.[121] Until the middle of the eighteenth century the singing remained unaccompanied, though a cello or bassoon was often employed to establish pitch and play along. Only in the last quarter of the century do other instruments commonly begin to be added to the ensemble – typically two to six of them, including a bassoon to strengthen the bass, and treble instruments such as a violin, flute, oboe or clarinet. Most such ensembles started to disappear after the 1830s, with the changing ecclesiastical outlook introduced by the Oxford Movement, though a few lingered on for several decades.[122] Thomas Hardy depicts them nostalgically in *Under the Greenwood Tree* (1872), though his fictional Mellstock band was perhaps untypical in having only string instruments and the singers being all male. For many, as Hardy portrays, music formed a core element in a village's social life, and in places the choir (with or without instruments) became semi-independent of the church – after all, they had no official position within it. Some might move around different places of worship in the neighbourhood, including Nonconformist chapels, as is evident from the repertoire of surviving music books.[123] They were clearly appreciated by their congregations, if not always by the clergy, some of whom evidently resented an alternative attraction to the sermon.[124]

Professional musicians predictably condemned the music of country psalmody as incompetent. The charity children singing teacher William Riley commented that 'such composers are not acquainted with the first principles of harmony ... as their tunes mostly consist of what they call Fuges [sic], or (more properly) Imitations, and are, indeed, fit to be sung by those only who made them'.[125] James Nares, a Chapel Royal organist who endeavoured to 'preserve the true character of church music, without regard to ... diversities of fancy',[126] noted in 1788 that 'having often been an auditor in country churches, where what they called anthems were sung in parts, I own I have been usually mortified by the performance, though at the same time I pitied the performers, who had against them not only their own inexperience, but the badness of the music'.[127] Others, including the clergy, criticized the sounds of the singers. The Wiltshire parson, William Bowles, wrote in 1828 that:

> In country churches, singing to the *'praise and glory of God,'* in general, is little better than singing to the annoyance of all who have any ear or heart for harmony. Two clarinets, out of tune, and a bassoon, which hurtles one note most sonorously, which three abortive blasts succeed: a man, for treble, with long hair, and eyes out of his head; a tenor higher than the treble, which completely mars the harmony; and a quavering bass, quavering as for life; and all those voices only agreeing in one point, as to which shall be heard longest and loudest; such voices, and such instruments, not unfrequently make up the musical part in country churches, of the church service.[128]

And just as the behaviour of cathedral choirs had repeatedly been the subject of complaint, so now the same strictures were commonly applied to the country singers by their clergy – they would turn up irregularly and without notice, create noise, and argue amongst themselves. Their full open-throated singing, without any attempt at subtlety of dynamics and subject to individuals improvising their own ornaments, was never going to satisfy those used to more refined sounds. But very few of these singers would have heard a cathedral choir, whose own singing by present-day standards would almost certainly be considered rough and ready; to them and fellow villagers it was simply the natural way to sing, just as they would have done in the local inn. The idea of uniform pronunciation of vowels as a prerequisite for good choral tone would have been quite foreign to them. The Mancunian Thomas Moore, in *The Psalm-Singer's Divine Companion* of 1750, already singled out pronunciation as the greatest fault encountered in village psalmody.[129] Nor, apart from the clergy and perhaps some of the local gentry who may have ventured to attend the occasional music festival, would their listeners have been acquainted with more conventional music-making. This music has recently enjoyed a revival by enthusiastic groups in the West Gallery Music Association. It must be admitted that their performances tend to be more restrained and polished than most of their eighteenth-century predecessors would have produced, especially, and understandably so, when the performances are committed to the permanence of recordings.[130]

The practice of country psalmody does not appear to have developed evenly throughout the country, but was particularly strong in certain areas, notably the north-west round Lancashire, Yorkshire and Cheshire, the West Country, East Anglia, and southern England around Sussex – at least these are the areas for which we have most evidence of activity.[131] Nor should we assume that raucous tones were prevalent everywhere, as will become evident when we come to the important story of Lancashire choralism. It is also the case that the boundary between town and country practices could be quite fluid; many publications, such as the popular *Book of Psalmody* compiled by John Chetham, a curate of Skipton, contained material suited to both types. Compiled and first published in 1718, it went through numerous editions and revisions, and included chants for the canticles (with full settings of the Jubilate and Nunc dimittis) as well as metrical psalms and anthems.[132] Certainly some parish churches, even early in the eighteenth century, on occasions attempted something more like the cathedral type of choral service, and surviving manuscript books show that simple settings of the evening canticles, often locally composed, were being sung by some village choirs towards the end of the century.[133] So, although the broad differentiation of town and country parish music may be valid, considerable exceptions and variety were also to be encountered, as local clergy and musicians were free to make their own decisions.

As for Scotland, the mid-eighteenth century witnessed a dissatisfaction in the Lowlands with the ultra-slow free-for-all style into which the singing of metrical psalms had fallen. Starting in Aberdeen, and closely followed by Edinburgh, around the year 1755 Presbyterian parishes began once again to assemble choirs to lead the singing, often in four-part harmony, and singing classes were organized.[134] As the Edinburgh author and publisher Robert Bremner reported in the second edition of *The Rudiments of Music* (1762): 'An universal spirit diffused through all ranks. Men of seventy and boys of seven years old were at school together, and equally keen of instruction. Their diligence enabled the teachers to produce very fine concerts [i.e. unanimity] in a few weeks ... so that in a few months the former erroneous manner of singing was entirely forgot.' But he also noted the danger of backsliding, especially in the habit of adding ornaments: 'but with grief I hear many of you are falling into the same error with your predecessors; and depend upon it, the consequence will be, that in a few years church-music will be as ridiculous as ever.'[135] The reform movement, however, does appear to have been successful, since the old style of psalm singing had been generally eliminated in Lowland towns by the end of the century. As with the country psalmody movement in England, the choirs also provided an important social element in the community, especially for young people.[136]

Georgian Cathedral Music

Unlike the previous two centuries, the cathedral music world of the eighteenth century saw nothing in the way of dramatic change. The Georgian era is generally regarded as reflecting a low point in the state of the established church. Preserving the status quo certainly characterized the behaviour of cathedral chapters; the evils of plurality of offices and absenteeism, although by no means new, were particularly prevalent. In these circumstances it is unsurprising that their ill-rewarded choirs were also affected, and if there were perhaps fewer reports of outright brawling and inebriation than in the past, shortage of personnel and absenteeism continued to be a major impediment. The early eighteenth-century anthem saw increased emphasis on writing for solo voices, including the rise of anthems for a single voice, and corresponding diminution of chorus sections. Influenced by the popularity of Italian opera, the melodic writing tended towards the florid, far removed from the principle of 'for every syllable a note'. This is seen in the works of London composers at the Chapel Royal, Westminster Abbey and St Paul's, such as William Croft and Maurice Greene, both of whom published substantial collections of their anthems,[137] setting a trend for putting cathedral music into print for the first time since the Restoration, and one which became increasingly common as the century advanced. Although the opportunities for vocal display doubtless offered satisfaction to the soloists, the new style of anthem also found favour for practical reasons in provincial choirs, where it could alleviate or disguise the problem of absenteeism, as well as reducing the quantity of music needing to be taught to the choristers. The fashion for solo anthems was fairly short-lived, but anthems incorporating passages for solo voices continued to dominate the rest of the century. The full anthem, however, still retained its place, being considered by some as the only appropriate style for true church music, being free of the temptations for personal display, and many composers, including Croft and Greene continued to contribute to both types.

While the physical state of cathedrals was often neglected and choir morale at a low ebb, the quantity of music that continued to be written was substantial, if rarely rising above mediocre quality. The size of individual institutions' repertoires varied enormously. At Bangor choral services were confined to Saturday Evensong, Sundays and important feast days. Its small choir knew only four service settings at the beginning of the century, and in 1718 the organist was ordered to teach two new anthems every year.[138] A century later, at Ely in the 1820s 94 anthems and 25 service settings were being sung, which still represents frequent repetition of items in the course of around 700 services a year.[139] Much of such a repertoire must have been virtually sung from memory, especially by the men. At Oxford, the surviving eighteenth-century partbooks from New College point to a substantial repertoire there, and one being continually added to. The vast majority was contemporary, with little representation of the Elizabethan/Jacobean period, and that only of the plainer kind, such as Tallis's 'Dorian' Service, Gibbons's Short Service in F, and anthems like 'I call and cry to thee' of Tallis and Richard Farrant's 'Call to remembrance', all now generally accompanied on the organ. The Restoration composers too were fast going out of fashion, though Purcell and Blow still made a modest appearance. Overall, it was the service settings of the sixteenth and seventeenth centuries which were retained in use rather than the anthems. One curiosity in the New College books is the inclusion of a substantial excerpt from Part One of *Messiah*, serving as an anthem, and copied as early as the mid-1740s, when the work was still very new[140] – a clear reflection of Oxford's early enthusiasm for Handel, and perhaps of the ability of William Hayes, the music professor, to gain early access to a copy of the score – he was to

Figure 3   Henry Purcell, Service in B flat, from William Boyce: *Cathedral Music*, vol. 3 (London, 1773). Humorous decoration of blank spaces could also be found in choirs' manuscript partbooks, perhaps echoing medieval illumination.

give a complete performance of the work in 1749 (see p. 85). It would, however, be the 1790s before Handel's oratorio choruses began to be generally brought into the anthem repertoire.

Although new music dominated in the quire, notable musicians in the eighteenth century were also concerned with the preservation and transmission of older repertoire. Between 1714 and 1720 Thomas Tudway, professor of music at Cambridge, was commissioned by Lord Harley to compile a six-volume anthology of services and anthems from the Reformation onwards, which includes lengthy prefaces on their history.[141] The anthology was never published, but may have influenced Maurice Greene, who in the 1750s began to work on a collection for publication, while John Alcock at Lichfield was having similar ideas, but abandoned them on hearing of Greene's plan. Greene died in 1755 with the project unfinished, but it was taken over by William Boyce, his successor as Master of the King's Music, and *Cathedral Music* appeared in three large folio volumes between 1760 and 1773. Subtitled 'a collection in score of the most valuable and useful compositions for that service, by several English masters of the last 200 years', it was destined to become a landmark publication.[142] Boyce's preface expressed the desire to provide choirs with more accurate editions of older music than the frequently corrupt copies currently in use. At the same time he commended the idea of singing from full scores rather than individual voice parts, so that the singers were more aware of their role within the composition – something earlier advocated by Croft.[143] Although Boyce was disappointed by sales, the list of subscribers shows that fourteen cathedral and similar choirs did buy sets sufficient for each of the lay clerks to have (or at least see) a copy, while most of the others did acquire one or two copies, from which works could have been transferred to their partbooks; it would certainly have encouraged choirs to expand their repertoire of older music. A second edition, posthumously published in 1788, achieved better sales, being subscribed to by many individuals and 'societies of singers', spreading interest far beyond the cathedral close. Further similar anthologies were issued at the turn of the century by Samuel Arnold and John Page,[144] but Boyce's compilation remained the best known, and even received two new editions in 1849, when it was also made available in separate partbooks as well as in score. Up to the early twentieth century, cathedral choirs came to rely heavily on Boyce for what little pre-1750 music they continued to perform. At Durham the original eighteenth-century copies were so beloved that the lay clerks were still singing from them in the 1970s.

As for performance standards, it is unsurprising to find few favourable reports of the regular round of daily cathedral services. By the eighteenth century, outside London the organist was almost always also Master of the

Choristers, and, as ever, an essential element in the quality of the choir lay with his skill and how conscientiously he trained his charges. The number of accounts we have is quite small, so we must beware of generalisations, but for Roger North writing in the 1720s, the only good choirs were those of the Chapel Royal and St Paul's.[145] Certainly the Chapel Royal continued to have the best available voices, since the current strength of twenty-six Gentlemen (ten of whom were priests) earned about ten times as much as in any provincial cathedral, quite apart from the fact that many of them held posts in plurality (including membership of Westminster Abbey choir) as well as opportunities for freelance engagements. The number of boys was reduced to ten in the early eighteenth century, and still sometimes drew in older boys from other choirs.[146] The Master of the Children was generally separate from one of the two organists' posts, and that the boys were well trained, especially under Bernard Gates's thirty-year period of office from 1727, is evident from the fact that Handel regularly employed them for his oratorio performances. Yet there is a distinct feeling that the Chapel Royal was now becoming something of a backwater compared with its prominence in earlier times. The increasing number of secular attractions, with their employment possibilities, meant that the court no longer played the central role it once did. Nor did the Georgian monarchs show any particular interest in their Chapel. Although its membership continued to contain leading musicians of the day, and some of them were granted a 'double place' to retain their services, none of them could compare with the greatest composers or singers of previous generations – even Handel's association with the Chapel being a tangential one. Fine voices were certainly to be found in their ranks, but, unlike the opera singers, they remained comparatively unknown to the public. Thanks to the length of George III's sixty-year reign the Chapel Royal also had no opportunity between 1761 and 1821 to appear in its most public role at a coronation. And throughout the nineteenth century, although its personnel would contribute to large-scale joint events, its activity at its by now permanent home in St James's Palace, where it now sang regularly only on Sundays, attracted no attention.

The splendours of the new St Paul's ensured it was the venue of choice for big occasions, from the Sons of the Clergy festival and state thanksgivings to Nelson's funeral in 1805. Maurice Greene was organist here from 1718 to his death in 1755, though, like the Chapel Royal, the boys had a separate master. The memoirs of Richard Stevens, a chorister in the 1760s under William Savage, provide a vivid account of his life there:

It may not be uninteresting to give some account of the education of a chorister of the cathedral. We rose at six o'clock, in the spring and summer half year; at seven o'clock from Michaelmas to Lady day. Our summons to our singing duty was the tolling of the cathedral bell to morning prayers at a quarter before six-o'clock from Lady day to Michaelmas, and a quarter before seven from Michaelmas to Lady day. We sung our solfeggi (or solfaing lessons) and singing exercises for the improvement of the voice, for an hour; the head boy accompanying us on the spinnet. Then came the writing master, who in the summer half year, staid two hours with us; and one hour in the winter half year. At nine o'clock we breakfasted upon a porringer of water gruel; excepting on Sunday and Thursday, when we had bread and butter, and small beer. At half past nine we went to the cathedral, and before eleven, we had returned to Paul's Bakehouse Court. We then practised singing till one o'clock, the head boy still accompanying us upon the spinnet; sometimes we sang together, sometimes singly, as our preceptor chose. At one o'clock we generally dined; and at three o'clock, again, went to the cathedral. We returned home by four o'clock; and from that time till six o'clock, we practised singing, accompanied upon the spinnet by the head boys. From six to seven o'clock we were permitted to exercise ourselves in a large yard; except on Wednesdays and Saturdays, when we had sometimes an hour, sometimes two hours allowed us to fetch our clean linnen from our parents' houses. At seven o'clock we supped upon bread and cheese and small beer; again exercised ourselves after supper till eight o'clock, when we invariably went to bed, unless engaged for the evening at concerts or other musical performances. The two head boys only, were permitted to sit up later, to practise from eight to ten o'clock upon the spinnet, various lessons, thoro' base, services, or anthems, or to improve themselves in the theory of music. Twice or three in a week (generally in a morning) Mr. Savage used to hear the progress that each boy had made in his singing.[147]

This degree of training suggests that it was done with an eye more to outside engagements than to what would have been the modest demands of the cathedral services. Savage seems to have been true to his name, for Stevens, while admitting his teaching ability, noted that 'he was violent and impatient in his temper to the greatest degree, and his impetuosity sometimes drove him into chastising the boys almost to cruelty'.[148] At the start of the nineteenth century, however, it was not the boys' musical ability, but their general welfare and education which gave rise to concern on the part of a redoubtable lady, Maria Hackett, whose story belongs in Chapter Five. As for Westminster Abbey, its music seems to have attracted little attention. Most of the vicars choral were also Gentlemen of the Chapel Royal, and a month on, month off system was in operation, with the men even being permitted to leave Abbey services early (before the sermon) in order to fulfil Chapel Royal duties. While the Abbey attracted numerous visitors to view the monuments, few probably stayed for services, and neither for here nor St Paul's do we have any contemporary accounts of the quality of the singing at this period.

Outside the capital, the music of the provincial cathedrals seems to reflect the general apathy and worldliness of the ecclesiastical hierarchy of the day. Whereas previously lack of attendance by the public would have been viewed as of little importance – the clergy and choir were there to carry out the *opus Dei*, regardless – now it was seen as symptomatic of a decline in the church as a whole. Thomas Tudway in 1720 complained of 'that contempt which Cathedral Service is fall'n into',[149] while at the end of the century John Byng (later 5th Viscount Torrington), although commending the quality of the singing at Lincoln – 'The service was nobly perform'd; ... a choir of 10 boys, and 5 men, of whom one boy and two men appear'd to have good voices; ... When this duty is well done, it becomes the best spiritual concert' – regretted how few were present in the congregation and gloomily predicted, 'Any attendance will soon cease and I shall live to see when none will be present at a cathedral service but a reader, a verger and two singing boys, who will gallop it over in a few minutes.'[150] In the middle of the century William Hayes blamed the 'mean and scandalous salaries annexed to the office of lay-clerk in every cathedral, except a very few' for the stalls 'being filled with mechanics, and in consequence of that, the miserable performances which we generally hear in country cathedrals'.[151]

Accounts of the situation in individual institutions are not numerous, and must be treated with caution, since standards naturally change with the personnel involved. At Salisbury, for example, when John Corfe was organist around 1720, the choirmen complained 'that it appeared to them that the boys, by the ill performance of their parts in the singing, were very much neglected'.[152] Yet later in the century, at a subscription concert in 1780, John Marsh commented that 'the boys were ... so well instructed at Sarum, and so polished in their style of singing.'[153] Marsh (1752–1828) in fact offers us a rare wide-ranging picture of the state of cathedral music at the turn of the eighteenth and nineteenth centuries. Living first in Salisbury and then briefly in Kent before settling in Chichester in 1787, Marsh was a skilled non-professional musician, who played both violin and organ as well as composing. His copious journals portray not only the musical life of his neighbourhood, but that of his travels, which took him as far north as Durham and Carlisle and as far west as Exeter. In contrast to his high opinion of Salisbury, he found much to criticise in Chichester, where the small choir (six boys and eight men) suffered in the 1780s from lack of interest on the part of the organist, William Walond junior (son of the Oxford organist of the same name) as well as from absenteeism of the men. He considered that, of two of the lay clerks,

> one of them was good for very little, Prince, a bass-singer who pleaded a stomach complaint that prevented his making the least exertion in singing, and another, Silverlock, an old man, the only tenor voice, was *worse than none* at all, every note he sang being so flat and out of tune as to mar, instead of improve or add to the general effect. So that the only two efficient singers were Barber, a pretty good but weak counter tenor and Luffe, a good choral bass.[154]

At Canterbury in 1802 he 'found so great a falling off in this choir, from what it used to be that even Mr Drew thought it much worse than Chichester, which choir he sho'd now, he said, speak up for more than he had usually done; the whole service at Canterbury, both morning and evening (except the readers part) being now gabbled over in such a hurryscurry way, the boys being very badly taught (or rather scarce taught at all)'. This he attributed to failings on the part of the elderly organist Samuel Porter, 'who in fact ought to be superannuated', but also blamed the authorities, since 'it appeared as if none of the prebendaries etc. now troubled themselves about the choir, but left every thing to take its chance'.[155] By then the Chichester choir had evidently improved under a new organist, James Targett. Marsh heard about a dozen cathedral choirs over the years, and though any judgments made on attending on a single day must be treated warily, it is clear that there were places which, in his view, generally maintained a good standard, including by the 1820s Durham, Exeter, Lichfield, Salisbury and Winchester.[156] He had been pleased too by what he heard at Norwich in 1794, where he singled out for approval the custom that when there were three or more psalms to be sung, a different chant was used for the middle ones, thus avoiding the monotony of singing everything to one chant,[157] which was clearly the norm – so different from modern practice, where frequent changes of chant have increasingly become the order of the day. If Marsh found Canterbury's choir in poor shape, then so also was that of York, which was to remain in sharp contrast to the magnificence of its building for much of the nineteenth century. According to Dean Markham, when he arrived in 1809 'the choir could scarcely perform the choruses in the anthems, which were therefore omitted'.[158] While the boys continued to be reproved for their frequent irreverent behaviour, absenteeism among the men appears to have been the principal cause for complaint. Even

Figure 4   Pencil portrait of three Winchester lay clerks in 1820; Hampshire Record Office: DC/D8/2/3/3/1; reproduced with permission of the Dean and Chapter of Winchester Cathedral.

Durham, which generally through the centuries maintained a good reputation, had problems with its men in the 1790s, when the chapter decided to bribe them with the offer of an extra shilling a day if they attended both services, while in 1795 one Samuel Marlor was suspended from his duties 'in consequence of gross and disorderly behaviour at church in a state of great intoxication by loud talking and the most shocking imprecations by which the reader was prevented for a considerable time from proceeding in the Service'.[159]

But perhaps we should conclude with John Byng again, who, like Marsh, toured the country. Although not a musician, he did attend cathedrals and other churches, and his diaries contain a variety of remarks on the quality of the music-making, both good and bad. While he found at Worcester in 1781 'the psalms were slurr'd over most irreverently',[160] yet at Southwell in 1789 'the organ was excellently play'd; and four singing men, and eleven boys, sang as carefully as if at the Antient Concert! – The anthem of 3 parts, 'Sing O heavens', by Mr Kent was capitally perform'd; and I was told that one of the boys was reckon'd to have the finest voice in England, and that the men has been sent for to the Abbey-musick'.[161] Moreover, before the service he was even given a choice of anthem by one of the clergy.[162] Byng, however, was also sympathetic to the country psalmody he encountered, though sensing that it was already on the decline. On hearing of the state of psalmody at Bottesford, Leicestershire in 1789, he declared:

> Nothing shou'd be more encouraged as drawing both young and old to church, than church melody, tho' profligacy and refinement of the age has abandon'd and ridiculed it: but were I a squire of a country village I wou'd offer such premiums and encouragement … as wou'd quickly rear an ambitious, and laudable desire of psalm-singing, and put forth a little chorus of children; than which nothing is more elevating and grateful and sublime, hearing innocence exert their little voices in praise of their Creator.[163]

Evidence of choirs in Roman Catholic worship occurs only for a few London foreign embassy chapels from the middle of the eighteenth century; earlier such chapels appear to have had only congregationally-sung plainsong accompanied by the organ.[164] But from around the 1760s three of the principal chapels, the Portuguese, Bavarian, and Sardinian, began to employ small mixed-voice choirs, including, at least later, some of the Italian opera singers, who sang settings of the Ordinary of the Mass. Their organists included some of the leading musicians of the day such as Thomas Arne, the elder Samuel Webbe, Samuel Wesley, and Vincent Novello, the founding father of the publishing firm, all of whom composed for the chapels' worship. By the early nineteenth century their repertoire also included the music of Haydn and Mozart, performed with organ rather than orchestral accompaniment. The Bavarian and Sardinian chapels were turned from embassy into public chapels towards the end of the eighteenth century, and all three became highly fashionable places of resort, in much the same way that the Catholic Queen Henrietta Maria's Chapel Royal had been in Charles I's time. The Bavarian chapel in particular gained the nickname 'the shilling opera' from the presence of opera singers, and its charging for admission to the galleries.[165] But although some of them were, at their best, seemingly capable of performing works such as Wesley's 'Dixit Dominus' and 'In exitu Israel',[166] their flowering was brief and had come to an end by the time the Portuguese chapel closed in 1829. The Roman Catholic Relief Act of 1791 had enabled Catholic churches to be legally set up, but it would be the latter part of the century before elaborate music was heard again in English Roman Catholic circles.

Musical Societies and the Evolution of the Choral Society

The regular coming together of people in a formal society for the purpose of making music dates from the late seventeenth century and took varying forms. Amongst the earliest recorded appears to be a 'music club' established in Oxford about 1690 at the Mermaid Tavern, whose original list of rules is still extant.[167] Like most societies, it had a mixture of performing and non-performing members. The former included lay clerks from the choral establishments, who probably formed the majority of the performers.[168] From what little we know of the music performed, it consisted mainly of instrumental and solo vocal items – many of the lay clerks were probably also proficient instrumentalists.[169] They may, however, have included the occasional choral item, especially perhaps the Latin oratorios and motets of Giacomo Carissimi, then becoming admired in England, particularly by the dean of Christ Church, Henry Aldrich, who transcribed many of them. This mix of repertoire was to be typical of such music societies of the day. Their music-making was an essentially private affair, but with members being permitted to introduce a limited number of guests. They flourished predominantly in the cathedral cities, where a pool of skilled musicians was available – indeed, in many cases it would have been the cathedral men who initiated their establishment. The societies developed in various ways – sometimes key professional members would be paid, and initially private meetings might evolve into a series of subscription concerts, soliciting a wider audience. This happened, for example, at Oxford in the mid-eighteenth century, when the 'Musical Society' as it officially became, was responsible for the erection of the Holywell Music Room, opened in 1748, and the oldest existing purpose-built concert room in the world.[170] The society employed a small regular orchestra, and subscriptions were open to both town and gown. One concert each term (then four in number) was reserved for choral music, when, above all, Handel's oratorios came to the fore, with the chorus being supplied from the college choral foundations. Occasional choral nights were a common feature of many other music societies, especially when a local cathedral choir could be called upon. Whatever their precise nature, in most places such institutions were known simply as the 'Musical Society', and, especially when their activities moved more into the public sphere, the tavern might be replaced as a venue by some civic building such as a guildhall or assembly room. Only in London, understandably, did societies require more distinctive names, such as the Castle Society, meeting at the Castle Tavern, or the Academy of Ancient Music, at the Crown and Anchor in the Strand. The latter, founded in 1726 as the Academy of Vocal Musick, changed its name in 1731, and was an exception among these southern music societies in being largely devoted to exploring choral and other vocal ensemble music of the past – a pioneer of the revival of 'early music' – much of it by Italian as well as English composers from the early seventeenth century onwards. Its membership included most of the men of St Paul's, Westminster Abbey and the Chapel Royal choirs; boys for its meetings were originally provided from Westminster Abbey and St Paul's, but they were replaced from 1734 by four boys specially trained by the leading figure in the Academy, John Christopher Pepusch. In this way many of London's lay clerks and choristers, like members of the early Oxford music club, were enabled to sing plenty of Latin sacred music, but outside any liturgical context. The Academy went on to include Handel's oratorios and other choral music, and its concerts, at first given for the membership and guests, soon became semi-public occasions, continuing until its demise in 1802.[171] Its later years were mostly devoted to more miscellaneous programmes with less choral content, as happened also in Oxford, as taste moved increasingly in the direction of the new instrumental music of Haydn, Pleyel and others.

Another London institution emerging from an interest in 'antiquarian' music was the Madrigal Society, founded in 1744,[172] and still in existence today. Its early membership of about twenty was unexpected in its makeup. Sir John Hawkins (himself a member for some years) described it as initially consisting of 'a few persons who had spent their lives in the practice of psalmody; and who, with a little pains, and the help of the ordinary solmisation, which many of them were very expert in, became soon able to sing almost at sight, a part in an English, or even an Italian madrigal. They were mostly mechanics; some, weavers from Spitalfields, others of various trades and occupations'.[173] Some doubt has been cast on the details of these 'mechanics',[174] but if the account is basically correct, they had most likely learnt their psalmody in those young men's religious societies. They were, however, soon joined by professional musicians, and certainly by the early nineteenth century the society moved towards a distinctly higher class of membership.[175] The music at their weekly meetings centred on the performance of both English and Italian madrigals, and appears at first to have been sung by men only – a note of January 1745 states that two altos, two countertenors, four tenors and six basses took part,[176] but from 1756 the treble parts were supplied by a few St Paul's boys.[177] The important thing about the Madrigal Society, certainly in its early days, was that it was essentially a gathering in which all the members were expected to join in the singing, and it thus established the idea of madrigals as a 'choral' genre, rather than being sung one to a part as originally conceived. So firmly did this idea take root, that by the early nineteenth century it was commonly asserted that a madrigal could only achieve its fullest effect when sung by a multi-voiced choir. Such were the views of Edward Taylor (1784–1863), an influential member of the Madrigal Society who toured the country giving lectures on English vocal music.[178] The later history of madrigal singers and societies will be explored in due course, but this choral treatment stands in contrast to the practice of clubs dedicated to the cultivation of catches and glees, the age's other favourite kind of communal secular music.

Catches – humorous rounds, often with indecorous (or worse) texts, and intended for three or four male voices – had been sung informally in taverns since Elizabethan times. More formally organized clubs sprang up in the second half of the eighteenth century, of which the Noblemen and Gentlemen's Catch Club, founded in 1761, was the most prominent, and usually known simply as the Catch Club.[179] As its full name implies, this was a club for the elite of society, in which (like the Madrigal Society) the conviviality of wining and dining was as important as any musical entertainment, which was principally provided by professional singers – male, of course – who were designated 'privileged members'.[180] Despite its title, catches formed only a small proportion of the music-making, which was dominated by the glee, a term used since the later seventeenth century to denote part-songs of various kinds, but now really coming to the fore. Like the catch, the glee at this period was composed in three or four parts for unaccompanied alto, tenor and bass voices, but it moved more to an SATB texture from around the end of the century, boys, as usual, supplying the top part in the clubs. Piano accompaniment also then began to feature. The glee was essentially a modern successor to the madrigal, but, while the latter was now often being sung chorally, the glee was really designed for solo voice performance, though where there was a refrain, some communal singing may well have occurred. The composition of catches and glees was greatly stimulated by annual prizes offered by the Catch Club from the outset. Composers like the Samuel Webbes, father and son, were prolific providers, and numerous collections were published, especially by Thomas Warren, the Catch Club's first secretary. Many similar clubs (if on a lower social level) flourished in London and throughout the country, under various names such as the Anacreontic Society, the Harmonists Society, or the Apollo Catch and Glee Society, some of which may have gone in for more of a choral approach to the singing.[181] With the development of choral societies in the nineteenth century, the glee was gradually transformed into a choral genre, with female participation. The term itself gave way to the more general 'part-song' in the latter part of the century, but survived in the names of clubs, as it does to the present day in American school and university circles, including such famed institutions as the Harvard and Yale Glee Clubs, both definitely large choruses rather than solo voice ensembles. Harvard, reflecting its eighteenth-century heritage perhaps, still remains an all-male choir, whereas Yale became mixed in 1970.

Lancashire, the Cradle of the Modern Choral Society

The type of musical society so far discussed was mainly to be found in the southern part of England. In the north, the term 'Musical Society' was used for a very different institution, but one which was to have far-reaching consequences for the future of choral music. The geographical split is significant, for the great majority of cathedrals and other choral foundations were to be found in the south. Only five cathedrals were located north of the Wash: Carlisle, Chester, Durham, Lincoln, and York, and of these only the choir of Durham had anything like a reasonably stable reputation for efficiency in the eighteenth century. In Manchester there was a small choral foundation at the Collegiate Church (later to become the cathedral), though it had only four boys and four men.[182] But in Lancashire and the immediate surrounding areas of Yorkshire, Cheshire and Derbyshire, the country psalmody movement took a strong hold from the end of the seventeenth century thanks in particular to two singing teachers, Abraham Hurst (or Hirst) and Elias Hall, based in Oldham, where already in 1701 a formal society was established containing thirty-six men (a number which perhaps included boys), but also, significantly, three women.[183] The participation of both sexes was to characterize these northern groups, with important markers for the future. Hall established numerous classes in an area ranging from Manchester to Prestwich and Ashton-under-Lyne,[184] and perhaps had an advantage over those singing teachers who only stayed for a few weeks before moving on. The method of basic music reading taught by Hurst and Hall was based on a simplified sol-fa system which had been known for at least a century. It was evidently highly effective and resulted in competent sight-readers, who by the middle of the century were in a position to tackle far more than the average country psalmody singer. Because of its success in the area, the method became known as the 'Lancashire Sol-fa', and still had its advocates over 150 years later.[185] (It should be noted that, unlike the tonic sol-fa system of the nineteenth century, it was a method which taught people to sing from normal staff notation). The foundations laid down in the early years of the century really began to bear further fruit from the 1740s onwards, thanks mainly to the activities of musical societies associated with churches and chapels of the Oldham area, especially those of the Shaw and Hey (or Lees) chapels. These were not Nonconformist places of worship, but 'chapels of ease', created to cater for the growing population unable to be accommodated in, or living too far from the old parish church. That of Hey (now a suburb of Oldham) opened in 1742 and could hold 500. A 'Musical Society' was started there in 1747, encouraged by the vicar; it was initially all male, but admitted women after a few years. Remarkably for such a church, in 1761 they not only installed an organ, but also employed a paid organist and provided him with accommodation. The first organist, Thomas Stopford, in his five years before moving to Halifax Parish Church, clearly built on an already keen foundation just at the time when Handel's music was being taken up more widely. 'Zadok the priest', together with Purcell's Te Deum and Jubilate, had been sung at the organ's opening, and it was Handel above all which would be responsible for the Society's fame.[186] Weaving was the mainstay of the Lancashire economy and at this time it was still a home-based activity, with weavers being paid by piecework. This gave them some freedom as to their working time, making it easier to assemble for music-making. The Society, which included instrumentalists as well as singers, was soon performing beyond Hey, generally combining with members of Shaw and Oldham. Stopford had previously been at the Shaw chapel, whose musical society was actually older than Hey's, dating from 1740,[187] and though we know less about it, as with that of Oldham itself, it was also ambitious in its aims, with a similar high reputation. In 1763 the combined forces took part in the first performance of *Messiah* in the north of England, given at the theatre in Manchester.[188] Such was their quality that Hey was to produce at least two nationally famous soprano soloists, Mary Russell (née Radcliffe) and Sarah Harrop, later Mrs Joah Bates.[189] Early outside engagements were almost entirely within Lancashire itself – mostly one-day special festivals, celebrating perhaps the opening of an organ, and these occasions were often termed an 'oratorio', whether or not an actual oratorio was sung. Such 'oratorios' might also be given to benefit the society's own funds. Following an initial visit across the county boundary to Halifax in 1766, the Lancashire singers increasingly took the Handelian choral message into western Yorkshire. They also provided vital support for larger-scale festivals in the north, as at Chester, Liverpool and York, filling the role that the cathedral choirs of the south did when they helped out at festivals away from home.[190]

Wider fame, however, awaited sopranos from these Oldham area choirs. By the 1770s the Three Choirs Festival acknowledged there was a lack of balance in the chorus, with insufficient sound from the boy trebles. News of the 'Lancashire sound' having reached the south, at the Gloucester festival of 1772 were engaged 'for the first time, to assist the trebles in the choruses, Miss Radcliffe and others, of the celebrated female chorus singers, as they were called, from the North of England'.[191] So successful was the experiment that the 'Lancashire Chorus Singers', probably numbering six to eight, were henceforth regularly employed by the southern music festivals, and were also engaged in London by the Concert of Ancient Music (founded in 1776).[192] Thus, this select group of singers became, at least seasonally, a semi-professional touring outfit. It can be readily imagined what impact the sound of just half a dozen such voices had on the soprano line of festival choirs, even if it had been the custom for soprano soloists to join the boys in the choruses. Nor was it just a passing phenomenon, for succeeding generations carried on the tradition, and as late as 1834 the Oxford Grand Music Festival advertised that 'The choruses will be sustained by the celebrated Female Singers from Lancashire, by gentlemen from the King's Concerts of Ancient Music, [singers from] Birmingham, [and] by members of the Oxford choirs &c.'[193] More importantly, it marked the beginning of the acceptability of mixed-sex choral bodies in the southern part of England, slow though it would be to develop. Such choirs were not entirely unknown earlier – in Bath 'several ladies and gentlemen of the first distinction' were involved in a performance of *Acis and Galatea* in 1757, and ladies continued to sing in oratorio choruses there over the following decades.[194] But being then the preeminent spa town of the leisured classes, it is perhaps not too surprising that they should have occupied some of their time in such pursuits, exceptional as it was, both in terms of sex and class. For choral singing throughout the kingdom was overwhelmingly still the preserve of males from the lower classes and would remain so until a broadening of appeal in the second half of the next century. And if women were gradually taking part – as for example in the chorus for the premiere of Thomas Arne's *Judith* at Covent Garden Theatre in 1773[195] – it was only as sopranos; the alto part in choruses would remain firmly reserved for men until mid-Victorian times.

Returning to the north, the visits of the Lancashire singers to Yorkshire in the late 1760s in turn stimulated local societies to be set up there in both villages and towns. The area was fortunate in having a number of good organists in the more important towns, including Thomas Stopford at Halifax, John Crompton at Leeds, and George Hartley at Sheffield, all imports from Lancashire, as well as the nationally known figure of Edward Miller at Doncaster. By the mid-1770s *Messiah* had received numerous performances throughout the region, while *Judas Maccabaeus* was the next most popular work.[196] The singer and composer Charles Dibdin, who travelled the country with his musical entertainments – he is now best remembered for his song 'Tom Bowling' – wrote in 1788:

> Halifax ... is said to be the most musical spot for its size in the kingdom: ... children lisp 'For unto us a child is born', and cloth-makers, as they sweat under their loads in the cloth-hall, roar out 'For his yoke is easy and his burden is light.' I have been assured, for a fact, that more than one man in Halifax can take any part in the choruses of the *Messiah*, and go regularly through the whole oratorio by heart; and, indeed, the facility with which the common people join together throughout the greatest part of Yorkshire and Lancashire, in every species of choral music, is truly astonishing.[197]

The spread of these northern musical societies and their keenness is also evident in the large number appearing in the subscription lists for musical publications of sacred music, including the second edition of Boyce's *Cathedral Music* anthology of 1788. Alongside 'Musical Society' the designation 'Society of Singers' or simply 'Singers at ...' was also popular, while the term 'Choral Society' already begins to make an occasional appearance.[198] Not all such societies were necessarily associated with a parish church. One body subscribing to Handel oratorios in the 1770s was the 'Musical Society at the Old Cock, Halifax'. Nonconformist denominations were also a fast growing force in the north throughout the eighteenth and nineteenth centuries, and some of their chapels also had associated musical societies, notably the Larks of Dean (or 'Deighn Layrocks'), connected with Baptist chapels in the Dean area of Rossendale in Lancashire; established about 1740, they survived until around 1870.[199] Although the music of Baptist, Methodist and other Nonconformist services was normally wholly congregational in nature, so that the function of any choir would have been to lead the singing, the occasional anniversary festival service or charity sermon would have offered scope for some special music, and, as with the parish choirs, 'practices' after the Sunday afternoon service could turn into long sessions of music-making.

The Lancashire village music tradition faded somewhat from the end of the eighteenth century, as the domestic weaving industry gradually gave way to factory working and a drift towards the towns, into which many villages became increasingly absorbed. In Yorkshire, where wool rather than cotton reigned, the shift came somewhat later, but in both counties domestic working was still to be found in the 1830s. George Hogarth could still write in 1835:

> In the densely peopled manufacturing districts of Yorkshire, Lancashire, and Derbyshire, music is cultivated among the working classes to an extent unparalleled in any other part of the kingdom. Every town has its choral society, supported by the amateurs of the place and its

neighbourhood, where the sacred works of Handel, and the more modern masters, are performed with precision and effect, by a vocal and instrumental orchestra consisting of mechanics and work people; and every village church has its occasional holiday oratorio, where a well-chosen and well-performed selection of sacred music is listened to by a decent and attentive audience of the same class as the performers, mingled with their employers and their families.[200]

Already too, Yorkshire men in particular were beginning to fill lay clerks' posts in cathedrals throughout the country, including the capital, a tradition that continued well into the twentieth century.[201] The nineteenth century was to see enormous industrial and social changes in the north, yet deep choral roots had been established, which would eventually see the creation of its famous large choral societies later in the century.

The Growth of the Festival Movement

For about three decades the Three Choirs Meeting remained the only regular festival lasting more than one day. But imitation was not long in coming. Salisbury led the way; having been accustomed to hold one-day St Cecilia celebrations since the beginning of the century,[202] in 1748 they began an initially two-, and later three-day annual festival along Three Choir lines, when local cathedral forces were regularly augmented by singers from Bath, Oxford and London.[203] The Salisbury-born philosopher and music patron James Harris was the driving force, and the music of his friend Handel was naturally predominant. Neighbouring Winchester was not slow in following with its own festival from 1756 (annual from 1761), which turned into the Hampshire Music Meeting and then the Hampshire Musical Festival, using similar choral resources to Salisbury.[204] But the cathedral cities were not the only locations to host festivals. In Leicestershire the eccentric village rector of Church Langton, Rev. William Hanbury, organized short-lived two-day choral festivals in an attempt to create a charitable foundation to benefit the village as a whole. Held from 1759 to 1761 and then transferring for a year each to Leicester and then Nottingham, they mainly employed performers returning from the Three Choirs.[205]

Far more significant was that held at Birmingham in 1768 in aid of completing the General Hospital; it was a large-scale three-day event with the standard mixture of oratorios, miscellaneous concerts and a service. Further occasional festivals followed in 1778 and 1780 before it was established on a triennial basis in 1784, still in support of the hospital.[206] Apart from the Three Choirs, it was to prove the longest-lived of all the festivals, and the most prestigious of the nineteenth century, surviving until 1912. Most importantly, at Birmingham the provision of modestly priced tickets was deliberately aimed at the growing middle classes of tradesmen and small manufacturers, which distinguished it from the gentry-dominated Three Choirs, and which augured well for its future support.[207] In common with the southern festivals, midlands Birmingham initially used a gathered chorus, assembled from various cathedral choirs and the town's own St Philip's Church, which was also a principal venue. Like the Three Choirs, whose own members contributed heavily to the Birmingham and other midlands festivals at this period, Birmingham began to employ the Lancashire chorus singers, but it was also eventually to lead the way in creating an independent festival chorus.[208]

Two- or three-day festivals also made an occasional appearance further north from the 1770s onwards, including at Chester, Derby, Leeds, Liverpool, Manchester and Newcastle. The oratorio – and that meant almost exclusively Handel – lay at the heart and success of any festival, becoming the focus of the choral interest formerly held by the festival service. Although the latter continued to be an essential feature of those festivals involving a church charity, elsewhere it increasingly fell by the wayside.[209] The oratorio also offered opportunities for organists in all manner of places, large and small, to mount festivals of one or more days as 'benefits' for themselves,[210] or as commercial events; the receipts from attracting a good-sized audience to a 'grand occasion' hopefully outweighed the costs involved. Such enterprise was more characteristic of the north than the south; in 1770, for example, John Crompton of Leeds took performers on an oratorio tour of Skipton, Otley and Knaresborough, three places which may never heard anything of the sort before, *Messiah* and *Judas Maccabaeus* being on the programme.[211] In Scotland, choral activity appears understandably to have been minimal, although the Edinburgh Musical Society (dating from the end of the seventeenth century) did for a while in the middle of the century manage to perform Handel oratorios with men from its own members and boys from George Heriot's Hospital, who had presumably benefitted by the reform movement in parish church psalm singing mentioned earlier.[212] But the society had ceased to exist in 1798, and when a first Edinburgh Musical Festival was held in 1815, many of the 58 chorus singers had to be imported from England, as so few were to be found locally.[213]

The 1784 Handel Commemoration and its consequences

In the mistaken belief that Handel was born in 1684 rather than 1685, a commemorative festival was held in London in May and June 1784, with concerts in Westminster Abbey and the Pantheon, involving forces vastly larger than anything hitherto attempted. Special galleries were erected in Westminster Abbey at the west end, together with an organ, at which the conductor, Joah Bates, presided, thanks to a special mechanism permitting the keyboards to be at a distance from the pipes. 513 performers were involved, of whom 257 formed the chorus, drawn chiefly from the choirs of the capital and elsewhere. In essence, therefore, the chorus was no different from that of festivals throughout the southern part of the country. Thanks to Charles Burney's official account of the festival, published the following year,[214] we have a complete list of the singers – establishing a custom that would be followed elsewhere. 47 boy trebles were supplemented by six female sopranos – they are visible on the left in the illustration published in Burney's account (Figure 5). Although we know one (Maria Parke) was from London, it is tempting to think that some of the others may have been from the Lancashire singers, especially as the wife of the conductor had herself once been among their number.[215] There were 45 altos – all male, of course – 80 tenors and 79 basses. It is not known where they all came from - presumably many cathedral choirs were severely depleted while the Commemoration was on – but it would seem that there were also probably more amateur choral singers around than might be imagined at this date. They were accompanied by an orchestra of 238, including 12 French horns, 6 trombones and a double bassoon, demonstrating that altering or adding to Handel's original orchestration was already under way before Mozart and others got to work on modernising his soundworld. With such forces, the balance cannot have favoured the treble chorus line, though it would have been heavily doubled by the oboes in particular. As the illustration shows, however, they were placed as usual with the soloists in front of the orchestra – sub-conductors at the side helped communication with Joah Bates. The contribution of the vast orchestra to the 'grand' sound should not be underestimated – 'Zadok the priest', after all, would still be impressive without the singers.

The choice of choral music was understandably confined to well-known pieces – a miscellaneous selection of sacred music for the first Abbey concert, and *Messiah* for the second, while the Pantheon concert featured further oratorio choruses and a coronation anthem in addition to operatic arias and instrumental music. A preliminary chorus rehearsal took place the week before (at which just a couple of unsuitable voices were weeded out); otherwise, just a single general rehearsal (open to the public) was held for each concert.[216] To the surprise of many, Burney included, the end result was remarkably well together. Perhaps the unanimity should not unduly surprise us, since to a certain extent, a Handel chorus, once started, can more or less look after itself. Under royal patronage – George III attended

Figure 5 Charles Burney, *Account of the Musical Performances in Westminster Abbey, and the Pantheon, May 26th, 27th, 29th; and June the 3d, and 5th, 1784. in Commemoration of Handel* (London, 1785); Oxford, Bodleian Library, Douce B subt. 272, Pl. VII.

all three concerts – the proceeds, after expenses, were donated to the picturesquely named Fund for Decayed Musicians (now the Royal Society of Musicians) and Westminster Hospital, over £7,000 being distributed. So great was the demand for tickets, that the two Abbey concerts were repeated a few days later, with a few changes to the programme of the first, the King again being present. A taste for the grandiose had been acquired, and it is not surprising that it was decided to repeat the event, resulting in further festivals in 1785, 1786, 1787, 1790 and 1791, with the number of performers increasing each time to 616, 640, 806, 'more numerous than on any former occasion' in 1790, and (an unlikely) 1067 for the final one; there is a limit to the idea that bigger must be better.[217] We have comparatively little information on these later performances – from where, for example, did all these additional performers originate? – but, with much the same music being repeated each time, combined with the troubled political situation in the wake of the French Revolution, by 1791 it was evident that this particular type of celebration had run its course, and no further extravaganzas took place. At the King's suggestion, however, an annual *Messiah* was instituted in 1792 at St Margaret's, Westminster, adjacent to the Abbey, with 300 performers, again in aid of the musicians' charity; it continued there for another two years before transferring for a while to the Whitehall chapel (the Banqueting House, which was fitted up as a chapel after the former Whitehall chapel had perished in the 1698 palace fire).[218]

The influence of the 1784 Commemoration was soon felt in many parts of the country, and there was a noticeable spread of festivals, usually on a small scale, held not only in the more obvious places like Norwich and Wells, but in towns as varied as Andover, Axminster, Farnham and Portsmouth.[219] The average size of festival choruses had probably been no more than about 25–30, partnered perhaps by the same number of instruments. Although the Three Choirs was always likely to have had more singers than the average, given their particular combination of forces, even here there were no more than 50 singers for the 1788 Worcester meeting which was attended by the King himself – 16 boys, 4 female sopranos, and 10 each of altos, tenors and basses.[220] Late eighteenth-century Birmingham festivals probably had 80–90 performers, not breaking the 100 barrier until 1802.[221] The Handel Commemoration inevitably created a desire for emulation elsewhere. Among the southern festivals, however, the scope for assembling larger forces was limited, given their continuing reliance on the cathedral choirs, and it was the north that offered more opportunity. Here the number of performers had already begun to grow in size before 1784 – Sheffield in 1770 mustered 60, while neighbouring Leeds, not to be outdone, fielded 70 in the same year. Both were surpassed by the Chester festival of

1783 with a total of over 100 performers, while Liverpool's own 1784 festival, held a couple of months after the London event, had 130.[222] Sheffield in 1786 advertised 150, and the following year no fewer than 257, including a chorus of 160, 118 of whom came from Sheffield itself.[223] Festivals now increasingly began to advertise themselves as 'Grand'. It was, however, not so much the number of performers, but the programme of the first Abbey concert, the miscellaneous selection from Handel's works, which was to prove most influential, albeit in a rather negative way. The 'Selection', as it became known, was immediately copied more or less exactly elsewhere, beginning with the Three Choirs that year, and it was generally advertised in being 'as performed at Westminster Abbey'. It was to become a staple element in festival programmes for the rest of the century. By the 1780s the enthusiasm for performances of complete oratorios (*Messiah* excepted) was already diminishing considerably, and the Abbey 'Selection', or something similar, tended to become a standard replacement. Handel's domination of the choral side of festivals was complete, but it was an extremely limited part of his output that most audiences would ever encounter, and in a manner far removed from the composer's conception of his oratorios as dramatic works. This was despite the fact that the first attempt at publishing a complete edition of his works was made by Samuel Arnold between 1787 and 1797.[224] Apart from *Messiah*, when complete or substantial parts of his large-scale works were given, they rarely ventured beyond the familiar favourites of *Acis and Galatea*, *Alexander's Feast*, *Judas Maccabaeus*, and *Samson*. Enterprise was shown from time to time, as at Sheffield, where the *Occasional Oratorio* was performed in 1787, and *Joseph* in 1788.[225] New oratorios or similar large-scale works by other composers were seldom encountered, and never established themselves in the repertoire – nobody now remembers Samuel Arnold's *The Prodigal Son* (1773), Felice Giardini's *Ruth* (1768) or John Stanley's *The Fall of Egypt* (1774). Of earlier works, William Boyce's serenata *Solomon* of 1743 was a rare exception in retaining some popularity. One apparently new work which did appear frequently in programmes was Samuel Arnold's *Redemption* (1787), but this was merely a compilation of various Handel pieces (including those of the 'Selection') turned into a convenient format for festival performances, with Arnold contributing only new recitatives. Late eighteenth-century audiences were not seeking novelty when it came to oratorios. It would take another foreigner to inject new life into the British choral repertoire.

On his first visit to London in 1791/2, Joseph Haydn attended a performance at the Westminster Abbey 1791 Handel Commemoration and was deeply affected.[226] He was to hear more Handel on his second visit of 1794/5, and the experiences provided the direct inspiration for *The*

Creation, completed in 1798. Composed as *Die Schöpfung*, the German libretto was actually based on an English model, and the full score, published by the composer himself in Vienna in 1800, had a title-page and text in both German and English.[227] In addition, the list of subscribers was headed by both the Empress of Austria and the King and Queen of England, showing clearly that Haydn intended it as much for England as for the German-speaking world. The first English performance was given in London by John Ashley in April 1800 in one of the concerts of the long-established Covent Garden Lenten Oratorio season, just ahead of one by Johann Peter Salomon, who had led the orchestra on Haydn's visits to London.[228] Ashley, originally a Covent Garden bassoonist, had been an assistant conductor at the Handel Commemorations. Between 1788 and 1793 he, together with his sons, organized a series of commercial festival tours, which took him from Portsmouth to Newcastle, but were concentrated in midlands and northern towns, mostly those for whom a festival was a novelty. His programmes offered largely the usual Handel fare, with a heavy representation of the Abbey 'Selection'. Ashley engaged leading London soloists and generally took at least the nucleus of his chorus (including Chapel Royal boys and Concert of Ancient Music singers), as well as orchestra, from the capital, supplementing them with local musicians. They proved highly popular, not least because they gave many an opportunity to hear the leading singers of the day, who rarely ventured to northern climes.[229] After his first performance of *The Creation*, Ashley (and following his death in 1805, his sons) continued to conduct the work in London and elsewhere. Whatever initial suspicions audiences may have had of this intruder into their traditional repertoire, its qualities quickly won over both singers and listeners, and it became a regular festival item. But it also importantly marked the introduction of foreign works into the repertoire, which increased steadily in the early decades of the nineteenth century, finally breaking the Handelian stranglehold. Mozart's Requiem was first heard in 1801, again through Ashley, while Beethoven's *Christus am Ölberge*, rendered into English as *The Mount of Olives*, made its debut under Sir George Smart, in 1814, and both works rapidly established themselves on British soil.[230] Haydn's successor to *The Creation*, *The Seasons* again had English roots in John Thomson's poem; although completed in 1801 and published in a German and English score in 1802, it apparently did not find even a partial English performance until a selection from 'Spring' was given at the 1817 Birmingham festival.[231] Despite its abundant attractive moments, it never acquired the same popularity as its predecessor, individual seasons being favoured over complete performances when it did appear on programmes.

The influence of the 1784 Commemoration was not confined to Britain. A German translation of Burney's 1785 account was published in the same year and led to a similar desire in Germany to emulate the grandeur of large choral forces as well as stimulating interest in Handel's works. The Berlin Singakademie, founded in 1791, had about 150 members by 1800; festivals held at Frankenhausen in Thuringia from 1810 to 1815 had 200–250 performers, while the Lower Rhine Music Festival, taking place in various towns along the river from 1817, regularly had 400–600 participants.

The music festival suffered something of a decline in popularity in the closing years of the eighteenth century, occasioned in part by the uncertain political and economic situation in the wake of the French Revolution. Some well-established regular festivals, such as those at Salisbury and Winchester, disappeared, and while the Three Choirs continued unbroken, it too ran into financial difficulties, with the 1798 Hereford meeting almost being cancelled. An increased number of 'stewards' was created in order to spread the cost of meeting the deficits, which continued for most of the next half-century.[232] A significant reason for the survival of the Three Choirs in the face of problems which ended many other festivals, must have been the relationship of the three cities involved. Local pride ensured that, whatever the financial situation, no city wanted to incur the odium of being responsible for breaking the tradition.

In the North, Halifax and Sheffield both managed to hold a large-scale festival in the 1790s,[233] but it was the early decades of the new century before there was an upturn in such activity throughout much of the country as the economy improved. This included John Ashley (with his sons) resuming his touring festivals, which again took them to places unused to such events, such as Boston, Ipswich, King's Lynn and Market Harborough, in some of which *The Creation* was performed;[234] meanwhile Charles Hague, professor of music at Cambridge, organized a similar series in the eastern counties between 1802 and 1814.[235] Although the later Georgian years saw much continuity in the choral world, they also experienced fresh developments which went hand in hand with the changes wrought by the evolving Industrial Revolution, all of which will traced in the next chapter.

Chapter 4
The Musical Festival and Choral Society in the Victorian Era

The Festival World up to 1850

As George IV and William IV brought the Hanoverian succession to an end, and Queen Victoria came to the throne in 1837, so significant developments were under way in the choral life of the country. On the festival scene, while the Three Choirs continued in its by now traditional way, others were being more experimental, although few festivals managed to survive on a long-term basis.[1] Three centres in particular, Birmingham, Norwich and York, attracted national attention, and of these Birmingham would turn out to be the most significant. York had held occasional festivals from 1769, including a four-day celebration in 1791, but it was the 1820s that saw it attempt grandiose affairs on a scale to match the magnificence of the Minster. For the first 'Yorkshire Musical Festival' in 1823 a choir of 273 was accompanied by an orchestra of 180 – easily the largest forces seen since the London Handel Commemorations, and mostly coming from the North.[2] Of the choir's 64 sopranos, only 13 were boys, reflecting the long northern tradition of women's participation in choral activity; the 55-strong alto line, however, was still an all-male preserve.[3] Handel continued to dominate the choral offerings, although parts of *The Creation*, *The Seasons*, and Mozart's Requiem also featured.[4] Three further festivals followed in 1825,[5] 1828 and 1835, with even larger numbers of performers – shades of London again – but there was severe criticism of the standard of the choir in 1835. *The Times* reported that 'the trebles were often inclined to take a time of their own, and run riot'.[6] A letter to the editor claimed that the poor performance was 'entirely owing to the inattention of the conductors in the selection of the chorus singers and the total neglect of rehearsals'.[7] Taken together with problems of positioning so many performers, this may have been one factor in bringing the series to an end, and it would be 1910 before York again experienced another large-scale festival.

A contrasting picture is offered by Norwich, where again, after isolated events from 1788 onwards, a triennial festival was inaugurated in 1824, the moving spirit of which was the Norwich-born Edward Taylor, who, starting as a local ironmonger, rose to become a nationally known bass soloist, lecturer, and writer on music.[8] In preparation for the festival, Taylor founded the Norwich Choral Society to provide the core of a festival choir. 150 singers took part in the1824 festival, of whom 101 were from Norwich.[9] The Norwich Choral Society, however, in common with others of the period, was all male, and although the festival's 45 sopranos included 7 females, it was decided afterwards that the top line needed strengthening. As a result, before the 1827 festival (for which the choir grew to 237), a separate Ladies Choral Society was established, which contributed 26 singers to a top line of 40 females and 31 boys.[10] The two choral societies continued in existence between festivals, rehearsing separately, but combining for annual concerts. Not before the late 1830s do they appear to have finally amalgamated, when it evidently was decided that it was safe for both sexes to practise together.[11] Taylor was a firm advocate of the music of Louis Spohr, and in 1830 Norwich gave the English premiere of *Die letzte Dinge*, translated by Taylor as *The Last Judgment*. It was to prove Spohr's most popular work in England, retaining a modest place in the repertoire for the rest of the century. Further works of his were given at later festivals, including, in 1839, *Des Heilands letzten Stunden* (*Calvary* in English), when Spohr himself came to conduct,[12] but none equalled the success of *The Last Judgment*. Taylor was also active in arranging other foreign works, often in bizarre forms. Perhaps most extreme was his arrangement of Mozart's Requiem for the 1836 festival, when, besides translating it into English as *Redemption* (Latin being unacceptable to local Protestant sentiment), he prefaced it with part of the overture to *Don Giovanni*, and added items from two other Mozart operas, Spohr's *Faust*, and a Bach Passion![13] The accident-prone nature of the early festivals is clear from the annotated programmes of George Smart (who conducted from 1824 to 1836), with their last-minute changes of singers, missing orchestral parts and the late arrival of players in the hall,[14] a state of affairs no doubt encountered at other festivals. Despite very variable standards – the poor quality of both chorus and orchestra was a common complaint, along with the notoriously long programmes – the festival rarely made a loss, and, unlike York, was long-lived, with a continuous history until 1911, and then being revived sporadically after the First World War. The boost given to local trade was evidently substantial, and, rather like the Three Choirs, 'county' patronage continued to be important in this comparatively isolated area of the country, which was reflected in the retention of a ball as an indispensable part of the festival until 1875.[15]

The undoubted leader of the festival movement in the nineteenth century, however, was Birmingham. The triennial festival's eighteenth-century beginnings have already been described in the last chapter, but its rise to prominence started with the appointment of Joseph Moore to manage the 1799 festival. Moore, a button manufacturer, had just the right skills to steer the festival in a new direction, with a professional approach far removed from the 'county' stewards of the Three Choirs, and in his hands the festival was able to return much larger profits to the General Hospital than previously. Recognizing that a core of regular local singers would greatly strengthen the base of the festival chorus, in 1806 he established the Birmingham Oratorio Choral Society, from which selected singers would be invited to participate in the festivals.[16] Initially its meetings followed the southern tradition of being all male, with boy trebles, though for the festivals the female Lancashire singers were amongst those forming the chorus, which continued to be gathered from many places, and whose numbers rose from 134 in 1820 to 217 in 1834, and 271 in 1846.[17] By the 1820s the Choral Society itself had a mixed-sex top line, with its sopranos soon contributing singers to the Three Choirs chorus,[18] and in 1843 it changed its name to the Birmingham Festival Choral Society, promoting its own concert season as well as forming the base of the Festival chorus.[19] At the festival itself, boy trebles, though not extinct, contributed only 7 to the 79-strong soprano line in 1846. In that year the 60 altos remained wholly male, but the barriers were about to begin to fall; in 1849 17 female contraltos joined the 60 men,[20] and then steadily replaced them as the century advanced, as they did throughout the country. As at Norwich, the Choral Society remained in existence between festivals, giving its own occasional concerts, mostly for charity.

Perhaps Moore's greatest service to Birmingham and its festival was to initiate the building of the Town Hall. St Philip's Church had long been recognized as inadequate for festival purposes, especially as the number of performers increased.[21] Construction began in 1832 and the Parthenon-inspired building, seating 3,000, was ready for the 1834 festival, complete with the second largest organ in the country, built by William Hill, in whose design Moore himself was involved.[22] It was to prove a model for similar halls throughout the country, especially in the north of England, providing large public meeting rooms not only for music, but for political, religious and other social gatherings.[23] Moore was also influential on the festival repertoire, promoting the emerging trend to move beyond Handel-dominated programmes. Birmingham was the first to commission new works for its festivals, and willing to look abroad to do so, starting with Sigismond Neukomm's *David* in 1834, and then most famously with Mendelssohn, whom Moore first met in Germany in 1836. This led to an invitation to conduct his new oratorio *St Paul* at the 1837 festival, and to compose his Second Piano Concerto for it. (*St Paul* had received its English premiere in November 1836 at the Liverpool Festival under Sir George Smart.) Mendelssohn was naturally the star at Birmingham and was to return for the next festival in 1840, which included the first English performance of his *Lobgesang* (*Hymn of Praise*). But Moore's biggest coup came when in 1845 he commissioned *Elijah* for the 1846 festival. Mendelssohn had been contemplating its composition ever since 1836, but it was Moore's request which finally provided the impetus for its execution. Given Mendelssohn's early death in little more than a year after the premiere, it is sobering to reflect that, but for Moore, the world might never have had *Elijah*. Its premiere on 26 August 1846 with four principal and six minor soloists, a choir of 271 and an orchestra of 125, was a predictable triumph; according to *The Times* 'the last note of "Elijah" was drowned in a long-continued, and unanimous volley of plaudits, vociferous and deafening'.[24] Odd as it may seem today, the practice of demanding encores extended to oratorios, and no fewer than eight numbers (four solos and four choruses) had to be repeated. Birmingham would hear the work again under the composer in a revised version the following spring, when he came to England for the last time, conducting it also in Manchester as well as giving four performances at Exeter Hall in London with the Sacred Harmonic Society, at one of which Queen Victoria and Prince Albert were present.[25] *Elijah* was immediately widely taken up, starting with the 1847 Three Choirs at Gloucester, and although *St Paul* also retained a fair degree of popularity, it inevitably lost out to the superior qualities of its successor. *Messiah* and *Elijah* were to form an indispensable core of most major festivals for the rest of the century, and not just for the financial stability they supplied; being so familiar to the performers, they could be given with minimal, or even no rehearsal time, so freeing up that precious commodity for the 'novelties'. Although *Elijah* has at times not lacked for disparaging remarks on the part of critics, notably the anti-religious George Bernard Shaw accusing the composer of 'despicable oratorio mongering',[26] for choirs it has constantly proved an exhilarating and immensely gratifying sing.

Important as the progress made by Birmingham was, its festival still had problems. The most common complaint, shared by virtually all festivals of more than one day, was the insufficiency of rehearsal time, aggravated when Birmingham (followed by others) increased its length from three to four days in 1820.[27] Mendelssohn expressed his frustration at the 1837 festival, when he commented in his diary: 'For all four festival days, all seven performances, just one day of rehearsal. That is how calves are led to the slaughterhouse, and it also leads to just such a feeling of misery and misfortune.'[28] While the broad massive choruses of *St Paul* went well, anything

BIRMINGHAM MUSICAL FESTIVAL.
1846.

ELIJAH,
A SACRED ORATORIO;

COMPOSED EXPRESSLY FOR THIS FESTIVAL BY

DR. FELIX MENDELSSOHN BARTHOLDY.

(The English Version by W. Bartholomew, Esq.)

And a Selection;

TO BE PERFORMED IN THE TOWN HALL,

ON WEDNESDAY MORNING, THE TWENTY-SIXTH OF AUGUST.

SOLD FOR THE BENEFIT OF THE GENERAL HOSPITAL.

PRICE ONE SHILLING.

BIRMINGHAM:
JOSIAH ALLEN AND SON, PRINTERS, 3, COLMORE ROW.

MDCCCXLVI.

Figure 6 Birmingham Musical Festival, 1846: programme for the première of *Elijah*; Oxford, Bodleian Library, Deneke 301.

demanding more delicacy left much to be desired. Mendelssohn's judgment would probably apply to performances at every festival of the era. It was very different in Germany, where provision for adequate rehearsal was the rule, even at such 'gathered' events as the Lower Rhine Music Festival, where Mendelssohn often conducted.

Most of the other towns with festivals in the early nineteenth century, such as Chester, Derby, Liverpool, Manchester and Newcastle, held no more than one or two. Apart from the Three Choirs, only Salisbury had a substantial long run, but even its festivals ceased in 1828. Although Liverpool and Manchester – already developing a rivalry – mounted the occasional festival, they found that a regular series of subscription concerts appealed more to the burgeoning middle-class audiences, despite a festival's draw of famous singers. The Three Choirs continued to attract national interest, but this was more by virtue of its long history and social caché – it enjoyed royal patronage from 1827, and a royal visit in 1830[29] – than for its musical quality. Whereas Birmingham was engaging the leading conductors of the day, such as George Smart and Thomas Greatorex, at the Three Choirs the organist of the hosting cathedral presided, however ill-equipped for the task. It wasn't slow, however, to take up the more important 'novelties' of the day – *The Creation* was heard in the year of its publication (1800), and *St Paul* and *Elijah* within a year of their premieres – but, unlike Birmingham, it never at this period had the funds (or inclination) to commission new works. Between 1834 and 1842 the morning oratorio performances were transferred from the quire to the nave of the cathedrals.[30] With a larger space to fill, the size of chorus increased, reaching over 200 by the 1850s.[31] At the same time the greater number of audience seats meant cheaper areas could be made available, enabling a wider class of attendance. This accorded well with the conviction of the time that experiencing 'good' music had an improving effect on the morals of the lower classes, though most would have considered such high-class entertainment was not for the 'likes of them'.[32]

Festivals were to benefit considerably from the transport revolution brought about by the creation of the railways, Birmingham being the first when the London to Birmingham line opened in 1838 – Mendelssohn would first use it when attending the 1840 festival.[33] The Three Choirs cities naturally took longer to become connected, starting with local lines in the 1840s, but eventually linking up with London. The result was a substantial increase in audiences, and special trains were soon being laid on. But before dealing with the later history of the provincial festivals, we need to step back and trace the rise of choral societies in London and elsewhere.

The Choral Society in London

It has to be admitted that we know little about how much non-liturgical choral activity was taking place in London at the turn of the eighteenth and nineteenth centuries. There were the continuing Lent 'oratorios', and the Academy of Ancient Music's concerts usually involved a chorus; the requisite singers for both would have come largely from the Chapel Royal, Westminster Abbey and St Paul's choirs, and free-lance theatre singers. Yet the large number of singers at the Handel Commemorations, increasing at each event, suggests that there were plenty of other keen choralists in the capital, even allowing for a substantial number coming from beyond London. A *Musical Directory* of 1794 lists three institutions meeting 'to practise choral music' – the Choral Fund (partly an 1791 amalgamation of two other bodies, the Handelian Society and the Surrey Chapel Society), the Cecilian Society, and the Portland Chapel Society – the last also acting as the chapel choir, singing anthems and services, then practising oratorios and church music in the evening.[34] Throughout the country many small choral groups almost certainly existed, of whose presence we are unaware, since they functioned within a largely private sphere, and never attracted public attention. It was, however, the 1830s which gave London its first substantial choral societies, the first being the 30-strong Classical Harmonists in 1831, members of which left in 1833 to form a larger body, the Choral Harmonists.[35] More importantly there followed the Sacred Harmonic Society in 1832, which was to be the capital's leading large choir for the next five decades. From 1834 it had the new 3,000-seat Exeter Hall in the Strand as its home,[36] and going against the fashion of presenting miscellaneous selections, it pioneered the restoration of performing complete oratorios.[37] Plenty of Handel, of course, but it was at Exeter Hall that Londoners first heard Mendelssohn's oratorios, on some occasions conducted by the composer. Like many choral societies of the day, the Sacred Harmonic Society included instrumentalists as well as singers, and from an initial membership of about 30, by 1850 it had a performing force of 700; the singers were all amateurs, while the orchestra mixed amateurs and professionals. Mendelssohn, who first heard them in 1837, noted that it was 'an amateur society drawn from the working classes, whose principal director, Mr Bowley, is a shoemaker'.[38] He was evidently unaware how typical this was for English choirs, for it was in strong contrast to the Berlin Singakademie, in which Mendelssohn had grown up, whose members came from the upper echelons of Berlin society. Nonconformity, with its enthusiastic hymn-singing, was a strong background of many of its members, and though artisans may have predominated, some certainly came more from the middle classes, and in 1840 royalty began to attend its concerts.[39] Standards in the early years were variable – Mendelssohn declared the orchestra 'deficient'[40] – which in 1848 led its first conductor, Joseph Surman, to be replaced (in rather acrimonious circumstances) by Michael Costa, conductor at the Royal Italian Opera and Philharmonic Society, who brought in far tighter discipline and with it artistic and financial success.[41] Costa's arrival signifies the rise of the more autocratic choral conductor, responsible for generally improving standards from the 1850s onwards. He remained in charge until the society's dissolution in 1882, partly caused by a forced move from Exeter Hall in 1881.[42] Since the early nineteenth century *Messiah* had regularly been given in Britain with Mozart's 'additional accompaniments' – producing the sound of a classical period orchestra, and further 'additions' continued to be made by others.[43] George Perry, the leader of the Society's orchestra from the outset, himself provided additional accompaniments to other works of Handel,[44] but Costa took the process a great deal further, and re-orchestrated a whole raft of them, with a particular penchant for plenty of brass.[45]

From May to September 1851 the Society capitalized on the great crowds being drawn to London for the Great Exhibition at the Crystal Palace in Hyde Park by performing an oratorio every week at Exeter Hall – *Messiah*, *Elijah* and *The Creation* in rotation – leaving it in a happy financial position.[46] After the Crystal Palace had been rebuilt in enlarged form at Sydenham in 1854, the Society's secretary, Robert Bowley, undertook the musical arrangements there, and with the centenary of Handel's death due in 1859, planned a festival with massed forces which put the eighteenth-century Commemorations in the shade. (A Handel festival conducted by George Smart in Westminster Abbey in 1834 on the occasion of the 75th anniversary of his death, had fielded a modest chorus of 356 and orchestra of 222.)[47] Bowley reflected 'the bigger, the better' approach when he stated: 'it was felt that a Commemoration of Handel in 1859 in any existing building in London, whether Exeter Hall, Westminster Abbey, St Paul's, or even Westminster Hall, would fail to afford a complete exhibition of Handel's colossal genius, and would prove unworthy the choral advance of the age in which it was undertaken.'[48] In preparation, and conscious of the potential problems of the vast building, a preliminary festival took place over three days in 1857, with a mere 2,000 singers (800 of whom came from outside London) and an orchestra of 400, conducted by Costa.[49] The *Musical Times* commented that 'The "Hallelujah Chorus" could be distinctly heard nearly half a mile from Norwood'.[50] Afterwards, the London constituents of what became known as the 'Handel Choir' were kept in training, and for the centenary itself there were 2,765 singers and 457 in the orchestra.[51] According to Bowley, the composer Giacomo Meyerbeer, who was present, 'described the performance of *Israel in Egypt* as the most wondrous display of choral power he had, with even his vast experience, ever witnessed'.[52] Commenting on the 1859 festival, the critic and antiquarian, John Edmund Cox, thought that increasing the size of choirs in Handel could serve 'only to enhance the grandeur of construction and the sublimity of conception'.[53] An audience of over 81,000 attended over the three days, yet with tickets prices at a guinea for centre seats and half a guinea for the side, these were concerts for the affluent, not the masses.[54] Such was the success with the public that the festival became a more or less triennial event, with over 3,000 voices in 1862 and 4,000 in 1923, only coming to an end in 1926 after 21 festivals.[55] The programmes themselves became predictable and fairly unchanging, with *Messiah* and *Israel in Egypt* the natural obvious oratorio choices, while a Selection day offered excerpts from other works. For the audience it certainly lacked nothing in the way of spectacle, not least the sight of Distin's Monster Bass Drum, originally made for the 1857 festival, but as critics quickly pointed out, the building was totally unsuited to oratorio, since the solo voices were audible only to those in the front rows,[56] and though the massed sound of the big choruses must have been spine-tingling to those close to the performers, even the grandest chorus sounded muffled and distant to many in the vast space. Already in 1857 it was noted that 'the music sounded as if the assemblage, performers and audience, were all singing and listening in the open air'.[57] Also, unlike the reverent silence in which modern concerts are heard, a nineteenth-century audience was not one to refrain from chatter, especially in the quieter moments of a performance. In the circumstances it is unsurprising that *Israel in Egypt* was generally thought the most successful oratorio for the building, owing to it consisting largely of choruses. Acoustic improvements, however, were made over the next decade, creating more of an enclosed space for concerts, and enabling at least experienced soloists to project their voices better. It would remain a popular, if still imperfect venue for large-scale musical events until its spectacular destruction by fire in 1936.[58] Costa conducted the Handel festivals up to 1880, and his orchestrations for them included adding six side drums to 'See the conquering hero comes' from *Judas Maccabaeus*.[59] His disciplined approach certainly helped keep the unwieldy forces together, though his successor, August Manns, who conducted up to 1900, was reckoned to achieve better musical results through more attention to rehearsals, including holding preliminary regional ones for provincial choirs taking part.[60]

Whatever their disputed musical merits, the Handel festivals proved lucrative for the Crystal Palace Company. They were, in fact, the only regular festival events held in London in the nineteenth century, except for the continuing annual Sons of the Clergy meetings. With the old aristocratic and gentry dominated 'season' giving way to all-year round musical activity, and with its attraction for international artists, the capital did not have the same need for festivals as the provinces. One result was that major choral works were much more likely to receive their first (or first British) performance at a provincial festival than in London, *St Paul*, *Elijah*, *The Dream of Gerontius*, and *Belshazzar's Feast* being just four examples.

Apart from the Handel centenary events, the 1850s were notable for the first English performances of Bach's St Matthew Passion under William Sterndale Bennett, whose youthful talent as pianist and composer had led to a close friendship with both Mendelssohn and Schumann. Bennett, with others, established a Bach Society in London in 1849 to collect a library of his works and to promote performances.[61] The Passion was given (in English of course) after much labour in April 1854 in a shortened form modelled on that of Mendelssohn's famous 1829 revival of the work in Berlin. Among those singing treble was the young John Stainer, who later commented on how much trouble Bennett had taken over it,[62] while the Evangelist was the leading tenor, Sims Reeves, who took the liberty of altering many of Bach's 'unvocal' lines.[63] That first performance achieved only partial success, but the Society persevered with it, and repeated the work with improving results later that year, and again in 1858 and 1862.[64] They also explored parts of the B Minor Mass and the *Christmas Oratorio*, but it was to fall to other organisations to bring Bach's major works properly into the British repertoire.[65]

'Rough and ready' might be a fair description of most choral performances at this time – the Sacred Harmonic Society, for example, presented no fewer than 14 concerts in 1860, with ten different programmes, besides practising seven further works.[66] But in 1856 Henry Leslie's Choir made its appearance, after this minor composer had taken over the conductorship of an amateur madrigal group and renamed it. With around sixty singers it specialized initially in an unaccompanied repertoire of part-songs and madrigals (which by now were firmly associated with choral performance), but also took on the Bach motets and, in 1879, even Tallis's 'Spem in alium', though this left its hearers rather baffled.[67] What distinguished the choir was the care and attention to detail in rehearsal, which quickly set new standards and drew warm plaudits from the critics, though some found the dynamic effects contrived: 'The singing under Mr. Leslie was marked by a refinement so elaborated and by devices so measured as to make the effect somewhat mechanical. We refer especially to the abuse of the *crescendo* and *sforzando*, which were employed with tiresome frequency, and often with exasperating regularity.'[68] Leslie later sometimes augmented the choir up to as many as 240 with a 'second division' set of singers in order to perform larger choral works with orchestra. He dissolved his choir in 1880, only for it to be resurrected for a few further years. The *Musical Times* summed up his achievement:

> Undoubtedly Mr Leslie has done incalculable good by showing us that a choir can be trained in this country to a state of absolute perfection, and the legacy he has left us will not be forgotten; but it is in the rendering of the great choral compositions that the fruits of this teaching should now be exhibited, for audiences will no longer rest satisfied with such chorus-singing as might often have been heard before the establishment of 'Mr Henry Leslie's Choir.'[69]

Leslie, however, was not the only person to run a choir bearing his own name. 'Mr Joseph Barnby's Choir' was created in 1867 by the composer of 'Sweet and low', with the chief aim of performing works, particularly modern ones, not being taken up by others. Their first programmes were of unaccompanied pieces, but they soon moved on to works with orchestra, especially promoting works published by the Novello firm, for whom Barnby had been music adviser since 1861. At a time when the Sacred Harmonic Society was playing safe in its repertoire (and suffering decline in the process), there was ample scope for Barnby's new choir, which in 1869 changed its name to the 'Oratorio Concerts'. Among their early achievements was perhaps the most successful British performance to date of Beethoven's *Missa Solemnis* in March 1870, the enthusiastic reception of which by the audience surprised many. Previous attempts, going back to partial ones in 1839 and 1844, and a complete one by Costa at a Philharmonic Society concert in 1846,[70] had often foundered on lack of rehearsal; it had last been tackled by the Sacred Harmonic Society in 1861. Barnby's performance also avoided the common strategy of altering some of the high-lying passages.[71] Equally significant were Barnby's performances of the St Matthew Passion, which in contrast to Bennett's efforts, really started its general revival in Britain. He began with a performance in Exeter Hall in April 1870, by which time the choir was 500 strong. It was repeated in 1871 at St James's Hall, when it was reported that 'it was with the utmost difficulty that Mr. Barnby could at all adhere to his determination to avoid encores, a resolution which, however, was compelled to give way before the simultaneous demand for a repetition of the overpowering chorus, "Have lightnings and thunders in clouds disappeared?" which was sung with marvellous precision and effect.'[72] Encores in the St Matthew Passion! He was then invited to give it in Westminster Abbey on Maundy Thursday 1871 within a liturgical setting – there was even a sermon between the two parts. The authorities did not at that time permit women to sing in the Abbey, so Barnby could use only the men from his choir, the soprano parts (including the solos) being sung by boys from various choirs, including the Abbey, St Paul's, Chapel Royal, the Temple Church, Windsor and Eton.[73] Such was the favourable reception, that it was repeated there in 1872, the year in which he also gave the first London performance of a cut version of the St John Passion at the Hanover Square Rooms, a work which, however, for long remained rarely heard. In February 1873 Barnby conducted four performances of the St Matthew Passion on consecutive evenings in the new Royal Albert Hall, in which the audience joined in the chorales (somewhat tentatively at first), supported by cornets,[74] while a large bass drum added reality to 'Have lightnings and thunders'.[75] The work can then be said to have truly arrived in the repertoire – the Three Choirs had also performed it for the first time at Gloucester in 1871 under Samuel Sebastian Wesley, who not only gave it complete, but then totally exhausted both performers and audience by following it with W.G. Cusins's oratorio *Gideon*, and excerpts from Spohr's *Cavalry*. The degree of under-rehearsal can be imagined, but fortunately the Passion still managed to make enough of an impression that it was given again the following year at Worcester.

With the opening of the Royal Albert Hall in 1871 came the creation of the Royal Albert Hall Choral Society. Interest in joining was enormous – over 5000 were auditioned and 1400 selected, of whom 1134 sang at the first concert.[76] Initially conducted, rather surprisingly and controversially, by Charles Gounod, it almost did not survive its first year. Gounod having resigned, Barnby took charge, securing its future by amalgamating it with his Oratorio Concerts, and reducing the size to what was considered a more manageable 850.[77] In 1888 Queen Victoria approved a new and now familiar name, the Royal Choral Society. Among the early years' highlights was the British premiere of Verdi's Requiem in 1875, conducted by the composer. In 1899 it had 242 sopranos, 174 contraltos, 174 tenors and 236 basses.[78] It enjoyed the stability of having just one change of conductor before 1922 – Sir Frederick Bridge, organist of Westminster Abbey, took over on Barnby's death in 1896, and proved popular and effective in controlling such a force. It rehearsed on Mondays in the hall itself to organ accompaniment.[79] Financial stability was maintained partly by virtue of its size (plenty of relatives and friends to supply an audience) and partly through a judicious programme of mixing standard favourites with more adventurous repertoire, including the British premiere (in concert form) of Wagner's *Parsifal* in 1884.[80]

The social make-up of choral societies saw gradual change in the second half of the nineteenth century. From a situation of singers having come largely from the artisan and lower end of the middle classes, a process of gentrification got under way as it became more acceptable for the professional middle classes to take up choral singing. Already the quality of Leslie's choir was attributed to the ladies having had 'the excellent education afforded them by schools for the upper middle class', while 'the gentlemen also were not far behind the ladies in general culture'.[81] Class issues certainly intruded into the choral scene in the second half of the century, and were very much to the fore in the early years of the Bach Choir, whose early history deserves attention for both musical and social reasons.

Founded in 1875, the Bach Choir was the brainchild of the lawyer Arthur Coleridge and the pianist, composer and conductor Otto Goldschmidt, who with his wife, Jenny Lind, had been settled in England since 1855.[82] Their initial objective was to the give the first substantially complete performance of the B Minor Mass in Britain. This took place in St James's Hall in April 1876, to a favourable reception, and encouraged them to make the choir permanent. The intention was to perform not only Bach, but other works neglected by most choirs. It was at first recruited from the Goldschmidts' friends, setting its upper-class tone, and one of Queen Victoria's daughters was among the early members. Early reviews were on the whole positive, and by 1880 it had a membership of 200 – modest in comparison with many other societies of the day. In many ways it is surprising that it survived its early years. Rehearsals, for example, started at 4.45 or 5 p.m., which naturally resulted in a shortage of men, so that professional reinforcement had regularly to be drafted in for concerts. Before the full rehearsal the sopranos and contraltos used to practise separately with Jenny Lind at her house. The choir's recruitment procedure resembled that of an exclusive club. Applicants had to be proposed and seconded by two members, then pass an audition before being elected by the committee. As time went on, criticism began to make itself felt, and concerts often produced unfavourable observations on the choir for its lack of impact. In 1884 the *Musical Times* commented on a mixed programme: 'The Choir has yet much to learn and to perfect, and will do well to tend earnestly towards improvement ere the advent of its next season.'[83] Enforcing regular attendance at rehearsals proved problematic given the social position of its members. Goldschmidt, who conducted for the first ten years, was not a forceful leader and prone to slow tempi. His successor, Charles Villiers Stanford, somewhat surprisingly, proved equally ineffective, at least in Bach and Handel – George Bernard Shaw found both Goldschmidt's and Stanford's performances of the B minor Mass 'intolerably slow'[84] – though to his credit the latter was responsible for commissioning Hubert Parry's *Blest Pair of Sirens* in 1887. But a performance of Parry's *Judith* in 1889 produced the criticism: 'There was here and there some uncertainty, as if the singers had not gained the requisite confidence for the fulfilment of the arduous duties required of them.'[85] The nadir was probably reached in 1894 with a performance of the St Matthew Passion in German: 'The well-meant use of the original German text was evidently embarrassing to the choir, the singing being feebler and more uncertain than at any previous concert of this estimable association within our remembrance.'[86] Things appeared to be no better at a performance of the same work in 1897, when 'to those who were familiar with this language the various modes of pronunciation by the English singers were disturbing'.[87] Both choir and audience numbers declined, leading to financial trouble, and by 1900 the future of the choir was in doubt. Following Stanford's resignation that year, a reorganisation took place, and rehearsals finally moved to the early evening. Under Henry Walford Davies a gradual revival of the choir's fortunes began, but it was not until the arrival in 1908 of the energetic Hugh Allen, organist of New College, Oxford, and conductor of the Oxford Bach Choir, that the choir had a charismatic leader, who could bring in the needed discipline, and for the first time a strict rule about attendance at rehearsals was successfully introduced. Allen also cultivated a fruitful symbiotic relationship between the Oxford and London choirs, with the Oxford singers frequently providing extra voices for the London concerts, and some of the undergraduates would have found a home in the Bach Choir after their student days.

Similar in many respects to the Bach Choir, though with a far less conspicuous public profile, was the Handel Society, founded in 1882 by no less a person than the future prime minister Arthur Balfour and friends, primarily to explore the whole of Handel's oratorio output, most of which was totally ignored by choral societies of the day. Surviving until 1939, it was an amateur body, which came to have about 130 singers and 80 orchestral players from very much the same social background as the Bach Choir. Its concerts were often private invitation affairs, though one public concert per year was usually given, latterly in the Queen's Hall. It made a point of sticking to Handel's original orchestration, and enthusiasm rather than high performance standards appear to have been the order of the day – even the vocal soloists were amateurs, though a few professionals strengthened the orchestra. It was directed by a series of mostly short-term conductors, including Samuel Coleridge-Taylor, Vaughan Williams and Reginald Goodall – for most, about four years appears to have been the limit of their musical tolerance.[88]

London, which in the course of the nineteenth century grew from 1,000,000 to 6,500,000 inhabitants, saw the rise and fall of many other choral societies from the mid-century onwards, especially in the developing suburbs. At the Alexandra Palace – North London's answer to the Crystal Palace – the Alexandra Palace Choral and Orchestral Society was formed soon after its opening in 1873, but really blossomed from 1901 under Allen Gill, when the choir had a strength of 500 (second only to the Royal Choral Society); it had a fine reputation and continued into the 1930s.[89] In central London one other important choir emerged before the First World War, the London Choral Society, formed in 1903; it would take its place with the Bach Choir and Royal Choral Society as a survivor to the present day, albeit changing its name to the London Chorus in 2004.

What was destined to become one of the most popular choral works in the first half of the twentieth century had its premiere not with one of these established choral societies, but at the Royal College of Music. This was Samuel Coleridge-Taylor's cantata *Hiawatha's Wedding Feast*, given in November 1898 under Stanford's baton – Coleridge-Taylor having been a recent pupil of his at the College. An immediate success, it was joined over the next two years by *The Death of Minnehaha* and *Hiawatha's Departure* to form the trilogy of *Scenes from 'The Song of Hiawatha'*. Published by Novello, it would prove highly profitable for the firm as it was quickly taken up by choirs, who, amongst other things, appreciated its straightforward choral writing.[90] It would later find further fame in a dramatized version (see p. 244).

The Sight-Singing Movement

Few things would appear more unlikely than Victorian Britain seeing mass enthusiasm for people spending their leisure hours attending sight-singing classes. That, however, is what happened in the 1840s, and at the same time major developments were taking place in music publishing, which were to have profound effects on choral life. The sight-singing story is quite involved, as rival systems and personalities came into play. In 1841 London found itself with two singing teachers offering free or cheap classes in sight-singing, both of which proved highly popular. One was run by a German, Joseph Mainzer, who had started classes for artisans in Paris in 1835, which attracted international attention. Mainzer's method used sol-fa names in conjunction with staff notation and followed the continental custom of 'doh' having the fixed pitch of C. Coming to London, he published a tutor, *Singing for the Million*, and organized classes in association with Mechanics' Institutes, schools and other bodies, initially teaching them himself. But he also made tours in the provinces, giving lectures and leaving it for local teachers to conduct classes using his tutor. He subsequently moved to Edinburgh and then Manchester, aiming everywhere to produce competent pupils who could then hold classes themselves. Mainzer's programme, however, did not long outlast his early death in 1851.[91] The other teacher was the composer John Hullah, who in 1839 had encountered the method and teaching of a Parisian rival of Mainzer, Guillaume Wilhem, and was encouraged by the educational authorities, anxious to see singing in schools, to introduce it in England, where he started classes in 1841, just before Mainzer. Held at Exeter Hall, these were initially for teachers, but were soon extended to the general public and Hullah published his own edition of Wilhem's method.[92] Attendees, like most singers of the day, came largely from the lower echelons of society, and by July 1842 it was claimed there were 50,000 learning from Hullah or from those he taught.[93] Part of the attraction would appear to have been the sheer volume of sound produced by massed voices.[94] Wilhem's method, as adapted by Hullah, was similar to Mainzer's, employing the same fixed 'doh' concept. However, while suitable and successful in the early stages, it quickly proved over-complicated when moving beyond the key of C, and both methods soon lost out to a third, based on radically different principles, which was to become the most powerful and lasting force in promoting musical literacy on a large scale for the rest of the century.

The tonic sol-fa method dispensed with a five-line stave and conventional notation in favour of alphabetical sol-fa syllables combined with the idea of a 'movable doh', which represented the home note (tonic) of any key. It was developed by a Congregationalist minister, John Curwen, and based on a method devised in the 1830s by a Norwich vicar's daughter, Sarah Glover, who had trained an excellent children's choir for her church, and published her *Scheme for Rendering Psalmody Congregational* in 1835. Some of its principles were in fact not so different from the old 'Lancashire Sol-fa' (see Chapter Three). It proved both easy to master and flexible in its capacity to deal with musical developments. Curwen's initial aim was to provide a method for teaching music to children in Nonconformist Sunday schools, which he did first in *Singing for Schools and Congregations* (1842). He did not come to it as a trained musician, but as a learner himself, and it was his profound understanding of the learning process which ensured that interest was maintained, by having a notation which enabled quick progress to be made in actual singing without the need to absorb details of musical grammar (clefs, crotchets, etc.). Curwen's aim was to harness singing to serve moral and religious causes, not to promote music for its own sake.[95] Hence his concern over the nature of texts to be sung – madrigals coming under particular censure. He delighted in encouraging congregations to sing in four parts, and was suspicious of the role of choirs in church: 'To have anthems sung by a choir, for show, is one of the most fearful desecrations of God's worship that could be invented,' he wrote in 1843.[96] Unlike Hullah, Curwen did not conduct classes himself, but relied on propagation through lectures and a series of publications, which gradually refined the method, which obtained its final form in the 1850s. From 1844 Curwen became his own publisher, and in addition to instruction manuals and music for choirs (not entirely in sol-fa notation), a monthly periodical, *Tonic Sol-fa Reporter and Magazine of Vocal Music*, priced at one penny, provided a principal vehicle for advancing the cause, which really took off in the 1850s. An estimated 2,000 pupils in 1853 rose to 186,000 a decade later.[97] Certificates of competence were awarded to both pupils and teachers, and to raise the standard of the latter, Curwen created the Tonic Sol-fa College in the 1870s to provide courses for them. The movement's success can be gauged from the Juvenile Festivals held at the Crystal Palace from 1857, when 3,000 children demonstrated their achievements.[98]

Rivalry between the systems of Hullah and Curwen continued into the 1870s. The official support obtained by Hullah meant that the fixed doh method was that authorized in teacher training establishments. But once in schools, teachers quickly abandoned it in favour of the practical superiority of tonic sol-fa. This pressure from below eventually led to the latter being granted official recognition alongside Hullah's method, which soon fell into oblivion. In 1885 the Lords of Admiralty even adopted tonic sol-fa for use in training ships.[99] The professional musical establishment, however, was largely dismissive of tonic sol-fa, seeing it as limiting pupils' horizons compared with traditional staff notation, as well as being suspicious of its moralistic basis.[100] To a certain extent, Curwen himself was responsible for this attitude. In the early days he had seen the method only as an initial way into music-making, with the intention that pupils should then progress into reading from staff notation. But he increasingly came to see sol-fa as a self-sufficient system – especially as publishers began to issue works like *Messiah* and *The Creation* in sol-fa editions – and he even (unsuccessfully) explored applying it to instrumental music. His missionary zeal meant he failed to perceive its limitations. Nevertheless, the method was not without influential supporters, for both John Stainer and Charles Villiers Stanford saw its value as an introductory tool, kindling musical enthusiasm, which could then be channelled into the demands of reading staff notation.[101] And tonic sol-fa was indeed to prove the path into music for generations of both schoolchildren and adults (who learnt it in evening classes) up to at least the 1920s. Although for many singers it was a stepping stone to reading staff notation, others found sol-fa sufficient for their needs, especially in Wales and northern England. Prejudiced professional musicians assumed that in choirs with singers using both sol-fa and staff notation, the former would be carried by the latter. In practice, however, the reverse tended to be the case, for the sol-fa readers had a much securer sense when it came to negotiating intervals, since sol-fa inculcated from the outset an association between the seen interval (doh-mi) and the aural experience of singing it. Even sceptics among school music inspectors had to admit that sol-fa readers performed much better in sight-reading exercises than did those brought up on staff notation. A striking and surprising example of the flexibility and adaptability of sol-fa is Walton's *Belshazzar's Feast*, for which Oxford University Press issued a sol-fa edition in 1933 – surely the most complex and advanced work to appear in the notation, with the key changing every few bars. That the publisher considered it worthwhile issuing, indicates that members of northern choral societies in particular were still demanding major works in sol-fa up to the Second World War.

Although Hullah's method failed ultimately to find popular favour, his work and influential position with the educational authorities was able to ensure music a role in the school curriculum. It became an obligatory component in teacher training colleges, even if the tuition was often inadequate, and the 'payment by results' system, in force in elementary schools in the latter part of the century, was eventually extended to include music. From 1883 to 1900 schools received 6d. per child for those who could sing songs by rote, and a further 6d. for those who could sing at sight by whatever method.[102] A downside of the scheme, however, was that, in concentrating on sight-reading, teachers paid little attention to the quality of vocal production.[103]

Music Publishing and the Choral World

Along with growth of the sight-singing movement and the number and size of choirs of all types, went hugely important developments in music publishing. While by the end of the eighteenth century, scores of much choral music were available in print, with few exceptions (such as Boyce's *Cathedral Music*), they were not used directly to perform from. Up to the middle of the nineteenth century all choirs continued to sing from separate voice parts, mostly in manuscript, and soloists in choral works also sang from individual parts. Small choirs would have mostly produced copies locally amongst themselves, but when we come to the increasingly large numbers involved in festival performances, then professional music copyists must have played an important part. The amount of copying involved for the Handel Commemorations was clearly enormous. We unfortunately have very little detail on exactly how or by whom such work was executed. But we know from the York festivals of 1823 and 1825 and the Gloucester one of 1826 that one John Hedgley, who had a London music business in Pimlico, was clearly the 'go-to man' for provincial festivals to obtain choral and orchestral parts.[104] Whether such copies were purchased outright or were available as 'hire library' material is unknown. Unlike continental music publishers, English ones were slow to go in for printing chorus parts, though in the mid-1830s they did begin to appear for some popular works, including *St Paul*, and a set was specially printed for the first performance of *Elijah* in 1846, before any publication of the work.[105]

One man above all was to be responsible for changing the face of choral music publishing in Britain. Alfred Novello (1810–96) was the son of the organist, composer and all-round musician, Vincent Novello, who had anticipated the creation of the family publishing business when, in the first decades of the nineteenth century, he published at his own expense scores or vocal scores of choral music, including the Masses of Haydn and Mozart, and sacred music by Purcell. Alfred set up his music shop in Soho in 1829, and in the 1830s became the main publisher of Mendelssohn's works in Britain. It was Novello's publication of *St Paul* in 1836, followed by *Lobgesang* (*Hymn of Praise*) in 1841, which greatly helped stabilize the firm's finances in its early years, though a dispute over the latter work led Mendelssohn to transfer his allegiance to the rival firm of Ewer in 1840 for almost all his later works, including *Elijah*.[106]

It was the 1840s which saw Novello's greatest innovations. Although Joseph Mainzer's activities and influence were short-lived, he did in 1841 launch a journal, *The National Singing Class Circular*, which he renamed in 1842 *Mainzer's Musical Times and Singing Circular*. Following financial difficulties, in 1844 it was taken over by Alfred Novello as *The Musical Times and Singing Class Circular*.[107] Novello had already experience in journal publication, for in 1836 he had founded *The Musical World*, which reported widely on the events and musical topics of the day, though he passed it on to other ownership after a couple of years.[108] The early monthly issues of the *Musical Times*, which cost just 1½d., consisted largely of short choral pieces, printed in score in a convenient octavo format.[109] The amount of textual content soon increased, and for the best part of the next century and a half it was the leading (and most influential) chronicler of the musical scene, ensuring that the whole country was covered. It remained close to its choral roots by continuing to include a musical supplement in every issue until 1977 (and then less frequently up to 1979) – all of which naturally functioned as advertisement for the firm's publications – and a section was always devoted to 'Church and Organ Music' until 1992. Novello sold the journal in 1988, and in other hands it has become more of a specialized musicological publication. Regrettably, its former long-time role as a recorder of the musical life of the country has no equivalent today.

It was the evident popularity of the *Musical Times* which led Novello onto his most important development, that of publishing vocal scores of complete choral works in cheap octavo format. He started predictably enough with *Messiah*, issued in twelve monthly instalments from August 1846, and then sold complete and bound for 6s 6d, with an edition of just the choruses also being available. *Messiah* was soon followed by other works such as *The Creation* and *Judas Maccabaeus*. Rival publishers were quick to imitate, and this forced prices down further in the following decades, aided by the repeal of taxes on paper, for which Alfred Novello had long campaigned. He also fought battles with the printing community, and from 1847 established his own printing works. Although he used the traditional method of printing music from engraved plates for small editions, when a large demand was expected then he favoured typeset music – for which he designed two new improved fonts – which enabled many thousands of copies to be run off with the aid of stereotyping.* Choirs quickly turned over to singing from vocal scores rather than separate parts, and as the tonic sol-fa movement gained popularity, works were issued in both staff and sol-fa notation, the latter usually in a small squarish format. For some the transition may have brought its own initial problems; it was no longer necessary to count out bars of rest, as you could see how your part fitted in with others and the accompaniment, but you now had to ensure your eye found the correct next stave as you reached the end of a line of music. Larger choral works, old and new, were rapidly embraced by 'Novello's Original Octavo Edition', as it was named, and generations of singers would later become familiar with its distinctive red and yellow cover with its 'great composers' border introduced in the 1870s – a few changes were made to the names over the decades, though Purcell was not included in the pantheon until 1933 and Elgar not until 1954. Singing from individual parts did not cease completely – Novello's still had chorus parts for *Messiah* available in the 1860s,[110] and newly commissioned works for festivals would have had to be sung from manuscript parts, if they had not been published beforehand in vocal score (which Novello sometimes managed to do). Popular works were also issued in 'pocket editions', intended more for an audience to bring

---

* Once a set of pages had been set up in type, a plaster impression was taken, which was then used to produce a metal plate, from which the actual printing was done – and which (like engraved plates) could then be stored for future use.

along and follow than for singers themselves to use. George Bernard Shaw, reviewing the 1891 Handel Festival, remarked that in massive choruses like 'See the conquering hero comes' or the Hallelujah Chorus 'the impulse to sing spreads even to the audience; and those who are old hands at choral singing do not always restrain it'.[111] One result of the move to vocal scores was that members of choral societies started purchasing their own copies of the music, whereas hitherto sets of individual voice parts would have been owned by the society. The possibility of hiring sets of vocal scores, either from the publisher or a library, would be a later development.

Taken together with many other series, such as 'Novello's part-song book', 'Novello's octavo anthems', 'Novello's parish choir book' and 'Novello's school songs', the firm would dominate choral music publishing in Britain for the next century. Other firms, like Boosey & Co., Chappell, and Curwen provided some competition in the nineteenth century, but it was not until well into the twentieth century that more serious challenges came from the likes of Stainer & Bell, and Oxford University Press. Alfred Novello's prime importance was that he ushered in an era of genuinely cheap but high-quality editions, affordable by singers who still predominantly came from the lower classes. Not for nothing was the first history of the firm in 1887 entitled *A Short History of Cheap Music*.[112]

Novello's were often called upon to print special choral selections for festivals, as they did for the Crystal Palace Handel festivals from 1859. And by the time the coronation of Edward VII took place in 1902, it is no surprise that the firm was the appointed official publisher of the book containing the music, a role that they fulfilled for every subsequent coronation up to that of Elizabeth II. However, although Novello's became an obvious publisher of choice for any composer of choral music, not every prominent Victorian composer was drawn firmly into the fold – Parry and Elgar certainly were, but Sterndale Bennett, Stanford and Sullivan less so, and in the twentieth century there was a distinct tendency for major composers such as Britten, Holst, Maxwell Davies, Tippett, Vaughan Williams and Walton to generally publish with other firms.

Provincial Choral Societies and Later Festival Developments

We have seen that the early nineteenth century saw the emergence of a few choral societies created with the specific aim of providing at least a core of prepared singers for festival purposes, as happened at Birmingham and Norwich, and that these societies could develop a life independent of the festivals. But if some societies came into being this way, there was a more general upsurge in the creation of choral societies in the years following the

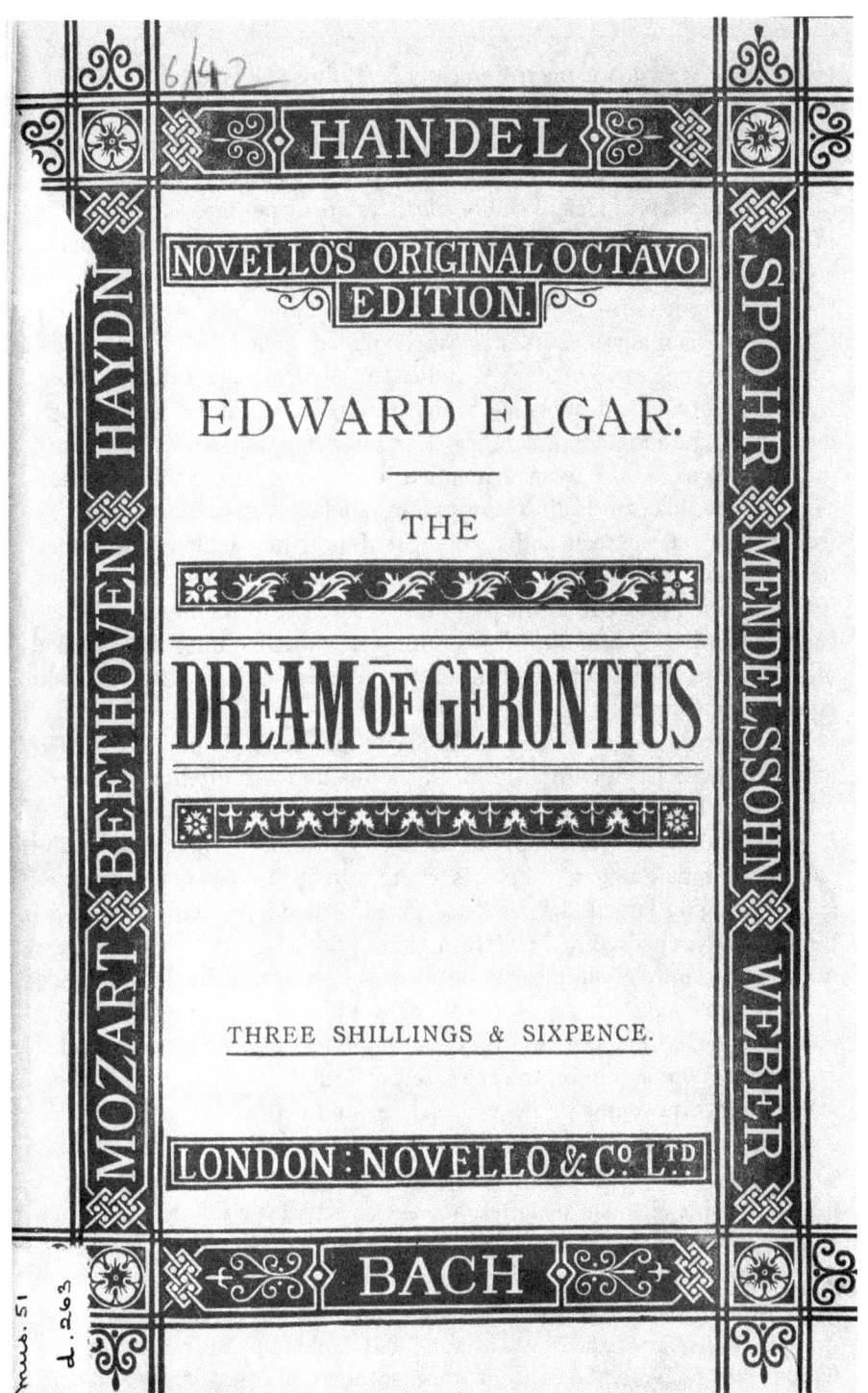

Figure 7　Edward Elgar: *The Dream of Gerontius*, vocal score (London, Novello, 1900).

Napoleonic Wars. So came the emergence of those like the Halifax Choral Society in 1817, Oxford Choral Society in 1819, Bradford Choral Society in 1821, and the Derby Choral Society by 1831. Unsurprisingly, their fortunes varied widely, and some were short-lived; initial enthusiasm could wear off, there might be a lack of suitable leadership, or perhaps simply clashes of personalities. Even a city like York could find it difficult to sustain a good-quality choral society over the decades.[113] As previously noted, among the many eighteenth-century 'music societies' appearing in subscription lists, we occasionally encounter a few who already called themselves 'choral societies' or 'societies of singers', indicating a specialized interest. Many were northern village societies, which tended to disappear in the early decades of the nineteenth century as industrialization saw people move into the towns, or the towns expanded to embrace surrounding villages. While some, like the Halifax and Oxford societies, gave public concerts from the outset, the main activity of most of these new societies continued to be that of their eighteenth-century predecessors – singers assembling for the mutual pleasure of making music together. In the first half of the century fortnightly or monthly meetings were more common than weekly ones, and pieces would have been run through rather than what we would consider rehearsed.

Choral societies of the time were very much male-dominated, indeed often wholly male in composition. Music-making was often preceded or followed by bread, cheese and ale – 'society' and 'social' as ever went hand in hand. So how were the soprano parts of SATB music catered for in the absence of female singers? In places where suitable boys were locally available – meaning largely the cathedral cities – then use could be made of them, as happened with the Oxford Choral Society, where women were not admitted until about 1852.[114] The all-male York Choral Society, founded in 1833, employed six boys, who could be troublesome, as shown in a letter to a boy's father in 1837: 'Sir, the Committee feel under the disagreeable necessity of complaining of the extremely disorderly conduct of your eldest son during this evening's rehearsal, as he would neither properly sing this own part, nor allow others to sing theirs by his interruption. The Committee, therefore, hope you will take measures to prevent such annoyance in future.'[115] Some all-male societies, however, opted for a different solution, at any rate for normal rehearsals. Unlikely as it may seem to modern ears, the men themselves sang the treble part, either in falsetto and/or with their normal voices in the tenor register. Such was the practice in the early societies at Bradford and Nottingham.[116] If it came to public performances, women singers would be engaged, though the men apparently would continue to sing the treble part at both pitches – the effect must have been not unlike that of hymn singing in church, where a choir in harmony combines with congregational singing of the melody in octaves. How widespread this practice was is unknown, but the fact that it existed in the North, where there had been a long tradition of women participating in choral music, is significant. But by the 1840s there was a strong move towards the integration of women into those societies which had been all-male domains, and the tradition of the Lancashire female chorus singers travelling widely to boost choral performances came to an end. However, although the women sang, the societies continued to be wholly under male control. The Sacred Harmonic Society is just one example where right through to its end in 1882, only men were listed as official members, as the lists in its Annual Reports show. Likewise, the rules of the Norwich Choral Society in 1857 set the membership limit at 230, to consist of '60 basses, 55 tenors, 55 altos, and a band of 60 instrumentalists'.[117] Although a chief motivation on the part of middle-class advocates of choral singing was to persuade the working classes to spend leisure time away from drinking establishments, and the temperance movement often played a significant role in the creation of choral societies,[118] the result was not only a growth in their number and size, but a gradual process of gentrification, as it became respectable for at least the lower end of the professional classes to participate. So not only did teachers, bank employees and the like join the ranks, but their wives and daughters too. Inevitably management of the societies tended to move into the hands of the professional class, with consequent increases in ambition and emphasis on public performance. In turn, families and friends came to constitute a significant proportion of the audience, as they still do today.

Like the Sacred Harmonic Society in London, choral societies elsewhere commonly included instrumentalists, who would be supplemented as necessary for public performances. Just how long they participated in the regular choral rehearsals is unknown, but certainly in the early days, when pianos were still comparatively weak in tone, their assistance would have been advantageous. It is an arrangement which could work well enough while rehearsals consisted of little more than running through pieces, but when a more sophisticated approach to choral practice developed from mid-century onwards, then many societies began to dispense with the orchestra as an integral part of the organisation, and to engage players for specific performances; alternatively the instrumentalists could be split off as a separate body for rehearsal purposes. The idea of a joint choral and instrumental body, however, persisted in places, the Huddersfield Choral Society being one example which still had instrumental members at the beginning of the twentieth century.[119]

Aside from festival choruses, the size of provincial choral societies remained quite modest in the first half of the century – certainly nothing comparable to that of the Sacred Harmonic Society. What was eventually to become the famed Huddersfield Choral Society was probably fairly typical in its early decades. Meetings were held monthly, with quarterly public performances. Like the older Halifax Choral Society, its origins were working class – it was established at a gathering in the Plough Inn in June 1836. Equipped with strict rules and regulations from the outset, within a year it had 62 performing members (including instrumentalists), eight of whom were female and did not have to pay a subscription.[120] Growth in numbers was steady rather than dramatic – by the 1860s it still had only around 100 performers, the decade in which rehearsals became fortnightly.[121] A dip in its fortunes occurred in the 1870s – probably due to conductor problems – before a great expansion took place following the opening of the 2,250-seater Town Hall in 1881; by 1885 concerts were featuring 400 performers.[122] This corresponded closely with the growth of greater middle-class involvement; the older tradition of the gentry and middle-classes listening to music performed by their social inferiors was giving way to less of a divide between platform and audience. 200–400 members would become typical of the biggest societies in the larger industrial towns by the end of the century; lesser centres might expect choirs of 100–150, while suburban societies generally mustered 60–100 – all of course highly variable, dependent on the degree of local enthusiasm and the merit or otherwise of the conductor.

The growth was fuelled by many factors – the stimulation provided by the sight-reading movement, the educational opportunities offered by the Mechanics' Institutes, which themselves often hosted singing classes,[123] and not least, a greater degree of leisure time following the 1847 Act giving employees a maximum ten-hour day – twelve hours having hitherto been common in the new industrial landscape. As for the vocal constituents of choral societies, the period from mid-century sees the total domination of the soprano line by females, with the virtual exclusion of boys, while for the first time, female contraltos appear on the alto line and progressively oust the male falsettists, who by the beginning of the twentieth century have become a rarity in choral society ranks. To some extent this was the result of the rise in tessitura of the alto line, particularly initially on the part of continental composers, including Mendelssohn, who were accustomed to writing for female contraltos. For the Sacred Harmonic Society's performances of *Elijah* under the composer in 1847, a number of boys were employed to help out the altos in the often high-lying part.[124] The Society itself began to include female contraltos from the following year, after Costa had assumed control.

The choral society's engagement with the public also altered from mid-century onwards. The early decades had seen various approaches; many started as singing clubs, the music heard only by any non-performing members present, with perhaps more ambitious 'quarterly meetings', which could be restricted to subscribers and their friends. Such a series was offered by the Liverpool Choral Society from 1817 to 1828, though it was unusual in giving whole oratorios rather than the miscellaneous programmes generally favoured.[125] Other bodies, such as the Oxford Choral Society, founded in 1819, were giving public concerts from an early date, sometimes on their own initiative, sometimes for a special occasion such as the opening of a building, and sometimes contributing items to the concerts of others. By mid-century the 'club' mentality had largely disappeared, and societies' meetings were orientated towards preparation for public concerts. With more emphasis on rehearsal in the modern sense, as opposed to just singing their way through works, most societies now aimed to give no more than three concerts a year – in which financial considerations increasingly played a part.

Although choral societies were ubiquitous throughout England by 1850, it was the northern choirs which were set to become pre-eminent. The rival towns of Liverpool and Manchester both held festivals in the 1820s and 1830s (five in Liverpool, two in Manchester), but neither continued on the festival road after 1836, when both towns featured one. Liverpool's festival chorus, however, continued in existence until 1860, while the Liverpool Philharmonic Society, founded in 1840 had its own hall from 1849. It was a mixed choral and orchestral body, which promoted a subscription series including choral concerts.[126] Manchester, preoccupied with making money, was slower to seriously indulge in the arts, but 1841 saw the creation of the Hargreaves Choral Society, which, in a short eight-year life, established a reputation for excellence, and Mendelssohn himself conducted it in one of the early performances of *Elijah* in 1847. The arrival in Manchester of Charles Hallé in 1848 not only eventually produced his orchestra, but also, in 1858, the Manchester Choral Society (whose female members, according to John Curwen, were known as 'Charles Hallé's mill-girls');[127] it would eventually become the Hallé Choir. Like many societies giving public concerts, it consisted of a mixture of unpaid higher-class 'amateurs' and mostly lower-class 'professionals' (such as the mill-girls) who were modestly compensated for their choral labour, ostensibly to cover their travel costs.[128] An initial 200 members quickly turned into 280, putting it firmly among the largest societies in the country, and having the great advantage of a permanent association with a professional orchestra. (Liverpool's Philharmonic orchestra was at that time only partly professional.) On a different scale was the Manchester Vocal Society, a carefully selected group of 60, founded in 1860 by Henry Wilson, which specialized in mainly unaccompanied repertoire, introducing Manchester to works like the Bach motets, Byrd's Masses, and Tallis's 'Spem in alium'. It survived into the twentieth century, giving an average of seven concerts a year; from 1885 it was under Henry Watson, the collector of an immense music library, which was bequeathed to the city and formed the foundation of the public library's Henry Watson Music Library.[129] Flourishing as Manchester and Liverpool's choralism was, the real fame of northern choral music in the second half of the century was to be found in the West Riding of Yorkshire, with its urban cluster of Bradford, Halifax, Huddersfield, Leeds and Sheffield, all of which had important choral societies, which were not devoid of local rivalries. But as their activities are closely bound up with festival developments of the period, we should first consider those.

By mid-century the Birmingham Musical Festival's influential position was to serve as a model for newly established festivals over the following decades. From 1849 to 1882 it had the stability of just one conductor in charge, Michael Costa, who was also to take on the Bradford and Leeds festivals as well as the Crystal Palace Handel festivals.[130] Birmingham had demonstrated both commercial viability and the advantages of having a festival chorus with a base drawn from local resources under the leadership of a skilled chorus master. In particular, the appointment of William Stockley in 1855 heralded several decades when its chorus was highly regarded. He was in the vanguard of a number of chorus masters who would revolutionize the sound of festival choruses in the Midlands and the North. Birmingham, having initiated the custom of commissioning new works, continued to do so, and the festivals regularly included far more 'novelties' in the programmes than did others – another sign of its financial stability. These imposed considerable demands on the chorus, and it was only possible with it being locally-based and so able to be adequately rehearsed – it would not work with the old 'gathered' festival chorus. The signs, however, are that Birmingham's choral heyday was over by the later 1880s, and the chorus's reputation faded somewhat in Stockley's latter years up to his retirement in 1895.

Birmingham's greatest embarrassment came at the 1900 festival, with the premiere of Elgar's *The Dream of Gerontius*, which was a festival commission.[131] Stockley's successor as chorus master suddenly died a few weeks before the event, and Stockley was brought out of retirement to undertake the rehearsals. Neither an ailing Stockley nor the chorus were prepared for the unusual difficulties of the work, which they had to sing from individual voice parts.[132] Coupled with late arrival of the music and the equal unpreparedness of the festival conductor, Hans Richter, the premiere was little short of a disaster. Nevertheless, Elgar's association with the festival continued, and Birmingham redeemed itself with the premieres of *The Apostles* in 1903 and *The Kingdom* in 1906, both conducted by the composer, as well as that of *The Music Makers* at the last festival in 1912.[133] Richter's years as festival conductor (1885–1909) did see a remarkable broadening of its contemporary choral repertoire, even if his own heart lay more in the orchestral realm. Berlioz's *Messe des morts*, and Brahms's *German Requiem* were introduced, as well as the commissioning of Dvořák's *The Spectre's Bride* (1885) and Requiem (1891), alongside British works of Stanford, Parry and Granville Bantock, not to mention many lesser lights. The Birmingham festival was not resumed after the First World War, and declining profits were already sending warning signals in the first decade of the century. But if the festival ceased, the Festival Choral Society did not, and has continued under the same name to the present day.

Birmingham's success in the festival sphere gave rise to emulation in the fast-growing northern industrial towns, especially in the West Riding of Yorkshire, whose choral strength led to a reputation surpassing that of Birmingham. Spurred on by civic pride, a series of magnificent town halls on the Birmingham model was erected throughout the region, designed in part with the needs of local choral societies in mind – hence the provision of substantial organs, instruments which of course also served for religious meetings and solo recitals. Bradford, recently raised to borough status in 1847, was the first, when the opening of St George's Hall in 1853 was celebrated with a music festival. Both schemes were initiated by the businessman and alderman, Samuel Smith, and designed in part to show that Bradford was more than just a grimy, damp industrial town.[134] The 229-strong choir was drawn almost entirely from the West Riding,[135] and Michael Costa, who conducted, brought his Royal Italian Opera orchestra. Of the chorus, according to William Spark, 'he was at once struck, not only with their enormous power, but with the rich tone of their voices, and their remarkable aptitude for reading music at first sight'.[136] Following this initial success, Bradford decided to embark on a triennial series à la Birmingham, and after the 1856 festival an official Bradford Festival Choral Society was inaugurated to maintain the chorus as a permanent body. Such was its immediate fame that it was 'commanded' to sing at Buckingham Palace in 1858, when it also impressed Londoners by a performance at the Crystal Palace. The third festival in 1859 turned out to be the last – unlike Birmingham they were not proving financially viable – but the festival chorus lived on, starting a subscription concerts series in 1865, and continuing to draw singers from the whole area – out-of-town singers being rewarded for their journey by a coffee and bun before the fortnightly meetings.[137] And like the Birmingham society, it has survived (and retained its name) to the present day, despite many vicissitudes. Unlike some later festival choirs, it was not a fiercely auditioned élite body, but it was divided into 'first-class' and 'second-class' singers, with the former being 'competent to sustain their part in choruses of moderate difficulty' and paying a subscription of one shilling a year, whereas the second-class members, who were 'not so far advanced, yet competent to answer questions respecting the time and mode of pieces of music' paid one shilling per quarter – an enterprising way of encouraging improvement.[138] Alongside the Festival Choral Society, which in the 1880s had 350 members,[139] the old Bradford Choral Society continued to prosper, and by 1894 had 300 voices.[140]

Following in the wake of Bradford, Leeds was the next place to celebrate the opening of its town hall with a festival in 1858. For the occasion, the Yorkshire-born William Sterndale Bennett, Principal of the Royal Academy of Music and Professor at Cambridge, was commissioned to compose and conduct *The May Queen*, a cantata, which, although now forgotten, was a rare native example of a commission which enjoyed life beyond the festival. Predictably *Messiah* and *Elijah* were the other two main works on the programme. Robert Senior Burton, organist of Leeds Parish Church since 1849 and conductor of the Leeds Choral Society, was the chorus master, selecting a choir of 245, almost all from the West Riding, although he considered only 80 residents of Leeds itself to be of sufficient standard, much to the disgust of many local choristers.[141] Burton was not an easy man to work with, and often ruffled feathers, but the outstanding results he obtained from the various societies he was associated with, made him the most influential choral trainer of the third quarter of the century. The *Times* reviewer commented on the 1858 festival: 'Such vigorous, powerful, and full-toned voices as these Yorkshire choristers possess, it rejoices the heart of the jaded Londoner to hear. The trebles and basses especially, are unrivalled anywhere.'[142] For this festival Burton introduced formal auditions for would-be singers he was unacquainted with, which caused dismay for some middle-class girls taking lessons from singing teachers, who considered it beneath them, and whose sight-reading ability often proved inadequate[143] – another sign that the composition of choirs was gaining a wider social spread. What tends to be forgotten is that festival choruses at this time were still routinely being paid, even if the individual sums were modest (usually between £2 and £3) – a few singers described themselves as 'amateurs' and did not require payment, but most classified themselves for festival purposes, however tenuously, as 'professionals' – even though in the choral societies in which most normally sang, they would have been paying a subscription for the privilege. For the 1858 Leeds festival the chorus bill was £880 10s.[144] Towards the end of the century the proportion of 'amateurs' increased, but the practice continued until the First World War.

One sidelight demonstrated at Leeds was that no fewer than ten soloists were involved in the *Messiah* performance.[145] The employment of more soloists in oratorios than strictly needed from the score goes right back to Handel himself, but was particularly prevalent in the festival world. The reason was quite simple – festivals were expected to engage a substantial number of prominent (and expensive) soloists as a draw for the public, which in turn expected to hear as many of them as possible at each concert. This also accounts for the habit of adding miscellaneous items after an oratorio, so as to make use of singers for whom no role had been found in the oratorio itself, as happened, for example, at the 1846 premiere of *Elijah*. So, the solos in *Messiah* were divided up, with the star singers doubtless being allotted their favourite numbers. Having ten singers, however, was exceptional, six or seven being more usual on such occasions. Present-day oratorio soloists have to work considerably harder, though it must be remembered that at eighteenth- and nineteenth-century festivals the soloists would have been involved in most of the concerts, including the miscellaneous evening programmes.

The 1858 festival was not the immediate start of a series in Leeds. Burton, however, capitalized on the success of the festival chorus by forming the Yorkshire Choral Union with singers from Leeds and neighbouring towns,[146] which, following the precedent of Bradford, was commanded to sing at Buckingham Palace in June 1860. Such 'choral unions' were to feature strongly in the high reputation of Yorkshire choralism in the following decades. It was 1874 before Leeds inaugurated a triennial festival, which remarkably managed to survive (with wartime breaks) until 1985. It gradually took over the mantle of the country's premier festival, with Arthur Sullivan its conductor for seven festivals from 1880.[147] Its many commissions and premieres up to the First World War included Dvořák's *St Ludmila*, Elgar's *Caractacus* and Vaughan Williams's *Sea Symphony*, and they were not afraid to at least occasionally omit *Messiah* and/or *Elijah* to make room for lesser known works.[148] The 273 singers in the Festival Chorus of 1874, now trained by James Broughton, came wholly from the West Riding,[149] and in addition to preliminary rehearsals, two full rehearsal days were allowed in the festival week – a true luxury compared with the much criticized single one encountered elsewhere.[150] The result was unanimous press praise. Ebenezer Prout wrote: '...Never in my life do I remember having heard chorus-singing to equal it. The splendid resonance of the voices, and their rich, pure tone, the perfect accuracy of their intonation, the preciseness and decision of their "attack", and the delicacy of their piano singing, were alike marvellous.'[151] In contrast to Birmingham, however, the festival chorus was not kept together between festivals, but recruited afresh each time, and from 1880 all singers were auditioned – 600 applied for 300 places that year, which saw a successful performance of Beethoven's *Missa Solemnis*.[152] 'Amateurs' were an increasing proportion of the choir, helping to keep down costs, though of course, the chorus costs were dwarfed by the sums paid to the soloists. But the absence of a permanent festival chorus was to some extent compensated for by the existence since 1870 of the Leeds Philharmonic Society, which, with 300 singers, rapidly became the town's leading choir, and which, in addition to supplying many singers for the festival chorus was also the source of the 'Leeds contingent' which helped strengthen several other festival choruses in the closing decades of the century, including that of the Three Choirs.[153] From 1897 Stanford was its conductor, while chorus masters took care of routine rehearsals. But from 1895 Leeds also had another large choir of over 300 members, the Leeds Choral Union, which prospered thanks to its wealthy founder, Henry Cawood Embleton.[154] There was very little overlap in membership of the two choirs, testifying to the strength of choral interest in the locality, as we have already seen with Bradford.[155] The emergence of new choral societies appears to have been particularly strong in the last two decades of the century.

The reputation of Leeds choral societies lasted up to the end of the century; but a certain falling-off in standards was noted by critics in the following decade, at the same time that another Yorkshire town, with a hitherto unremarkable choral history, suddenly began to astonish the world. Up to the final decade of the nineteenth century, Sheffield had experienced music-making similar to towns like Halifax and Bradford, with the occasional modest festival, the opening of a 2,200-seat Albert Hall in 1873, and a number of competent choral societies, but lacking the distinction of its northern neighbours. That this underwent dramatic change was due entirely to one extraordinary man, whose life deserves to the outlined in some detail.

Henry Coward

Born in Liverpool in 1849, Henry Coward spent almost his entire life in Sheffield, where, during an impoverished childhood he joined the Band of Hope, learning temperance songs and subsequently attending a tonic sol-fa class, being dedicated to self-improvement to an astonishing degree.[156] After being apprenticed as a cutler and working in the trade, he trained as a pupil teacher, and having qualified, eventually ended up as headmaster of the Free Writing School in 1879.[157] But music dominated his interests. In his spare time he held tonic sol-fa classes, and his penchant for conducting developed first with the Sheffield Tonic Sol-fa Association from 1876. He was soon being called upon to conduct massed choirs like the 3,000 voices assembled for a Band of Hope gala in 1878. He decided to leave teaching and take up music full-time in 1887, and seeking to advance his musical education, he prepared and obtained the Oxford B.Mus. degree in 1889 – taken externally, as was then usual – and even more remarkably followed it up by the D.Mus. in 1894, all self-taught. It was his association with the Sheffield Triennial Festival, established in 1896, which was to bring Coward national fame and make him the foremost chorus master of his time. The 350-strong festival chorus was rigorously auditioned by singing teachers from behind a screen, with Coward placing emphasis on sight-reading. Coward would remark on the choir's inclusivity: 'We know of no social distinctions. A manufacturer will stand side by side with one of his workmen; a manufacturer's daughter next to one of her father's work-girls; a lady of high degree beside a dressmaker.'[158] Singers from Coward's own Sheffield Musical Union (as the Tonic Sol-fa Association had become) naturally formed the core. His autocratic nature, combining the firm discipline of a schoolteacher with memorable aphorisms and great attention to detail, proved ideal. Coward was not conductor at the Sheffield festivals (though he had conducted *Elijah* at a 'trial' one in 1895), but press reports singled him out for praise, as in 1899: 'An unrivalled Festival Choir and a genius Chorus-master – Henry Coward ... Attack, vigour, phrasing, articulation, perfect ensemble, and unsurpassable tone.'[159] It is therefore no surprise that when *The Dream of Gerontius* was performed at the 1902 festival under Henry Wood, Elgar was able to hear his oratorio as he intended for the first time. Quite what the Nonconformist Coward made of Cardinal Newman's text is unknown, but he would have relished the challenges of the choral effects demanded by Elgar, not least in the Demons' chorus.

As a result of these festival successes, Coward was in demand as a chorus trainer throughout the North, taking over most of the big choirs in the early years of the twentieth century, and resulting in a huge amount of travel. A typical week in the winter season could be: Monday, Leeds Choral Union; Tuesday, Newcastle and Gateshead Choral Union; Wednesday, Glasgow Choral Union; Thursday, Sheffield Musical Union; Friday, Huddersfield Choral Society[160] – all made possible, of course, by the railway. Choral societies at Barnsley, Derby, Hull and Preston were among those he also conducted at some time. In addition, he was active as a lecturer, examiner, adjudicator at competitive festivals, singing master at two Sheffield schools, and music critic for local papers. But he nevertheless remained a regular

Sight Test (Tune) unaccompanied

The tests may be sung from either notation to the solfa syllables or to any vowel sound.

Sight Test (Time) unaccompanied

The Time Test will consist of 5 bars in common time and will include no difficulties beyond those included in the following specimen:

Figure 8   Specimen sight-reading tests for the Sheffield 1896 Festival; J.A. Rodgers, *Dr. Henry Coward* (London, 1911), p. 29.

member of the Queen Street Congregational Chapel (in whose choir he had sung as a boy), and his family life produced eight children by the first of three marriages, the eldest son, Henry, becoming a choral scholar at King's College, Cambridge.[161]

The Sheffield Musical Union, however, was the choir which remained at the heart of Coward's activity, and with which he would achieve his most notable feats, making the Sheffield choral sound known to the world at large. Felix Weingartner conducted them at a 1904 London Elgar Festival in *Gerontius*, Beethoven's Ninth Symphony and the *Missa Solemnis*, declaring that 'we shall have to send our German conductors to Sheffield to be taught how to train choruses'.[162] Two years later Coward took a combined choir from the Sheffield Musical Union and the Leeds Choral Union to Germany itself on a triumphant tour of Düsseldorf, Cologne and Frankfurt, featuring *Messiah* and *Gerontius*. 200 singers were taken on an eleven-day Canadian tour in 1908, and a second visit made to Germany in 1910.

But undoubtedly the outstanding event was a six-month Round the World Tour from March to September 1911, when Coward recruited a choir of 200 under the 'Sheffield' name, but with singers from the whole West Yorkshire area and even a few from places as far as London, Newport and Glasgow.[163] The whole was planned and financially guaranteed by a Canadian organist and composer Charles Harriss, who had already organized Coward's Canadian tour. (Harriss, who was born in England, had married a wealthy widow in 1900.) Among the major works in a huge repertoire of 160 pieces were *Messiah, Elijah, Gerontius, The Creation*, Sullivan's *The Golden Legend*, Berlioz's *The Damnation of Faust*, Verdi's Requiem and Beethoven's Ninth Symphony – quite apart from part-songs, folk song arrangements and madrigals. Coward's preparations were predictably meticulous, with around 300 rehearsals (including sectionals), and each singer was issued with a diary in which to record daily practice – inspected by Coward himself! The tour took in Canada, the USA, Australia, New Zealand, and South Africa, and everyone knew in advance their ship berth number, hotel room or private host. Nine soloists accompanied the party, and local orchestras were engaged, with local choirs sometimes joining them in Australia and New Zealand. Elgar himself conducted *Gerontius* in Canada and the USA, while a young Leopold Stokowski conducted Beethoven's Ninth in Cincinnati. Everywhere there were welcome parties and receptions (when the choir would also sing). Arrangements appear to have worked smoothly, though disaster nearly overtook the whole party when a huge wave almost sank the ship on the crossing from Sydney to Auckland. Coming at the height of the imperial era, the national prestige represented by the enterprise produced a general willingness of local authorities to grant teachers leave of absence and manufacturers to release their employees. The 200 singers included just five married couples, and 93 of the 117 women were single. All travelling expenses were covered, and even a small gratuity of five guineas given to each member at the end. Astonishingly the tour did not make a loss, to Dr Harriss's great relief. It remained an extraordinary and unique event, never likely to be repeated, but one wonders how many members of the choir were not on speaking terms with one another after six months together.

Coward's fame was such that a biography was published that same year, describing him as 'the pioneer chorus-master',[164] and official recognition came with a knighthood in 1926. Although the post-First World War years were uneventful, he continued to conduct the Sheffield Musical Union until 1933 and died at the age of 94 in 1944. Coward can be seen as following in the steps of successful chorus masters like Stockley and Burton, but it was his attention to the detail of choral technique that marked him out, and his motto, 'Method is the secret of success' derived obviously from his initial absorption in tonic sol-fa instruction.[165] He certainly did not lack self-belief as is clear from his *Reminiscences*, and his style did not suit everyone; some choristers complained he talked too much at rehearsals rather than allowing them to sing.[166] His overall interpretation could encounter criticism, with some finding his constant dynamic changes and special effects overdone. The movement by movement analysis of the *Messiah* choruses in his 1914 book *Choral Technique and Interpretation* conveys a precise and invaluable impression of how an Edwardian performance of the work may have sounded. The treatise has been influential on later generations of choir trainers, and some of his many aphorisms, such as 'If your neighbour can hear you, it is too loud'[167] remain in circulation.

Developments outside the North

If the northern area of England had claim to be the most stimulating place chorally as the century advanced, there was certainly no lack of activity throughout the rest of the country. The Three Choirs Festival continued in its old ways, though increasingly seen as a backwater musically. While other festivals were employing conductors of national repute, the Three Choirs continued with the tradition of the local organist being in charge. The problem was that a cathedral organist of the time was not even accustomed to conducting his own choir – he always presided at the organ, leaving the choir to follow in his wake. In the days when Handel dominated the festival repertoire, a conductor needed no great technical ability. But nineteenth-century music soon demanded much more from a conductor – increasingly so as the century advanced, and few cathedral organists were equipped for the task. S.S. Wesley at Gloucester from 1865 to 1876, for all his eminence, was no conductor, reluctant to raise his eyes from the score.[168] There were exceptions, such as Wesley's successor, Charles Harford Lloyd, who conducted the St Matthew Passion in 1877 and the first Three Choirs *Missa Solemnis* in 1880, but this was the last festival he conducted before leaving for Oxford in 1882.[169] It would be the turn of the century before a new generation of organists like Ivor Atkins at Worcester and Herbert Brewer at Gloucester would bring a generally higher standard of conducting to the Three Choirs.

Although from mid-century all three cities had local choral societies which rehearsed for the festival, for long they constituted only a minority of the festival chorus, which continued to be drawn from many parts of the country, but increasingly relying on strong contingents from the Bradford and Leeds choirs, the whole chorus not coming together until the day before the festival opened.[170] However good the northern singers were (and they did rehearse in their home territory beforehand), the result was far from satisfactory, especially with works which were new to the festival, and breakdowns in performance were not uncommon.[171] The Three Choirs choral sound could not begin to compete with that of the northern festivals, with their small area of recruitment, well co-ordinated rehearsals and chorus masters of a quality unknown down south. Only in the 1890s did the Three Choirs begin to rely entirely on local singers, a process not fully accomplished until the beginning of the next century. Nevertheless, it was a measure of progress when purely local forces successfully gave the first Three Choirs performance of *The Dream of Gerontius* at the 1902 festival.

'Novelties' were increasingly regarded as indispensable at the Three Choirs as at other major festivals in order to attract national press interest, even though, particularly with oratorios, they often failed to draw large audiences. Some works were modest commissions – the Three Choirs did not have the resources of Birmingham and the northern festivals to approach notable foreign composers – while others were offered by composers in the hope of raising their profile. Most novelties failed to make a lasting impression, but one noteworthy coup was the first British performance of three of Verdi's *Quattro pezzi sacri*, given at Gloucester in 1898 under Brewer, just five months after their Parisian premiere.[172]

Unlike the northern festivals, the Three Choirs remained very much involved with the church, which continued periodically to raise problems. There were certainly those still opposed to using the cathedrals as concert venues, to charging admission, and to the expense of highly-paid soloists. And a quite different atmosphere from other festivals existed simply because no applause was permitted in the cathedrals, and where performances began and ended with a prayer.[173] The most notorious case of conflict arose in 1875, when the dean and chapter of Worcester forbade the use of the cathedral for the customary morning performances. As a result, that year's festival (designated the 'Mock Festival') was reduced to what amounted to little more than miserably attended extended choral services, much to the dismay of the city's traders amongst others.[174] Fortunately, pressure by the county set saw that normality was restored by the time Worcester's turn came round again in 1878. Overall, however, clerical support was generally forthcoming, not least because the collections at the festival still supported clergy widows and their dependents. As might be expected, there was considerable concern over the 1902 *Gerontius* on account of its heavy leavening of Roman Catholic doctrine. After much argument, the dean and chapter of Worcester secured changes to the text, including deleting all references to the Virgin Mary, and omission of the Litany of the Saints, to which Elgar (who conducted the work for the first time) reluctantly agreed.[175] The press condemned the changes – 'a deplorable blunder', declared the *Musical Times*,[176] – but it wasn't long before the work in its original state became a staple of the Three Choirs. Elgar's other two oratorios, *The Apostles* and *The Kingdom* were also heard soon after their premieres, alongside many of his orchestral works. Together with the later works of Parry and Stanford, and joined in time by figures like Vaughan Williams and Holst, the Three Choirs Festival in the early twentieth century was at last able to create a distinctive identity for itself promoting British music, which would see it survive the vicissitudes of the era. The familiar problem, common to all festivals, of far too little full rehearsal time for the amount of music, remained, with only partial amelioration until late in the twentieth century. But festivals were, and still are, not only about the music; especially at the Three Choirs it was a social highlight of the year for the upper echelons of the area's society, even if the balls had been terminated in 1874.[177] It had an audience which tolerated the 'novelties', so long as *Messiah* and (usually) *Elijah* were on the menu.

Festival activity elsewhere in the country included a triennial cathedral-based series at Chester (1879–1900), a more-or-less triennial festival at Bristol from 1873 to the First World War, notable for its large chorus of 300–400 being purely voluntary,[178] and a surprisingly enterprising one at Hovingham in Yorkshire (held irregularly, 1887–1906), financed by the local squire and which avoided much over-familiar repertoire.[179] Many southern seaside resorts also briefly dipped their toes into festival waters between the 1870s and the First World War.[180] But special mention should be made of one area of the country not immediately associated with choral activity, the Pottery towns of North Staffordshire.[181] In 1888 the acoustically splendid Victoria Hall was opened in Hanley, and a North Staffordshire Festival Choir was formed by the Birmingham organist and conductor Swinnerton Heap from nine local choral societies. Their programmes in the course of the next eleven years included the premieres of Elgar's *King Olaf* (in 1896) and Samuel Coleridge-Taylor's *The Death of Minnehaha* (in 1899), both conducted by their composers, the performances marred only by orchestral inadequacies – as so often, there was a reluctance to spend money on mere instrumentalists![182] Even at the Sheffield festivals, unfavourable remarks were made when assessing the orchestral as opposed to the choral contribution.

The Potteries had, in fact, been prominent since the 1860s in the early development of a new type of choir – that which specialized in competitions, sometimes to the virtual exclusion of other activity. The idea of competitive singing had its roots in the tonic sol-fa movement, which in 1860 held its first Tonic Sol-fa Competition at the Crystal Palace, and one of the five choirs then taking part came from Staffordshire, the Burslem Tonic Sol-fa Choir, conducted by Josiah Wolstancroft Powell, which came third.[183] Choirs such as the Hanley Glee and Madrigal Society, run by a local potter, John Garner (a protégé of Powell), in the 1880s regularly won prizes for its unaccompanied singing, though it also expanded into cantatas and oratorios.[184] It was, however, another choir, the North Staffordshire District Choral Society, under the charismatic James Whewall, which at the beginning of the twentieth century took on the Welsh and for several years triumphed at the Welsh National Eisteddfod.[185] After their victory in 1906, the dates of the Eisteddfod were changed to ones inconvenient for the Potteries. Aside from competitions, that society went on to have particular associations with the big choral works of Elgar and Delius – Elgar himself conducted highly praised early performances of *The Dream of Gerontius*, *The Apostles* and *The Kingdom*, while Thomas Beecham conducted Delius's *Sea Drift* at Hanley in 1908, repeating it with the choir in London in February 1909, and he then had them give the first English performance of *A Mass of Life* at the Queen's Hall later that year – both works sung to considerable acclaim from tonic sol-fa notation.[186] If proof were needed of the advantages of tonic sol-fa training in creating secure aural perception of intervals, then these works certainly provided it. So, it was not just the crack Yorkshire choirs who in these years opened the ears of Londoners to the qualities of choral sound outside the capital. Asked why he had used the Hanley choir for *A Mass of Life*, Beecham is said to have replied, 'Because I couldn't get a good enough choir in London.'[187]

The heyday for competitive choir festivals came in the last quarter of the century; they could be either specifically choral contests, or choral classes within more general musical competitions, some purely local in nature, others creating national interest. They proved particularly popular with choirs in the Midlands, the North and Wales[188] and were certainly facilitated by the comprehensive and inexpensive rail travel then available – in 1885 the Inventions Exhibition at the Royal Albert Hall included a three-day choral competition which brought choirs from as far as Scotland and Wales. Blackpool, Morecombe and Glasgow were among the leading festivals where choirs sought glory, and for those involved in school music, they could provide an invaluable incentive to improvement.[189] Competitions typically involved a choir performing not only one or two short prepared pieces, but also a sight-reading test – testimony to the skills that the tonic sol-fa movement had developed, though not one that could be imagined in a modern competition.

Beginning also in 1885, up in Kendal, a competitive choral festival was devised by an accomplished amateur singer, Mary Wakefield, on rather different lines from elsewhere. This involved her encouraging the formation of, and often training herself, choirs in local villages (where she had already given lectures on music), choirs which deliberately ignored both class and religious divisions and did much to promote social harmony. At the Kendal festivals, they not only competed against each other, but concluded the proceedings by a combined performance of some prepared work. Wakefield's enterprise served as a model and was quickly imitated by others, notably Mary Egerton in Yorkshire and Lady Mary Trefusis, at first at Madresfield, near Worcester, and then in Cornwall.[190]

The competitive movement had its advocates and detractors. On the positive side, it had the potential to encourage improvements in technique, so much so that where specially commissioned test pieces were introduced, composers, impressed by the standard of singing, were tempted to write increasingly challenging works – as witness some of the part-songs of Elgar and especially Granville Bantock. Brass band competitions followed a similar trajectory. Other benefits included stimulating regular attendance at rehearsals, the opportunity to listen and learn from other choirs, and a general increase in *esprit de corps*. While this was admirable for choirs for whom competing was just one part of their activities, it also led to the creation of 'pot-hunting' choirs, whose sole or main purpose was to aim for medals, and increasingly, towards the end of the century, prize money, which could be substantial at major events. Such choirs were particularly associated with Wales, whose musical culture now claims attention.

Wales, 'the Land of Song'

Wales's predominantly rural nature meant that its choral scene only emerged in the wake of the industrialization of the south and north-east of the country, and not properly until the middle of the nineteenth century. Among early manifestations were the creation of a choral society based at the Tabernacle, Aberystwyth, singing oratorio choruses in the early 1850s, while Swansea had a choral society with 140 members from 1861. The earliest traced full performance of *Messiah* was at a North Wales Musical Festival at Rhuddlan Castle in 1850, and that was by English performers; it was another decade before the Welsh themselves put on a similar performance.[191] In the background was the strong hold that Nonconformity – in particular, Methodism, with its vigorous hymn-singing – had taken throughout the principality, with which the temperance movement was also closely associated, giving rise to temperance choral unions. Indeed, the popular image of the country as 'The Land of Song' owed just as much to its communal hymn-singing as to its choirs. 'Singing practice' for congregations were commonly held after services, which led in the late 1850s to hymn-singing festivals (cymanfa canu), involving the whole congregation singing in four-part harmony.[192] Although tonic sol-fa became the most common way for people to learn to read music in the principality, there continued to be a strong element of non-readers within choirs, who relied on repetition for mastering the music.[193] Competitive choirs proved especially suitable for such singers, since they concentrated on preparing a few short pieces for months on end, and rarely gave public concerts. The main focus of competition for the Welsh was the Eisteddfod, either local, or national – the latter not necessarily taking place in Wales, since both the Royal Albert Hall and Liverpool were also favoured venues. While solo singing had always featured as part of the Bardic tradition, choral classes began to feature in the national eisteddfodau from 1859.[194] Nowhere was the competitive instinct more alive than in Wales and there developed fierce local partisanship, with large crowds of supporters travelling to events. It was a brave adjudicator who dared make an unpopular decision, or offer serious criticism of a performance, and there were cases where adjudicators had to be given protection to see them safely out of a hall.[195] Echoing the sporting world, fighting between rival supporters was not unknown, as happened at the Swansea National Eisteddfod in 1891.[196] In the circumstances it is not surprising to find choirs 'playing to the gallery', and the choice of test pieces tended to be narrow, with the same works appearing repeatedly – again, providing no incentive to learning to read music. The sight-reading test, which at one time formed part of an eisteddfod competition, fell by the wayside, to the regret of those wishing to improve standards.

If the industrial north of England became particularly noted for its brass bands, then Wales became equally so for its male-voice choirs, which developed primarily in the mining communities of the south and north-east of the country from the 1860s onwards. This is not to deny that Wales too had strong brass bands, just as the north of England had many male-voice choirs. The competitive streak was common to both institutions and an important element in the strong social bonding that characterized them. Again, the chapel hymn-singing provided a clear background to the Welsh male-voice tradition, and hymn arrangements and similarly textured pieces, backed up by organ accompaniment, formed a core of the repertoire, with native composers and arrangers finding a prominent role. 'Battle' pieces were another favourite genre, offering strong dynamic contrasts (though little in the way of more subtle expression) and opportunities for vivid, if naïve, description. Perhaps best known was Laurent de Rille's *The Martyrs of the Arena*, one of many pieces the Welsh took over from the French male-voice *Orphéoniste* tradition. First published in Britain in 1872, it was apparently inspired by its composer seeing a picture of a lion ready to devour praying Christians in a Roman arena. Its melodramatic quality was such that it has remained in the male-voice repertoire to the present day.

Soft singing was not a prominent feature of nineteenth-century Welsh choirs. Vigour and volume were apparently the order of the day when awarding prizes at eisteddfodau, 'the Welsh notion, at that time, being power and still more power in singing choruses' according to Henry Coward.[197] It was argued that there was a distinct Welsh aesthetic when it came to choral singing, which valued power and passion above all, and that choirs should be judged accordingly. This was certainly what Welsh audiences appreciated, and what made the most immediate impact when their choirs were heard in England, as demonstrated by the 450-strong South Wales Choral Union, when it claimed the cup at a National Music Meeting at the Crystal Palace in 1872, conducted by the well-known 'Caradog' (Griffith Rhys Jones) from Aberdare.[198] Not until around the turn of the century did the adjudicators, many of them English, start demanding more subtle choral virtues.[199] Compared to English choral societies, knowledge of the oratorio repertoire in Wales was quite limited – most people would have sung only selected choruses of even *Messiah* and *Elijah*. There were, however, exceptions such as a long series of annual complete oratorio performances by the Aberdare Choral Union under Rees Evans from 1874, and those in the Rhondda Valley at the start of the twentieth century, particularly associated with the choir of the Noddfa Chapel, Treorchy, which in 1910 even managed Bach's St Matthew Passion, though it was not appreciated by the audience, many of whom left before the end.[200] The general level of sight-reading, even from sol-fa, was low, according to both English and Welsh critics, and local eisteddfodau were particularly seen as a block to progress by retaining the same familiar old test pieces, with only the National Eisteddfod introducing new works. As the composer David Jenkins declared in 1888: 'It was full time for their musical committees to leave that beaten track and lead the choirs into a new path. Prizes should be offered to choirs for reading at first sight.'[201]

Welsh choirs were never afraid of an emotional punch or a certain sentimentality, exemplified in another work from the 1870s, the part-song 'Myfanwy', by the most eminent Welsh composer of the day, Joseph Parry, and one still familiar to Welsh choirs. The self-belief in their choral culture was to encounter a major shock at the 1900 National Eisteddfod in Liverpool. Entry to the competition was not limited to the Welsh, and on this occasion English choirs took all the major prizes, except for the male-voice award. The Welsh came to refer to it as the 'Liverpool massacre'.[202] Nor was it an isolated incident, for English choirs, especially Staffordshire ones, continued to take prizes at eisteddfodau over the next few years, though they generally withdrew from the fray from around 1905. It was sufficient, however, to cause the Welsh to begin to take to heart some of the criticism that had been accumulating for more than a decade. Neglect of intonation, poor breath control and phrasing, and forced tone were all aspects which commonly came in for comment. With male-voice choirs especially, there was the habit of allowing tenors to force their chest tone up to the top notes, instead of developing the 'mixed voice' fostered by skilled trainers. The result was often a harshness as well as a tendency to flatten as tiredness set in.[203] A chief problem was that most conductors were self-taught with little opportunity to learn from a wider musical culture. Such was Dan Davies, the pugnacious and highly competitive conductor of, first, the Dowlais Harmonic Society, and then the Merthyr Philharmonic Choir in the last decades of the nineteenth century, and with whom he won numerous contests. Noted for his flamboyant conducting style and love of exaggerated effects, he was not slow in challenging adverse verdicts and rejecting criticism. When the Merthyr choir suffered defeat, as it did in 1896 and 1897 at the Llandudno and Newport National Eisteddfodau, his outburst of unsporting behaviour proved too much and effectively brought his period of fame to an end, though be continued to conduct into the next century.

Wales did have a minority of successful conductors with a more conventional and thorough musical education, such as Roland Roberts, organist of Bangor Cathedral, who trained the Penrhyn Choral Union,[204] and in particular the young Harry Evans, who, coming from a humble but musical background, became a professional musician, achieving his Fellowship of the Royal College of Organists in 1897. In 1893 he founded the Dowlais Philharmonic Society, followed up by a 50-strong Dowlais Ladies' Choir, and a 100-stong male-voice choir, which was the only Welsh choir to win at the 1900 Liverpool debacle.[205] To think of Welsh choirs wholly in terms of working-class culture, would be a mistake, for Evans's women were, unusually, recruited from the middle class, privately educated, and able to read music, so that he was able to perform more in the way of complete works than most others. But Evans was not destined to remain in Wales; in 1902 he accepted the conductorship of the Liverpool Welsh Choral Union. Enlarging it to 300 auditioned members, and moving to the city in 1906, he presented a wide repertoire, including the St Matthew Passion, *Gerontius* and *The Apostles*, being much admired by Elgar.[206] Ironically then, the finest Welsh choir of the pre-war years was found outside the country, though Evans himself died in 1914 at the early age of 41. But, as will emerge later, the choir was to enjoy its greatest glory days after the First World War. And in Wales itself, the twentieth century would see a general expansion of the choral repertoire, as wider musical influences came to permeate its native culture, so that by the 1920s audiences were becoming increasingly acquainted with the works of Bach, Coleridge-Taylor, Elgar, Stanford and others.

Scotland and Ireland

If nineteenth-century Wales could be said to have been bursting with song of one sort or another, a very different picture was to be found in Scotland. Here the Calvinist distrust of music, especially any sacred music apart from metrical psalms, made for a slow development of choral music. We have already seen that when Edinburgh held a festival in 1815, the chorus had to be mostly brought in from England. Three further festivals were held there, with ad hoc choruses, and by the time of the last, in 1843, greater local forces were in evidence, since, of the festival choir of 125, only 36 were from outside the capital.[207] A number of societies, such as the Edinburgh Harmonic Association, sprang into being, in part a reflection of a gradual change of attitude to music within the Church of Scotland, which would eventually allow in organs to support the singing, as well as growing Episcopalian influence within the city.[208] Of those choral societies established in the second half of the century, the Edinburgh Choral Union, founded in 1858 (adding 'Royal' to its title in 1911) would become the most important – its repertoire would include the Scottish composers, Hamish MacCunn and Alexander Mackenzie, and it was an early performer of *Gerontius* in 1903.[209] The city had at least four societies by 1900, but it would be the next century before the Scottish capital would really blossom chorally. Elsewhere in Scotland, Dundee apparently had a choral society as early as 1813 judging by a concert given for charity,[210] Aberdeen held festivals in 1828 and 1834, the latter very much on 'county' lines and both including *Messiah*,[211] and a whole crop of choral societies began to emerge around mid-century in towns such as Greenock, Kirkcaldy, and Perth, partly the result of enthusiasm generated by the sight-singing movement.[212]

But it was Glasgow which was the period's most prominent musical centre in Scotland, helped by its rapid population growth and wealth, however unevenly spread. A Glasgow Choral Society came into existence in 1833, followed by the Glasgow Musical Association in 1843, which gave the city its first *Messiah* in 1844.[213] The sopranos in its early days appear to have been rather tentative, for when a new conductor arrived in 1852, he found that they were being led by a tenor.[214] Changing its name to the Glasgow Choral Union in 1855, it became the city's most prestigious choir, and with its 400 members under the leadership of Albert Lambeth, it lay behind Glasgow's first venture into the festival world in January 1860 – a rare month for such an event. Remarkably, a new work was commissioned for the occasion, Charles Horsley's *Gideon*, partnered by *Messiah* and *Elijah*, with the orchestra supplied by the Philharmonic Society of London. The chorus was praised – 'finer choral singing could not be heard in London'[215] –

but the festival failed financially, attributed in part to continuing religious objections to 'sacred' entertainment.[216] It would be 1873 before another festival took place, by which time attitudes had changed, and attendance ensured that a profit for local charities was made. (That religious sensibilities still had to be considered is seen in the attempt by the festival committee to forbid applause of sacred works, which met with only partial success.)[217] But although the choral singing was again praised,[218] other problems revealed themselves. The City Hall was an inadequate and uncomfortable venue, and Lambeth, although a thorough and much-admired choral trainer, in common with many, lacked experience with orchestras – again the Londoners came up – and the choir itself was evidently unused to collaborating with one. Understandably the best performance was of Michael Costa's *Eli*, conducted by the composer himself.[219] No further festivals were forthcoming, but it did prompt the creation of the Glasgow Choral Union Orchestra in 1874 (a forerunner of the Scottish National Orchestra), and in 1877 the city acquired a worthy concert venue in the St Andrew's Halls (burnt down in 1962), while the Glasgow Choral Union itself became one of those societies which Henry Coward would take under his wing in 1908.[220]

It was to be a very different choir which would make the city's name known musically in the early twentieth century. In 1901 the 25-year-old Hugh Roberton, who had started adult life in the family's undertaking business, took over as conductor of the Toynbee House Musical Association, which in 1906 became the Glasgow Orpheus Choir. With this vehicle and a highly disciplined approach, Roberton soon brought Scottish choralism to the attention of English and ultimately international audiences, starting with a visit to the Queen's Hall, London, in 1908. Later they broadcast regularly, made recordings, sang for royalty and prime ministers, and toured both Europe and North America. Their repertoire consisted mostly of part-songs and traditional Scottish songs, arranged largely by Roberton himself. He also composed many works for them, most famously 'All in the April Evening', which became almost their signature tune. The choir was notable for its rich warm tone, which combined well with its unashamedly sentimental approach. Roberton, who was a much sought-after adjudicator, was knighted in 1931. When he announced he was stepping down from the Orpheus in 1951, the choir itself decided to disband, only for many members to reform as the Glasgow Phoenix Choir, which has continued its tradition to the present day.[221]

Over in Ireland, the spirit of its eighteenth-century enthusiasm for Handel lived on, and an annual commemoration of the composer, initiated in 1787 by the Irish Musical Fund Society in the wake of the London ones, continued in Dublin into the 1820s, though not confining its music to Handel – in 1801 *The Creation* was given, just a year after publication, if in a rather under-rehearsed performance.[222] Successive generations of the Robinson family were to be a leading force in Dublin's choral life for almost a century, and from 1810 Francis Robinson appears to have directed the Sons of Handel, a small society dating from the 1780s, which concentrated on his oratorios.[223] It seemingly folded in 1824, but had a successor in the Antient Concerts Society founded in 1834 by Francis's son, Joseph, who also became the first conductor of the University of Dublin Choral Society in 1837.[224] Both of these were still very much private institutions, admitting only members and their guests to the concerts.[225] Joseph Robinson would prove a particular champion of Mendelssohn's works, introducing many of them to Dublin audiences soon after their English premieres; furthermore, he personally persuaded the composer to produce an orchestral accompaniment for 'Hear my prayer', which was then first heard at an Antient Concert in 1848. The social structure of Ireland, however, was changing, as after the Act of Union 1801 many of the old Anglo-Irish aristocracy and gentry left for England, so that the middle classes increasingly took the lead in cultural affairs. In Dublin too, music could provide common ground for both Protestants and Catholics, so much so that Catholic churches could host oratorio and other sacred music performances in aid of parochial charities, which Protestants would also attend.[226] From mid-century an effort was made to embrace a wider audience for choral music, exemplified by the founding of the Royal Choral Institute in 1851 by the Catholic John William Glover, whose advertisements proclaimed that 'one of the leading objects of the Society is to give ALL classes an opportunity of hearing the best productions of the most celebrated composers.'[227] Its performers numbered 150–200, and with four concerts a year, besides the expected *Messiah*, *The Creation*, and *Elijah*, it ventured to include Handel's *Samson*, and in 1854 even Schumann's *Paradise and the Peri*. But standards were variable, and the Society did not survive beyond 1855. It would be 1875 before Dublin found itself with a choral society on the scale of many English ones, when the tireless Joseph Robinson created the Dublin Musical Society, with 250–350 participants, giving around three concerts a year, which were very much open to the public at large, and which survived until 1902.[228] By this time also, the tonic sol-fa movement had begun to exert its beneficial influence on choral recruitment.

Understandably, the regular festival movement never took off in Ireland – the Handel commemorations were only single-concert affairs. In the first half of the century there was a solitary six-day Grand Musical Festival in 1831, just before the coronation of William IV, when Irish musicians were augmented by singers from the Liverpool Festival Choral Society and players from the Philharmonic Society in London to produce a choir of 172 and orchestra of 74.[229] After 1850 the occasional mammoth choral assembly occurred, as when Joseph Robinson gathered 1,000 performers for the opening of the Great Industrial Exhibition of 1853, and a similar number for the Dublin International Exhibition of Fine Art and Manufactures in 1865, while St Patrick's Day was celebrated for several years in the 1870s with 500 performers rendering one of the few oratorios by an Irish composer, the above-mentioned Glover's *St Patrick at Tara*.[230] As in other cultural spheres, Ireland tended to lose many promising young musicians to emigration, as happened with the Dublin-born and educated Charles Villiers Stanford. Even more so than in England, orchestras tended to be the Achilles heel of choral life, especially as choirs grew larger; they often had to be assembled from diverse sources, including expensive importation from England, and the results were predictably unsatisfactory and reflected in press criticism.[231]

Outside Dublin, significant choral activity was found mainly in Cork and Belfast. Cork displayed a conservative nature, where an Antient Concerts Society was established in 1846 after its Dublin namesake, with its choir and orchestra of 100 giving two or three concerts a year to a subscribing membership and their friends, as did the slightly larger Cork Musical Society, founded in 1869.[232] Belfast, with its fast growth and increasing wealth in the second half of the century, was nevertheless slow in developing chorally. In the 1830s it had seen the local Catch and Glee Club combining with the instrumental Anacreontic Society for choral performances,[233] while the Belfast Classical Harmonists started life in 1851.[234] The opening of the 2,000 seat Ulster Hall in 1862 gave the city a large venue to match the new English town halls, though in its early days its size proved rather challenging to choirs and orchestras,[235] while conservative tastes among Belfast audiences would also prove an impediment to artistic ventures.[236] Later concern to revitalise the music society scene led in 1874 to the creation of the Belfast Philharmonic Society, formed from an amalgamation of the Classical Harmonists with a recently established Belfast Musical Society.[237] The resulting choir of 200–400 (still in existence) ensured the city could hear the standard repertoire with the size of forces that by now was customary in large centres across the Irish Sea, and provided a foundation to develop the flourishing choral scene for which Northern Ireland would become known in the twentieth century.[238]

A Choral Miscellany

The male-voice choir tradition in England developed in more varied ways than in Wales. In part they reflected the manner of the older catch and glee clubs. Whereas the Welsh male choirs all had a TTBB constitution, the use of the falsetto alto on the top line continued to be a basis for many English choirs, in some cases right up to the 1930s, so that an ATBB formation was commonly found as well as TTBB. Competitions had separate classes for each group, and many new part-songs continued to be composed for ATBB voices into the twentieth century. Unlike the Welsh, unaccompanied singing was the norm among English male choirs. As in Wales, it was the industrial areas of Lancashire, Yorkshire and Staffordshire which provided the most fertile areas of growth, offering alternative male-centred musical opportunities to those not attracted or suited to the brass band. And, like the latter, in addition to competing, the male-voice choirs found themselves in demand locally for civic occasions, charity events and the like. The Welsh migration to England, in the face of the poverty caused by the inter-war decline of the South Wales coalfields, saw the emergence of at least one 'exile' male-voice choir in the Oxford Welsh Glee Singers.[239]

Although workplace choirs have recently attracted much attention, thanks largely to Gareth Malone's television series, their history extends back to at least the late nineteenth century, when they were all-male institutions, existing on various levels of society.[240] The Cooperative Wholesale Society choir in Manchester gave its first concert in 1903, having evolved from a singing class formed in 1899.[241] In London, the Civil Service Vocal Union, the Stock Exchange Orchestral and Choral Society, and the Bar Musical Society ('consisting of Members of the Inns of Court') were all flourishing before 1900, pointing towards participatory interest amongst the upper middle classes, in part no doubt reflecting the older more exclusive type of glee club – all three were ATB based, and 'smoking concerts' and Ladies Nights featured in their activities.[242] Police choirs, too, have a long history, going back to 1872, when the Metropolitan Police Minstrels, a blackface vocal and instrumental group, began giving concerts, mainly in aid of the Metropolitan and City Police Orphanage. They prompted the creation of similar troupes and male-voice choirs in other police forces, and continued in existence until 1933,[243] being succeeded by the Metropolitan Police Male Voice Choir, which in 2016 became the mixed-voice Metropolitan Police Choir, with membership extending also to ancillary staff. Among other groups, postal and railway workers have likewise formed choirs, and such public performances as they give have tended to be for charity.[244]

While male- and mixed-voice choirs attracted most attention, there were also certainly many female-voice choirs created in the second half of the nineteenth century, as witness the classes for them at competitive festivals, as well as the considerable amount of music published. In the complete Novello catalogue of *c.* 1900, sixteen pages are dedicated to secular vocal music 'for female and boys' voices' as against eleven for male voices.[245] But their activities are sparsely documented – at least before the emergence of the Women's Institute choirs in the 1920s, and there is scope for research here. The example of the Dowlais Ladies Choir suggests that they came more out of the leisured middle classes than most choral societies of the time. Apart from those choirs which competed, their public appearances probably lay mainly in providing entertainment at local social events. On the subject of class, an interesting sidelight is provided by those choirs which used the term 'Amateur' in their title. In this context it did not serve to distinguish unpaid practitioners from professionals, as it usually did with the 'amateur orchestra', or the 'amateur operatic society'. Rather it sought to imply that their members were true 'lovers' of music, as opposed to the supposedly cruder tastes of other choirs. Such, for example, was the Sheffield Amateur Musical Society, founded in 1864 from among 'heads of well-known firms and businessmen and their wives'.[246] Their concerts tended to be private affairs for invited audiences or exclusive subscribers, and many would not have outlasted the enthusiasm of their founders. An extreme example is seen in the following advertisement from the *Musical Times* for 1866: 'To ladies and gentlemen having a taste for vocal music – A private society is being formed, consisting solely of amateurs occupying good social positions. There will be none of the elements of the ordinary choral society'.[247] Whether this exclusive group ever materialized is unrecorded. Not every choir incorporating the amateur name was of this nature, but it was sufficiently common to constitute a distinct type, and such societies continued to be created into the 1890s.[248]

A minor phenomenon was the appearance of a number of new madrigal societies after the London model, and like it, generally all male, employing boy trebles. Many were founded as a result of a series of illustrated lecture tours on old English vocal music by Edward Taylor (of Norwich Festival fame) in the 1830s.[249] Most societies were short-lived, with a tendency to diversify their repertoire into modern glees and part-songs, but one, the Bristol Madrigal Society, founded in 1837, has survived to the present day, having changed its name to the Bristol Chamber Choir. It even retained the use of boys until 1945.[250] Like the catch and glee clubs, they were private organisations, meeting for mutual enjoyment, though Bristol, for one, soon had an annual 'Ladies Night' open to the public, attracting an audience of 1,400 in 1854.[251] Among the founder members of the Bristol society was the amateur composer Robert Lucas Pearsall, during one of the brief periods he spent in this country. Pearsall wrote over twenty modern madrigals, mostly inspired by his Bristol experience, demonstrating that he had absorbed the contrapuntal techniques of the Elizabethan era to an astonishing degree (far more so than professional composers who occasionally imitated the style). Combining this with more contemporary harmonic language, resulted in some splendid works which have endured, not least the outstanding 'Lay a garland'.[252]

A discussion of school music will be left until a later chapter, but despite the lack of any formal teaching or encouragement in public schools for most of the Victorian era, there was sufficient musical talent and interest at Oxford and Cambridge for music societies to take root. The Cambridge University Musical Society (CUMS) dates back to 1844 (emerging from the Peterhouse Musical Society created a year before) and had a choral element in its twice-yearly concerts. Boys sang the soprano part until 1872, when Stanford (at that time still an undergraduate organ scholar at Queen's) turned it into a mixed choir, presumably with town involvement, and introduced a more contemporary repertoire.[253] By the first decade of the twentieth century CUMS was introducing undergraduates to the B minor Mass and the St Matthew Passion. Other mixed town and gown choirs also made their appearance, notably a Festival Chorus formed by Dr A.H. Mann of King's, initially to celebrate Queen Victoria's Golden Jubilee in 1887. It went on to become the Cambridge Choral Society in 1904 and the present Cambridge Philharmonic Society in 1924.[254] At Oxford, in addition to the old Oxford Choral Society, dating from 1819, a Philharmonic Society was started in 1866 by John Stainer, then organist at Magdalen. Although mostly town based, both societies had university members; they amalgamated in 1890, and in turn were incorporated in 1910 into the recently created Oxford Bach Choir.[255] Taking its cue from the London choir, this was founded in 1896 by Basil Harwood, organist of Christ Church, to similarly promote the music of Bach in the first place. It was conducted for over twenty years from 1901 by the fiery and enthusiastic Hugh Allen, one of whose declared aims was to give every generation of undergraduates the opportunity to sing either the St Matthew Passion or the B minor Mass.[256] Although including town membership, it became the nearest thing Oxford had to a university chorus, reaching a peak of 400 members in the 1920s, and tackling the whole standard choral repertoire.[257] At a more intimate level, a number of colleges formed glee and madrigal societies in Victorian times, and doubtless kept their proceedings well provided with liquid refreshment.[258]

Questions of pitch increasingly concerned choirs as the nineteenth century advanced. A general rise in the pitch of instruments took place in the first half of the century, as the desire for a more 'brilliant' sound developed, with the result that a common pitch standard was about a quarter tone sharp of the modern standard of $a'=440$, and Victorian organs can still be encountered at this high pitch. Bearing in mind that, in Handel's day, pitch in England was about a semitone below modern pitch, it is no surprise that singers, especially from the 1860s on, began to complain – all the more so when they were faced with the demands of the B minor Mass, the Choral Symphony, or the *Missa Solemnis*.²⁵⁹ The French had already begun to confront the problem in 1859 by laying down a new lower standard (*diapason normal*) about a quarter-tone below a'=440, which quickly won favour on the continent. The first attempt to introduce it in England was by Joseph Barnby for his Oratorio Concerts at St James's Hall in 1869, when a new organ tuned to the *diapason normal* was installed. Yet although vocalists welcomed the change, there was a long battle over the question for the rest of the century (especially as changing the pitch of organs was expensive) and the Royal Albert Hall organ remained at high pitch until 1923.²⁶⁰

Also related is the question of choirs failing to maintain pitch in unaccompanied singing, usually meaning they ended up flat. This took on special importance with the growth of competitive festivals, where it became the custom at the end of an unaccompanied item for the final chord to be sounded on the piano. No doubt a round of applause greeted those choirs which ended in the correct key, but it was a source of embarrassment for others. Some musicians felt that testing pitch in this way was in danger of attaching undue importance to the matter. A choir which gave an artistic performance, with generally good internal tuning, but sank a little in pitch – to the extent that very few people would notice – could find themselves over-penalized. The piano test was eventually abandoned to general relief. Of course, flattening is still with us, though we have plenty of potentially helpful remedies to hand these days. But the infamous 'Since by man came death'/ 'For as in Adam all die' chorus in *Messiah* remains an anxious moment for many conductors. Victorian choirs were usually untroubled by this particular passage, since it was common for it to be sung by the soloists, and even when sung chorally, the 'Mozart' accompaniments included instrumental support.²⁶¹

As the nineteenth century closed, not everyone was in favour of the additional accompaniments of Mozart and others, which had accrued to *Messiah* in particular. Already in 1883 Sir George Grove had called for them to be discarded,²⁶² and in December 1885 C.S. Macpherson conducted a performance of *Messiah* in Westminster Town Hall, using a chorus of about a hundred, with just strings, oboes, trumpets and timpani; a harmonium substituted for the organ and a 1771 Shudi harpsichord was used for the recitatives. The *Monthly Musical Record*, while describing the effect as 'fairly good', called it a 'historical curiosity'.²⁶³ At Cambridge, Dr A.H. Mann, the scholarly organist of King's, found the original instrumental parts from Handel's Foundling Hospital performances. In 1894 he used these as the basis for a performance in King's Chapel, although the size of his forces was hardly Handelian, with 200 in the choir and 63 in the orchestra.²⁶⁴ Mann, however, followed this up in 1906 with a truly Handelian-size performance using a chorus of 24 and 32 instrumentalists, though his purpose was merely illustrative of what Handel had available, rather than a model to be followed.[265] More significant was the work of Frederick Bridge as conductor of the Royal Choral Society, when in 1889 he too adopted the Foundling Hospital orchestration, albeit with 100 players, but these were still pitted against 800 singers, rendering the oboes and bassoons in particular more or less inaudible. Nevertheless, this remained the Society's practice to the end of Bridge's conductorship in 1922.[266]

The most important *Messiah* development at the turn of the century, however, was the Novello publication in 1902 of a new edition by Ebenezer Prout, well known as teacher and author of standard musical treatises. He examined the original sources, and successfully purged the oratorio of many mistakes in the vocal parts, which were found in every edition to date. He also introduced the idea of double dotting certain rhythms in accordance with eighteenth-century practice. On the other hand, he considered Handel's own sparse instrumentation unsuitable for the size of modern choirs, and so retained many of the by now traditional 'Mozart' additional accompaniments, with other modifications of his own, so this was still *Messiah* with flutes, clarinets and trombones. Prout sought to present a single version of the work, so he offered no alternative versions of arias, and relegated rarely sung numbers to an appendix.[267] It was destined to become the standard edition for twentieth-century singers until a new revolution was started by Watkins Shaw in 1959.

Participation in choral activities reached its peak in the decades immediately preceding the First World War. Never again would 300–400 be the norm for larger societies, for in the post-war situation choirs of all types would find recruitment a growing problem. But the seeds of decline had already been sown in the early years of the century, as alternative sources of entertainment began to make inroads into both choir membership and audiences. Even within the musical sphere tastes were changing (or at least broadening), with opera and orchestral concerts claiming increasing attention. The consequences will be explored in Chapter Six.

Chapter 5
Church and Cathedral Choirs in the Nineteenth Century

As seen in Chapter Three, the general condition of cathedral music at the end of the eighteenth century was at one of its lowest points, while at parish level the developments of country psalmody had certainly enlivened music in rural churches, even if it was strongly disapproved of by many clergy and professional musicians. Meanwhile, most town churches still relied on local charity children to support their music, although voluntary mixed choirs were appearing in some more adventurous parishes. By the end of the nineteenth century a major transformation had taken place, particularly in parish churches where what we have come to consider as the typical church choir emerged. The cathedrals had begun to awake from their somnolent state, and both Nonconformist and Roman Catholic churches also developed choral cultures. In the course of that change, various issues would periodically arise. One of the most significant was the relationship between choir and congregation, which confronted not only parishes, but on occasions the cathedrals too, as their Sunday congregations grew. The question of female participation, whether as sopranos or contraltos, produced an assortment of practices, both within the Church of England, as the divisions of churchmanship became more pronounced, and in the Roman Catholic Church.

Standards of church music in the early decades of the century were probably no worse than in the preceding period, but its plight was heightened by the increased amount of criticism that began to make its way into print. In 1831 John Antes La Trobe began his idiosyncratic survey *The Music of the Church* by stating, 'It is impossible for a man of observation to flatter himself, that our church-music is in a healthful and vigorous condition. He must acknowledge, if he has given the subject the slightest consideration, that the end for which music was introduced into our services, is not generally attained.'[1] And William Thoms in 1837 commented in an article in the *Musical World*, 'The choirs of our cathedrals, with some few exceptions only, are in a most crippled and enfeebled condition. They are the living skeletons of what were once vigorous and effective bodies.'[2] The state of cathedral music will be examined more closely in due course, but criticism was well under way before that emanating from what was to prove the major catalyst for church reform generally, the so-called Oxford Movement.

The Oxford Movement

In 1833 a group of high churchmen in Oxford, including John Keble, John Henry Newman, and Edward Pusey, initiated a public attack on the state of the Church of England in sermons and a series of publications called *Tracts for the Times*, as a result of which, early supporters were known as Tractarians. Their concern was to reassert the validity of the State Church and its priesthood as part of the universal church, in the light of recent repeal of the laws discriminating against Roman Catholics and Nonconformists. Associated with this was respect for the Book of Common Prayer and interest in reviving certain practices and features of the medieval church – thus a strong tinge of the escapism inherent in Romanticism attaches to the movement. On the practical side, their main concerns were for greater dignity in worship, to reinstate the altar in place of the pulpit as the focal point of the church, to stress the importance of the Sacraments, and for priests to take their responsibilities seriously and so enhance their authority. There was, however, a wide range of opinion within the Movement. Some wished to embrace more Roman Catholic practices, either medieval or modern, which in certain cases, notably that of Newman, led to them converting. But most remained to exercise influence within the Church of England. An immediate and important effect was on would-be ordinands of all shades of churchmanship at the universities – the Movement's ideas quickly spread also to Cambridge – inspiring enthusiasm which they took into their early curacies in villages and towns throughout the country. They were not necessarily all high churchmen, but the new generation of priests were certainly endowed with a new sense of responsibility.

Music was hardly a concern of leaders of the Oxford Movement like Newman and Pusey. But it did become the main focus of a number of its adherents, who, like the theologians, were not necessarily of one mind in the direction reform ought to take. Some sided with those Tractarians, who wanted to see greater active congregational involvement in worship, including the singing. Since it was generally acknowledged that Anglican chant was unsuited for congregational singing of the psalms, there was advocacy for employing plainsong instead, it being thought that participation could be more easily encouraged. 'Gregorians', as plainsong was commonly called, also neatly fitted in with the 'medievalizing' spirit of the Oxford Movement.

Among the influential musical figures was Thomas Helmore (1811–90), who from 1842 was vice-principal and precentor (i.e. in charge of music) at St Mark's College, Chelsea, a newly-created teacher training institution. Here he initiated daily choral services in which the (wholly male) student body sang the psalms and canticles in plainsong, together with a choir (including boy trebles from the associated 'Model School') which sang unaccompanied service settings and anthems from the sixteenth and seventeenth centuries, including English adaptations of Palestrina.[3] The newly trained teachers subsequently went out to church schools throughout the country, hopefully able to assist musically in the reforms desired by the new generation of Tractarian-inspired clergy emerging from the universities. Thomas Helmore went on to produce various standard plainsong publications, and was a leading figure in the Motett Society. Founded in 1841, it aimed to demonstrate through publications and public performances the merits of mainly sixteenth-century music (including continental works in translation) it considered suitable for use in worship.[4]

Meanwhile, a younger brother, Frederick, aided the cause as a travelling choirmaster, recruiting and training mainly village choirs, rather in the tradition of the eighteenth-century itinerant singing masters. He did, however, also spend time in 1850–1 establishing the choir in the new St Ninian's episcopal cathedral in Perth.[5] He would typically work intensively with a choir for one to two months, rehearsing boys perhaps four or more times a week on their own, who then joined the men on two or more evenings. A small core repertoire, including simple anthems like Richard Farrant's 'Lord, for thy tender mercies sake', would be established before he moved on to another parish. In the early years he aimed to revisit a choir annually in order to 'refresh' them. Quite how the choirs were led once he had left, and how many prospered in the long term, is unrecorded, but he did cover many villages, especially in the North, and his work in one place probably stimulated other efforts in the neighbourhood.[6]

Frederick Helmore's endeavours were certainly one factor in a fast growth in the number of village choirs in the middle years of the century. This was very much bound up with the development of village schools, from which boys – and it was predominantly boys – could be recruited. At times this would have involved dispensing with an existing west gallery vocal and instrumental group, replacing it with a body of singers seated (usually) in the chancel. The bringing back into use of chancels was one of the major reforms of the Tractarian movement. The previous century had often seen them more or less sealed off as the main body of the church became a 'preaching box', focused on a three-decker pulpit. The Cambridge Camden Society (founded in 1839 and known from 1845 as the

Ecclesiological Society) was the Tractarian body concerned with architecture and church furnishings. It promoted the building of new churches (or the remodelling of existing ones), taking the fourteenth-century Decorated style as its model, and deliberately designed longish chancels to accommodate the new generation of choirs.[7] It is one of the ironies of the movement that the chancels of medieval parish churches were in fact not filled with choristers, but with various ranks of clergy, which in places where they were numerous (as in the case of some churches with chantries), occasioned chancels of substantial length.[8] Placing the choir in the chancel, decently clad in surplices – cassocks came later in the century – was one measure which itself helped promote the greater sense of decorum now desired by the clergy. Particularly in rural parishes, Tractarian priests (or at least the more sensitive of them) must often have had to compromise their reformist ideas in the face of conservatively-minded congregations. Getting rid of the old gallery singers and instrumentalists understandably sometimes provoked rifts, even if by mid-century it was becoming clear that their day was past, though they would linger on in a few places into the 1890s.[9] The old village structure, headed by squire and parson, may have been slow to break down, but growing competition from Nonconformists in even the smallest communities meant that incumbents needed to take note of the opinion of their parishioners, and not least the local squire, who was unlikely to favour radical change. However much Tractarian country priests may have wanted to stress the importance of Holy Communion, in practice Matins and Evensong remained the bedrock of most Sunday village services, albeit conducted in a more seemly way than previously.

There were indeed examples where a keen village priest managed to create choral life far beyond the norm, as happened at Kemerton near Tewkesbury, where the high church incumbent and curate introduced a surpliced choir of boys and men, which by the early 1850s was singing daily choral services, the church having been rebuilt according to the Ecclesiological Society's principles.[10] One suspects, however, that initial enthusiasm may have soon waned. Likewise, despite the advocacy of 'Gregorians' by the Helmores and other early Tractarians on the grounds that they were easier for a congregation to join in, they proved in practice to be no more suitable than Anglican chants in most parochial situations, as well as being less appealing to Victorian musical taste. The people may have taken to neo-Gothic church architecture, but when it came to the austerities of Gregorian chant, medieval idealism gave way to belief in the progress of musical composition. By the 1860s plainsong was increasingly found only in the more Anglo-Catholic ritualistic churches, where its performance was essentially confined to the choir.

The growth of new-style village choirs manifested itself clearly also in the creation of annual diocesan choral festivals. The first was held in Lichfield Cathedral in 1856 with about twenty-six choirs taking part, and it was soon widely imitated elsewhere in England and Wales.[11] The Welsh, in particular, took preparations for their festivals seriously, and in 1865 advertised in the *Musical Times* for a choir organizer to spend several months going round rehearsing choirs for the Llandaff festival,[12] where by 1866 there were a thousand participants from forty choirs.[13] The music selected for early festivals was understandably kept very simple – single chants for psalms and canticles, and easy anthems – but gained in ambition as time passed. The tradition has managed to continue in many areas to the present day, typically taking the form of a full cathedral-style choral Evensong, giving many choirs the opportunity of experiencing a form of service they would not normally encounter in their own parishes.

Placing a surpliced choir in the chancel may have been satisfying aesthetically and liturgically, but from the point of view of the Tractarian desire to have the choir lead congregational singing it was the worst possible position, especially if there was a substantial chancel arch or screen to impede the sound reaching the nave. It also raised the problem of where to site the organ, which many churches were now acquiring for the first time. The Ecclesiologists would gladly have done without organs, as they regarded them as obtrusive, and architects rarely took the organ into consideration when designing new or re-ordered buildings.[14] As far as villages were concerned, where only small instruments were involved, they were generally tucked away on one side of the chancel – often backing into a vestry or special chamber – which may have suited the choir, but produced an inadequate sound in the nave. Alternatively, the organ could be placed in the nave, often at the back of the church at ground level (for galleries tended to be done away with in the nineteenth century); this certainly made for audibility by the congregation, but was a disadvantage for the choir trying to fulfil the role of leading the singing. This was an era in which a whole raft of new hymns was rapidly replacing the old familiar metrical psalms. *Hymns Ancient and Modern* (first published in 1861) would soon become the nearest thing the Church of England had to an official hymnbook, and so there was plenty of leading for choirs to do, especially given the reluctance of most Anglican congregations to sing. Even those town churches which could afford larger and more powerful instruments often found it difficult to site them satisfactorily.

Village choirs would have varied enormously in their constitution, competence and ambition. Perhaps the greatest factor in their development was the availability of a skilled trainer, always a matter of luck, especially in rural parishes. The schoolmaster may have been in a position to fulfil that role, particularly if he had been come through a college like St Mark's, Chelsea, but training boys could be time-consuming and far from easy. And it was boys who formed the foundation of these new-style choirs. Unlike the old urban choirs from charity schools, where both boys and girls commonly participated, though separated, girls were now rarely recruited. In part this reflected Tractarian views, which saw the chancel as a male preserve, and it was to create a trend in which a parish church choir of boys and men became regarded as standard by late Victorian times.[15] Although the influence of the tonic sol-fa movement may have encouraged more people to learn to read music, many choirs, especially rural ones, would have still largely relied on singing by rote, repetition being the key to mastering new material. The role of women in the choir will be examined a little later.

Town Choirs

In urban settings church choral life developed in more varied ways. Differences between evangelicals, the broad middle ground, and high church Anglo-Catholics came into sharper focus in the second half of the century. As a result, in towns with several parishes, people could find themselves with a choice of very different styles of worship – quite apart from Nonconformist chapels – so that the traditional attachment to one's own parish church began to diminish. In 1858 there appeared a *Guide to the Church Services in London and its Suburbs*, helping to simplify finding a church to one's taste.[16] Apart from theological considerations, music could obviously be a factor in determining allegiance. On the high church wing there was no consensus on its role. Not all were in agreement with the early Tractarian desire to encourage congregational singing and the use of plainsong. There were many, particularly among professional musicians, who considered plainsong, with its modal base, as a relic of a bygone age and unsuited to the aesthetic taste of Victorian Britain, which favoured the modern harmonies of Anglican chant. They also adhered to the traditional high church concept of the 'beauty of holiness', believing that only the best quality of musical performance should be offered in worship. Not for them the rough singing of a congregation, but a well-trained choir, imitating cathedral music at its (theoretical) best, was their ideal. Models of this approach began to appear in the 1840s. One was at Leeds Parish Church. Here there had actually been a surpliced paid choir since 1818, supported by parish funds, and by the 1820s singing to Anglican chants.[17] The arrival of Walter Hook as vicar in 1837 soon led to the replacement of the existing dilapidated church with a large new one, consecrated in 1841. Hook held high church views without being a Tractarian, and for musical advice relied on John Jebb, a member of the cathedral chapter of Limerick in Ireland, who had made an extensive study of the choral service and was to publish his criticisms and proposals for reform in 1843.[18] Jebb was no supporter of congregational chanting of the psalms – at best they should join in very softly – nor did he like plainsong.[19] As a result, the re-established choir at Leeds sang daily cathedral-style services – not without some initial opposition – and in 1842 no less a figure than Samuel Sebastian Wesley was invited to become organist. Wesley, who came from a post at Hereford Cathedral, and was to return to that world at Winchester in 1849, naturally shared Jebb's views. His presence in Leeds drew national attention to developments there, and he composed some challenging music for the new choir, including his Service in E, still very much in the repertoire. With its daily choral services, Leeds was perhaps exceptional in setting itself up virtually as a cathedral music-wise, but it did find imitation on Sundays at other churches with musical ambition; one such was St Philip's, Sheffield, which had cathedral-style services by the 1850s.[20]

In London too there were influential models of the evolving liturgical/choral scene. On the high church wing, Tractarian principles were first conspicuously demonstrated at the unpretentious Margaret Chapel in the West End, when Frederick Oakeley, fresh from being chaplain at Balliol College, Oxford, became vicar in 1839. He re-ordered the 'preaching box' building, restoring the altar to prominence, and instituting a sober, dignified liturgy. Musical himself, he recruited a sympathetic organist, Richard Redhead, and a small choir of boys, who were soon chanting, initially using single Anglican chants. Oakeley quickly switched to 'Gregorians', himself editing a pointed psalter, which was distributed to the congregation, with the idea of encouraging them to sing – how successfully is unknown – and he also introduced full choral Communion services.[21] Although the musical quality was unremarkable, visiting priests were impressed by the atmosphere of the services, and were inspired to go off and imitate.[22] But Oakeley's innovations, such as wearing a surplice rather than a gown when preaching, and placing candles on the altar – modest as they would soon seem – provoked ructions within the diocese as being dangerously 'popish', and Oakeley himself converted to Roman Catholicism in 1845.[23] The Margaret Chapel itself was soon replaced by a new church, All Saints, Margaret Street. Consecrated in 1859 in all its richly adorned neo-Gothic splendour, it became a leading and popular centre of ritualistic Anglo-Catholic worship with a musical style very different from that of Oakeley. It had its own boarding choir school – Laurence Olivier would be a twentieth-century chorister – and the continental Masses of Haydn, Mozart and others, in

English adaptations, became standard fare at the Eucharist, with a high standard of singing soon being achieved. While remaining true to the Prayer Book texts, Anglo-Catholic establishments like All Saints began to add other elements to bring them closer to the Catholic Mass, including the Benedictus following the Sanctus, and the Agnus Dei, neither of which were in the Book of Common Prayer. As there had never been reason to set these texts in English before, continental works were the obvious source until native composers got round to including them in their settings.[24] As the Eucharist gradually became the main focus of high church Sunday worship, Matins was usually reduced to a hastily performed said service immediately preceding it.

A similar change of music direction took place in another fashionable Tractarian church, St Andrew's, Wells Street. When it opened in 1847, congregational participation alongside the choir was the order of the day, and plainsong was employed; yet within a few years Anglican chant had been substituted, and, also having its own choir school, daily choral services were being sung. With the appointment in 1863 of Joseph Barnby as organist, musical taste moved even more in a contemporary direction, and in 1866 he introduced his English adaptation of Gounod's *Messe solennelle en l'honneur de Sainte Cécile* (composed in 1855), including the use of a harp in addition to the organ.[25] Such arrangements could be managed by only a handful of churches, but the influence was felt generally in Anglo-Catholic circles. For choirs which could not aspire to Viennese Masses and the like, John Marbeck's setting of Holy Communion (republished in 1843 for the first time since 1550) often became a standard item, though with a regular metrical structure and harmonization imposed on its plainsong-style melodies. Proving suitable for congregational participation, it achieved a popularity which has in places been retained through liturgical changes to the present day. An English adaptation of the plainsong *Missa de angelis* also found considerable favour.

Outside the high church orbit London was also to provide a model for a very different style of choral service. The Temple Church is the chapel of two of the Inns of Court, the Inner and Middle Temple, just off the Strand. It consists of the twelfth-century Round Church (originally the home of the Knights Templar), which came to serve as a sort of ante-chapel to the added thirteenth-century Quire. Musically it had been distinguished since the end of the seventeenth century for its Bernhard ('Father') Smith organ, which was placed on the screen separating the Round Church from the Quire. Here the blind organist John Stanley, organist to the Inner Temple, played for over fifty years in the middle of the eighteenth century. Chorally, however, matters were far from remarkable; there was no choir at all until

1827 – the parish clerk leading what little singing took place – when two women, soon joined by two men were engaged to lead the singing from the organ gallery. Initially introduced to encourage the congregation to sing, they quickly took it upon themselves to perform chants and anthems. (Such quartets were also common in American churches at this time.)[26] According to Edward John Hopkins, a curtain at the front of the gallery 'would be drawn aside for a few minutes, the singers would sing, and everybody would turn west to look at them; then the curtain was banged to with a rattle of brass rings'.[27] But that situation was short-lived, since the church was in a poor state of repair and was closed in 1841 for restoration and re-ordering. The opportunity was then taken to radically alter the musical arrangements. The organ was moved to a chamber on the north side of the Quire, which was furnished with facing stalls like a cathedral or college chapel, though it also had box pews down the centre. When it reopened in 1842, in place of the quartet, a surpliced choir of boys and men was established, which after some initial experimentation in both numbers and placement, settled down to eight boys (later increased to twelve, plus four probationers) and six men,[28] most of whom also held posts in the Chapel Royal or Westminster Abbey. They occupied the stalls on both sides of the Quire by the organ – a gap in the central box pews being left at this place so the two sides could see each other. The Temple authorities had decided that the services should now be conducted chorally after the cathedral manner, and in 1843 the 25-year-old Edward John Hopkins was appointed organist, and soon after also became Master of the Choristers.[29] He had been a chorister at the Chapel Royal and approached the task with youthful enthusiasm. A similar establishment, though on a smaller scale, was created at this time at Lincoln's Inn Chapel, and the two sets of boys would eventually share schooling.[30]

By the late 1840s the choir was already highly regarded. Hopkins paid special attention to the voice training and blend of the boys, and above all he concentrated on the psalm singing, personally marking each copy of the psalms in their prayer books.[31] As a result, *The Guardian* reported in 1848 that at the Temple people 'may hear psalm chanting in its utmost perfection … no slovenly hurrying or clipping of words, but all as it should be … every word distinctly pronounced, every sentence clearly and reverentially enunciated'.[32] The style of chanting, however, was far removed from the 'speech rhythm' method developed in the twentieth century. The notes of the chant following the reciting note were still sung and played slowly in strict time. Yet, although the Temple took cathedral worship as its model, including monotoning parts like the Confession, in one important way it differed from the cathedrals: there were no daily choral services, and so it is easy to see how refinement could be achieved, and why its choristers were soon in demand to assist at major events like the Duke of Wellington's funeral at St Paul's in 1852 in addition to taking part in concerts.[33] The churchmanship of the Temple was firmly central and non-ceremonial, much to the disappointment of Tractarians; it had a candle-free altar, and its Sunday morning service had the traditional form of Matins, Litany and Ante-Communion; full choral Communion was not celebrated.[34] This was still the pattern for the great majority of parish churches, as well as the cathedrals, throughout the country. In another respect also, the Temple resembled the cathedrals, in that Hopkins's authority over the choir at first extended only to the boys; the men were answerable to the Choir Committee of the Benchers, and though comparatively well rewarded, were not totally immune to the diseases of unpunctuality and absenteeism. Only in 1869 was Hopkins given complete control over the choir,[35] and the Temple was to prove a congenial post, for he remained in office for 55 years until his death in 1898. His successor, Henry Walford Davies, was to serve 25 years, giving the choir remarkable stability and consistency, so that in the pre-First World War years it was still regarded by many as finest in the country. Walford Davies updated and broadened the repertoire – more Bach and Brahms in place of many of the minor Georgian and early Victorian composers still favoured by Hopkins. His chief innovation was the introduction of a monthly cantata or oratorio segment in place of the anthem at Evensong, which then saw the choir tackle parts of the *Christmas Oratorio* and Brahms's *German Requiem*.[36] But equally important was his further refining of the choir's psalm singing in such a way that he can be seen as one of the pioneers of 'speech rhythm'. And Walford Davies would in turn be succeeded in 1923 by the phenomenal 27-year-old George Thalben-Ball, who would outdo both his predecessors in length of service, retiring only in 1981.[37]

The Temple Church has merited special consideration since it was certainly influential – more so than Leeds Parish Church or the cathedrals – in determining the direction musical arrangements would take in many of the larger non-Tractarian churches, particularly in the more affluent areas. Musicians flocked to hear the choir (and Hopkins's renowned accompanying and improvisation), taking inspiration back to their own parishes, struck also no doubt by the popularity of the crowded services with a fashionable congregation. Among the most conspicuous London churches to have followed the Temple model was St Anne's, Soho, to which Joseph Barnby moved as organist from Wells Street in 1871. Here he had a huge all-male choir of 32 trebles, 8 altos (half of them boys), 12 tenors and 12 basses. The boys came mostly from the local National School, and like the Temple boys, rehearsed daily.[38] They sang to a large congregation, drawn from afar, whose only musical contribution was soft singing in the hymns; many of them apparently made a hasty exit after the anthem.[39] For Barnby the anthem was the musical highlight, 'a kind of musical sermon',[40] although critics labelled the church the 'Sunday opera',[41] echoing descriptions of the Bavarian Embassy Chapel earlier in the century. Although of a somewhat higher churchmanship than the Temple, the same morning service of Matins, Litany and Ante-Communion prevailed. In addition, from 1873 Barnby introduced occasional oratorio services, which included the Bach Passions that he had already performed with his choral society.[42]

Just as a surpliced choir of boys and men rapidly became a feature of Anglican parish churches of all levels of churchmanship, except perhaps the most evangelical, so did lighted candles on the altar and the processing in and out of the choir and clergy. The size of Barnby's choir may have been exceptional, but there was a general increase in choir numbers as the century progressed, and thirty or so filling the stalls would become common in large town churches (and indeed in some villages), especially where choirs were essentially voluntary. The result was a considerable demand for boy choristers, the supply of which was helped by the introduction of universal elementary education under the 1870 Education Act. Choirboys still tended to come from the artisan and lower middle classes; much as choirmasters would have liked the sons of the professional class, their parents would rarely have encouraged them joining such a social mix, doubtless suggesting that their sons had too much homework to permit attendance at the three or four rehearsals a week that was common practice. There was also a market for already trained choristers, as seen in this typical advertisement from the *Musical Times* for April 1880:

> Leading treble required immediately for a Church Choir. Previous experience indispensable. Liberal salary to a Boy with a really good voice.[43]

The need for boys was also eventually met commercially. In 1894 the London Training School for Choristers (later the London College for Choristers) was established by James Bates when choirmaster at Christ Church, Lancaster Gate. Initially held as an evening class five days a week, it turned into a regular school in 1907 and made trained boys available to cathedrals and affluent churches. This was usually as deputies in cases of illness or holidays, but it would also fill permanent posts as well as furnishing choirs or soloists for weddings, funerals and numerous concert engagements. Five of the boys sang in the coronation choir of 1902.[44] It survived until the Second World War, but from 1915 it faced competition from the London Choir School, whose history will be considered later.[45]

As choirmasters found, training boy choristers was never a straightforward task from both disciplinary and musical points of view. The later Victorian period unsurprisingly saw the publication of several books on vocal technique for boys, notably by George Martin, organist of St Paul's (*The Art of Training Choir Boys*, 1892) and John Varley Roberts, organist of Magdalen College (*A Treatise on a Practical Method of Training Choristers*, 1898). The desired vocal quality was the result of cultivation of the so-called 'head voice', so as to achieve a pure tone, free from the coarseness encountered when a boy's normal 'chest' voice, as used in speech, was forced upwards. It would constitute the model that would survive virtually unchallenged until the second half of the twentieth century. Such sophisticated training was chiefly confined to certain town churches. Village boys would rarely benefit from any instruction in voice production, and consequently, as the organist of Canterbury Cathedral noted in 1883:

> It is rather to be regretted that certain High Church authorities will recognise no high-pitched voices save those of rough country lads, who may have had, during several weeks, no other mode of practising their vocal organs than that obtained by screaming in the cornfields and orchards as living scarecrows. By an infusion of female voices, the rough tone of these country lads would be greatly ameliorated, and the congregation most grateful for such a real blessing; saving them all the ear-splitting which is, in some of the rural districts, truly distressing.[46]

In addition to singers, it became clear that organists and choirmasters themselves needed a more professional approach to training. The old articled pupil model was no longer adequate for the times, and whereas earlier in the century most parish church organists would have had few or no responsibilities for whatever choir may have been present, they now usually found themselves in charge of the new surpliced chancel choirs.[47] The first change came with the creation of the College of Organists (later Royal College of Organists) in 1864, which began to offer examinations in organ playing leading to the granting of diplomas. Then, in order to promote the training of church musicians more generally, in 1872 the Rev. George Henry Bonavia Hunt initiated the Church Choral Society, soon renamed the College of Church Music and then Trinity College, London. It was a modest start, with probably limited success – the college went on to become a general music conservatoire, now the Trinity Laban Conservatoire of Music and Dance in Greenwich – but it anticipated more fruitful developments in the next century.

It would, however, be an exaggeration to imagine that the introduction of surpliced choirs was found everywhere in later Victorian times.

A survey of 953 London Anglican churches in 1884 revealed that 790 had choirs of some sort, of whom only two thirds were surpliced.[48] In several parishes the old charity children arrangement persisted into the 1880s.[49] Although the absence of a choir would have been in many cases the lack of resources, there were parishes with large congregations, which out of choice remained wholly congregational. One notable example was the low church St Pancras, where the famous organist Henry Smart presided from 1864, producing hearty unison congregational singing of hymns and canticles, accompanied by varied harmonies – there was no choir apart from 20 boys leading the congregation from near the organ in the gallery.[50]

A curious offshoot of the Romantic side of the Oxford Movement was the creation by a few of the gentry of new private chapels on their estates, almost harking back to pre-Reformation times. In at least two cases this led to choirs being formed to sing daily cathedral-style services. The Duke of Buccleuch's chapel at Dalkeith Park, Midlothian, was in need of an alto and a tenor in 1859, offering £72 a year,[51] while another Scottish laird in 1866 advertised as follows:

> Wanted an Under Gardener, possessing an Alto, Tenor, or Bass Voice, for a Private Chapel in Perthshire. Must be a Communicant of the Church of England. Terms 14s. per week and £5 per year, with lodging.[52]

Perhaps most impressive was the choir of six boys and six men established at mid-century at the Tractarian chapel of Rowland Egerton-Warburton at Arley Hall near Northwich in Cheshire; the boys, recruited nationally, boarded with the organist and wore livery of blue velvet suits and red stockings. Astonishingly, the set-up was maintained until the First World War.[53] The Duke of Newcastle at Clumber Park, Worksop, also maintained a choir school from 1893 for his magnificent private chapel, which lasted until his death in 1928.[54]

What role did women play in Victorian parish choirs? Tractarian misogyny certainly saw the chancel as an all-male preserve, and although women had often formed part of the country west gallery choirs and the voluntary or professional choirs supporting town psalmody, as at the old Temple Church set-up, they increasingly fell out of official favour in many places in the new religious climate. In 1850, a survey of church music in Liverpool in the Tractarian journal *The Parish Choir*, while acknowledging the 'exceedingly good' singing of a choir of two women and five men at St George's, added that 'the admission of women into the choir seems to me as unbecoming as it is unnecessary'.[55] In practice, however, an efficient boys' choir was not easily obtained. Already in 1849 S.S. Wesley echoed the thoughts of Roger North more than a century earlier (see p. 72), when he considered that boys' voices 'at their best, are a poor substitute for the vastly superior quality and power of those of women'[56] – not an opinion likely to have been shared by his fellow cathedral organists. Churches, especially of broad churchmanship, having set up choirs of boys and men, often found it necessary to call upon women (and sometimes, girls too) to strengthen the top line, especially in places with musical ambition; they might also be employed on the alto line, when male altos were in short supply. The question arose as to where they should sit and what they should wear. As ever, the solutions varied. In some churches they were kept out of the chancel and occupied the front pew in the nave; if in the chancel, they tended to be in the back rows. In 1886 a female correspondent in the *Musical Times* advocated their use, and commented: 'In nearly all churches where there is a chancel screen, one or two rows of women could be placed behind the surpliced choir where they would not be obtrusively visible.'[57] Surplices were then for males only, so the women initially just wore their normal clothing, but from the 1880s gowns and a cap began to be introduced.[58] A flurry of correspondence in August 1889 in the *Daily Telegraph* on the subject of female participation produced a predictable variety of opinion from musicians, clergy and members of congregations, with the majority supporting their use.[59] Stainer, in his inaugural lecture as Professor of Music at Oxford in 1889, was strongly in favour of their introduction where adequately trained boys were not available.[60] Even though the early Tractarians advocated all-male choirs, their Anglo-Catholic successors, seeking to adorn worship sumptuously, including its music, often found that their boys alone were inadequate to the demands of Mozart or Gounod Masses, and so admitted women to at least supplement them. While this would not have been the case at the likes of All Saints, Margaret Street, it certainly applied to similar establishments lacking its resources. The danger of having strong female support for the treble line, however, was that it could disincentivise the boys from exerting themselves fully, leading them to become more ornamental than musically useful. But despite the trend towards all-male parochial choirs, it is clear that women continued to sing in Anglican choirs in later Victorian times to a far greater extent than the popular image would suggest. Advertisements for them regularly appeared in the musical press, and according to official figures, in 1891/2 there were roughly 62,000 voluntary and 2,400 paid female singers in English parish churches, as against 198,000 voluntary and 32,500 paid males.[61] Far from there being a uniform picture of all-male surpliced choirs, the Victorian era saw the widest variety in parochial choral arrangements. The virtual silence of the Prayer Book on musical matters left ample room for local decisions, especially as the higher authorities expressed little interest in the subject, unlike the Roman Catholic hierarchy.

The issue of choir and congregation relations continued to reverberate in some churches. Commenting in 1880 on the music at St Anne's, Soho, where the congregation hardly sang apart from 'a quiet hum' in hymns, John Spencer Curwen, who headed the tonic sol-fa movement after his father's death that year, regarded it as 'an illustration of the saying the better the choir the worse the congregational singing'.[62] As a counter to this, a wide survey of music in London churches in the early 1880s reported many examples of places where the congregation did join in heartily regardless of the presence or absence of a choir.[63] Nevertheless, vigorous congregational singing was most characteristic of evangelical parishes and of the Nonconformist denominations, where religious fervour dominated, and choirs, where they existed, were mainly just leading the congregation. Most Anglican churches, however, lay within the broad church spectrum, where church-going was often more a matter of social convention than firm conviction and where middle-class attitudes regarded hearty singing as unbecoming; in consequence they were quite content to play a subsidiary musical role to the choir. Naturally, there might be factions who expressed discontent, especially where the choir's quality left much to be desired.[64] As the cleric H.R. Haweis, author of the popular *Music and Morals*, cynically noted: 'the majority of the congregation seems to belong to one of two classes – those who look upon the anthem as an unwarrantable interloper, and those who regard it simply in the light of a show-off for the choir.'[65] But on the whole people went along with the situation, and friction was more likely to occur between choir or organist and clergy. That said, congregational hymn singing was almost certainly better in most places in 1900 that in 1850, owing to the general adoption of *Hymns Ancient and Modern*, which resulted in congregations becoming familiar with a range of standard hymns, some of which became firm favourites.

Cathedrals in the Early Nineteenth Century

Among examples of particularly poor cathedrals which occasioned comment in the early decades of the nineteenth century were Lincoln and York. In 1848, a letter in *The Guardian* on a service in Lincoln noted that:

> To say that the boys couldn't sing, and the organ couldn't play, and the boys and organ could not go together, would only half describe it. It was sluggishness and torpor personified. It crawled like a wretched lame insect from beginning to end. Its excessive feebleness was such

that it seemed every moment on the point of stopping from mere want of breath. I was surprised that it went on at all. At no one point in the service did the organ rise to the substance or dignity of a street barrel ... The voices of the choir were in keeping. I dare say there were good voices among them, but it did [not] seem to be expected that they should exert themselves in the slightest degree. I could not help feeling sincere and unfeigned astonishment at the exhibition, which was going on, and asking myself repeatedly – what are these people doing? Is this Cathedral service, or is it something else?[66]

In 1819 the already mentioned John Marsh visited York, where there was 'nothing remarkable, except the trebles appeared weak, and an overpowering bass'.[67] And in *The Guardian* in 1849, another correspondent reported on the choristers of York: 'I can truly affirm that I never saw anything so disgraceful as their conduct. They were laughing, talking, pinching each other, and pulling each other's hair during the greater portion of the divine service. The eldest boy, instead of setting a good example, seemed to be the ringleader of all the mischief.'[68] Opinions, of course can vary between individuals, and circumstances can change quickly. Salisbury, for example, was well thought of by John Marsh in the early nineteenth century,[69] and commended by Maria Hackett in 1830, when she considered 'the service is performed with great solemnity in its most attractive form';[70] but recollections by John Harding, a chorister who left the choir in 1833, was less complimentary on weekday services:

> The psalms ended, the head boy left his place to inquire of the Dean, or in his absence of the canon in residence present, what service and anthem he wished to be sung. Having got an answer, he turned towards the boys who were waiting for the information, and gave out in a loud whisper the name of the author and the key of the service chosen; he then passed on under the red curtain and through the Choir doors and gates round to and up the staircase to the organ loft, to acquaint the organist, which done, he retraced his steps back to his seat. Sometimes when the first lesson was a short one, or the Canon took a long time to make up his mind, an awkward pause would ensue, accompanied by a good deal of tumbling about of music books, turning over of leaves, anxious whisperings between Choristers and Singing-men etc.; but in general, all went off smoothly. Sometimes too, but not often, the organist would play the wrong anthem or service, through having mistaken what the head boy had told him.[71]

Arthur Corfe was organist for 59 years from 1805, so ups and downs were perhaps only to be expected, despite his reputation for conscientiousness.

The arrival in 1841 of a new canon, Walter Hamilton, marked the start of major improvements, and he successfully pressed for reform in the conduct of services.[72] He was eventually to become bishop of the diocese. At Windsor too, things were in a poor state with only seven boys and a dearth of able men. Like Salisbury, the music was decided upon at the last minute, the senior boy having to go up to the organ loft just before the service to find out what was to be sung.[73] (It should be noted, however, that other places were already setting out weekly music plans early in the nineteenth century, including Chichester, Exeter, Hereford, Wells, and Winchester.)[74] But things changed with the appointment in 1835 of the 19-year-old George Elvey as organist, who in the course of 47 years' service was to transform the choir into one of the best; it earned him a knighthood in 1871, making him the first organist to be so honoured.

Meanwhile Durham, Exeter, Lichfield and Norwich were among cathedrals which generally avoided much in the way of criticism at this period, though in common with virtually all choirs, they had at least occasional problems with absenteeism on the part of the men. In Wales, services at Bangor's modest establishment were admired for being performed 'with reverential decorum and a true solemnity of devotion',[75] while Norwich was notable for the organistship of Zechariah Buck from 1819 to 1877. Unusually for the time, Buck's main interest was in cultivating boys' voices rather than organ playing, taking Italian singing methods as his model, concentrating on the 'head' voice and devoting particular attention to trills ('shakes') and grace notes. Intensively and eccentrically trained – boys were given phials of port before important solos – he reputedly had the best treble line in the country at mid-century, albeit performing in a style – indulged in also by the choirmen – which seemed increasingly old-fashioned.[76] As one lay clerk remembered: 'Everything was in the most florid style, viz., grace notes, cadenzas, 'shakes' (single, double and triple), while time was not much considered. Indeed, some of the treble solos were nearly sung <u>ad libitum</u> ... In the anthems I have heard three boys making 'shakes' simultaneously, and not only the boys but the lay-clerks used to 'shake' most extensively.'[77] As a result, Buck's boys were much in demand as soloists beyond Norwich, and two of them were engaged for Barnby's St Matthew Passion performance in Westminster Abbey in 1872.[78] In contrast to other choirs, Norwich singers complained that they were over-rehearsed![79] But the real historical importance of Buck lay in the fact that one of his later choristers and subsequently organ apprentice was Arthur Henry Mann, the future organist of King's College, Cambridge, and the famous 'King's sound' can be seen to trace its lineage back to nineteenth-century Norwich.[80]

In the capital, comparisons were inevitably made between Westminster Abbey and St Paul's, with many people able to assess both places. A mixed picture emerges at the Abbey. The boys – ten in number in the 1830s – appear to have been well trained under James Turle, organist and Master of the Choristers from 1831, often having soloists who were lent to other churches for special occasions.[81] While Sunday services generally met with approval, the American Lowell Mason, visiting on a Sunday in May 1837, may have encountered a bad day when he noted in his diary: 'They sang an anthem by Dr. Croft. But it was poorly done – the choir was inefficient. The harsh tone of the Boy's Soprano was disagreeable.'[82] Walter Macfarren, a chorister in Turle's early years, also had very critical comments about the weekday services: 'There were supposed to be three men on each side, but very often the service was sung with only an alto on one side and a bass on the other!'[83] *The Times* reported in 1837 that 'a correspondent complains of the incessant and indecorous behaviour of the singing men at Westminster Abbey, who, he says, totally neglect that part of their functions which consists in answering the responses, which duty, therefore, devolves upon the choir boys'.[84] The choir could certainly rise to the occasion, as it did for a Commemoration of Purcell in 1848, and the Abbey repertoire under Turle included more Tudor/Jacobean music than most other choirs, with Friday becoming a day for unaccompanied music.[85]

In the City, St Paul's choir had clearly reached a nadir, which effectively lasted until the 1870s. A combination of extreme indifference on the part of the dean and chapter, neglect of their duties by the choirmen, an equally neglectful Master of the Choristers in William Hawes (a man with many other interests), and less than forceful, if distinguished, organists in Thomas Attwood and his successor John Goss, did not make for quality music-making at what was seen as the nation's premier cathedral. St Paul's was unusual by this time in still having separate posts of organist and Master of the Choristers, while in common with other cathedrals, the overall control of the music remained the clerical responsibility of the precentor (delegated here to his deputy, the succentor). So it is hardly surprising to encounter anecdotes like that of 1837 that 'the beautiful treble duet in the anthem by Dr Nares, "The Eyes of the Lord", was on Wednesday in last week omitted, in consequence of incapacity to perform',[86] or that in Goss's time the 'Hallelujah Chorus' was sung with only two men present.[87] When the King of Prussia visited England in 1842 and expressed a wish to attend a service at St Paul's, a large number of 'extras' was hastily drafted in, to give the King a more favourable impression of the choir.[88]

There was, however, one person who took a deep interest in St Paul's and its choir over many years, and that was Miss Maria Hackett.[89] Her connexion began in 1810, when she had a 7-year-old orphaned cousin enrolled in the choir, and was soon appalled by the neglect of supervision, lack of education and the exploitation of boys being hired out for evening engagements. Well-educated and in a reasonably secure financial situation, Hackett began to bombard the dean and chapter, and even the bishop, with demands that they fulfil the obligation to its choristers laid down in the old medieval statutes – her knowledge of Latin enabled her to read these, no doubt much to the astonishment of the authorities. Repeatedly ignored, she even threatened legal action, and in 1814 did at least obtain the appointment of a schoolmaster to provide some education. While continuing her St Paul's campaign – the sight of yet another letter from her must have caused dismay in the recipient – she widened her interest and investigated the condition of choristers' welfare and education in cathedrals and similar institutions throughout the country, the results of which she had printed and circulated in 1827.[90] Much of her information was gathered by means of a questionnaire, the answers to which doubtless portrayed the institution in as favourable light as possible, but they do reveal wide variation in conditions. Hackett was to make regular personal visits to choirs for over half a century, aiming to see each one every three years; she brought small gifts for the boys, earning herself the title of the 'Choristers' Friend'. If evidence for the direct impact of her activity in securing improvements is hard to assess, she certainly ensured the issue was kept alive round the country, and at St Paul's she lived to see a splendid new choir school under construction, which was opened in 1875, the year after her death at the age of ninety.[91]

The Stirring of Reform

In the later 1830s Parliament began an investigation into the state of the cathedrals of the nation's Established Church, which culminated in the Ecclesiastical Commissioners Act of 1840 (also known as the Dean and Chapter, or Cathedrals Act). Although music was not its concern, the resulting reduction in the number of canons and minor canons did have some impact, both in the number of clergy available to conduct services, and in cathedrals like Hereford, where, unusually, all the choirmen were still in holy orders and classified as minor canons – they also all had local benefices, so that they were mostly on duty in their parishes and absent from the main service on Sunday mornings.[92] But the 1840s also saw musicians themselves bring forward proposals to deal with problems. In 1840 a 'Memorial' was addressed to deans and chapters from twenty-two organists of cathedrals and similar institutions, supported by a large number of other musicians and clergy.[93] It advocated a minimum of twelve lay clerks, with provision for pensions, a dedicated practice room, and the organist being paid sufficiently to enable him to devote all his time to cathedral work, where he should be much more in overall charge of the music than was then the case. Inevitably perhaps, nothing came of these ideas, not least because the authorities were able to plead poverty, especially in view of the reduction of revenue brought about by the 1840 Act. In 1849 S.S. Wesley, who was not a signatory to the petition, published *A Few Words on Cathedral Music and the Musical System of the Church, with a Plan of Reform*. Like others, Wesley bemoaned the present state of cathedral music, condemning unmusical clergy, showy verse anthems, and service settings that were 'more like *glees* than church music'.[94] In common with the 1840 petition he wanted a minimum of twelve men, and a high salary for cathedral organists, 'the *bishops* of their calling'.[95] But he did not expect the organist to descend to basic voice training of the boys: 'The organist, if a man of eminence in his art, should hardly be teazed with the tuition of the singing boys. The rudiments of an art may be better taught by those from whom nothing is expected in the higher branches'.[96] He admits that, had it been possible, rather than boys' voices, he would prefer 'the vastly superior quality and power of those of women'.[97] In common with some other would-be reformers, Wesley had a Utopian view of the past, when he imagined church music had enjoyed a 'golden age', which, as we have seen, is hard to discern. Wesley's own strengths lay in his highly regarded organ playing and compositions; in his various cathedral posts (Exeter, Hereford, Winchester, and Gloucester) his own conduct was hardly a model for others, and often gave cause for complaint. He seemingly craved an important London position, but his character ultimately meant that he had to be content with the provincial circuit.[98]

At least two Americans were also disillusioned by their experiences of cathedral services. Stephen Tyng, rector of St George's, New York, visited England in 1842, and predictably, perhaps, given his evangelical and anti-Catholic stance, declared that 'I saw enough of these singing, formal services, in the cathedrals and the chapels of England, to disgust me with the system completely. With but few exceptions, this whole plan of worship is irreverent and light, the deportment of the choristers almost uniformly very exceptionable, and the influence of the system very unedifying.'[99] At a service in Westminster Abbey, 'There seemed to be no one engaged in it who felt the least concern in the whole matter, except in the desire to get through it as quickly as possible. To expect any religious influence or effect from mummery like this is preposterous. ... In this case there was not even the compensation of tolerable music.'[100] At Durham, however, 'There was a vast improvement in the method of performance here, in comparison with the last which I had heard. The swelling notes of the organ, as they rolled through the long aisles and lofty arches, mingled with the clear and sweet tones of the responsive chants, which were performed with great harmony, affected me with feelings of solemnity, and excited my heart to praise; – certainly, I heard no cathedral music in England equal to this evening's worship. ... I wandered round afterwards, and admired greatly the size and simple magnificence of the building; but I formed no new opinion of the importance or advantage of these cathedral services.'[101] Then, Lowell Mason, a Congregationalist choirmaster from Boston, on a return visit in 1852–3, while more sympathetic to cathedral worship, found at Worcester that:

> The chanting was poor enough, at least, for three reasons: 1st. Great rapidity of utterance. 2d. No two members of the choir kept together. 3d. The enunciation of the words was so careless, that it was with difficulty one could keep the place and follow the performance, even with book in hand. ... The great leading object seemed to be to hurry on, and get through as quickly as possible.[102]

This was, however, Matins in an unheated building at the beginning of January! But at St Paul's, 'the same irreverent hurrying prevails,'[103] while at York, 'we find the same rapid style of chanting, or nearly so, and the terrible roughness of boys' voices. Of course, boys' voices must be relied upon for such establishments, but it is enough to tear out one's soul to hear them.'[104] For Mason, boys' voices were problematic. He had been to Berlin, where he was greatly impressed by the cathedral choir, which he considered 'much in advance of such of the English cathedral choirs as we have heard', but in his view, even their boys failed to blend perfectly with the men.[105] In short, he expressed surprise 'that good people from America, ministers and others, should write in such glowing terms of the cathedral music of England.'[106]

Cathedral choirs soon came under the eye of another Royal Commission on the state of cathedrals and choral foundations, which was set up in 1852. Its report, published in 1854–5, contains a mine of information provided by institutions about their establishments and revenues, though some of its recommendations regarding music were rather odd.[107] Some members at least seemed to be unaware of the basic nature of cathedral choral services, when they recommended that most of the music should be suited to congregational participation.[108] They did, however, urge cathedrals to fully maintain their choral provision, and indeed perhaps increase it, with adequate remuneration for organists and lay clerks, and, if possible, provision for pensions. They also pressed for the abolition of the old corporations of minor canons, vicars choral or lay clerks in the small number of establishments where they still existed. As far as the choristers were concerned, they pointed to the need of proper general educational facilities, evidently having been impressed by those then provided at Salisbury.[109] But that apart, there was scarcely any indication that the choirs of cathedrals were in a sorry state. Unlike the previous Commission, which had resulted in the 1840 Act, the recommendations of the new one remained just that, and unsurprisingly produced no instant reforms. The individuality and independence of cathedrals and their diverse constitutions, allied to a legalistic mindset intent on defending its customs, were long an obstacle to substantial change.

Sir Frederick Ouseley and St Michael's College, Tenbury

One man in the 1840s was so appalled by the current condition of cathedral music that he was determined to make a personal contribution to its improvement. Frederick Ouseley, son of the music-loving Orientalist and diplomat, Sir Gore Ouseley, was born in 1825, and showed extraordinary musical precocity, composing prolifically from the age of three; an opera featured among over 200 juvenile works.[110] Educated at home, he went up to Christ Church, Oxford in 1843, and succeeded to his father's baronetcy the following year. At Oxford he was dismayed by the state of music at the cathedral, which was also his college chapel – its choir was described by the *Parish Choir* in 1847 as 'miserably deficient, possibly the worst in England'.[111] After graduation he sought ordination, and eventually became curate at the new Tractarian church of St Barnabas, Pimlico, where he gave the organ and paid for a choir of boys and men. But following 'anti-popery' riots at the church in 1850, Ouseley and the vicar resigned, and the choir was disbanded. Ouseley, however, kept the boys together, boarding them in Langley, Buckinghamshire, where they sang daily services under the care of an ex-St Barnabas chorister, John Hampton; for he already had in mind the creation of a model institution to demonstrate how cathedral worship ought to be conducted. On a visit to Germany in 1851 he was highly impressed by the all-male choirs of the Thomaskirche in Leipzig and Berlin Cathedral; he considered the tone of the boys superior to anything in England, and attributed it to their coming from a higher class than most English choirboys.[112] Back in England, he settled upon the outskirts of Tenbury Wells in rural Worcestershire as the site for his miniature choral foundation. A new parish was created, and Ouseley paid for the erection of the church, as well as the college buildings. St Michael's College was finally dedicated in 1856, with Ouseley as warden and vicar of the parish. It was to educate boys who would sing cathedral-style Matins and Evensong every day, with a devotional atmosphere as important as high musical standards. The boys from Langley (or at least those still singing treble) formed the nucleus of the new choir, complemented by four lay clerks and assistance from teachers and local volunteers. Ouseley appointed John Hampton as choirmaster, a decision which would prove important for the college's eventual survival. A complement of ten boys was aimed at, who paid no fees; numbers were hard to maintain, but through Ouseley's personal contacts they included sons of clergy and other friends, so his desire for a higher class of chorister began to be met, and was the beginning of a trend which would slowly gain ground over the following decades – the creation of adequate provision for general education being the key to recruiting from the children of the middle classes. And in turn St Michael's did, as Ouseley hoped, see some of its former choristers turn into musical clergy as well as conscientious church musicians.[113]

Ouseley's own brand of high churchmanship was not at all ritualistic – one reason for his leaving Pimlico – and he certainly did not share the Tractarian enthusiasm for congregational participation and 'Gregorians'. He was a Jebbite rather than a follower of Helmore; his ideal lay in the tradition of cathedral worship, which he wanted to be executed in the best possible manner, both liturgically and musically. The repertoire at St Michael's was wide-ranging, with a sprinkling of sixteenth- and seventeenth-century music to leaven the usual diet of Georgian and later works, and an increasing preference for the 'full' over the 'verse' style, as was a general trend of the time.[114] Walmisley, S.S. Wesley and other contemporaries were sung, as, of course, were Ouseley's own numerous compositions. Unfortunately, like so many young prodigies, his inventiveness in adulthood failed to match his early promise, and the result was, like so much Victorian church music, merely solid and 'worthy', with devotional spirit winning over vitality. Nor did Tenbury occupy the whole of Ouseley's time; he had taken the Oxford D.Mus. degree in 1854, and in 1855 was appointed Professor of Music there – a role not requiring constant residence, but one in which he would be responsible for important reforms in the granting of music degrees. In addition, he also served as non-resident precentor at Hereford Cathedral from 1855, whose choir he found in a woeful state.[115]

Although St Michael's soon took in fee-paying non-choristers, Ouseley had to continue personally financing an annual deficit. Following his death in 1889, John Hampton succeeded him as warden, but immediately faced a financial crisis, and its closure was averted only by the fortuitous arrival of a large legacy.[116] It enabled the college to survive into the twentieth century, preserving its unique, if idiosyncratic character – for the choir sang morning and evening to an empty church, except for Sundays, when it was joined by the parish congregation and the non-choristers. It also managed to attract some first-rate musicians as its organist and choirmaster, who produced a standard of singing enabling them to feature in BBC choral Evensong broadcasts from 1937 onwards.[117] But inevitably, social and demographic change eventually brought about the closure of the college in 1985, just as it did with many boarding prep schools at this time. The remarkable thing was that St Michael's lasted as long as it did – almost 130 years.

How much influence did it really have on improving the standards of cathedral worship? Thanks to his social contacts, Ouseley attracted many illustrious visitors to Tenbury, musical and non-musical, particularly for the annual dedication festival. But, given its isolated situation, its services were likely to have been experienced by only a small number of visiting musicians or clergy. In reality, perhaps its most significant influence was an indirect one, for in 1857 Ouseley invited the 17-year-old John Stainer to become his organist, after hearing him deputise at St Paul's Cathedral. Stainer had been a chorister there and had sung at the Duke of Wellington's funeral in 1852; he had also benefitted from Maria Hackett's generosity when she paid for organ tuition. He spent over two years at Tenbury and acknowledged that these were decisive in shaping his own future reforming work at Magdalen and St Paul's.[118] Sharing Ouseley's devout high churchmanship, the standards set at Tenbury must have offered the greatest contrast to what he had experienced at St Paul's. At the same time, he was not blind to Ouseley's limitations as a composer; while admiring his great skill in improvisation, he noted: 'Yet when this talented man took up his pen to *write* a composition it seemed as if some evil genius stood by to damp his invention and wreck his originality.'[119]

Reform Gathers Pace

If Tenbury was one attempt to inspire improvement in cathedral worship, then it was not quite alone at mid-century. As we have seen, Canon Walter Hamilton at Salisbury and George Elvey at Windsor had already embarked on reforms, and there were other places where things were changing for the better. At Ely, for example, the arrival of a new dean in 1839, and particularly a new precentor in 1858, saw an increase in both choir numbers and morale, with the lay clerks' remuneration being increased; in the 1860s it was reckoned to be amongst the best in the country.[120] And at York, so long in an appalling state, it was the appointment in 1859 of a high church dean together with a new organist, Edwin George Monk, that marked the beginning of a steady recovery which would continue under the distinguished organistships of Thomas Tertius Noble, Edward Bairstow and their successors.[121] It was the eventual arrival in the cathedral closes of clergy influenced by the Oxford Movement which tended to be the catalyst in promoting reform as much as any change of musical personnel. Nowhere was this clearer than in the case of St Paul's.

The great transformation in the music of the nation's metropolitan cathedral which occurred in the 1870s was very much the result of a coming together of key new figures, clerical and musical. First was the arrival between 1868 and 1871 of a new high church dean, Richard Church, and two similarly-minded canons, for whom a seemly performance of the liturgy was all-important. One early sign was the introduction in 1869 of the choir entering in procession.[122] Then in 1872 came the retirement as organist of the aged John Goss and the appointment of John Stainer, fresh from twelve successful years at Magdalen College, Oxford. In addition, came two more significant postholders: in 1874 George Martin, a former composition and organ pupil of Stainer from his Oxford days,[123] took over the training of the boys, becoming also sub-organist in 1876, while in the latter year a new succentor was appointed, William Sparrow Simpson, with whom Stainer happily collaborated.[124]

One of the first actions following Stainer's arrival was the enlargement of the choir. In 1860 the cathedral had been opened up by the removal of the old screen, with the organ placed initially on the north side of the quire before being divided between the two sides at a major rebuild in 1872. No longer was the choir singing in a comparatively intimate semi-enclosed space, and it became obvious that the numbers were now both visually and sonically inadequate. In 1873 the boys were increased from 12 to 24 and the men from 10 to 18 (with 12 required to attend on weekdays). Fortunately for Stainer, only two of the traditional six freehold vicars choral were still active singers, so he had relatively little trouble in his dealings with the men, and, with his tactful manner, was able to introduce a weekly full practice – officially he was still only organist, with no statutory authority over the choir.[125] With the opening of the new choir school in 1875, all the boys became boarders,[126] and (like Ouseley's at Tenbury) in future came predominantly from the middle classes, now that educational provision was seen to be taken seriously.[127] The number of boys was then increased to 38 (comparable to Barnby's array at St Anne's, Soho)[128] – the whole choir must have been an impressive sight when processing. A major change also took place in 1873 when a full weekly choral Communion on Sundays was introduced, replacing the previous Ante-Communion which had followed on from Matins. St Paul's was the first to do so regularly,[129] and the practice was only gradually adopted elsewhere, full choral Communion being generally introduced only at major festivals, or once a month at best.[130]

The St Paul's repertoire was increasingly orientated towards the nineteenth century – out went most of the verse anthems of Greene, Boyce and others, so long a staple, now seen as ineffective in the enlarged space as well as less to the taste of the times. Likewise, Sparrow Simpson was not fond of contrapuntal music, also considered unsuitable in the vast acoustic. Besides modern English compositions, which naturally included Stainer's own works, Gounod, Mendelssohn and Spohr made prominent appearances, and St Paul's music was regarded as 'colourful.'[131] Occasional services with orchestra were introduced, including annual performances of the St Matthew Passion from 1873, with a greatly enlarged choir, although all the soloists came from within St Paul's.

Already in 1858, St Paul's, following the Abbey,[132] had started to hold Sunday evening services of a congregational character, led by an enormous voluntary choir of 500 mixed voices under the dome. Stainer, who, unlike some organists, was also keen on congregational singing, quickly reorganized the choir for these services, reducing its size to about 70 singers, made up of the St Paul's boys and a contingent of voluntary men placed in the quire.[133] Such Sunday evening congregational services also proved popular elsewhere in the late nineteenth century, and large voluntary choirs, almost always of boys and men, were commonly recruited – Westminster Abbey had 60, Worcester 70, Gloucester nearly 100 and Chester 150, the last including women from the start in 1867; in time these choirs would also be employed for other special services.[134]

The Stainer, Martin and Sparrow Simpson partnership, for that is what it essentially was, ensured that St Paul's acquired a fine reputation for its music within a dignified liturgy that would have been unthinkable a couple of decades earlier. Following Stainer's resignation in 1888 – he went on to become Professor of Music at Oxford – Martin took over, and unlike his predecessor, continued in charge of the boys, becoming the author of a standard textbook on training them.[135] Although cultivating 'head' voice production, Martin apparently aimed to give it a cutting edge especially suited to the St Paul's acoustic.[136] The repertoire continued to expand, with both new music and some reinstatement of older works, so that at the end of the century it was probably the largest in the country. An American organist from Baltimore, Miles Farrow, toured seventeen English cathedrals in 1900, and though not as disappointed as Lowell Mason and Stephen Tyng half a century earlier, did not find choirs living up to his expectation, with the exception of Magdalen, King's, Cambridge, and St Paul's, which 'offered the best examples in the world of the possibilities, the beauty, the perfection of vested choirs of men and boys.'[137] Cathedral choirs, however, rarely run trouble-free for long, and St Paul's 'golden age' faded somewhat around the turn of the century, when Martin was encountering the problem of the voices of what had been a new cohort of younger men in the 1870s, coming to the end of their useful lives. This was particularly noticeable at men's only services, which became more numerous as the boys gradually gained a total of six weeks' annual holiday, when they were able to all be absent together, instead of, as previously, having only part of the treble line away at any one time.[138]

Tenbury and St Paul's provide two well-documented examples of choral reform, but from the 1870s there is evidence of steady improvement elsewhere – the cathedrals were being shamed into action by changes widely occurring in the parishes. In 1875 the 30-year-old Frederick Bridge, already an Oxford D.Mus., arrived at Westminster Abbey, nominally as deputy to the aged James Turle, though in practice taking over his duties, and officially becoming organist on Turle's death in 1882 at the age of 80. Although he found the Abbey boys well trained, Bridge encountered problems with the entrenched vicars choral, among whom absenteeism was common and who resisted the idea of full rehearsals. As he recalled: 'I soon made a move to get regular rehearsals established, but this was stoutly opposed by some members of the choir, one of whom, a man approaching seventy, told me that when he was appointed he undertook to obey the laudable customs of the Abbey, and he did not find that the laudable customs of the Abbey included any rehearsals!'[139] Nor was he always supported by the authorities in such disputes. Nevertheless, there were important changes; the number of boys was eventually increased from 16 to 24 and, like St Paul's, they began to board, while six assistants were added to the men. As with St Paul's, the Abbey repertoire became vast, with Bridge noting that in 1913 they sang 437 different anthems and 140 different services, wide-ranging in character, including continental sixteenth- and seventeenth-century music, naturally in English translation.[140]

Bridge was to preside over the music for two coronations. That of Edward VII in 1902 was the first the Abbey had seen for more than 60 years, and Bridge planned for the music to reflect British music over five centuries.[141] The 430 singers, in addition to the traditional core choirs of the Abbey, St Paul's, the Chapel Royal, and Windsor, included representatives from every cathedral and choral foundation, as well as from other important churches and choral societies, plus various well-known amateurs.[142] It was to create a blueprint for all subsequent twentieth-century coronations. As a special concession, he admitted one old man from Wells, who as a Windsor chorister had sung at the coronation of William IV in 1830. The chief novelty of

1902 was Parry's 'I was glad', whose impact was such that it joined 'Zadok the priest' as a staple of future coronations; it was provided with a new introduction for that of George V in 1911. In those pre-broadcasting days, at least some of the general public were able to get an impression of the music by being admitted (for a fee to charity) to the final rehearsals held in Church House. In the Abbey the singers were placed in galleries either side of the quire screen, which accommodated the orchestra.[143] Despite the use of sub-conductors, not all the singers were able to see any beat, but the overall coordination was reported to have been remarkable.[144]

The increase in choir size seen at Westminster Abbey and St Paul's was mirrored throughout the country. No longer did the typical provincial cathedral choir of eight boys and six men, found in the earlier part of the century, appear adequate at the height of Victorian imperialism, especially when compared with the forces many principal town churches were now mustering. So, by the final decades of the century the boys of cathedral choirs were commonly increased to sixteen, a number which may or may not have included probationers. And whereas six men remained standard on weekdays (not least for financial reasons), numbers often doubled on Sundays. A choir of around thirty was obviously more in keeping with the size of the buildings, especially those like Durham, Hereford, Lichfield, Peterborough, Salisbury and Worcester, which, like St Paul's, had removed the quire screen.[145]

Even with larger choirs, potential choristers appear to have been fairly numerous. Chester at the beginning of the twentieth century had 16 full choristers and 8 probationers,[146] while in Edinburgh, the newly established St Mary's Cathedral (1879) soon had 36 boys, enough to split and have half on daily duty in alternate weeks, with 24 being employed on Sundays.[147] At Durham in 1873 there were about 50 at the voice trial for 4 places, and in 1913 no fewer than 99 applicants, of whom 9 were eventually selected for admittance when vacancies occurred.[148] But if the front stalls became well filled, the age-old problem of the boys' general education was never far from the surface, and came more into focus with the increased numbers. The introduction of universal elementary education under the 1870 Act also highlighted the necessity for the cathedrals to improve their provision, and various solutions, sometimes short-lived, were tried. Having a single master, teaching either just the three Rs, or more of a classical syllabus, in an odd room in the cathedral precincts, such as had been the practice at places like Canterbury, Chichester or Winchester, generally proved ineffective, and far too dependent on the ability and commitment of individuals. Salisbury by the late 1840s had a decently run school, boarding its choristers, but lack of finance, despite taking in fee-paying non-singers, led to its decline a decade later, and recovery began only in the 1880s.[149] Few institutions had the will or money to follow the example of St Paul's and the Abbey in the 1870s, and bear the costs of boarding schools catering just for the choristers. Attempts to include boys in the old grammar schools (often 'King's Schools') associated with some cathedrals almost always proved unsatisfactory – the time spent on cathedral duties was incompatible with the routine of the schools, quite apart from the fact that the typical chorister still came from social classes where an apprenticeship rather than academic success was the goal. Peterborough, however, was a rare exception, where a relationship with the grammar school was made to work.[150] But if the cathedrals were to seek more middle-class choristers, as they often did, then educational provision would be the key. However, it needed the changes in patterns of worship which followed the First World War before satisfactory solutions could gradually emerge.

Modest improvements were also made in the lay clerks' remuneration. Although some cathedrals made attempts to do away with the old statutory corporations where they existed, they came to nothing, so they remained a block to proper reform. But some progress was made towards providing pensions, which could ease the way to retirement of worn-out voices. Among provincial cathedrals, Lichfield offered some of the best pay and conditions of service, so that vacancies there attracted plenty of applicants.[151] The reputation of Yorkshire singers was such that they were found in choirstalls round the country. Rumour had it that when Charles Hylton Stewart arrived as organist at Rochester in 1916, his greeting the lay clerks as 'you men of Kent' produced the retort, 'Eh, lad, we all come from Yorkshire'.[152] As with the boys, it was the post-war years which would bring about the biggest changes in a lay clerk's life.

In the course of the Victorian era, cathedral organists experienced something of a rise in status. The creation of the College of Organists in 1864 was intended to increase professionalism by holding examinations for its diplomas of Associate and Fellow. At the same time written examinations were introduced into the requirements for music degrees at Oxford and Cambridge, qualifications which were especially sought after by aspiring organists – they were still mostly taken externally, though some lectures and provision for tuition were gradually provided by the universities for those who chose to reside.[153] As a result, cathedral organists equipped with such qualifications gained more academic respect in their communities, and competition for posts could be fierce. 168 applied in 1885 to succeed Buck at Norwich,[154] while in 1889 at Hereford George Sinclair was selected from 50 candidates,[155] and 79 applied at York in 1897 to succeed John Taylor, with Thomas Tertius Noble being chosen.[156] These, though, do not compare with the 312 hopefuls who applied for Leeds Parish Church in 1905, when Edward Bairstow was successful.[157] There does appear to have been something of a glut of organists and professional musicians in general around the turn of the century.[158] Although no alteration was made to the organist's official position within cathedral establishments – the precentor or succentor still had overall responsibility for the music – his musical authority generally gave him more influence over the whole choir and the choice of repertoire than would have been the case in earlier generations. Disputes could, of course, still arise – Sinclair had problems with both the succentor and the vicars choral at Hereford,[159] but the general impression at the end of the century is of greater harmony than for many a day.

Over in Dublin, the two Church of Ireland cathedrals were no quicker than their English counterparts at instituting reform. The practice of the lay clerks singing at both cathedrals continued; it declined slightly but did not cease completely until after re-organisation following the Irish Church Act of 1871, which disestablished the Church of Ireland. The generous salaries continued to attract good singers from England. St Patrick's was the more fashionable at mid-century, despite the precarious state of the building before major reconstruction in the 1860s, and was popularly known as 'Paddy's opera', owing to the prominent solo displays prevalent on Sunday afternoons, which attracted large congregations. According to Stanford, who heard them as a boy in the late 1850s,

> As soon as the anthem began ... the bulk of the congregation walked out of their seats and stood under the desks and the noses of the singers, with all the air of a concert audience, only stopping short at applause. I remember wondering if they would clap after a well-sung solo, and why my mother had not brought her opera-glasses so that we may see better from our stage-box. After the anthem there was a general stampede out of the church.[160]

At Christ Church things were more decorous, and although suffering, as in the past, from neglect of attendance by the men on weekdays, the boys had the reputation of being well-trained. Its repertoire at mid-century was decidedly old-fashioned and rooted in the eighteenth century, even though 135 different anthems were sung in 1849.[161] Like Westminster Abbey, however, it was also singing more sixteenth- and seventeenth-century music (largely from Boyce's *Cathedral Music*) than most choirs of the day.[162] Disestablishment was to substantially weaken the financial position of all Ireland's Protestant cathedrals, and outside Dublin, by the end of the nineteenth century, most held choral services only on Sundays, with female sopranos generally having replaced, or at least supplemented, boys.[163]

The Cathedral Repertoire

If William Boyce was disappointed by sales of his collection of *Cathedral Music* in his lifetime, then, had he been able to see how widely it was in use in the nineteenth century he would have considered his efforts finally justified. For Boyce's collection, together with the later supplementary collections of Samuel Arnold and John Page, as well as anthem publications of individual composers like Maurice Greene and James Nares, formed the bedrock from which much of the cathedral repertoire in the first half of the nineteenth century was drawn. So, the eighteenth century, represented by the likes of Boyce, Greene, James Kent, Charles King, James Nares and John Travers, continued to dominate the repertoire, with verse anthems still enjoying favour – not least for their giving opportunities for the egos of various soloists to be massaged, as well as demanding little of the full choir. It was music which rarely rose above the workmanlike at best; Blow, Purcell and Croft made only modest appearances, while the music of the Tudor/Jacobean composers was confined to a handful of its simpler works – the 'short' services of Richard Farrant, Gibbons, and Tallis in particular, continuing to be found useful. Although the early Tractarians valued the latter for their simple devotional quality, they were regarded by many musicians, including S.S. Wesley, as representative of a more primitive and imperfect stage of the country's musical development. Little of Handel's true church music found its way into the daily repertoire, but oratorio excerpts certainly did, joined by those of Haydn, Beethoven, and Louis Spohr, as well as anthems adapted from the Masses of Haydn, Mozart and Hummel.[164] Such 'intrusions' into traditional church repertoire were criticized, particularly by Tractarians, though their popularity with both singers and congregations could not be denied. The most prominent British names contributing to cathedral music in the early nineteenth century were the deservedly forgotten John Clarke-Whitfield, organist of Trinity and St John's colleges, Cambridge and then of Hereford Cathedral, and the far more accomplished Thomas Attwood, one-time pupil of Mozart and organist of St Paul's, whose 'Teach me, O Lord' and 'Turn thy face from my sins' remain familiar today. From the middle years of the century compositions of George Elvey, Goss, Ouseley, Walmisley and S.S. Wesley were prominent among those finding general adoption. Mendelssohn, however, was the great new arrival in music lists, although he composed only one work specifically for cathedral use – a morning and evening service written at the request of Vincent Novello. It was widely sung in Victorian Britain, though its somewhat awkward word-setting and stolid rhythms eventually led to a fall from favour. English translations of his shorter German and Latin sacred pieces were popular, as of course were excerpts from the oratorios. The one work above all which associates Mendelssohn's name with cathedral music, 'Hear my prayer', was not conceived with it in mind. Instead it originated from a request in 1844 by William Bartholomew, the English translator of many of his works, for a piece to be included in a series of concerts of sacred music organized by Bartholomew's sister-in-law, the organist Elizabeth Mounsey, at Crosby Hall in London. Bartholomew himself provided the text, a paraphrase of Psalm 55, and it was premiered in January 1845.[165] The solo part was intended not for a boy, but for a female soprano, which helps explain the dramatic nature of the first part. Nevertheless, as early as November 1845 there is evidence that it was in the repertoire of Worcester Cathedral,[166] though its general incorporation into the cathedral repertoire appears to date from the 1860s onwards, eventually becoming the 'dream' solo of every aspiring chorister (the story of its twentieth-century fame will be reserved for the next chapter). Incidentally, although Mendelssohn did also publish it in German as 'Hör mein Bitten', it has been known for English choirs recently to perform it in German under the misapprehension that they were singing the original version.

The spirit of Mendelssohn and Spohr would hang over much church music of the third quarter of the century, in which composers like Stainer and Barnby came to the fore. Here it is opportune to deal with Stainer's most popular and lasting work, albeit one not intended for cathedral use. *The Crucifixion* was composed in 1887, towards the end of his time at St Paul's, to a libretto by W.J. Sparrow Simpson, the son of the St Paul's succentor. While Stainer could annually raise the forces necessary to perform the St Matthew Passion during Holy Week at St Paul's, he designed *The Crucifixion* as a work for parish choirs, needing just two soloists and organ accompaniment in addition to a four-part choir, with the intention that ordinary church congregations could gain something of the devotional experience that the Bach offered at the cathedral. He chose not to imitate the dramatic nature of Bach, but sub-titled the work a 'Meditation' on the Passion. Critical opinion has always been divided on its merits, but what sometimes appears to a later generation sometimes as sentimental, was by no means so perceived by its Victorian listeners.[167] If the solo sections are generally considered the least successful parts, then the choruses immediately endeared themselves to choirs, while the interpolated hymns – all newly written and composed – equally found favour with the congregations that were intended to join in singing them (as Stainer had done with the St Matthew Passion chorales). The hymn tunes are indeed among Stainer's happiest inspirations. The work clearly met a need and achieved enormous popularity, being taken up by Nonconformists as well as Anglicans, notwithstanding the high church tone of the hymns. Inevitably it gave rise to imitations, notably John Henry Maunder's *Olivet to Calvary* (1904), which, though lacking the memorability of Stainer's melodies, was widely sung for many years, often alternating annually with its predecessor. Remarkably, *The Crucifixion*, despite being composed in 1887, did not come out of copyright until 2023, since Sparrow Simpson lived on until 1952.

If the generation of Stainer and Barnby was of a conservative mind compositionally, then a breath of fresh air entered the choirstalls from about 1880, when Charles Villiers Stanford, organist at Trinity College, Cambridge from 1874, began publication of church music, in particular service settings, which were soon joined by anthems. With their melodic attractiveness and rhythmic liveliness, memorability being enhanced by the use of repeating motifs, they were immediately taken up everywhere and provided models for others such as Parry and Charles Wood. The Dublin-born Stanford had the advantage of not coming from the narrow cathedral stable; a musician of the widest interests, his church music benefitted correspondingly and was only ever a small part of his compositional output.

Although the old eighteenth-century verse anthem, with little for the full choir to do, had largely fallen out of favour by the mid-nineteenth century, there was still plenty of opportunity for solo voices to be heard, since Victorian cathedral anthems, such as S.S. Wesley's 'The Wilderness', frequently involved solo passages. Sundays increasingly attracted large congregations to cathedrals, especially at Evensong, and there was a natural tendency to offer more popular fare then. As a precentor of Norwich admitted: 'On Sundays we used more of modern music, passages from oratorios, and compositions in which there was a greater abundancy of beautiful and expressive melody. It seemed hard upon the greater number of the congregation to give them music which for them had no attraction, and which did not interpret to them the meaning of the words.'[168] 'Hear my prayer' was definitely a Sunday Evensong anthem.

From around the 1860s cathedral choirs began to abandon their old separate manuscript partbooks in favour of singing from the new octavo vocal scores, which Novello and other firms were issuing in great quantities. Including both contemporary works and new editions of older repertoire, the demand was really led by the more ambitious parish churches, for the cathedrals by themselves hardly constituted a market for standard cathedral fare. Besides service settings and anthems, the remainder of the choir's musical duties consisted of the responses, psalms and the Litany. Treatment of the responses appears to have varied considerably between cathedrals; the plainsong-style responses of Marbeck's time had been handed down orally over the centuries, acquiring variation as they did so, and from the later eighteenth century they were increasingly being sung in various local harmonisations, with or without organ. These were the so-called 'ferial' responses, which served for day-to-day use. John Jebb had collected and published the many varying versions in two volumes in 1847–57, as well as including other harmonised settings from the sixteenth and seventeenth centuries.[169] Of the latter, only Tallis's was in common use; in reality it was a version drawn from the two sets he composed, and they were used on the more important feast days (the so-called 'festal' responses).[170] Other composers' settings would await the twentieth century before being revived. Likewise, the Litany, which was customarily performed on Wednesday, Friday and Sunday mornings, was sung either to an adaptation of the Sarum plainsong (harmonized or not) or to Tallis's setting.

Psalm singing in cathedrals also underwent change. A number of pointed psalters began to appear in the first half of the century, but they were aimed at parish churches – the first was J.E. Dibb's *Key to Chanting* (London, 1831), originating in practice at St Saviour's, York.[171] Cathedrals, routinely singing the whole psalter every month, felt no pressing need to reform their traditional rule-of-thumb method. Hurrying through the recitation without regard to keeping together, and then observing strict time from the final syllables before the change from the reciting note remained standard practice. At Ely, however, the organist, Robert Janes, published a pointed psalter in 1837, which, although intended to appeal to parishes, was presumably in use in the cathedral. Its title-page is worth quoting:

> The Psalter, or, Psalms of David. Carefully marked and pointed, to enable the voices of a choir to keep exactly together, by singing the same syllable to the same note; and, the accents as far as possible made to agree with the accents in the chant; and also to remove the difficulty which individuals generally find who are not accustomed to the chanting of the Psalms

But it was the effect of the care shown over the psalms by E.J. Hopkins at the Temple Church which was probably most influential in setting an example that eventually rubbed off elsewhere. 1875 saw the publication of *The Cathedral Psalter*, which, despite its title, was designed, like its predecessors, to appeal to the parish church market. With Stainer, Turle, and E.J. Hopkins as the musical editors, it rapidly became as standard a book in the choirstalls as *Hymns Ancient and Modern*. But its preface gives a clue to the way cathedral practice was developing, when it stated that 'the words should be deliberately recited'. The rest of the chant, though, was still to be sung in strict slow time – the idea that all the notes of a chant could be rhythmically flexible had yet to emerge. A new development was the employment of separate chants for each psalm (and even changes of chant within a psalm), in place of the previous common practice of singing all the psalms of a service to the same chant.[172] This was made clear in the 1878 edition of *The Cathedral Psalter*, which was the first to print chants at the head of the psalms.

The University Choral Foundations

In Oxford, we have already noted the pitiful state of the cathedral choir at Christ Church at mid-century. Elsewhere in the city, the services at New College appear to have been considered the most satisfactory, if not of a high order. The organist, Stephen Elvey (elder brother of the Windsor organist, George), was evidently conscientious, and in 1856 published a pointed psalter, which was used in the chapel.[173] New College was also the first to attempt to supplement its lay clerks with undergraduate choral scholars. A scheme was initiated in 1858, planning to recruit between eight and ten, but it proved premature, and was run down after 1863. There was simply not the supply of applicants with the necessary combination of musical and academic ability, for music played little part in the public schools from which almost all undergraduates came (and New College's sister foundation, Winchester College in particular). Only twelve scholars were recruited in that time, all of whom eventually became priests;[174] it would be 1920 before the college tried again in very different circumstances. The rest of the century saw no dramatic changes, though in common with some other colleges, from 1867 daily choral Matins was shortened by omitting the canticles[175] – this was, after all, a time when attendance at chapel was compulsory for all students. Choral standards were reportedly only 'adequate' during the 35-year organistship of James Taylor (1865–1900),[176] but rose considerably after 1901 under Hugh Allen. In his eighteen years in post, he revitalized its repertoire and set the choir on a road to excellence, which it would continue to enjoy for the rest of the century and beyond.[177]

It was, however, Magdalen that was to experience the greatest change of fortune in the nineteenth century. Around 1840 the choir's standard was mediocre. John Rouse Bloxam, a Fellow of the college, noted 'the wretched state of the choir', owing to irregular attendance by the lay clerks, some of whom also sang in other choirs. The college took action from 1841 to remedy the situation, by finding extra money for the clerks, and things were certainly better under the organistship of Benjamin Blyth (1845–59).[178] The potential for improvement was also there in the form of Magdalen College School, which both took in boarders and provided a classical education, which could lead pupils on into the university itself. As a result, the sixteen choristers were recruited from a wide area and chiefly from the sons of clergy and other middle-class professions. (To some extent the university connexion also helped recruitment at New College and Christ Church as well.) A problem, however, lay in the fact that choristerships were entirely in the gift of the college's President, who, at that time, was in the habit of often bestowing them on boys he favoured, regardless of musical ability.[179] There were good voices among them – they managed to introduce Mendelssohn's 'Hear my prayer' in 1849[180] – but also a number of virtual non-singers. The state of the school was also far from satisfactory at the time, with ill-discipline and bullying common.[181] All that was to change with the arrival in 1860, as organist and *Informator choristarum*, of the still only 19-year-old John Stainer, from St Michael's College, Tenbury, chosen against far more experienced applicants. In the twelve years he spent at Magdalen before his departure for St Paul's, his enthusiasm and personal charm would win over all sides – even persuading the lay clerks to rehearse – with resulting great improvement in standards.[182] Like New College, Magdalen also experimented with choral scholars (termed 'academical clerks') in Stainer's time, though running into similar problems of recruitment. The college, however, persisted with the idea in a low-key manner, with just two or three undergraduates supplementing the six or seven professional lay clerks right through to the 1950s.[183] The college was also fortunate in Stainer's successors. First came the Huddersfield-born Walter Parratt, a formidably gifted chess player in addition to having a phenomenal musical memory. When he left for Windsor ten years later, he was followed in 1882 by another Yorkshireman, John Varley Roberts, who came from Halifax Parish Church, already holding the Oxford D.Mus. degree. An eccentric character, who retained his strong Yorkshire accent, he was an indifferent organist, but a superb choir trainer, who published *A Practical Method of Training Choristers* in 1898.[184] Firm cultivation of the 'head voice' was his method (like Martin at St Paul's); his musical taste remained distinctly high Victorian with a style tending, as with many others, to the over-expressive. But during his 36-year reign Magdalen choir was generally judged as among the finest in the country, and both choristerships and lay clerks' posts were highly sought after.[185]

Meanwhile things certainly changed for the better at Christ Church as the century progressed, particularly under the organistships of C.H. Lloyd (1882–92) and Basil Harwood (1892–1909). Less is known about other Oxford college choirs before the First World War, though St John's, which, having maintained a small choral foundation in the seventeenth and eighteenth centuries, enlarged the choir in the 1850s after the rebuilding of the chapel; about twelve boys and six lay clerks (who also sang elsewhere) sang a daily Evensong.[186] But as the century progressed, a growing number of colleges at both Oxford and Cambridge created modest voluntary choirs of undergraduates, sometimes supplemented by boys from the town.

If at Oxford choir personnel could be found singing at more than one college, then in Cambridge the sharing of resources was at least equally prevalent. For in the first half of the nineteenth century the six lay clerks of King's also sang at Trinity and St John's, as well as at the University Church, while from 1819 to 1856 Trinity and St John's also shared their 8–10 boys and the organist.[187] The last two colleges held choral services only on Sundays and important feast days (so-called 'surplice days'). King's had its statutory sixteen choristers, all local boys from the artisan classes, whose duties included serving in the college hall – Magdalen choristers had ceased to do this in 1802.[188] Unlike Oxford, no college had a dedicated school for them, but King's nevertheless had a steady supply of applicants. The choir, however, was considered the least efficient of the three throughout the middle of the century, mainly owing to the failing powers of John Pratt, organist from 1799 to 1855. As one former Trinity chorister remembered:

> King's suffered for many years from an old and almost laudable complaint, called the anti-resignation fever. Venerable Mr. Pratt sickened and partially recovered, I dare not say how many times. He survived two or three younger occasional deputies, yet the college authorities, with almost pardonable remissness, would not move a finger to break the oppressive and traditional spell. No, it was the custom, and a cleric or other official must only exchange his gown or surplice for a garment of a more sepulchral character.[189]

The choir's saving grace was the chapel's famous acoustic, which so successfully disguised vocal failings that the large, undiscerning congregation which assembled on Sunday afternoons thought they could experience nothing finer. The atmosphere was hardly devotional, as an ex-chorister from the 1830s admitted:

> No standing room was allowed in the Choir, but the space under the organ got most uncomfortably and unseemly filled [by people from the ante-chapel] by the time the Anthem commenced, and immediately it was over a general stampede was made, and the space, with most part of the Ante-Chapel (where there were no seats, other than the stone benches round the North, South, and West walls), soon became nearly clear; some few would remain at the West end to hear the closing Voluntary.[190]

Tuneful offerings of Handel, Haydn, Mozart, and Hummel were reserved for Sundays, in contrast to more restrained music on other days. Better musical standards were to be found at Trinity and St John's, especially under the organistship of Thomas Attwood Walmisley, who arrived at the age of nineteen in 1833, and, as with Stainer at Magdalen, the enthusiasm of youth proved efficacious.[191] It was for these colleges that his evening service in D minor was composed, and Walmisley, who also became Professor of Music in 1836, remained in post until his early death in 1856.

Although King's in 1852 had added four supernumerary lay clerks for weekend and festival duties, dissatisfaction with the state of the choir was still felt, and in revising its statutes in 1862, proposals were made for reverting to services throughout the year – they were currently mainly limited to term times – and for boarding the choristers. But it would be 1871 before the former was implemented, and only in 1876 did boarding start, while a dedicated choir school opened two years later.[192] 1876 in fact was to mark the start of a new era, for that was when Arthur Henry Mann took up the reins and began to set King's choir on the road to its subsequent fame.[193] With his Norwich background under Zechariah Buck, King's at last had a dedicated choir trainer. Like Stainer, his manner encouraged ready cooperation from the lay clerks, and full rehearsals were soon established. As at St Paul's, the creation of boarding for the choristers quickly changed the intake to that of offspring of clergy and other middle-class parents, taking advantage of the classical education provided. In this way Cambridge came to offer boys similar opportunities to those at Magdalen, Oxford. King's was also to follow Oxford in introducing choral scholars. A proposal to do so in 1873 was voted down – the aged Provost being aghast at the idea of young gentlemen singing next to lay clerks who may have also been college servants. After all, at the time, half of its undergraduate intake of around fifty students still came from its sister college at Eton.[194] In 1880, however, thanks to a private benefaction, the plan was agreed to, and the first choral scholar was elected the following year. As at Oxford, finding suitable candidates sometimes proved impossible, but the college persisted with the scheme, and by 1900 three scholars at a time were regularly to be found in the choirstalls, a number which was to increase steadily over the following three decades (apart from the war years) until it was decided in 1926 to phase out the lay clerks and rely entirely on choral scholars, whose numbers were set at twelve plus two volunteers.[195] King's was the first Oxbridge college to do so, and the implications of this radical move will be explored later.

Mann's rehearsals were passionate and intense, with an emphasis on tuning and round tone; uniquely for the time he rehearsed unaccompanied.[196] Tempi were deliberately on the slow side in order to accommodate the chapel's echo as far as possible, and performances were highly expressive with wide changes of dynamics, mirrored in Mann's own colouristic organ-playing. In this he continued to reflect his Norwich inheritance, but even within his lifetime – and he remained at King's until his death in 1929 – his interpretations were considered old-fashioned and exaggerated.[197] Fortunately we have aural evidence of this in a recording of two Bach sacred songs from the *Schemelli Gesangbuch* he made in his final year. While being cautious in judging from such a small sample (and with consideration for Mann's age and the limitations of recording), they do seem to confirm the above impressions. The firm smooth boys' tone, tuning and ensemble are fine, but the already slow tempi are subject to further conspicuous slowing down at the end of each verse, while there is no attempt to stagger breathing in the middle of long phrases.[198] Nevertheless, by the turn of the century King's reputation stood alongside Magdalen and St Paul's at the top of the choral tree. Wednesday was an unaccompanied day, and, unusually for the time, Mann did sometimes conduct during a service, standing at one end of the choirstalls.[199] Despite producing an edition of Tallis's 'Spem in alium',[200] his interest in performing pre-eighteenth century music was slight, and though Byrd and Palestrina made their appearances, the repertoire remained based round Boyce's *Cathedral Music* and Victorian music from Walmisley onwards. As the universities, under the dispensation of Queen Elizabeth, were permitted to use Latin in services, King's took advantage of this to sing the anthem in Latin on Tuesdays – often the Benedictus of a Mass by Schubert or Hummel.[201]

Change came also to the other two Cambridge choral foundations. Following Walmisley's death in 1856, the arrangement of a shared choir at Trinity and St John's came to an end, and each formed its own choir, though Trinity continued to use the King's lay clerks until 1871.[202] Trinity was to appoint the 21-year-old Stanford as its organist in 1874,[203] who, despite his many other preoccupations, raised the choir to a high state of efficiency;[204] his compositions for them included the service in B flat, and the three Latin motets, 'Justorum animae', 'Coelos ascendit hodie' and 'Beati quorum via'. On his resignation in 1892, his good work was continued by Alan Gray (a noted composer of descants), who retired in 1930. Meanwhile, Walmisley's successor at St John's, George Garrett, an articled pupil of S.S. Wesley at Winchester, saw the consecration of a new large chapel in 1869, and in 1888 a benefaction enabled the college to follow King's and recruit four choral scholars to assist its four lay clerks.[205] Under Garrett, who died in office in 1897, its repertoire was dominated by contemporary Victorian music, but the arrival of Cyril Rootham in 1901 marked a complete turnaround, and within a few years three quarters of the music dated from before 1750.[206] A bright future awaited both choirs as the twentieth century progressed.

Besides Oxford and Cambridge there was one other university in the nineteenth century which featured a chapel choir, and that was King's College, London. Founded in 1829 as an Anglican counterpart to the non-denominational University College, it had its chapel, which by around 1840 at the latest had a choir of boys and men,[207] establishing a still-continuing choral tradition, with the present-day mixed choir ranking among the best of its kind.

Roman Catholic Choirs

At the beginning of the nineteenth century, little music, apart from plainsong, appears to have been heard in Roman Catholic circles in mainland Britain outside the London embassy chapels featured in Chapter Three. Their decline in the second and third decades corresponded, however, with the start of a big expansion in the Catholic population, particularly through immigration from Ireland, and to a lesser extent by conversions from Anglicanism. This was accompanied by significant legal and administrative changes – notably the 1829 Catholic Emancipation Act, which removed the bar on Catholics sitting in Parliament, and the restoration of the episcopal hierarchy in England in 1850 (Scotland followed in 1878), creating new Roman Catholic dioceses under the Archbishop of Westminster. The outcome was the building of a large number of new churches – typically in the Victorian neo-Gothic style or as neo-classical Roman basilicas. New cathedrals, though, were slow to emerge, St George's, Southwark and St Chad's, Birmingham being the first in the 1840s. There being no tradition of congregational singing in Catholic churches, any music apart from such intoning and plainsong as might be sung by the priest and assistants had to be provided by choir and organ. Information is scanty as to how widespread the existence of choirs was, but, where present, they were mostly mixed and amateur, singing from a gallery – women would not have been allowed in the chancel. Non-Catholics might also be involved, as shown by an attack on their employment in 1841 by Nicholas Wiseman, President of Oscott College (and later Archbishop of Westminster).[208] As early as the 1850s the hierarchy was advocating the use of plainsong and Renaissance (or Renaissance-style) polyphony as being the most fitting for worship, and deprecating the singing of Viennese Classical Masses as being too secular in style – all this half a century before the famous papal bull *Moto proprio* of 1903, affirming these principles.[209] Choirs, and one suspects their congregations, were, however, not generally willing to abandon their Haydn,

Mozart, Hummel and the like, and this continued to be the preferred fare in most places for the rest of the century. Particularly given the voluntary nature of the choirs, priests who might have wanted to fall in line with official wishes were in practice faced with the prospect of having no choir at all if they forced the issue. So, the young Elgar in Worcester, where his father was organist at St George's Roman Catholic Church, was brought up on a spiritual diet of Pergolesi, Haydn, Mozart, Beethoven and Hummel.[210] At St Chad's Cathedral, Birmingham, however, which had a paid choir of boys and men, the authorities did succeed in imposing plainsong and polyphony in the mid-1850s.[211] Similarly, Wiseman's successor as Archbishop, Henry (later Cardinal) Manning, urged a battle against the use of women in choirs, but his attempt to ban them was widely ignored.[212] For there was simply no tradition of training Catholic boys to sing, and few persons competent to do so. Wiseman and Manning were both pursuing the papal agenda, aiming to bring the whole Church into line with Roman doctrine and practice. This included the introduction of the office of Benediction and increased devotion to the Virgin Mary, as well as the promotion of plainsong and polyphonic music. As far as plainsong was concerned, there was a desire to standardize its form and performance from the great variety of practice then current – a process which would eventually lead to the official sanctioning of the version which resulted from the researches of the monks of Solesmes, with the chant sung smoothly in equal note values. But in Britain throughout the nineteenth century, it was sung with longer and shorter notes to organ accompaniment and quite slowly;[213] there was general agreement that it was sung badly, even at somewhere like Brompton Oratory.[214] The most satisfactory performances were probably by the choirs of seminaries like Oscott, and schools like Downside and Ampleforth, associated with monasteries which emerged in the second half of the nineteenth century.

Despite the large-scale church building programme, the great majority of Catholic parishes were poor, and could spend little on their music. There were, nevertheless, wealthy churches created in fashionable areas with resources to support substantial music programmes. The Brompton Oratory established a choir of boys and men soon after its foundation in 1849 (before the present church was consecrated in 1884), and became noted for its opulent music, employing an orchestra for festivals, but also singing Palestrina and Carissimi as well as Viennese Classical and later music.[215] The boys came from its own Oratory School. In similar vein, the Jesuits at their Church of the Immaculate Conception in Farm Street, Mayfair, opened in 1849, also managed an all-male choir, with boys drawn from various schools; they also had orchestral Masses on great feasts until the

Moto proprio of 1903 put an end to them. Its all-male choir tradition, however, continued through until the Second World War, achieving particular renown in the inter-war period under Fr John Driscoll.[216] Across the river, at St George's Cathedral in Southwark, a paid mixed choir existed until 1890, when it was abruptly abolished.[217] The authoritarian nature of the Catholic Church, in which the laity had no voice, made choirs particularly subject to the whims of the clergy. It would be replaced by a choir of boys and men.[218] A similar situation would later develop at St Anne's, Edge Hill, Liverpool, where the former Leeds organist and choirmaster Alfred Benton spent the end of his career from about 1913, having converted to Roman Catholicism. The church had a strong musical tradition and Benton brought the choir up to broadcasting standard in the 1920s, specialising in Renaissance polyphony. But a new priest in 1928 suddenly ordered that only plainsong was to be sung in future, and had virtually the whole choir library burnt.[219] Liverpool also had at least one other musically active Catholic church in St Francis Xavier, opened in 1848, where a mixed choir, at times professional, sang Haydn, Gounod and the like until after *Moto proprio*, when it became all-male – the church also having already had a separate boys' choir, singing Vespers from as far back as 1866.[220] St Wilfrid's in York, dating from 1802, also had a long musical tradition; orchestrally accompanied Masses were sung on special occasions from 1815 onwards, with the assistance of singers from the Minster and elsewhere. The famous soprano Clara Novello sang in its choir as a girl in the 1820s, and at the beginning of the twentieth century the choir was still very active and enjoyed success in a local choral competition.[221] It is hard to establish just how common such flourishing activity was, but it suggests that there was more musical activity in parts of the Roman Catholic church in mainland Britain than is often assumed. The major development that occurred with the opening of Westminster Cathedral for worship in 1903 will be left until the next chapter.

Emerging chiefly out of nineteenth-century Catholic Germany came the 'Cecilian movement', aiming to reform church music away from secular influences in the direction of promoting the performance and composition of (preferably) unaccompanied works, especially those in the Palestrina tradition approved by Rome. It was at its most active in the second part of the century, but had only limited influence and imitation in England.[222] While it many have produced modest new additions to the repertoire, there was no great appetite for new compositions within Catholic circles, and no significant Catholic composers emerged from nineteenth-century Britain until the arrival of Elgar, whose own contribution to the Catholic repertoire were limited to a few youthful pieces for St George's, Worcester, where he was briefly organist in the 1880s – all his later liturgical music was written for

Anglican use. Over in Ireland, where full celebration of the Catholic liturgy had been legally permitted since the 1780s, the early nineteenth century had seen the appointment of several foreign musicians to posts such as Dublin's St Mary's Pro-Cathedral, where the Viennese classical Masses would be standard fare.[223] With Ireland's strongly conservative-minded priesthood, the Cecilian movement had more effect in the last quarter of the century, and an Irish Cecilian Society was created,[224] though even there the taste for elaborate orchestral Masses was by no means eliminated before the 1903 *Moto proprio*.

Nonconformist Choirs

From its beginning in the 1740s the Methodist movement had no use for choirs or organs, relying entirely on unaccompanied singing. In this they were at one with older dissenting bodies like the Congregationalists (then known as the Independents) and the Baptists, although Methodist singing was from the outset marked by its fervour and liveliness. But as the century progressed and the quantity of new hymns, written by the likes of Isaac Watts and Charles Wesley, mushroomed, then all three denominations found choirs emerging from their congregations, often by way of singing classes, in order to help them become acquainted with the growing repertoire. The choirs, once established, began also to sing anthems, thereby adding an element of variety to the hymn/metrical psalm diet which otherwise was the sole musical content of Nonconformist worship. Organs were long regarded with suspicion, and the Methodist Conference only permitted them officially in 1820, but like the Anglican 'gallery choirs', the early Nonconformists often used a cello, and possibly other instruments, to support the choir.[225] With the great expansion of Nonconformity in the nineteenth century came the building of numerous new chapels. They typically assumed the traditional 'preaching box' form, with the centrally placed pulpit at the front, but now with an organ behind it in a gallery which also seated the choir. As the century advanced the influence of the Oxford Movement was also felt in Nonconformist circles, and new chapels, particularly in the more affluent areas, were increasingly built in the neo-Gothic style, even with elements of a 'chancel' in which to accommodate the choir, which began to be decorously kitted out in gowns.

In Scotland, although fierce opposition to organs prevailed in Church of Scotland (Presbyterian) circles until at least the 1860s, choirs to aid the singing of metrical psalms, and an increasing variety of other hymns, were often found, and that of Paisley Abbey under the direction of Robert Archibald Smith, precentor (i.e. music leader of the church) from 1807, encouraged the congregation away from the 'old' extremely slow style of singing still prevalent in many places, as well as broadening the range of music heard there.[226] The charm of Anglican chant also sometimes added to the musical mix in Nonconformist churches (even Presbyterian ones), where they were commonly set to metrical texts. Yet suspicion of choirs continued in many places into the second half of the century, nowhere more than among the Free Presbyterians, who in a report in 1852, while concerned to improve their psalmody, ruled out choirs 'on the ground of their concentrating *all* the good singers, and tempting the congregation to sit and listen to them'.[227]

Although Nonconformist choirs were almost all voluntary, there were examples where payment occurred. In York, Albion Street Methodist chapel was paying singers and a singing master from 1818 to 1856, while at Lendal Congregational chapel in the 1850s singers received annual payments of £10.[228] In Birmingham, Carr's Lane Congregational church choir had an excellent reputation at the end of the century under William Stockley (choirmaster of the Birmingham Festival Choral Society, 1855–95), and some of its members were paid.[229] In the Nonconformist strongholds of Lancashire and Yorkshire, chapel choirs were often reckoned as the best in the area, and their members contributed substantially to the famed northern choral societies. Some could mount cantata or oratorio performances themselves, perhaps calling on the assistance of fellow chapel singers, and waiting lists for membership of good choirs existed.[230] Virtually all Nonconformist choirs appear to have consisted of adult mixed voices; one Congregational church, Christ Church in Enfield, had a choir of boys and men in the 1890s, though this was probably unique.[231] But however ubiquitous choirs may have become, congregational singing remained at the heart of Nonconformist worship, even though concerns were sometimes expressed that they were not singing as well as formerly. Congregational participation in anthems was not unknown, especially where there was a tradition of singing classes. In North Wales, for example, from the 1840s evening chapel congregations were regularly singing anthems,[232] and composers produced a steady stream of simple 'congregational anthems', hardly more demanding than a hymn tune. The success of the tonic sol-fa movement probably contributed to their growth. The most spectacular example was at the Union Chapel (Congregational), Islington, where Henry Gauntlett and then Ebenezer Prout were organists. A weekday singing class began in 1848 and was still going 40 years later, with 200–300 members paying to be taught. Congregational anthems were then sung in services, even including parts of *Messiah* on Christmas Day, and a book of anthems was published in 1872.[233]

Just as the Anglicans developed diocesan festivals, Nonconformist choirs too came together to celebrate. The Nonconformist Choir Union (later the Free Church Choir Union) was found in 1888 by Ebenezer Minshall, organist of the City Temple in London, and an annual festival was held – from 1889 at the Crystal Palace, where up to 8,000 participants took part in the years before the First World War. Minshall would travel round the country taking preliminary local rehearsals, and the programme extended beyond services, to include both choral and solo voice competitions.[234] It was to be a period which marked the peak of Nonconformist choral activity.

Chapter 6
World War to World War, 1914–1945

Change Beckons in the Cathedrals

The immediate effect of the outbreak of the First World War on the daily round of cathedral life appears to have been minimal. Some lay clerks would have enrolled in the forces, but given that most were beyond call-up years, serious disruption to choral services was unlikely. The university choral foundations would have lost most of such choral scholars as they were accustomed to have, but all still relied mainly on lay clerks. It would be the aftermath of the war, with its economic and social upheavals, which ushered significant changes in the world of cathedral music, minor as these were in comparison with what would occur in the latter part of the century.

Among the most important developments of the inter-war years was the gradual abandonment in most cathedrals of weekday choral Matins. Its continuation was becoming a major impediment to both the engagement of lay clerks and the education of the choristers. What had still been manageable in late Victorian Britain became increasingly anachronistic after the First World War. With the employment uncertainties of the period, the opportunities for lay clerks to find suitable work outside singing duties were far fewer than earlier – not many employers would now be prepared to allow an hour's absence in the middle of the morning – for Matins was still usually at 10 a.m. – as well as early release for a 3 p.m. Evensong. Work round the cathedral might be provided for a few, but some form of self-employment, which could be precarious, is likely to have been the most common way to supplement an average singing man's salary of £100–150 per year.[1] But the biggest impact of abandoning Matins was to be on the choristers' education. The disruption of the school day had been of concern to many since late Victorian times – unwelcome even in small chorister-only schools, but a particular problem where the boys attended schools with others. With an increasing desire of organists to attract more middle-class choristers, such as were now filling the stalls of St Paul's, Westminster Abbey, and the university choral foundations, the quality of education would clearly be important for prospective choir parents. A more normal school day would become an essential factor, and this was to be aided, not only by abandoning Matins, but by putting back the time of Evensong, which typically gradually moved to 4 p.m. and eventually to 5 p.m.[2] (The universities had a rather different pattern, with Evensong at 5 p.m. or later, to fit in with the academic day.) Boys began to benefit from a full school day, although, with an early morning pre-school practice becoming normal, it was a long one. Few people lamented the loss of choral Matins, which in most places is likely to have been sung without any congregation, and so hardly conducive to either good musical or behavioural standards. Evensong at least usually had a core congregation from among the local retired or leisured. In short, weekday Matins had become regarded as a chore, breaking up the working day, while Evensong provided an aesthetically, and, for many, a spiritually satisfying end to it. Nevertheless, there were traditionalists among senior church musicians who deplored the loss of Matins as late as 1940.[3] Some saw it as signifying the end of the last trace of the medieval idea of regular sung worship throughout the day, and fear was expressed for the whole future of cathedral music, especially given the precarious financial prospects of many cathedrals by the time the Second World War arrived.[4] Of particular regret was the loss of the whole psalter being sung through each month. Many clerks and organists, like their predecessors going back to medieval times, could probably have sung the whole of the psalms off by heart. Henceforth choirs would be familiar with little more than half of them.

The disappearance of weekday Matins was not a sudden occurrence; it tended to begin as a reduction in the number sung each week, and the Second World War was often the point at which it ceased completely, not to be restored in peacetime. St Paul's and Westminster Abbey were among the few to continue with the service after the war, only to abandon it in 1981.[5] St Michael's, Tenbury, kept it going until 1976,[6] while the only cathedral in the British Isles to maintain the tradition into the twenty-first century is St Patrick's, Dublin, latterly sung, however, by the boys only. Matins, however, continued as a main Sunday morning service, even when a weekly choral Eucharist was introduced, and is still sung by a declining number of cathedrals. It offers an opportunity to retain at least some of the better settings of the morning canticles in the repertoire.

Cathedrals were to struggle with solutions to the choristers' education for much of the twentieth century. Those with chorister-only choir schools found them increasingly untenable on both financial and educational grounds. Some expanded by taking in non-choristers, as did Salisbury from around 1900, developing into more standard prep schools;[7] others made (or already had) arrangements for the boys to be educated at other schools. Chester was perhaps the last to close its small choir school (which also had non-choristers) in 1975,[8] and today Westminster Abbey is the only remaining establishment with a school catering solely for its singers. One major change has been that, whereas up to the twentieth century the choristers' education was free, parents now began to be asked to pay fees, subsidized by scholarships, which varied greatly in their generosity. This naturally increased the trend towards a middle-class intake, and, particularly where the school had a good academic reputation, some parents doubtless saw a choristership as a means for their child to acquire a private education on the cheap. This gentrification of choristers was a gradual process and varied widely between institutions – at York, for example, up to the 1940s, most of the boys were sons of engine drivers, farm labourers, teachers and shopkeepers,[9] while at Lincoln around 1930 'the boys were a mixed bunch and, in some cases, pretty wild'.[10] By way of contrast, many Salisbury boys in the first decade of the century were going on to public schools.[11] Still, regardless of educational opportunities, there appears to have been no shortage of applicants for choristerships in the inter-war years. But with a gradual shift to prep school education, which generally only catered for them up to thirteen, the choirs often lost boys when at their vocal best – delighted though their next school's music department would have been to receive them. The age at which a boy's voice changed in the past and any relationship to training methods, nutrition and so on, is still a matter of dispute, and would have varied considerably, but anecdotal evidence suggests that more fourteen- and fifteen- year-olds were then still capable of singing treble than nowadays.

Some change also came the way of lay clerks. Those remnants of the communal life of medieval times, the corporations or 'colleges' of the Old Foundation cathedrals, so often a thorn in the side of chapters, were finally brought to an end by the Cathedrals Measure of 1931, as a result of which the Wells corporation was wound up in 1933 and Hereford's held its last meeting in 1937.[12] Associated with the corporations (but not confined to them) was the continuing freehold status of lay clerks in many institutions. Except for serious misdemeanours, they could not be dismissed, and with no compulsory retirement age, they could remain in post regardless of the condition of their voice. An extreme example was Henry Dutton, who was still singing alto at St Paul's in 1943 at the age of 90, despite having been asked to retire in 1913.[13] Cathedrals were beginning to make some provision for pensions, but they were by no means universal or adequate, so chapters were often reluctant to press the issue on compassionate grounds, however much the organist might have desired action, though financial inducements were sometimes forthcoming. A 1941 report issued by the Church Music Society, recommended a general retirement age of 65 if not earlier, as well as contributory pension schemes.¹⁴ Although the practice of appointing lay clerks to freehold posts was declining, its demise was gradual, and the last three freeholders at Westminster Abbey were only persuaded to retire in 1977.¹⁵

Lay clerks were perhaps inherently traditionally minded, and the habits, good and bad, of the older members tended to be passed down to the next generation. Unpunctuality, reluctance to rehearse, scepticism towards new repertoire and a general casualness certainly often remained evident, as, in the London choirs especially, was an over-fondness for employing deputies.¹⁶ Yet there were undoubtedly many conscientious and devout among their numbers, with a real dedication to the daily round. Lay clerks were still engaged principally for their individual vocal quality. Sight reading ability may have been regarded as comparatively unimportant, and the idea of seeking voices which would fit in with other singers was of little concern – the ideal of a 'blended' choir was slow to emerge, and came, as we shall see, from the university choral foundations. The boys, with their daily rehearsal, could be welded into a more uniform vocal unit, and a fine treble line helped mask infelicities below, especially in a resonant acoustic. Idiosyncrasy was certainly common among the lay clerks. Melville Cook, organist of Hereford Cathedral between 1956 and 1966, recalled that in his days as a Gloucester chorister in the mid-1920s the six lay clerks were 'probably the most eccentric set of singers to be found in any cathedral',¹⁷ while Lionel Dakers's verdict on the Windsor lay clerks around 1950 was that 'they sang badly all day, with nearly everything unaccompanied dropping a semitone in pitch. They certainly are a queer and awkward bunch and quite unaccountable'.¹⁸ Choristers were quick to discern vocal peculiarities in the back rows. A Lincoln boy from around 1930 recalled their enjoyment of a certain Yorkshire bass's rendition of a verse anthem by William Boyce: 'I 'ave surely built thee an 'ouse to dwell in. Be'old the 'eaven of 'eavens cannot contain thee, 'ow much less the 'ouse that I 'ave builded. I 'ave 'allowed this 'ouse.'¹⁹ It would be the second half of the century that gradually saw the real transformation of the men's side of cathedral choirs.

Between 1876 and 1927 nineteen new dioceses were created in England, mainly taking over (at least initially) existing parish churches as their cathedrals. As such, they did not have the weight of ancient choral tradition to contend with, and in consequence most felt no obligation to institute daily choral services. Truro and Liverpool, however, did so early in their existence (even before their buildings were completed), and all would eventually seek to offer at least a couple of weekday choral Evensongs, notwithstanding financial constraints. In Ireland, a new cathedral, St Anne's, Belfast, was consecrated in 1904, built around the existing parish church, which was demolished as building proceeded. Here the mixed-voice church choir of around 50 (including 20 boys) became the cathedral choir, but it remained very much a parish church cathedral, singing for many decades only on Sundays.[20]

Richard Terry and the new Westminster Cathedral

The most interesting development in liturgical music in the early twentieth century came not from the Church of England but from the opening of the Roman Catholic Westminster Cathedral in 1902 and the appointment of Richard Terry as choirmaster.[21] Terry, from an Anglican family, spent two years in the 1880s as an alto choral scholar at King's under A.H. Mann, which fundamentally influenced his approach to choir training.[22] Converting to Catholicism, he taught from 1896 at Downside School, where he explored hitherto unknown Renaissance music with its choir, bringing it to such a state of excellence that, on a visit to London, it was noticed by Cardinal Vaughan, who subsequently recruited Terry for his new cathedral, where a choir school was started in 1901. Terry initially had a choir of about twenty boys and fourteen men, with whom he quickly developed a wide repertoire centred on unaccompanied Renaissance music – Palestrina, Lassus, Victoria and other continental composers, but he also increasingly revived Latin Tudor music, including Taverner, Tallis and especially Byrd. His interests extended to the plainsong reforms of Solesmes, which influenced his approach at Westminster. This and unaccompanied polyphony were very much in tune with the reforms desired by the papal *Moto Proprio* of 1903. Terry brought to life music that many of the time thought was only fit for antiquarian study, and his work soon attracted the attention of musicians, who came to hear this exciting new music, so different from what was to be experienced in either Anglican or Catholic churches.

There was clearly an element of the showman and publicist in Terry, who did not confine himself to reviving older music, but also encouraged contemporary composers, Catholic or not, to contribute new works in the spirit of the Renaissance masters. Stanford, Holst and especially the young Howells, among others, all wrote for Westminster, but Terry rightly reckoned the greatest work to be Vaughan Williams's Mass in G minor, first heard there in 1923.[23] Unfortunately, not all these works have survived – Westminster appears to have been particularly negligent in preserving its choir library.[24] With such a large and developing repertoire – the choir sang Mass and Vespers daily – Terry insisted on the boys rapidly becoming good sight readers. Their tone was seemingly formed on the King's/Magdalen head voice model, to judge by a few recordings made from 1909 onwards[25] – for once we enter the twentieth century, we begin to have aural evidence of the choral sounds of the time, however imperfect early recordings may be. Terry certainly did not appreciate what he considered the 'raucous and horrible' tone of continental boys,[26] and so remained very much within the Anglican tradition in this respect; this was in contrast to what was to happen to the choir's sound after the Second World War.

Besides their cathedral duties, Terry also had the choir participate in charity concerts and provided the treble line for the Western Madrigal Society, much as his Anglican counterparts were accustomed to do. Financial problems at the cathedral soon saw the number of men in the choir whittled down – to nine in 1906 and six in 1912, much to Terry's dismay.[27] Only one remained in place during the First World War and Terry had to manage the post-war years with just five for the weekday services, extras being employed for Sundays and special occasions. Terry himself, like some other gifted choir trainers, had uneasy relationships with the authorities, not helped by what became frequent personal absences, and he eventually resigned in 1924, continuing to pursue a wide range of activities including adjudicating and collecting sea shanties. Succeeded at Westminster by priests, less exciting times ensued, even if a good standard was maintained. Unlike the situation in the early years, a stipulation was made that only Catholics should be engaged as choirmen.[28]

Terry's lasting influence within Catholic circles appears to the been limited, though it is noteworthy that Leeds Roman Catholic Cathedral choir was singing works by Byrd, Tye, Palestrina and others in the 1920s.[29] More significant was his demonstration of the vitality of Tudor sacred music, and this was an important factor in the securing of funding from the Carnegie United Kingdom Trust to enable the publication between 1922 and 1929 of a ten-volume edition of *Tudor Church Music* by Oxford University Press, from which individual items were soon issued, adapted for practical use. These were to play a decisive role in the general revival of the music by cathedral and other choirs. Terry initially led the team of editors but was found temperamentally unsuited to the detailed demands of the task and retired from the editorial board in 1922.[30] Much of the subsequent editing was undertaken by Edmund Fellowes, a minor canon of Windsor, Oxford educated (including a BMus degree) and a fine violinist. His Windsor duties were light, and family money meant he could devote himself on an astonishingly industrious scale to the editing of Tudor and Jacobean music, starting with the complete works of the madrigalists (*The English Madrigal School*), followed by the lute songs (*The English School of Lutenist Song Writers*), and in due course by the complete vocal works of Byrd. His editorial methods aimed to combine scholarship with practical needs, and it is primarily his editions (and those of his fellow editors like Percy Buck and Alexander Ramsbotham) that provided for the revival of

Tudor music in the cathedral repertoire.[31] Present-day editors would not be so liberal with dynamic indications and other editorial interpretative marks, but such practical advice was considered essential at the time, and certainly helped bring the music to life for the many choirs, sacred and secular, who otherwise might have rendered the bare notes in a dull and uncomprehending manner.

Transformation at the University Choral Foundations

It was at Oxford and Cambridge in the inter-war years that we begin to see changes that would, in the second half of the century, eventually produce a very different sound, not only in the cathedral choirs, but in the secular professional choral world as well. And one institution above all would lead the way – King's College, Cambridge.[32] The latter years of Mann's tenure as organist (he remained in post until 1929) saw an innovation which would in time catapult the choir worldwide fame. It was a new dean, Eric Milner-White, who, as the First World War came to end in 1918, introduced the Festival of Nine Lessons and Carols on Christmas Eve. The idea was not original; he adapted it from a service first created at Truro in 1880 by Bishop Edward Benson and others for the cathedral of the new diocese. It proved immediately popular and was imitated elsewhere.[33] Milner-White had a fine feeling for liturgy and liturgical language, and the incomparable Bidding Prayer was wholly his creation. The service successfully belies its late Victorian origin and manages to give the impression that it is quite ancient. In fact, there are faint medieval echoes in the presence of nine lessons, as were found in the pre-Reformation office of Matins on Sundays and major feast days.[34] By the time of its introduction, Mann was in his late sixties and not prone to welcome innovation – he disliked the dean's introduction of occasional Eucharists in place of Sunday Matins[35] – but the service predictably found great favour, not least with the town population, for whom Milner-White saw it as an offering on the part of the college. A few minor modifications were made to the service over the next few years before it settled down to its present form. Although the service opened with 'Once in royal David's city' from 1919, the 'traditional' singing of the first verse by a solo boy dates only from the time of the Second World War.[36] Mann kept to simple carol arrangements, and congregational participation was greater than was later the case. The fledgling BBC had already transmitted an Evensong from the chapel in 1926, and in 1928 the Festival of Nine Lessons and Carols was broadcast for the first time, becoming (except for 1930) an annual fixture, listening to which was soon regarded throughout the land as a Christmas tradition. The quality of Mann's choir had long been familiar to generations of students, local residents and visitors; now its fame was to increase enormously, all the more so when the service gradually began to be relayed on short-wave radio to the world at large from 1932 onwards.[37]

The 1928 carol service was Mann's last, for he died the following year. His successor was also to become something of a legend. Boris Ord did not come to the post with any cathedral experience. After school at Clifton College and war service, he studied at the Royal College of Music before moving to Cambridge with an organ scholarship at Corpus Christi College. A research fellowship at King's followed in 1923, but he also spent a year working at the Cologne Opera House, and a strong interest in opera and madrigals continued through his life. Taking over at King's at the age of 32, he was in a perfect position to capitalize on what he inherited from Mann – a choir which had just done away with the last of the lay clerks, and henceforth consisted of sixteen boys and fourteen choral scholars. In many ways it was more like a school choir than the cathedral choirs of the day, and had some similarities to the Leipzig Thomanerchor and Dresden Kreuzchor, which drew solely on their respective schools. They, however, were much larger ensembles and used unbroken boys' voices on the alto line. But Ord now had an instrument he could mould to his liking, with malleable young men on the back rows, and all the advantages of having a full choir rehearsal before every service, as well as a light schedule compared with that of cathedrals. In addition to the refined tuning that was already a mark of Mann's choir, Ord's professionalism secured a precision in ensemble that was unprecedented, and with this went a concern for a real choral blend, in which any tendency for a voice to stand out was suppressed. Yet the alchemy by which it was achieved is not easily discerned. Like other organists of the time, during services Ord played for the psalms and other accompanied music himself, descending only to conduct unaccompanied pieces. This he did in the most discreet manner possible from the end of the cantoris boys' stall, using no more than the tap of a finger of his left hand and the occasional nod of the head. Such discretion was, however, typical of the time – more flamboyant conducting would have been condemned. What he instilled in the choir was the need to listen to each other, so that the whole body behaved rather like a string quartet. Watching across had, of course, always been the means by which cathedral choirs attempted to keep themselves together, but it was Ord's insistence on looking and listening, coupled with proper rehearsal, which produced the outstanding results. There is a remarkable demonstration of this in a recording of the television broadcast of a version of the 1954 carol service – not the actual Christmas Eve event, but a live broadcast on 23 December, mirroring in abbreviated form the following day's service.[38] At the start of the last verse of the unaccompanied carol 'A Virgin most pure', Ord stops tapping his finger and walks calmly towards the lectern in order to read the next lesson, leaving the choir to finish the carol of their own, which they do immaculately. Ord's conducting style may have been minimal, but there is no doubt about the authority he exercised over the whole choir. And his broad musical interests continued to find an outlet outside the chapel, especially as conductor of the Cambridge University Musical Society, with which he undertook both choral and operatic work.[39]

The qualities of Ord's choir became increasingly familiar to the public through broadcast Evensongs, especially during the Second World War, when the choir would certainly have been identifiable to many, despite the broadcasts being anonymous for security reasons. Recordings, however, only began to appear with a couple of 78 rpm records of carols, issued for the Christmas market in 1949.[40] In 1950–51 the choir contributed several items to Columbia's *Anthology of English Church Music* series, but it was the LP era that cemented its fame, when in the mid-1950s discs of Gibbons, a Festival of Lessons and Carols, an Evensong and *An Easter Matins* were issued.[41] The last, in particular, demonstrated what a fine ensemble he was to bequeath to his successor, David Willcocks, in 1958.

In place of much of the Georgian and Victorian repertoire favoured by Mann, Ord introduced far more sixteenth- and seventeenth-century music, English and foreign, often facilitated by Fellowes's new editions. Ord's choir, with its liberal rehearsal time, was much better equipped to tackle the greater technical demands of such music than others. Comparatively little contemporary music was featured, though easily the most significant new work was Howells's 'Collegium Regale' service. The morning and evening canticles dated from 1944–5, with the Holy Communion setting being added in 1956. Howells was always conscious of the aura of the place he was composing for, and the unforgettable soaring treble line of the evening canticles' Gloria was undoubtedly composed with the King's acoustic in mind. The idea for commissioning the Te Deum and Jubilate may have come from Howells's friend, Harold Darke, who deputized for Ord during the war, while the college's Dean, Eric Milner-White appears to have instigated the evening set.[42] The work was the first of more than twenty canticle sets that Howells would be commissioned to write for particular cathedrals and choral foundations over the next thirty years – everyone wanted their own 'Coll. Reg.'

In contrast to later developments, Ord's choice of carols, like that of Mann, favoured the simple and straightforward, although it included several which would become King's 'classics', like Robert Lucas Pearsall's 'In dulci jubilo' and Peter Cornelius's 'The three kings'. Ord's own inimitable 'Adam lay ybounden' dates from his final years; it was his only published composition and was also destined to become an annual fixture. The recordings of Ord's choir in the 1950s suggest that in some ways the sound was closer to that of Mann's of 1929 than to King's at the end of the century – the generally slow speeds in older music, big changes of dynamics in a Bach chorale, breathing in the middle of phrases, and rallentandi (often with a rapid diminuendo) at the end of verses, are all echoes of the earlier age, even if on a less exaggerated scale. But the undoubted musicality of it all shines through and continues to be a source of wonder.

The psalm singing under Ord was certainly distinctive, and illustrative of how varied and individual styles could be within a 'speech rhythm' approach. We don't know how Mann's choir chanted, but Ord is reputed to have quickly changed it on taking over.[43] There was no lingering around – speeds were generally brisk, and, instead of proceeding in a smooth flow, little words are rather hurried over – though, of course, sung perfectly together and with admirably clear diction. And, far from observing the old tradition of the notes after the reciting note being sung steadily in strict time, Ord moves quickly through to the end of the verse. Notable too is that verses follow each other immediately without any hint of a break. Interesting comparisons can be made with Willcocks's treatment on his famous *Psalms of David* recording, issued in 1969, little more than a decade after Ord's retirement.[44] It provides a clear illustration that the psalms are the part of a service on which the choir director can most obviously stamp his personal mark.

King's choir was also heard on the continent in 1936, when Ord took them on a tour of Sweden, Denmark, the Netherlands and Germany, where their singing was enthusiastically received for its perfection of intonation, delicacy and precision.[45] It wasn't quite the first English cathedral-type choir to have been abroad, for Sydney Nicholson, whose career will shortly be discussed, had already taken a choir of twelve boys from Westminster Abbey and the men of St George's, Windsor on a seven-week tour of Canada and the United States in 1932 – the current Windsor boys being considered too young, while the Abbey choir was large enough to allow a dozen senior boys to tour.[46]

Down the road at St John's, there were also only two organists in the first half of the century, Cyril Rootham (1901–38) and Robin Orr (1938–51), for whom Herbert Howells deputized during the Second World War. Neither man can be considered innovative in their choir work, although St John's actually beat King's in producing the first Cambridge recording, when a disc of Byrd's verse anthem, 'Have mercy upon me', was issued in

1927 – notable for being one of the first occasions on which HMV's new mobile recording van was used.[47] Accompanied by a string quartet, the performance, however, is extremely slow and lugubrious (about two-thirds of the speed of modern performances) with all the boys singing the verse sections. On this evidence, Fellowes's ideas on the vitality of Tudor music had yet to bear fruit here. While the boys sing smoothly enough, the men (half lay clerks and half choral scholars) belong distinctly to the old lay clerk school with heavy vibrato. Unlike King's, St John's was still singing only at weekends and on important feast days, and although Orr laboured to improve the choir, and succeeded in his final years in replacing the last lay clerks with choral scholars,[48] St John's era of choral fame lay firmly in the future. Trinity College's choir was in a very similar position, with Hubert Middleton succeeding Alan Gray in 1931, and the choir being reorganized after his resignation in 1957. Its rise to prominence would come a little later than St John's. Elsewhere in Cambridge, a few college choirs, such as Jesus, recruited boys,[49] but most would have had just male students, run by ever-changing undergraduate organ scholars, who had gradually become a regular feature of Oxbridge college life since the late nineteenth century.

Over at Oxford, Magdalen choir lost some of its pre-eminence under Varley Roberts's successors, H.C. Stewart (1919–38), William McKie (1938–41) and Philip Taylor (1941–57); it was New College which was generally reckoned as the city's best choir in the post-First World War period. Following Hugh Allen's resignation in 1918 on taking up the Music Professorship, the choir was directed by a series of fine musicians in William Harris, John Dykes Bower, Sydney Watson and H.K. Andrews. In 1927, just before St John's made their recording, New College took to the microphone to record two discs, containing four anthems from Byrd to Stanford, with Harris conducting.[50] His most famous anthem, 'Faire is the heaven', for unaccompanied double choir, was written for the college in 1925, and its difficulties testify to the choir's ability. None of the three Oxford choral foundations followed King's in relying entirely on choral scholars at this time, and only Magdalen would eventually do so, and not until 1960.[51] In 1944 H.K. Andrews actually managed to replace the two New College choral scholars with an extra lay clerk.[52] Preference for more mature voices may have been one reason for the retention of lay clerks, but it was probably also due to the fear of not being always able to find choral scholars with the necessary vocal and academic abilities. King's, given its fame, would naturally always tend to attract the best candidates; none of the other choirs had anything like the same allure in the first half of the century. Although both King's and New College broadcast their Evensongs during the Second World War, no-one could have mistaken one for the other. Surviving excerpts of New College broadcasts from 1940 and 1942 reveal very much an old-style lay clerk sound among the men, and, to us today, a decidedly ponderous style of performance (especially in S.S. Wesley's 'Thou wilt keep him in perfect peace'), reminiscent of Mann.[53] Yet the choir, still under Andrews, underwent something of a transformation in the post-war years, since performances of Byrd on a broadcast Evensong in 1955 are splendidly alive, with a sound quite equal to its Cambridge rival.[54]

At Christ Church, the choir seems to have attracted little attention at this time. The young William Walton was a chorister there from 1912 under the noted organist Henry Ley (1909–26), while the versatile Thomas Armstrong (1933–55) was also an important figure generally in Oxford music, including conducting the Oxford Bach Choir. Other colleges operated much like their Cambridge counterparts. Boys were to be found at Exeter, Hertford, Queen's, St John's and Worcester, though only Queen's had a permanent organist, while among the women's colleges, Lady Margaret Hall was active chorally from the 1920s when the chapel choir was run by Margaret Deneke, a highly successful fundraiser for the college and prominent figure in Oxford's musical life.

The Impact of Broadcasting and Recording

Reference has already been made to broadcasts by Oxbridge choirs. From its beginnings in the early 1920s, the BBC had as its general manager (later director-general) John Reith, a man of Scottish Presbyterian stock, under whom religion came to have an important role in the broadcast output. The short 'Daily Service' began in 1928, with singing provided by the recently formed Wireless Singers (renamed the BBC Singers in 1937), a group of eight professionals, half of whom sang at each service – later the number was increased to sixteen, with eight singing at a time.[55] The music was simple – a hymn and a psalm, with an occasional short anthem. The studio had a small organ, at which George Thalben-Ball regularly presided. The high standard of singing, with good blend, provided something of a model for ordinary church choirs, and speech rhythm chanting of the psalms was usefully promoted to the country at large. But the BBC also broadcast services directly from cathedrals and other choral establishments, confronting the numerous technical and acoustical problems involved. Sunday evening services were heard from around the country (and included those of denominations other than the Church of England), while weekly Thursday choral Evensongs from Westminster Abbey started in 1926 – transferred to St Paul's in 1936 because of coronation preparations at the Abbey.[56]

By the 1930s, however, disquiet was being expressed in BBC management at the low standard exhibited at many provincial cathedrals.[57] Particular embarrassment was caused by the situation at York Minster, where the eminent but tetchy Sir Edward Bairstow was still in charge. A weekly Tuesday Evensong was broadcast on the North Regional wavelength, and according to internal reports in 1936 'the choir [was] often out of tune', and 'singing, judged by many broadcasts, is definitely below par'.[58] Apparently, after tactful approaches to Bairstow by the dean and others, some improvement was made.[59] It was perhaps partly the common problem of an organist being in post too long – Bairstow had been at York for over twenty years, and the quality of the Minster music, admired in the post-war years, was no longer a priority given his, by now, many other commitments. But it is also the case, that, when broadcasts were live, and before the availability of recordings of them, the participants themselves would have been unaware of how they sounded on air. The microphone was unforgiving in what it picked up, and in those early experimental days could be unflattering even to first-rate performers. The listener at home also lacked any of the visual distractions and general atmosphere offered to the worshipper in the building itself; they were totally reliant on the sound of the choir, and even this was a pale reflection of the effect in the building, for the microphone would pick up little of its acoustic. York may have been a particularly bad example, but there was a general feeling in the BBC that most cathedral choirs could not compare with the quality of the Wireless Singers and were unworthy of being on the air. It would, however, be the 1950s before the issue of standards of broadcasting such choirs would be seriously confronted.

Occasional reference has already been made to early recordings, and they do provide some insight into choral practice, though a very imperfect one – ideas of tempo, the use of vibrato, and the general tone of the boys' voices are certainly conveyed, but the overall sound of the choir in its natural environment is lost, even when the recordings were made *in situ* rather than in a studio, as was the case with the earliest. The temptation to try and capture choirs on disc went back to the early 1900s – there is an extraordinary studio recording of Matins by the choir of St Andrew's, Wells Street, made in 1908 with harmonium accompaniment.[60] The singing gives anything but a favourable impression of a supposedly leading choir of the capital, but it certainly illustrates the old pre-speech rhythm method of chanting, with its rushing through the recitation, swallowing words galore, followed by rigidly metrical cadences. There was even a ludicrous attempt to record an abbreviated *Dream of Gerontius* in 1924, with a choir of eight and an orchestra including just nine strings![61] Things improved markedly after the introduction of electrical recording in 1926, which also enabled choirs to be recorded *in situ*, and a flurry of discs of church music by various choirs appeared around 1930. But thereafter, interest on the part of recording companies waned, and did not revive until the dawn of the LP era in the 1950s.

One recording of 1927, however, would take the world by storm, and give its choir fame on a quite unexpected scale. Ernest Lough at the Temple Church was fifteen at the time he recorded Mendelssohn's 'Hear my prayer' – one of the early electrical recordings made in the church itself. As was always his custom, George Thalben-Ball played the organ himself and there was no conductor – soloist and choir just communicated amongst themselves with remarkable precision. Lough did not produce the stereotypical 'pure white' choirboy sound, for he sang with plenty of vibrato, and Thalben-Ball was quite happy for his treble line to take on something of the natural vibrato heard from the men. But Lough's quality immediately caught the public's fancy, so much so that the choir was obliged to re-record it a few months later in 1928, since the original masters were worn out.[62] It is this latter recording, with Lough almost sixteen, that was continually reissued in various formats over the following decades. What few listeners, apart from those who may have sung the piece themselves, would have realized is that they were not hearing the complete anthem. As with so many works at the time, it had to be abbreviated to fit onto the available disc space – in this case by making a cut in the 'O for the wings of a dove' section. By chance, St George's, Windsor had itself recorded the piece under Walford Davies just a month or so before the Temple, but in a far more mutilated form, and with a less accomplished soloist – it was no competition for Lough's. It would be the 1950s before 'Hear my prayer' was heard complete on disc. Meanwhile sentimental myths grew up about the recording – notably that Lough had expired on singing the last note – and the curious flocked to the Temple to hear the choir.[63] The cult of the solo boy treble went back to late Victorian times, when advertisements regularly appeared from fashionable London choirs for a 'Solo Boy', and commercial training establishments like the London College of Choristers furnished soloists as well as complete treble lines.[64] Lough's success came about, at least in part, because he happened to come along at a particularly opportune moment in the development of recording techniques, for the sound is remarkably good. Needless to say, in his wake, numerous other solo boys – often operating in the popular concert sphere of sentimental songs – made recordings, in the hope of emulating Lough's sales.[65] Lough himself never profited from 'Hear my prayer' (or a couple of other things he recorded before his voice changed), and in due course he returned to the choir as a bass, with his own son, Robin, eventually becoming a Temple chorister.[66]

But despite this anthem having long been a favourite, not everyone considered it a suitable solo for a boy, on account of its sentiments. Even that arch-advocate of boy choristers, Sydney Nicholson, noted that 'no healthy choirboy longs for "The wings of a dove"; he much prefers the wings of an aeroplane'.[67] Nevertheless, choristers continue to love to soar.

The Cathedral Repertoire

As the Victorian era receded, at least its more mediocre music gradually fell into disuse; in future, that of the likes of Stanford and Charles Wood would increasingly set the standards by which 'worthiness' would be determined. The period, however, saw little in the way of new compositions which immediately marked them out as 'classics'. One early twentieth-century anthem which did find ready acceptance was John Ireland's 'Greater love hath no man'; it was composed before the war, in 1911, but its text was to make it peculiarly appropriate for the mood of the inter-war period. Another 'standard', Bairstow's 'Blessed city, heavenly Salem', also just pre-dated the outbreak of the war. As in all generations, there were plenty of 'jobbing' composers among cathedral musicians, producing modest works, which publishers were still happy to issue, but most of them were quickly given a decent burial, although canticle settings by composers such as Herbert Brewer and George Dyson quickly found general take-up, as did Harold Darke's Communion Service in F. Except for their fleeting involvement with Westminster Cathedral choir in Terry's time, most of the leading composers like Vaughan Williams and Holst wrote mainly 'occasional' works for the church, rather than contributing to the regular repertoire. Changes in cathedral repertoire focussed not so much on the introduction of contemporary works as on the revival of earlier music. This included not only the Tudor/Jacobean works now being made available through the work of Edmund Fellowes and others, but Renaissance continental music, and more Bach as well, still mostly in English translation, though Latin was beginning to be heard in some cathedrals.[68] In part this reflected the growth of a generation of organists who were increasingly university-educated, with a wider musical outlook than many brought up under the old articled pupil system. The shift, however, was a gradual one and by no means uniform throughout the country. Among older organists, George Bennett at Lincoln from 1895 to 1930 was early in modestly promoting Tudor music in place of Victorian repertoire.[69] And there was no discrimination in singing style between music of different eras: as recordings testify, the soundworld of Parry and Elgar was never far away. Compared with today, there was a distinct limit on the amount of new repertoire that most choirs could absorb. The sight-reading ability of many lay clerks could be quite poor, and with a cathedral typically having just six of them, learning new works necessarily proceeded at the pace of the least competent – added to which, most establishments had no more than one full rehearsal with the men each week. The simple necessity of filling up the service lists also meant the retention in the repertoire of many works past their sell-by date.

Cathedrals in the World Wars

The outbreak of the First World War saw little change in the daily round of cathedral life, especially when the popular expectation was that 'it will be all over by Christmas'. Comparatively few lay clerks were of military service age, and where they did volunteer to enlist, deputies were generally not hard to find. Difficulties did increase as the war continued, when conscription was introduced in 1916 covering men up to 41. At St Paul's, for example, the number of boys'-only services was increased in 1916,[70] and some curtailment of choral services took place, ostensibly as a temporary measure, but in places a foretaste of future developments. Ripon's organist, Charles Moody, a renowned trainer of boys, kept the services going by bringing back some retired lay clerks, employing boys with changing voices as altos and persuading musical clergy to sing.[71] Westminster Cathedral was unusual in having five of its six men join up,[72] but this was probably a reflection of them being a more youthful group in a new establishment. Of course, personal loss of family and friends would have been felt throughout the cathedral community, and the cathedrals themselves drew large crowds for special services of prayer and commemoration. At the universities, those choirs including choral scholars would have seen most of them disappear into the forces, but, depleted or not, the choral foundations survived the war fundamentally unchanged.

Things were very different in September 1939 at the start of the Second World War. The immediate perceived threat of air attack, especially on the south-east of the country, led to the large-scale evacuation of children from London. The St Paul's boys were sent to Cornwall on the day war broke out and the school was to remain there for the duration. They maintained their own identity within Truro Cathedral School, usually singing in the cathedral separately from the Truro choir. The occasional return to London was made, and those with homes in or near London sometimes sang back at St Paul's during the holidays, especially at Christmas and Easter. Some recruitment of new choristers continued,[73] though there were only 17 (out of an establishment of 38) when a final return was made in 1945,[74] very few of whom would have been in the choir in 1939, even though boys normally stayed singing until 14½.[75] Meanwhile at St Paul's itself, the choirmen, depleted by call-ups and with the organist, John Dykes Bower, himself enrolled in the RAF, maintained a reduced number of services, held mostly down in the crypt, with much use of plainsong.[76] In addition to the occasional appearance of the St Paul's boys, those of St Mary's Choir School, Reigate also sang about once a month.[77]

Despite all the difficulties, at least the St Paul's choir managed a continuity of existence, which was to ease its post-war recovery. Less fortunate was Westminster Abbey, which, after an initial evacuation of its boys to Christ's Hospital, Horsham, disbanded them entirely in 1940, some boys transferring to the choirs of King's, Magdalen and New College.[78] Although fear was expressed that this might prove permanent, the choir school was re-established, though not until 1947. During the war, apart from the men, temporary local boys were recruited in 1943 to provide some singing on Sundays and special occasions.[79] Westminster Cathedral's choir school was closed in 1939, and not reopened until 1946.[80] The Chapel Royal choir ceased operation, to be replaced by adult volunteers until its restoration near the end of the war.[81] At the Temple Church, the boys, educated at the City of London School, went with the school to Marlborough, but continued to sing during the holidays until the destruction of the church in an air raid in May 1941. It would be 1955 before the choir was reborn in the rebuilt church, still with George Thalben-Ball as organist.[82] Central London churches virtually all lost their boys, although the London Choir School, evacuated to Kent, remarkably continued to supply a few, including the Savoy Chapel, throughout the war.[83] Canterbury too, especially vulnerable to air raids, evacuated its boarding choristers to Cornwall until January 1945, though local dayboys kept some singing going in the cathedral. Rochester and Portsmouth also reportedly lost their boys,[84] but elsewhere full-voice choirs continued, even if in a depleted state and with a reduced number of services. At King's, Cambridge, Boris Ord's organ scholar, David Willcocks, was called up in 1940 and the following year Ord himself enlisted in the RAF, in which he had fought during the First World War. Harold Darke (organist of St Michael's, Cornhill since 1916) was called upon to deputize for him. Likewise, at St John's, Herbert Howells substituted for the enlisted Robin Orr, while in Oxford William McKie left Magdalen for the RAF. A reduced number of lay clerks at Oxford was shared between New College, Magdalen and Christ Church by staggering the times of Evensong.[85]

Although several cathedrals, including St Paul's, were subject to damage from air raids, only Coventry in November 1940 suffered complete destruction, and its choir had retained its parish church character since the elevation of St Michael's Church to cathedral status in 1918. The general mood among cathedral organists, however, was pessimistic, fearing that wartime economies would be made permanent, with the future of choir schools being particularly threatened.[86] Little could they have imagined that the true 'golden age' for the performance of cathedral music lay in the future.

Choirs in Parish Churches

The immediate pre-First World War era witnessed the 'traditional' parish church choir at its greatest numerical strength. By then, a chancel choir of boys and men was seen as standard in churches of virtually every degree of churchmanship in both towns and villages, even if, in practice, women (and to a lesser extent girls) often played a more significant role than many would care to have admitted. The arrival of the war was to bring more disruption to parish choirs than to cathedrals; not only did organists and choirmen enlist (or were conscripted), but boys, too, would find themselves dragooned into helping with war work of one sort or another, which they may well have found more rewarding than choir activity. In addition to which, the newly created scout movement was rapidly proving a rival attraction. As in other spheres, women took over some of the roles vacated by the male sex. Parish choirs did successfully struggle on, but in the post-war world many would never regain their former prominence. But if pre-war choirs were strong in numbers, concern had already been expressed at the quality of the music they sang, and the standards exhibited. Back in 1906, a small group of establishment figures in the musical world formed the Church Music Society to address these issues. Although the cathedrals were not ignored, their main focus came to be on parish music. Over the following decades a series of booklets was produced, offering advice on matters including the choice of music, including hymns, and psalm singing to both Anglican and Gregorian chant. In particular, a distinction was drawn between what was suitable for parish churches as opposed to cathedrals, and criticism was made of parish church choirs whose offerings were a poor imitation of cathedral practice.[87] It was a sentiment which would find increasing support in the inter-war period. The necessity for some degree of reform in worship practices came to the fore, exemplified in the 1928 proposed revision of the Book of Common Prayer, which, although Parliament ultimately refused to grant it legal sanction, nevertheless found widespread unofficial adoption, at least in part. There was a general desire for shorter services – something emphasized by the experience of army chaplains during the war.[88] The typical Victorian broad church Sunday morning pattern of Matins plus communion (full or otherwise), with or without the Litany, was no longer in favour. In its place, the period saw the emergence of a

'Parish Communion', usually starting before 10 a.m. and wholly congregational in character, with the music consisting of hymns and (if sung) Marbeck or some similar setting, such as Martin Shaw's *Anglican Folk Mass* (published in 1918). Matins, with choir, would then become a later morning service. Although this splitting of the main morning congregations initially probably resulted in decent-sized numbers for both services – there were clearly strong advocates for each – in time 'Parish Communion' proved the greater attraction, especially after the Second World War. This would naturally have implications for the choir, which will be considered in due course. The more evangelical parishes, however, with their emphasis on the biblical authority and preaching, continued with Matins as their most suitable Sunday morning vehicle, while a choral Eucharist had long been the focus of Anglo-Catholics, who now often openly termed it 'Mass'.

There was no precipitative decline in parish choir activity in the interwar years, despite a lessening sense of obligation to attend church by the middle classes – the working classes had, by and large, never been regular attendees.[89] Sunday was still a 'day of rest', with cinemas and other places of entertainment closed; as yet, comparatively few people owned cars, so weekend excursions were exceptional. The all-male choir continued to be considered the norm, however modified by local circumstances. Urban churches with a musical reputation could still expect boys to attend up to three practices a week – something that worked against the involvement of the more academic boy. Recruitment was certainly more difficult than earlier, but many choirstalls remained well filled, even if not always with a choirmaster's ideal material.

There was one part of the country, however, which encountered significant problems, aggravated by changing demography, which led one choirmaster to write in 1925 that 'in the west end of London and in the City, it is frequently a real difficulty to obtain boys for church choirs at all'.[90] It was to partly meet this need – at least for the wealthier churches – that the London Choir School arose in 1920. Initially created in order to provide a treble line for the King's Chapel of the Savoy (which had closed its own school in 1919), it was a day and boarding school in South London, catering, in theory at least, for the 'sons of gentlemen'.[91] Under its proprietor, Carlton Borrow, it prospered with up to 125 boys, and would supply complete treble lines of a dozen boys to several churches such as St Peter's, Eaton Square, St Luke's, Chelsea, All Souls, Langham Place, and Holy Trinity, Brompton. In return, the churches defrayed the costs of the boys' tuition. The boys were also much in demand for weekday fashionable weddings, funerals and memorial services at other churches, from which they often derived generous tips. Their reputation grew rapidly and they contributed additional voices for the St Paul's annual oratorio services, as well as providing the choir for the British Legion's Festival of Remembrance in the Royal Albert Hall, and being engaged for film work. Most extraordinary, however, was a series of lengthy tours to Canada and the United States, undertaken by a select dozen boys from 1930 onwards, usually under the title 'The English Boy Choristers'. Sometimes extending to six or eight months, there was certainly an element of commercial exploitation involved, and the mixed sacred and secular programmes were of a predictably sentimental nature. Although the boys' general education was supposedly catered for during these tours, it would appear that the 'school of life' played a major part in it. The leading soloist from 1930 was a Welsh boy, Iwan Davies, who already had a national reputation when he joined the school at the late age of fourteen, and whose voice would last until he was seventeen. In his own way, he was as well-known as Ernest Lough. As already noted, although the school was evacuated to Kent at the outbreak of the Second World War, boys continued to travel into London to sing on Sundays. Post-war, however, a scandal involving a subsequent proprietor in the 1950s ultimately sealed its fate, and it finally closed in 1958, with St Peter's, Eaton Square being the last church to use its services.

During the Second World War, church choirs outside Central London, endeavoured to maintain activity as best they could. Although there was less mass enlistment into the armed services than in the First World War, the demands of war-work at home, such as air-raid wardens, volunteer firemen, or the Home Guard, could all contribute to lack of personnel in the choir stalls. Naturally it was the absence of an organist/choirmaster which was most problematic, for though suitable keyboard players might not be too difficult to find – even if they used manuals only – competent choir trainers were much rarer. One unexpected oasis of enterprise during the war, however, was to be found at St Matthew's, Northampton. This unassuming suburban Anglo-Catholic church, dedicated in 1893, had as its vicar from 1937 Walter Hussey, who saw it his life's mission to bring contemporary arts into the Church of England by means of commissions to composers, artists and poets, with funds partly provided by himself.[92] The first result, at a festival to celebrate the church's fiftieth jubilee in 1943, was that minor masterpiece, Britten's 'Rejoice in the Lamb', as well as Henry Moore's sculpture of 'Madonna and Christ'. In the years following, in addition to poetry and sculpture, further musical commissions included works from Edmund Rubbra, Lennox Berkeley, Gerald Finzi ('Lo, the full final sacrifice') and others. In 1955 Hussey left Northampton to become Dean of Chichester and continued his endeavours there, with Bernstein's *Chichester Psalms* and Walton's Chichester Service chief among the many musical offerings, while John Piper, Graham Sutherland, and Marc Chagall were just the most prominent figures whose contributions adorned the cathedral in other ways.

Sydney Nicholson and the School of English Church Music

Although the Church Music Society had been attempting to stimulate improvements through its modest publications since the early years of the century, it was to be its chairman who would take decisive steps in the 1920s to give real practical impetus to the cause. At first sight, Sydney Nicholson appeared to be an improbable champion of parish church musicians.[93] One of the newer breed of university-educated organists, Oxford had led to appointments at Carlisle and Manchester cathedrals, before he took over at Westminster Abbey in 1919. As early as 1924 he had organized a section of the Westminster Abbey Special Choir to demonstrate a simple sung Evensong in various London churches. He considered, however, that the key to improvement lay in the training of choir directors, and in 1927, with the blessing of the Church Music Society and the support of Cosmo Lang, Archbishop of Canterbury, he established the School of English Church Music (SECM), relinquishing his Abbey post the following year. Thanks to family money, he bought, largely with his own resources, a suitable place at Chislehurst as headquarters for the School, together with its associated College of St Nicolas to cater for full-time students. It opened in 1929 and was set up rather like an Oxbridge college. It included a chapel with a resident boys' choir, the initial intake of which came in part from the last-surviving private aristocratic chapel, that of the 7th Duke of Newcastle-under-Lyne at Clumber Park, which had closed on the death of the duke in 1928. Just four students (three men and one woman) constituted the first intake, and, in fact, there were never more than a handful at any one time. To Nicholson's disappointment, it was never destined to become a major training ground for church musicians as he envisaged, and the College proved a continual monetary drain, relying on Nicholson's own financial support, though even this was not limitless. Visiting tutors, including distinguished names, provided instruction not only in organ and choir matters, but also in church history and liturgy. Twice daily services of a varying nature were held in the chapel, with students and staff providing the lower parts, while on Sunday mornings the boys went to sing at the Church of the Holy Sepulchre in London, a church with which the SECM maintained a close relationship.

Alongside the College, the SECM established the idea of having 'affiliated' choirs, and it is in its work of providing resources, courses, and

Figure 9 Choir of Child Okeford, Dorset in 1930. It was the first choir to affiliate to the School of English Church Music. The three ladies provided the alto part; *English Church Music*, vol. 1, no. 1 (1931).

encouragement to parish choirs that the institution would find its real purpose. These activities would only develop gradually during the 1930s – indeed, the modest annual affiliation fee was seen initially mainly as a means of supporting the residential College. Nicholson was very much a traditionalist, and a prime objective was to promote his 'ideal' of all-male choirs in both village and town churches. Despite the growing presence of female singers in many places – especially in the villages – he viewed them very much as inferior options, to be resorted to only when a supply of boys proved impossible to find. He did, however, go so far as to consider that women could usefully function on the alto line where good male specimens were not available.[94] Apart from the appeal to 'tradition' (however suspect), outwardly he justified his position on the grounds that boys were the future occupants of the rear choir stalls, and that they had 'exactly that impersonal and unemotional quality which is so valuable in music designed to voice the sentiments of a general congregation'.[95] Mixing women and boys was unsatisfactory, for the women would dominate, leaving the boys feeling they had little to contribute. Girls scarcely entered into Nicholson's argument, but this was an age when it was generally felt that boys and girls should not mix in groups – witness the separate entrances and playgrounds for each in most schools. More personally, Nicholson evidently just enjoyed the sound of boys' voices and found himself most comfortable dealing with them. In a way he may be viewed as the Robert Baden-Powell of the choral world. However out-of-step his attitude might seem in the twenty-first century, it was widely shared by many of his generation.

Nicholson's principal concerns were to encourage choirs to sing music appropriate to their abilities, and to improve psalm singing by adopting 'speech rhythm' methods. Particular attention was also directed at matters like processing and choir decorum, as being conducive to general efficiency. Modern technology was quickly embraced in the form of demonstration records made by the College choir, focussing especially on the psalms.[96] Nicholson himself edited *The Parish Psalter*, published in 1928,[97] which, with its simple pointing, rapidly achieved a popularity which had eluded many other recent attempts.

The public profile of the SECM was increased through the holding of large-scale festivals for affiliated choirs, starting with one for a thousand singers at the Royal Albert Hall in 1930, sponsored by no less than the *Daily Mail*.[98] Its success resulted in further festivals at the Crystal Palace, accommodating no fewer than 4,000 singers in 1933 and 1936, while, following the destruction of the Crystal Palace in 1936, a final pre-war festival was held back in the Royal Albert Hall in 1939.[99] Significantly, while women were welcomed at these festivals, boys' voices predominated, and any choir which had both women and boys was expected to include some of the latter. Nicholson was perhaps in his element at such 'broad brush' gatherings and succeeded in securing remarkably coherent sounds from the massed forces – in his cathedral days, he had proved outstanding neither as an organist nor as a practitioner of the finer points of choir training.[100] The festivals also probably helped to spread the introduction of that peculiarly British supplement to hymn-singing, the descant. The addition of a soaring treble line to a unison verse was unknown before the twentieth century, and really developed after Alan Gray, organist of Trinity College, Cambridge, published 133 examples in *A Book of Descants* (1920) and they began to enter hymnals with *Songs of Praise* in 1925. Descants have been variously considered a glorious enhancement or an unwelcome distraction – good examples are difficult to write and rare – and nowadays are principally associated with Christmas hymns, thanks to David Willcocks's unsurpassed examples.

The 1930s also saw the introduction of popular residential courses for boys – making use of the facilities of public schools out of term. But the most significant activity long-term was the introduction of assessment and advisory visits to individual choirs (at their request), carried out by Nicholson himself and various 'commissioners', often the local cathedral organist, which could offer real encouragement to those finding themselves struggling with the many problems that can beset choirs. A number of Anglican churches in the Empire, keen to maintain links with Britain, also became affiliated, and in 1934 Nicholson made a tour of Australia, New Zealand and Canada to establish more personal contact; it was the start of overseas outreach which would develop further in the post-war years.

Nicholson's vision for the SECM was admittedly limited. Despite a growing inter-war emphasis on congregation participation in singing, his interest lay solely in the choirs – and it was the choir which was affiliated, not the church. Although he advocated the idea of congregational practices, little did he realise the impracticality or the reluctance of congregations to engage in them; and he quite misjudged the ability of most organists (especially in rural areas) to cope with the many challenges of training boys in the twentieth century.

Although the College of St Nicolas closed in 1939 at the start of the war, Nicholson kept the SECM alive, occupying temporary offices, first at Tenbury, then at Leamington; he continued to make visits to choirs, and run choirboy courses and local festivals. The number of affiliations actually increased during the war, from 1,500 in 1939 to 2,072 by 1945.[101] From 1942 he even managed to organize Evensongs in Westminster Abbey for several hundred boys, mainly from London suburban choirs, and the same year saw the first 'cathedral course', where a choir sang the daily services for two weeks during the summer at Gloucester Cathedral – the first time an outside choir had filled in on weekdays during a cathedral choir's holiday, something that would become commonplace later in the century.[102]

With the end of the war, the SECM relocated to Canterbury in 1945, when, by royal command, its name changed to the Royal School of Church Music (RSCM) – much to the relief of the non-English parts of the kingdom. The College of St Nicolas reopened, but now without a resident boys' line in its choir – local boys were recruited instead. The number of students remained small, though David Willcocks was one who spent a year there after war service. Nicholson, who had been knighted in 1938, died in 1947, and the next few years were precarious financially – grants from the Hymns Ancient and Modern Trust helped keep the RSCM afloat, but it was not until 1952 that a new full-time director could be appointed, which was to usher in its most fruitful decades.

Choirs in Other Churches

Like Anglican choirs, those of the Nonconformist churches had been at their strongest before the First World War. Ready information of later activity is thin on the ground, especially beyond England and Wales, but when the Nonconformist Choir Union (from 1926 The Free Church Choir Union) resumed its annual festivals at the Crystal Palace in 1924, there was initially a considerable falling-off in numbers from pre-war days, perhaps due to economic factors like the cost of travelling.[103] By 1927, however, they were back to about 4,000 participants.[104] The Nonconformists would be subject to the same general decline in churchgoing as other denominations, though at the first festival in 1945 after the Second World War held in Westminster Central Hall, it managed to muster about 700 voices from 57 choirs.[105] Choral activity certainly remained strongest amongst the Methodists, particularly in areas such as the North, Cornwall and Wales. One Barrow-in-Furness choir in 1917 had a long waiting list for entry,[106] while Fulwood Wesleyan Methodist in Sheffield, whose choir had long been regarded as one of the best in the city, was still paying seven singers in 1946 to supplement its volunteers.[107] The lack of elaborate formal liturgy in Nonconformist churches meant that, apart from leading the hymn singing, the choir's own contribution was chiefly focussed on an anthem, although in some churches chanted canticles, and even psalms, also featured, at least from time to time. As a result, the more musically ambitious choirs were able to explore choral society repertoire and to offer occasional oratorio performances, perhaps drawing in extra assistance from other local churches, and even employing well-known soloists. These could extend beyond the predictable *Messiah* and *The Crucifixion*. In the 1920s the choir of Elland Congregational Church in West Yorkshire performed Handel's *Samson* and *Judas Maccabaeus* as well as Mendelssohn's *St Paul*.[108] Most northern towns of any size could probably still have furnished at least one chapel choir of note in the area and Nonconformist voices continued to play a big role in the large northern choral societies.

If Nonconformist choirs were still very much in business, the choral landscape of the Roman Catholic church can only be described as dismal. The unintended repercussions of Pius X's *Moto Proprio* of 1903, with its advocacy of plainsong and Renaissance (or Renaissance-style) polyphony, were that competent choirs (probably never that many), which had been accustomed to subsisting on a mainly nineteenth-century musical diet, faded away, rather than converting to a very different repertoire. There were probably members of the hierarchy who retained a soft spot for Haydn, Mozart and Gounod, and who were less than assiduous in pursuing the papal agenda,[109] but choral music disappeared from many places, as we have seen in the case of St Anne's, Edge Hill, Liverpool (p. 212). A few willing practitioners of plainsong with organ accompaniment was probably all that could be generally expected at the principal Mass on a Sunday morning. Given that both Anglo-Catholic and Roman Catholic churches were often located in poorer neighbourhoods, it was the former that could 'put on a good show' musically. Apart from the cathedrals, only a few places like the Brompton and Birmingham Oratories or the Jesuits at Farm Street, Mayfair, and the Sacred Heart Church, Wimbledon, had the resources to maintain anything like a strong musical tradition. Indeed, the Oratories did not entirely discard the old repertoire, though the Classical and Romantic Masses were subjected to considerable abridgement, turning them more into *missae breves*, in order not to unduly hold up the action of the Mass.[110] The two Jesuit churches in the inter-war period enjoyed excellent choirs of boys and men under the direction of Fr John Driscoll, and were much admired – Farm Street's accomplishment being all the more remarkable from having to bring the boys together from across London.[111]

The Inter-War Festival Scene

With the outbreak of the First World War, all festival plans were naturally abandoned. For Birmingham, the 1912 festival proved to be its last; declining interest and finances pre-war meant there was no enthusiasm to resurrect it after 1918. But most of the other leading festivals were revived. Predictably the Three Choirs was the first, when it held its meeting at Worcester in 1920, and resumed very much along its traditional lines. One improvement made that year was to engage the London Symphony Orchestra *en bloc*, rather than assembling players individually from that orchestra and elsewhere, as had been the practice.[112] But the question of the adequacy of the local conductors, although acknowledged, remained unresolved, and the concerts continued to be largely conducted by the cathedral organists with varying success, although composers frequently conducted their own works. Percy Hull, organist at Hereford since 1918, was reckoned to be the most competent, known for his lively tempi, especially in the B minor Mass – criticized by some, although they would most probably be considered sedate by comparison with many present-day performances.[113] Herbert Sumsion, at Gloucester from 1928, was also well regarded as a conductor. The post-war years were notable for the frequent presence of Elgar, conducting his own works: here, not only *Gerontius*, but *The Apostles* and *The Kingdom* were frequently heard, and *The Kingdom* was to be the last work Elgar conducted, at Hereford in 1933. The festival continued to be committed to presenting new British music by younger composers, commissioned or otherwise, and premières of works by Vaughan Williams, Howells, George Dyson and countless others regularly featured, while Ethel Smyth came to conduct her Mass in D – just the Kyrie and Gloria in 1925, but the complete work in 1928.[114] A few important modern foreign works were also heard, like

Honegger's *King David* and Kodály's *Psalmus Hungaricus*, both in 1928, the latter conducted by Kodály himself.[115] The conservative audience continued to demand their familiar favourites, but even here change was on the way. *Elijah* was dropped in 1930 and increasingly so in later years. The old problem of far too much music for the very limited rehearsal time, and general overloading of the festival chorus, still endured, with its inevitable lack of first-rate performances and occasional near disasters. But the overall social atmosphere and the array of well-known faces to be encountered ensured both its financial viability and continued attention in the national press.

From the musical point of view, Leeds had long been regarded as the premier festival in the country, based above all on the quality of its choral singing, and its employment of leading soloists and conductors. Yet its post-war revival in 1922 was by no means inevitable. For all the kudos and trade it brought to the city, local support was apparently lukewarm, and fears were expressed that weakness in the finances, already evident in the pre-war years, could now lead to serious losses. The festival chorus had to be recruited from a wider local area than before, since the two leading Leeds choral societies declined to take part officially, though many of their members did so individually.[116] (There may have been good reasons for their reservation, for festival obligations tended to disrupt the societies' regular seasons.) In the event, the 1922 festival proved financially successful, if musically unadventurous, and the chorus, trained by Albert Tysoe, was widely praised.

So, the triennial pattern was resumed, with the 1925 festival featuring the première of Holst's demanding *Choral Symphony*, which the Festival Chorus apparently spent about a year learning.[117] But the highlight of the inter-war festivals was undoubtedly the first performance of Walton's *Belshazzar's Feast* under Malcolm Sargent on 8 October 1931, the one indisputable choral masterpiece to emerge from this period. With its jazzy rhythms, pungent discords and general exuberance, it was as far from the conventional festival work as could be imagined. Understandably the choir found the work a severe challenge, especially rhythmically. There are disputed accounts as to how well it took to the work,[118] but the end of the première on 8 October saw enormous enthusiasm on the part of both audience and choir.[119] Frank Howes's review commented on 'the certainty and power of the singing of a choir which at first mistakenly thought that displaced accents and harmonies were too difficult for it'.[120] One must feel sorry for Eric Fogg, whose substantial cantata *The Seasons* was also premiered in the same concert. For Sargent it was a personal triumph and would lead to lasting engagement with northern choirs. Despite its challenges, *Belshazzar's Feast* was soon being tackled by a number of choral societies throughout the country, reaching both Edinburgh and Belfast in 1933.[121] It even made it to the National Eisteddfod at Neath in 1934, performed, together with Elgar's *The Music Makers*, by a specially convened Eisteddfod Choir – probably aided by the publication of the tonic sol-fa edition published by Oxford University Press the previous year (see p. 137).[122] The remaining two Leeds festivals before the interruption of the Second World War were uneventful by comparison.

Among other festivals, the Norfolk and Norwich resumed its triennial course in 1923, unremarkable for the most part, though it gave the première of Arthur Bliss's *Morning Heroes* in 1930, and that of Vaughan Williams's *Five Tudor Portraits* in 1936 – no festival, however, was held in 1933 for economic reasons.[123] The gargantuan Handel festivals continued at the Crystal Palace until declining attendance brought them to an end in 1926. Oxford saw several intermittent celebrations, involving a wide variety of the city's choral forces, including a Bach festival in 1914, and a commemoration of the 250th anniversary of the births of Bach and Handel in 1935. The last was notable for an exhibition at the Bodleian Library, at which the autograph manuscripts of the St Matthew Passion (from the Berlin State Library) and *Messiah* (from the British Museum Library) were brought together for the first time.

Choral Society Activity in London

Although the First World War certainly saw a diminution of choral activity, increasingly so as the war progressed, it is surprising to see just how much singing continued throughout the country – in part, no doubt, being seen as helping to sustain morale. As might be expected, concerts were frequently given by choirs large and small to raise money for war charities – *Messiah* being an obvious choice, as guaranteeing a large audience. The recently formed London Choral Society did suspend operation from 1916 to 1920,[124] but most prominent societies managed to stay singing, and not just with easy repertoire. The Huddersfield Choral Society tackled the Verdi Requiem for the first time in 1915,[125] while the challenges of *The Dream of Gerontius* no longer deterred choirs judging by the many performances featured, particularly around 1916. At St Anne's, Soho a complete performance of the *Christmas Oratorio*, with orchestra, could be heard in a pair of concerts in the winter of 1915/16.[126] No doubt there were often instruments missing from the orchestras – wind and brass players could be hard to find, even in peacetime – but a clear determination to keep making music is evident.

For the capital's leading choral societies, the years following the war proved an unsettled time. Sir Frederick Bridge gave up the conductorship of the Royal Choral Society in 1922 after 26 years,[127] and for a few seasons a variety of conductors was engaged before Malcolm Sargent took permanent charge in 1928,[128] remaining in post until his death in 1967. With 800 singers, it had rapidly regained its pre-war numbers and was easily the country's largest society. It could certainly produce a sound to fill the Royal Albert Hall, but its somewhat unwieldy nature required the strong hand of Sargent to keep everything under control. It also became the most financially secure, following years when audiences were often poor except for the annual *Messiah* performances and the popular carol concerts held since 1912. It was the creation of staged performances of Samuel Coleridge-Taylor's *Hiawatha* which was keep the society's treasurer happy. First held as a charity event at the Royal Albert Hall in May 1924, it was devised by the pageant producer Thomas Fairbairn, who involved 500 members of the Royal Choral Society, 200 dancers and the Philharmonic Society's orchestra, conducted by Eugene Goossens, in a spectacular extravaganza – a real waterfall was featured – and the chorus (who, of course, already knew the music well) were dressed in home-made costumes as squaws and braves. Such was the success of a week's performances that Fairbairn repeated it in a fortnight's sold-out run the following year, and so it continued, except for 1926 and 1927, until the Second World War.[129] From 1928 Sargent was its regular conductor, revelling in the showmanship which the occasion offered. For the Royal Choral Society, unlike most choirs, it meant it did not have to worry about the financial implications of programme planning, though it was never particularly adventurous in this respect. Its finances would be further enhanced by royalties from gramophone recordings it began to make from 1926 onwards.[130] Fairbairn found the dramatized *Hiawatha* could be exploited elsewhere, and saw it produced in the 1930s in places like Leicester, Pickering and Sheffield,[131] while in 1939 it even made it as far afield as Melbourne, Australia.[132] But it proved very much a phenomenon confined to the inter-war years, when even titled members of the Royal Choral Society could literally let their hair down. After the war, a revival was mounted in the coronation year, 1953, by a specially formed London Coronation Choir, but it was clear that it no longer fitted the times.[133]

The Bach Choir also managed to maintain concerts during the First World War, though some were economical 'private' affairs for friends rather than full-scale public ones. After the war, the ebullient Hugh Allen stood down as conductor in 1921 owing to pressure of other work, and Vaughan Williams took over.[134] It was perhaps a frequent failing on the part of the Bach Choir's committee that, in selecting conductors, they tended to opt for established names instead of seeking the best choral trainer. In Allen they had been fortunate, but Vaughan Williams proved less successful, judging by the respectful rather than enthusiastic reviews of their concerts. He certainly promoted the music of the choir's namesake, performing many of the cantatas and motets in addition to the big works. His approach, however, was decidedly old-fashioned, with, for example, addition of clarinets and trombones to the orchestra, and rejection of such instruments as the oboe d'amore and the high so-called 'Bach trumpet' which the Bach Choir had come to regularly employ.[135] He asserted that a choir of 350 needed a large modern orchestra. At its most extreme, perhaps, was his treatment of the bass solo 'Quoniam' in the B minor Mass, which in 1926 he had sung by all the chorus basses, with the horn solo played by four horns.[136] Vaughan Williams was succeeded in 1928 by Adrian Boult, who, in a brief four-year reign, did help revitalize the choir, but it was with the appointment of Reginald Jacques in 1932 that it acquired what was really needed, a real choral specialist, able to make a long-term commitment to its development. Jacques was to remain until 1960, and 1936 saw the introduction of its annual carol concerts, rivalling those of the Royal Choral Society.[137] These, together with safe programme planning, helped stabilize the choir's financial position, which had hitherto remained precarious.

The other large established London choir, the Alexandra Palace Choral and Orchestral Society was still receiving good reviews in the early 1920s under Alan Gill, but, as age took its toll on him, the choir's fortunes declined until it was taken over by the 25-year-old Charles Proctor in 1931, who gave it renewed life, though it ceased operation at the start of the Second World War.[138] Proctor and the Alexandra name, however, were to re-appear during the war. At least two significant new societies emerged in the inter-war years. In 1919, encouraged by Henry Wood and Thomas Beecham, Charles Kennedy Scott created the Philharmonic Choir, partly in response to a need of the Royal Philharmonic Society ('Royal' since 1912) for a good-quality chorus for some of their concerts. The choir, which came to have 300 carefully selected singers, partly professional (especially tenors),[139] had an association with the Society, though it remained an independent body, also promoting its own concerts. Scott, who in 1904 had already formed the 100-strong Oriana Madrigal Society, was perhaps the nearest thing London had to a Henry Coward. Seeking perfection in detail, he drove himself and his singers hard, with long rehearsals, and having, like Coward, a tendency to talk too much. But the result was the best choral sound to be heard in the capital. It was a choir keen to tackle and able to deal with demanding new works such as Stravinsky's *Symphony of Psalms*, Hindemith's *Mathis der Maler* and Holst's *Hymn of Jesus*, as well as doing full justice to the *Missa Solemnis* and Ninth Symphony of Beethoven.[140] It even sprouted a younger body, the Junior Philharmonic Choir, of some 200–300 girls and young men not considered old enough to join regular choral societies, who were able to tackle works like the B minor Mass.[141] The Philharmonic Choir was disbanded at the outbreak of the Second World War, although some members would form the basis of a new London Philharmonic Choir in 1946.[142] The other notable newcomer was the Goldsmiths Choral Union, which was founded in 1932 in South London at Goldsmiths College by Frederick Haggis. It quickly achieved renown, performing major works at the Royal Albert Hall and elsewhere.[143] Managing to continue through the war, it remains active today, remarkably having had just two conductors up to Brian Wright's retirement in 2022.

With a strength in the 1930s of over a hundred, the Goldsmiths Choral Union was of only moderate size for a major London choir of the period. Although the overall numerical strength of choirs recovered after the First World War – and the creation of new choirs showed a continuing enthusiasm for choral singing – there were persistent laments about the understandable shortage of men. In the 1926/7 season, for example, the Bach Choir had only 75 tenors and basses against 282 sopranos and altos.[144] Balance in the big choirs had always favoured the upper voices, but it was now very evident, though the appetite for some judicious pruning was rarely found. And amongst the men, the lack of tenors was especially felt. What had happened to them all? It is striking that in chorus listings for nineteenth-century festivals, tenors and basses were generally more or less equal in numbers. At the 1784 Handel Commemoration there were 83 tenors and 84 basses;[145] at Birmingham in 1846 there were 60 tenors and 72 basses;[146] Glasgow in 1873 had 93 tenors and 110 basses,[147] while Huddersfield in 1881 had 68 tenors and 62 basses.[148] The 826 members of the Royal Choral Society in 1899 included 174 tenors and 236 basses,[149] while the 1911 Three Choirs at Worcester had 56 tenors and 65 basses.[150] Yet in 1920 William McNaught commented: 'A new "choral problem" seems to have arisen for the bewilderment of choral conductors – the problem of manpower. The evidence of its urgency is visible and audible at every choral concert. It is of course nothing new to see the women vastly outnumbering the men, but the brave little group of tenors that used to battle successfully with superior odds, now dwindle hopelessly out of the combat, and the basses follow closely behind in this reduction of personnel.'[151] While the overall number of men recovers somewhat in the following years, tenors were especially sought after, all the more so after the Second World War, when advertisements like 'immediate vacancies for tenors' were common.[152]

One possible explanation for the decline in tenor numbers lies, at least in part, in the attitude towards the development of adolescent voices around the turn of the century, when the prevailing wisdom began to decree that boys' voices should be rested for some years after they change.[153] Now the majority of untrained men's voices tend to have a natural range of a baritone, and most end up as tenors or basses by developing the upper or lower ends of their range. It is much easier to do this if the changing voice has been kept judiciously 'in practice' during adolescence, especially if the tenor register is to emerge. A man coming to singing for the first time, or after resting his treble voice, will naturally find it easier to deal with bass parts, relaxing down to low notes, rather than discover a potential tenor range. This situation may have become particularly noticeable in the wake of the First World War, when so many young men would not have sung (at any rate chorally) for several years. In the post-war period, attitudes towards resting the voice rather changed – both Arthur Somervell and Sydney Nicholson were advocates of keeping boys singing, and the growing importance of choral singing in public schools was also a factor.[154] But a general decline in the number of boys singing in choirs was also under way, and combined with the effects of another World War, this may have adversely affected the emergence of a healthy number of tenors in the next generation.

For many musicians of the inter-war period, the ideal secular choral sound was produced by a big chorus of several hundred singers, regardless of the music performed. In 1922 the editor of the *Musical Times*, Harvey Grace, who was also an adjudicator at competitive festivals, spoke for many when he declared:

> Bach used a small force not from choice, but necessity. Had the result of his limitations been music suited only for a small choir there would have been one Bach problem the less. But we are hit in the face by the fact that most of his choral music is of a character that can not only carry a large body of tone; it even demands such resources. Nobody suggests that the B minor Mass should be sung by a small choir, yet it is certain that Bach never heard any of it sung by a large one. Are we therefore to attempt it with a handful of picked singers? Although much of the music of the Cantatas is of an intimate character, many of their choruses are on too big a scale for a small choir – *e.g.*, the tremendous opening number of *Ein' feste Burg*. But the most convincing argument is to be found in the Motets. What sized choir sang them under Bach? Just a little group of boys and men. Shou'd we care to hear (say) *Sing ye to the Lord* performed by a choir of thirty? A few exceptional singers to a part might get through it flawlessly, but only a big choir can give us all there is in the music, and (what is even more important) do it without the sense of effort that is always present in a performance by a choir of less than a hundred and fifty to two hundred voices.[155]

Astonishing as that statement may appear to us today, it was shared by leading conductors of the day such as Henry Wood, Sargent and Beecham, as well as Vaughan Williams. And the size of the chorus also served to justify their attitude towards re-orchestrations of Bach and Handel – as it had their Victorian predecessors. His fame resting above all on the Proms, Wood is not immediately thought of as a choral conductor, but he did a considerable amount of such work throughout the country, especially in the first three decades of the century. Indefatigable, and a sought-out singing teacher himself, he was noted for the very detailed instructions he would send to singers in advance of his arrival for a concert. Wood conducted many of the early performances of *The Dream of Gerontius*, including the successful Sheffield one of 1902. He introduced Rachmaninoff's *The Bells* at Liverpool in 1921,[156] and succeeded Henry Coward as conductor of the Sheffield Musical Union in 1933, though a chorus master was also employed.[157] His treatment of Bach and Handel, however, was controversial even at the time, as was his approach to revised orchestration. Although with the St Matthew Passion in 1908 he more or less left the orchestration intact, even employing oboi d'amore, oboi da caccia, and a gamba, he doubled up heavily, and demanded exaggerated dynamics from the chorus, all in the name of expressiveness.[158] Flexibility of tempo was common among conductors, Coward included, but Wood was perhaps its most extreme exponent. At a Birmingham Festival *Messiah* in 1912, his tempi in the Hallelujah Chorus ranged from 46 to 120 crotchet beats per minute, with a critic commentating on the performance, 'When it was over not a few in the hall felt wounded'.[159] Two decades later, a Good Friday performance of the St John Passion in 1934 with the Philharmonic Choir and BBC Orchestra was commended for the excellence of the choral singing, though 'the work is not improved by the addition of trombones and the less reputable instruments of percussion'.[160]

Wood's great rival in these decades was Thomas Beecham – so much so that Wood's wildly inaccurate autobiography, *My Life of Music*, omitted all mention of him.[161] Although his choral engagements were nothing like as numerous as Wood's, since his heart lay more in the opera house and purely orchestral music, Beecham was highly influential, and his performances could be electrifying. Noted as a champion of Delius (which Wood also claimed to be), he had given the first English performance of *A Mass of Life* in 1909.[162] Ethel Smyth, too, benefited from his advocacy, including a performance of her Mass for her 75th birthday in 1934.[163] But Bach he virtually ignored, and many other 'standard' works received only a single performance. In the 1920s he often used the Philharmonic Choir, with whom in 1928 he performed Handel's *Solomon*, completely rescored, with the orchestra including piccolo, trombones, tuba, triangle and cymbals.[164] Harvey Grace, commenting on the choir noted:

> The chorus – the Philharmonic Choir – rose well to Sir Thomas's excited demands. The delicate singing of 'Let no rash intruder' was, for many of us, the best thing of the evening. The grandly expressive 'Draw the tear' was perhaps the next best. No choir in the world, however, could have done all that Sir Thomas asked in some of the quick choruses, for the practical reason that there is a speed limit beyond which rapid eight-part florid choral writing simply cannot 'come off', and the limit was passed in several numbers. Still, there was no mistaking Beecham's extraordinary power of compelling his forces to pull out that little extra bit beyond their normal, which makes a performance effervesce.[165]

Messiah was to be subject to similar treatment. Unlike Wood, Beecham was notorious for his lax attitude to rehearsal, though he marked up the parts carefully. He expected performers to know the notes, and it was his sheer personal magnetism which could produce extraordinary results. As a review of a *Messiah* with the Philharmonic Society in 1932 stated, the choir 'caught fire from the conductor, and its performance was sheer virtuosity'.[166] Judging by the recording Beecham made in 1927 with the smallish BBC Choir, 'virtuosic' might well have described this too.[167] His speeds cover both extremes – very slow in 'Behold the Lamb of God' and many solos like 'Come unto him', staid in 'And the glory of the Lord', but quite frantic in 'For unto us', 'He trusted in God', and 'Let us break their bonds asunder' – almost as if Sir Thomas was mischievously challenging his singers to keep up with him. All this was combined with dramatic rallentandi at the end of choruses. The orchestration on the recording, however, is quite restrained – more or less the 'Mozart' version – though this may have been due to the restrictions of the recording process, which can also have limited the size of the choir. Beecham was to record *Messiah* twice more. In 1947 he experimented with using the Luton Choral Society together with a smaller professional choir, allotting the latter the sections with florid runs, though his fast speeds are nothing like as extreme as in 1927.[168] We are, however, back to 'grand', which is even more evident in his famous last recording made in 1959 at the age of 80 with the Royal Philharmonic Orchestra and Chorus, and using an orchestration he had commissioned from Eugene Goossens.[169] Still with some of his earlier mannerisms, it nevertheless illustrates just how exhilarating his music-making could be. Here the Hallelujah Chorus comes complete with piccolo, trombones, and cymbal clashes – magnificent in its Beechamesque way!

Beecham's younger rival was Malcolm Sargent, himself a protégé of Henry Wood. Like Wood, he took on an enormous amount of conducting of all sorts throughout the country in the 1920s, and his exceptional rapport with choirs first brought him the conductorship of the Bradford Festival Choral Society in 1925 – a post he retained until 1951. He was thus the ideal person to take over the Royal Choral Society in 1928, and his success with the première of *Belshazzar's Feast* at Leeds in 1931 led to him being the obvious successor to Henry Coward when the latter finally resigned as conductor of the Huddersfield Choral Society in 1932 at the age of 81. It was a post Sargent would retain until his death in 1967, and his work with it will be considered later. He also took on the Liverpool Welsh Choral Union from 1940; nor did he neglect Wales itself, for he regularly conducted the Three Valleys Festival at Mountain Ash from 1930, with up to a thousand singers drawn from choirs in the Rhondda Valley.[170] His immaculate appearance and suave manner were all part of his showmanship, though it did nothing for his relationship with orchestral players, whom he had misguidedly slighted in 1936,[171] and his best work was done in the early decades rather than after the Second World War. The results could be exciting, as William McNaught commented on the Royal Choral Society in 1931: 'Persuading and exhorting, he makes the enormous choir sing as no one in the old days ever thought it could.'[172] Yet it was felt that he often failed to get to the heart of the music – his performances of the B minor Mass were often criticized for their incessant drive.[173] But in view of his ability to secure unanimity from a body like the Royal Choral Society, even at speed, and to produce sheer beauty of tone, it is understandable that Beecham should declare that 'he is the greatest choirmaster we have ever produced. ... He makes the buggers sing like blazes!'[174] Although he embraced the modern orchestra in Bach and Handel, it was on a less extravagant scale than Wood or Beecham, as demonstrated in his *Messiah*, which he recorded complete no fewer than four times between 1946 and 1964. Sargent's tempi in the faster numbers, as reflected in these recordings, seem quite slow to us today, so used have we become to fleet-footed performances with small forces, while the slow arias and choruses now seem interminably drawn out. But the fact that so little criticism of these speeds appears in contemporary reports suggests that they were then regarded as normal; it was an age which was content to let sacred music take its time.

Not everyone in these years, however, was in favour of over-inflating baroque music. In 1926, Hubert Foss, the first head of Oxford University Press's new music department, established the Bach Cantata Club and invited Charles Kennedy Scott to direct it.[175] Scott, already conducting the Oriana Madrigal Society and the Philharmonic Choir, created a select choir of about 40 voices. He explored not only the cantatas, but, for example, performed the St Matthew Passion in St Margaret's Church, Westminster, in 1930 with 37 singers (plus the St Margaret's choirboys for the ripieno part) and 26 in the orchestra. It was much admired for its clarity and for 'giving Londoners the chance of hearing Bach's choral work under ideal conditions and on the scale planned by the composer'.[176] Only his very quiet treatment of the chorales was questioned. The Club's performance of the B minor Mass at the same venue in 1931 was equally successful, with tempi 'naturally (and rightly) a little quicker than those usually adopted'.[177] But Scott was not a lone pioneer. Up in Newcastle upon Tyne, the Bach enthusiast W. Gillies Whittaker had already formed the Newcastle Bach Choir of 40 voices back in 1915 to perform the cantatas and all the major works with similarly small forces. Moving to Glasgow in 1930 as Professor of Music at the university and Principal of the Scottish Academy of Music, he continued his work by creating a Bach Cantata Choir there, and by 1936 had done all the cantatas.[178] In London, the 36-strong Harold Brooke Choir, formed about 1925, although not specializing in baroque music, also performed Bach cantatas as well as Handel's *Semele* and *Acis and Galatea* with the original orchestration in its short five-year existence.[179] Interestingly, while by the 1920s many choirs were becoming relatively comfortable with Bach's vocal writing, soloists employed for their concerts often came in for criticism for their lack of understanding of the style, something that would only really change after the Second World War. As a counterblast to the large 'madrigal choirs', the six voices of the English Singers, formed as a professional group in 1920, were early users of Fellowes's madrigal editions, singing at times seated round a table.[180] With a repertoire which also included folk songs and sacred music, they were in many ways the precursors of the King's Singers and other modern professional vocal ensembles.

Outside the Capital

The fame of the northern choirs, especially those of Yorkshire, was set to continue in the inter-war years, even though it was felt in the 1920s that there had been some falling-off in quality, and particularly in sight-reading ability.[181] Impressive choirs were certainly brought together for festivals, as the reviews from Leeds and Sheffield testified, but individual societies suffered setbacks, and many smaller ones folded or amalgamated. The financial downturns of the period, combined with increasing competition for leisure time from the cinema and radio affected both choir recruitment and audience size, and festivals themselves could have a negative effect on the finances of local choral societies as competitors for audiences' money.[182]

Even before the war, societies were finding it difficult to fill a hall for anything other than *Messiah*. And amongst the musically inclined, there was a steady increase in interest in orchestral concerts, helped by a growth in professional orchestras nation-wide.[183]

Henry Coward was still in charge of the big Huddersfield, Leeds, and Sheffield choirs, finally relinquishing his baton between 1929 and 1933, by which time he was 82. The later years had seen less in the way of the exaggerated choral effects (and vagaries of tempo) that sometimes characterized his pre-war activity, to the advantage of the music, critics felt, and there was probably less drive in his performances. At any rate, when Sargent took over at Huddersfield in 1932, the choir was surprised by the brisker speeds he took in the B minor Mass.[184] Huddersfield was to be the big gainer of the era, thanks to Sargent's presence. New younger voices were attracted to the choir – many older ones had departed with Coward[185] – and Sargent's charisma was to produce good audiences and lucrative recording contracts, so that the society never suffered the financial problems that beset many. But on the artistic side, it was not exactly adventurous, though it did commission Vaughan Williams's *Dona nobis pacem* to celebrate its centenary in 1936. The renowned quality of the choir's sound was by no means all down to Sargent; Herbert Bardgett, the newly appointed chorus master, did much of the week-by-week work – and indeed often had to conduct concerts in the early years, owing to Sargent's treatment for tuberculosis. Bardgett, already conductor of the Leeds New Choral Society, was, like Coward, to take on many choirs throughout the region and would remain with the Huddersfield for thirty years.[186] He was universally regarded as one of the top choral trainers of his generation. Regardless of other notable choirs of the area, including the Bradford Festival Choral Society, also under Sargent's wing, for the public at large, northern choralism came to mean one thing, the Huddersfield Choral Society. The biggest loser of the 1930s was Sheffield, for the one-time preeminent Musical Union failed to rejuvenate after Coward's retirement in 1933, despite Henry Wood taking over as conductor. Falling numbers resulted in its amalgamation with the recently created Sheffield Philharmonic Society in 1938.[187] With the last Sheffield Festival being held in 1933, the city's choral reputation faded.

Activity in London and the North, however, should not lead us to ignore noteworthy centres elsewhere. Among many deserving of mention may be singled out three with mid-nineteenth century origins: the Nottingham Harmonic Society (where Bardgett was conductor from 1937 to 1960),[188] the 400-strong Leicester Philharmonic Society (conducted by Wood from 1921 to 1934),[189] and the Luton Choral Society, for a time Beecham and Boult's recording choir of choice in the late 1940s and early 1950s.[190] Over in the

West Country, Bristol Choral Society lacked nothing in numbers, with its annual *Messiah* in 1911 fielding a choir and orchestra of 550.[191] Oxford and Cambridge continued to introduce its academic youth to the choral repertoire via the Oxford Bach Choir and the Cambridge University Musical Society – both bodies, incidentally, giving performances of *Messiah* in the 1930s with the original orchestration and harpsichord continuo (Cambridge under Cyril Rootham in 1932, the Oxford under Hugh Allen in 1935).[192]

That there was generally felt to be a difference between northern and southern approaches to choral singing, and not in the latter's favour, was expressed by William McNaught in 1920, when he declared: 'A weekly meeting of an hour-and-a-half or two hours for a "run through," with a seventy-five per cent. attendance, is a poor approach to the task, but in southern regions it is frequently considered as fulfilling the whole duty of a choral society. In Lancashire and Yorkshire we used to hear of choirs rehearsing daily for weeks in preparation, not for a competition but for a concert.'[193] A dart aimed at genteel southerners, including no doubt some well-known choirs, though certainly not those under Kennedy Scott's baton.

If many London choral societies appeared to be largely middle-class in constitution, that is not the whole story, for, from the early twentieth century, determined efforts were made to promote singing as a leisure activity among the working classes, many of whom could have already gained elementary, if not particularly artistic, ability through singing lessons at school. In particular, the London County Council (LCC) Evening Continuation Classes included 'Choral Unions', of which there were seven by 1913.[194] Besides singing for their own pleasure, they gave occasional concerts. Most overtly political was the London Labour Choral Union, led from 1924 to 1929 by Rutland Boughton, though its popularity soon faded before the attractions of the cinema and football.[195] In South London, Morley College had been opened in 1889 to promote adult working-class education; Gustav Holst headed its Music Department from 1907 to 1924, and the enthusiasm he generated with the choir and orchestra resulted in performances that attracted wide attention, and which were notable for their revival of Purcell's dramatic works. A later director was Michael Tippett, who from 1940 to 1951 again explored repertoire, old and new, far beyond the norm. This included not only the first London performance of *A Child of Our Time*, but, most significantly, in 1946, the first modern revival of the Monteverdi *Vespers*, in Hans Redlich's edition.[196]

The competitive music festival was still very much an attraction for choirs up to the Second World War. In 1925 there were no fewer than 288 choirs at the Glasgow Festival,[197] and concert giving was apt to come to a halt once a competition was approaching. One advocate that same year declared: 'It is to such contests that we must look for the preservation and development of chorus-singing in the future, for during the last ten years there has been a marked falling off in the number and quality of the non-competitive choral society.'[198] The frequent downside, of course, was the concentration on a narrow range of repertoire by choirs who chose to let the competitive ethos dominate. The North, especially, took delight in such festivals, with Blackpool and Morecombe hosting large-scale events in the inter-war years, whose choral sections included classes for both church and secular choirs.

But festivals on a lesser scale could be found in every corner of the country. One such event in particular found an exceptionally happy blend of competitive and non-competitive elements, the Leith Hill Musical Festival. Founded in 1905 to bring village choirs in the Dorking area of Surrey together, it had Vaughan Williams, a local resident, as its conductor from the outset.[199] The involvement of all social classes in a village was evident here – so close to Vaughan Williams's egalitarian heart. The Abinger Choral Society, for example, in 1925, included the rector, a schoolmistress, the postmistress, a builder, a plumber, a wheelwright, a milkman and two gardeners.[200] It closely followed the principles established by Mary Wakefield, when she developed her festivals in Kendal in the 1880s, in which the competing choirs also joined in singing together. Leith Hill made the latter activity as important as the competitive one, with the choirs spending months learning choral works to perform in concerts with well-known soloists and increasingly professional orchestras, all of whom came to find a welcoming atmosphere to which they were very content to return regularly. From 1922 local town choirs were also permitted to join, and by the 1930s the choirs were even able to tackle works like *The Dream of Gerontius*. Alongside the festival itself, Vaughan Williams had the choirs learn the St Matthew Passion. First performed in 1931 in his own inimitable and idiosyncratic style, it eventually became an annual event, and, having retired as festival conductor in 1953, Vaughan Williams continued to direct the work until the year of his death in 1958.[201]

School Music

The standard of singing in the nation's elementary schools was probably at its best in the first decades of the twentieth century. Although 'payment by results' had disappeared, singing was still one of the skills assessed by school inspectors, with tonic sol-fa easily the dominant method of tuition. As might be expected, the North could dramatically demonstrate what could be achieved and the dedication involved. In May 1926, for example, the 13th Annual Festival of Massed Singing was held in St George's Hall, Liverpool, organized by the local Committee of the Teachers' Association. Two sets of preliminary sectional rehearsals, involving thirty-six schools, had been held in eight centres in the previous November, all personally directed by the festival's conductor. Out of more than 3,000 attendees, 700 were selected to appear at the final event, when the repertoire included music by Handel, Elgar, Holst, Warlock and others, all sung from memory. As a reviewer noted, the singers 'had received a directional sense for the future, and one envisaged them as skilled and enthusiastic members of the choral and operatic societies of to-morrow'.[202] But there is audible proof of what children could achieve at this time in the famous recording made in 1929 of the Manchester Children's Choir singing Purcell's 'Nymphs and shepherds' and a duet from Humperdinck's *Hansel and Gretel* with the Hallé Orchestra, conducted by Sir Hamilton Harty.[203] The choir of 250 voices (60 boys and 190 girls) was formed in 1925 by Gertrude Riall, assistant music advisor to the Manchester Education Authority, and all were from local elementary schools. The freshness and vitality of the sound, their agility and the ease with which they soar up to high G (not to mention the final top B of the Humperdinck) remain a complete delight. What a contrast to the attempts at massed school singing encountered at the end of the century! Yet the North was not alone in demonstrating its youthful talent, and that experienced adjudicator and editor of the *Musical Times*, Harvey Grace, in 1925 was of the opinion that the best school singing, elementary and secondary, was to be found in London, Bedford and Kent.[204]

Yet this proved to be something of a false dawn, for the advocates of tonic sol-fa had not completely won the educational battle, despite its proven success. Its chief opponent in the 1920s was the composer, Arthur Somervell, who was the Board of Education's Chief Inspector of Music, and in 1928 he used his position to abolish its teaching in schools. The result was a rapid decline in the standard of sight-singing, which Harvey Grace (himself a convert to sol-fa after initial scepticism) lamented in 1943, noting that 'as far as a very large part – perhaps the greater part – of the country is concerned, two generations of children have left school musically illiterate'.[205] In a letter to the editor, Marmaduke Conway, organist of Ely Cathedral, remarked that 'the lack of sight-reading ability makes it all but impossible to keep our local choral society going … Our practices during last season have consisted of 75 per cent learning by ear and repetition, and 25 per cent instruction in sight-reading and rudiments'.[206] In the event, future choralists would emerge from rather different patterns of music education.

In the public school world, music had begun to find a respected niche, even if sport and the cadet corps still dominated the ethos in many places.

There had been early pioneering efforts from the 1850s onwards, including the appointments of Joseph Barnby at Eton,[207] Paul David (son of Ferdinand David, Mendelssohn's friend and leader of the Gewandhaus Orchestra in Leipzig) at Uppingham, W.S. Bambridge at Marlborough, and John Farmer at Harrow,[208] while at Winchester a pupil initiated a Glee Club in 1864.[209] A choral society was found in many schools by the final decades of the century, giving pupils at least a taste of the most popular oratorios,[210] while full-time musicians were generally starting to appear on the staff, and in 1903 they formed their own professional association, the Union of Directors of Music in Secondary Schools – later the Music Masters' Association – with Paul David an early president. More ambitious music in the school chapel began to feature alongside increasingly adventurous choral society offerings, and the *Musical Times* had a regular report on 'Music in the Public Schools' from 1923. Perhaps exceptional was Loretto School at Musselburgh near Edinburgh, which in 1880 was offering a scholarship of 90 guineas a year 'open to boys with a good treble voice, able to take solo and verse parts in oratorio and anthem music and preferentially the sons of graduates in need of such assistance'.[211]

The outstanding example came from Oundle. In 1921 under Clement Spurling, its choral society put on a performance of *Messiah*, which also made use of the rest of the school as a unison choir to join in selected passages, such as 'Wonderful, Counsellor' in 'For unto us'. This was followed up more spectacularly the following year, when most of the B minor Mass was performed in a similar manner, with the orchestra boosted with a dozen players from the London Symphony Orchestra and well-known soloists – helped by the soprano's son being a pupil.[212] Such performances became an annual tradition, with further B minor Masses, but also Bach cantatas, the *Christmas Oratorio*, and Handel's *Saul*. Bradfield followed suit with a B minor Mass of its own in 1930,[213] while in 1938 we find schools tackling works like the Mozart and Verdi Requiems, and *Hiawatha's Wedding Feast*. An interesting joint enterprise took place back in 1927, when Bradfield, Radley and Wellington combined to sing the Brahms *German Requiem* in the Sheldonian Theatre at Oxford.[214] The gradual trend of cathedrals to recruit middle-class choristers, many of whom would move on to public schools, would also prove a boon to their choral societies. Yet it would be true to say that in 1930, thanks to tonic sol-fa, the average state school pupil would have outshone their public school counterpart in sight-singing.

Choral Society Repertoire

The most conspicuous development of the repertoire in this period was the rapidly increasing popularity of Bach. One sign was the number of new 'Bach Choirs' which sprang into life, including Newcastle (1915), Bognor (1928), Leicester (1930) and Glasgow (1930). Like their older London and Oxford namesakes, they sang other music as well, though Bach remained a constant focus of their activity. But works like the B minor Mass and the St Matthew Passion were now being tackled by choirs everywhere, even in schools. The Passion was increasingly sung in the new English edition originally produced by Elgar and Ivor Atkins for the 1911 Worcester Festival. With Atkins having revised the translation again in 1938, it would survive into the twenty-first century, although Neil Jenkins's translation of 1997 has found increasing favour, including with the Bach Choir. Compromises with the orchestration were often inevitably made – and performances of the Passions with just organ and/or piano accompaniment were common, especially in churches. Surprisingly perhaps, the challenging double-choir motet *Singet dem Herrn* (as *Sing ye to the Lord*) achieved considerable popularity, especially with northern choirs, for whom a successful performance was reckoned a 'tour de force'.[215] The Bradford Festival Choral Society, for example, had demonstrated its qualities in this work on a visit to London for a Philharmonic Society concert in 1906.[216] Seldom encountered before the 1920s, the *Christmas Oratorio* began to feature in programmes, as to a lesser extent did the Magnificat, surely one of the most audience-friendly of Bach's works (and available from Novello's since 1874).[217] Appearances of the St John Passion, however, remained a rarity.

The increasing cultivation of Bach did not at this time lead to a more general revival of baroque sacred music. There was not even any real expansion of Handel's representation in the repertoire – if anything, he had to make way for more Bach. *Judas Maccabaeus* was still encountered, but otherwise, performances of his other oratorios, such as Beecham's *Solomon*, were very much the exception. The Victorian oratorio quickly disappeared, though Sullivan's *The Golden Legend* was a survivor; out too went Spohr and Gounod. So too did much of Parry's choral output after his death in 1918. *Elijah*, of course, continued to appear, and attempts were made to produce dramatic versions from 1912, including a production by the Moody-Manners Opera Company in 1920.[218] Thomas Fairbairn, capitalizing on the success of his *Hiawatha* spectaculars, in 1932 produced a dramatic *Elijah* with additional dialogue for Southampton Musical Society;[219] he subsequently had it revived professionally at the Royal Albert Hall with Albert Coates as conductor, where, like *Hiawatha*, it was performed annually for some years.[220] *Hiawatha* itself continued to enjoy regular non-dramatic performances by choral societies everywhere up to mid-century, while another Coleridge-Taylor cantata, *A Tale of Old Japan* (premiered by the London Choral Society in 1911),[221] also proved immensely popular throughout the inter-war period. As for Elgar, *The Dream of Gerontius*, after its uncertain start, was quickly widely embraced by societies, who soon appeared to make light of its difficulties. *The Apostles* and *The Kingdom* were never able to compete with it for popularity, though they had their advocates, notably the excellent Croydon Philharmonic Society under their founder, Alan Kirby.[222] In addition, even early works like *King Olaf* and *Caractacus* continued to attract enterprising societies. By way of contrast, Delius's works, such as *A Mass of Life* and *Sea Drift*, despite the continued enthusiasm of conductors like Beecham, failed to kindle popular approval. Even works like Vaughan Williams's *Sea Symphony* and Holst's *Hymn of Jesus* were not that frequently performed, though the former's smaller pieces such as the folk-song arrangements and the *Fantasia on Christmas Carols* were eagerly taken up. Two now forgotten works which did enjoy brief periods of fame were Walford Davies's *Everyman* (1904) and John Foulds's *A World Requiem* (1921), which was incorporated into the British Legion's Festival of Remembrance from 1923 to 1926. Among later works, Constant Lambert's *The Rio Grande* (1927) and George Dyson's *The Canterbury Pilgrims* (1931) quickly won acceptance, though the former's virtuosic instrumental demands limited early amateur performances; Arthur Bliss's choral symphony, *Morning Heroes* (1930), was born out of his own experiences in the war but was destined to receive greater appreciation in the second half of the century than it immediately received. Few contemporary European works made it across the Channel, exceptions being Rachmaninoff's *The Bells*, Kodály's *Psalmus Hungaricus* and Honegger's *King David*, which were heard by a few audiences. One slightly older novelty for the public was the Fauré Requiem. Although it had reached its final version in 1900, it was only introduced into Britain by Nadia Boulanger in November 1936.[223] Just a handful of performances occurred before 1945, after which it quickly established itself in the repertoire. The inter-war years perhaps produced only one work which could rank as a masterpiece alongside *Gerontius*, and that was Walton's *Belshazzar's Feast*. Rather like the Elgar, its technical difficulties were soon seen as a challenge to be met by any ambitious choral society. Among smaller-scale works, Edmund Fellowes's madrigal editions certainly encouraged small choirs to explore this repertoire, and composers continued to pour out part-songs and the like – in part stimulated by the continuing popularity of competitive festivals – which publishers were still content to bring to market. But alongside traditional choral fare, societies began to feature concert performances of operas with substantial choral content, such as Bizet's *Carmen*, Edward German's *Merrie England* and Gounod's *Faust*. The occasional Gilbert and Sullivan operetta appears in concert programmes, but they were more the property of a growing number of amateur operatic societies.

Choral Society Activity during the Second Word War

The first artistic casualty of the Second World War was the 1939 Three Choirs Festival at Hereford, set to open on 3 September, the day war on Germany was declared, and cancelled just a few days previously.[224] It would be 1946 before it was resumed. The only festival to maintain some activity was the Leith Hill at Dorking, where Vaughan Williams conducted *Judas Maccabaeus* and *Elijah* in March 1940,[225] and at least one work in each of the following years, including the St Matthew Passion annually from 1942 – performed initially with an accompaniment of just strings, organ and piano.[226]

Among major London choral societies, the Alexandra Choral and Orchestral Society and the Philharmonic Choir ceased to exist at the outbreak of war,[227] and the London Choral Society suspended activity in 1940.[228] Yet the Bach Choir, the Goldsmiths Choral Union, and the Royal Choral Society continued to operate, and in 1940 there was even a new select 200-strong choir born at Henry Wood's urging, initially to sing at the Proms – the Alexandra Choir, formed by Charles Proctor, who had previously conducted the old Alexandra Choral and Orchestral Society.[229] It was to find much acclaim. There was, in fact, far more choral activity around than might have been expected. In 1940 London you could still have heard four St Matthew Passions, the St John Passion, the B minor Mass, and *The Dream of Gerontius*, as well, of course, as *Messiah*. Later in the war, in 1943 the Croydon Philharmonic Choir gave *The Kingdom*,[230] and the Royal Choral Society *Belshazzar's Feast*.[231] The Southwark Cathedral Special Choir also managed to continue its established Saturday afternoon series throughout the war, with five or six concerts a season.[232] The morale-boosting abilities of choral music, for both performers and audiences, was clearly in evidence, however rough and ready the results may have been in the circumstances. A major blow to London's musical life, however, came in May 1941 with the destruction of the Queen's Hall in an air raid, which left the Royal Albert Hall, with all its acoustic problems, as the capital's sole large concert venue, and one which fortunately remained intact, apart from minor damage caused in October 1942. It was to here that the Proms were transferred from the Queen's Hall, and it became their permanent home. Only with the opening of the Royal Festival Hall in 1951 would London acquire a new concert hall.

In the country at large, choral activity was maintained in most places, even with depleted ranks of tenors and basses. Adequate orchestral accompaniment would often prove the biggest obstacle, so performances with organ or piano were common. Wind and brass being the departments hardest to fill, a compromise was often to have a string orchestra together with an organ supplying essential other parts, a solution not unique to wartime. On the whole, northern choirs, situated where there was generally at least less constant risk of air raids, enjoyed the more normal existence. It was now that the Huddersfield Choral Society really came to national prominence, for under Sargent they went on to become frequent broadcasters on the national network, starting with a *Messiah* in December 1940.[233] With the Hallé Society it also broadcast *Belshazzar's Feast* in December 1942, and, supported by the British Council, went on the record the work the following January, with Walton himself conducting the Liverpool Philharmonic Orchestra. A further enterprising recording, with the same support, came with that of Holst's *Hymn of Jesus* in 1944, Sargent conducting, which was followed up with *The Dream of Gerontius* in 1945.[234] But the Society's fame was cemented by their first *Messiah* recording in 1946, 83,000 copies of which were sold within weeks of release.[235]

Although choral societies understandably mostly stuck to standard fare in wartime conditions, there was a notable exception when the Leicester Philharmonic Society gave the first provincial performance of Tippett's *A Child of our Time* in December 1944, under the composer, just seven months after he had conducted the première in London with an augmented Morley College Choir. Many of Tippett's vocal lines must have presented considerable challenges, but compensation was to be found in the five spirituals, so evocatively arranged, which soon found their own life outside the oratorio. Tippett's inspiration had come from the events surrounding the pogrom of Kristallnacht in Germany in 1938, and despite weaknesses in the text (the composer's own), the work's strong humanitarian appeal helped it to gradually make its way into the repertoire of enterprising choirs. Significantly, it also received European performances in the immediate post-war years, even including an Italian radio performance under Herbert von Karajan in 1952.[236]

In Scotland too, choral societies remained in action. Although Edinburgh, and especially Glasgow, were not immune to air attacks, the damage was minor in comparison with what London experienced. The Edinburgh Royal Choral Union still had a choir of nearly 300 in its 1941/2 season, when it gave eight concerts, with a repertoire from *Messiah* to *The Dream of Gerontius*, while the Glasgow Orpheus Choir continued to bring comfort to many with its concerts and broadcasts of its own very individual repertoire.

We saw earlier how the Carnegie United Kingdom Trust subsidized the publication of the *Tudor Church Music* edition in the 1920s. It was to play an even more important role in supporting amateur choirs, when from 1935 onwards it made funds available through the National Federation of Music Societies, specifically to help small music societies employ professional artists for their concerts. This proved invaluable, both in the depressed conditions of the inter-war years and through the war itself, keeping many societies in existence which would otherwise have folded. Carnegie funding would eventually be superseded by that from the Arts Council of Great Britain, created in 1945, which, through the National Federation, would continue to assist societies until the 1980s. So, traditional choral societies emerged from the war perhaps in a better state than they might have feared, but in the next half-century they were to encounter a far more diverse choral culture.

Chapter 7
Into the Second Elizabethan Era

The Cathedral Scene

The pessimism about the future of cathedral music expressed by senior musicians in the early years of the war turned out to be unjustified, at least in part. As men were gradually demobilized, organists and lay clerks returned to their posts, including John Dykes Bower to St Paul's, Gerald Knight to Canterbury, William McKie to Westminster Abbey, and Boris Ord to King's. Of course, not all lay clerks wanted to return to the choirstalls, and recruitment would prove an increasing problem for choirs outside the capital, since remuneration generally remained pitifully small, and both accommodation and suitable day-time work were in short supply. The cathedrals themselves faced severe financial problems, not least on the fabric front; even if they had not suffered war damage, inability to carry out much routine maintenance during that time, inevitably created a post-war backlog of work. Music could hardly be a priority in the circumstances. Chorister recruitment remained a lesser issue, although the declining viability of small dedicated choir schools increasingly confronted the authorities, a problem to which they would find varying solutions as the century advanced.

The post-war years were dedicated to the restoration of traditional routines, even if it was now generally admitted that, outside London, the final knell for weekday choral Matins was being sounded – Chester, Durham, Worcester and York were among a handful still singing Matins on some weekdays (usually no more than two) in the 1950s.[1] With the exception of the more recent 'parish church' cathedrals, they would remain rather inward-looking institutions until the stirrings of liturgical reform in the 1960s began a slow process of transformation. It is hardly surprising, then, that performance of the music often left much to be desired. None of the supposedly leading establishments of St Paul's, Westminster Abbey, Windsor and York had choirs of any distinction, even if they could rise to special occasions. Outside the limelight, however, there were places where higher standards prevailed. Stanley Vann, arriving at Peterborough in 1953 to find a very run-down choir, was to transform it into one whose psalm singing in particular was regarded as unsurpassed in the country.² Allan Wicks, succeeding Norman Cocker at Manchester in 1954, built on his predecessor's renowned boys' sound to produce a lively choir with an adventurous modern repertoire before his move to Canterbury in 1961.³ Although at Ely for only five years from 1953, Michael Howard cultivated a forthright boys' tone, as well as new repertoire, and was in the vanguard of what was to become standard practice, whereby the organist conducted in the choir-stalls, leaving an assistant to provide the accompaniment. Howard, despite his innovations, was not entirely suited to Ely, and a fondness for the bottle ultimately led to his departure; he was perhaps best known for his work with his London choral groups, the Renaissance Singers and Cantores in Ecclesia.⁴ More significant was the appointment in 1947 of the 27-year-old David Willcocks to the organistship of Salisbury, following distinguished war service and having completed his studies as organ scholar under Boris Ord at King's. His stay was brief, for in 1951 he was offered the Worcester post with its Three Choirs responsibilities. In his seven years there, the sense of discipline, inherited from the army and Ord, combined with remarkable musical gifts, saw him revitalize a choir which had become decidedly slack by the end of Sir Ivor Atkins's 52-year tenure; in addition, he was to bring much needed new expertise to the Three Choirs Festival. Willcocks was a demanding master, who used to say to his choir that 'Worcester's best day is equal to Cambridge's worst' – perhaps not the most diplomatic way to enthuse singers, but standards certainly rose, and Worcester was soon on the BBC Choral Evensong circuit, even if, as at Salisbury, he often had to contend with lay clerks with old-fashioned habits.⁵ Such were the efforts of some among a younger cohort of organists to inject new vigour into their establishments. More general improvement in the cathedrals, however, would only begin to emerge later, and the catalyst would be the Oxbridge choral foundations, whose achievements need to be considered before the remarkable late-twentieth century flowering of music in the cathedrals themselves can be chronicled.

The University Choral Foundations

The 1950s marked a decisive time of change for the choral foundations of Oxford and Cambridge, as a new generation of organists took over. This also coincided with the onset of the LP era, which was to dramatically increase public awareness of their choirs. One college above all was to benefit from this – King's, Cambridge. As already noted, a few recordings were issued in Boris Ord's last years, but it was Willcocks, taking over in 1957, who was to exploit the medium to the full, making it easily the most famous choir of its kind in the world. Inheriting Ord's already highly disciplined and well-tuned choir, Willcocks was to refine it further. His singers recall an extreme emphasis on keeping major thirds sharp, while it was a grave sin to 'sing out'; a homogenous blend of voices was the goal.[6] The result was a Rolls Royce sound, the envy of many choir directors worldwide. And the choir could certainly be heard everywhere, for quite apart from the Christmas Eve service and broadcast Evensongs, it took full advantage of LP recording, releasing far more discs than any comparable choir. There were popular 'best sellers' of hymns and carols, of course, but the repertoire extended far beyond Anglican church music and included the St John Passion, Haydn Masses, Handel's *Dixit Dominus*, the Fauré Requiem and much else. A *Messiah* also appeared, though not until 1972. All this was made possible by a schedule which allowed for plenty of rehearsal time – and to this end (and to permit more touring) singing of normal services outside term time was reduced, especially around Christmas. Two recordings may be singled out, beginning with the first volume of 'The Psalms of David', recorded in 1968, with Willcocks himself providing the inimitable organ accompaniments. It was an exquisite and influential demonstration of King's psalm singing, all the more remarkable for being virtually unrehearsed and recorded in Trinity College Chapel, since King's was closed for renovation.[7] The other was the 1963 recording of Allegri's *Miserere* with the twelve-year-old Roy Goodman soaring effortlessly up to the high Cs with the purest of treble tones, having apparently just rushed in from the rugby field.[8] In its own way it was as iconic in the sixties as Ernest Lough's 'Hear my prayer' in the twenties, though Goodman's name was not given prominence – in later life, he would become a noted violinist and conductor. The recording itself was to make a frequent appearance among 'Desert Island Discs' choices. Despite the work itself being entirely atypical of Anglican cathedral repertoire, it represented for many the embodiment of its sound.

King's may have been an early beneficiary of the LP, but its arrival was a pivotal moment in attitudes to choral standards generally. Not only could twenty or more minutes of music now be heard on disc uninterrupted – invaluable for many choral works – but the vastly improved sound quality was coupled with the development of hi-fi systems and tape editing which offered the possibility of creating 'note perfect' performances. To this was also added the introduction to the UK of FM radio in 1955. As a consequence, a new critical ear arose in both performers and listeners, for whom many pre-war standards of performance now seemed inadequate, and served as a wide stimulus to improvement.

King's fame was such that the choir could attract many of the best applicants for choral and organ scholarships, and numerous prominent musicians would emerge from its ranks over the following decades – including Andrew Davis, Simon Preston, Robert Quinney and Thomas Trotter from among the organ scholars, and Bob Chilcott, James Gilchrist, Brian Kay and Robert Tear from the choral scholars. The sound of King's in the Willcocks era was a rigorously controlled one, so much so that, for all the technical perfection, there was often a limited emotional range in performances where sometimes sheer exuberance is called for, especially when they stepped outside the Anglican repertoire. Their Byrd and Gibbons was certainly beautiful, but more recent choirs and vocal ensembles have demonstrated how much more can be found in the music. As with many choirs, the King's sound was also one very much tailored to its chapel – and not only in choice of speeds; elsewhere it could appear not quite so special. Half a century on, too, the Willcocks vowels can now often sound rather precious (as of course do BBC announcers of that era) – the public school ethos being very much in evidence.

King's, however, was not without competition on its own doorstep. George Guest, having just finished as organ scholar (or 'student' as the college termed it) at St John's, was offered the organistship of the college on Robin Orr's retirement in 1951. It was to prove a 'job for life', lasting 40 years, but, unlike so many cases of long tenure, he was to retire in 1991 with the choir in excellent form. Guest's own particular brand of magic, as usual, defied close analysis, but at its heart lay an emphasis on verbal stress and sense of musical line.[9] Starting with a choir which was still to find its feet after the war – though Orr had seen the retirement of the last of the lay clerks – Guest was, during his first decade, to transform it into a real rival of King's. Not releasing its first LP until 1958, the 1960s would see no fewer than twenty-one recordings, including five of the late Haydn Masses. Guest cultivated a freer, more open sound from the trebles than King's. Influenced only a little by George Malcolm's Westminster Cathedral boys, he let them sing more naturally, as he did the choral scholars, who in consequence often had the more mature sound of the two choirs. The distinctive quality of the St John's boys is perhaps nowhere better captured than on the 1964 recording of Britten's *A Ceremony of Carols*, where they make a superbly fresh sound.[10] Although St John's never drew the regular large crowds that King's did, the discerning often preferred it as their favourite choir. Like King's, notable organ scholars like Stephen Cleobury, David Hill and Andrew Nethsingha would carry Guest's influence far and wide, just as the choral scholars would produce voices like Andrew Carwood, Mark Deller, Simon Keenlyside and Michael Rippon. St John's also did an immense amount of touring, both at home and abroad, particularly to The Netherlands, the USA and Canada, where they predictably proved great ambassadors for the English cathedral tradition. Following Guest's retirement, the choir's reputation was to be fully maintained by Christopher Robinson, David Hill and Andrew Nethsingha.

Although initially less in the public eye, over in Oxford, similar changes were under way, as a younger generation began to take charge. In 1957 Bernard Rose became organist and *Informator choristarum* at Magdalen, while at New College David Lumsden arrived in 1959, after H.K. Andrews had been briefly succeeded by Meredith Davies (1956–9), who left to pursue his conducting career. They were the first of a series of Cambridge-educated organists, who would dominate all three Oxford choral foundations over the following decades. New College retained a mixture of choral scholars and lay clerks, whereas Bernard Rose quickly saw a transformation to choral scholars only. Magdalen enjoys the best acoustic of any Oxford chapel (closely followed by Merton), and Rose's choir developed a vibrant full-bodied sound – mirroring Rose's own ebullient nature – that made it perhaps the most admired of the Oxford choirs in the 1960s, though New College's more restrained approach also had its advocates. Certainly, a big updating of repertoire occurred, and Rose's own scholarly enthusiasm for Thomas Tomkins resulted in two discs of his music. But although both choirs recorded in the 1960s and early 1970s, it was on nothing like the scale of their Cambridge counterparts.

Oxford's choral scene, however, was soon set to attract far greater attention. At Christ Church, 1970 saw the retirement of Sydney Watson (best known for his Evening Service, which he affectionately referred to as 'me in E'), and the arrival of Simon Preston from his post as assistant organist at Westminster Abbey. The ex-King's organ scholar already had a fine reputation as a recitalist and was now to demonstrate his ability to dramatically revitalize a choir. A demanding and volatile personality, Preston soon had the choir producing the most exciting sound in Oxford, even if his idiosyncratic treatment of the psalms – with exaggerated lengthening of important syllables – was an acquired taste. Repertoire was expanded, sometimes in unusual ways – Stravinsky's Mass with wind instruments was introduced at the Sunday Eucharist. And for the first time Christ Church made recordings, including Handel's *Israel in Egypt* and Vivaldi's Gloria; it was also the choir Christopher Hogwood used for his much lauded *Messiah* (1980), which decisively raised its public profile. Preston departed in 1981 to return to Westminster Abbey as organist, to be replaced by another ex-King's organ scholar, Francis Grier. He left the world of church music four years later, and Stephen Darlington took over the reins of the place where he had once been organ scholar under Preston. He would remain in post for thirty-three years, retiring in 2018, during which time the choir produced over fifty recordings of the most diverse character – from the Eton Choirbook to the music of Howard Goodall (including his theme music for *The Vicar of Dibley* TV series), as well as undertaking numerous world-wide tours. Christ Church's biggest hindrance was the unhelpful dry acoustic of the cathedral, with the result that all their recordings were made elsewhere.

The 1970s also saw an important change at New College, when the 29-year-old Edward Higginbottom arrived in 1976 to spend no fewer than thirty-eight years in charge. His interest in all things French saw the choir make frequent visits to that country in particular, among what became a world-wide touring schedule, while, like Christ Church, a large recording programme, totalling some 120 CDs (including some notable commercial successes), brought the choir critical acclaim for its exceptionally flexible and mature sound, not least from the boys, who were one of the first to have individual singing lessons.[11] Meanwhile at Magdalen, Rose's successors, John Harper and Bill Ives, maintained the choir's reputation, even if it had a lower profile than their neighbours. Although the choral foundations of both universities were singing excellently and recording copiously by the closing decades of the century, it was Oxford which was offering the widest and most adventurous choice of repertoire. And like Cambridge, many well-known professionals would emerge from the ranks of its choral and organ scholars, including Robin Blaze, James Bowman, Anna Lapwood, Dudley Moore, Christopher Robinson, Toby Spence and Roderick Williams. On the secular side too, a notable event was the arrival at Merton College in 1960 of the outstanding choral conductor László Heltay, a refugee from the Hungarian revolution of 1956. He quickly established the Collegium Musicum Oxoniensis as a select chamber choir, which won great acclaim and was able to tackle the most demanding repertoire with complete assurance. Renamed the Schola Cantorum of Oxford after Heltay's departure in 1964, it has continued to flourish under a series of first-class conductors, while Heltay himself, among other activities, would go on to create the Brighton Festival Chorus and the Chorus of the Academy of St Martin in the Fields.

The old choral foundations, however, tell only part of the story of post-war chapel music at Oxford and Cambridge. Even before co-education began to seep into the colleges in the 1970s, some of the men's colleges had started to introduce female voices from the women's colleges and elsewhere (such as the then popular secretarial colleges) into their chapel choirs and college choral societies, as Queen's, Cambridge did in the early sixties.[12] Once co-education took hold, mixed-voice choirs, with choral scholarships open to both sexes, were established in many colleges, of which the most prominent at Cambridge became those of Clare, Gonville & Caius, and Trinity, with qualities which came to rival those of King's and St John's. At

Oxford the emergence of such premium quality choirs was slower, but in time Keble, Merton and Queen's in particular would become noted for their choirs – all joining the Radio 3 Choral Evensong list. Thanks to successful fund-raising, Merton's choir was actually turned into a choral foundation in 2008, on the initiative of the Tallis Scholars' Peter Phillips, who co-directed it with Benjamin Nicholas in its formative years. It notably commissioned fifty new works, forming the *Merton Choirbook*, to celebrate the college's 750th anniversary in 2014. The decisive factor in all this transformation was placing the choirs under a permanent 'director of music' rather than transient organ scholars – only at Trinity, Cambridge and Queen's, Oxford had there hitherto been such a person (though termed 'organist'). Although the appointees were usually also organists, they were chosen for their choral direction skills, and the organ scholars assumed a mainly accompanimental role, though also given opportunities to participate in choir training. Many other colleges would gradually go some way down the same route, perhaps having a senior figure who would at least have general oversight of the chapel music without necessarily regularly directing the choir. There was perhaps some merit in the old ways whereby organ scholars were solely in charge and learned to 'sink or swim', occasionally experiencing youthful disasters within the confines of a generally supportive community. But, particularly in view of the increasing academic pressures of the age, some change was inevitable.

Summer touring, at home and abroad, became a regular (and social) attraction of these choirs, as did recordings, the best of which offered a quality at least on a par with the all-male choirs. In addition, a fresh supply of experienced singers would enter the London choral scene, which was offering increased professional opportunities to those coming from a choral environment.

Change comes to the Cathedrals

From the 1960s onwards, there began a general stirring of reform in the cathedral closes, leading to a more outward-looking attitude. Driven in part by financial pressures, they increasingly set out to welcome visitors and to cultivate their own regular congregations. There was also the introduction of more special services. Christmas carol services, usually on the King's model, had long drawn the crowds, but they were now joined by an Advent Carol Service, which also proved highly popular, especially given its opportunity for symbolic and dramatic use of candles – Exeter was a pioneer here in the late 1950s under the influence of the reform-minded Canon Ronald Jasper.[13] (King's itself had introduced an Advent Carol Service in 1934 to alleviate the demand on places at the Christmas Eve service.[14]) Liturgical reform was very much in the air in the 1960s, and although this initially mainly affected the parishes, some of its principles and practices would eventually percolate through to the cathedrals. In all this the cathedral choir came to play an important role, leading to its being increasingly regarded as one of a cathedral's prime assets in promoting its image and relevance, as opposed to being just a drain on its financial resources, as had been a common view of many chapters. Nevertheless, as the century progressed there was increasing anxiety among organists about the future sustainability and relevance of cathedral music.[15] A desire not to leave cathedral worship without music when its choir was not present – and its 'holiday' periods had inevitably become more numerous – led to greater use (or creation) of a local voluntary adult choir as well as welcoming visiting choirs. The evolution, of course, was gradual and varied greatly in direction and pace, but increasingly the post of organist was being occupied by a generation which had experienced at university the high standards widely offered by its choirs, which they sought to emulate.

As ever, outside the capital, the recruitment of lay clerks continued to be a problem, especially given the demands of the expanded and more varied repertoire that organists now aimed at, together with a move towards holding full choir rehearsals before each service, as the university choirs were able to do. Those cathedrals with nearby universities began to explore the idea of offering choral scholarships as one way to alleviate a shortage of men. Exeter and York were probably the earliest to do so in the 1960s;[16] Chelmsford, Durham and Norwich were among those who have followed.[17] Organists naturally also began to look for ex-university choral scholars to fill lay clerk vacancies, though in practice, outside the London area, it was hard to attract them.[18] A place like Southwell Minster, just too far from Nottingham to benefit from its university, was particularly prone to recruitment difficulties.[19]

Although the number of boys coming forward for choristerships was declining, most cathedrals in the 1960s were still finding sufficient for their needs, despite isolated local problems. They increasingly now came from the middle and professional classes, and the cathedral authorities typically provided subsidized education in the independent sector – either in a 'cathedral school' now made financially viable by taking in more non-choristers (as at Durham, Salisbury and Winchester) or by making arrangements with other schools. At a time when selective education was coming under attack in the 1970s, there was even a threat to the existence of choir schools, which was successfully countered, in part by stressing their role in developing musical talent – the re-orientation of Wells Cathedral School as one for the musically gifted dates from this period.[20] Some cathedrals, particularly those of more recent creation, did not take responsibility for their choristers' education, but drew them from various local schools, state and private, which may have given them a wider social mix. Such arrangements placed considerable burden on parents in assisting with transport, but cathedrals like Coventry, Derby, Leicester and Liverpool were all of this type. Fewer weekday Evensongs were the rule in such circumstances.

One new cathedral, however, was quick to create a remarkable choral reputation for itself, and that was Guildford. A start on the building had been made in 1936, but with the war and its aftermath intervening, it was 1961 before it was consecrated. It was the inspired gamble of appointing the 25-year-old Barry Rose as organist, which was to be the key to its musical future. Rose had no cathedral background, and, indeed, no formal musical qualifications, but his work as organist and choirmaster at the London suburban church of St Andrew's, Kingsbury since 1957 had resulted in the boys of the choir becoming well-known locally and even taking part in BBC broadcasts. Like George Guest, Rose just had that inexplicable charisma when it came to choir training. With very little money available, his enthusiasm and determination saw him establish a choir at Guildford that within a couple of years was singing a live broadcast Evensong, with recordings soon following. The 18–20 boys were educated at a local prep school, Lanesborough, while it was necessary to have a very flexible rota of men, many of whom, often travelling from London, could manage only a couple of services a week. But such was Rose's attraction, that they were happy to come for little reward, and even singers like the young Robert Tear and John Shirley-Quirk could be seen in the stalls from time to time. For, uniquely among the newer cathedrals, Guildford set out to have a sung Evensong on six evenings a week. Rose's choir became renowned for the sheer beauty of the boys' tone and for its sensitivity to word setting, not least in the psalms, to which Rose devoted much practice time. Compared to other cathedrals, the Guildford repertoire was not large, and Rose did not despise some unfashionable Victorians – their first recording was of Maunder's *Olivet to Calvary*! – but quality of performance was always uppermost in his mind. Rose's achievement in creating so much with few financial resources was to be an inspiration to other cathedrals in similar situations.[21]

In 1974 Barry Rose left Guildford for St Paul's, where he was nominally sub-organist, but he was soon effectively running the choir, whose quality increased dramatically. A few years later, in 1981, Simon Preston was back at Westminster, effecting equally impressive improvements in the Abbey choir, so that in the 1980s the capital at last had choirs of distinction in its two most iconic churches. Since 1971 Rose had also been Music Advisor to the Head of Religious Broadcasting at the BBC (in succession to George Thalben-Ball), with duties that included direction (with others) of the music of the Daily Service, to which was soon added the responsibility for editing and producing Choral Evensong broadcasts – a post with considerable influence on standards. In 1969/70 there had been a move by the BBC to abolish (or at least substantially reduce) its Evensong broadcasts, but strong public opposition forced an abandonment of the policy.[22] At St Paul's, Rose's highlights were the Silver Jubilee service for Queen Elizabeth in 1977 and the marriage of the Prince of Wales and Lady Diana Spencer in 1981, but his personal relationship with the organist, Christopher Dearnley, and the cathedral authorities deteriorated, as he was prone to pursue his own path without consultation, including making unauthorised recordings with the choir; it was ultimately to lead to his bitter dismissal in 1984.[23] During his last week there, the choir sang five different settings of 'There is no rose' at Evensong.[24] At the heart of the problem lay the unsatisfactory definition of his status vis-à-vis the organist. A calmer period would set in as John Scott was appointed sub-organist, taking over as organist when Dearnley retired in 1990, and maintaining the choir's excellence.[25]

Girls Arrive at the Cathedrals

The 1990s were to see one of the most controversial developments in the traditional cathedral world of all-male choirs. Girls had, in fact, been found in the choirstalls of a few cathedrals since the 1960s; tiny St David's had introduced a mixed treble line under Peter Boorman in 1966, following a severe shortage of boys,[26] while Harrison Oxley at Bury St Edmonds went the same way from 1971 until the early 1980s (when the girls were phased out after the arrival of a new Provost), and Leicester had a separate girls' choir from 1974.[27] More conspicuously, at St Mary's Cathedral, Edinburgh, Denis Townhill in 1978 introduced a mixed boy and girl treble line, which was widely admired, and Townhill became a firm advocate for the cause.[28] Manchester also followed suit in the 1980s.[29] Nevertheless, the real catalyst came when Richard Seal at Salisbury, after consultation with Townhill, persuaded the chapter to establish a separate girls' choir, which came into being in September 1991.[30] It was the arrival of girls at one of the ancient English cathedrals that attracted considerable media attention and generated controversy which lasted for the rest of the decade. But Salisbury's innovation was quickly and widely copied in varying ways, and by the end of the decade about a dozen further English cathedrals had introduced girls.

In every case the girls were set up as separate groups, unlike the Edinburgh/Manchester model; while keen to see girls given the same opportunity

Figure 10   Girl choristers of Salisbury Cathedral in 1991; reproduced with kind permission of Salisbury Museum ©.

to experience the joys and benefits of participating in cathedral music, organists generally did not want to lose the particular qualities of an all-boy treble line. The arguments over the differences between the voices of boys and girls were rehearsed at length. It was admitted that they could be trained to sound like one another – and nowadays it is often difficult to identify the sex of a treble line, especially when a degree of vibrato has been introduced into the sound. But it remains true that it is also possible for both boys and girls to produce distinctive sounds of their own, which merit preserving and exploiting. Quite apart from the rather extreme example of George Malcolm's Westminster Cathedral boys, there is an unmistakeable boys' sound to be heard on George Guest's 1964 recording of Britten's *A Ceremony of Carols* already mentioned, or on the 1998 'Begone Dull Care' disc by the Lichfield boys under Andrew Lumsden.[31] So, while welcoming the fresh possibilities offered by the introduction of girls, organists have been anxious to ensure that the best of traditional practices were not sacrificed. Given the individuality of cathedrals, it is no surprise that the make-up of girls' choirs has varied; some, like Salisbury, have recruited girls with the same age range as the boys, whether educated at the same school (as at Salisbury) or not. Others, like Winchester, have gone for an older girls' line, perhaps in the 12–18 age group, which naturally gives them a different timbre from the boys. Once firmly established, the girls generally sang one or two weekday services, either on their own or with the lay clerks, and shared the Sunday services with the boys on a rota basis. Only for special occasions, such as major feasts, might the choirs be combined. For better or worse, boys and girls at that age tend to have a natural preference to associate in single-sex groups, and a little friendly competition between them has proved a useful stimulus. The lighter service schedule of girls in part reflected the fact that fewer financial benefits were generally available to them. For cathedral chapters, the additional demands occasioned by the new choirs were considerable, at a time when their finances were coming increasingly under strain. Even where the girls were essentially voluntary, there were extra administrative and training costs to be taken on board. Wells was one cathedral which soon found that it had been over-optimistic in its initial provision for them. Having been introduced in 1994, a financial crisis in 2000 threatened their continuation, until a solution was found, initially involving a reduction in the subsidy of school fees.[32] It is no wonder that one of the criticisms made by opponents of the innovation was that it would be the thin end of the wedge, which could see chapters seeking to save money by combining boys and girls into one treble line. Controversy was to continue for the rest of the decade, giving birth to a Campaign for the Defence of the Traditional Cathedral Choir, though its support never appears to have been substantial.[33] It is hardly coincidental that the 1990s was also the decade which saw the equally controversial introduction of women priests into the Church of England. And just as most people began to see the positive aspects of women's ministry, so too, as the confidence of the girls' singing grew, did an appreciation of their additional contribution to a cathedral's music.

While recruitment of suitable girls proved relatively easy, as the end of the millennium approached several cathedrals, including Guildford, were finding it increasingly hard to find their boy choristers.[34] Changing religious and social habits were clearly making themselves felt. The traditional annual chorister auditions day was no longer adequate, and the cathedrals had to resort to more proactive methods to search out new recruits. One popular idea has been the 'Chorister for a Day' activity, allowing both boys and girls a chance to experience life on the inside of a choir, in the hope that some would be enthused enough to apply to join. Another initiative has involved chorister visits to schools, while, more broadly, cathedrals have seen the necessity of keeping their choir in the public eye locally. The introduction of girls may even have aided the recruitment of boys. Exeter, for example, noted that when a girl joined the choir, it sometimes prompted a male sibling to do the same.[35] But, more importantly, the reduction in the service load on the boys helped persuade parents concerned about the effect on academic work (a particular concern with day boys) that it need not suffer – and indeed evidence strongly supports the view that the discipline and concentration of choir work can benefit a child in other spheres.

So, as the millennium closed, there were actually many more children singing in cathedral and collegiate choirs than a generation previously. Despite financial pressures, no cathedral had abandoned its choir. There had, however, been one notable casualty. St Michael's College, Tenbury finally closed its doors in 1985 after 120 years. Although it had maintained its musical standards to the end, demographic and financial factors brought about its demise – a remote corner of Herefordshire was ill-suited to such an institution in an age when prep school boarding was rapidly going out of fashion. From its financial assets the Ouseley Trust was created in 1989, which over the following decades has provided invaluable support for cathedral music in diverse ways.

The Cathedral Repertoire

The post-war cathedral repertoire was to experience the biggest changes and expansion in its history. Paradoxically, it occurred at the same time as the number of weekly services was being reduced. Although fewer cathedral organists were now inclined to compose regularly, there were still significant practitioners, some of whose compositions achieved general circulation – including Francis Jackson and his successor at York, Philip Moore, while Herbert Sumsion continued to compose long after his retirement from Gloucester in 1967, including one modern 'classic' anthem in 'They that go down to the sea in ships'. Among mainstream composers, Howells's continuing contributions to the choral repertoire included (besides his service settings) *A Hymn for St Cecilia* (1960), and the powerful motet in memory of President Kennedy, 'Take him, earth for cherishing' (1964). From Britten came the *Festival Te Deum* (1945), Jubilate in C (1961) and the *Missa brevis* for the Westminster Cathedral boys (1959), while Michael Tippett, commissioned to write something for the choir of St John's, Cambridge in 1961, produced an arresting setting of the Evensong canticles far removed from Anglican tradition in its modernity and dissonance, but which has been widely taken up. Kenneth Leighton made substantial contributions to both the cathedral and parish church music, of which the Magdalen and Second services, together with the Passiontide motet 'Solus ad victimam', have particularly anchored themselves in the repertoire. A few other potential modern classics emerged towards the end of the century, including Jonathan Dove's 'See him that maketh the seven stars', Jonathan Harvey's 'I love the Lord' and 'The dove descending', James

MacMillan's 'A new song' and Richard Shephard's 'And when the builders'. There has also been a striking increase in recent decades of the amount of (mostly contemporary) music by female composers being sung – surely related in part to the arrival of girls in cathedral choirstalls. At King's, Stephen Cleobury, taking over in 1982, developed a tradition of commissioning a new carol every year for the Christmas Eve service, among which Judith Weir's 'Illuminare Jerusalem' (1985) has found lasting popularity.[36] Here too, perhaps, should be mentioned surely the most significant (and for the publisher most profitable) choral anthology of the century, used by choirs and choral societies of every kind, *Carols for Choirs*. Published in 1961 by Oxford University Press, the first volume of fifty carols, edited by Reginald Jacques, just retired as conductor of the Bach Choir, and David Willcocks at King's, made available for the first time many of the carol arrangements from the repertoire of those two famous choirs. It inevitably promoted numerous clones of the King's Christmas Eve Festival – especially as the text of the nine lessons was included in the volume – not to mention many an embarrassing solo rendition of the first verse of 'Once in royal David's city'. Five further volumes have built on the first volume's success.

When it comes to contemporary music, the university choirs have the considerable advantage over the cathedrals of relatively generous rehearsal time, so often necessary for such works. It is therefore understandable that cathedral choirs, despite the presence nowadays of more skilled and adaptable lay clerks, have tended to sing little of the more demanding types of present-day music, although most would seek to have one or two such items under their belt.

One of the biggest changes in the cathedral repertoire was in the amount of Latin being sung. Before the Second World War, although Latin anthems at Evensong were beginning to gain a place, Communion settings remained strictly in English. Works originally in Latin, like a Palestrina Mass or a Byrd motet, were routinely sung in translation – even Vaughan Williams's Mass in G minor was published in an English version as well as the original Latin. But post-war attitudes gradually changed, particularly as the cathedrals moved towards a weekly sung Eucharist as the main Sunday morning service. There simply were not enough good English Communion settings, and singing a Palestrina Mass in translation increasingly felt an anachronism. Christ Church, Oxford had been singing Latin Masses since 1946, but it would be the 1960s before the practice became commonplace. The repertoire then came to include not only English and continental Renaissance examples, but the shorter Viennese classics, as well as more modern examples from Widor onwards.

The introduction of modern language liturgies from the 1970s initially affected mostly parish churches, as we shall see, but the cathedrals eventually adopted them for their Eucharists, while firmly retaining the Prayer Book services for Matins and Evensong. For the Eucharist, the new services fortunately allowed the choirs to continue singing the traditional repertoire in English and Latin – few composers have felt inclined to provide cathedral-style settings of the modern language texts. The blend of traditional and modern language texts no longer seems odd, and congregations have generally resisted any attempted updating of the language of well-loved hymns.

One conspicuous post-war innovation has been in the treatment of the Preces and Responses at Matins and Evensong. Although an edition of Tudor/Jacobean settings had been published back in 1933,[37] it was only after the war that they began to replace the usual Ferial or so-called 'Tallis' Festal responses, and for settings to be regularly changed, usually on a weekly basis. In addition, many composers began to write new settings (often also including the Lord's Prayer), of which those by Humphrey Clucas, Kenneth Leighton and Bernard Rose have found particular favour. The novelty has even extended to giving the priest's part more than the traditional inflected monotone to recite – creating difficulties for some. It must be admitted that some composers appear to have set out to challenge choirs (and worshippers) with over-elaborate and discordant settings, leaving the essential simplicity of the genre far behind.

In Roman Catholic musical circles, the post-war era saw interest once more focussed on Westminster Cathedral. George Malcolm, then making his name chiefly as a harpsichordist, took charge of the music there in 1947, and proceeded to radically change the sound of the boys, inspired partly by what he had heard John Driscoll achieve at Farm Street and Wimbledon.[38] The resultant forthright quality – characterized by Malcolm himself as 'controlled shouting' – was quite unlike any Anglican choir, but produced a vigour and passion in the choir's singing that had both admirers and detractors, though it seemed well suited to the building's acoustics. Britten was certainly impressed and wrote his *Missa brevis* for the boys in 1959, which was to be Malcolm's last year there. Boys were also used on the alto line in conjunction with one adult countertenor. Unfortunately, little evidence of the choir's sound has survived, since only a single LP recording was made – of Victoria's *Tenebrae* Responsories, plus a BBC recording of the Britten (later released commercially), owing to the cathedral authorities' opposition to such activity.[39]

The boys' tone remained distinctive, though modified, under Malcolm's successors, who included, in more ecumenical times, two non-Catholics in Stephen Cleobury and David Hill, both of whom achieved excellent results and were able to finally bring the choir wider fame through recordings, as did their successor in 1988, the Catholic James O'Donnell, who then moved on to equally distinguished work at the Abbey in 2000. The repertoire remained very Catholic and Latin – the more extreme effects of the post-Vatican II introduction of vernacular liturgy were resisted – but some cross-fertilization from the riches of Anglican music occurred. As so often in the short history of the cathedral, financial problems arose in the inflation-afflicted 1970s, which threatened the choir's existence; it was avoided thanks to a successful appeal, enabling it to survive into the new millennium in good shape.

Elsewhere, at a generally dispiriting time for Catholic church music, one bright spot was the creation of the all-male choir for the new Liverpool Metropolitan Cathedral. It began life in 1960 in the crypt of the still to be erected main edifice, which was finally opened in 1967. With few financial resources and no choir school, the choir, initially under Christopher Symons and subsequently (from 1966 to 1996) led by Philip Duffy (with his brother Terence as organist), the music was soon highly regarded, and it enjoyed an excellent relationship with its Anglican counterpart just down the road, whose repertoire it happily incorporated.[40] Also in the North, Leeds Catholic Cathedral, after a period without a choir following its disbandment in 1968 in the wake of Vatican II reforms, re-established one in 1988. It was aided by a funded scheme of encouraging singing in Catholic schools in the diocese, which proved remarkably successful, resulting in keen competition for cathedral chorister places by the early 2000s.[41] In contrast, down in Bristol, the new Clifton Cathedral, built in the spirit of Vatican II, opened in 1973 and formed an adult mixed choir as the main basis for its music,[42] a step also taken by St Chad's Cathedral, Birmingham, when recruitment difficulties forced the abandonment of its all-male choir by 2003.[43]

The overall standard of singing being delivered by cathedral choirs of all types at the end of the twentieth century would have astonished any worshipper half a century earlier. Naturally, with inevitable ever-changing personnel and with heavy dependence on the character and ability of their directors, not every establishment excelled, and ups and downs could occur even among the best. John Sanders, returning to Gloucester as organist in 1967, after earlier having been assistant there, noted that it needed time to build up standards, which he successfully did. Previously at Chester, he had found the situation dispiriting, with little prospect of quick improvement – the following decades, however, would eventually see a transformation of its fortunes too.[44] As late as 1992, the Archbishops' Report on church music, *In Tune with Heaven*, remarked that 'there are cathedrals in this country with feeble standards', but if so, they were a distinct minority.[45] Certainly by 2000, the fears of the 1941 report by organists that the post-war prospects for cathedral music were bleak, could not have been further from reality.

Music in Parish and Other Churches

Parish church choirs in the post-war years saw no immediate alteration to their accustomed routines, though the decline in membership, already in evidence in the 1930s, was set to continue, with recruitment of boys predictably becoming more difficult. Yet the 'traditional' model of the all-male parish choir as the norm persisted, even if in practice girls and women were in many places increasingly appearing in the choirstalls.[46] In central London, however, which had seen most of its choirs disappear during the war, a rather different pattern arose. Although All Saints, Margaret Street brought its evacuated boys back to its choir school, and all-male choirs were re-established at St Margaret's, Westminster and Holy Trinity, Sloane Square, others tended to go for a small adult professional choir, singing a cathedral-type repertoire. This was the case at St Bartholomew-the-Great, Smithfield where its pre-war choir of 20–24 boys and 6 men was replaced by an SATB quartet, later doubled in number.[47] Such arrangements were to become commonplace in London and were sometimes found in more affluent parishes elsewhere.

Most parish choirs still expected to turn out twice on a Sunday, and their day revolved around this. But change was in the air in the 1950s. Among the centre-ground churches, a more family-orientated 'Parish Communion', already appearing in the 1930s, now really began to take root, usually starting life as an additional service held earlier than Matins, with only the latter service involving the choir. Such a division in itself could impact on choir recruitment, as families with children gravitated towards the earlier service. The trend became more pronounced with the arrival of the new 'alternative' liturgies in the 1960s – at first still employing traditional language, but with modern language forms from 1973. By this time there was a general move towards the abandonment of Matins, except in evangelical parishes, which still tended to embrace at least a Matins-based framework. By the 1970s most choirs were moving towards singing at a Sunday morning Communion service, and with the modern language Communion service completely new settings were necessary; given the trend of the times, in most churches they had to be basically singable by the whole congregation. The new linguistic style came in for much criticism from musicians, but settings were quickly forthcoming, amongst which John Rutter's was a much-used early example.[48] The 1960s onwards were certainly disturbing times for the more traditionally minded choir member, all the more so as 'pop-style' hymn tunes (initiated by the Twentieth Century Light Music Group) were promoted by various members of the clergy, followed by the arrival of 'worship songs', few of which involved four-part harmony for a choir. Indeed, a 'music group' often began to replace (or at least supplement) the traditional choir, and it favoured electronic keyboard and guitar band accompaniment in place of the organ. Added to this was the fact that Evensong congregations rapidly declined, leading to its abandonment in many churches, at least as a regular service. As a result, the singing of the psalms to Anglican chants vanished in many places. Although a short psalm had an optional place in the new Communion services, it was often sung in responsorial form rather than to Anglican chant or plainsong.

In these circumstances it is not surprising that the supply of competent organists/choir directors became a growing problem, which in turn affected choir recruitment. More than ever, it would be the personality and enthusiasm of its leader which could see a choir flourish. Children in particular make considerable demands on time if they are to be properly trained, and with recruitment becoming ever more challenging, participation of both boys and girls in church choirs decreased markedly, so that by the end of the century they had disappeared entirely from many choirs.

Village choirs, especially, were to suffer. Before the Second World War the village choir was still an important social element in many villages, even if its musical accomplishments were often modest. In the second half of the century, the changing nature of villages, with many residents working elsewhere, tended to fracture community life, church attendance included. The real blow came as financial factors and clergy shortages forced groups of parishes to be served by a single incumbent. This usually meant that an individual church, especially in the smaller villages, was no longer guaranteed to be able to hold a main service every Sunday. For many choirs, which rely on a regular round of practices and services to flourish, this proved fatal. There would be exceptions, of course, where local skill and determination kept the flame alive, but by the end of the century village choirs were becoming something of a rarity in many parts of the country.

The history of the Royal School of Church Music over this period can be seen as a barometer of parish choir life. It was also the time when it did some of its most useful work. At the beginning of 1953, Gerald Knight left Canterbury Cathedral to become its Director, coinciding with a move into the grand surroundings of Addington Palace, Croydon (a former residence of the Archbishops of Canterbury).[49] Although it continued to cater for a small number of full-time students from home and abroad, usually enrolled for a year, it boosted its always precarious finances by also providing accommodation for a few students at the London music colleges. Three choirs of trebles (each singing twice a week) were recruited locally to form the 'house' choir, so daily services could be maintained and experience in choir training provided. The RSCM continued to hold occasional large-scale festivals in London, but from the 1960s the emphasis shifted more to regional events, beginning with a Northern Festival in Leeds Town Hall in 1961.[50] Residential weeks for choristers held round the country proved increasingly popular, but it was 1966 before such a course for girls was introduced;[51] under Knight the RSCM was slow to move on from Nicholson's ideal of all-male parish choirs. One important and lasting innovation, however, was the introduction in 1965 by Martin How of the Chorister Training Scheme, adapting an idea developed by Geoffrey Holroyde at St Mary's, Warwick.[52] Through the use of cards with boxes to be ticked on achievement of musical and teamwork goals, children could progress through the ranks from probationer to full chorister, with various coloured ribbons and medals to denote their status. It did, of course, make increased demands on the choir director's time, but for those able to institute it, it provided valuable incentives to capture and retain the enthusiasm of both boys and girls. The scheme was eventually extended to cover older teenagers and revamped as 'Sing Aloud' and 'A Voice for Life'.

It would be the final abandonment of the full-time students and the arrival of Lionel Dakers (from Exeter Cathedral) as Director in 1974 that marked the beginning of much needed modernization of the organisation.[53] An emphasis was put on decentralization, with local area committees becoming primarily responsible for promoting activity, such as three-day courses during school holidays, and festivals at an archdeaconry or diocesan level, while at Addington itself, short courses and day events were expanded, including the popular 'reluctant organist' courses of Janette Cooper. Various ideas were tried out, some inevitably more successful than others. Dakers's fifteen years as Director certainly saw the RSCM begin to address the real needs of parish choirs coming to terms with the new liturgical environment, and its expanding publications department, which had hitherto concentrated mainly on issuing festival music books, began to publish music for the new liturgies.

The success of these new policies could be seen in the fact that choir affiliations actually reached their highest number at this time, at around 8,000–9,000, including about 1,000 overseas affiliations – for successive Directors had continued to make regular visits to churches in the Commonwealth and the USA which looked to uphold the traditions of English church music. It was, however, to be a false dawn, since from the late 1980s there began a steady decline in affiliations – they were down to around 6,000 by the end of the century and under 5,000 by 2014.[54] The social and religious changes were to prove too hard to resist in many places, and although the RSCM recognized that it now had a duty to assist with the music of churches without choirs – especially as in 1996 the General Synod had made it the Church of England's 'official agency for music'[55] – it was quite hard to do in practice. The dramatic decline in the number of boy choristers saw a gradual abandonment of boys' only residential courses. Despite the efforts of later Directors like Harry Bramma and John Harper, the RSCM underwent retrenchment, moving out of Addington Palace in 1996 to the modest Cleveland Lodge near Dorking, before finally settling in 2006 in the Close at Salisbury, where it shares facilities with Sarum College and basically has just office accommodation. Nevertheless, although its most influential days appear to be past, it has continued to do its best to sustain choirs through turbulent times.

In some way complementary to the work of the RSCM have been the week-long high-powered choral courses for older teenagers initiated by Ralph Allwood in the 1980s, held first at Uppingham School and then at Eton College, where he became Precentor and Director of Music in 1985, and where they went under the name of the Eton Choral Course. They have increasingly become regarded as providing valuable experience for those considering applying for university choral scholarships. As an offshoot, the Rodolfus Choir, formed by Allwood mainly from participants in the courses, has become one of the leading youth choirs in the country. Although many course members have come from the independent school sector, bursaries have been made available in order to encourage applications regardless of financial situation. Latterly the scope of courses, now known as Rodolfus Choral Courses, has been extended under the auspices of the Rodolfus Foundation, which has an aim to promote choral activity widely among children and young people.[56]

If the 1960s onwards ushered in an era of often unwelcome change for many Anglican choirs, they were at least continuing to sing in the same language, whereas for Roman Catholics, the introduction of the vernacular following Vatican II brought about complete musical confusion, especially as it took several years for the authorities to issue firm guidance as to what was permitted in the new liturgies.[57] Given that, in the minority of churches which cultivated any appreciable musical tradition, choir members would tend to have been even more conservative than their Anglican counterparts, it is not surprising that choirs disappeared entirely in many places. In 1964, even that musical stronghold at Farm Street in Mayfair lost the professional mixed choir it had had since 1945, and it would be the 1970s before one was restored.[58] There was a widespread assumption that singing in Latin was ruled out in ordinary churches in the interests of encouraging congregational participation – only in some cathedrals and the two oratories was it still to be cultivated. Gradually, however, it was acknowledged that such widespread abandonment of the Catholic church's vast musical inheritance was not really intended by Vatican II reforms, and the use of Latin crept back discreetly into churches which had managed to retain (or re-establish) their choirs thanks to local enthusiasm. By the end of the millennium there were Catholic churches where the Viennese Classical Masses could be heard again (as they were also in Anglican churches). Such choirs were almost inevitably mixed adult groups – although a few churches in the 1960s cultivated boys' choirs attached to the international 'Pueri Cantores' movement, their existence tended to be fairly short-lived.[59] For the majority of churches at the end of the century, their music most commonly relied on a solo cantor (often amplified) attempting to lead the congregational singing, or else a guitar-based music group.

In the Nonconformist churches too, the post-war years were ones of gradual retrenchment, which saw the closure of many chapels (especially marked in Wales), and there was a general move to purely congregational singing. The larger Methodist churches tended to retain their choirs, particularly in their traditionally strong areas, even if they were on a smaller scale than previously, and, like the Anglicans, the tradition of 'twice on a Sunday' faded as the century neared its end. As elsewhere, modern hymnody and worship songs had their impact upon traditional choral culture.

The Church of Scotland experienced a dramatic fall in numbers in the latter decades of the century, in most places extinguishing what choral activity there may have been. Two notable exceptions have been St Giles Cathedral, Edinburgh, and Paisley Abbey, both of which may be termed 'high' churches by Presbyterian standards, with liturgies closely following Anglican patterns – in Paisley's case including a monthly 'choral Evensong'. St Giles, with its 30-strong adult mixed choir, indeed goes so far as to sing Latin Mass settings at its Holy Communion service – what the church's Calvinist Reformation minister, John Knox, who is buried in the churchyard, would make of that, can only be imagined.[60] Paisley, where George McPhee began to direct the choir in 1963 and, remarkably, was still in post in 2023, has enjoyed an excellent reputation and, exceptionally, still has a sizeable section of boys and girls in addition to adult sopranos.[61] But these two stand out in an otherwise bleak landscape.

Before leaving the sphere of church music, one event of the second half of the century demands attention – the 1953 Coronation of Queen Elizabeth II. Ceremonially and musically, it was closely modelled on the previous three coronations of the century, and, like the 1951 Festival of Britain, it provided, with all its pageantry, an uplift to the mood of the nation in the difficult post-war years. Under the musical direction of the Abbey organist, William McKie, the choir of 400 included, besides the traditional full choirs of the Abbey, Chapel Royal, St Paul's and Windsor, representatives of cathedrals, choral foundations and leading parish churches throughout the country.[62] A number of singers from the Commonwealth were also invited; these included some women – the first time they had featured since a group of about forty females had sung at Queen Victoria's coronation in 1838.[63] Rehearsals were intensive – the boys spent a month boarded at the RSCM headquarters, Addington Palace, beforehand[64] – and the result was probably the most successful performance of the music in the ceremony's history up till then – all the more important since the service was televised live for the first time. 'Zadok the Priest' and Parry's 'I was glad' were by now fixtures, the former in the 're-orchestrated' version made for the 1937 coronation by Gordon Jacob, who now also retouched the Parry; but notable amongst the new music were Vaughan Williams's little motet 'O Taste and See' and his stirring arrangement of the Old Hundredth – the first time a congregational hymn had been included – as well as Walton's exuberant setting of the Te Deum and his march *Orb and Sceptre*, conducted, as with the rest of the orchestral music, by Adrian Boult.

The Festivals Revive

Although post-war physical and economic conditions would hardly have seemed favourable to a resumption of festival life, there was a determination to see 'normal service' restored. The Three Choirs, predictably, was the first with the Hereford Festival of 1946, and Leeds and Norwich followed in 1947. But the latter year also saw the birth of both the Edinburgh International Festival and the Llangollen International Musical Eisteddfod. Like virtually all of what would become a growing number of new festivals, Edinburgh was not chorally centred, but it soon acquired an excellent Festival Chorus, which, combined with eminent visiting orchestras and conductors, made for many an outstanding concert. Llangollen was a competitive event, with the choral classes playing a major role, and was unique in attracting many foreign choirs from the outset – indeed, the promotion of reconciliation between nations was one of its founding principles. For many years, winning at Llangollen was a highly prestigious achievement.

The Three Choirs largely resumed its traditional pattern, with all the problems of too much music for too little rehearsal time. As Martin Cooper wrote of the 1950 Festival:

> No series of concerts maintains with less alteration the aesthetic, and even a remnant of the social, traditions of the late Victorian and Edwardian eras. Among the tail-coats and top-hats, the occasional feather boa and the faded lace, the ghosts of Sir Hubert Parry and Sir

> Edward Elgar walk with less visible displeasure, less palpable indignation, than among the grey flannels and the cotton frocks of the Albert Hall, or the more spivvish elegances of Covent Garden. Experiment of any kind is out of place in such a setting and programmes are designed to give familiar delight rather than to provoke discussion. ... The sheer quantity of music sung would go far to explain a certain tiredness and lack of resilience which characterized all the choral singing.[65]

It would, however, be during the 1950s, when figures like Meredith Davies and David Willcocks were in charge, that real measures were taken to improve the situation.[66] More generous rehearsal time was allotted, and the non-choral orchestral concerts were gradually handed over to professional orchestral conductors. Howells's *Hymnus Paradisi* had a notable premiere in 1950, while in 1957 Willcocks persuaded the Worcester authorities to finally allow a Three Choirs' performance of Walton's *Belshazzar's Feast* – hitherto the goings-on of Belshazzar and his concubines had been considered unfit for a cathedral. A general rise in standards, coupled with discreet modernization, occurred over the following decades; the annual inclusion of *Messiah* (inevitably still scarcely rehearsed) was broken in 1964 – it would be 1977 before it was heard again;[67] applause at cathedral concerts began in 1969, and in 1984 the traditional Opening Service was dropped in favour of a Festival Dedication. The Three Choirs was still providing the major opportunity for British composers to have premieres of new large-scale works, while it also continued to give the first British performances of many foreign compositions. Few were destined to achieve a more permanent place in the repertoire, but that is the fate of innumerable works, and the festival's blend of tradition and adventurousness was to attract an increasingly large audience from beyond the locality. At a time when the burgeoning number of festivals throughout the country were tending to become rather copycat affairs, the Three Choirs retained its distinctive ethos, the social atmosphere, with old friends reuniting each year, being as essential an element as ever.

1960 saw the important revival of the Southern Cathedrals Festival – last held in 1932 – when the choirs of Chichester, Salisbury and Winchester came together for two (later increased to three) days, rotating among the cities, and firmly based round the three choirs themselves, though not without its 'Fringe' events.[68] Newly commissioned works regularly provided novelty, including, in 1965, Leonard Bernstein's *Chichester Psalms*. In some ways, its modest form resembled the early days of the Three Choirs Festival itself. A successful niche festival has also been offered since 1956 at Edington Priory in Wiltshire, specifically celebrating 'music within the liturgy', with singers, now in three different ensembles, drawn from cathedral and similar choirs.

Leeds was to experience difficulty in recreating a festival chorus comparable in quality to its pre-war ones, and, as a temporary measure in 1953, resorted to five individual Yorkshire choirs sharing the concerts, of which seven out of eight were choral, including a performance of Stravinsky's *Oedipus Rex* with the Colne Valley Male Voice Choir.[69] Deficits, however, were becoming unacceptably high and the festival was threatened with closure.[70] But it survived until 1985, having celebrated its 125th anniversary in 1983, and remained a high profile affair, with conductors including Carlo Maria Giulini, Charles Mackerras and Pierre Boulez. In the 1970s the Festival Chorus, under Donald Hunt, was reconstituted as a smaller and younger body of about 200. After the festival closed, the Chorus (like the Birmingham Festival Chorus earlier in the century) continued as an independent body, having already become self-governing in 1976.[71]

At Norwich, the first post-war festival of 1947 had Malcolm Sargent and the cathedral organist, Heathcote Statham, sharing the conducting, with Kathleen Ferrier as the Angel in *The Dream of Gerontius* a notable highlight. But although a morale booster, it became apparent that problems with venues and attracting audiences were threatening the festival's future. A decision to delay the next festival (due in 1950) by a year so as to coincide with the 1951 Festival of Britain and to integrate it with other artistic events in the city would see the beginning of its evolution into a general arts festival, rather than a primarily musical one, and certainly less chorally orientated. From 1988 it switched to become an annual event, and the Festival Chorus, though continuing in existence, did not appear every year; despite financial ups and downs, the festival successfully saw its way into the next millennium.[72]

Choral Societies Evolve

Although, as we have seen, many choral societies suspended activity during the war, others kept singing as best they could. In the post-war situation, with its continuing hardships, the old societies soon revived, although an understandable shortage of men was a frequent complaint. Remarkably, the Bach Choir was back to its pre-war strength by 1948, and in 1954 capped its numbers at 400, with a waiting list.[73] It tackled *Belshazzar's Feast* for the first time in 1949, and its annual St Matthew Passion became so popular that from 1952 there were two performances a year, on Passion and Palm Sundays. Reginald Jacques continued as conductor until his retirement on health grounds in 1960 and was succeeded by David Willcocks. With his customary disciplined approach, Willcocks gave the choir a more lithe and rhythmically responsive sound, which helped counter the growing awareness that to perform Bach with 300 and more singers was anachronistic.

The choir also toured abroad for the first time in 1963, the year in which it had (together with the LSO Chorus) made the definitive first recording of Britten's *War Requiem*, conducted by the composer. Recordings and tours were now to become a regular part of its activities. Willcocks was to remain in charge until 1998, when he was succeeded by David Hill. Like all the big societies, it would slim down as the century advanced, and settled at around 200 members – a musically more manageable number.[74] It still retained something of its upper-class image – minor royalty was to be found among the membership and it was invited to sing at the wedding of Prince Charles and Lady Diana Spencer in 1981 – although in recent years it has tried to widen its social make-up.

The Royal Choral Society had a chequered post-war history. Sargent continued as its conductor up to his death in 1967, still capable of producing that beautiful tone from it, but without some of the earlier vitality. No long-term successor followed, and the choir had a series of conductors until Richard Cooke took over in 1995. It continued with its annual favourites of *Messiah* and carol concerts, and in addition to the standard choral repertoire, it embraced more popular fare in the shape of selections of film and operatic music, singing for charity events, as well as giving concerts outside the capital. It never returned to its vast pre-war strength of 800 – perhaps thankfully – and by the end of the century it was similar to the Bach Choir, with around 200 members. But, in an ever more competitive choral landscape, it had survived and was still able to draw an audience.[75]

The Huddersfield Choral Society under Sargent enjoyed a post-war reputation in the popular mind as the choral society *par excellence*, a reputation burnished by critical acclaim for performances at the 1948 Edinburgh Festival and at the Festival of Britain in 1951. Moreover, it became well known to the country at large in the 1950s through television broadcasts of the Christmas music from *Messiah*, and for decades it was easily the most travelled choir of its type, fulfilling many 'out of town' engagements, including numerous visits to London. Not overly adventurous in repertoire, it did, however, commission Walton's Gloria to celebrate its 125th anniversary in 1961.[76] But difficulties in recruitment were already beginning to appear in that decade and, like the Royal Choral Society, after Sargent's death in 1967 it had an unsettling period, before happier times returned in 1980 with Owain Arwel Hughes.[77] By the end of the century it was still a choir of around 200, smaller, but not dramatically so, than in Sargent's day; less of a household name, but still a prime cultural asset of the town.

If traditional choral societies generally resumed their activities fairly promptly after the war, competition for both singers and audiences would grow steadily as the century advanced, with its many alternative ways of people spending their leisure time, beginning with the general invasion of television into homes in the 1950s. This was reflected in the average size of societies; whereas 300 plus members were commonplace for large societies before 1939, by the end of the century 150 singers would be regarded as a large choir. Just such a choir was a distinguished newcomer into the choral scene, the North London based Crouch End Festival Chorus (originating in, but outliving, the Crouch End Arts Festival in 1984) which has gone on to wide acclaim for its concerts and recordings, often serving as the supporting chorus for famous solo artists in both the classical and popular music fields. In Scotland there was a post-war upsurge in Gaelic choirs, as well as the creation of groups like the Aberdeen Bach Choir and the Scottish Chamber Choir, while in Wales, notable arrivals have included Bach choirs in Cardiff and Swansea and the BBC National Chorus of Wales.

Choirs saw an enrichment of their repertoire, not in the widespread take-up of contemporary works (a continuing rare phenomenon), but in the discovery of older foreign repertoire which had hitherto eluded the attention of British choral societies. Reference has already been made to the late introduction of the Fauré Requiem; from 1947 on it would quickly find ready acceptance. The later Requiem it inspired, that of Maurice Duruflé, did not begin to reach British ears until 1957 and remained relatively unknown until more recent decades.[78] The Monteverdi Vespers of 1610 was pioneered by Morley College Choir under Walter Goehr in 1946 in an edition by Hans Redlich, but Goehr was to publish his own edition in 1957, which then encouraged many choirs to take up the work. At the time it was assumed the work was 'choral' in the modern sense, but few works have produced more controversy as to how they should be performed, questions which are still unresolved today, though most scholars now incline to think that only solo voices were originally involved.[79] Carl Orff's *Carmina Burana* received its British premiere in 1951[80] and Janáček's *Glagolitic Mass*, despite a pioneering performance by Henry Wood at the Norwich Festival in 1930, only began to register on the British choral scene after it was heard at the 1953 Leeds Festival.[81] The now universally popular Vivaldi Gloria was first published in wartime Italy and was not discovered by British choirs until the late 1950s, when the late Haydn Masses (particularly the 'Nelson') also began to achieve wider circulation; the Bruckner Masses, however, had to await the 1970s before audiences could become familiar with them, while the Rachmaninoff Vespers received its first complete British performance in 1971 by Wyn Morris and the Mahler-Bruckner Choir.[82] .

The one undisputed British choral masterpiece to emerge in the second half of the century was Britten's *War Requiem*, composed to celebrate the consecration of the new Coventry Cathedral in 1962. It was quickly taken up by those who could muster the necessary substantial choral and orchestral resources and received its Three Choirs premiere in 1963. The same composer's *Spring Symphony* with its important choral element, first heard in England in 1950, also came to find regular, if not frequent, performances. Making more modest demands, and with average choirs in mind, John Rutter, in addition to numerous anthems, carols and part-songs, has also composed on a larger scale, including a Gloria (1976) and Requiem (1986). Fauré's Requiem found a reflection in Andrew Lloyd Webber's 1985 work, while David Fanshaw's *African Sanctus* (1972), offering a fusion of classical, pop and traditional African music, achieved international success, with a particular appeal to youth choirs.

An important development in the world of larger choral societies in the post-war era was the creation of specialized symphony orchestra choruses. In the North, Liverpool and Manchester had long had choruses associated with the Philharmonic and Hallé orchestras, but that was not the case with the independent London orchestras. The BBC, it is true, had its own amateur chorus from 1928, which operated under various names before finally becoming the BBC Symphony Chorus in 1977. Well trained by Leslie Woodgate from 1934 to 1961, it has contributed most notably to the Proms. Otherwise, the nearest thing in the earlier part of the century had been Charles Kennedy Scott's Philharmonic Choir, formed in 1919, partly to provide a choir for Royal Philharmonic Society concerts, though it remained independent. That choir was dissolved in 1939, but some of its members would sing in a new London Philharmonic Choir, formed in 1946 specifically to work with the (Beecham-created) London Philharmonic Orchestra, with which it made a formal agreement. With Frederick Jackson as its first conductor, it was 300-strong, including professional strengthening of 30 – a feature typical of such choirs. They would normally sing for two of the orchestra's concerts per season, as well as promoting their own.[83]

In 1957 Walter Legge founded the Philharmonia Chorus to complement his already established Philharmonia Orchestra, bringing in Wilhelm Pitz, chorus master of the Bayreuth Festival to train it. His highly disciplined approach soon marked out the choir as exceptional, and a tradition of it having German chorus masters lasted until 1992.[84] Last among the capital's symphonic choirs to emerge was the LSO Chorus (now the London Symphony Chorus), formed in 1966 and destined to achieve an equally fine reputation. Elsewhere, the City of Birmingham Symphony Chorus dates from 1973, and, with Simon Halsey as its chorus master since 1983, it has proved itself at least the equal of its London counterparts. What distinguishes these symphony choruses from other choral societies are the frequent intensive periods of rehearsal shortly before concerts, as well as considerable touring schedules. As a result, the time commitment is substantial, and the choirs tend to be relatively youthful with a fairly high turnover.[85] The compensation is the incomparable experience of singing with some of the world's greatest soloists and conductors.

Small is Beautiful

Post-war London began to see the emergence of an assortment of smaller-size choirs with specialist interests, all essentially the creation of their conductors. A number were professional (or at least included professional singers), taking advantage of growing opportunities in the recording, film and broadcasting industries. These were to provide professional choral singers a career beyond that of the opera house and the like. Such were Denis Stevens's Ambrosian Singers (1951), Michael Howard's Renaissance Singers (1944) and his later Cantores in Ecclesia, Henry Washington's Schola Polyphonica, and Bruno Turner's Pro Musica Sacra. Most specialized in pre-Baroque music, bringing a wide range of little-known British and continental Renaissance music into the concert hall and recording studio, though the highly regarded John Alldis Choir was an exception in focussing on modern music. Seventeenth-century interests were served by Roger Norrington's Schütz Choir, founded in 1962, while Kennedy Scott's pre-war Bach Cantata Club found a post-war successor in Paul Steinitz's London Bach Society (originally the South London Bach Society). Formed in 1946, they initially sang Bach in English, moving over to German in 1951. Giving the St Matthew Passion with a mixed amateur and professional choir of about 60, they continued Scott's advocacy of smaller-scale performance of the work. Their annual performances with an appropriately-sized orchestra (later the Steinitz Bach Players) were eagerly anticipated, offering a complete contrast to that of the Bach Choir.[86] Like all such choirs, they did not limit themselves to Bach, but in Steinitz's 41-year reign, he worked through all the cantatas. His insistence on the essential dance-like nature of Bach's music gave his performances a particular sparkle, and the choir often appeared at festivals outside London, and made trips abroad.

At the same time as Steinitz was proclaiming the merits of smaller-scale Bach Passions, John Tobin in 1950 with the London Choral Society was showing a new approach to *Messiah*. Using about 60 voices, including a mixed male and female alto line for greater incisiveness, he gave the work complete – still an unusual occurrence at the time. Having consulted the original source material, he introduced some of the alternative versions of arias, including giving the countertenor Alfred Deller 'But who may abide' and 'Thou art gone up on high' – arias which hitherto were firmly associated by the public with a bass. Novel too was the introduction of a certain amount of ornamentation.[87] Tobin gave further performances with other revisions in subsequent years, but the real *Messiah* revolution started in 1959, when Novello's published Watkins Shaw's edition, intended to replace their old 1902 one, edited by Ebenezer Prout. Shaw not only included the main alternative versions, but also made various amendments and recommendations, especially concerning matters like double dotting and word setting. For old-time choristers, wedded for decades to their Prout, the innovation was naturally controversial and often resisted – the Huddersfield Choral Society did not change over until 1986.[88] So far as the choruses were concerned, however, the changes were not so radical as to prevent singers from continuing to use their old Prout copies, suitably annotated, and for many years a mixture of editions would be seen in use by choirs before Shaw eventually prevailed.

The arrival of Shaw's edition also coincided with choral societies abandoning the 'Mozart' additional accompaniments and reverting to Handel's original orchestration. This corresponded also with a gradual change of attitude towards the nature of the orchestras that played for them. Society committees, while happy to spend considerable sums on vocal soloists (regarded as an audience draw), tended to display little regard as to the quality of the orchestra, and were reluctant to see money spent on players. 'We sing for nothing, why should players have to be paid?' was a not uncommon, if illogical, opinion. As a result, most choral societies operated with amateur orchestras, supplemented as necessary with a few professionals. While this could work well in Romantic and later repertoire, with their generally richer orchestral texture, the more exposed and transparent lines of Baroque and Classical works quickly revealed weaknesses of ensemble and intonation. But the emergence of first-class recordings in the LP era made more obvious the inadequacies of many choral society concerts on the instrumental side, with the result that choirs, where possible, began to use professional orchestras – either an established ensemble, or one recruited ad hoc – at least for earlier repertoire. By this one expedient, the overall quality of many an amateur choral concert in 2000 was vastly different from that of fifty years previously.

A New Choral Ideal

It was to be the universities of Oxford and Cambridge in the 1960s that would provide the catalyst for a radical shift in concepts of choral tone, particularly as it affected early music. As early as 1961, while still a student at Magdalen College, David Wulstan brought fellow choral scholars and others together to form the Clerkes of Oxenford, with the intention of performing elaborate sixteenth-century polyphony, from that of the Eton Choirbook to Tallis and John Sheppherd (the subject of Wulstan's research). It began as a men's only ensemble, but women were soon added, and it was these who were to give the choir its most distinctive sound. For Wulstan believed that the music of this period was sung at a high pitch – a theory which was controversial – so that the treble line often soared to and remained at stratospheric heights. The women cultivated a pure vibrato-free tone such as the boys of Magdalen and King's were producing. The result was that the Clerkes sounded quite unlike any other choir, exotic even, and combined with the intensity of Wulstan's interpretations – though he aimed to let the music speak for itself – they attracted widespread admiration and served as an inspiration to others. Both Peter Phillips, who founded the Tallis Scholars in 1973 and Harry Christophers (a one-time member of the Clerkes), who founded The Sixteen in 1977, acknowledged their influence.[89] The Clerkes themselves would survive until the early 1980s, and although they made a number of recordings, they never migrated to being a true professional ensemble.

In Cambridge, a rather different revolution took place, when in 1964 a 20-year-old history student at King's, with a burning desire to enliven what he saw as an over-restrained approach to early music in Cambridge, mounted a performance of the Monteverdi Vespers in King's Chapel. Creating an immediate impact and attracting critical acclaim, thus was born John Eliot Gardiner's Monteverdi Choir, consisting then of choral scholars from King's and elsewhere and undergraduate sopranos.[90] It would evolve into a fully professional choir, usually of 30–40 singers, which set new standards for flexibility and virtuosity, with a repertoire extending from the sixteenth century to the present day, and equally at home in Percy Grainger as in Purcell. With its clear-cut tone, supplied largely by the graduate products of the Oxbridge college chapels and their like, it would usually be partnered by one of Gardiner's period instrument orchestras, the English Baroque Soloists, or (for later music) the Orchestre Revolutionnaire et Romantique. Bach was to become a particular focus, culminating in its 'Bach Cantata Pilgrimage' of 2000, performing and recording almost all the sacred cantatas in churches throughout Europe.[91] Great attention to the expressiveness of the texts has characterized its performances, typically given a firm rhythmic drive at speeds, which sometimes could be taken to excess by the demanding Gardiner. But its world-wide touring provided an excellent showcase for British choral singing at its best. The trend towards faster speeds in late baroque music became marked among all groups as the century advanced (and not confined to Britain), and while the ensuing liveliness was welcome, something of the 'grandeur' of the music could often be lost – it could take conductors like Charles Mackerras to find the happy balance.

Gardiner's pioneering work would be followed by other similar-sized and equally accomplished groups, each formed by an individual keen to pursue their own vision of how they wanted to create music. Often starting with a narrow focus, many have gradually broadened their repertoire. Notable among them have been Andrew Parrott's Taverner Choir and Consort (1973), Peter Phillips's Tallis Scholars (1973), Paul McCreesh's Gabrieli Consort and Players (1982), Robert Hollingworth's I Fagiolini (1986) and the Birmingham-based Ex Cathedra (1969), created by Jeffrey Skidmore, whose enthusiasm for the Baroque music of Latin America has revealed rich pickings. Most of these groups are quite flexible in constitution, operating anything from a full choir down to a small consort. Their clear-cut sound was complemented by the instrumental forces they employed in accompanied repertoire – formed from a new generation of historically aware players with appropriate instruments, who would appear in various ensembles, either specifically associated with a choral group, or in bodies such as the Academy of Ancient Music and the Orchestra of the Age of Enlightenment.

It was the growth of (usually) one-to-a-part vocal ensembles which would mark out the late decades of the century. Such a group had its predecessors, as witness The English Singers in the 1920s, but the new era started when a six-man ensemble emerged out of the mid-1960s King's choral scholars, already used to providing out-of-chapel entertainment at college feasts and madrigal parties on the river. In 1968 they took part in a concert at the Queen Elizabeth Hall under the name of The King's Singers, and their reception suggested that it might be possible to make a career out of it.[92] It took a couple of years for the group's membership to settle – women were occasionally involved in early concerts – but by 1972 they were touring internationally and appearing on popular television shows. The link with the college diminished over time as any vacancies were filled by the most suitable voice available, regardless of origin. Their secret was to generally present mixed programmes, starting with serious fare, sacred and secular, old and new, and finishing with arrangements from musicals and popular music of all types, many created explicitly for the group by the best in the business; they never forgot that they were there to entertain the audience. The sound was an amalgam of the precise, immaculately tuned and blended tone with its roots in the stalls of Willcocks's King's, together with the rhythms and jazz-influenced world of close harmony groups.[93]

The King's Singers have had few real imitators – not least in their unusual make-up of two countertenors, one tenor, two baritones and a bass – but their success was to lead others to hope that small professional ensembles could be made financially viable. So, from the 1970s onwards, we see a number of groups come into existence, mostly specializing in medieval and Renaissance music, exemplified in Gothic Voices, the Hilliard Ensemble, the Cardinall's Musick and the Brabant Ensemble. With all these small groups we are in a grey area when it comes to defining a choir and choral music. The medieval music sung by groups like Gothic Voices was certainly intended to be sung one voice to a part. For sacred music of the sixteenth century, when polyphony began to be sung with at least more of the whole choir participating, there must have been many occasions on which pieces were still sung one to a part, or with minimal doubling (especially by the lower voices), so modern ensembles who perform it that way can claim historical justification for it, quite apart from the arguments that it allows complex textures to be more clearly discerned, or that, in the right hands, the music works well that way to modern ears.

The singers in these new professional choirs and ensembles came predominantly from the Oxbridge chapel tradition – in which women had begun to play an increasingly conspicuous role as the colleges become mixed – and were thus fully 'ensemble trained' by the time they left university. This contrasted with many who had undergone the more soloist-orientated conservatoire curriculum, though many of these would have supplemented their student finances by singing in church choirs. With the exception of the King's Singers, none of these new groups offered full-time employment, though the Monteverdi Choir was busier than many. As a result, the same singers would be found in more than one ensemble, and it must be admitted that, given the similarity of their basic sounds, it is often difficult to tell individual groups apart. Above all, the modern professional ensemble singer needs to be flexible, not only in availability, but also vocally. Directors will have different wishes regarding vibrato, for example, and in addition to these specialized singing commitments, other income streams may involve such diverse areas as opera chorus work, church choirs, strengthening symphonic choruses or teaching, quite apart from non-musical forms of employment. It is clear, however, that far more singers were able to make a living – even if often a precarious one – from the musical profession in the latter decades of the century than had been the case hitherto. Two factors have played an important part in this: firstly, the large growth in the number of festivals throughout the country and abroad, for which small ensembles in particular were economically attractive and increasingly popular with the public, either in a main spot or as extra late-night entertainment. Secondly, these decades, with the transition from the LP to the CD, were a boom time for the recording industry and provided a vital element in the financial viability of these ensembles.

School and Youth Choirs

The post-war years saw major educational change in the state sector, following the passing of the 1944 Education Act, with its confirmation of a division between primary and secondary education at age eleven, and its raising of the school leaving age, initially to fifteen. With music, emphasis soon shifted away from singing to playing instruments. For many at primary level, this was to be the age of the recorder rather than the singing class. Sight-singing instruction, already in decline in the 1930s, was to largely disappear as new curricula were developed. With a gradual fall-off in daily Christian assemblies, fewer children would even experience communal hymn singing. From the sixties onwards, the voices of pop singers, and later rappers, dominated by the microphone, tended to form young people's idea of singing techniques; most were never taught to find the upper registers of their voices. The results were painfully evident in many a concert by massed junior school choirs towards the end of the century, when children were routinely struggling with any notes above D on the fourth line of the treble stave. At its root often lay the lack of any practical training of teachers themselves, who were just not equipped to impart vocal technique to their pupils. Nevertheless, even though those responsible for music at primary level are unlikely to be professionally trained musicians, the basics of good vocal production can be taught quite simply to non-specialists, and some encouragement to this end would be forthcoming in the next century.

There were, of course, excellent state school choirs to be found, when a charismatic figure was in charge. At secondary level they were naturally more common among girls – and in mixed schools, junior boys would seldom be found singing treble with them, resulting consequently in a lack of young tenors and basses. But boys could be found singing in state schools, most notably in the Wandsworth School Choir, created in 1954 by its 23-year-old director of music, Russell Burgess. He was the classic example of how one person could produce extraordinary results out of very ordinary material. For Wandsworth School was then in a predominantly working-class area of South London, and though a grammar school at the time of Burgess's arrival, it would soon mutate into a comprehensive. Within a few years the trebles were being employed to sing in concerts with the leading London orchestras, and boys were wanting to join the school for the sake of its music.[94] The 'Wandsworth Sound' was an unmistakeable strong and open one. Their entry of 'Sumer is icumen in' in Britten's *Spring Symphony*, cutting easily through the full orchestra, made an unforgettable impression on audiences. Unsurprisingly, Britten was much taken by their sound and musicianship, and used them for his recording of *The Golden*

Vanity in 1970. Nor did Burgess neglect the changed voices in the school, for he directed a fine SATB choir (and proficient orchestra), even if it did not have the same public exposure. Burgess was to die prematurely in 1979 at the age of forty-eight, and though choral activity at first continued strongly, outside engagements soon fell away, and the school itself lost its name on amalgamation with another in 1986.

Also in the state sector, the Tiffin School, Kingston, a selective grammar school, has had a similarly strong choral culture since 1957, and the Tiffin Boys' Choir has regularly fulfilled engagements with major orchestras, at Covent Garden, and in the recording studio, including film soundtracks.[95] Likewise, more recently, the Cardinal Vaughan Memorial School Schola Cantorum has had a similar range of activity. The capital's other two prominent boys' school choirs of the period were both in the independent sector. That of Highgate School (which numbered John Taverner and John Rutter among its pupils) was frequently used by the BBC, and most notably was chosen by Britten for the boys' choir in his 1963 recording of the *War Requiem*. Then at Trinity School, Croydon, David Squibb founded the Trinity Boys' Choir in 1964, which went on, like the Tiffin boys, to become well-known in the opera house as well as in concerts and recordings.[96] Fine choirs in girls' schools were doubtless also to be found, but with fewer calls by composers specifically for girls' voices, they had less opportunity to make their name in public. In general, the independent schools, with their inherently traditional nature, maintained choral singing as an important element of school life when the state sector was rapidly discarding it. One part of the UK which ran somewhat counter to the general trend was Northern Ireland, where school choirs continued to flourish, even through the 'troubles', and not least at the Methodist College, Belfast, which had a long tradition of choral excellence.

But if singing in state schools was in decline, then efforts were being made by enthusiasts to run local junior choirs in various parts of the country. Among the best known were the Orpington Junior Singers, a girls' choir formed in 1949 by Sheila Mossman, which went on to win many competitions; it would survive Mossman's early death in 1971 but ceased to exist soon after the millennium. Equally renowned has been the Southend Boys' Choir, formed in 1970, which, like the London boys' choirs, has been much in demand on the professional concert and recording scene. It has subsequently been joined by the Southend Girls' Choir and other young ensembles, which continue to thrive to the present day.[97] Other groups which have risen and fallen, enjoying fame for a while, have included the London Boy Singers (1961–74), the New London Children's Choir (1991–2022) and the Manchester Boys' Choir (1981–2009). The various County Music Services, which sprang into existence in the post-war period have focussed mainly on orchestral and other instrumental ensembles, often reaching impressive standards; such choral activity as some have cultivated has been a side-line.

Choral Diversity Reigns

One of the most striking developments of the latter part of the century was the growth in the variety of choirs coming into existence. On the professional side, we have already seen the emergence of small expert vocal ensembles, but mention should also be made of full-time opera choruses. Before the Second World War, opera seasons at both Covent Garden and Sadler's Wells were short and highly dependent on financial conditions, so that freelance chorus singers were engaged according to need.[98] Only with the resumption of opera performances after the war and the introduction of state subsidies from the newly created Arts Council was there a move to create permanent choruses, which soon distinguished themselves by their quality – with Sadler's Wells moving from Islington to the Coliseum in 1968 to become English National Opera. Welsh National Opera began life as a part-time amateur company in 1946 without a permanent base, only gradually moving into the professional world; its chorus, much praised even in the early days, began to turn professional in 1968, completing the process in 1973 when the company settled into in its Cardiff home.[99] Similarly strong choruses have been characteristic of the later creations of Opera North and Scottish Opera, while Glyndebourne Festival Opera's chorus has, apart from its own merits, proved a valuable training ground for future operatic stars. Post-war opera choruses have had to develop their acting and dancing skills far more than their predecessors, as the modern curse of 'director's opera' has taken hold. 'Stand and deliver' is no longer the order of the day.

The chorus, of course, has had an important role in the many amateur operatic societies found throughout the country. Some, like that of Halifax, began to emerge at the beginning of the century,[100] often then combined with a dramatic society. Opera in this context generally came to mean the comic operas of Gilbert and Sullivan or works like Edward German's *Merrie England*.[101] The real growth, in both numbers and ambition, came after the Second World War, when Gilbert and Sullivan tended to give way to modern Broadway and West End musicals from *Oklahoma* and *My Fair Lady* to *West Side Story*, *Oliver*, *Sweeny Todd* and beyond. The standard of many productions became increasingly professional, and the societies have often successfully attracted young members.

In the provinces, post-war urban choral societies began to experience competition from within the choral community. Notably, there was a development of smaller choirs of around 20–40 singers, often tending to specialize in particular repertoires, whether unaccompanied Renaissance polyphony or challenging contemporary music. By their very nature, such choirs demanded more proficiency in sight-reading than might be expected from the average choral society member – there was no room for 'passengers'. As a consequence, they could contribute to the weakening of the larger bodies, as better singers often preferred the stimulus offered by a chamber choir, especially if the large choral society was stuck in the rut of well-known classics. Such choirs tended to be spared the expenses involved in employing large orchestras and soloists, which helped offset the fact that overheads had to be covered by a smaller number of singers, and that there was a smaller pool of 'family and friends', who typically constitute a substantial part of choral society audiences. Among specialized choirs the revival of 'country psalmody' by groups in the West Gallery Music Association, founded in 1990, has already been noted in Chapter Three.

Yet a further type of choir which has sprung into existence towards the end of the century is one specializing in visiting cathedrals to sing services when the resident choir is absent. These have thus supplemented the work of cathedrals' own voluntary choirs and of competent parish choirs accustomed to take over cathedral duties. Members of these new groups might also sing in their parish choirs, but welcome the opportunity to tackle more ambitious repertoire, while others may have abandoned a parish choir (or failed to find a suitable one). Some choirs have quite local membership, rehearsing regularly, whereas others draw singers from a wide area and only come together at the venue itself. Most visits involve singing only at the weekend, but sometimes a whole week's residence is undertaken, combined with other holiday activities. The cathedrals themselves have come to value their contribution, which helps to keep their buildings musically alive throughout the year.

Still within the sacred music sphere has been the rise of Gospel Music choirs. Their origins lay in post-war immigration from the Caribbean, which led to the formation of black church communities, whose services, typically of a Pentecostal nature, are characterized by fervent singing from a choir (usually with a lead singer), often amplified, with or without instrumental support. The more general appeal of this style of music has resulted in the creation of gospel choirs operating outside church networks. Thus were born groups such as the London Community Gospel Choir (1982) and the London International Gospel Choir, which draw their membership from all attracted to the sounds of gospel music, regardless of cultural background. By way of contrast, the well-known London Adventist Chorale, formed in 1981, requires membership of the Seventh Day Adventist Church. Gospel music itself covers a wide range of material but is typically based on a rich vibrato-laden sound. Often operating on the amateur/professional borderline, many of these choirs have developed a strong commercial presence, offering entertainment for weddings, conferences and the like, in addition to their recordings.

Among choirs which have emerged to cater for particular segments of society, one of the most conspicuous is the London Gay Men's Chorus, born in 1991 out of the repercussions of the Aids crisis. Rejoicing in the immense therapeutic and social value of bringing people together in song, and with some 200 members, it has provided Londoners with high-quality fun entertainment. With a history going back to Victorian times, workplace choirs still flourish in many places, of which the British Museum Choir and the Parliament Choir are but a couple of examples. On the negative side, the fortunes of the old male-voice choir movement have continued to wane in many areas, with the gradual disappearance of the traditional industries around which many of them revolved. Unlike their one-time stable mates, the brass bands, which have in many cases managed to revitalize themselves and involve new generations of players, the male-voice choirs have struggled with an ageing membership and an unadventurous sentimental repertoire of 'old favourites'. Female-voice choirs have continued to find modest support, but both types are heavily outnumbered by the mixed-voice variety, which present-day would-be choral singers have generally found most congenial.

For all types of choir, one institution, which had been so prominent in pre-war times, was now in decline – the competitive festival at both local and national level. In the 1970s there still appeared to be an appetite for them, especially in the North, but by the 1990s even the Llangollen festival could only attract a handful of entries in the main competitions. In areas such as the North West, where those traditional competitors, the male-voice choirs, still had a healthy presence, some enthusiasm for local contests remained, if on a smaller scale than formerly. The spirit of choral competition, however, was not entirely lost, but shifted more towards the broadcast media, with choirs stimulated by the prospect of fleeting appearances on national radio and television. Back in 1957, BBC radio began its 'Let the People Sing' competitions, initially confined to British choirs, but in the 1960s becoming international in scope.[102] From 1984 came the biennial 'Choir of the Year' event, sponsored by Sainsbury's until 2002; it proved a considerable draw, with some 300 choirs entering the preliminary rounds in 1990.[103] The greatest contrast with competitions of earlier eras was in the sheer variety of presentation. No longer were choirs expected to stand still in formal ranks; they were at liberty to show real exuberance and *joie de vivre* as appropriate to their chosen repertoire, particularly when it came to the more popular genres. Seeing choirs obviously enjoying themselves in such competitions may even have encouraged more youthful recruitment – certainly they demonstrated that choral singing could embrace the widest variety of tastes.[104] Alongside this have been organisations like Sing for Pleasure, founded in 1964, offering courses and other resources for singers and conductors.

One popular late twentieth-century development, and probably largely a British phenomenon, has been the 'Come and Sing' event, whereby choral singers are invited to assemble to sing through a well-known work, either straightaway or after a preliminary rehearsal, with an audience of friends and others being welcome to listen in. *Messiah* is clearly the most commonly favoured choice, but works such as the Mozart and Fauré Requiems, or Haydn's 'Nelson' Mass have proved suitable, as on a more ambitious scale has even something like the Verdi Requiem. Such events have often been put on for charitable causes, and they could range from a homely affair in a local church to a vast gathering for several thousand at the Royal Albert Hall. As an offshoot, many choral societies have taken to holding 'Come and Sing' workshop days, inviting non-members to join them in studying a work and ending with an informal performance – events also serving as potential recruitment opportunities.

The British, however, were also becoming aware as never before of other nations' choral traditions, both through recordings and at competitions. The Bach recordings of Karl Richter and his Munich Bach Choir from the 1950s onwards, with their finely drilled articulation and choice of tempi – his B minor Mass of 1961 remains something of a classic – quickly influenced the younger generation of British conductors. But it was perhaps the fine choral sounds coming from Scandinavia, the Baltic States, and Hungary which surprised most, revealing deeply rooted choral cultures, crucially supported by the state, which not only cultivated singing in schools, but subsidized it at a professional level too. It was little wonder that these choirs would regularly win top prizes in competitions. In a different way, the Red Army Choir, with its renowned deep basses, was very much a showpiece (and propaganda tool) of the Soviet Union. Nor was the influence of American choral pedagogy to be ignored. With courses in choral conducting widely available in its conservatoires and universities, it showed a professional approach to the subject far removed from British practice, which still relied on acquiring the skills by a combination of singing under and observing other conductors, followed by trial and error. American choralism at its best has been characterized by great discipline and care over detail, and it was principally from America that the idea of beginning rehearsals with 'warm-ups' was introduced to British choirs.

All choirs have benefitted in recent decades from greatly increased access to music scores. Physical music shops may have dwindled, but music is readily available from online specialists and publishers, and can often be supplied either in hard copy or as downloads. In addition, contemporary composers now frequently self-publish from their websites, while out-of-copyright music is freely available from the Choral Public Domain Library. Obtaining rarities has never been easier, while on the downside, illegal use of the photocopier has severely affected the economics of traditional choral music publishing.

British Choral Traditions Abroad

The penetration of British choral influence abroad is a subject that can only be touched upon here. Its full treatment could form a study in itself, for which much basic research remains to be done. Most obviously, the colonization of large areas of the world by the British, especially from the eighteenth century on, brought with it the establishment of Christian communities of both settlers and their descendants, and, through missionary activity, among the native population, particularly in Africa and the Caribbean. As the larger urban areas developed, church choirs and choral societies emerged. In Australia, it was claimed that Christ Church St Laurence, Sydney had a surpliced choir of boys and men from 1845 – an exceptionally early date.[105] But, apart from the cathedrals (and not always there), a treble line of boys was to prove very much the exception abroad, and, understandably, women dominated church choirs, as well as often providing an alto line in cathedrals. As Sydney Nicholson found to his dismay when touring Australia in the 1930s, although there was an 'almost frightening readiness to look to England as a model', when boys were introduced in mixed choirs, they received little training and were openly regarded as 'ornamental'.[106] Nevertheless, the efforts of Nicholson and others saw a rapid rise in affiliations to the School of English Church Music, reflecting a desire for improvement. And there were fine cathedral choirs around by the 1930s – in Australia especially, those of St Andrew's, Sydney and St Paul's, Melbourne, the latter the only one to have a daily choral Evensong,[107] while in New Zealand that very English city of Christchurch had its cathedral choir (complete with a choir school) from 1881,[108] and in South Africa, St George's, Cape Town had a choir that could perform the St Matthew Passion in 1933, with boys executing the solos.[109] A steady stream of organists moving from Britain had provided continuing links with British practice since the nineteenth century, but with a general loosening of ties with the 'mother country' in the post-Second World War era, there was less looking toward it in cultural and religious matters.

Africa, and South Africa in particular, was where British choral traditions interacted most with those of the black population. Through Christian hymns introduced into schools and churches by missionaries in the nineteenth century, Africans came to absorb Western harmonies and textures into their traditional musical styles found in work and ceremonial songs, with all their rhythmic sophistication.[110] In time, however, wider influences, notably American Gospel music, would become predominant among African choirs. Meanwhile British choral traditions were maintained in the private schools, which in South Africa gradually became multi-racial as apartheid was dismantled at the end of the century. One unique example has been the Drakensberg Boys Choir School, founded in 1967 in the mountainous Drakensberg area. Admitting its first black pupil in 1988, its various choirs have toured internationally, now with a repertoire heavily slanted towards musical and other popular genres.[111]

The USA has naturally been subject to many diverse influences in its singing traditions, in which the British play only a minor part. Given the seventeenth-century Puritan origin of British immigration, choral music had no real foothold in the churches until the nineteenth century. The eighteenth-century country psalmody movement in England, however, was a strong influence on the singing schools and small musical societies that arose to provide sociable activity as well as improved singing in church, and which was promoted in the latter part of the century by native composers like William Billings. Desire to perform large choral works led to the creation of the Boston Handel and Haydn Society in 1815, which gave its first *Messiah* three years later, and is still in existence today. It should not, however, be regarded as wholly inspired by British traditions, since one of the principal founders was of German origin.[112] In the ecclesiastical sphere, English influence became most prominent as the Episcopal (Anglican) Church cultivated more elaborate music, especially on the high church wing in the wake of the Oxford Movement. Both all-male and mixed choirs flourished in a church, which, though numerically relatively small, tended to have fairly affluent middle-class congregations. Nineteenth-century Americans were accustomed to have an idealized picture of the standards of British choirs, and, as we have seen in Chapter Five, at least some of those who travelled to England were rather disillusioned by what they frequently found. The best known American instance of English cathedral-style music was (and is) to be found at St Thomas Church, Fifth Avenue, New York, a consciously Anglophilic church in the Anglo-Catholic tradition. In 1913 it succeeded in attracting Thomas Tertius Noble from York Minster to become its organist. He went on to establish the choir's reputation and to found the country's only residential choir school in 1919 for the boys of its fully professional choir. Even so, as throughout America, daily choral services were never to become a characteristic. Achieving international renown under Gerre Hancock (1971–2004), its strong British links were reinforced when John Scott moved from St Paul's Cathedral to succeed him.

In Canada, too, influences on the choral scene were naturally mixed, with its most famous institution, the Toronto Mendelssohn Choir, being founded in 1894 by Augustus Stephen Vogt, who was of German and Swiss parentage; its repertoire, however, was typical of British societies and included the Canadian premiere of *Belshazzar's Feast* in 1936.[113] Healey Willan, another English émigré who went to Toronto in the same year as Noble arrived in New York, became perhaps Canada's best-known composer, whose wide-ranging compositions included many short finely-crafted choral works in a fairly conservative idiom. They were mostly written for the Anglo-Catholic church of St Mary Magdalene, where Willan was organist from 1921 to his death in 1968, and whose small choir included many students, who were to carry the influence of Willan's high standards to all parts of the country.[114]

From the second half of the twentieth century onwards, other avenues opened up to display British choral traditions to the world at large. Most obviously it was helped by the enormous growth in recordings, but choirs of all types would themselves undertake visits abroad, to increasingly far-flung shores. So, places like Australia would hear choral foundations like King's and St John's, the Bach Choir would visit Hong Kong, and the City of Bath Male Choir would go to Japan, while the numerous small professional vocal ensembles are in demand world-wide. The author recalls a Leipzig performance of *Elijah* in 2009, conducted by Kurt Masur, when, judging by the audience reaction, the stars of the evening were the City of Birmingham Symphony Chorus, brought over for the occasion. But perhaps the most surprising phenomenon of recent decades has been the interest shown in the British cathedral choral tradition by choirs in the Netherlands, where groups such as the Kampen Boys Choir and the Roden Boys Choir, both of which are full SATB ensembles clad in cassocks and surplices, can be found singing choral Evensong complete with Stanford and Howells – indeed a case where 'imitation is the sincerest form of flattery'.

Chapter 8
Enter the New Millennium

The Lull before the Storm

The opening years of the twenty-first century brought no sudden change to music in the cathedrals and choral foundations, but rather a continuation of trends set in motion in the previous few decades. The participation of girls, in varying ways, was to spread to virtually every cathedral by 2020; opposition to them virtually disappeared, at least in any formal way.[1] The fear that chapters would see a single mixed-sex treble line as a means of saving money has, so far, not been realized. A few places have gone down that route since 2000, but difficulty in finding sufficient boys has often been the chief cause. For virtually all cathedrals and similar institutions have found their recruitment a continuing challenge in modern times, requiring ever more effort to fill the choirstalls. One institution, Leeds Parish Church (since 2012 Leeds Minster), for long musically a cathedral in all but name, has exemplified the problem in a particularly stark manner. Whereas the church had for over 150 years maintained a large all-male choir with around 30 boys, singing several weekday services in addition to Sundays, by 2000 the organist, Simon Lindley, was struggling to find 14 boys; in 1997 a separate girls' choir, about a dozen strong in the 11–16 age range, had also been started.[2] But recruitment problems continued, resulting in the abandonment of both boys and girls in 2015 and their replacement by an adult mixed choir of 24, singing just a Thursday Evensong and two Sunday services.[3]

Financial concerns, however, were certainly preoccupying many cathedrals at the start of the millennium. The situation at Truro in 2005 was such that its choir was in danger of at least radical change,[4] though a successful appeal avoided drastic action, and the choir, always 'batting above its weight', has gone on to be among the very best in the country, with a separate girls' choir having been created in 2015.[5] Another sign of financial distress came at Llandaff in 2013, when all the lay clerks and the assistant organist were made redundant, being replaced by per service payments.[6] Yet, on the whole, chapters continued to support their choirs well in the circumstances; in particular, music staff often increased in number, in part to meet safeguarding requirements and to assist with outreach projects in the community. It was also becoming common (following initial introduction at some of the choral foundations) for specialist vocal coaches to be employed to give individual (or small group) vocal tuition to the choristers – in the universities this could also extend to the choral scholars. One-year organ scholarships – for either pre- or post-university students – which were already on offer at some places like Southwell Minster before the millennium, have become common, and some cathedrals have developed pre-university choral scholarships – with notable success, for example, at Portsmouth.[7] Sunday congregations in cathedrals appear to have enjoyed some increase in numbers in recent decades, for which the music may be reckoned to have played some part. In many places the choir at weekday Evensongs understandably continues to heavily outnumber the congregation, although a few of the many tourists now visiting cathedrals do find themselves remaining for spiritual refreshment at the end of the day.

Alongside this has gone a gradual transformation of the position of the traditional 'cathedral organist'. As the role has progressively changed into being principally concerned with conducting the choir, leaving the organ playing to an assistant, so the official title has tended to evolve into that of 'Director of Music'. And for chapters seeking to appoint to that position, it is a candidate's skills in choir training and all-round communication, rather than at the organ console, which now figures foremost in their deliberations. Although most will still come from an organ background, it is no longer a pre-requisite, as seen most conspicuously in the appointment of a non-organist, Andrew Carwood, director of The Cardinall's Musick ensemble, to run the music at St Paul's in 2007.[8]

The other major innovation at cathedrals has been the opening up of alto lay clerkships to women. Their employment in the role was not totally unprecedented, as Chichester had used them out of necessity during the Second World War, though this had ceased by the early 1950s. In Wales, they had appeared at both St David's and Brecon, and Coventry too had introduced them, while Peterborough was the first ancient English cathedral to appoint a female lay clerk in 2010.[9] More in the headlines was St Paul's, which appointed Carris Jones as its first permanent female lay clerk in 2017, having already used female deputies since 2012.[10] They have now become common in many places, and indeed, the combined male and female alto sound can often help provide a better blend between the top line and the lower voices of the choir. In the same way, chamber choirs have found a mixed alto line can offer clearer, more incisive tone than contraltos on their own. Although female tenors are by no means unknown in choral societies and parish church choirs, they remain unlikely to find a place in cathedral choirstalls.

If musical standards in cathedrals and similar institutions remained at a high level, the same cannot be said about parish choirs, where the decline already well under way in many places was set to continue. Not only did boys singing in parish choirs become an increasingly rare sight, but the participation of any children in the choir often ceased, with them becoming wholly adult in composition. The reasons may be various – training children is inevitably demanding on a choir director's time, which many do not have available in twenty-first century Britain; parents may also be more reluctant than previously to let their children out to evening rehearsals; and lastly, the new regulations regarding safeguarding, however necessary, impose an additional administrative burden. It may be regarded as somewhat ironic that provisions designed to protect children taking part in such activities have often led to their complete disappearance, as choirs have found it more expedient to manage without them. Where there is provision for children to sing, it is often in the form of a separate children's choir, making its own contribution to services on an occasional basis. Better than nothing, perhaps, but their repertoire tends to be of a more juvenile nature, denying them exposure to the world of quality church music and the experience of singing on an equal basis with adult singers. Of course, the picture is not all gloomy, and there are plenty of places, particularly in the larger urban areas, where at least one church may be found with a flourishing choir of children and adults. In such cases, it will inevitably be the dedication and hard work of a particular choir director which keeps the ship afloat. The same may be said of the adults only choirs which now predominate; given the right leadership, results can be excellent, though one wonders where future generations of church choir members will come from.

In the universities, general improvement in the standard of chapel choirs continued to make headway. One contributing factor may be the passing into the university system of the first cohorts of girls to have experienced membership of cathedral choirs. The number of university choirs deemed worthy of being heard on BBC choral Evensongs increased significantly – and not just those of Oxford and Cambridge, but King's College, London and Royal Holloway are amongst those whose choirs were attracting first-class singers, with expert direction from the likes of David Trendell, Lionel Pike and Rupert Gough. University choirs, including the old choral foundations, have also benefitted from the recent large expansion in graduate students, whose more mature voices provide a welcome bonus. Up in Scotland, St Andrews has since 2009 supported choirs in its two chapels with over-subscribed choral scholarships.[11] Outreach activities have led to the creation of separate choirs of school-age girls at St Catharine's and Pembroke, Cambridge[12] and at Merton, Oxford,[13] typically singing one service a week during term-time, while also at Oxford, a girls' choir, Frideswide

Voices, rotated for three years a term at a time between the three old choral foundations before finally settling in 2019 as the girls' choir of Christ Church Cathedral.[14] On the mildly negative side, the ambition of many university choirs, together with the liberal provision of choral scholarships, has tended to produce problems of choirs competing for the best singers, particularly amongst the men, where the results of the increasing scarcity of those with a choral background as boys is becoming evident. Singing in the choir of a college other than one's own has become commonplace.

Although the standard of singing at university level was often very impressive, that in schools – at least in the state sector – continued to appal musicians. By the start of the twenty-first century, however, there were stirrings amongst various bodies and individuals to find ways of rescuing the situation. The Association of British Choral Directors was among those in the forefront of reform, realising that first of all you had to 'train the trainers'.[15] In 2000 Truro Cathedral and the Cornwall Music Service started a programme of taking choristers to sing in primary schools to provide stimulation to their pupils, an initiative which was quickly copied in several other dioceses.[16] The message that getting children singing well had educational benefits far beyond the activity itself did eventually percolate through to government, which began to support it with grants through its Music and Dance Scheme. In 2007 it went further and provided funding for a four-year project, 'Sing Up', to promote singing for primary school children on a national scale. It was spearheaded by the creation of a National Ambassador for Singing in the person of Howard Goodall, and the cathedral Chorister Outreach Programme became an official part of 'Sing Up' with no fewer than 45 institutions taking part.[17] Much valuable stimulation resulted, but it was only a four-year project, whose funding stopped in 2010, and insufficient to really lay foundations for any permanent resurrection of singing in schools. Nevertheless, many of the Outreach programmes did find means of continuing their work, often with the assistance of charitable trusts. Some choral societies and professional vocal ensembles also began to take an interest in the problem, creating projects for schools and youth groups – the Bach Choir, The Sixteen, Gabrieli, and Voces8 were among many taking initiatives, as well as various organisations founded by Suzi Digby, including the Voices Foundation. But they necessarily remain very haphazard in their reach and are no substitute for long-term properly funded support for all schools. Unfortunately, in the second decade of the century, official educational policy resulted in the demotion of music (and other creative arts) within the National Curriculum, which, combined with the effects of financial stringency on many local authority music services, produced anything but a favourable climate for developing singing among the young, despite the creation of Music Education Hubs in 2012 to coordinate provision. In these circumstances it has taken exceptional personalities and devotion to maintain singing in state schools. A new National Plan for Music Education, produced in 2022 looks promising on paper, but as ever, the resources made available to realize it will determine its fate.

The elite end of youth choirs, exemplified in the various National Youth Choirs of Great Britain or the Rodolfus Choir can give a false impression of the health of young people's singing outside the cathedral tradition. For these choirs, meeting only for a few intensive sessions each year, tend to be drawn heavily from the independent schools sector, despite bursaries being available for those in financial need. Below this, however, there is a network of regional children's and youth choirs, some run under local authority music services, others independent set-ups, such as the Only Boys Aloud organisation in Wales, established in 2010 with local groups for boys aged 11 to 19, and since joined by Only Girls Aloud and Only Kids Aloud.[18] Geographical distribution is inevitably uneven, as is the level of ambition and achievement. Only a few make specific provision for boy trebles. Since it is generally agreed that boys are most easily encouraged to sing with other boys, it is an area which is most in need of attention for the sake of the long-term health of choral singing. It may well be that most young people's introduction to the world of choral music comes in future from organisations such as these, rather than the hitherto traditional paths of church and school choirs.

On a more positive note, one significant development since the millennium has been the provision of choral conducting courses. Taking their cue from the United States, many higher education bodies now offer courses, finally bringing a professional approach to the subject, so long dominated by the 'pick it up as you go along' tradition. Although full-time choral conducting jobs are few in number, there is certainly the potential for a new level of expertise to be brought into choral societies and youth choirs generally.

For traditional choral societies the new millennium brought no immediate surprises. Financial concerns generally kept the choice of repertoire conservative, allowing only occasional forays into concerts with works guaranteed to make a substantial loss. The main exception would be the symphony choruses, who were more likely to be presented with challenging contemporary works, such as James MacMillan's St John Passion, by innovative conductors. It is perhaps a sad reflection that no new large-scale choral work within the classical music tradition has arisen to capture public imagination to the same degree as Britten's *War Requiem* of 1962. Leading composers are certainly commissioned to write shorter works by the professional vocal ensembles, but they are by and large tailored to the exceptional abilities of those groups – György Ligeti's *Nonsense Madrigals* (1988–93) for The King's Singers being an extreme example – and unlikely to find their way into more general choral circles.

One major development which took off in the early years of the century has been the emergence of 'community choirs'. In essence, the idea was not new. Many old village choirs, in particular, could have been so labelled. The basic characteristics are that they are open to anyone without audition and do not require an ability to read music. The prime aim is simply for people to enjoy making music together, without necessarily having any public performance in mind. Although they vary widely in nature, for many the concentration is on the light/pop end of the repertoire and learning tends to be by rote rather than from scores. Although most have been initiated by purely local enthusiasts, the movement has also seen more commercial interests involved, such as the Rock Choir and Popchoir organizations, with their many local groups. The community choir movement was given an important boost by the choral conductor Gareth Malone's TV series *The Choir*, which first appeared in 2007. Going into a school, workplace or other community, Malone recruited a choir from scratch, which was then trained up to take part in some conspicuous public event, competitive or otherwise.[19] Although the scenarios were rather obviously artificially fashioned to make 'good' television, and though many may have taken part only for their 'fifteen minutes of fame', the series clearly inspired a take-up of community singing round the country. As ever, having the right person in charge, is essential to success, and the qualities necessary to lead a community choir are in some ways more demanding than those for conventional choirs, for musical competence must be combined with tolerance of human imperfection.

Of Malone's subsequent TV series, perhaps the most significant was that featuring the Military Wives Choir in 2011. It followed on from the creation at Catterick in 2010 of a choir of military wives and girlfriends by two of their number, as a means of providing moral support when their men were deployed to Afghanistan, and they turned to Malone for advice. He then went on to form choirs at two other military bases for the purpose of the TV series. The subsequent success of their song 'Wherever you are', sung at the Festival of Remembrance in 2011 and released as a recording, taken together with the TV series, led to the wide take-up of choirs at other bases – 75 by 2022 – and the formation of a charitable trust, with individual groups coming together to record albums, all of which allowed them to function with professional direction.[20]

Another striking development from around the turn of the century has been the emergence of a seemingly endless succession of new professional ensembles, several of which have rapidly achieved international fame, though the fear is that there now may be too many for the market to sustain. Among the most prominent have been the Dunedin Consort (1995, conducted by John Butt from 2003), Suzi Digby's ORA Singers (2016), Nigel Short's 16-strong Tenebrae (2001), the 12 voices of Stile Antico (2001) and Voces8 (2005), the last two operating (like The King's Singers) on a co-operative, non-conducted basis. With the exception of the Edinburgh-based Dunedin Consort, and an older Scottish group, Cappella Nova (1992), most of these ensembles are almost inevitably based in London, drawing on the capital's large pool of freelance singers. There has been a tendency for them to move away to some extent from the pure vibrato-free tone sought by some of the earlier groups under the influence of the 'Willcocks blend' to more varied voice production. But the 'British choral sound' remains one of relatively restrained vibrato, compared with many other traditions on both sides of the Atlantic.

One remarkable and surprising feature of the various ensembles which sprang up in the latter part of the last century has been their longevity. David Willcocks's opinion at the outset of The King's Singers that 'they should give it a go, but it won't work',[21] of course proved spectacularly wide of the mark, but the Monteverdi Choir, Tallis Scholars, The Sixteen, the Gabrieli Consort, I Fagiolini and Ex Cathedra also continue to flourish at the start of the third decade of the twenty-first century, and all six were still being led in 2023 by their founders. Most, too, have had their existence threatened by financial crises in the course of these decades. Nor should the long-established BBC Singers be forgotten – alongside The King's Singer's the country's only full-time secular group, whose versatility is shown particularly in its promotion of contemporary music. Meanwhile, a few other prominent groups from that era decided that it was time to call a halt as their personnel grew older, including the Hilliard Ensemble and Gothic Voices who retired in the early years of the new century.

The turn of the millennium also marked something of a watershed in the recording industry. The boom which followed the advent of the CD in the 1980s, from which the new groups certainly profited, had now passed, and recording companies were beginning to be far more cautious and less generous. Many of the groups responded by asserting their independence and creating their own labels – the Tallis Scholars had been a forerunner in this, with their Gimell label back in 1980. Choral foundations like New College and King's would also go down this route, as indeed would some leading orchestras. The arrival of streaming services has further revolutionized the recording industry, and many foresee the demise of the CD, but for many small ensembles in particular, having a physical object to sell at concerts remains a useful source of revenue – quite apart from the fact physical CDs may stand more chance of being reviewed than streamed recordings.

And Then It All Stopped …

In February 2020 the choral life of the country was following its usual annual course; cathedral and church choirs were moving into Lenten repertoire, while choral societies were preparing Bach Passions or other seasonal fare for their Spring concerts. Although there was general awareness of the spread of the Covid-19 virus from China to Europe and of a serious situation in Italy, there was as yet little inkling of what was to come. Expert voices were certainly warning that it was inevitable that a major outbreak would soon occur in Britain, but by the end of February there were fewer than 25 recorded cases.[22] As we entered March, however, apprehension grew and when the government advised against indoor gatherings and theatres and cinemas began to close, a mood of uncertainty rapidly took hold. The author himself was present at the last concert to be given before lockdown at the Royal Festival Hall on the afternoon of Sunday 15 March. It was a Philharmonia Orchestra promotion, reconstructing the marathon four-hour concert that Beethoven gave of his own works in 1808, which, besides the Fifth and Sixth Symphonies and the Fourth Piano Concerto, included amongst other works the Choral Fantasia and excerpts from the C major Mass, sung by the Philharmonia Voices and the Rodolfus Choir, all conducted by Esa-Pekka Salonen. Sold out in advance, about three-quarters of the ticket holders actually turned up. Brilliantly compered by Stephen Fry, himself wondering when we might meet again, there was certainly something of a surreal atmosphere in the hall for what was a memorable and strangely moving experience. Even as halls and theatres all cancelled performances in the following week, few anticipated just how draconian the lockdown measures ushered in on 23 March would be or how long they would last. Perhaps nothing emphasized the seriousness of the situation more than the closure of all church buildings for the first time in history. In addition to the anxiety produced by the threat of infection and possible death, came that of enforced isolation and the financial repercussions of the pandemic for both individuals and institutions. Cathedral staff, salaried orchestral musicians, conservatoire teachers and the like were able to be furloughed – a word new to most of the population – which offered some temporary security, but so many of the music profession were freelance and self-employed, and fell outside the scope of any government relief measures, at least at the outset.

Choral singing being essentially a social activity, its cessation hit particularly hard. Singing, involving as it does projection of the voice, was viewed throughout the pandemic by medical professionals as a hazardous activity, with an increased risk of spreading the virus. They could point to the fact that some of the first group outbreaks in early March had been among the Skagit Valley Chorale in Washington State, the Berlin Cathedral Choir and the Amsterdams Gemengd Koor.[23] This consideration would lead, even after congregations were allowed back into churches for public worship, to a continuing ban on their participation in singing. It is a matter of dispute, however, as to whether it was the singing, or just the close interaction of choir members (in those early pre-distancing days) which was responsible for the spread of the virus among them. Initiated in part by two lay clerks at Salisbury, scientific investigation at Porton Down sought to clarify the dangers over the summer of 2020,[24] which eventually enabled at least professional groups to establish conditions under which they could resume limited activity.

Although all normal choral activity was brought to a sudden halt, enterprising heads were soon intent on finding ways to maintain choir members' voices and spirits in the absence of physical meeting. It was here that modern technology really came to the rescue. A video conferencing facility, virtually unknown outside the business community, was suddenly to become a household word – Zoom. This and social media platforms were to permit choir directors to organize online quizzes, music theory lessons, vocal coaching and the like. It was even possible to hold virtual choir practices, even though the director could not hear the individuals singing. With the aid of backing files, individual church choir members could record hymns and simple anthems, which were then (laboriously) edited into a 'performance' and could be incorporated into Zoom online services. There were problems and limitations, of course, especially with audio quality, and it needed someone with technical expertise to bring everything together. Perhaps only a small minority of church choirs could manage this, and many simply went into hibernation for the time being, but it demonstrated the determination of some to 'keep the show on the road'.

Various professional groups took on the challenge of creating virtual performances of ambitious repertoire for YouTube. The Oxford Bach Soloists and guests, including distinguished names, produced a remarkable complete St John Passion,[25] while Stile Antico's twelve singers managed to record the 40-part 'Spem in alium'![26] Other early projects invited general participation from those at home, including Gareth Malone's The Great British Home Chorus, the Stay at Home Choir, and the Self-Isolation Choir (later Choir of the Earth), which created a virtual *Messiah*.[27] The latter two were to continue beyond the pandemic as subscription-based online choirs.

Technically impressive as these enterprises were, and an invaluable boost to the participants' morale, singing alone into a microphone just emphasized how unreal and removed from normal choral experience it all was. For senior cathedral choristers, about to enjoy their last months in the choir, the lockdown would have hit particularly hard, since it brought their period of service to an abrupt end, without any of the traditional farewells and memories of their final services.

But Life Begins to Resume

As the first wave of the virus subsided over the summer of 2020, there were hopes that the worst was over, especially with the prospect of a vaccine becoming available far sooner than might have been thought possible. Schools and universities were reopened in the autumn, albeit operating under strict 'social distancing'. The provision for children to be grouped into 'bubbles', however, did enable both school choirs (mainly in the independent sector) and cathedral-type choirs to resume some activity. Church buildings were allowed to reopen in June 2020, initially only for private prayer and funerals. It was now that the sudden development of 'livestreaming' of services, made available on platforms like YouTube and Facebook, came into its own. Audio 'webcasting' had been pioneered by St John's, Cambridge and New College, Oxford in the first decade of the century,[28] offering remote listening to selective college services, but livestreaming was a totally different and most effective way of enabling a church's congregation (and others) to participate in their own homes.

Livestreaming was initially confined to the main Sunday morning Eucharist, and continued as limited congregations were allowed back from July 2020, for many were naturally reluctant to resume their seats in church. Congregational singing was not permitted and only a very small number of choir singers allowed – in most cases, when music was provided, a lone cantor presided. The professional set-ups of cathedral-type institutions were able to function with something resembling a normal choir, at least where the trebles were already in a school bubble. Only a bare minimum of lay clerks, however, were initially to be seen on broadcasts (presumably no longer on furlough), and while the trebles might be grouped together, the men were suitably distanced from one another, so that the choir was often seen positioned away from their normal stalls. From comparatively crude beginnings, some of the livestreaming from cathedrals became very sophisticated with the use of multiple cameras (invading even the organ loft!), and the best could rival television broadcasts in visual quality, as, for example, those from Truro and Winchester. Inevitably, however, sound quality was rarely on a par, emphasized by the limits of internet technology. Nevertheless, so useful has livestreaming been found as a way of communicating to the world outside the church building, that many institutions have continued with it after the official end of the pandemic. It has certainly made it easy to view and compare choirs at work, and, like the BBC choral Evensong broadcasts, has promoted the maintenance of standards, not to mention decorum in the choirstalls.

Further shorter, and partly local, lockdowns were imposed over the winter of 2020/21 as new variants of the virus took hold, though churches remained open. Unexpected setbacks could occur; the recording of the 2020 television programme of Carols from King's was imperilled when the choral scholars had to withdraw with a case of Covid. The situation was rescued by the imaginative step of drafting in The King's Singers. While the choristers sang as normal from the stalls, the Singers stood, socially distanced, in the centre of the chapel.

The swift introduction of the vaccination programme at the end of 2020[29] meant that by July 2021 restrictions on congregational singing and choir numbers were relaxed, though social distancing and the wearing of face masks continued in many situations. It would also be the signal for choral societies to start up again in the autumn. Understandably they did so in a somewhat tentative manner, and numbers returning were initially well down on pre-pandemic levels. Although many were delighted to be able to get back to making music together again, for some older members, the lockdown break would have provided a suitable opportunity to conclude their singing years. The usual annual pattern of recruiting new members having also been interrupted, most societies found that it took at least a year before a feeling of normality prevailed. Audiences, too, gradually returned, perhaps in larger numbers than feared, glad to be able to hear live music once again.

For church choirs, already facing a continuing period of decline before the pandemic, recovery has in many cases been slow, and more than ever dependent on the abilities of the choir director. This is also reflected in the post-pandemic figures for RSCM choir affiliations, which stand at about 3,500 – a drop of 1,500 from 2014.[30] Particular hurdles have been encountered by that minority who have continued to work with children on the top line. The regular recruitment of new blood, so essential for their flourishing, had naturally been halted, as had the ongoing training of those using the Voice for Life scheme. Some will have surmounted these problems, but a further fall-off in the participation of children in church choirs appears to be an inevitable consequence of the pandemic.

In the cathedral music world, as restrictions were eased, so choirs returned to their close formation in the stalls with a full complement of lower voices, and, remarkably, most were soon singing as well as ever. Whatever the disruption to the choristers' training, it was quickly made good. Recruitment, of course, had been affected, and while finding boys had become increasingly challenging in recent years, most choirs returned to adequate, if not comfortable, numbers. There were, however, problems which came to the fore in some of the newer cathedrals and made public news. Sheffield, which had experienced frequent changes of music director in the years preceding the pandemic, suddenly announced the dismissal of its choir in the summer of 2020, and its intention to restructure its music in more diverse ways[31] – in mid-2023, still evidently a work in progress. Equally dramatically, financial pressures caused St Anne's Cathedral, Belfast in the summer of 2022 to disband its paid adult choir and full-time director of music, to be replaced by a volunteer choir and part-time director.[32] This was particularly disturbing in view of the high reputation that the cathedral's music had long enjoyed, and which had only recently been enhanced by new ventures promoted by Matthew Owens, who had moved there from Wells in 2019. Although the Cathedral Choirs' Emergency Fund (created during the pandemic by a number of charities) helped alleviate immediate problems, the state of all cathedrals' finances in the post-pandemic era is giving cause for concern, especially as the expense of the music now constitutes a major proportion of the budget for many of them.

There have also been recent developments in the treble lines of a number of establishments. St Paul's announced in 2023 that it would create a girls' choir by 2025, with the girls boarding, like the boys, in an enlarged choir school.[33] Most institutions continue to run separate boys' and girls' choirs, but a few, post-pandemic, have moved to having a mixed treble line. Rochester in September 2020 merged its two choirs into a single body.[34] Then, more surprisingly, in October 2021 St John's, Cambridge announced that it would introduce girls into its top line from 2022, intending to eventually increase the total number of trebles to 25, as well as opening up the alto part to female as well as male choral scholars.[35] Also in 2022 Chichester, Hereford and St George's, Windsor,[36] announced that girls would begin to join their all-male treble lines. A varying mixture of equal opportunity considerations, financial prudence and recruitment problems probably lay behind the decisions in most cases. Such arrangements may be fine, so long as it is not considered that all choirs should follow that model – diversity in the constitution of choirs is something to be valued. The soprano Lesley Garrett's comment in 2018, disapproving of the all-male nature of the King's College choristers, would probably find little popular support.[37]

Much public attention has been focussed in recent decades on the admission of girls to the world of cathedral music, giving them opportunities long enjoyed by boys. Yet in the 2020s, while their recruitment appears to be relatively easy, boy choristers are increasingly seen as an endangered species, and their preservation is generally considered best guaranteed by having them operate for the most part as single-sex groups.[38]

May 2023 was to witness one national occasion in which music played a major role: the coronation of King Charles III and Queen Camilla. For the great majority of the population, this was the first coronation they would have experienced. Compared to that of Queen Elizabeth in 1953, it was a slimmed-down affair, not only in length, but in the size of the congregation and the choral forces. No special galleries were constructed this time to accommodate hundreds of singers. Instead, the choir sang from their accustomed place in the quire, and consisted of just the Abbey and Chapel Royal personnel, with the treble line supplemented by small contingents of girls from Truro Cathedral and the Methodist College, Belfast, and the men by eight members of the Monteverdi Choir. These singers were directed by the recently appointed Abbey organist, Andrew Nethsingha. Modern communication techniques ensured perfect coordination with the orchestra up in the organ loft, conducted by Antonio Pappano. The result was probably the most polished rendition of the music in the ceremony's history. The now indispensable 'Zadok the priest' and Parry's 'I was glad' naturally found their place, and there were no fewer than twelve new commissions in assorted styles from composers including the Master of the King's Music, Judith Weir. Guest soloists in the ceremony itself included Bryn Terfel and Roderick Williams, while an eight-voice gospel group, the Ascension Choir, and the Byzantine Chant Ensemble added to the eclectic mix. The pre-service music opened with a contribution of Bach and Bruckner from the Monteverdi Choir and English Baroque Soloists, before proceeding to orchestral and organ selections and two arias from the South African soprano Pretty Yende. The overall judgment was that the occasion had provided a superb display of British music-making at its best – it was also an affirmation that, artistically at any rate, the country had made a remarkable recovery from the pandemic years.

As we approach the second quarter of the twenty-first century, it is too early to assess the full impact of the pandemic on the British choral landscape. Outwardly, most activity has rebounded from the disruption remarkably well – audiences at concerts, understandably hesitant at first to return, are back in healthy numbers, and musical standards have recovered. Choir websites were already universal before 2020, and invaluable in promoting their activities, but, together with other social media, they really came into their own as a communication tool for members during the pandemic. Committee meetings and the like, then conducted online out of necessity, have often continued in that format out of choice. The internet also provides useful learning tools in the form of rehearsal tracks for individual voice parts of popular choral works, helping those with limited sight-reading skills.

While most cathedral and university choirs are flourishing again, ordinary voluntary church choirs continue to give cause for concern, though how far this is due to the pandemic as opposed to more general trends in church life is debatable. Beyond musical considerations, however, one post-pandemic concern affects choirs of almost every description – finance. The effects of the sharp rise in inflation and energy costs, on top of the pandemic, pose a threat to institutions generally. Opera choruses and the cathedral choirs are amongst those at greatest risk, and St Anne's, Belfast may be just a foretaste of radical restructuring that others may be forced to undertake in the future. It should, however, be pointed out that Lionel Dakers was predicting that the 'whole cathedral system' would be 'snuffed out through economic reasons' back in 1960.[39] Yet, whatever vicissitudes may face the choral community, somehow the desire for people to preserve Britain's immensely diverse singing culture will win through in the end. That, at least, must be our hope.

Further Reading

Chapter 1

The best general account of the musical institutions and developments of the medieval era remains Frank Harrison's *Music in Medieval Britain*, while Roger Bowers's numerous publications offer detailed investigations of various establishments. A clear exposition of the complexities of the liturgy is provided by John Harper's *The Forms and Orders of Western Liturgy*, and an excellent short introduction to plainchant is David Hiley's *Gregorian Chant*, complementing his longer work *Western Plainchant: A Handbook*. The niceties of Sarum Use are set out in Nick Sandon's *The Use of Salisbury*. Studies of the cathedrals are to be found in Stanford E. Lehmberg's *English Cathedrals: A History*, and Kathleen Edwards's *The English Secular Cathedrals in the Middle Ages*, while the classic account of medieval monastic life is David Knowles's *The Religious Orders in England*. John Caldwell's *The Oxford History of English Music* provides the most comprehensive overview of the music for this and later periods. Alan Mould's *The English Chorister* likewise covers the whole history of boys' contribution to the choral tradition, though it confines itself to cathedral-type establishments.

Chapter 2

Peter Le Huray's *Music and the Reformation* provides the best general overview of both musical and institutional life for the whole period. Diarmaid MacCulloch's *Thomas Cranmer* supplies essential background information on the Reformation years, while Kenneth Fincham and Nicholas Tyacke's *Altars Restored: The Changing Face of English Religious Worship, 1547–c.1700* covers later developments. Stanford E. Lehmberg's *Cathedrals under Siege: Cathedrals in English Society 1600–1700* continues on from his *The Reformation of Cathedrals*, and much valuable material on puritan attitudes is found in Percy Scholes's *The Puritans and Music*. Parochial music in all its aspects from Reformation times up to the mid-twentieth century is the subject of Nicholas Temperley's magisterial study *The Music of the English Parish Church*.

Chapter 3

General surveys are offered by vols 3 and 4 of *The Blackwell History of Music in Britain* (*The Seventeenth Century*, ed. Ian Spink; *The Eighteenth Century*, ed. Harry Diack Johnstone and Roger Fiske). Of various accounts of the Three Choirs Festival, the most recent is Anthony Boden and Paul Hedley's *The Three Choirs Festival: A History*, though Watkin Shaw's *The Three Choirs Festival* remains useful. For the festival movement as a whole Brian Pritchard's 1968 dissertation, 'The Musical Festival and the Choral Society in England in the Eighteenth and Nineteenth Centuries', is of fundamental importance. Donald Burrows's *Handel and the English Chapel Royal* provides valuable background information on the Chapel Royal in addition to Handel's association with it. The St Cecilia celebrations are comprehensively covered in Bryan White's *Music for St Cecilia's Day: from Purcell to Handel*. Glee culture is the subject of Emanuel Rubin's *The English Glee in the Reign of George III*, while Simon McVeigh's *Concert Life in London from Mozart to Haydn* covers many aspects of London music-making in the second half of the eighteenth century. A valuable study of country psalmody is Sally Drage's dissertation, 'The Performance of English Provincial Psalmody c.1690–1849', and the development of Anglican chant is comprehensively discussed in Ruth Wilson's *Anglican Chant and Chanting in England, Scotland, and America, 1660–1820*.

Chapter 4

Vol. 5 of *The Blackwell History of Music in Britain*, *The Romantic Age*, edited by Nicholas Temperley, offers a good survey. Percy Scholes's *The Mirror of Music* presents the history of the period as reflected in the pages of *The Musical Times*. For the festival scene, in addition to Brian Pritchard's dissertation (see Chapter Three), Pippa Drummond's *The Provincial Music Festival in England, 1784–1914* has useful material. The two main protagonists in the sight-singing movement are portrayed in Frances Hullah's *The Life of John Hullah, Ll.D*, and John Spencer Curwen's *Memorials of John Curwen*, while two leading conductors are the subject of John Carnelley's *George Smart and Nineteenth-Century Concert Life*, and John Goulden's *Michael Costa: Britain's First Conductor*. Michael Hurd's *Vincent Novello – and Company* is a good introduction to the developments in music publishing, and Michael Musgrave's *The Musical Life of the Crystal Palace* deals with music in that extraordinary building. Basil Keen's *The Bach Choir: The First Hundred Years* includes much valuable information on other choral societies of the time in addition to its main subject. Male-voice choirs are comprehensively studied in Christopher Wiltshire's dissertation 'The British Male Voice Choir: A History and Contemporary Assessment'. Among regional studies may be singled out Roy Johnston and Declan Plummer's *The Musical Life of Nineteenth-Century Belfast*, E.D. Mackerness's *Somewhere Further North: A History of Music in Sheffield* and Reginald Nettel's *Music in the Five Towns 1840–1914* and *North Staffordshire Music: A Social Experiment*, while Gareth Williams's *Valleys of Song: Music and Society in Wales 1840–1914* provides the most comprehensive picture of musical life in the principality.

Chapter 5

Vol. 5 of *The Blackwell History of Music in Britain*, *The Romantic Age*, edited by Nicholas Temperley, and Percy Scholes's *The Mirror of Music* are as useful in the sacred field as in the secular. Temperley's *The Music of the English Parish Church* is particularly comprehensive in its coverage of this period, while Bernarr Rainbow's *The Choral Revival in the Anglican Church (1839–1872)* is chiefly focussed on Tractarian developments. Philip Barrett's *Barchester: English Cathedral Life in the Nineteenth Century* includes a wealth of information on the music, if in rather indigestible form. Timothy Day's *I Saw Eternity the Other Night: King's College, Cambridge, and an English Singing Style* ranges far wider than its title suggests, dealing extensively with choral reform from the mid-nineteenth century onwards. David Lewer's *A Spiritual Song: The Story of the Temple Choir* chronicles the important story of the Temple's music, and Thomas Muir's *Roman Catholic Church Music in England (1791–1914); A Handmaid of the Liturgy?* is a valuable contribution to a neglected area.

Chapter 6

Continuing treatments of their respective subjects from earlier periods are provided by Nicholas Temperley's *The Music of the English Parish Church*, Timothy Day's *I Saw Eternity the Other Night*, Basil Keen's *The Bach Choir* and Anthony Boden and Paul Hedley's *The Three Choirs Festival*. Peter Doyle's *Westminster Cathedral: 1895–1995* is the best history of that institution's music, while the early years of the School of English Church Music are covered in John Henderson and Trevor Jarvis's *Sydney Nicholson and the College of St Nicolas: The Chislehurst Years*. An analysis of changing cathedral choir repertory in the twentieth century is provided by John Patton and Steve Taylor's *A Century of Cathedral Music 1898–1998*. Modern biographies of three principal conductors of the time are found in

Hannah French's *Sir Henry Wood: Champion of J.S. Bach*, Alan Blackwood's *Sir Thomas Beecham: The Man and the Music*, and Richard Aldous's *Tunes of Glory: The Life of Malcom Sargent*.

Chapter 7

In addition to the continuing relevance of many of the works cited for Chapter Six, the later history of the Royal School of Church Music is found in John Henderson and Trevor Jarvis's *The Royal School of Church Music: the Addington Years*. A personal view of church music developments in the period is Lionel Dakers's *Places Where They Sing*, while the creation of Guildford Cathedral choir is well told in Simon Carpenter's *The Beat is Irrelevant*. An account of one of the new symphony choruses is Daniel Snowman's *Hallelujah! An Informal History of the London Philharmonic Choir*.

Notes

Chapter 1

1. Hiley, *Western Plainchant* (1993), 487–8.
2. Even after the Reformation, the early editions of the Book of Common Prayer of 1549, 1552 and 1559, have a note that 'to the end the people may better hear, lessons *shall be sung* in such places where they do sing'.
3. Knowles and Hadcock, *Medieval Religious Houses* (1971), 45, 494.
4. Lehmberg, *The Reformation of Cathedrals* (1988), 38.
5. Edwards, *The English Secular Cathedrals* (1967), 33.
6. Dobson, 'The English Vicars Choral', in Hall and Stocker (eds), *Vicars Choral* (2005), 5. Hereford was an exception, apparently owing to financial constraints (Edwards, *The English Secular Cathedrals* (1967), 258–9).
7. Edwards, *The English Secular Cathedrals* (1967), 255.
8. Ibid., p. 253. Initially, in theory, the vicar was supposed to be in the same order as his canon.
9. Bowers, 'Choral Institutions' (1976), 2007.
10. Edwards, *The English Secular Cathedrals* (1967), 268–9.
11. Ibid., 256–7.
12. Jong, *In Samuel's Image* (1996).
13. Bowers, 'Choral Institutions' (1976), 2013.
14. Orme, 'The Medieval Clergy' (1982), 88–9; Boynton, 'Boy Singers', in Boynton and Rice (eds), *Young Choristers* (2008), 37–48.
15. Orme, 'The Medieval Clergy' (1982), 88.
16. Ibid., 91–4.

17 Edwards, *The English Secular Cathedrals* (1967), 312.

18 Ibid., 167–8.

19 Watkin, *Dean Cosyn* (1943), 29.

20 Harper, *The Forms and Orders* (1991), 38.

21 For details of the Sarum Use see Sandon (ed.), *The Use of Salisbury* (1984–99); for liturgy in general see Harper, *The Forms and Orders* (1991).

22 Knowles, *The Religious Orders* (1948), i, 285.

23 Oxford, Bodleian Library, MS Bodl. 775; Cambridge, Corpus Christi College, MS 473.

24 Hiley, *Western Plainchant* (1993), 370.

25 Harper, 'The Vicars Choral in Choir', in Hall and Stocker (eds), *Vicars Choral* (2005), 20.

26 Hiley, *Western Plainchant* (1993), 341.

27 Caldwell, 'Plainsong and Polyphony' in Kelly (ed.), *Plainsong* (1992), esp. 7–14; Hiley, *Western Plainchant* (1993), 373–85; Sheer, 'The Performance of Chant', in Kelly, *Plainsong* (1992), 179.

28 McGee, *The Sound of Medieval Song* (1998), 28, 117–20.

29 Harrison, *Music in Medieval Britain* (1963), 113.

30 London, British Library, Add. MS 25031; Oxford, Bodleian Library, MS. Lat. liturg. d. 20; Worcester Cathedral Library, Add. MS. 68.

31 Edwards, *The English Secular Cathedrals* (1967), 57.

32 Orme, 'The Medieval Clergy' (1981), 86.

33 Dobson, 'The English Vicars Choral', in Hall and Stocker (eds), *Vicars Choral* (2005), 5.

34 Edwards, *The English Secular Cathedrals*, (1967), 268.

35 Ibid., 271–2; Robertson, *Sarum Close* (1938), 51–8, 96–102.

36 Bowers, 'Music and Worship', in Owen (ed.), *A History of Lincoln Minster* (1994), 55–6.

37 Robertson, *Sarum Close* (1938), 56–7.

38 Bowers, 'Choral Institutions' (1976), 2025–7.

39 Watkin, *Dean Cosyn* (1943), 22.

40 Ibid., 11–14.

41 Ibid., 22–4.

42 Robertson, *Sarum Close* (1938), 104.

43 Caldwell, *The Oxford History of English Music* (1991), i, 53–7.

44 Edwards *The English Secular Cathedrals*, (1967), 311.

45 Nichols (ed.), 'Sermon of the Child Bishop' (1875), 24–5. The original is in London, British Library, Cotton MS Vespasian A XXV, pp. 173–9.

46 The quoted sermon belonged to the years of the brief return to Catholicism under Queen Mary, though she had died in November 1558 before it was delivered.

47 Harrison, *Music in Medieval Britain* (1963), 219.

48 Bowers, 'Choral Institutions' (1976), 2028; Bowers, 'Music and Worship' in Owen (ed.), *A History of Lincoln Minster* (1994), 53.

49 Edwards, *The English Secular Cathedrals* (1967), 258–9; Harper, 'Music and Liturgy' in Aylmer and Tiller (eds), *Hereford Cathedral* (2000), 384.

50 Bowers, 'Choral Institutions' (1976), 3020–1.

51 Ibid., 4085–4100.

52 Bowers, 'An Early Tudor Monastic Enterprise' (2007), 25.

53 Bowers, 'The Musicians and Liturgies' (2003), 37–43.

54 Bowers, 'Choral Institutions' (1976), 4040.

55 Lehmberg, *English Cathedrals* (2005), 88.

56 Bowers, 'Choral Institutions' (1976), 4048.

57 Kisby, 'The Royal Household Chapel' (1996), 83–4.

58 Ibid., 106–10.

59 Bowers, 'The Cultivation and Promotion of Music' (1991), 189.

60 Kisby, 'The Royal Household Chapel' (1996), 169–71.

61 London, British Library, Add, MS 57950.

62 Caldwell, *The Oxford History of English Music* (1991), i, 114–15.

63 Bowers, 'To Chorus from Quartet', in Morehen (ed.), *English Choral Practice* (1995), 18.

64 Harrison, *Music in Medieval Britain* (1963), 416–17.

65 Bowers, 'To Chorus from Quartet', in Morehen (ed.), *English Choral Practice* (1995), 19.

66 Storey, 'The Foundation', in Buxton and Williams (eds), *New College, Oxford* (1979), 3–4.

67 Woodman, *The Architectural History of King's College Chapel* (1986), 1–2.

68 Harrison, *Music in Medieval Britain* (1963), 19. St George's was only incorporated in 1352, although its letters patent are dated 1348.

69 Bowers, 'Choral Institutions' (1976), 6097–8.

70 Bowers, 'The Cultivation and Promotion of Music' (1991), 179–80.

71 Harrison, *Music in Medieval Britain* (1963), 197.

72 Atchley, 'The Halleway Chauntry' (1901), 75, 83.

73 On Boston, see Williamson, 'Liturgical Music' (2006), 192–3; on Louth, Williamson, 'The Role of Religious Guilds' (2001); on Ludlow, Smith, 'Elizabethan Church Music' (1968).

74 Williamson, 'Parish Music' (2017), 218.

75 Harrison, 'The Repertory of an English Parish Church' (1969), 143–7.

76 Williamson, 'Liturgical Music' (2006), 224–42.

77 Kisby, 'The Royal Household Chapel' (1996), 382.

78 Baillie, 'A London Church' (1955), 59–61.

79 Kisby, 'The Royal Household Chapel' (1996), 330–42.

80 Williamson, 'Liturgical Music' (2006), 217–18.

81 Ibid., 210–13.

82 Trowell, 'Faburden and Fauxbourdon' (1959).

83 Morley, *A Plain and Easy Introduction* (2003), 223.

84 Bowers, Choral Institutions' (1976), 6002.

85 Ibid., 6097.

86 Eton, Eton College Library, MS 178.

87 Doe (ed.), *Early Tudor Magnificats* (1964), vii.

88 Although the statutes stipulated 10 chaplains, 10 clerks and 16 choristers, it appears that only 5–7 chaplains, 5–7 clerks and 10–11 boys were in office at any one time between 1467 and 1520, and initially only four of the clerks were required to be skilled in polyphony. Extra men's voices when required may have been provided by suitably musical chaplains and/or ex-choristers from King's, St George's and Eton itself at the College (Williamson, *The Eton Choirbook* (2010), 7–9).

89 Bowers, Choral Institutions' (1976), 6021.

90 Bowers, 'Canterbury Cathedral' (1995), 420.

91 Bowers, 'To Chorus from Quartet', in Morehen (ed.), *English Choral Practice* (1995), 31.

92 Caldwell (ed.), *Early Tudor Organ Music* (1966), vii.

93 Parrott, 'Falsetto Beliefs' (2015), on which much of the following depends.

94 Curwen, *The Boy's Voice* (1909), 98–100.

95 Parrott, 'Falsetto Beliefs' (2015), 94.

96 Harrison, *Music in Medieval Britain* (1963), 56.

97 Bowers, 'The Vocal Scoring' (1987), 54; Bowers, 'An Early Tudor Monastic Enterprise' (2007), 30–1.

98 *Calendar of State Papers … existing in … Venice* (1864), ii, 247. *Giubilavano* is considered as probably referring to the florid style of singing as found in the Eton Choirbook (Blackburn, 'Music and Festivities' (1992), 16).

99 Bowers, *English Church Polyphony* (1999), Appendix to reprint of 'Music and worship to 1640 [at Lincoln Cathedral]', 6–7.

100 'hi lascivis hinnitibus & mobili gutture Deum placari credunt',

Erasmus, *Opera omnia* (1703), vi, 732C (comments on a passage in I Corinthians 14); translated in Miller, 'Erasmus on Music' (1966), 339.

101 Oxford, Bodleian Library, MSS Mus. Sch. E. 376–81.

102 Bowers, 'To Chorus from Quartet', in Morehen (ed.), *English Choral Practice* (1995), 34.

103 However, in the early sixteenth century, a more nationalist spirit was displayed in the Aberdeen Breviary, which had been promoted by King James IV and printed in 1509/10. It included many Scottish saints and followed Roman rather than Sarum liturgy (Cowan, *The Scottish Reformation* (1982), 2).

104 Everist, 'From Paris to St Andrews' (1990).

105 Preece, *Our Awin Scotts Use* (2000), 82–3.

106 Harper, 'Music in Worship', in Herbert, Clarke and Barlow (eds), *A History of Welsh Music* (2023), 53.

107 Boydell, *Music at Christ Church* (1999), 15.

108 Yardley, *Performing Piety* (2006), 109–11, who cites three other possible examples.

109 Yardley, 'The Musical Education of Young Girls', in Boynton and Rice (eds), *Young Choristers* (2008), 49–67. After the Black Death, even a large nunnery would appear to have had no more than 50 members (Power, *Medieval English Nunneries* (1922), 3, 214–16).

110 Bowers, 'The Music and Musical Establishment' (2001), 199–200.

Chapter 2

1 Le Huray, *Music and the Reformation* (1967), 2.

2 Lehmberg, *The Reformation of Cathedrals* (1988), 195–9.

3 Ibid., 194.

4 Expressed in a letter to Henry VIII, 7 Oct. 1544, quoted in MacCulloch, *Thomas Cranmer* (1996), 330.

5 Following legislation in 1547.

6 For the fate of Fotheringhay see Skinner, 'Music and the Reformation' (2008).

7 Lehmberg, *The Reformation of Cathedrals* (1988), 113.

8 Bowers, 'Canterbury Cathedral' (1995), 433; Simpson, *Chapters in the History of Old St Pauls'* (1881), 57; Atherton and Morgan, 'Revolution and Retrenchment', in Atherton *et al.* (eds), *Norwich Cathedral* (1996), 544.

9 Oxford, Bodleian Library, MSS Mus. Sch. E. 420–22. A comprehensive study of the manuscripts is Wrightson, *The Wanley Manuscripts* (1989), who also edited a complete edition (1995).

10 Even this set is not complete, lacking one of the four partbooks (the tenor book).

11 As in the Lincoln injunctions of 1548: 'They shall from henceforth sing or say no anthems of our Lady or other Saints, but only of our Lord, and then not in Latin; but choosing out the best and most sounding to Christian religion, they shall turn the same into English, setting thereunto a plain and distinct note for every syllable one: they shall sing them and none other.' (Frere and Kennedy (eds), *Visitation Articles* (1910), ii, 168).

12 Milsom, 'English-texted Chant' (1992), 91.

13 Robin Leaver's introduction to the facsimile edition of Marbeck, *The Booke of Common Prayer Noted* (1980), 31.

14 Le Huray, *Music and the Reformation* (1967), 28–9; Willis, *Church Music* (2010), 55.

15 Le Huray, *Music and the Reformation* (1967), 29.

16 Lehmberg, *The Reformation of Cathedrals* (1988), 130–1; Knowles, *The Religious Orders* (1948), iii, 424–34.

17 Page, 'Uniform and Catholic' (1996), 101.

18 Frere and Kennedy (eds), *Visitation Articles* (1910), iii, 23.

19 Ibid., iii, 319.

20 For example, Lowe, *A Short Direction* (1661).

21 Le Huray, *Music and the Reformation* (1967), 161–3.

22 Bowers, 'Canterbury Cathedral' (1995), 439.

23 Le Huray, 'The English Anthem' (1959/60), 7.

24 Ashbee and Harley, *The Cheque Books* (2000), i, 61–2.

25 Gasquet and Bishop, *Edward VI* (1928), 113–14.

26 The full title was *Cantiones, quae ab argumento sacrae vocantur, quinque et sex partium*.

27 A description of the impressions of the Russian ambassador and the Duke of Bracciano on a visit in 1601 is to be found in Hotson, *The First Night* (1954), 188–91.

28 Clay, *The Book of Common Prayer Illustrated* (1841), 192–3; *Liber precum publicarum* (London, 1560), royal imprimatur. In the 1662 Prayer Book Westminster School was added to the institutions permitted to use Latin.

29 This is doubted by some scholars, such as Roger Bowers and Richard Turbet (letters to the editor in *Cathedral Music*, April 2003, 54–5).

30 Harley, *Thomas Tallis* (2015), 149; Milsom, 'The Nonesuch Music Library' (1993), 168. There were also two octagonal towers with suitable first-floor rooms.

31 London, British Library, Egerton. MS 3512.

32 Burney, *A General History of Music* (1776–89), iii, 74–5; Hawkins, *A General History of... Music* (1853), i, 456–7.

33 Salisbury Cathedral Archives, CO/CH//2/2/1.

34 Robertson, *Sarum Close* (1938), 155.

35 James, *An Account of the Grammar School* (1927), 55.

36 Morley, *A Plaine and Easie Introduction* (1597), 179; modern edn (2003), 182.

37 Welch, *Two Cathedral Organists* (1957), 2–5; Brown, *Thomas Weelkes* (1969), 33–43. At an archiepiscopal visitation in 1615, however, all six of the choirmen had admired Weelkes's skill as their organist (Fincham, 'Contemporary Opinions' (1981)).

38 Bowers, 'Music and Worship', in Owen (ed.), *A History of Lincoln Minster* (1994), 71–2.

39 Simpson, *Registrum Statutorum* (1873), 275–6.

40 Field and Wilcox (1572), sig. B6.

41 *A Request of all true Christians to the Honourable House of Parliament*, quoted in Neal, *The History of the Puritans* (1732–8), i. 480. Copies of the original pamphlet appear not to have survived. A variant form of the text is found in Peel (ed.), *The Seconde Part of a Register* (1915), ii, 211: 'where the time and place of God's service, preaching and prayer is most filthily abused in piping with organs, singing, ringing and trowling of psalms from one side of the choir to another, with the squeaking of chanting choristers, disguised (as are all the rest) in white surplices; some in corner caps and filthy copes … imitating the manners and fashion of Antichrist, the Pope, that man of sin and child of perdition, with his other rabble of miscreants and shavelings.' The title of the pamphlet is given there as *The Request of all true Christians to the moste Honourable High Courte of Parliament*.

42 Earle, *Micro-cosmographie* (1628), sig. F9–10v.

43 Shaw, *The Succession of Organists* (1991), 199–201.

44 Boston, *The Musical History of Norwich Cathedral* (1963), illustration following p. 30.

45 Green (ed.), 'Life of Mr William Wittingham' (1870), 22–3.

46 Smith, 'The Practice of Music' (1967), 429–35; Lehmberg, *The Reformation of Cathedrals* (1988), 155; Payne, *The Provision and Practice of Sacred Music* (1993), 54.

47 The so-called 'Hamond' partbooks in the British Library (Add. MSS 30480–4) apparently began life in a London or East Anglian choral institution in the early Elizabethan years, before being added to in a domestic environment (Butler, 'From Liturgy' (2019)).

48 Aplin, 'The Origins of John Day's "Certaine Notes"' (1981), 297.

49 It is possible, however, that in certain cases a Chapel Royal composer may have lent his personal score for the purpose.

50   Le Huray, *Music and the Reformation* (1967), 237.

51   Harley, *William Byrd* (1997), 302.

52   Edward Kellie, sent from Edinburgh to London in 1630 to recruit personnel for the Scottish Chapel Royal, reported that he had brought back 'two boyes for singing divisions in the versus' (Rogers, *History of the Chapel Royal of Scotland* (1882), clxvii).

53   Oxford, Bodleian Library, MS Tenbury 791. Batten's authorship has been questioned, and other candidates proposed include two of Thomas Tomkins's sons, Giles and John, of whom the latter may have the best claim. See Evans, 'John Tomkins' (1987/8).

54   London, British Library, Harleian MS 7033, fol. 151, quoted in Plummer, *Elizabethan Oxford* (1887), 199.

55   Nichols, *The Progresses* (1823), i, 538; 2014 ed., ii, 344; see Parrott, '"Grett and solompne singing' (1978), 183 (and reprint in *Composers' Intentions* (2015), 369): 'She entered into the church with great and solemn singing and music with cornetts and sackbuts.'

56   Bowers, 'Canterbury Cathedral' (1995), 446–7.

57   Ashbee and Harley, *The Cheque Books* (2000), i, 94.

58   Boydell, *Music at Christ Church* (1999), 80.

59   Bowers, 'Canterbury Cathedral' (1995), 445.

60   Crosby, 'The Choral Foundation' (1993), 193–4.

61   Fincham and Tyacke, *Altars Restored* (2007), 82–3.

62   McCulloch, 'Music Reconciled to Preaching' (2013), 122.

63   Needham and Webster, *Somerset House* (1905), 104–6.

64   Crosby, 'The Choral Foundation' (1993), 169–72.

65   Costin, *The History of St John's College, Oxford* (1958), 67–70; Harley, *Orlando Gibbons* (1999), 160. In 1620 the College also commissioned an 'Anthem of St John' ('As they departed') from the Lichfield Cathedral organist Michael East (Costin, *The History of St. John's College* (1958), 68).

66 Caldwell, *The Oxford History of English Music* (1991), i, 506.

67 Cheverton, 'English Church Music' (1985), 231–3; Crosby, 'A 17th-Century Durham Inventory' (1978).

68 Crosby, 'The Choral Foundation' (1993), 221–67.

69 Ibid., 177–90.

70 On Barnard's book see Bamford, 'John Barnard's *First Book of Selected Church Musick*' (2009).

71 Morley, *A Plaine and Easie Introduction* (1597), 151; modern ed. (2003), 154.

72 Smith, 'The Practice of Music' (1967), 272–3.

73 Fincham and Tyacke, *Altars Restored* (2007), 95–8.

74 Smith, 'Elizabethan Church Music' (1968).

75 Smith, 'The Practice of Music' (1967), 300–3.

76 Cornish-Dale, 'Migrations of the Holy' (2018), 185.

77 Reynolds, 'Middleton's Household Chapel' (2000); Harper, 'Music in Worship', in Herbert, Clarke and Barlow (eds), *A History of Welsh Music* (2023), 68–71.

78 Frere and Kennedy (eds), *Visitation Articles* (1910), iii, 23; see also p. 40.

79 Temperley, *The Music of the English Paris Church* (1979), i, 63.

80 Ibid., i, 86; Marsh, *Music and Society* (2010), 426–8, who also challenges the idea that the psalms were initially sung briskly and only slowed down as the years passed (430–3).

81 Ashbee, *The Cheque Books* (2000), 114: 'Admonition was given to all the Gent[lemen] general that at all times of waiting, they bring their psalters into the Chapel, and sing at the psalmody, and not be silent when it is their duties to use their voices.'

82 Parker, *The Whole Psalter* (1567), sig. W4.

83 Byrd, *Psalmes, Sonets, and Songs of Sadnes and Pietie* (1588), [preface].

84 Weston, *William Weston* (1955), 71.

85 Milsom, 'Sacred Songs', in Morehen (ed.), *English Choral Practice* (1995), 164–70.

86 Two of the Masses (those for three and four voices) went through two editions, and both books of *Gradualia* were reissued in 1610, using unsold sheets of the original issues with new title-pages – cf. Clulow, 'Publication Dates' (1966), 2–3; Smith, *Thomas East* (2003), 170–2.

87 Gibbons, *A Collection of the Sacred Compositions* (1873), [iii]; Ouseley's conclusion was already challenged in his lifetime by reference to analysis of old pipes; see Johnstone, '"As it was in the beginning"' (2003), 519–21.

88 Johnstone, '"As it was in the beginning"' (2003); Parrott, 'Falsetto Beliefs' (2015).

89 Phillips, 'Treble or Soprano' (2005), 499.

90 Le Huray, *Music and the Reformation* (1967), 14–17.

91 Bowers, 'The Vocal Scoring' (1987), 48, gives 14 or 15 as normal in the fifteenth century. The problem of ascertaining the age is complicated by the fact that boys could be kept 'on the books' for educational or other reasons after a change of voice.

92 Greenslade (ed.), *A History of the County of Stafford* (1970), 168; Lehmberg, *The Reformation of Cathedrals* (1988), 204.

93 Bowers, 'Music and Worship', in Owen (ed.), *A History of Lincoln Minster* (1994), 65.

94 Lehmberg, *The Reformation of Cathedrals* (1988), 200–1.

95 Rashdall and Rait, *New College* (1901), 116.

96 Bowers, 'Music and Worship', in Owen (ed.), *A History of Lincoln Minster* (1994), 66.

97 Ibid., 68.

98 Crosby, 'The Choral Foundation' (1993), 132.

99 Robertson, *Sarum Close* (1938), 148; Shaw, *The Succession of Organists* (1991), 259.

100 Butler, *The Principles of Musik* (1636), 203, quoted in Parrott, '"Grett and solompne singing"' (1978), 186. Bowers,

'Canterbury Cathedral' (1995), 445, cites an account entry in 1626/7 at Canterbury for a book of '*cantiones*' intended 'for the viols', suggesting they may have been used for verse anthems there.

101 For an account of choirboy actors see Mould, *The English Chorister* (2007), 113–25, and Hillebrand, *The Child Actors* (1926).

102 Preece, *Our Awin Scottis Use* (2000), 294–8; Johnson, *Music and Society in Lowland Scotland* (2003), 9, 171–8.

103 Rogers, *History of the Chapel Royal of Scotland* (1882), lxxix–lxxxiii.

104 Ibid., cxxi–cxxvi.

105 Preece, *Our Awin Scottis Use* (2000), 299–303.

106 Rogers, *History of the Chapel Royal of Scotland* (1882), clxiv–clxix.

107 Ibid., cxcvii–cci.

108 Evans, 'A Short History' (1984/5), 53–60.

109 Cheverton, 'English Church Music' (1985), 101–2.

110 Boydell, 'The Establishment of the Choral Tradition' (2000), 239, 245–6.

111 Le Huray, *Music and the Reformation* (1967), 53.

112 Boydell, *Music at Christ Church* (1999), 50.

113 Scholes, *The Puritans and Music* (1934), 142.

114 Vicars, *God's Arke* (1646), 184.

115 Le Huray, 'Towards a Definitive Study' (1960), 170.

116 Scholes, *The Puritans and Music* (1934), 142, 148–9.

117 Smith, 'The Practice of Music' (1967), 233–5.

Chapter 3

1 e.g. Pepys, *The Diary* (1970), 12 Aug., 2 Sept., 7 Oct., 14 Oct. 1660; 25 Dec. 1662; 1 Mar., 22 Nov. 1663; 25 Nov. 1666; Spink, 'Music, 1540–1649', in Keene, Burns and Saint (eds), *St Paul's* (2004), 392.

2   Burrows, *Handel and the English Chapel Royal* (2005), 441–3.

3   Harley, *Music in Purcell's London* (1968), 90.

4   Locke, *The Present Practice* (1673), 19.

5   Parrott, 'Falsetto Beliefs' (2015), 77–9.

6   Pepys, *The Diary* (1970), i, 195.

7   Ibid., i, 265.

8   Range, *Music and Ceremonial* (2012), 58.

9   Pepys, *The Diary* (1970), iv, 393–4.

10 Holman, *Four and Twenty Fiddlers* (1993), 282–4.

11 Ibid., 397–9.

12 Ibid., 403–5.

13 Evelyn, *The Diary* (1955), iii, 347.

14 Holman, *Four and Twenty Fiddlers* (1993), 394.

15 Spink, *Restoration Cathedral Music* (1995), 97.

16 Lehmberg, *English Cathedrals* (2005), 222.

17 Thistlethwaite, 'Music and Liturgy', in Meadows and Ramsey (eds), *A History of Ely Cathedral* (2003), 245.

18 Crosby, *Durham Cathedral Choristers* (1980), 22.

19 Boyer, 'The Cathedral' (1999), 66–7.

20 Lowe, *A Short Direction* (1661), sig. A2.

21 Griffiths, *A Musical Place* (1994), 14.

22 Hereford Cathedral Library, Claviger's accounts for 1661, quoted in Iles, 'Music and Liturgy', in Aylmer and Tiller (eds), *Hereford Cathedral* (2000), 403–4.

23 Eward, *No Fine* (1985), 135.

24 Diary, 28 Feb. 1664: Pepys, *The Diary* (1970), v, 67.

25 Michael Honeywood to William Sancroft (Oxford, Bodleian Library, MS Tanner 130, fol. 17), quoted in Bowker, 'Historical Survey', in Owen (ed.), *A History of Lincoln Minster* (1994), 195.

26 Boyer, 'The Cathedral' (1999), 91–3.

27 Ibid., 337–47.

28 Diary, 26 Feb. 1666 (Pepys, *The Diary* (1970), vii, 58).

29 Spink, *Restoration Cathedral Music* (1995), 255.

30 Eward, *No Fine* (1985), 130.

31 Spink, *Restoration Cathedral Music* (1995), 399.

32 Crosby, 'The Choral Foundation' (1993), 193–5.

33 Spink, *Restoration Cathedral Music* (1995), 206

34 North, *Roger North on Music* (1959), 40.

35 Recorded in a 1728 version of his manuscript treatise *The Musicall Grammarian* (North, *The Musicall Grammarian* (1990), 212).

36 Cheverton, 'Cathedral Music in Wales' (1986).

37 Wilson, *Anglican Chant* (1996), 44, 59. Wilson provides a comprehensive picture of the early development of Anglican chant.

38 Ibid., 138.

39 Ibid., 91–2.

40 Alcock, *Divine Harmony* (1752), preface.

41 Beckwith, *The First Verse* (1808), 7.

42 Mace (1676), 22–3.

43 Hayes (1753), 100–2.

44 'Dr B—'s answer to H—P—', in Brown, *A Continuation or Second Part of the Letters* (1703), 266.

45 York Minster appears to have acquired a set (Aston, *The Music of York Minster* (1972), 9).

46 Ashbee, *Records of English Court Music* (1986), viii, 337.

47 Spink, *Restoration Cathedral Music* (1995), 207, 230.

48 Dexter, *A Good Quire of Voices* (2002), 199.

49 Preface to vol. 6 of his collection of services and anthems

for Lord Harley (London, British Library, Harleian MSS 7337–42), transcribed in Spink, *Restoration Cathedral Music* (1995), 445.

50 Lehmberg, *Cathedrals under Siege* (1996), 189–90.

51 Wetenhall, *Of Gifts and Offices* (1678), 489.

52 9 Dec. 1660 (Pepys, *The Diary* (1970), i, 313); 29 Dec. 1661 (Ibid., ii, 240).

53 Boyer, 'The Cathedral' (1999), 337.

54 Sharp, *Memoirs* (1820), 454.

55 Clifford, *The Divine Services* (1663), 'To the Reader'. The idea of such participation was even suggested by Francis Close, dean of Carlisle, in the nineteenth century (Close, *Thoughts on the Daily Choral Services* (1865), 7–8).

56 Granville, *The Life* (1902), 249, quoted in Crosby, *Durham Cathedral Choristers* (1980), 25.

57 Lefkowitz (ed.), *Trois masques* (1970), 47.

58 McGuinness, *English Court Odes* (1971).

59 White, *Music for St Cecilia's Day* (2019), 168, 182–5.

60 As specified in Purcell's hand in the autograph score (Oxford, Bodleian Library, MS Mus. c. 26).

61 White, *Music for St Cecilia's Day* (2019), 219–307.

62 Trowles, 'The Musical Ode' (1992), 352–4.

63 Baldwin and Wilson, 'Purcell's Stage Singers' (1996), 126–7.

64 16 May 1674: Ashbee, *Records of English Court Music* (1986), i, 138.

65 Range, *Music and Ceremonial* (2012), 7.

66 Ibid., 89–91.

67 Pearce, *The Sons of the Clergy* (1904) is the standard history of the Corporation.

68 Burrows, 'Orchestras in the New Cathedral', in Keene, Burns and Saint (eds), *St Paul's* (2004), 401.

69 Holman, *Before the Baton* (2020), 70.

70   Ibid., 109–10; McVeigh, *Concert Life* (1993), 209.

71   The name of the charity, after amalgamation with another, has changed to the more prosaic Clergy Support Trust, but the festival retains its old name.

72   Marsh, *The John Marsh Journals* (1998), i, 623.

73   The first history of the festival was by Daniel Lysons, *Origin and Progress of the Meetings of the Three Choirs of Gloucester, Worcester and Hereford* (1812); the latest is by Anthony Boden and Paul Hedley, *The Three Choirs Festival* (2017).

74   White, *Music for St Cecilia's Day* (2019), 277–8.

75   Shaw, *The Three Choirs Festival* (1954), 24.

76   Handel was also writing the occasional non-ceremonial anthem for the Chapel Royal at this period, and there is a fair bit of to-and-fro borrowing between the Chandos and Chapel Royal works.

77   Range, *Music and Ceremonial* (2012), 155–6. The number of instrumentalists, in particular, is uncertain.

78   Ibid., 178, quoting a note from Boyce to the Lord Chamberlain of 9 Sept. 1761 (London, National Archives, LC 2/32).

79   Burrows, *Handel and the English Chapel Royal* (2005), 264.

80   Johnson, '"Giant Handel"', (1986). Even larger forces, estimated at between 140 and 180 were employed in 1738 for Handel's funeral anthem for Queen Caroline, 'The ways of Zion do mourn' (Range, *British Royal and State Funerals* (2016), 172).

81   The standard work on Handel's oratorios is Winton Dean's *Handel's Dramatic Oratorios and Masques* (1959); it does not, however, include *Messiah*.

82   Dean, *Handel's Dramatic Oratorios and Masques* (1959), 81–2.

83   His fine alto soloist, Walter Powell, was a lay clerk at Christ Church, but had already sung for Handel earlier that year in London.

84   Wollenberg, *Music at Oxford* (2001), 23–31. Hayes had

attended the 1733 Act, when he was still organist of Worcester Cathedral.

85 Smith had several assistants in his copying workshop. Contemporary copies in hands other than those of the Smith circle do exist but would have ultimately derived from the Smith business.

86 Or perhaps through Dublin musicians such as Matthew Dubourg – see Burrows, *Handel* (2012), 340–1.

87 Ibid., 341. The oboe and bassoon parts, doubling chorus lines, date from later London performances.

88 *Dublin Journal*, 27 March 1742, quoted in Handel, *Collected Documents* (2013), iii, 801.

89 An advertisement stated 'the gentlemen of the choirs of both cathedrals will assist' (*Dublin Journal*, 27 Mar. 1742, quoted in Handel, *Collected Documents* (2013), iii, 801).

90 Burrows, 'Handel's Dublin Performances', (1996), 56.

91 Ibid., 56. It is unclear whether the soprano solos were all sung by the same singer.

92 Dean, *Handel's Dramatic Oratorios and Masques* (1959), 640.

93 O'Regan, *Music and Society in Cork* (2018), 48.

94 Hogwood, *Handel* (1984), 156–7, 180–1; Dean, *Handel's Dramatic Oratorios and Masques* (1959), 134.

95 Wollenberg, *Music at Oxford* (2001), 29, 62–6.

96 Knight, *Cambridge Music* (1980), 50–2.

97 Pritchard, 'The Musical Festival' (1968), 52.

98 Burrows, 'Lists of Musicians' (2010), 88–102; Burrows, '"Before him stood sundry sweet Singers of this our *Israel*"' (2020).

99 Dean, *Handel's Dramatic Oratorios and Masques* (1959), 640.

100 *Jackson's Oxford Journal*, 28 June 1755, quoted in Dean, *Handel's Dramatic Oratorios and Masques* (1959), 106.

101 Temperley, *The Music of the English Parish Church* (1979), i, 124.

102 Ibid., i, 103–4.

103 *A New and Easie Method to Learn to Sing by Book* (1686), Preface, [viii–ix].

104 Temperley, *The Music of the English Parish Church* (1979), i, 104–5.

105 Ibid., i, 127.

106 Ibid., i, 131–2.

107 Ibid., i, 129.

108 Riley, *Parochial Music Corrected* (1762), 26–7.

109 Landon, *Haydn* (1976), iii, 173–4.

110 Temperley, *The Music of the English Parish Church* (1979), i, 219–20.

111 Ibid., i, 222–3.

112 Ibid., i, 225–31. A common tradition in many places was for the *Gloria Patri* at the end of a psalm to be sung to a chant after the psalm itself had been said. Originally sung by the charity children, the congregation now increasingly took part.

113 Ibid., i, 145–6.

114 There were many later editions (to 1730), entitled *An Introduction to the Skill of Musick*.

115 Drage, 'The Performance of English Provincial Psalmody' (2009), 84–92.

116 Temperley, *The Music of the English Parish Church* (1979), i, 185.

117 Ibid., i, 165.

118 Drage, 'A Reappraisal of Provincial Church Music', in Wyn Jones (ed.), *Music in Eighteenth-Century Britain* (2000), 172; Gammon, 'The Performance Style of West Gallery Music', in Turner (ed.), *Georgian Psalmody I* (1997).

119 Temperley, *The Music of the English Parish Church* (1979), i, 162.

120 John Crompton (*The Psalm-Singer's Assistant* (1778), ix) was among those who warned against excluding congregations from participation.

121 Drage, 'The Performance of English Provincial Psalmody' (2009), 94–8.

122 Temperley, *The Music of the English Parish Church* (1979), i, 148–50, 196–200.

123 Ibid., i, 240.

124 Gammon, '"Babylonian Performances"' (1981) offers a sympathetic, if rather one-sided, class-orientated assessment of their rise and fall.

125 Riley, *Parochial Music Corrected* (1762), 1.

126 Nares, *Twenty Anthems in Score* (1778), preface.

127 Nares, *A Morning & Evening Service* (1788), preface, p. 2.

128 Bowles, *The Parochial History of Bremhill* (1828), 203–4.

129 Moore, *The Psalm-Singer's Divine Companion* (1750), ii, 17.

130 Gammon, 'Problems in the Performance' (2006) attacks the over-refined performances featured in many recordings, which treat it like art music rather than the natural style of rural musicians.

131 Temperley, *The Music of the English Parish Church* (1979), i, 158; MacDermott, *Sussex Church Music* (1923).

132 Temperley, *The Music of the English Parish Church* (1979), i, 144.

133 Ibid., i, 168–70.

134 Marr, *Music for the People* (1889), xv–xvi.

135 Bremner, *The Rudiments of Music* (1762), xiii–xiv. Bremner's publication, first published in 1756 as a deliberate response to the reforms, was intended to be useful to the growing number of Episcopalian churches as well as to Presbyterians, since the selection of music following the rudiments, included not only metrical psalm tunes, but Anglican chants for the canticles, as well as anthems and canons, which might have been used recreationally by all.

136 Johnson, *Music and Society in Lowland Scotland* (2003), 175–81.

137 William Croft, *Musica sacra: or, Select Anthems in Score*, 2 vols (London, 1724–5); Maurice Greene, *Forty Select Anthems in Score*, 2 vols (London, 1743).

138 Clarke, *Bangor Cathedral* (1969), 62.

139 Thistlethwaite, 'Music and Liturgy 1660–1846', in Meadows and Ramsey (eds), *A History of Ely Cathedral* (2003), 255.

140 Oxford, Bodleian Library, MSS Mus. d. 156, 158, 161, 166.

141 London, British Library, Harleian MSS 7337–42. The prefaces are printed in Spink, *Restoration Cathedral Music* (1995), 434–49.

142 Johnstone, 'The Genesis of Boyce's "Cathedral Music"' (1975).

143 Croft, *Musica Sacra* (1724), preface to vol. 1.

144 *Cathedral Music*, ed. Samuel Arnold, 4 vols (London, 1790); *Harmonia sacra*, ed. John Page, 3 vols (London, 1800).

145 North, *Roger North on Music* (1959), 268–9.

146 Burrows, *Handel and the English Chapel Royal* (2005), 445–7.

147 Stevens, *Recollections* (1992), 4–5.

148 Ibid., 13.

149 Preface to vol. 2 of his collection of services and anthems for Lord Harley, transcribed in Spink, *Restoration Cathedral Music* (1995), 437.

150 Byng, *The Torrington Diaries* (1934), ii, 346, 400.

151 Hayes, *Remarks on Mr. Avison's Essay* (1753), 96, 98, quoted in Heighes, *The Lives and Works of William and Philip Hayes* (1995), 84.

152 Robertson, *Sarum Close* (1938), 232.

153 Marsh, *The John Marsh Journals* (1998), i, 211.

154 Ibid., i, 408.

155 Ibid., i, 753.

156 Ibid., ii, 312–13, 369.

157 Ibid., i, 554.

158 Griffiths, *A Musical Place* (1994), 19.

159 Durham Cathedral Act Book 20 Nov. 1796 and 11 Apr. 1795, quoted in Southey, *Music-Making in North-East England* (2006), 98–9.

160 Byng, *The Torrington Diaries* (1934), i, 44.

161 Presumably the Handel Commemorations in Westminster Abbey (see p. 114).

162 Byng, *The Torrington Diaries* (1934), iv, 141–2.

163 Ibid., iv, 139–40.

164 Olleson, 'The London Roman Catholic Embassy Chapels', in Wyn Jones (ed.), *Music in Eighteenth-Century Britain* (2000), 105–6.

165 Ibid., 117.

166 Ibid., 113–14.

167 Oxford, Bodleian Library, MS Top. Oxon. a. 76

168 Crum, 'An Oxford Music Club' (1974), 85.

169 Ibid., 92–5.

170 Mee, *The Oldest Music Room in Europe* (1911).

171 Johnstone, 'Westminster Abbey and the Academy of Ancient Music' (2014), 329–32. In the 1790s the chorus was nominally 32 strong, with 8 of each voice (Doane, *A Musical Directory* (1794), 81).

172 Not 1741 as given by Hawkins, cf. Hobson, 'Musical Antiquarianism' (2015), 44.

173 Hawkins, *A General History of … Music* (1853), 887.

174 Hobson, 'Musical Antiquarianism' (2015), 24

175 Ibid., 91.

176 Ibid., 60.

177 Ibid., 63.

178 Hobson, 'Three Madrigal Societies' (2012), 44–5.

179 Robins, *Catch and Glee Culture* (2006) provides an excellent survey of the culture of the clubs.

180 Rubin, *The English Glee* (2003), 115.

181 Ibid., 91–8.

182 Gastrell, *Notitia Cestriensis* (1849), 57, quoted in Spink, *Restoration Cathedral Music* (1995), 407.

183 Drage, 'Elias Hall' (2000), 627.

184 Andrew, 'Musical Renascence' (1902), 262.

185 Andrew, Abraham Hurst' (1903), 183–7; Greenwood, *The Sol-fa System* (1880).

186 Andrew, *A Souvenir* (1905), 15–19.

187 Pritchard, 'The Musical Festival' (1968), 120.

188 Ibid., 124.

189 Ibid., 144.

190 Ibid., 130–1, 140–2.

191 Lysons, *Origins and Progress* (1812), 203, quoted in Boden, *The Three Choirs Festival* (2017), 48.

192 Pritchard, 'The Musical Festival' (1968), 144–5.

193 *Jackson's Oxford Journal*, 7 June 1834.

194 James, 'Concert Life in Eighteenth-Century Bath' (1987), 42.

195 McVeigh, *Concert Life* (1993), 92.

196 Pritchard, 'The Musical Festival' (1968), 124–9, 133–8.

197 Dibdin, *The Musical Tour* (1788), 196.

198 Burchell, 'Musical Societies' (1998).

199 Buckley, 'The "Deighn Layrocks"', (1928–9); Drage, 'The Larks of Dean', in Cowgill and Holman (eds), *Music in the British Provinces* (2007), 195.

200 Hogarth, *Musical History* (1835), 430.

201 Hodgson, *Choirs and Cloisters* (1995), 28.

202 White, *Music for St Cecilia's Day* (2019), 261–8.

203 Pritchard, 'The Musical Festival' (1968), 41–3.

204 Ibid., 76–9, 111–13; Dale, 'The Provincial Musical Festival', in Cowgill and Holman (eds), *Music in the British Provinces* (2007), 327.

205 Pritchard, 'The Musical Festival' (1968), 55–7, 106.

206 Ibid., 24–8.

207 Ibid., 178–9.

208 Ibid., 114–15.

209 Ibid., 51.

210 Ibid., 61–4.

211 Ibid., 74.

212 Marr, *Music for the People* (1889), xvi; Johnson, *Music and Society in Lowland Scotland* (2003), 35–6.

213 Marr, *Music for the People* (1889), lvi; Crosse, *An Account of the Grand Musical Festival* (1825), 92.

214 Burney, *Account of the Musical Performances* (1785).

215 Drage, 'The Larks of Dean', in Cowgill and Holman (eds), *Music in the British Provinces* (2007), 208.

216 Burney, *Account of the Musical Performances* (1785), 12–13.

217 Crosse, *An Account of the Grand Musical Festival* (1825), 41, 45–6.

218 Ibid., 50–2.

219 Pritchard, 'The Musical Festival' (1968), 150.

220 Shaw, *The Three Choirs Festival* (1954), 18.

221 *Aris's Birmingham Gazette*, 2 Sept. 1802, quoted in Pritchard, 'The Musical Festival' (1968), 274.

222 Pritchard, 'The Musical Festival' (1968), 162–3.

223 *Sheffield Register*, 25 Aug. 1787, quoted in Pritchard, 'he Musical Festival' (1968), 164.

224 *The Works of Handel in Score, Correct, Uniform, and Complete*, ed. Samuel Arnold, 32 vols (London, [1787–97]).

225 Pritchard, 'The Musical Festival' (1968), 165.

226 Rice, 'Did Haydn attend the Handel Commemoration?' (2012) surveys the various pieces of evidence for his attendance. The assumption that he heard *Messiah* is unproven.

227 The score was also issued in a German/French edition.

228 Salomon is also said to have been involved in Haydn being given the English model libretto of the oratorio.

229 Pritchard, 'The Provincial Festivals of the Ashley Family' (1969).

230 Olleson, *Samuel Wesley* (2003), 141–4.

231 Crosse, *An Account of the Grand Musical Festival* (1825), 399.

232 Boden, *The Three Choirs Festival* (2017), 54–6.

233 Pritchard, 'The Musical Festival' (1968), 258, 272.

234 Ibid., 245; Pritchard, 'The Provincial Festivals of the Ashely Family' (1969), 67–70.

235 Pritchard, 'The Musical Festival' (1968), 239.

Chapter 4

1 Drummond, *The Provincial Music Festival* (2011) surveys the period 1784 to 1914, and is particularly useful for including those of many minor centres.

2 A complete account is in Crosse, *An Account of the Grand Musical Festival* (1825). For the York festivals as a whole see Griffiths, *A Musical Place* (1994), 83–98.

3 Crosse, *An Account of the Grand Musical Festival* (1825), 6–12.

4 Ibid., 310, 322, 400.

5 An extensive review is in [Anon.], 'Grand Musical Festivals', *The Quarterly Musical Magazine and Review*, 7 (1825), 413–44.

6 *The Times*, 11 Sept. 1835.

7 *The Times*, 30 Sept. 1835.

8 The history of the Norwich Festival is recorded at length in Legge and Hansell, *Annals* (1896).

9 Pritchard, 'The Musical Festival' (1968), 409.

10 Ibid., 476.

11 Ibid., 479–80.

12	Legge and Hansell, *Annals* (1896), 77–81.
13	Ibid., 62.
14	London, British Library, Case 61.g.16.
15	Legge and Hansell, *Annals* (1896), 215.
16	Pritchard, 'The Musical Festival' (1968), 296–302.
17	Ibid., 340 and 476; *Birmingham Musical Festival, 1846* programme book, 6–8.
18	Shaw, *The Three Choirs Festival* (1954), 53.
19	Deakin, *History of the Birmingham Festival Choral Society* (1897), 22; the years 1841–5 saw disputes among competing choral societies in the town (ibid. 18–22).
20	Pritchard, 'The Musical Festival' (1968), 706.
21	[Anon.], 'Grand Musical Festivals', *Quarterly Musical Magazine and Review*, 8 (1826), 286.
22	The largest organ was in York Minster.
23	Birmingham Town Hall was closed for very necessary restoration in 1996, reopening in 2007 with a reduced seating capacity of 1,200.
24	*The Times*, 27 Aug. 1846. Edwards, *The History of Mendelssohn's Oratorio 'Elijah'* (1896) provides a detailed history.
25	Edwards, *The History of Mendelssohn's Oratorio 'Elijah'* (1896), 123–9.
26	*The Star*, 23 Feb. 1893, reprinted in Shaw, *Shaw's Music* (1989), i, 565.
27	Pritchard, 'The Musical Festival' (1968), 340.
28	Mendelssohn Bartholdy, *The Mendelssohns on Honeymoon* (1997), 109.
29	Boden, *The Three Choirs Festival* (2017), 58, 74–6.
30	Shaw, *The Three Choirs Festival* (1954), 31.
31	Ibid., 54.
32	Hogarth, *Musical History* (1835), 431.

33 Todd, *Mendelssohn* (2003), 403.

34 Doane, *A Musical Directory* (1794), 84–5.

35 Charles Mackeson, 'Choral Harmonists Society', in Grove, *A Dictionary of Music* (1879), i, 362.

36 Until 1836 the Society used the building's smaller hall.

37 Bowley, *The Sacred Harmonic Society* (1867), 7–12.

38 Mendelssohn Bartholdy, *The Mendelssohns on Honeymoon* (1997), 88.

39 Bowley, *The Sacred Harmonic Society* (1867), 14, 39.

40 Mendelssohn Bartholdy, *The Mendelssohns on Honeymoon* (1997), 104.

41 Goulden, *Michael Costa* (2015), 176–8.

42 A new society, under the same name, took over, but struggled, and ended its existence in 1889 (Scholes, *The Mirror of Music* (1947), 25–7).

43 Although described as Mozart's, the published edition of 1803, upon which everyone relied, in fact combined the work of Mozart with that of Johann Adam Hiller, who had produced his own version in 1786, even before Mozart, whose work dated from 1789.

44 Bowley, *The Sacred Harmonic Society* (1867), 14.

45 Musgrave, 'Changing Values', in Bashford and Langley (eds), *Music and British Culture* (2000), 185–7. The Royal College of Music Library has several of Costa's arrangements.

46 Bowley, *The Sacred Harmonic Society* (1867), 35.

47 Carnelley, *George Smart* (2015), 199.

48 Bowley, *The Sacred Harmonic Society* (1867), 40.

49 Pritchard, 'The Musical Festival' (1968), 712–13.

50 *Musical Times*, 8 (1857), 72.

51 *Musical Times*, 9 (1859), 75. For an overall history of the festivals see Musgrave, *The Musical Life of the Crystal Palace* (1995), 27–57.

52 Bowley, *The Sacred Harmonic Society* (1867), 42.

53 Cox, *Musical Recollections* (1872), ii, 340.

54 Musgrave, *The Musical Life of the Crystal Palace* (1995), 46.

55 Scholes, *The Mirror of Music* (1947), 179.

56 *Illustrated London News*, 47 (8 July 1865), 18.

57 *Illustrated London News*, 30 (27 June 1857), 640.

58 Piggott, *Palace of the People* (2004), 200–2.

59 [Anon.]: 'The Great Handel Festival at the Crystal Palace', *Musical Times*, 9 (1859), 75–83; at 78: 'In the chorus, the effect was greatly increased by the addition of half-a-dozen side drums; and this pleasing composition was never heard to greater advantage.' Handel himself had employed one side drum in the March which follows the chorus.

60 Musgrave, *The Musical Life of the Crystal Palace* (1995), 50–1.

61 Bennett, *The Life of William Sterndale Bennett* (1907), 203–4.

62 Ibid., 233–4.

63 Reeves, *My Jubilee* (1889), 179.

64 Parrott, 'William Sterndale Bennett' (2006), 34–6.

65 Keen, *The Back Choir* (2008), 9.

66 *Twenty-eighth Annual Report of the Sacred Harmonic Society* (London, 1861).

67 Cole, *Thomas Tallis* (2008), 120–2.

68 *Musical Times*, 23 (1882), 443.

69 *Musical Times*, 22 (1881), 15–16.

70 Goulden, *Michael Costa* (2015), 171.

71 Scholes, *The Mirror of Music* (1947), 31–2.

72 [Anon.], 'The Oratorio Concerts', *Musical Times*, 15 (1871), 10. That chorus appears to have ended Part One, since Barnby was criticised for omitting Bach's concluding chorus 'O Lamb of God'. The Westminster Abbey performances had the same cut ([Anon.], 'Bach's Passion-Music at Westminster

Abbey', *Musical Times*, 15 (1871/3) [May 1871], 74): Walford Davies also favoured this cut (Boult and Emery, *The St. Matthew Passion* (1949), 5). Barnby was known for his general opposition to encores (Palmer, *Conductors in Britain* (2017), 119).

73 [Anon.], 'Bach's Passion-Music at Westminster Abbey', *Musical Times*, 15 (1871/3) [May 1871], 74.

74 *Musical Times*, 16 (1873/5) [May 1873], 73.

75 [Anon.], 'Royal Albert Hall Choral Society', *Monthly Musical Record*, 3 (1873), 38.

76 Klein, 'The Jubilee of the Royal Albert Hall' (1921), 393.

77 Ibid., 394.

78 [Anon.], 'A Royal Choral Society's Rehearsal', *Musical Times*, 40 (1899), 22–3; at 22.

79 Dibble, *John Stainer* (2007), 204.

80 Klein, 'The Jubilee of the Royal Albert Hall (1921), 394–5; Palmer, *Conductors in Britain* (2017), 105–14 provides an account of Barnby's tenure and the profitability or otherwise of his concerts.

81 *Musical World* 58 (1880), 481.

82 The choir's history is admirably dealt with in Keen, *The Bach Choir* (2008), to which the following is indebted.

83 *Musical Times*, 25 (1884), 336.

84 *The World*, 24 Dec. 1890; in Shaw, *Shaw's Music* (1981), ii, 236.

85 *Musical Times*, 30 (1889), 343.

86 *Musical Times*, 35 (1894), 240.

87 *Musical Times*, 38 (1897), 1312.

88 On the Society see Reißfelder, 'Jenseits des Crystal Palace' (2021).

89 Elkin, *Queen's Hall* (1944), 69–70; [Anon.], 'The Alexandra Palace Choral Society, Performance of Parry's *Judith*', *Musical Times*, 44 (1903), 809. 'Palace' was eventually dropped from its name, after it ceased to sing there during the First World War.

90 Green, *Samuel Coleridge Taylor* (2011), 63.

91 Scholes, *The Mirror of Music* (1947), 3–10.

92 Hullah, *Wilhem's Method of Teaching Singing* (London, 1841).

93 Hullah, *The Life of John Hullah* (1886), 35; Rainbow. *Music in Educational Thought* (2006), 191.

94 Bennett, 'Some Recollections' (1898), 452, quoted in Rainbow, *Music in Educational Thought* (2006), 201.

95 Curwen, *Memorials of John Curwen* (1882), 73–4.

96 Curwen, *Singing for Schools and Congregations* (1985), 114.

97 Curwen, *Memorials of John Curwen* (1882), 153.

98 Ibid., 139.

99 Curwen and Graham, *The Tonic Sol-fa Jubilee* (1891), 24.

100 See McGuire, *Music and Victorian Philanthropy* (2009) for a study of the moral aspect of the tonic sol-fa movement.

101 Dibble, *John Stainer* (2007), 176–7, 222–5; Stanford, *Studies and Memories* (1908), 49–51.

102 Lynch, 'Towards the Abolition' (2001), 187.

103 Ibid., 190.

104 Griffiths, *A Musical Place* (1994), 97; Boden, *The Three Choirs Festival* (2017), 71. Hedgley, who died in 1831, was also assistant librarian and copyist for the Concert of Ancient Music for 53 years, so may well have been at least partly responsible for the copying at the Handel Commemorations (Matthew, 'The Ancient Concerts' (1906/7), 69).

105 Philip Knapton, a York music publisher involved in the 1825 festival, did experiment with printed parts for a few works on that occasion, but it was not repeated (Griffiths, *A Musical Place* (1994), 97). Vincent Novello also made chorus parts available for his editions of Haydn and Mozart Masses, but whether these were printed or in manuscript is uncertain. Curiously, none of these, nor any chorus part of a Handel oratorio, including *Messiah*, has apparently survived to the present day.

106 Ward Jones, 'Mendelssohn and his English Publishers' (1992), 245–50.

107 Cooper, *The House of Novello* (2003), 122–6.

108 Hurd, *Vincent Novello* (1981), 129–30.

109 Musical supplements had also featured in Mainzer's publication.

110 Cooper-Deathridge, 'The Novello Stockbook' (1987/8), 243, 249.

111 *The World*, 1 July 1891; in Shaw, *Shaw's Music* (1981), ii, 381.

112 Bennett, *A Short History* (1887).

113 Griffiths, *A Musical Place* (1994), 147–54, 163–70.

114 *Jackson's Oxford Journal*, 24 Dec. 1852, noted with approval the inclusion of several female singers at a recent concert.

115 Rose, *The History of the York Musical Society* (1948), 21.

116 Pritchard, 'The Musical Festival' (1968), 483, after Cudworth, *Musical Reminiscences of Bradford* (1885), 7.

117 Pritchard, 'The Musical Festival' (1968), 646–7.

118 Russell, *Popular Music in England* (1997), 29.

119 Edwards, *And the Glory* (2011), 85.

120 Ibid., 11–16.

121 Ibid., 47, 54.

122 Ibid., 67.

123 Mackerness, *A Social History of English Music* (1964), 147–51.

124 Edwards, *The History of Mendelssohn's Oratorio 'Elijah'* (1896), 123–4.

125 Pritchard, 'The Musical Festival' (1968), 448–9.

126 Taylor, *Two Centuries of Music in Liverpool* (1976), 10–11.

127 Ludlow and Jones, *Progress of the Working Class* (1867), 193–4, quoted in Pritchard, 'The Musical Festival' (1968), 748.

128 Beale, *Charles Hallé* (2007), 103–7. Members of the Hargreaves Choral Society had apparently all been paid.

129 Scholes, *The Mirror of Music* (1947), 40.

130 For an assessment of Costa's predominant role in the festival world in the third quarter of the century see Goulden, *Michael Costa* (2015), esp. 187–90.

131 Moore, *Edward Elgar* (1984), 256, 290–1.

132 Bennett, '"Gerontius"' (1933), 34–5, gives a chorus member's view of the premiere and its preparation.

133 Only parts 1 and 2 of *The Apostles* were ready in 1903, but the complete work was given in 1906 alongside *The Kingdom* (Moore, *Edward Elgar* (1984), 413–17, 504).

134 Russell, '"Awaking to the Reality"' (1992), 5–10.

135 Sewell, *A History of the Bradford Festival Choral Society* (1907), 34, which provides an extensive account of the festivals.

136 Spark, *Musical Memories* (1909), 3.

137 Sewell, *A History of the Bradford Festival Choral Society* (1907), 45; Russell, 'Provincial Concerts in England' (1989).

138 Sewell, *A History of the Bradford Festival Choral Society* (1907), 46.

139 Pritchard, 'The Musical Festival' (1968), 758.

140 Scholes, *The Mirror of Music* (1947), 40.

141 Spark and Bennett, *History of the Leeds Musical Festivals* (1892), 15.

142 *The Times*, 13 Sept. 1888.

143 Spark and Bennett, *History of the Leeds Musical Festivals* (1892), 15.

144 Ibid., 33.

145 Ibid., 12.

146 Ibid., 51.

147 Sullivan's reign at Leeds and his rather old-fashioned approach to conducting (seated on a high chair) is discussed in Palmer, *Conductors in Britain* (2017), 115–25, 131–4, 141–3.

148 Spark and Bennett, *History of the Leeds Musical Festivals* (1892), 344.

149 Ibid., 79–81.

150 Ibid., 82.

151 *The Academy*, 6 (1874), 444.

152 Spark and Bennett, *History of the Leeds Musical Festivals* (1892), 186–7.

153 Demaine, 'Individual and Institution' (2000), 97.

154 Ibid., 111–16. An earlier manifestation of a Leeds Choral Union had occurred in 1880, which survived only briefly.

155 Ibid., 126–7.

156 Rodgers, *Dr. Henry Coward* (1911) supplies biographical detail, supplemented by Coward's own *Reminiscences* (1919); see also Mackerness, *Somewhere Further North* (1974), esp. 81–121.

157 Coward, *Reminiscences* (1919), 85.

158 [Anon.], 'The Sheffield Festival Choir: A Talk with Dr. Henry Coward', *Musical Times*, 40 (1899), 731.

159 [Anon.], 'The Sheffield Musical Festival', *Musical Times*, 40 (1899), 737.

160 Rodgers, *Dr. Henry Coward* (1911), 57.

161 Ibid., 56.

162 Ibid., 91.

163 The tour is described in Coward, *Round the World on Wings of Song* (1933).

164 Rodgers, *Dr. Henry Coward* (1911).

165 Ibid., 60.

166 Ibid., 54.

167 Ibid., 72.

168 Boden, *The Three Choirs Festival* (2017), 80–1.

169 Ibid., 123.

170 Shaw, *The Three Choirs Festival* (1954), 72–3.

171 Boden, *The Three Choirs Festival* (2017), 157–8.

172 Ibid., 165–6.

173 Shaw, *The Three Choirs Festival* (1954), 81.

174 Ibid., 54–8; Boden, *The Three Choirs Festival* (2017), 96–101.

175 Hunt, *Elgar and the Three Choirs Festival* (1999), 73–4; Boden, *The Three Choirs Festival* (2017), 177.

176 [Anon.], 'The Worcester Musical Festival', *Musical Times*, 43 (1902), 676.

177 Boden, *The Three Choirs Festival* (2017), 133.

178 Drummond, *The Provincial Music Festival* (2011), 123–5, 149–50.

179 Pritchard, 'The Musical Festival' (1968), 805–7, 810–12.

180 Ibid., 812–13.

181 Nettel, *Music in the Five Towns* (1944), 37, 40–7.

182 Ibid., 51.

183 *Musical Times* 9 (1860), 356; Nettel, *North Staffordshire Music* (1977), 9, 15.

184 Nettel, *Music in the Five Towns* (1944), 14–22; Nettel, *North Staffordshire Music* (1977), 15.

185 Nettel, *Music in the Five Towns* (1944), 56–9.

186 Ibid., 100–4; Ship, *A History of the North Staffordshire District Choral Society*, (1909), 16–49 *passim*.

187 Reid, *Thomas Beecham* (1961), 59.

188 Scholes, *The Mirror of Music* (1947), 641.

189 Galloway, *Musical England* (1910), 177–8.

190 Wiltshire, *The Festival Movement* (1997), 18–25.

191 Williams, *Valleys of Song* (1998), 202.

192 Ibid., 29–30.

193 Griffiths, 'Musical Communications' in Herbert, Clarke and Barlow eds), *A History of Welsh Music* (2023), 201–6.

194 Griffiths, 'The Eisteddfod Tradition' in ibid., 108.

195 Bennett, *Forty Years of Music* (1908), 400, quoted in Williams, *Valleys of Song* (1998), 102.

196 Williams, *Valleys of Song* (1998), 3.

197 Coward, *Reminiscences* (1919), 119.

198 Williams, *Valleys of Song* (1998), 45–8; Herbert, 'Popular Nationalism', in Bashford and Langley (eds), *Music and British Culture* (2000), 264–71. Admittedly, in 1872 they were the only competing choir in their class (for choirs of 300–500 members), but at next year's meeting, another choir entered, whom they beat.

199 Coward, *Reminiscences* (1919), 119–20.

200 Williams, *Valleys of Song* (1998), 141.

201 [Anon.], 'Music in Monmouthshire and South Wales', *Musical Times*, 29 (1888), 550.

202 Williams, *Valleys of Song* (1998), 108.

203 Ibid., 147–8.

204 Ibid., 154–5.

205 Ibid., 106–9.

206 Ibid., 110–11.

207 Marr, *Music for the People* (1889), xcix. A short-lived Institution of Sacred Music to train more local singers was initiated after the 1815 festival (ibid., lix–lx).

208 Ibid., and Farmer, *A History of Music in Scotland* (1947), 456–81 give a good overall survey of choral society development in Scotland in the nineteenth century.

209 Waddell, *History of the Edinburgh Choral Union* (1908), 182–3; Waddell provides the standard early history of the society, which started modestly with about 50 singers.

210 *Dundee Courier*, 27 Jan. 1813.

211 *Aberdeen Journal*, 23 Jan. 1828; 1 and 8 Oct. 1834; Farmer, *A History of Music in Scotland* (1947), 470.

212 Marr, *Music for the People* (1889), xcvi, civ–cv.

213 Craig, *A Short History of the Glasgow Choral Union* (1944), 15–17.

214 Marr, *Music for the People* (1889), cvii.

215 *Musical World*, 11 Feb. 1860, 95.

216 [Anon.], 'Glasgow Musical Festival, *Musical Times*, 16 (1873), 307.

217 [Anon.], 'Glasgow Musical Festival', *The Times*, 8 Nov. 1873.

218 [Anon.], 'Glasgow Musical Festival', *The Athenaeum*, issue 2403 (8 Nov. 1873), 603–4.

219 *Monthly Musical Record*, 3 (1873), 158.

220 Rodgers, *Dr. Henry Coward* (1911), 46.

221 On the choir, see Roberton, *Prelude to the Orpheus* (1946) and Roberton and Roberton (eds), *Orpheus with his Lute* (1963).

222 Hogan, *Anglo-Irish Music* (1966), 79; Beausang, '"For the Support of Decayed Musicians"', (2019), 177–8.

223 Ferris, 'The Music Collections' (2006), 22–3.

224 Boydell, 'Music, 1700–1750' (1986), 609; Rodmell (2002), 211–33.

225 Fleischmann, 'Music and Society' (2010), 501.

226 Hogan, *Anglo-Irish Music* (1966), 63.

227 *Freeman's Journal*, 30 Jan. 1852.

228 Fleischmann, 'Music and Society' (2010), 509.

229 Boydell, 'Music, 1700–1750' (1986), 612.

230 Fleischmann, 'Music and Society' (2010), 509.

231 Ibid., 510–11; Johnston, *The Musical Life of Nineteenth-Century Belfast* (2015), 272, 282.

232 Fleischmann, 'Music and Society' (2010), 503, 511.

233 Boydell, 'Music, 1700–1750' (1986), 616.

234 Johnston, *The Musical Life of Nineteenth-Century Belfast* (2015), 163.

235 Johnston, 'Concert Auditoria' in Murphy and Smaczny (eds), *Music in Nineteenth-Century Ireland* (2007), 246–8.

236 Johnston, *The Musical Life of Nineteenth-Century Belfast* (2015), 11.

237 Ibid., 247–8.

238 Fleischmann, 'Music and Society' (2010), 510.

239 Bedwin, *Fifty Years of Song* (1978).

240 An earlier example was a choir started in the 1830s by John Strutt, a musically inclined cotton manufacturer in Belper, who conducted it himself and allowed his employees time off *in lieu*. In contrast to later workplace choirs, Strutt's motive was, in part, to improve the musical taste of his workers (Gardiner, *Music and Friends* (1838), ii, 12–13).

241 Wiltshire, 'The British Male Voice Choir' (1993), 107–8.

242 Kidner, *How to Start a Men's Choir* (1900), 34–9.

243 Cowgill, 'On the Beat', in Rodmell (ed.), *Music and Institutions in Nineteenth-Century Britain* (2012), 229–42.

244 For the Great Western Railway Musical Society, supported by the directors, see Galloway, *Musical England* (1910), 133–4.

245 Novello & Co., *The Complete Catalogue of Music* (c.1900).

246 Pritchard, 'The Musical Festival' (1968), 755.

247 *Musical Times*, 12 (Feb. 1866), 217.

248 Pritchard, 'The Musical Festival' (1968), 756–7.

249 Hobson, 'Three Madrigal Societies', in Rodmell (ed.), *Music and Institutions in Nineteenth-Century Britain* (2012), 44–5.

250 Ibid., 50.

251 Ibid., 50.

252 Hobson, 'Musical Antiquarianism' (2015), 206–15.

253 Norris, *Stanford* (1980), 7, 23–4.

254 Knight, *Cambridge Music* (1980), 83–4; a full history is in Meadows, *Centenary Celebration* (1987).

255 George Thewlis, typescript notes on Oxford music (Bodleian Library, uncatalogued); for the Oxford Bach Choir's history see Darwall-Smith, 'The Oxford Bach Choir' (2023).

256 Ibid., 37.

257 Ibid., 35.

258 Wollenberg, *Music at Oxford* (2001), 184–6.

259 The tenor Sims Reeves sympathized with chorus singers (Reeves, *My Jubilee* (1889), 262).

260 Scholes, *The Mirror of Music* (1947), 406–9; Haynes, *A History of Performing Pitch* (2002), 346–9, 355–9.

261 Coward, *Choral Technique* (1914), 238; Crosse, *An Account of the Grand Musical Festival* (1825), 301.

262 Smither, 'Messiah and Progress' (1985), 347.

263 *Monthly Musical Record*, 16 (1886), 18.

264 Day, *I Saw Eternity* (2018), 119–20.

265 Scholes, *The Mirror of Music* (1947), 69.

266 Ibid., 68–9.

267 Preface to the full score (London, 1902), reprinted in *Musical Times* 43 (1902), May–Oct. issues. Later reprints of Prout restored the appendix numbers to their proper place.

Chapter 5

1 La Trobe, *The Music of the Church* (1831), 1.

2 Thoms, 'What it were Good to do for the Choirs' (1837), 115.

3 Rainbow, *The Choral Revival* (1970), 65–8.

4 Ibid., 64–5; Adelmann, *The Contribution of the Cambridge Ecclesiologists* (1997), 218–21.

5 Rainbow, *The Choral* Revival (1970), 138; Helmore, *Memoir of the Rev. Thomas Helmore* (1891), 62–3.

6 The preface to the 4th edition (1879) of Helmore's *Church Choirs* gives a valuable picture of the changes in both village choirs and cathedrals over the previous half century.

7 Rainbow, *The Choral Revival* (1970), 263–4; Hewett, *The Arrangement of Parish Churches Considered* (1848), 8.

8 Addleshaw and Etchells, *The Architectural Setting* (1948), 16.

9 Temperley, *The Music of the English Parish Church* (1979), i.

239; Galpin, 'The Village Church Band' (1893); Dickson, *Fifty Years of Church Music* (1894), 45–6, gives an account of one smooth transition in the 1850s.

10 Adelmann, *The Contribution of the Cambridge Ecclesiologists* (1997), 93–6; Rainbow, *The Choral Revival* (1970), 199.

11 Adelmann, *The Contribution of the Cambridge Ecclesiologists* (1997), 205–7.

12 *Musical Times*, 11 (1863–5), 449.

13 *Musical Times*, 12 (1865/6), 150.

14 Temperley (1979), i, 253–4.

15 Hillsman, 'Women in Victorian Church Music' (1990), 445–6.

16 L.A.M. and J.G.T., *Guide to the Church Services* (1858); further editions were issued in 1862 and 1863.

17 Temperley, *The Music of the English Parish Church* (1979), i, 225–6. The earliest introduction of a surpliced choir in a parish church appears to have been in 1814 at St Mary Magdalene, Newark-on-Trent (Turner, 'The Decline of the Gallery Tradition', in Turner (ed.), *Georgian Psalmody I* (1997), 76).

18 *The Choral Service of the United Church of England and Ireland* (London, 1843).

19 Rainbow, *The Choral Revival* (1970), 30.

20 Ibid., 28, 35.

21 Ibid., 17–20.

22 Ibid., 24.

23 Ibid., 25; Temperley, *The Music of the English Parish Church* (1979), i, 255–6.

24 Temperley, *The Music of the English Parish Church* (1979), i, 294–5.

25 Webb and Docker, *S. Andrew's Church* (1897), 104.

26 Mason, *Musical Letters from Abroad* (1854), 114.

27 Lewer, *A Spiritual Song* (1961), 84.

28 Ibid., 164–5.

29 Ibid., 117, 125.

30 Ibid., 140–1; *The Records … of Lincoln's Inn* (1897), iv, 209; v, 50.

31 Lewer, *A Spiritual Song* (1961), 137–8.

32 *The Guardian*, 13 Sept. 1848, quoted in Lewer, *A Spiritual Song* (1961), 138.

33 Lewer, *A Spiritual Song* (1961), 139.

34 Ibid., 182.

35 Ibid., 155–6.

36 Ibid., 217.

37 Thalben-Ball had in fact been sharing responsibilities with Walford Davies on a rather unsatisfactory basis since March 1919 (Rennert, *George Thalben-Ball* (1979), 56–60).

38 Curwen, *Studies in Worship Music* (1880), 179.

39 Ibid., 182.

40 Ibid., 182.

41 Rainbow, *The Choral Revival* (1970), 281.

42 Temperley, *The Music of the English Parish Church* (1979), i, 285; [Anon.], 'The Passion Services at St. Anne's, Soho', *Musical Times*, 16 (1873–5) [Apr. 1873], 41–3.

43 *Musical Times*, 21 (1880), 153.

44 [Anon.], 'The Coronation of King Edward the Seventh', *Musical Times*, 43 (1902), 585.

45 Curwen, *The Boy's Voice* (1909), 122–35; 'Tractarian Choir Schools' online at https://recordedchurchmusic.org/tractarian-choir-schools; and https://recordedchurchmusic.org/college.

46 W.H. Longhurst, quoted in Curwen, *Studies in Worship Music* (1901), 316–17.

47 The training of early Tractarian choirs was often undertaken by a curate, but increasingly handed over to the organist from the 1870s (Hillsman, 'Trends and Aims' (1985), 142).

Notes to Pages 183–186   361

48   Makeson, *A Guide to the Churches of London* (1884), 171, quoted in Hillsman, 'Trends and Aims' (1985), 152.

49   Box, *Church Music* (1884), 126ff.

50   Curwen, *Studies in Worship Muisc* (1880), 168.

51   *Musical Times*, 9 (1859), 17.

52   *Musical Times*, 12 (1865/6), 361.

53   Rainbow, *The Choral Revival* (1970), 225–6.

54   'Tractarian choir schools' online at https://recordedchurch music/tractarian-choir-schools.

55   [Anon. "A Native"], 'Church Music in Liverpool', *Parish Choir*, 3 (1849/51), 170.

56   Wesley, *A Few Words* (1849), 72.

57   [Anon. 'Cantatrice'], 'Employment of Female Voices in Church Choirs', *Musical Times*, 27 (1886), 742.

58   Blackmore, 'The "Angelic Choir"', (2016), 67–79.

59   *Daily Telegraph*, Aug. 1889; see Blackmore, 'The "Angelic Choir"' (2016), 41–2, 50–1.

60   Stainer, *The Present State of Music in England* (1889), 16–17.

61   Blackmore, 'The "Angelic Choir"' (2016), 13, quoting *The Official Year-Book of the Church of England* (1893), xxiv. No breakdown between children and adults is given.

62   Curwen, *Studies in Worship Music* (1880), 182.

63   Box, *Church Music* (1884).

64   See, for example, Crowest, *Phases of Musical England* (1881), 101.

65   Haweis, *Music and Morals* (1871), 121.

66   *The Guardian*, 23 Aug. 1848, p. 547.

67   Marsh, *The John Marsh Journals* (1998), ii, 280.

68   *The Guardian*, 22 Aug. 1849, p. 552.

69   Marsh, *The John Marsh Journals* (1998), ii, 369.

70 Letter dated 30 July 1827 in *Gentleman's Magazine*, 97 (Sept. 1827), 197.

71 Robertson, *Sarum Close* (1938), 279–80.

72 Ibid., 284.

73 Wridgway, *The Choristers of St George's Chapel* (1980), 63–4.

74 Barrett, *Barchester* (1993), 154.

75 Clarke, *Bangor Cathedral* (1969), 63.

76 One of his choristers in the 1820s, John Edmund Cox, hated Buck's severe discipline and thought his musical knowledge deficient (Cox, *Musical Recollections* (1872), i, 34–7).

77 Kitton, *Zechariah Buck* (1899), 24.

78 [Anon.], 'Bach's Passion Music at Westminster Abbey', *Musical Times*, 15 (1871/3) [Apr. 1872], 434.

79 Kitton, *Zechariah Buck* (1899), 9–10.

80 Day, *I Saw Eternity* (2018), 106–7, 116–17.

81 *Musical World*, 4 (1837), 159.

82 Mason, *A Yankee Musician* (1990), 30.

83 [Anon.], 'Mr. Walter Macfarren', *Musical Times*, 39 (1898), 10.

84 *The Times*, 2 Mar. 1837.

85 Knight, 'Nineteenth-Century Repertoire' (2002), 81–2.

86 *Musical World*, 4 (1837), 189.

87 Storey, 'Music, 1800–2002', in Keene, Burns and Saint (eds), *St Paul's* (2004), 404.

88 Bumpus, *The Organists and Composers* (1891), 16.

89 For an account of her life see Garrett, 'Miss Hackett' (1973–5).

90 Hackett, *A Brief Account* (1827).

91 Mould, *The English Chorister* (2007), 201.

92 Barrett, *Barchester* (1993), 85; Iles, 'Music and Liturgy from 1600', in Aylmer and Tiller (eds), *Hereford Cathedral* (2000), 400, 413.

93	Knight, 'Nineteenth-Century Repertoire' (2002), 90–3.
94	Wesley, *A Few Words* (1849), 39.
95	Ibid., 61.
96	Ibid., 73.
97	Ibid., 72.
98	Horton, *Samuel Sebastian Wesley* (2004), 32–4.
99	Tyng, *Recollections of England* (1847), 193.
100	Ibid., 260–1.
101	Ibid., 266.
102	Mason, *Musical Letters from Abroad* (1854), 12–13.
103	Ibid., 15.
104	Ibid., 309.
105	Ibid., 112.
106	Ibid., 15.
107	*First (-Third) Report of Her Majesty's Commissioners to Inquire into the State and Condition of the Cathedral and Collegiate Churches in England and Wales* (London, 1854–5).
108	*Third and Final Report*, xiv.
109	*First Report*, xxxiv; *Third and Final Report* (1855), xix.
110	For Ouseley's biography see Joyce, *The Life of Rev. F.A.G. Ouseley* (1896) and Bland, *Ouseley and his Angels* (2000).
111	[Anon. 'Jubal'], 'Church Music at Oxford', *Parish Choir*, 2 (1847), 46.
112	Letter to Wayland Joyce, 28 Oct. 1851, in Joyce, *The Life of Rev. F.A.G. Ouseley* (1896), 77.
113	Shaw, *Sir Frederick Ouseley* (1988), 42–4.
114	Ibid., 54–8.
115	Barrett, *Barchester* (1993), 173.
116	Shaw, *Sir Frederick Ouseley* (1988), 50–2.
117	Bland, *Ouseley and his Angels* (2000), 173.

118 Stainer, *The Present State of Music in England* (1889/90), 33–4.

119 Ibid., 36.

120 Dickson, *Fifty Years of Church Music* (1894), 55–66; Thistlethwaite, 'Music and Liturgy', in Meadows and Ramsey (eds) *A History of Ely Cathedral* (2003), 333–4.

121 Barrett, *Barchester* (1993), 147–8; Griffiths, *A Musical Place* (1994), 21–3.

122 Lichfield had started processing in 1842, and Wells in 1847 (Barrett, 'English Cathedral Choirs' (1974), 17–18).

123 Storey, 'The Music of St Paul's Cathedral' (1998), 39.

124 Ibid., 45.

125 Storey, 'Music, 1800–2002', in Keene, Burns and Saint (eds), *St Paul's* (2004), 406.

126 Storey, 'The Music of St Paul's Cathedral' (1998), 40.

127 Mould, *The English Chorister* (2007), 201.

128 30 choristers and 8 probationers: Storey, 'The Music of St Paul's Cathedral' (1998), 19.

129 Barrett, *Barchester* (1993), 118.

130 Ibid., 117–18.

131 Storey, 'The Music of St Paul's Cathedral' (1998), 48–50, with a detailed analysis in the appendices.

132 Barrett, *Barchester* (1993) 119, 359; for Westminster Abbey, which first held evening services from January to June 1858 with a voluntary choir, see also Stancliffe, 'Victorian Chapter', in Carpenter (ed.), *A House of Kings* (1966), 295–7.

133 Russell, *Musical Services in S. Paul's Cathedral* (1887), 37, quoted in Hillsman, 'Trends and Aims' (1985), 320.

134 Hillsman, 'Trends and Aims' (1985), 320; Bridge, Wyatt and Stockbridge, 'The Nave Choir' (2017), 38–9.

135 *The Art of Training Choir Boys* (1892).

136 Storey, 'The Music of St Paul's Cathedral' (1998), 62–3.

137 [Anon.], 'Church and Organ Music', *Musical Times*, 41 (1900), 464; quoted in Scholes, *The Mirror of Music* (1947), 531.

138 Storey, 'The Music of St Paul's Cathedral' (1998), 66–70.

139 Bridge, *A Westminster Pilgrim* (1919), 74.

140 Ibid., 333.

141 Range, *Music and Ceremonial* (2012), 227.

142 [Anon.], 'The Coronation of King Edward the Seventh ..', *Musical Times*, 43 1902), 578; Bridge, *A Westminster Pilgrim* (1919), 185–6.

143 [Anon.], 'The Coronation of King Edward the Seventh ..', *Musical Times*, 43 1902), 578.

144 [Anon.], 'Music in the Coronation Service', *Musical Herald*, issue 760 (July 1911), 214.

145 Storey, 'The Music of St Paul's Cathedral' (1998), 5; Dibble, *John Stainer* (2007), 147.

146 Whiteside, 'A Chester Cathedral Chorister' (1981), 109.

147 Townhill, *The Imp and the Thistle* (2000), 70.

148 Collinson, *The Diary of an Organist's Apprentice* (1982), 38; Crosby, *Come on Choristers* (1999), 64.

149 Robertson, *Sarum Close* (1938), 286–309.

150 Mould, *The English Chorister* (2007), 205.

151 Hodgson, *Choirs and Cloisters* (1995), 31.

152 Ibid., 28.

153 Williams, *A Short Historical Account* (1893), 42–3. Residence was only made compulsory in the early twentieth century.

154 Bates, *Reminiscences* (1930), 29.

155 Iles, 'Music and Liturgy', in Aylmer and Tiller (eds), *Hereford Cathedral* (2000), 430.

156 Barrett, *Barchester* (1993), 186, from *The Guardian*, 15 Dec. 1897, p. 1993.

157 Webster, *Church and Patronage* (1988), 77.

158 Ehrlich, *The Music Profession* (1985), 123–6.

159 Iles, 'Music and Liturgy', in Aylmer and Tiller (eds), *Hereford Cathedral* (2000), 430–1.

160 Stanford, *Pages from an Unwritten Diary* (1914), 37.

161 Boydell, *A History of Music at Christ Church Cathedral* (2004), 168.

162 Ibid., 170.

163 Grindle, *Irish Cathedral Music* (1989), 117.

164 Aston, 'Music since the Reformation' (1977), 417.

165 Todd, *Mendelssohn* (2003), 468.

166 The *Worcester Journal* of 27 Nov. 1845 has a review of special services at All Saints Church, Worcester, with a choir from the local choral society, assisted by men from the cathedral choir and with the organ played by the cathedral organist, William Done. Evensong concluded with Mendelssohn's anthem, 'delightfully sung by Master John Tirbutt, one of the Cathedral choristers'. Although no confirmation is available from the cathedral archives, this strongly suggests that it would also have been heard in the cathedral itself around this time.

167 For a useful discussion, see Gatens, *Victorian Church Music* (1986), 74–81, 170–1.

168 Kitton, *Zechariah Buck* (1889), 28.

169 Jebb, *The Choral Responses* (1847–57).

170 On the question of Tallis's responses, see Ben Byrom-Wigfield at the Ancient Groove Music website, https://ancientgroove.co.uk/freebies/responses.html.

171 Temperley, *Jonathan Gray* (1977), 19–20.

172 Norwich Cathedral, however, was changing chants in the late eighteenth century, as witnessed approvingly by John Marsh (*The John Marsh Journals* (1998), i, 554) and the organist John Beckwith's chant collection (*The First Verse of Every Psalm of David* (1808)).

173 Elvey, *The Psalter* (1856). It was frequently reprinted up to the early twentieth century.

174 Hale, 'Music and Musicians', in Buxton and Williams (eds), *New College* (1979), 280; 45–6; Day, *I Saw Eternity* (2018), 39–41.

175 Day, *I Saw Eternity* (2018), 281.

176 Deneke, *Ernest Walker* (1951), 46.

177 Hale, 'Music and Musicians', in Buxton and Williams (eds), *New College* (1979), 285–6.

178 Bloxam, *A Register* (1853), ii, pp. cciv-ccv; Dibble, *John Stainer* (2007), 77.

179 Tuckwell, *Old Magdalen Days* (1913), 17; Day, *I saw Eternity* (2018), 19–20.

180 Music lists in Magdalen College Archives, DD2/X2/2.

181 Stanier, *Magdalen School* (1940), 145–9.

182 Dibble, *John Stainer* (2007), 78.

183 Day, *I Saw Eternity* (2018), 61–2.

184 Baker, 'John Varley Roberts' (2017), 46–9. Venables, *Sweet Tones Remembered* (1947) and Hey, *Magdalen Schooldays* (1977), who were Magdalen choristers under Roberts, provide vivid descriptions of him.

185 Day, *I Saw Eternity* (2018), 65.

186 Hutton, *S. John Baptist College* (1898), 257–8; Knights, 'The History of the Choral Foundation' (1990), 446–7; Tyack, *St John's College* (2000), 27.

187 Dickson, *Fifty Years of Church Music* (1894), 17.

188 Ibid., 18; Case, *Memoirs* (1899), 12–13; Bloxam, *A Register* (1853), i, p. xiii.

189 Glover, *The Memoirs of a Cambridge Chorister* (1885), i, 247.

190 Case, *Memoirs* (1899), 24.

191 Adelmann, *The Contribution of the Cambridge Ecclesiologists* (1997), 49.

192 Day, *I Saw Eternity* (2018), 96–7, 100.

193 For a detailed account of Mann at King's see Marston, '"As

England knows it'", in Massing and Zeeman (eds), *King's College Chapel* (2014).

194   Day, *I Saw Eternity* (2018), 109.

195   Ibid., 104–5.

196   Ibid., 110, 113; Andrews, *Westminster Retrospect* (1948), 10–11.

197   Day, *I Saw Eternity* (2018), 119.

198   HMV B 3707; available on YouTube.

199   Day, *I Saw Eternity* (2018), 117.

200   Tallis, *Motet for 40 Voices* (1888).

201   Andrews, *Westminster Retrospect* (1948), 11.

202   Adelmann, *The Contribution of the Cambridge Ecclesiologists* (1997), 200.

203   While still an undergraduate organ scholar at Queen's, Stanford played recitals at Trinity in 1872, and moved to that college in April 1873, having being recruited as assistant organist in March, essentially taking over the organist's duties from John Larkin Hopkins who was on sick leave and died in April; Stanford was appointed his successor in February 1874 (Rodmell, *Charles Villiers Stanford* (2002), 38).

204   Dibble, *Charles Villiers Stanford* (2002), 102.

205   Morphet and Hill, 'St John's College, Cambridge' (2011), 52.

206   Adelmann, *The Contribution of the Cambridge Ecclesiologists* (1997), 214.

207   The records of Lincoln's Inn in 1841, preparing to set up its own choir of boys and men, mention a Mr. Jolley who 'supplies choristers to King's College': *The Records ... of Lincoln's Inn* (1897), iv, 209.

208   *The London & Dublin Orthodox Journal of Useful Knowledge*, 13 (1841), 67, cited in Muir, *Roman Catholic Church Music* (2008), 97.

209   Muir, *Roman Catholic Church Music* (2008), 112.

210   Butt, 'Roman Catholicism' (2004), 107.

211 *A History of St Chad's Cathedral, Birmingham* (1904), 122–8.

212 *Church Choirmaster and Organist*, 3 (1868), 134.

213 Muir, '"Full in the Panting Heart of Rome"' (2004), 161–2.

214 Blackburn, 'Music in the Roman Church' (1899), 12.

215 Washington, 'The Oratory Musical Tradition', in Napier and Laing (eds), *The London Oratory Centenary* (1984), 115. Even at the Oratory, however, there was a brief period in the 1850s when the choir was disbanded for lack of funds (ibid., 163; Downes, 'The Organs', in ibid., 173).

216 Farm Street website, www.farmstreet.org.uk/our-music.

217 Muir, '"Full in the Panting Heart of Rome"' (2004), 128.

218 Harper, 'Southwark's 'other' Cathedral' (2016), 45.

219 Webster, *Parish Past and Present* (1988), 67–8.

220 Taylor, *Two Centuries of Music in Liverpool* (1976), 63–4. The choir of St. Anne's had decamped to St Francis Xavier in the 1850s after the choirmaster had had a contretemps with the priest (Santley, *Student and Singer* (1892), 33).

221 Novello, *Clara Novello's Reminiscences* (1910), 37; Griffiths, *A Musical Place* (1994), 47–9.

222 Muir, *Roman Catholic Church Music* (2008), 222–7.

223 O'Donoghue, 'Music and Religion in Ireland' (1995), 126.

224 White, *The Keeper's Recital* (1998), 75–8; the most comprehensive account of the Irish Cecilian movement is found in Daly, *Catholic Church Music in Ireland* (1995).

225 See Gardiner, *Music and Friends* (1838), i, 3, for a choir being formed together with a 'bass-viol' in a Presbyterian church in Leicester about 1760. On the whole the Presbyterians long held aloof from choirs and even organs – the Leicester Presbyterians, however, acquired one in 1800 (ibid. i, 23).

226 Patrick, *Four Centuries of Scottish Psalmody* (1949), 193–4.

227 *Practical Suggestions for the Improvement of Church Music* (Edinburgh, 1852), quoted in Farmer, *A History of Music in Scotland* (1947), 375.

228 Griffiths, *A Musical Place* (1994), 45–6.

229 Sutcliffe Smith, *The Story of Music in Birmingham* (1945), 92.

230 Young, *Chapel* (1972), 93–5.

231 Lightwood, *The Story of the Free Church Choir Union* (1931), 6.

232 Williams, *Valleys of Song* (1998), 122.

233 Curwen, *Studies in Worship Music* (1880), 174–6; Scholes, *The Oxford Companion to Music* (1955), 245; *The Congregational Psalmist. 3rd Section: Church Anthems*, ed. Henry Allon (London, 1872).

234 Minshall, *Fifty Years' Reminiscences* (1910), 97–8, 101–3; Lightwood, *The Story of the Free Church Choir Union* (1931).

Chapter 6

1 Church Music Society, *Cathedral Music Today and Tomorrow* (1941), 32.

2 Ibid., 44–5.

3 Ibid., 7.

4 Mould, *The English Chorister* (2007), 229.

5 St Paul's: Storey, 'Music, 1800–2002', in Keene, Burns and Saint (eds), *St Paul's* (2004), 412, though Saturday Matins continued for a while; Westminster Abbey (Beeson, *Window on Westminster* (1998), 149).

6 Bland, *Ouseley and his Angels* (2000), 242.

7 Robertson, *Sarum Close* (1938), 351–2.

8 Chester Cathedral Choristers' Association website, https://occa.uk.

9 Roden, *The Minster School, York* (2005), 280.

10 Woodward, *Boy on a Hill* (1984) [unpaginated].

11 Robertson, *Sarum Close* (1938), 335.

12 Wells: Greenhalgh, 'The Nineteenth Century and After' (1982), 189; Hereford: Barrett, 'The College of Vicars Choral', in Aylmer and Tiller (eds), *Hereford Cathedral* (2000), 459.

13 Storey, The Music of St Paul's Cathedral' (1998), 69; *Musical Times*, 84 (1943), 123.

14 Church Music Society, *Cathedral Music Today and Tomorrow* (1941), 32.

15 Beeson, *Window on Westminster* (1998), 47.

16 Henderson and Jarvis, *Sydney Nicholson and his Musings* (2013), 105–6.

17 Cook, 'Close to Music' (1992), 663.

18 Dakers, *Places Where they Sing* (1995), 88.

19 Woodward, *Boy on a Hill* (1984) [unpaginated].

20 Grindle, *Irish Cathedral Music* (1989), 127–9.

21 For general details on Terry and Westminster see Andrews, *Westminster Retrospect* (1948) and Doyle, *Westminster Cathedral* (1995), to which this section is indebted.

22 Day, 'Sir Richard Terry' (1994), 302–3.

23 The Mass was first heard in a concert performance in Birmingham in 1922, and was dedicated to Gustav Holst, but the composer certainly wrote it with Westminster in mind (Kennedy, *The Works of Ralph Vaughan Williams* (1980), 158–60).

24 Patrick Russell, 'Sir Richard Terry and New Music at Westminster Cathedral, 1912–1922', RSCM Lunchtime Lecture, 5 Feb. 2021 (available on YouTube).

25 Terry, *Catholic Church Music* (1907), 98–9, himself recommended the books on training choristers by George Martin and Varley Roberts.

26 Day, 'Sir Richard Terry' (1994), 203.

27 Doyle, *Westminster Cathedral* (1995), 55.

28 Ibid., 59–60.

29 *Musical Times*, 64 (1923), 279.

30 Day, 'Sir Richard Terry' (1994), 302.

31 Fellowes, *Memoirs* (1946), 82.

32   For a thorough account of the rise of King's, see Day, *I Saw Eternity* (2018).

33   Routley, *The English Carol*, (1958), 228–31, 245–52; Hart-Davis, *Hugh Walpole* (1952), 5; Nash, '"A Right Prelude to Christmas"', in Massing and Zeeman (eds), *King's College Chapel* (2014), 323–43.

34   Hiley, *Western Plainchant* (1993), 26; Routley, *The English Carol* (1958), 147 points out a possible relationship to the Holy Week service of Tenebrae, which also had nine lessons.

35   Henderson, *A History of King's College Choir School* (1981), 62.

36   Day, *I Saw Eternity* (2018), caption to Pl. 14 and p. 273. The innovation may have been due to the acting organist, Harold Darke. Before 1919, there was already a tradition of starting Christmas Eve Evensong with 'Once in royal David's city' in procession, with the boys singing the first verse and the men joining in the second (James, *Eton and King's* (1926), 238–9).

37   Nash, '"A Right Prelude to Christmas"; in Massing and Zeeman (eds), *King's College Chapel* (2014), 342.

38   Available on YouTube. Information from 'The Story of Nine Lessons & Carols' on the Archive of Recorded Church Music website.

39   Radcliffe, *Bernhard (Boris) Ord* (1962), 14–15.

40   Columbia DX 1611; DB 2608.

41   Argo RG 39; RG 80; RG 99; RG 100.

42   Andrews, 'Herbert Howells' (1999), 376–9. The details of the commissioning and first performances are rather confused and contradictory, especially considering that Ord's war service took him abroad in 1944–5 (Radcliffe, *Bernhard (Boris) Ord* (1962), 16). Howells's own recollections appear to be unreliable – cf. Palmer, *Herbert Howells* (1992), 400–1.

43   Radcliffe, *Bernhard (Boris) Ord* (1962), 10.

44   EMI, CSD 3656.

45   Day, *I Saw Eternity* (2018), 131.

46   Wilkinson, *Westminster Abbey* (2003), 119.

47 Day, *A Century of Recorded Music* (2000), 18.

48 Day, *I Saw Eternity* (2018), 184.

49 Boys at Jesus were first introduced in 1846 (Adelmann, *The Contribution of the Cambridge Ecclesiologists* (1997), 56).

50 Anon., 'Lord, for they tender mercies' sake' and S.S. Wesley, 'O Lord, my God', HMV B2446; Byrd, 'Justorum animae' and Stanford, 'Beati quorum via', HMV B2448.

51 Day, *I Saw Eternity* (2018), 187.

52 Ibid., 182.

53 Available on YouTube.

54 Available on YouTube.

55 Frost, 'English Cathedral Music and the BBC' (2011), 79, 199.

56 Ibid., 135.

57 Ibid., 188.

58 Ibid., 219.

59 Jackson, *Blessed City* (1997), 188.

60 Made available by the Archive of Recorded Church Music on YouTube. As the recording had to have been made in the recording studio, a harmonium was the substitute for the church's organ.

61 Batten, *Joe Batten's Book* (1956), 158.

62 Beet, *The Better Land* (2005), 144–5.

63 Lewer, *A Spiritual Song* (1961), 350–1.

64 Curwen, *The Boy's Voice* (1909), 122–35.

65 Beet, *The Better Land* (2005); many can be heard on *The Better Land* series of CDs.

66 Channel 4 documentary, 'The Boy who sang O for the wings of a Dove', written by Robin Lough, 1993. Available from the Archive of Recorded Sound on YouTube.

67 Nicholson, 'The Choirboy' (1943/44), 68–9.

68 Church Music Society *Forty Years of Cathedral Music* (1940), 17.

69 Kirwan, *The Music of Lincoln Cathedral* (1973), 12–13; Thistlethwaite, 'Music and Worship, 1660–1980', in Owen (ed.), *A History of Lincoln Minster* (1994), 109–10.

70 Storey, 'The Music of St Paul's Cathedral' (1998), 80.

71 Beer and Crawshaw, *Music at Ripon Cathedral* (2008), 62.

72 Andrews, *Westminster Retrospect* (1948), 138, from Terry in the *Morning Post*, 9 Apr. 1924.

73 Storey, 'The Music of St Paul's Cathedral' (1998), 106, 113.

74 Storey, 'Music, 1800–2002', in Keene, Burns and Saint (eds), *St Paul's* (2004), 409.

75 Storey, 'The Music of St Paul's Cathedral' (1998), 118.

76 Ibid., 111–12.

77 Storey, 'Music, 1800–2002', in Keene, Burns and Saint (eds), *St Paul's* (2004), 409.

78 Pine, *The Westminster Abbey Singers* (1953), 247.

79 Ibid.

80 Doyle, *Westminster Cathedral* (1995), 64.

81 Baldwin, *The Chapel Royal* (1990), 390–2.

82 Lewer, *A Spiritual Song* (1961), 454–7; Rennert, *George Thalben-Ball* (1979), 106–11.

83 Norris (ed.), *London Choir School* (2008), 171, 215.

84 *English Church Music*, 10 (1940), 3.

85 CD booklet of *New College Choir: Archive Recordings (1927–1951)*, New College Choristers' Association, 1997 (CHASS 971), p. 5.

86 Church Music Society: *Cathedral Music Today and Tomorrow* (1941), esp. 7, 39–42.

87 Armstrong, *Church Music Today* (1946), 11.

88 Temperley, *The Music of the English Parish Church* (1979), i, 318.

89 Official figures reveal Anglican choir membership in England in the mid-1930s of about 300,000, much the same as at

the end of the nineteenth century, though of course the population had increased in the meantime. By 1939 this was down to about 276,500 (*The Official Year-Book of the National Assembly of the Church of England*, 1938–41).

90 Toop, *The Organist and his Choir* (1925), 8.

91 Norris (ed.), *London Choir School* (2008) presents a vivid portrait of the school's history, drawn largely from the memories of former pupils, on which this account depends.

92 Webster, *Church and Patronage* (2017) provides a full picture of Hussey's activity.

93 This account relies mainly on Shaw, *Vocation and Endeavour* (1997), Henderson and Jarvis, *Sydney Nicholson and the College of St Nicolas* (2011) and Henderson and Jarvis, *Sydney Nicholson and his Musings* (2013).

94 Nicholson, 'Principles and Recommendations' (1941), 91.

95 Nicholson, *Quires and Places where they Sing* (1932), 68–9. Others would favour mixed choirs just because they could display a wide range of emotion. Charles Cleall considered that 'the mixed choir is the only true voice of mankind: it is the voice of suffering, of shame, of humiliation, of purification, of clear seeing, of courage, of humble access' (Cleall, *The Selection and Training of Mixed Choirs* (1960), 75).

96 [Anon.], 'Church Music on the Gramophone', *English Church Music*, 1/1 (1931), 24–5.

97 This was a 'words only' edition; one with chants followed in 1932.

98 Henderson and Jarvis, *Sydney Nicholson and his Musings* (2013), 170–1.

99 Ibid., 174.

100 Shaw, *Vocation and Endeavour* (1997), 10.

101 Henderson and Jarvis, *Sydney Nicholson and his Musings* (2013), 206.

102 Choirs from the diocese had begun to sing Sunday services at Hereford during the summer from 1936 (Iles, 'Music and Liturgy', in Aylmer and Tiller (eds), *Hereford Cathedral* (2000), 433).

103 Lightwood, *The Story of the Free Church Choir Union* (1931), 12.

104 *Musical Times*, 68 (1927), 747.

105 *Musical Times*, 86 (1945), 309.

106 Young, *Chapel* 1972), 93.

107 Mackerness, *Somewhere Further North* (1974), 154.

108 Young, *Chapel* (1972), 93.

109 Terry, *A Forgotten Psalter* (1929), 111–13 describes the confused situation in the wake of the *Moto proprio* and the continuing performance of Viennese Masses.

110 Washington, 'The Oratory Musical Tradition,' in Napier and Laing (eds), *The London Oratory Centenary* (1984), 165.

111 'History of Music at Farm Street', Farm Street website, www.farmstreet.org.uk.

112 Boden, *The Three Choirs Festival* (2017), 195.

113 Ibid., 199, 217.

114 Ibid., 208, 212.

115 Ibid., 212.

116 Thompson, 'The Leeds Musical Festival' (1922), 796.

117 *Musical Times*, 66 (1925), 1007–8.

118 Bedford, 'Belshazzar's Feast' (2018), 52, which contradicts the account in Aldous, *Tunes of Glory* (2001), 51–2; cf. also Reid, *Malcolm Sargent* (1968), 201.

119 Aldous, *Tunes of Glory* (2001), 52; Bedford, 'Belshazzar's Feast' (2018), 53.

120 *Musical Times*, 72 (1931), 992.

121 *Musical Times*, 74 (1933), 173, 366.

122 Griffiths, 'The Eisteddfod Tradition,' in Herbert and Barlow (eds), *A History of Welsh Music* (2023), 114; *Musical Times*, 75 (1934), 815. Performances of major contemporary choral works were a feature at some of the National Eisteddfodau in the early decades of the century, including *The Dream of Gerontius* in 1918 and Delius's *A Mass of Life* in 1933 (Griffiths, ibid.).

123 Mitchell, *Festival for a Fine City* (2021), 127.

124 Keen, *The Bach Choir* (2008), 102.

125 Edwards, *And the Glory* (2011), 89.

126 *Musical Times*, 57 (1916), 90.

127 Keen, *The Bach Choir* (2008), 122.

128 Reid, *Malcolm Sargent* (1968), 156.

129 Keen, *The Bach Choir* (2008), 123; Green, 'Requiem: "Hiawatha" in the 1920s and 1930s' (2001), 283–5.

130 Reid, *Malcolm Sargent* (1968), 163–8.

131 *Musical Times*, 73 (1932), 1937 (Leicester); 74 (1933), 364 (Pickering), 552 (Sheffield).

132 *Musical Times*, 81 (1940), 40.

133 *Musical Times*, 94 (1953), 231.

134 Keen, *The Bach Choir* (2008), 106.

135 Ibid., 113.

136 Ibid., 119.

137 Ibid., 139–40.

138 Ibid., 141. 'Palace' was dropped from the choir's name by the 1930s.

139 Elkin, *Queen's Hall* (1944), 65. Henry Balfour Gardiner largely paid for the professional element.

140 Taylor, 'Charles Kennedy Scott' (1951), 494–6.

141 *Musical Times* 71 (1930), 451; Elkin, *Queen's Hall* (1944), 66.

142 Snowman, *Hallelujah!* (2007), 15.

143 Keen, *The Bach Choir* (2008), 140.

144 Ibid., 121.

145 Burney, *Account of the Musical Performances* (1785), 'Commemoration of Handel', 19–21.

146 Birmingham Musical Festival 1846 programme book.

147 [Anon.], 'Glasgow Musical Festival', *The Athenæum*, issue 2402 (8 Nov. 1873), 103.

148 *Musical Times*, 22 (1881), 568.

149 [Anon.], 'A Royal Choral Society's Rehearsal', *Musical Times*, 40 (1899), 22.

150 Boden, *The Three Choirs Festival* (2017), 186.

151 *Musical Times*, 61 (1920), 41.

152 E.g. for the South London Bach Society *Musical Times*, 90 (1949), 331.

153 Williams and Brewer, *Church Music* (1918), 13.

154 Hunt, 'Singing for Boys' (1945), 237; Day, *I Saw Eternity* (2018), 181.

155 Grace, 'London Concerts', *Musical Times*, 63 (1922), 251.

156 *Musical Times*, 62 (1921), 510.

157 A comparison of Coward and Wood as choral trainers is found in Rodgers, *The New Choralism* (1911), 5–7.

158 Wood, *My Life of Music* (1938), 285–95. For assessment of and reaction to Wood's interpretations of Bach's choral works, including specimens of his annotated scores see French, *Sir Henry Wood* (2019), esp. 185–238.

159 [Anon.], 'The Birmingham Musical Festival', *Musical Times* (1912), 723–7, which includes detailed criticism of *Messiah*. Cf. also a review of a 1933 *Messiah* in *Musical Times*, 74 (1933), 167–8.

160 *Monthly Musical Record*, 64 (1934), 85.

161 London, 1938.

162 Nettel, *Music in the Five Towns* (1944), 102.

163 *Monthly Musical Record*, 64 (1934), 85.

164 Snowman, *Hallelujah!* (2007), 132.

165 *Musical Times*, 69 (1928), 449.

166 *Monthly Musical Record*, 63 (1933), 14.

167 Columbia, 9320/17; available on YouTube.

168 HMV, ALP 1077/80.

169 RCA, RE 25002/5.

170 Williams, *Valleys of Song* (1998), 194.

171 Aldous, *Tunes of Glory* (2001), 80–3.

172 *Musical Times*, 72 (1931), 261.

173 *Musical Times*, 72 (1931), 454; 83 (1942), 222.

174 As reported by Lord Boothby on the BBC 1 television programme 'Sargent at Seventy', 22 April 1965, quoted in Reid, *Malcolm Sargent* (1968), 202.

175 Keen, *The Bach Choir* (2008), 125.

176 *Musical Times*, 71 (1930), 66.

177 Howes, 'London Concerts', *Musical Times*, 73 (1932), 67–8.

178 *Musical Times*, 85 (1944), 255.

179 *Musical Times*, 67 (1926), 450; 71 (1930), 165.

180 Scholes, *The Mirror of Music* (1947), 53; Day, *I Saw Eternity* (2018), 132–5.

181 Mackerness, *Somewhere Further North* (1974), 141.

182 Jackson, *Blessed City* (1997), 68.

183 *Musical Times*, 83 (1942), 217–18.

184 Aldous, *Tunes of Glory* (2001), 53–4.

185 Edwards, *And the Glory* (2011), 97–8.

186 Bradbury, 'Pen Portrait: Herbert Bardgett' (1960).

187 Mackerness, *Somewhere Further North* (1974), 142.

188 *Musical Times*, 101 (1960), 424.

189 *Musical Times*, 87 (1946), 377.

190 Luton Choral Society website, www.lutonchoralsociety.org.uk.

191 *Musical Times*, 53 (1912), 45.

192 *Musical Times*, 74 (1933), 73; *Monthly Musical Record*, 65 (1935), 110.

193 'Choral Notes and News', *Musical Times*, 61 (1920), 104–6.

194 *School Music Review*, 22 (1913), 23.

195 Hughes and Stradling, *The English Musical Renaissance* (2001), 189.

196 Richards, *Offspring of the Vic* (1958), 164–8, 184–6, 193–6, 258–60, 268–70.

197 *Musical Times*, 66 (1925), 549.

198 Wilson, 'Choral Competitions' (1925), 937.

199 For a history of the festival see *Music Won the Cause* (2005).

200 Ibid., 59.

201 A recording of the 1958 performance is on YouTube.

202 *School Music Review*, 35 (1926), 32–3.

203 12" 78 rpm record, Columbia 9909. Available on YouTube.

204 *Musical Times*, 66 (1925), 322–5.

205 Grace, 'The Decline of Sight-Singing' (1943), 138.

206 *Musical Times*, 84 (1943), 188.

207 Eton had even engaged John Hillah to conduct sight-reading classes for 150 boys back in 1842, though the experiment was short-lived (*Musical World* 17 (1842), 341).

208 Rainbow, *Bernarr Rainbow on Music* (2010), 218–19.

209 Rannie, *The Story of Music at Winchester College* (1970), 33; Rainbow, *Music in Independent Schools* (2014), 11.

210 Rainbow, *Music in Independent Schools* (2014), 18–51.

211 *Musical Times*, 21 (1880), 265.

212 *Musical Times*, 64 (1923), 62–3.

213 *Musical Times*, 71 (1930), 160–1.

214 Howes, 'A Public School Concert' (1927), 354.

215 *Musical Times*, 61 (1920), 317.

216 Sewell, *A History of the Bradford Festival Choral Society* (1907), 224–6.

217 Costa had performed the Magnificat at the 1877 Leeds Festival, while Henry Wood introduced it at the Norwich Festival of 1908, evidently using Robert Franz's rescored edition; he also performed the *Christmas Oratorio* at the Westmorland Festival of 1910 (French, *Sir Henry Wood* (2019), 32).

218 Hennemann, 'Operatorio?', (2014), 83.

219 *Musical Times*, 73 (1932), 554.

220 Hennemann, 'Operatorio?' (2014), 82–4.

221 Elkin, *Queen's Hall* (1944), 64.

222 Bonavia, 'Alan Kirby' (1950), 49–51.

223 *Musical Times*, 77 (1936), 1127.

224 Boden, *The Three Choirs Festival* (2017), 225–6.

225 *Musical Times*, 81 (1940), 231.

226 *Musical Times*, 83 (1942), 154.

227 Snowman, *Hallelujah!* (2007), 15.

228 Keen, *The Bach Choir* (2008), 150.

229 *Musical Times*, 86 (1945), 16.

230 *Musical Times*, 84 (1943), 90.

231 *Musical Times*, 85 (1944), 29.

232 *Musical Times*, 85 (1944), 215.

233 Edwards, *And the Glory* (2011), 107.

234 Ibid., 111.

235 Ibid., 111.

236 Tippett, *Those Twentieth Century Blues* (1991), 192–6, 206; Soden, *Michael Tippett* (2019), 370–1.

Chapter 7

1. Mould, *The English Chorister* (2007), 224.
2. Mould, 'Stanley Vann at 80' (1990), 341; Vann and Ferguson, 'The Golden Opportunity' (1999), 220–3.
3. Kennedy, 'Pen Portrait: Allan Wicks' (1960), 629–30.
4. Howard, *Thine Adversaries Roar* (2001); Storey, 'Forty-one Years in the Fens' (2006), 13.
5. Newsholme (ed.), *Memories of Worcester Cathedral Choir* (1997), 32; Sandon, *Living with the Past* (1997), 63.
6. Day, *I Saw Eternity* (2018), 171.
7. Owen, *A Life in Music* (2008), 154; the disc was first released in 1969.
8. Ibid., 148.
9. John Scott, 'George Howell Guest', *Oxford Dictionary of National Biography*, online, www.oxforddnb.com.
10. *The World of Christmas*, vol. 2, Argo, SPA/A 164.
11. Higginbottom, 'Transcending Time and Place' (2014), 24.
12. Ratcliffe, 'Tradition' (1999), 38.
13. Dakers, *Places Where they Sing* (1995), 111.
14. Pare, 'Eric Milner-White' (1984), 8.
15. Particularly noticeable in the Annual Reports of the Friends of Cathedral Music in the late 1970s and 1980s.
16. Thurmer, 'Exeter Cathedral' (1983), 181; Aston, *The Music of York Minster* (1972), 13.
17. Barry, 'It shouldn't work' (2014), 8 [Chelmsford]; Evans, 'Conrad Eden'(1995), 29 [Durham]; Aston and Roast, 'Music in the Cathedral', in Atherton *et al.* (eds), *Norwich Cathedral* (1996), 702 [Norwich].
18. Chichester successfully did so in the 1960s (Foster, 'Music at the Cathedral' (2004), 111–13).
19. Dalgleish, 'Southwell Minster' (2001), 11.

20	Hamilton, 'Tradition, part 17' (2003), 37; Mould, *The English Chorister* (2007), 252–5.
21	For the early years of the choir see Carpenter, *The Beat is Irrelevant* (1996). Rose's personal account appears in Rose, *Sitting on a Pin* (2021).
22	Barry, 'Broadcasting Choral Evensong' (2007), 13.
23	Storey, 'Music, 1660–1800', in Keene, Burns and Saint (eds), *St Paul's* (2004), 410–12.
24	Rose, *Sitting on a Pin* (2021), 214.
25	A useful survey of the condition of cathedral-type music around 1980 as viewed by many organists is found in Phillips, 'The Golden Age Regained' (1980).
26	Phillips, 'The Introduction of Girl Choristers at St David's Cathedral' (2017), 44.
27	Derby Cathedral evidently had a mixed boys and adult soprano line from some time until 1983, when the new organist, Peter Gould, moved the sopranos to become the Voluntary Choir, and reinstated a wholly boy top line (Gould, 'This is Your Life' (2013), 13).
28	Townhill, *The Imp and the Thistle* (2000), 121.
29	Palmer, 'The Manchester Question' (1999), 15.
30	Mould and Seal, 'The Girls in Sarum Green' (1991), 22–8.
31	Lammas Records, LAMM 107.
32	Hamilton, 'Tradition, part 17' (2003), 38.
33	It changed its name to the Campaign for the Traditional Cathedral Choir in 2005 (Stewart, 'The Impact of the Introduction of Girl Choristers' (2020), 17).
34	Stevens, 'No Danger of Complacency' (2006), 47.
35	Barry, 'The Choirs at Exeter Cathedral' (2005), 19.
36	A study of the history and background of these commissions is in Williams, '"What Sweeter Music"' (2019).

37   *Six Settings of the Responses by Tudor Composers*, ed. I. Atkins and E.H. Fellowes (London, 1933).

38   Doyle, *Westminster Cathedral* (1995), 65.

39   Ibid., 66–7.

40   Duffy, 'Evening Office' (1967), 1617; Duffy, 'Music in the Metropolitan Cathedral' (1986), 347–8.

41   Saunders, 'A New Model' (2006), 11

42   Walker, 'Establishing a Musical Tradition' (1974), 31–5.

43   Saint, 'A Life at St Chad's' (2016), 18.

44   John Brooks, 'An Interview with Dr. John Sanders', on the Sanders Society website, www.sanderssociety.org.uk/Research.aspx.

45   *In Tune with Heaven* (1992), 216.

46   Official figures for 1956 suggest there were about 102,000 boys to 44,000 girls, and 68,000 men to 40,000 women (*Facts and Figures about the Church of England* [no. 1] ([London], 1959), 33). Such figures, especially with a membership that is largely voluntary, need to be treated with caution, since, amongst other things, they do not reflect regularity of attendance.

47   Morris, 'Music at St Bartholomew-the-Great' (1973).

48   John Rutter: *Communion Service: Text as proposed for Series III ... For Congregational Use with Optional S.A.T.B. Choir* (London, 1972).

49   For Addington Palace see Henderson and Jarvis, *The Royal School of Church Music* (2015).

50   Ibid., 217.

51   Ibid., 167.

52   Ibid., 142–5; personal communication from Edward Higginbottom.

53   Dakers, *Places Where they Sing* (1995), 152–3.

54   Henderson and Jarvis, *The Royal School of Church Music* (2015), 339; *Church Music Quarterly*, Sept. 2015, 29.

55   Henderson and Jarvis, *The Royal School of Church Music* (2015), 388.

56 See the Rodolfus Foundation website, www.therodolfusfoundation.org.uk.

57 Purney, 'Director's Letter' (1967), 3–4.

58 See a history of the church's music on the Farm Street website, www.farmstreet.org.uk.

59 See regular reports in *Church Music*, 1964–71.

60 See the Cathedral website, www.stgilescathedral.org.uk.

61 See the Abbey website, www.paisleyabbey.org.uk.

62 Hollis, *The Best of Both Worlds* (1991), 113.

63 [Anon. 'A Chorister'], Letter, *Musical Times*, 45/2 (Feb. 1848), 162.

64 [Anon.], 'A Day to Remember', *Church Music Quarterly*, Mar. 2013, 15.

65 Cooper, 'The Three Choirs Festival' (1950), 398.

66 See Boden, *The Three Choirs Festival* (2017), for a general account of developments.

67 Ibid., 252.

68 Kirkman, 'The Southern Cathedrals Festival' (1999), 110.

69 Ashworth, 'Leeds Triennial Musical Festival' (1953), 577–8.

70 Editorial, *Musical Times* 95 (1954), 467–8.

71 Leeds Festival Chorus website, www.leedsfestivalchorus.co.uk/about-us/who-we-are/.

72 Mitchell, *Festival for a Fine City* (2021) recounts the history up to 2020.

73 Keen, *The Bach Choir* (2008), 144ff. for most of the information in this paragraph up to the 1960s.

74 Bach Choir website, www.thebachchoir.org.uk/about/about-the-choir/.

75 Royal Choral Society website, www.royalchoralsociety.co.uk/history.htm.

76 Jacobs, 'Walton's "Gloria" at Huddersfield' (1962), 24.

77 Edwards, *And the Glory* (2011), 139.

78 One of the earliest British performances was at the King's Lynn Festival in 1957 by Ely Cathedral choir under Michael Howard, in the version with organ accompaniment, played by Arthur Wills (Howard, *Thine Adversaries Roar* (2001), 78).

79 Whenham, *Monteverdi Vespers (1610)* (1997), 82–9.

80 *Musical Times* 92 (1951), 371.

81 Simeone, *The Janáček Compendium* (2019), 80; *Musical Times* 94 (1953), 577–8.

82 *Musical Times*, 113 (1972), 167.

83 On the choir's history see Snowman, *Hallelujah!* (2007).

84 Pettitt, *Philharmonia Orchestra* (1985), 87–8; Philharmonia Chorus website, www.philharmoniachorus.co.uk/about/chorus-history.

85 Snowman, *Hallelujah!* (2007), 122.

86 Morris, 'The South London Bach Society' (1952), 107–9.

87 Howes, 'A Restoration' (1950), 153.

88 Edwards, *And the Glory* (2011), 156.

89 Day, *I Saw Eternity* (2018), 192–7. They started as an unnamed group, assuming their name in 1979 (the Sixteen website, www.thesixteen.com/page/3093/History).

90 Ibid., 204–6.

91 Details in the Wikipedia 'Monteverdi Choir' entry.

92 Day, *I Saw Eternity* (2018), 203–4.

93 On the early days see *The King's Singers* (1980).

94 1970 television documentary 'The Wandsworth Sound', available on YouTube.

95 Wikipedia entry on 'Tiffin School'.

96 Swinson, 'The School where Dreams still Happen' (2018).

97 'Southend Choirs' website, https://southendchoirs.org.uk.

98 The D'Oyly Carte Opera Company, with its more or less year-round Gilbert and Sullivan productions (in London and

touring), and the touring Carl Rosa Opera Company would have been the only ones with a permanent chorus line.

99   Leech, *Welsh National Opera* (2006), 12–13; Welsh National Opera website, www.wno.org.uk/about/our-history.

100   Established in 1902; see the Halifax Amateur Operatic Society website, www.haosproductions.com/history. Another group, the Halifax Light Opera Society, was established in 1907; see www.halifaxlightopera.co.uk/who-we-are. Both are still in existence.

101   Early amateur productions of Gilbert and Sullivan had appeared at the end of the nineteenth century, sometimes given by ordinary choral societies, the earliest recorded being of *H.M.S. Pinafore* at Kingston-on-Thames in 1879 by the Harmonists' Choral Society (Baily, *The Gilbert & Sullivan Book* (1956), 173).

102   Morris, 'Elusive Choirs' (1998), 52–3.

103   *Musical Times* 133 (1992), 61.

104   Maddocks, 'Choir of the Year 2010' (2010).

105   Babbington (ed.), *The Oxford Companion to Australian Music* (1997) 120; *English Church Music*, 5/1 (Jan. 1935), 11.

106   *English Church Music*, 5/2 (Apr. 1935), 40–3.

107   *English Church Music*, 5/1 (Jan. 1935), 11–12.

108   Thomson, *The Oxford History of New Zealand Music* (1991), 44.

109   *English Church Music*, 3/3 (July 1933), 73–4.

110   Malan (ed.), *South African Music Encyclopedia* (1978), ii, article 'Indigenous musics', 269–73.

111   Wikipedia article, 'Drakensberg Boys' Choir School' and the school website, https://dbchoir.com.

112   Perkins and Dwight, *History of the Handel and Haydn Society* (1883), 37–40, 68.

113   Kallmann, Potvin and Winters (eds), *Encyclopedia of Music in Canada* (1992), 1298–9.

114   Clarke, *Healey Willan* (1997), 77.

Chapter 8

1. Stewart, 'The Impact of the Introduction of Girl Choristers' (2020), and Stewart, 'Girl Choristers' (2021) provide a good summary of the current situation.
2. Stevens, 'Tradition, Part 8' (2000), 55–6.
3. Leeds Minster website, https://leedsminster.org.
4. Archive of Recorded Church Music: 'Saving Truro Cathedral Choir', on YouTube.
5. Association of English Cathedrals website, www.englishcathedrals.co.uk: New girls' choir at Truro Cathedral.
6. 'Llandaff – Stay of Execution for Choir', *Choir & Organ*, 22/1 (Jan–Feb 2014), 6; personal communication from Stephen Moore.
7. Pritchard, 'In Full Sail' (2019), 51–2.
8. 'Andrew Carwood', Wikipedia article.
9. Reid, 'Sweet Singing in the Quire' (2011), 5–6.
10. *Church Music Quarterly*, June 2017, 33; *Choir & Organ*, 30/6 (July–Aug. 2022), 33.
11. Hamilton, 'Ancient … and Modern' (2019), 29–33.
12. Pritchard, 'Pushing Horizons' (2018), 59–60.
13. Merton College website, www.merton.ox.ac.uk/merton-college-girl-choristers.
14. [Anon.], 'Girls' choir at Christ Church Cathedral in Oxford is formally adopted', *Oxford Mail*, 27 Sept 2019.
15. Association of British Choral Directors website, www.abcd.org.uk.
16. Capon, 'Thumbs up for Cathedrals' (2011), 41–5.
17. Ibid., 41–5.
18. Stevens, 'How Green is my Valley' (2020); The Aloud Charity website, www.aloud.cymru.
19. 'Gareth Malone' Wikipedia article.
20. 'Military Wives Choirs' website, www.militarywiveschoirs.org.

21   Brian Kay in Owen, *A Life in Music* (2008), 186.

22   'Timeline of the COVD-19 pandemic in the United Kingdom (January–June 2020)', Wikipedia article.

23   *The Observer*, 17 May 2020.

24   *Salisbury Journal*, 13 Sept. 2020.

25   'St John Passion from isolation', available on YouTube.

26   '40 parts for 40 days: Stile Antico sing Spem in Alium', available on YouTube.

27   The idea of virtual choirs was not new, but went back at least to Eric Whitacre's Virtual Choir, devised by the American composer in 2009.

28   St John's in 2008 ('Choir of St John's College, Cambridge', Wikipedia article), New College in 2010.

29   'COVID-19 vaccination in the United Kingdom', Wikipedia article.

30   Information from RSCM headquarters.

31   *Choir & Organ*, 28/7 (Sept–Oct 2020), 9.

32   *Choir & Organ*, 30/8 (Sept 2022), 3 and 6.

33   *Choir & Organ*, 30/6 (July–Aug 2022). 7.

34   Rochester Cathedral website, www.rochestercathedral.org.

35   St John's College, Cambridge website, www.sjcchoir.co.uk/news.

36   *Your Herefordshire* (htpps://yourherefordshire.co.uk), 4 Feb. 2022 [Hereford]; *Choir & Organ*, 30/2 (March 2022), 7 [Chichester and Windsor].

37   *The Guardian*, 6 Dec. 2018.

38   The whole matter of the physiology and psychology of modern boys' singing is the subject of Ashley, *How High should Boys Sing* (2009).

39   Dakers, 'The Great Heritage of Cathedral Music' (1960), 11.

Bibliography

Printed and Online Sources

Aberdeen Journal, 1747–
The Academy, 1869–1902
Addleshaw, G.W.O. and Frederick Etchells, *The Architectural Setting of Anglican Worship* (London, 1948)
Adelmann, Dale, *The Contribution of the Cambridge Ecclesiologists to the Revival of Anglican Choral Music 1839–62* (Aldershot, 1997)
Alcock, John, *Divine Harmony, or a Collection of Fifty-five Double and Single Chants, for Four Voices* ([Lichfield, 1752])
Aldous, Richard, *Tunes of Glory: The Life of Malcom Sargent* (London, 2001)
Andrew, Samuel, 'Abraham Hurst and Elias Hall, Exponents of the Old Lancashire Notation in Music', *Transactions of the Lancashire and Cheshire Antiquarian Society*, 21 (1903), 183–7
— 'Musical Renascence in Manchester during the latter portion of the seventeenth and the beginning of the eighteenth centuries', *Transactions of the Lancashire and Cheshire Antiquarian Society*, 20 (1902), 261–3
— *A Souvenir, Comprising the History of Hey* (Oldham, 1905)
Andrews, Hilda, *Westminster Retrospect* (London, 1948)
Andrews, Paul D., 'Herbert Howells: A Documentary and Bibliographical Study' (D.Phil. diss., University of Wales, Aberystwyth, 1999)
[Anon.], *A New and Easie Method to Learn to Sing by Book* (London, Printed for William Rogers, 1686)
— 'Grand Musical Festivals', *The Quarterly Musical Magazine and Review*, 7 (1825), 411–48
— 'Grand Musical Festivals', *The Quarterly Musical Magazine and Review*, 8 (1826), 263–95
— ['Jubal'], 'Church Music at Oxford', *Parish Choir*, 2 (1847), 46–7
— ['A Chorister'], Letter, *Musical Times*, 45/2 (Feb. 1848), 162
— ['Native'], 'Church Music in Liverpool', *Parish Choir*, 3 (1849/51), 168–71
— 'The Great Handel Festival at the Crystal Palace', *Musical Times*, 9 (1859), 75–83
— 'The Oratorio Concerts', *Musical Times*, 15 (1871/3) [Mar. 1871], 9–10
— 'Bach's Passion-Music at Westminster Abbey', *Musical Times*, 15 (1871/3) [May. 1871], 74

— 'Bach's Passion Music at Westminster Abbey', *Musical Times*, 15 (1871/3) [Apr. 1872], 433–4
— 'The Passion Services at St. Anne's, Soho', *Musical Times*, 16 (1873/5) [Apr. 1873], 41–3
— 'Royal Albert Hall Choral Society', *Monthly Musical Record*, 3 (1873), 38
— 'Glasgow Musical Festival', *The Athenæum*, issue 2402 (8 Nov. 1873), 603–4
— 'Glasgow Musical Festival, *Musical Times*, 16 (1873), 307
— 'Glasgow Musical Festival', *The Times*, 8 Nov. 1873
— ['Cantatrice'], 'Employment of Female Voices in Church Choirs', *Musical Times* 27 (1886), 742
— 'Music in Monmouthshire and South Wales', *Musical Times*, 29 (1888), 549–51
— 'Mr. Walter Macfarren', *Musical Times*, 39 (1898), 10–15
— 'A Royal Choral Society's Rehearsal', *Musical Times*, 40 (1899), 22–3
— 'The Sheffield Festival Choir: A Talk with Dr. Henry Coward', *Musical Times*, 40 (1899), 730–3
— 'The Sheffield Musical Festival', *Musical Times*, 40 (1899), 737–9
— 'Church and Organ Music', *Musical Times*, 41 (1900), 464
— 'The Coronation of King Edward the Seventh and Queen Alexandra in the Collegiate Church of St. Peter in Westminster, August 9, 1902, *Musical Times*, 43 (1902), 577–86
— 'The Worcester Musical Festival', *Musical Times*, 43 (1902), 675–6
— 'The Alexandra Palace Choral Society, Performance of Parry's *Judith*', *Musical Times*, 44 (1903), 809
— 'Music in the Coronation Service', *Musical Herald*, issue 760 (July 1911), 213–15
— 'The Birmingham Musical Festival', *Musical Times* (1912), 723–7
— 'Church Music on the Gramophone', *English Church Music*, 1/1 (1931), 24–5
— 'A Day to Remember', *Church Music Quarterly*, Mar. 2013, 15
— 'Girls' Choir at Christ Church Cathedral in Oxford is Formally Adopted', *Oxford Mail*, 27 Sept 2019
Aplin, John, 'The Origins of John Day's "Certaine Notes"', *Music & Letters*, 62 (1981), 295–9
Aris's Birmingham Gazette, 1741–1862
Armstrong, Thomas, *Church Music Today*, Church Music Society Occasional Papers, 17 (London, 1946)
Arnold, Samuel (ed.), *Cathedral Music*, 4 vols (London, 1790)
Ashbee, Andrew, *Records of English Court Music*, 9 vols (Snodland and Aldershot, 1986–96)
— and John Harley, *The Cheque Books of the Chapel Royal*, 2 vols (Aldershot, 2000)
Ashley, Martin, *How High Should Boys Sing? Gender, Authenticity and Credibility in the Young Male Voice* (Farnham, 2009)

Ashworth, A.H., 'Leeds Triennial Musical Festival', *Musical Times*, 94 (1953), 577–8

Aston, Peter, *The Music of York Minster* (London, 1972)

— 'Music since the Reformation', in G.F. Aylmer and Reginald Cant (eds), *A History of York Minster* (Oxford, 1977), 395–429

Atchley, E.G. Cuthbert F., 'The Halleway Chauntry at the Parish Church of All Saints, Bristol, and the Halleway Family', *Transactions of the Bristol and Gloucestershire Archaeological Society*, 24 (1901), 74–125

Atherton, Ian et al. (eds), *Norwich Cathedral: Church, City and Diocese, 1096–1996* (London, 1996); Ian Atherton and Victor Morgan: 'Revolution and Retrenchment: The Cathedral, 1630–1720', 540–75; Peter Aston and Tom Roast: 'Music in the Cathedral', 688–704

Atkins, Ivor and Edmund Horace Fellowes (eds), *Six Settings of the Responses by Tudor Composers* (London, 1933)

Aylmer, Gerald, and John Tiller (eds), *Hereford Cathedral: A History* (London, 2000); John Caldwell, 'Music before 1300', 363–74; John Harper, 'Music and Liturgy 1300–1600', 375–97; Paul Iles, 'Music and Liturgy from 1600', 398–440; Philip Barrett, 'The College of Vicars Choral', 441–60; Anthony Boden, 'The Three Choirs Festival', 461–9

Babbington, Warren (ed.), *The Oxford Companion to Australian Music* (Melbourne, 1997)

Baillie, Hugh, 'A London Church in Early Tudor Times', *Music & Letters*, 36 (1955), 55–64

Baily, Leslie, *The Gilbert & Sullivan Book*, 4th rev. edn (London, 1956)

Baker, David, 'John Varley Roberts and the Victorian Organ', *Journal of the Royal College of Organists*, 11 (2017), 45–66

Baldwin, David, *The Chapel Royal: Ancient & Modern* (London, 1990)

Baldwin, Olive and Thelma Wilson, 'Purcell's Stage Singers', in *Performing the Music of Henry Purcell*, ed. Michael Burden (Oxford, 1996), 104–29

Bamford, Daniel John: 'John Barnard's *First Book of Selected Church Musick*: Genesis, Production and Influence' (Ph.D. diss., York Univ., 2009)

Barnard, John (ed.), *The First Book of Selected Church Musick* (London, 1641); facsimile edn with introduction by John Morehen (Farnborough, 1972)

Barrett, Philip, *Barchester, English Cathedral Life in the Nineteenth Century* (London, 1993)

— 'English Cathedral Choirs in the Nineteenth Century', *Journal of Ecclesiastical History*, 25 (1974), 15–37

Barry, Michael, 'Broadcasting Choral Evensong', *Once a Chorister*, 6/10 (2007), 12–19

— 'The Choirs at Exeter Cathedral', *Once a Chorister*, 6/8 (2005), 16–25

— 'It shouldn't work, 5: A Profile of the Choirs of Chelmsford Cathedral', *Once a Chorister*, 7/7 (2014), 8–10

Bashford, Christina and Leanne Langley (eds), *Music and British Culture, 1785–1914: Essays in Honour of Cyril Ehrlich* (Oxford, 2000); Michel Musgrave, 'Changing Values in Nineteenth-Century Performance: The Work of Michael Costa and August Manns', 169–91; Trevor Herbert, 'Popular Nationalism: Griffith Rhys Jones ('Caradog') and the Welsh Choral Tradition', 255–74

Bates, Frank, *Reminiscences and Autobiography of a Musician in Retirement* (Norwich, 1930)

Batten, Joseph, *Joe Batten's Book: The Story of Sound Recording* (London, 1956)

Beale, Robert, *Charles Hallé: A Musical Life* (Aldershot, 2007)

Beausang, Ita, '"For the Support of Decayed Musicians and their Families": The Papers of the Irish Musical Fund Society, 1787–1979', in Kerry Houston, Maria McHale, and Michael Murphy (eds), *Documents of Irish Music History in the Long Nineteenth Century*, Irish Musical Studies, 12 (Dublin, [2019]), 167–81

Bebbington, Warren (ed.), *The Oxford Companion to Australian Music* (Melbourne, 1997)

Beckwith, John, *The First Verse of Every Psalm of David* (London, [1808])

Bedford, Stewart, 'Belshazzar's Feast', in David Lloyd-Jones (ed.), *The William Walton Reader: The Genesis, Performance and Publication of his Works* (Oxford, 2018), 47–63

Bedwin, Richard E., *Fifty Years of Song: A Brief History of the Oxford Welsh Glee Singers, 1928–1978* (Witney, 1978)

Beer, Malcolm S. and Howard M. Crawshaw, *Music at Ripon Cathedral: The People, the Building, the Instruments, the Music, 657 to 2008* ([Ripon], 2008)

Beeson, Trevor, *Window on Westminster: A Canon's Diary, 1976–1987* (London, 1998)

Beet, Stephen R., *The Better Land: In Search of the Lost Boy Sopranos* (Portlaw, Co. Waterford, 2005)

Bennett, J.R. Sterndale, *The Life of William Sterndale Bennett* (Cambridge, 1907)

Bennett, Joseph, *Forty Years of Music 1865–1905* (London, 1908)

— *A Short History of Cheap Music: As Exemplified in the Records of the House of Novello, Ewer & Co.* (London, 1887)

— 'Some Recollections', *Musical Times*, 39 (1898), 451–3

Bennett, William, '"Gerontius": the First Performance', *Monthly Musical Record*, 63 (1933), 34–5

Birmingham Musical Festival, 1846, [Programme book] (Birmingham, 1846)

Blackburn, Bonnie J., 'Music and Festivities at the Court of Leo X: A Venetian View', *Early Music History* 11 (1992), 1–37

Blackburn, Vernon, 'Music in the Roman Church', *The Chord*, no. 3 (Dec. 1899), 7–16.

Blackmore, Elizabeth Naomi, 'The "Angelic Quire": Rethinking Female Voices in Anglican Sacred Music c. 1889' (MA diss., Durham Univ., 2016)

Bland, David, *Ouseley and his Angels: The Life of St. Michael's College, Tenbury and its Founder* (Eton, 2000)

Bloxam, John Rouse, *A Register of the Presidents, Fellows, Demies, Instructors in Grammar and in Music, Chaplains, Clerks, Choristers, and Other Members of Saint Mary Magdalen College in the University of Oxford: from the Foundation of the College to the Present Time*, 8 vols (Oxford, 1853–85)

Boden, Anthony, *Three Choirs: A History of the Festival* (Stroud, 1992); rev. edn with Paul Hedley as *The Three Choirs Festival: a History* (Woodbridge, 2017)

Bonavia, F., 'Alan Kirby', *Musical Times* 91 (1950), 49–51

Boston, Noel, *The Musical History of Norwich Cathedral* (Norwich, 1963)

Boult, Adrian Cedric, and Walter Emery, *The St. Matthew Passion, its Preparation and Performance* (London, [1949])

Bowers, Roger, 'Canterbury Cathedral: The Liturgy of the Cathedral and its Music, c.1075–1642', in P. Collinson, N. Ramsey and M. Sparks (eds), *A History of Canterbury Cathedral* (Oxford, 1995), 408–450

— 'Choral Institutions within the English Church: Their Constitution and Development, 1340–1542' (Ph.D. diss., Univ. of East Anglia, 1976)

— 'The Cultivation and Promotion of Music in the Household and Orbit of Thomas Wolsey', in S.J. Gunn and P.C. Lindley (eds), *Cardinal Wolsey: Church, State and Art* (Cambridge, 1991), 178–218

— 'An Early Tudor Monastic Enterprise: Choral Polyphony for the Liturgical Service', in James G. Clark (ed.), *The Culture of Medieval English Monasticism* (Woodbridge, 2007), 21–54

— *English Church Polyphony* (Aldershot, 1999). [Reprint of previously published articles, with some addenda]

— 'The Lady Chapel and its Musicians, c.1210–1559', in John Crook (ed.), *Winchester Cathedral: Nine Hundred Years, 1093–1993* (Chichester, 1993), 247–56

— 'The Music and Musical Establishment of St George's Chapel in the Fifteenth Century', in C. Richmond and E. Scarff (eds), *St George's Chapel, Windsor, in the Late Middle Ages* (Windsor, 2001), 171–213

— 'The Musicians and Liturgies of the Lady Chapels of the Monastery Church, c.1235–1540', in Tim Tatton-Brown and Richard Mortimer (eds), *Westminster Abbey: The Lady Chapel of Henry VII* (Woodbridge, 2003), 22–57

— 'The Vocal Scoring, Choral Balance and Performing Pitch of Latin Church Polyphony in England, c. 1500–58', *Journal of the Royal Musical Association*, 112 (1987), 38–76

Bowles, William, *The Parochial History of Bremhill* (London, 1828)

Bowley, Robert K., *The Sacred Harmonic Society: A Thirty-Five Years' Retrospect, from its Commencement in 1832, to the Five Hundredth Concert in Exeter Hall, 13th December, 1867* (London, 1867)

Box, Charles, *Church Music in the Metropolis* (London, 1884)

Boyce, William (ed.), *Cathedral Music*, 3 vols (London, 1760–73; 2nd edn, 1788)

Boydell, Barra, 'The Establishment of the Choral Tradition, 1480–1647', in K. Milne (ed.), *Christ Church Cathedral, Dublin: A History* (Dublin, 2000), 237–51

— *A History of Music at Christ Church Cathedral, Dublin* (Woodbridge, 2004)
— *Music at Christ Church before 1800: Documents and Selected Anthems* (Dublin, 1999)
Boydell, Brian, 'Music, 1700–1750', in T.W. Moody and W.E. Vaughan (eds), *A New History of Ireland. IV, Eighteenth-Century Ireland, 1691–1800* (Oxford, 1986), 568–628
Boyer, Sarah P.M., 'The Cathedral, the City and the Crown: A Study of the Music and Musicians of St Paul's Cathedral, 1660 to 1697' (D.Phil. diss., Manchester Univ., 1999)
Boynton, Susan, and Eric Rice (eds), *Young Choristers, 650–1700* (Woodbridge, 2008); Susan Boynton, 'Boy Singers in Medieval Monasteries and Cathedrals', 37–48; Anne Bagnall Yardley, 'The Musical Education of Young Girls in Medieval English Nunneries, 49–67
Bradbury, Ernest, 'Pen Portrait: Herbert Bardgett', *Musical Times*, 101 (1960), 424–5
Bremner, Robert, *The Rudiments of Music*. 2nd edn (Edinburgh, 1762)
Bridge, Claire, Andrew Wyatt, and Paul Stockbridge, 'The Nave Choir at Chester Cathedral', *Cathedral Music*, 2017 no. 2, 38–9
Bridge, John Frederick, *A Westminster Pilgrim* (London, 1919)
Brooks, David, 'An Interview with Dr John Sanders, March 1994', Sanders Society website (www.sanderssociety.org.uk/Research.aspx#brooksinterview)
Brown, David, *Thomas Weelkes: A Biographical and Critical Study* (London, 1969)
Brown, Thomas, *A Continuation or Second Part of the Letters from the Dead to the Living* (London, 1703)
Buckley, Annie, 'The "Deighn Layrocks"', *Baptist Quarterly*, new ser., 4 (1928–9), 43–8
Bumpus, John S., *The Organists and Composers of St. Paul's Cathedral* (London, 1891)
Burchell, Jennifer, 'Musical Societies in Subscription Lists: An Overlooked Resource', *Handbook for Studies in 18th Century Music*, 9 (1998)
Burney, Charles, *Account of the Musical Performances in Westminster Abbey, and the Pantheon, May 26th, 27th, 29th; and June the 3d, and 5th, 1784: in Commemoration of Handel* (London, 1785)
— *A General History of Music*, 4 vols (London, 1776–89); ed. Frank Mercer, 2 vols (London, 1935)
Burrows, Donald, '"Before him stood sundry sweet Singers of this our *Israel*": The Chorus Singers for Handel's London Oratorio Performances', in John Cunningham and Bryan White (eds), *Musical Exchange between Britain and Europe, 1500–1800: Essays in Honour of Peter Holman* (Woodbridge, 2020), 265–81
— *Handel*, Master Musicians. 2nd edn (New York and Oxford, 2012)
— *Handel and the English Chapel Royal* (Oxford, 2005)

— 'Handel's Dublin Performances', in Patrick F. Devine and Harry White (eds), *Irish Musical Studies 4: The Maynooth International Musicological Conference 1995: Selected Proceedings: Part One* (Blackrock, 1996), 46–70
— 'Lists of Musicians for Performances of Handel's *Messiah* at the Foundling Hospital (1754–1777)', *Royal Musical Association Research Chronicle*, 43 (2010), 85–109
Butler, Charles, *The Principles of Musik* (London, 1636)
Butler, Katherine, 'From Liturgy and the Education of Choirboys to Protestant Domestic Music-Making: The History of the 'Hamond' Partbooks (GB-Lbl: Add. MSS 30480–4), *Royal Musical Association Research Chronicle* 50 (2019), 29–93
Butt, John, 'Roman Catholicism and being Musically English: Elgar's Church and Organ Music', in Daniel M. Grimley and Julian Rushton (eds), *The Cambridge Companion to Elgar* (Cambridge, 2004), 106–19
Buxton, John, and Penry Williams (eds), *New College, Oxford, 1379–1979* (Oxford, 1979); R.L. Storey, 'The Foundation and the Medieval College, 1379–1530, 3–43; Paul R. Hale, 'Music and Musicians', 268–92
Byng, John (5th Viscount Torrington), *The Torrington Diaries, Containing the Tours Through England and Wales of the Hon. John Byng (later Fifth Viscount Torrington) between the Years 1781 and 1794*, ed. C. Bruyn Andrews, 4 vols (London, 1934–8)
Byrd, William, *Psalmes, Sonets, and Songs of Sadnes and Pietie* (London, 1588)
Caldwell, John, *The Oxford History of English Music*, 2 vols (Oxford, 1991–9)
— (ed.), *Early Tudor Organ Music: I, Music for the Office*, Early English Church Music, 6 (London, 1966)
Calendar of State Papers and Manuscripts, Relating to English Affairs, existing in the Archives and Collections of Venice, and of other Libraries in Northern Italy, 38 vols (London, 1864–1947)
Capon, Jane, 'Thumbs up for Cathedrals!', *Cathedral Music*, May 2011, 41–5
Carnelley, John, *George Smart and Nineteenth-Century Concert Life* (Woodbridge, 2015)
Carpenter, Edward (ed.), *A House of Kings: The History of Westminster Abbey* (London, 1966): M.S. Stancliffe: 'Victorian Chapter: The Age of Reform', 273–99; William McKie: 'Music in the Abbey', 416–45
Carpenter, Simon, *The Beat is Irrelevant: Barry Rose and the Early Years of Guildford Cathedral Choir* (Guildford, 1996)
Case, Thomas Henry, *Memoirs of a King's College Chorister* (Cambridge, 1899)
The Cathedral Psalter, ed. S. Flood Jones *et al.* (London, 1875); edition including chants (London, 1878)
Chetham, John, *A Book of Psalmody* (London, 1718; 3rd edn, 1724)
Cheverton, Ian, 'Cathedral Music in Wales during the Latter Part of the Seventeenth Century', *Welsh Music*, 8/1 (1986), 6–17
— 'English Church Music of the Early Restoration Period, 1660–c. 1676' (Ph.D. diss., Univ. of Wales, Cardiff, 1985)
Choir & Organ, 1993–

Church Music Society, *Cathedral Music Today and Tomorrow* (London, 1941)
— *Forty Years of Cathedral Music, 1898–1938* (London, 1940)
Clarke, F.R.C., *Healey Willan: Life and Music* (Toronto, 1997)
Clarke M.L., *Bangor Cathedral* (Cardiff, 1969)
Clay, William Keatinge, *The Book of Common Prayer Illustrated* (London, 1841)
Cleall, Charles, *The Selection and Training of Mixed Choirs in Churches* (London, [1960])
Clifford, James, *The Divine Services and Anthems usually Sung in the Cathedrals and Collegiate Choires in the Church of England* (London, 1663; enlarged 2nd edn, 1664)
Close, Francis, *Thoughts on the Daily Choral Services in Carlisle Cathedral* (Carlisle, 1865)
Clulow, Peter, 'Publication Dates for Byrd's Latin Masses', *Music & Letters* 47 (1966), 1–9
Cole, Suzanne, *Thomas Tallis and his Music in Victorian England* (Woodbridge, 2008)
Collinson, Thomas Henry, *The Diary of an Organist's Apprentice at Durham Cathedral, 1871–1875* (Aberdeen, 1982)
The Congregational Psalmist: (Third Section), Church Anthems, ed. Henry Allon (London, 1872)
Cook, Melville, with Basil Ramsey, 'Close to Music', *Musical Times*, 133 (1992), 663–5
Cooper, Martin, 'The Three Choirs Festival', *Musical Times*, 91 (1950), 398
Cooper, Victoria L., *The House of Novello: Practice and Policy of a Victorian Music Publisher, 1829–1866* (Aldershot, 2003)
— [as Victoria Cooper-Deathridge], 'The Novello Stockbook of 1858–1869: A Chronicle of Publishing Activity', *Notes* [Music Library Association], 44 (1987/8), 240–51
Cornish-Dale, Charles, 'Migrations of the Holy: The Devotional Culture of Wimborne Minster, c.1400–1640' (D.Phil. diss., University of Oxford, 2018)
Costin, W.C., *The History of St. John's College, Oxford, 1598–1860* (Oxford, 1958)
Cowan, Ian B., *The Scottish Reformation: Church and Society in Sixteenth Century Scotland* (London, 1982)
Coward, Henry, *Choral Technique and Interpretation* (London, [1914])
— *Reminiscences of Henry Coward* (London, 1919)
— *Round the World on Wings of Song: (Reciprocity): An Account of the Tour of the Sheffield Musical Union through the British Dominions from 17th March 1911 to 30th September 1911* (Sheffield, 1933)
Cowgill, Rachel and Peter Holman (eds), *Music in the British Provinces 1690–1914* (Aldershot, 2007); Rachel Cowgill: 'Disputing Choruses in 1760s Halifax: Joah Bates, William Herschel, and the Messiah Club', 87–114; Sally Drage: 'The Larks of Dean: Amateur Musicians in Northern England', 195–221; Catherine Dale: 'The Provincial Musical Festival in Nineteenth-century England: A Case Study of Bridlington, 325–47

Cox, John Edmund, *Musical Recollections of the Last Half-Century*, 2 vols (London, 1872)

Craig, Robert, *A Short History of Glasgow Choral Union* (Glasgow, 1944)

Croft, William, *Musica Sacra: or, Select Anthems in Score*, 2 vols (London, 1724–5)

Crompton, John, *The Psalm-Singer's Assistant* (London, 1778)

Crosby, Brian, 'A 17th-Century Durham Inventory', *Musical Times*, 119 (1978), 167–70

— 'The Choral Foundation of Durham Cathedral, c.1350–c.1650' (Ph.D. diss., Durham Univ., 1993)

— *Come on Choristers: A History of Durham Cathedral Choristers School* ([Durham], 1999)

— *Durham Cathedral Choristers and Their Masters* (Durham, 1980)

Crosse, John, *An Account of the Grand Musical Festival, held in September 1823, in the Cathedral Church of York* (York, 1825)

Crowest, Frederick J., *Phases of Musical England* (London, 1881)

Crum, Margaret, 'An Oxford Music Club, 1690–1719', *Bodleian Library Record*, 9/2 (1974), 83–99

Cudworth, W., *Musical Reminiscences of Bradford: Reprinted from the Bradford Observer* (Bradford, 1885)

Curwen, John, *Singing for Schools and Congregations (1843: 3dn of 1852)*. [Reprint] introduced by Bernarr Rainbow (Clifden, 1985)

Curwen, John Spencer, *The Boy's Voice* (London, 1891; 5th edn 1909)

— *Memorials of John Curwen* (London, 1882)

— *Studies in Worship Music*, [first series] (London, 1880; 3rd edn 1901); second series (London, 1886)

— and John Graham, *The Tonic Sol-fa Jubilee: A Popular Record and Handbook* (London, [1891])

Dakers, Lionel, 'The Great Heritage of Cathedral Music – What of its Future?', *Church Music Society Annual Report 1960*, 10–17

— *Places Where They Sing: Memoirs of a Church Musician* (Norwich, 1995)

Dalgleish, Paul, 'Southwell Minster: A Medieval Treasure', *Cathedral Music*, Oct. 2001, 10–12

Daly, Kieran Anthony, *Catholic Church Music in Ireland, 1878–1903: The Cecilian Reform Movement* (Blackrock, 1995)

Darwall-Smith, Robin, 'The Oxford Bach Choir, 1896–1997' in Robin Darwall-Smith and Susan Wollenberg (eds), *Music in Twentieth-Century Oxford: New Directions* (Woodbridge, 2023), 31–53

Day, John, (ed.), *Certaine Notes Set Forth in Foure and Three Parts* (London, 1565)

Day, Timothy, *A Century of Recorded Music: Listening to Musical History* (New Haven and London, 2000)

— *I Saw Eternity the Other Night: King's College, Cambridge, and an English Singing Style* (London, 2018)

— 'Sir Richard Terry and 16th-Century Polyphony', *Early Music*, 22 (1994), 297–307

Deakin, Andrew, *History of the Birmingham Festival Choral Society: Together with some Notices of the Rise and Progress of Chorus Singing in Midlands Towns* (Birmingham, [1897])

Dean, Winton, *Handel's Dramatic Oratorios and Masques* (London, 1959)

Demaine, Robert, 'Individual and Institution in the Musical Life of Leeds 1900–1914' (Ph.D. diss., University of York, 2000)

Deneke, Margaret, *Ernest Walker* (London, 1951)

Dexter, Keri, *'A Good Quire of Voices': the Provision of Choral Music at St. George's Chapel, Windsor Castle and Eton College, c.1640–1733* (Aldershot, 2002)

Dibble, Jeremy, *Charles Villiers Stanford: Man and Musician* (Oxford, 2002)

— *John Stainer: A Life in Music* (Woodbridge, 2007)

Dibdin, Charles, *The Musical Tour of Mr. Dibdin* (Sheffield, 1788)

Dickson, William Edward, *Fifty Years of Church Music* (Ely, 1894)

Doane, J., *A Musical Directory for the Year 1794* (London, [1794])

Doe, Paul (ed.), *Early Tudor Magnificats: I*, Early English Church Music, 4 (London, 1964)

Doyle, Peter, *Westminster Cathedral: 1895–1995* (London, 1995)

Drage, Sally, 'Elias Hall, "the faithful chronicler" of Oldham Psalmody', *Early Music*, 28 (2000), 621–34

— 'The Performance of English Provincial Psalmody c.1690–1849' (Ph.D. diss., Leeds Univ., 2009)

Drummond, Pippa, *The Provincial Music Festival in England, 1784–1914* (Farnham, 2011)

Duffy, Philip, 'Evening Office, 1: Experiment at Liverpool Metropolitan Cathedral', *Church Music*, 2/17 (Feb. 1967), 16–17

Duffy, Terence, 'Music in the Metropolitan Cathedral, Liverpool', *The Old Chorister*, 4/9 (May 1986), 347–8

Dundee Courier, 1801–

Earle, John, *Micro-cosmographie, or a Peece of the World Discovered in Essayes and Characters* (London, 1628)

Edwards, Frederick George, *The History of Mendelssohn's Oratorio 'Elijah'* (London, 1896)

Edwards, Kathleen, *The English Secular Cathedrals in the Middle Ages: A Constitutional Study with Special Reference to the Fourteenth Century*, 2nd edn (Manchester, 1967)

Edwards, R.A., *And the Glory: A History in Commemoration of the 150th Anniversary of the Huddersfield Choral Society* (Leeds, [1985]); 2nd rev. edn as *And the Glory: A History in Commemoration of the 175th Anniversary of the Huddersfield Choral Society* ([Huddersfield?], [2011])

Ehrlich, Cyril, *The Music Profession in Britain since the Eighteenth Century: A Social History* (Oxford, 1985)

Elkin, Robert, *Queen's Hall, 1893–1941* (London, 1944)

Elvey, Stephen, *The Psalter, or Canticles and Psalms of David, Pointed for Chanting* (Oxford, 1856)

English Church Music, 1931–80

Erasmus, Desiderius, *Opera omnia*, ed. Jean Le Clerc (10 vols [in 11], Leiden, 1703–6)

Evans, David Burton, 'Conrad Eden', *Cathedral Music*, Nov. 1995, 29–31

Evans, David R.A., 'John Tomkins and the Batten Organ Book', *Welsh Music*, 8/7 (1987/8), 13–22

— 'A Short History of the Music and Musicians of St. David's Cathedral, 1230–1883', *Welsh Music*, 7/8 (1984/5), 50–66

Evelyn, John, *The Diary of John Evelyn*, ed. Esmond S. De Beer, 6 vols (London, 1955)

Everist, Mark, 'From Paris to St Andrews: The Origins of W_1', *Journal of the American Musicological Society*, 43 (1990), 1–42

Eward, Suzanne, *No Fine but a Glass of Wine: Cathedral Life at Gloucester in Stuart Times* ([Wilton], 1985)

Facts and Figures about the Church of England [no. 1] ([London], 1959)

Farmer, Henry George, *A History of Music in Scotland* (London, [1947])

Fellowes, Edmund Horace, *English Cathedral Music* (London, 1941, 5th edn, rev. by Jack Westrup, 1969)

— *Memoirs of an Amateur Musician* (London, 1946)

Ferris, Catherine, 'The Music Collections of the Anacreontic Society and the Sons of Handel Society and Music Making in Dublin c.1740–1865', *Brio*, 43 no. 1 (2006), 21–33

Field, John, and Thomas Wilcox, *An Admonition to the Parliament* ([Hemel Hempstead?], 1572)

Fincham, Kenneth, 'Contemporary Opinions of Thomas Weelkes', *Music & Letters*, 62 (1981), 352–3

— and Nicholas Tyacke, *Altars Restored: The Changing Face of English Religious Worship, 1547–c.1700* (Oxford, 2007)

First (-Third) Report of Her Majesty's Commissioners to Inquire into the State and Condition of the Cathedral and Collegiate Churches in England and Wales (London, 1854–5)

Fleischmann, Aloys, 'Music and Society, 1850–1921', in W.E. Vaughan (ed.), *A New History of Ireland. VI; Ireland under the Union, II: 1870–1921* (Oxford, 2010), 500–22

Foster, Paul, 'Music at the Cathedral: An Interview with John Birch and Alan Thurlow', in Paul Foster (ed.), *Chichester & the Arts, 1944–2004: A Celebration*, Otter Memorial Paper, 18 (Chichester, 2004), 110–29

Freeman's Journal, 1763–1924

French, Hannah, *Sir Henry Wood: Champion of J.S. Bach* (Woodbridge, 2019)

Frere, Walter Howard, and William McClure Kennedy (eds), *Visitation Articles and Injunctions of the Period of the Reformation*, Alcuin Club Collections, 14–16, 3 vols (London, 1910)

Friends of Cathedral Music, [*Annual Report*] (London, [1957?]–1990)
Frost, Rebecca Ruth, 'English Cathedral Music and the BBC, 1922 to 1939' (Ph.D. diss., King's College, London, 2011)
Galloway, William Johnson, *Musical England* (London, 1910)
Galpin, Francis William, 'The Village Church Band: An Interesting Survival', *Musical News*, 5 (1893), 31–2, 56–8
Gammon, Vic, '"Babylonian Performances": the Rise and Suppression of Popular Church Music, 1660–1870', in E. and S. Yeo (eds), *Popular Culture and Class Conflict, 1590–1914* (Brighton, 1981), 62–88
— 'Problems in the Performance and Historiography of English Popular Church Music', *Radical Musicology*, 1 (2006), [online at http:/www.radical-musicology.org.uk/2006.Gammon.htm]
Gant, Andrew, *O Sing unto the Lord: A History of English Church Music* (London, 2015)
Gardiner, William, *Music and Friends*, 3 vols (London, 1838–53)
Garrett, K.I., 'Miss Hackett of Crosby Square', *Guildhall Studies in London History*, 1 (1973–5), 150–62
Gasquet, Francis Aidan and Edmund Bishop, *Edward VI and the Book of Common Prayer*, rev. edn (London, 1928)
Gastrell, Francis, *Notitia Cestriensis* (Manchester, 1849)
Gatens, William J., *Victorian Cathedral Music in Theory and Practice* (Cambridge, 1986)
Gibbons, Orlando, *A Collection of the Sacred Compositions of Orlando Gibbons*, ed. F.A.G. Ouseley (London, 1873)
Glover, William, *The Memoirs of a Cambridge Chorister*, 2 vols (London, 1885)
Gould, Peter, 'This is Your Life', *Cathedral Music*, 2013 issue 1, 12–15
Goulden, John, *Michael Costa: Britain's First Conductor: The Revolution in Musical Performance in England, 1830–1880* (Farnham, 2015)
Grace, Harvey, 'The Decline of Sight-Singing', *Musical Times*, 84 (1943), 137–9
— 'London Concerts (The Newcastle Bach Choir; London Festival)', *Musical Times* 63 (1922), 250–1
Granville, Roger, *The Life of the Honble. and Very Revd. Dennis Granville, Dean and Archdeacon of Durham* (Exeter, 1902)
Green, Jeffrey, 'Requiem: "Hiawatha" in the 1920s and 1930s', *Black Music Research Journal*, 21 (2001), 283–8
— *Samuel Coleridge-Taylor: A Musical Life* (London, 2011)
Green, Mary Anne Everett (ed.), 'Life of Mr William Wittingham', Camden Miscellany VI (London, 1870), 1–48
Greene, Maurice, *Forty Select Anthems in Score*, 2 vols (London, 1743)
Greenhalgh, D.M., 'The Nineteenth Century and After', in L.C. Colchester (ed.), *Wells Cathedral: A History* (Shepton Mallet, 1982), 179–203
Greenslade, M.W. (ed.), *A History of the County of Stafford*, 3, The Victoria History of the County of Stafford ([London], 1970)
Greenwood, James, *The Sol-fa System of Teaching Singing as Used in Lancashire and Yorkshire* (London, 1880)

Griffiths, David, *A Musical Place of the First Quality: A History of Institutional Music-Making in York c.1550–1990* (York, [1994])

Grindle, W.H., *Irish Cathedral Music: A History of Music at the Cathedrals of the Church of Ireland* (Belfast, 1989)

Grove, George (ed.), *A Dictionary of Music and Musicians*, 4 vols (London, 1879–89)

The Guardian (London), 1846–1951

The Manchester Guardian (from 1959 *The Guardian*), 1821–

Hackett, Maria, *A Brief Account of the Cathedral and Collegiate Schools* (London, 1827; new edns [c.1860], [1873])

Hall, Richard, and David Stocker (eds), *Vicars Choral at English Cathedrals: Cantate Domino: History, Architecture and Archaeology* (Oxford, 2005); Barrie Dobson, 'The English Vicars Choral: An Introduction', 1–10'; John Harper, 'The Vicars Choral in Choir', 17–22.

Hamilton, Maggie, 'Ancient ... and Modern. [St Andrews University]', *Choir & Organ*, 27/1 (Jan-Feb 2019), 29–33

— 'Tradition, part 17. [Wells]', *Choir & Organ*, 11/5 (Sept.-Oct. 2003), 34–8

Handel, George Frideric: *George Frideric Handel: Collected Documents*, ed. Donald Burrows *et al.* (Cambridge, 2013–)

— *The Works of Handel in Score, Correct, Uniform, and Complete*, ed. Samuel Arnold, 32 vols (London, [1787–97]).

Harley, John, *Music in Purcell's London* (London, 1968)

— *Orlando Gibbons and the Gibbons Family of Musicians* (Aldershot, 1999)

— *Thomas Tallis* (Farnham, 2015)

— *William Byrd: Gentleman of the Chapel Royal* (Aldershot, 1997; rev. edn 1999)

Harper, John, *The Forms and Orders of Western Liturgy: From the Tenth to the Eighteenth Century* (Oxford, 1991)

Harper, Norman, 'Southwark's 'other' Cathedral', *Cathedral Music*, 2016 no. 2, 44–7

Harrison, Frank Ll., *Music in Medieval Britain*, 2nd edn (London, 1963)

— 'The Repository of an English Parish Church in the Early Sixteenth Century', in Jozef Robijns (ed.), *Reniassance-Muziek 1400–1600: Donum Natalicium René Bernard Lenaerts* (Leuven, 1969), 143–7

Hart-Davis, Rupert, *Hugh Walpole: A Biography* (London, 1952)

Haweis, Hugh Reginald, *Music and Morals* (London, 1871)

Hawkins, John, *A General History of the Science and Practice of Music*, 5 vols (London, 1776); new edn with author's posthumous notes, 2 vols (London, 1853)

Hayes, William, *Remarks on Mr. Avison's Essay on Musical Expression* (London, 1753)

Haynes, Bruce, *A History of Performing Pitch: The Story of "A"* (Lanham, 2002)

Heighes, Simon: *The Lives and Works of William and Philip Hayes* (London, 1995)

Helmore, Frederick, *Church Choirs* (London, 1865; 4th edn, 1879)
— *Memoir of the Rev. Thomas Helmore* (London, 1891)
Henderson, John, and Trevor Jarvis, *The Royal School of Church Music: The Addington Years* (Salisbury, 2015)
— *Sydney Nicholson and his Musings of a Musician* (Dorking, 2013)
— *Sydney Nicholson and the College of St Nicolas: the Chislehurst Years* (Swindon, 2011)
Henderson, R.J., *A History of King's College Choir School* (Cambridge, 1981)
Hennemann, Monika, 'Operatorio?', in Helen M. Greenwood (ed.), *The Oxford Handbook of Opera* (New York, 2014), 73–91
Herbert, Trevor, Martin V. Clarke and Helen Barlow (eds), *A History of Welsh Music* (Cambridge, 2023); John Harper: 'Music in Worship before 1650', 53–77; Rhidian Griffiths: 'The Eisteddfod Tradition', 100–20; Rhidian Griffiths: 'Musical Communications in the Long Nineteenth Century', 195–209
Hewett, John William, *The Arrangement of Parish Churches Considered* (Cambridge, 1848)
Hey, Colin G, *Magdalen Schooldays, 1917–1924* ([Oxford], 1977)
Higginbottom, Edward, 'Transcending Time and Place', *Cathedral Music*, 2014, no. 1, 22–5
Hiley, David, *Western Plainchant: A Handbook* (Oxford, 1993)
Hillebrand, Harold Newcomb, *The Child Actors: A Chapter in Elizabethan Stage History* (Urbana, 1926)
Hillsman, Walter, 'Trends and Aims in Anglican Church Music, 1870–1906, in Relation to Developments in Churchmanship' (D.Phil. diss., Oxford Univ., 1985)
— 'Women in Victorian Church Music: Their Social, Liturgical, and Performing Roles in Anglicanism', in W.J. Sheils and Diana Wood (eds), *Women in the Church: Papers read at the 1989 Summer Meeting and the 1990 Winter Meeting of the Ecclesiastical History Society*, Studies in Church History, 27 ([Oxford],1990), 443–52
A History of St Chad's Cathedral, Birmingham, 1841–1904, compiled by the Cathedral Clergy (Birmingham, 1904)
Hobson, James, 'Musical Antiquarianism and the Madrigal Revival in England, 1726–1851' (D.Phil. diss., Bristol University, 2015)
Hodgson, Frederic, *Choirs and Cloisters: Seventy Years of Music in Church, College, Cathedral and Chapels Royal*. 2nd edn (London, 1995)
Hogan, Ita Margaret, *Anglo-Irish Music, 1780–1830* (Cork, 1966)
Hogarth, George, *Musical History, Biography, and Criticism* (London, 1835)
Hogwood, Christopher, *Handel* (London, 1984)
Hollis, Howard, *The Best of Both Worlds: A Life of Sir William McKie* ([s.l.], 1991)
Holman, Peter, *Before the Baton: Musical Direction and Conducting in Stuart and Georgian Britain* (Woodbridge, 2020)

— *Four and Twenty Fiddlers: The Violin at the English Court 1540–1690* (Oxford, 1993)
Horton, Peter, *Samuel Sebastian Wesley: A Life* (Oxford, 2004)
Hotson, Leslie, *The First Night of Twelfth Night* (London, 1954)
Howard, Michael, *Thine Adversaries Roar: Autobiographical Observations, 1922–1999* (Leominster, 2001)
H[owes] F[rank], 'London Concerts (Bach Cantata Club)', *Musical Times*, 73 (1932), 67–8
— 'A Public School Concert', *Musical Times*, 68 (1927), 354
— 'A Restoration of "The Messiah"', *Musical Times*, 91 (1950), 153
Hughes, Meirion and Robert Stradling, *The English Musical Renaissance, 1840–1940: Constructing a National Music*, 2nd edn (Manchester, 2001)
Hullah, Frances, *The Life of John Hullah, Ll.D.*, by his wife (London, 1886)
Hullah, John, *Wilhem's Method of Teaching Singing* (London, 1841)
Hunt, Donald, *Elgar and the Three Choirs Festival* (Worcester, 1999)
Hunt, Reginald, 'Singing for Boys: The Adolescent Voice', *Musical Times*, 86 (1945), 237–8
Hurd, Michael, *Vincent Novello – and Company* (London, 1981)
Hutton, William Holden, *S. John Baptist College*, University of Oxford College Histories (London, 1898)
In Tune with Heaven: The Report of the Archbishops' Commission on Church Music (London, 1992)
Jackson, Francis, *Blessed City: The Life and Works of Edward C. Bairstow 1874–1946* (York, 1996; 2nd rev. edn 1997)
Jackson's Oxford Journal, 1753–1898
Jacobs, Arthur, 'Walton's "Gloria" at Huddersfield', *Musical Times*, 103 (1962), 24
James, Kenneth, 'Concert Life in Eighteenth-Century Bath' (Ph.D. diss., London Univ., 1987)
James, Montague Rhodes, *Eton and King's – Recollections, mostly Trivial, 1875–1925* (London, 1926)
James, W.A., *An Account of the Grammar School and Song Schools of the Collegiate Church of the Blessed Virgin Mary of Southwell* (Southwell, 1927)
Janes, Robert, *The Psalter, or, Psalms of David* (Ely, 1837)
Jebb, John, *The Choral Responses and Litanies of the United Church of England and Ireland*, 2 vols (London, 1847–57)
— *The Choral Service of the United Church of England and Ireland* (London, 1843)
Johnson, Claudia L., '"Giant Handel" and the Musical Sublime', *Eighteenth-Century Studies*, 19 (Summer 1986), 515–33
Johnson, David, *Music and Society in Lowland Scotland in the Eighteenth Century* (London, 1972; 2nd edn, Edinburgh, 2003)
Johnston, Roy with Declan Plummer, *The Musical Life of Nineteenth-Century Belfast* (Farnham, 2015)

Johnstone, Andrew, '"As it was in the beginning"; Organ and Choir Pitch in Early Anglican Church Music', *Early Music*, 31 (2003), 506–25

Johnstone, Harry Diack, 'The Genesis of Boyce's "Cathedral Music"', *Music & Letters*, 56 (1975), 26–40

— 'Westminster Abbey and the Academy of Ancient Music: A Library Once Lost and Now Partially Recovered', *Music & Letters*, 95 (2014), 329–73

— and Roger Fiske (eds), *The Eighteenth Century: Music in Britain*, The Blackwell History of Music in Britain, 4 (Oxford, 1990)

Jong, Mayke de, *In Samuel's Image: Child Oblation in the Early Medieval West* (Leiden, 1996)

Joyce, Frederick Wayland, *The Life of Rev. F.A.G. Ouseley, Bart.* (London, 1896)

Kallmann, Hellmut, Gilles Potvin and Kenneth Winters (eds), *Encyclopedia of Music in Canada*, 2nd edn (Toronto, 1992)

Keen, Basil, *The Bach Choir: The First Hundred Years* (Aldershot, 2008)

Keene, Derek, Arthur Burns and Andrew Saint (eds), *St Paul's: The Cathedral Church of London, 604–2004* (New Haven & London, 2004); Ian Spink: 'Music, 1540–1640', 312–16, and 'Music, 1660–1800', 392–8; Donald Burrows, 'Orchestras in the New Cathedral', 399–402; Timothy Storey: 'Music, 1800–2002', 403–12

Kelly, Thomas Forrest (ed.), *Plainsong in the Age of Polyphony* (Cambridge, 1992); John Caldwell, 'Plainsong and Polyphony 1250–1550', 6–31; Richard Sherr, 'The Performance of Chant in the Renaissance and its Interactions with Polyphony', 178–208

Kennedy, Michael, 'Pen Portrait: Allan Wicks', *Musical Times*, 101 (1960), 629–30

— *The Works of Ralph Vaughan Williams*, new edn (London, 1980)

Kidner, Walter James, *How to Start a Men's Choir*, 2nd edn (London, [1900?])

The King's Singers: A Self-Portrait: Nigel Perrin, Alastair Hume, Bill Ives, Anthony Holt, Simon Carrington and Brian Kay (London, 1980)

Kirkman, Tim, 'The Southern Cathedrals Festival', *Organists' Review*, 85/2 (1999), 110

Kirwan, A. Lindsey, *The Music of Lincoln Cathedral* (London, 1973)

Kisby, Fiona Luise, 'The Royal Household Chapel in Early-Tudor London, 1485–1547' (Ph.D. diss., Royal Holloway Univ., 1996)

Kitton, Frederic G., *Zechariah Buck ...: A Centenary Memoir* (London, 1899)

Klein, Hermann, 'The Jubilee of the Royal Albert Hall and the Royal Choral Society', *Musical Times*, 62 (1921), 229–35, 313–20, 393–400

Knight, David, 'Nineteenth-Century Repertoire and Performance Practice at Westminster Abbey', in Jeremy Dibble and Bennett Zon (eds), *Nineteenth-Century British Music Studies*, 2 (Aldershot, 2002), 80–98

Knight, Frida, *Cambridge Music* (Cambridge, 1980)

Knights, Francis, 'The History of the Choral Foundation of St John's College, Oxford', *Musical Times*, 131 (1990), 444–7

Knowles, David, *The Religious Orders in England*, 3 vols (Cambridge, 1948–59)

— and R. Neville Hadcock, *Medieval Religious Houses: England and Wales*, [new edn] (London, 1971)

Landon, H.C. Robbins, *Haydn: Chronicle and Works*, 5 vols (London, 1976–80)

La Trobe, John Antes, *The Music of the Church; Considered in its Various Branches, Congregational and Choral: An Historical and Practical Treatise for the General Reader* (London, 1831)

Leech, Caroline (ed.), *Welsh National Opera* (Cardiff, 2006)

Lefkowitz, Murray (ed.), *Trois masques à la cour de Charles Ier d'Angleterre* (Paris, 1970)

Legge, Robin H, and W.E. Hansell, *Annals of the Norfolk & Norwich Triennial Musical Festivals, MDCCCXXIV – MDCCCXCIII* (London, 1896)

Lehmberg, Stanford E., *Cathedrals under Siege: Cathedrals in English Society 1600–1700* (Exeter, 1996)

— *English Cathedrals: A History* (London, 2005)

— *The Reformation of Cathedrals: Cathedrals in English Society, 1485–1603* (Princeton, 1988)

Le Huray, Peter, 'The English Anthem, 1580–1640', *Proceedings of the Royal Musical Association*, 86 (1959/60), 1–13

— *Music and the Reformation in England, 1549–1660* (London 1967; 2nd edn, 1978)

— 'Towards a Definitive Study of Pre-Restoration Anglican Service Music', *Musica Disciplina*, 14 (1960), 167–95

Lewer, David, *A Spiritual Song: The Story of the Temple Choir and a History of Divine Service in the Temple Church* (London, 1961)

Liber precum publicarum (London, 1560)

Lightwood, James T., *The Story of the Free Church Choir Union* (London, [1931])

Locke, Matthew, *The Present Practice of Musick Vindicated* (London, 1673)

The London & Dublin Orthodox Journal of Useful Knowledge, 1835–1843

Lowe, Edward, *A Short Direction for the Performance of Cathedrall Service* (Oxford, 1661); 2nd edn as *A Review of Some Short Directions for Performance of Cathedral Service* (Oxford, 1664)

Ludlow, J.M. and Lloyd Jones, *Progress of the Working Class, 1832–1867* (London, 1867)

Lynch, Michael, 'Towards the Abolition of 'Payments by Results': The End of School Music or an Opportunity for Further Development as Reported in School Music Review 1892–1901?', *British Journal of Music Education*, 18 (2001), 187–93

Lysons, Daniel, *Origin and Progress of the Meetings of the Three Choirs of Gloucester, Worcester and Hereford, and of the Charity connected with it* (Gloucester, 1812); enlarged edn with John Amott (Gloucester, 1864) and with C. Lee Williams and H. Godwin Chance (Gloucester, 1895)

[M., L.A. and J.G.T.], *Guide to the Church Services in London and its Suburbs* [signed L.A.M. and J.G.T.] (London, 1858; 2nd edn, 1862; 3rd edn, 1863)

MacCulloch, Diarmaid, *Thomas Cranmer: A Life* (New Haven & London, 1996; rev. 2nd edn, 2016)
MacDermott, K.H., *Sussex Church Music in the Past* (Chichester, 1923)
Mace, Thomas, *Musick's Monument* (London, 1676)
Mackerness, E.D., *A Social History of English Music* (London, 1964)
— *Somewhere Further North: A History of Music in Sheffield* (Sheffield, 1974)
Mackeson, Charles, *A Guide to the Churches of London and its Suburbs for 1884* (London, 1884)
Maddocks, Fiona, 'Choir of the Year 2010', *The Observer*, 5 Dec. 2010
Malan, Jacques P. (ed.), *South African Music Encyclopedia*, 4 vols (Cape Town, 1978–86)
Marbeck, John, *The Booke of Common Prayer Noted* (London, 1550); facsimile edn with intro. by Robin A. Leaver (Oxford, 1980)
Marr, Robert A., *Music for the People: A Retrospect of the Glasgow International Exhibition, 1888, with an Account of the Rise of Choral Societies in Scotland* (Edinburgh, 1889)
Marsh, Christopher, *Music and Society in Early Modern England* (Cambridge, 2010)
Marsh, John, *The John Marsh Journals: The Life and Times of a Gentleman Composer (1752–1828)*, ed. Brian Robins (2 vols; vol. 1, Stuyvesant, NY, 1998, rev. edn Hillsdale, NY [2011?]; vol. 2, Hillsdale, NY, [2013])
Martin, George C., *The Art of Training Choir Boys* (London, ([1892])
Mason, Lowell, *Musical Letters from Abroad* (New York, 1854)
— *A Yankee Musician in Europe: The 1837 Journals of Lowell Mason*, ed. Michael Broyles (Ann Arbor, 1990)
Massing, Jean Michel, and Nicolette Zeeman (eds), *King's College Chapel, 1515–2015: Art, Music and Religion in Cambridge* (London, 2014); Roger Bowers: 'Chapel and Choir, Liturgy and Music, 1444–1644', 259–83; Nicholas Marston: '"As England knows it": "Daddy" Mann and King's College Choir, 1876–1929', 303–21; Nicholas Nash: '"A Right Prelude to Christmas": A History of *A Festival of Nine Lessons and Carols*', 323–43
Matthew, James E., 'The Ancient Concerts, 1776–1848', *Proceedings of the Musical Association*, 33 (1906/7), 55–79
McCulloch, Peter, 'Music Reconciled to Preaching: A Jacobean Moment?', in Natalie Mears and Alec Ryrie (eds) *Worship and the Parish Church in Early Modern Britain* (Farnham, 2013), 109–30
McGee, Timothy J., *The Sound of Medieval Song: Ornamentation and Vocal Style according to the Treatises* (Oxford, 1998)
McGuinness, Rosamond, *English Court Odes 1660–1820* (Oxford, 1971)
McGuire, Charles, *Music and Victorian Philanthropy: The Tonic Sol-fa Movement* (Cambridge, 2009)
McNaught, William, 'Choral Notes and News', *Musical Times*, 61 (1920), 104–6
McVeigh, Simon, *Concert Life in London from Mozart to Haydn* (Cambridge, 1993)

Meadows, Gwen, *Centenary Celebration: A History of the Contribution of the Cambridge Philharmonic Society to Music in the City* (Cambridge, 1987)

Meadows, Peter and Nigel Ramsay (eds), *A History of Ely Cathedral* (Woodbridge, 2003): Ian Payne, 'Music and Liturgy to 1644', 225–44; Nicholas Thistlethwaite, 'Music and Liturgy 1660–1846', 235–58; Nicholas Thistlethwaite, 'Music 1836–1980', 333–62

Mee, John H., *The Oldest Music Room in Europe: A Record of Eighteenth-Century Enterprise at Oxford* (London, 1911)

Mendelssohn Bartholdy, Felix and Cécile, *The Mendelssohns on Honeymoon: The 1837 Diary of Felix and Cécile Mendelssohn Bartholdy, together with Letters to their Families*, ed. and trans. Peter Ward Jones (Oxford, 1997)

Miller, Clement A., 'Erasmus on Music', *Musical Quarterly*, 52 (1966), 332–49

Miller, Edward, *The Psalms of David for the Use of Parish Churches* (London, 1790)

Milsom, John, 'English-texted Chant before Merbecke', *Plainsong and Medieval Music* 1 (1992), 77–92

— 'The Nonesuch Music Library', in Chris Banks, Arthur Searle and Malcolm Turner (eds), *Sundry Sorts of Music Books: Essays on the British Library Collections: Presented to O.W. Neighbour on his 70th Birthday* (London, 1993), 146–82

Minshall, Ebenezer, *Fifty Years' Reminiscences of a Free Church Musician* (London, 1910)

Mitchell, Bob, *Festival for a Fine City: 250 Years of the Norfolk and Norwich Festival* (Norwich, [2021])

The Monthly Musical Record, 1871–1960

Moore, Jerrold Northrop, *Edward Elgar: A Creative Life* (Oxford, 1984)

Moore, Thomas, *The Psalm-Singer's Divine Companion*, 2nd edn, 2 vols (London and Manchester, [1750])

Morehen, John (ed.), *English Choral Practice 1400–1650* (Cambridge, 1995); Roger Bowers, 'To Chorus from Quartet: The Performing Resource for English Church Polyphony c.1390–1559', 1–47; John Milsom, 'Sacred Songs in the Chamber', 161–79

Morley, Thomas, *A Plaine and Easie Introduction to Practicall Musicke* (London, 1597); modern edn, ed. Ben Byram-Wigfield (Great Malvern, 2003)

Morphet, David, and David Hill, 'St John's College, Cambridge', *Once a Chorister*, 7/4 (2011), 52–3

Morris, Andrew, 'Music at St Bartholomew-the-Great', *Musical Times*, 114 (1973), 941–3

Morris, Eleanor, 'The South London Bach Society', *Musical Times*, 93 (1952), 107–9

Morris, Norman, 'Elusive Choirs', *Choir & Organ*, 6/4 (July–Aug. 1998), 52–3

Mould, Alan, *The English Chorister* (London, 2007)

— and Richard Seal, 'The Girls in Sarum Green', *Cathedral Music*, Nov. 1991, 22–8

Mould, Simon, 'Stanley Vann at 80', *Musical Times*, 131 (1990), 341

Muir, Thomas, '"Full in the Panting Heart of Rome": Roman Catholic Church Music in England: 1850–1962' (Ph.D. diss., Durham Univ., 2004)

— *Roman Catholic Church Music in England (1791–1914); A Handmaid of the Liturgy?* (Aldershot, 2008)

Murphy, Michael and Jan Smaczny (eds), *Music in Nineteenth-Century Ireland*, Irish Musical Studies, 9 (Dublin, 2007); Roy Johnston: 'Concert Auditoria in Nineteenth-Century Belfast', 234–51; Paul Rodmell: 'The Society of Antient Concerts, Dublin, 1834–64', 211–33

Musgrave, Michael, *The Musical Life of the Crystal Palace* (Cambridge, 1995)

Music Won the Cause: 100 Years of the Leith Hill Musical Festival, 1905–2005 [by Shirley Corke et al.] ([Dorking?], 2005)

The Musical Times and Singing Class Circular (from 1904 *The Musical Times*), 1844–

Napier, Michael, and Alistair Laing (eds), *The London Oratory Centenary 1884–1984* (London, 1984); Henry Washington, 'The Oratory Musical Tradition', 152–71; Ralph Downes, 'The Organs of the Oratory', 173–80.

Nares, James, *A Morning & Evening Service ... together with Six Anthems in Score* (London, 1788)

— *Twenty Anthems in Score for 1.2.3.4. and 5. voices* (London, 1778)

Neal, Daniel, *The History of the Puritans*, 4 vols (London, 1732–8)

Needham, Raymond and Alexander Webster, *Somerset House* (London, 1905)

Nettel, Reginald, *Music in the Five Towns 1840–1914: A Study of the Social Influence of Music in an Industrial District* (London, 1944)

— *North Staffordshire Music: A Social Experiment* (Rickmansworth, 1977)

New College Choir: Archive Recordings (1927–1951), New College Choristers' Association, 1997 (CD: CHASS 971)

Newsholme, Richard. (ed.), *Memories of Worcester Cathedral Choir* (Worcester, 1997)

Nichols, John, *The Progresses and Public Processions of Queen Elizabeth*, new edn, 3 vols (London, 1823); new edn 'of the early modern sources', ed. Elizabeth Golding *et al.*, 5 vols (Oxford, 2014)

Nichols, John Gough (ed.), 'Sermon of the Child Bishop, Pronowsyd by John Stubs, Querester, on Childermas Day, at Glocester, 1558', in *The Camden Miscellany*, 7; Works of the Camden Society, new series, 14 (London, 1875), 14–29

Nicholson, Sydney H., 'The Choirboy and his Place in English Music', *Proceedings of the Musical Association* 70 (1943/44), 53–74

— 'Principles and Recommendations [of the School of English Church Music]', *English Church Music* 11/1 (1941), 89–94

— *Quires and Places where they Sing* (London, 1932)

Norris, Gerald, *Stanford, the Cambridge Jubilee, and Tchaikovsky* (Newton Abbot, 1980)

Norris, Michael (ed.), *London Choir School: An Anthology* ([s.l.], [2008])

North, Roger, *The Musicall Grammarian, 1728*, ed. Mary Chan and Jamie C. Kassler (Cambridge, 1990)

— *Roger North on Music: Being a Selection from his Essays Written during the Years c.1695–1728*, ed. John Wilson (London, 1959)

Novello, Clara, *Clara Novello's Reminiscences*, compiled by her daughter Contessa Valeria Gigliucci (London, 1910)

Novello & Co., *The Complete Catalogue of Music Published by Novello and Company Limited* (London, c.1900)

The Observer, 1791–

O'Donoghue, Patrick, 'Music and Religion in Ireland', in Gerard Gillen and Harry White (eds), *Music and Irish Cultural History* (Blackrock, 1995), 116–37

The Official Year-Book of the Church of England, [from 1922] *The Official Year-Book of the National Assembly of the Church of England* (London, 1883–1962)

Olleson, Philip, *Samuel Wesley: The Man and his Music* (Woodbridge, 2003)

O'Regan, Susan, *Music and Society in Cork, 1700–1900* (Cork, 2018)

Orme, Nicholas, 'The Medieval Clergy of Exeter Cathedral. I: The Vicars and Annuellars', *Transactions of the Devonshire Association for the Advancement of Science, Literature and Art*, 113 (1981), 79–102

— 'The Medieval Clergy of Exeter Cathedral. II: The Secondaries and Choristers', *Transactions of the Devonshire Association for the Advancement of Science, Literature and Art*, 115 (1982), 79–100

Owen, Dorothy, (ed.), *A History of Lincoln Minster* (Cambridge, 1994); Roger Bowers, 'Music and Worship to 1640', 47–76; Nicholas Thistlethwaite, 'Music and Worship, 1660–1980', 77–111; Margaret Bowker, 'Historical Survey, 1450–1750', 164–209

Owen, William, *A Life in Music: Conversations with David Willcocks and Friends* (Oxford, 2008)

Oxford Dictionary of National Biography, ed. H.C.G. Matthew and Brian Harrison, 20 vols (Oxford, 2004) and online.

Page, Daniel Bennett, 'Uniform and Catholic: Church Music in the Reign of Mary Tudor (1553–1558)' (Ph.D. diss., Brandeis Univ., 1996)

Page, John, (ed.), *Harmonia sacra*, 3 vols (London, 1800)

Palmer, Andrew, 'The Manchester Question', *Cathedral Music*, Oct. 1999, 15–18

Palmer, Christopher, *Herbert Howells: A Centenary Celebration* (London, 1992; rev. edn, 1996)

Palmer, Fiona M., *Conductors in Britain, 1870–1914: Wielding the Baton at the Height of Empire* (Woodbridge, 2017)

Pare, Philip, 'Eric Milner-White, born 23 April 1884', *The World of Church Music* (1984), 7–12

Parker, Matthew, *The Whole Psalter Translated into English Metre* (London, 1567)
Parrott, Andrew, *Composers' Intentions: Lost Traditions of Musical Performance* (Woodbridge, 2015)
— 'Falsetto Beliefs: the "Countertenor" Cross-Examined', *Early Music*, 43 (2015), 79–110; reprinted with additions in *Composers' Intentions*
— "Grett and solompne singing": Instruments in English Church Music before the Civil War', *Early Music*, 6 (1978), 182–7; reprinted in *Composers' Intentions*
Parrott, Isabel, 'William Sterndale Bennett and the Bach Revival in Nineteenth-Century England', in Rachel Cowgill and Julian Rushton (eds), *Europe, Empire and Spectacle in Nineteenth-Century British Music* (Aldershot, 2006), 29–44
Patrick, Millar, *Four Centuries of Scottish Psalmody* (London, 1949)
Patton, John and Steve Taylor: *A Century of Cathedral Music 1898–1998* (Winchester, 2000)
Payne, Ian, *The Provision and Practice of Sacred Music at Cambridge Colleges and Selected Cathedrals c.1547 – c.1646* (New York and London, 1993)
Pearce, Ernest Harold, *The Sons of the Clergy: Some Records of Two Hundred and Seventy-Five Years* (London, 1904; 2nd edn, 1928)
Peel, Albert (ed.), *The Seconde Part of a Register, a Calendar of MSS. under that Title Intended for Publication by the Puritans about 1593, and now in Dr Williams's Library, London*, 2 vols (Cambridge, 1915)
Pepys, Samuel, *The Diary of Samuel Pepys: A New and Complete Transcription*, ed. Robert Latham and William Matthews, 11 vols (London, 1970–83)
Perkins, Charles C. and John S. Dwight., *History of the Handel and Haydn Society, of Boston, Massachusetts* (Boston, 1883–93)
Pettitt, Stephen J., *Philharmonia Orchestra: A Record of Achievement 1945–85* (London, 1985)
Phillips, Benjamin, 'The Introduction of Girl Choristers at St David's Cathedral', *Cathedral Music*, 2017 no. 1, 42–5
Phillips, Peter, 'The Golden Age Regained', *Early Music*, 8 (1980), 3–16, 178–98
— 'Treble or Soprano?: Performing Tallis', *Early Music*, 33 (2005), 495–502
Piggott, J.R.: *Palace of the People: The Crystal Palace at Sydenham, 1854–1936* (London, 2004)
Pine, Edward, *The Westminster Abbey Singers* (London, 1953)
Playford, John, *A Breefe Introduction to the Skill of Musick* (London, 1654); later editions (to 1730) titled *An Introduction to the Skill of Musick*.
Plummer, Charles, *Elizabethan Oxford* (Oxford, 1887)
Power, Eileen, *Medieval English Nunneries, c. 1275 – 1535* (Cambridge, 1922)
Practical Suggestions for the Improvement of Church Music (Edinburgh, 1852)
Preece, Isobel Woods, *Our Awin Scottis Use: Music in the Scottish Church up to 1603*, with additional contributions by Warwick Edwards and Gordon J. Munro (Glasgow and Aberdeen, 2000)

Pritchard, Brian W., 'The Musical Festival and the Choral Society in England in the Eighteenth and Nineteenth Centuries: A Social History' (Ph.D. diss., Birmingham Univ., 1968)
— 'The Provincial Festivals of the Ashley Family', *Galpin Society Journal*, 22 (1969), 58–77
Pritchard, Stephen, 'In Full Sail, [Portsmouth Cathedral]', *Choir & Organ*, 27/5 (Sept. 2019), 51–2
— 'Pushing Horizons', *Choir & Organ*, 26/6 (Nov-Dec 2018), 59–60
Purney, Wilfrid, 'Director's Letter', *Church Music*, 2/18 (Apr. 1967), 3–4
Radcliffe, Philip, *Bernhard (Boris) Ord, 1897–1961: Fellow and Organist, University Organist and Lecturer in Music: A Memoir* (Cambridge, 1962)
Rainbow, Bernarr, *Bernarr Rainbow on Music: Memoirs and Selected Writings*, with introductions by Gordon Cox and Charles Plummeridge (Woodbridge, 2010)
— *The Choral Revival in the Anglican Church (1839–1872)* (London, 1970)
— *Music in Educational Thought and Practice: A Survey from 800 BC*, new edn with additional material by Gordon Cox (Woodbridge, 2006)
— et al., *Music in Independent Schools*, ed. Andrew Morris (Woodbridge, 2014)
Range, Matthias, *British Royal and State Funerals: Music and Ceremonial since Elizabeth I* (Woodbridge, 2016)
— *Music and Ceremonial at British Coronations: From James I to Elizabeth II* (Cambridge, 2012)
Rannie, Alan, *The Story of Music at Winchester College, 1394–1969* (Winchester, 1970)
Rashdall, Hastings and Robert S. Rait, *New College*, University of Oxford, College Histories (London, 1901)
Ratcliffe, Shirley, 'Tradition, [Queens' College, Cambridge]', *Choir & Organ*, 7/6 (Nov.–Dec. 1999), 38–41
The Records of the Honorable Society of Lincoln's Inn: The Black Books, ed. W. Paley Baildon *et al.* (London, 1897–)
Reeves, Sims J., *My Jubilee: Or, Fifty Years of Artistic Life* (London, 1889)
Reid, Andrew, 'Sweet Singing in the Quire: Agenda for Lay Clerks', *Cathedral Music*, May 2011, 5–8
Reid, Charles, *Malcolm Sargent: A Biography* (London, 1968)
— *Thomas Beecham: An Independent Biography* (London, 1961)
Reißfelder, David, 'Jenseits des Crystal Palace: Arthur James Balfour und die (zweite) Handel Society', *Göttinger Händel-Beiträge*, 22 (2021), 29–50
Rennert, Jonathan, *George Thalben-Ball* (Newton Abbot, 1979)
Reynolds, William, 'Middleton's Household Chapel: Church Music on the Welsh Border in the Seventeenth Century', *Welsh Music History*, 4 (2000), 111–22
Rice, John A., 'Did Haydn attend the Handel Commemoration in Westminster Abbey?', *Early Music*, 40 (2019), 73–9

Richards, Denis, *Offspring of the Vic: A History of Morley College* (London, 1958)
Riley, William, *Parochial Music Corrected* (London, 1762)
Roberton, Sir Hugh Stevenson, *Prelude to the Orpheus* (Edinburgh, 1946)
— and Kenneth Roberton (eds), *Orpheus with his Lute: A Glasgow Orpheus Choir Anthology* (Oxford, 1963)
Roberts, John Varley, *A Treatise on a Practical Method of Training Choristers* (London, 1898; 3rd edn, 1905)
Robertson, Dora H., *Sarum Close* (London, 1938)
Robins, Brian, *Catch and Glee Culture in Eighteenth-Century England* (Woodbridge, 2006)
Roden, John, *The Minster School, York: A Centenary History, 1903–2004* (York, 2005)
Rodgers, J.A., *Dr. Henry Coward, the Pioneer Chorus-Master* (London, 1911)
— *The New Choralism* (London, [1911])
Rodmell, Paul, *Charles Villiers Stanford* (Aldershot, 2002)
— (ed.), *Music and Institutions in Nineteenth-Century Britain* (Farnham, 2012); Rachel Cowgill, 'On the Beat: The Victorian Policeman as Musician', 221–45; James Hobson, 'Three Madrigal Societies in Early Nineteenth-Century England', 33–53
Rogers, Charles, *History of the Chapel Royal of Scotland, with the Register of the Chapel Royal of Stirling* (Edinburgh, 1882)
Rose, Barry, *Sitting on a Pin: A Musical Memoir* ([s.l.], 2021)
Rose, Reginald, *The History of the York Musical Society and the York Choral Society*, York Georgian Society, Occasional Paper, 4 (York, 1948)
Routley, Erik, *The English Carol* (London, 1958)
Royal School of Church Music, *Church Music Quarterly* (London, 1977–)
Rubin, Emanuel, *The English Glee in the Reign of George III: Participatory Art Music for an Urban Society* (Warren, Michigan, 2003)
Russell, Dave, '"Awaking to the Reality of our New and Loftier Position": The Bradford Triennial Music Festivals 1853–1859', *The Bradford Antiquary*, 3rd series, 6 (1992), 3–21
— *Popular Music in England, 1840–1914: A Social History*, 2nd edn (Manchester, 1997)
— 'Provincial Concerts in England, 1865–1914: A Case-Study of Bradford', *Journal of the Royal Musical Association*, 114 (1989), 43–55
Russell, W., *Musical Services in S. Paul's Cathedral: A Report to the Dean and Chapter of the Music and other Matters Connected with the Choir, from Easter 1885 to Easter 1887* (London, 1887)
Sacred Harmonic Society, *Twenty-eighth Annual Report of the Sacred Harmonic Society* (London, 1861)
Saint, David, 'A Life at St Chad's', *Cathedral Music*, 2016, no. 2, 14–18
Salisbury Journal, 1736–
Sandon, Henry, *Living with the Past* (London, 1997)

Sandon, Nick (ed.), *The Use of Salisbury*, 6 vols (Newton Abbot, 1984–99; 3rd edn, [2017]–)
Santley, Charles, *Student and Singer: The Reminiscences of Charles Santley* (London, 1892)
Saunders, Benjamin, 'A New Model for Children's Singing in English Cathedrals', *Cathedral Music*, May 2006, 10–11
Scholes, Percy A., *The Mirror of Music*, 2 vols (London, 1947)
— *The Oxford Companion to Music*, 9th edn (London, 1955)
— *The Puritans and Music* (London, 1934)
The School Music Review, 1892–1930
Sewell, G.F., *A History of the Bradford Festival Choral Society: From its Formation in 1856 to its Jubilee in 1906* (Bradford, 1907)
Sharp, Granville, *Memoirs of Granville Sharp*, ed. Prince Hoare (London, 1820)
Shaw, George Bernard, *Shaw's Music: The Complete Musical Criticism*, ed. Dan H. Laurence, 3 vols (London, 1981; 2nd rev. edn, 1989)
Shaw, H. Watkins, *Sir Frederick Ouseley and St. Michael's, Tenbury: A Chapter in the History of English Church Music and Ecclesiology* (Birmingham, 1988)
— *The Succession of Organists of the Chapel Royal and the Cathedrals of England and Wales from c.1538: Also of the Organists of the Collegiate Churches of Westminster and Windsor, Certain Academic Choral Foundations, and the Cathedrals of Armagh and Dublin* (Oxford, 1991)
— *The Three Choirs Festival: The Official History of the Meeting of the Choirs of Worcester, Hereford and Gloucester, c.1713–1953* (Worcester, [1954])
— *Vocation and Endeavour: Sir Sydney Nicholson and the Early Years of the Royal School of Church Music* ([s.l.], 1997)
Ship, Richard Walter, *A History of the North Staffordshire District Choral Society* (Hanley, 1909)
Simeone, Nigel, *The Janáček Compendium* (Woodbridge, 2019)
Simpson, William Sparrow, *Chapters in the History of Old St. Paul's* (London, 1881)
— (ed.), *Registrum Statutorum et Consuetudinum Ecclesiae Cathedralis Sancti Pauli Londiniensis* (London, 1873)
Skinner, David, 'Music and the Reformation in the Collegiate Church of St Mary and All Saints, Fotheringhay', in Clive Burgess and Martin Heale (eds), *The Late Medieval English College and its Context* (Woodbridge, 2008), 253–74
Smith, Alan, 'Elizabethan Church Music at Ludlow', *Music & Letters*, 49 (1968), 108–21
— 'The Practice of Music in English Churches and Cathedrals, and at the Court, during the Reign of Elizabeth I' (Ph.D. diss., Birmingham Univ., 1967)
Smith, Jeremy L, *Thomas East and Music Publishing in Renaissance England* (Oxford, 2003)
Smither, Howard E., 'Messiah and Progress in Victorian England', *Early Music*, 13 (1985), 339–48

Snowman, Daniel, *Hallelujah! An Informal History of the London Philharmonic Choir* (London, 2007)
Soden, Oliver, *Michael Tippett: The Biography* (London, 2019)
Southey, Roz, *Music-Making in North-East England during the Eighteenth Century* (Aldershot, 2006)
Spark, Frederick Robert and Joseph Bennett, *History of the Leeds Musical Festivals, 1858–1889* (Leeds, 1892)
Spark, William, *Musical Memories* (London, 1888; new edn, [1909])
Spink, Ian, *Restoration Cathedral Music, 1660–1714* (Oxford, 1995)
— (ed.), *The Seventeenth Century: Music in Britain*, The Blackwell History of Music in Britain, 3 (Oxford, 1992)
Stainer, John, 'The Character and Influence of the late Sir Frederick Ouseley', *Proceedings of the Musical Association*, 16 (1889/90), 25–39
— *The Present State of Music in England: An Inaugural Lecture Delivered in the Sheldonian Theatre, Oxford, November 13, 1889* (Oxford, 1889)
Stanford, Charles Villiers, *Pages from an Unwritten Diary* (London, 1914)
— *Studies and Memories* (London, 1908)
Stanier, Robert Spenser, *Magdalen School: A History of Magdalen College School, Oxford* (Oxford, 1940)
The Star, 1888–1960
Stevens, Clare, 'How Green is my Valley', *Choir & Organ*, 28/6 (Jul.–Aug. 2020), 48–51
— 'No Danger of Complacency', *Choir & Organ*, 14/1 (Jan.–Feb. 2006), 46–9
— 'Tradition, Part 8 [Leeds Parish Church]', *Choir & Organ*, 8/6 (Nov–Dec 2000), 55–7
Stevens, R.J.S., *Recollections of R.J.S. Stevens: An Organist in Georgian London*, ed. Mark Argent (London, 1992)
Stewart, Claire, 'Girl Choristers and the Anglican Choral Tradition', *Church Music Quarterly*, Dec. 2021, 43–7
— 'The Impact of the Introduction of Girl Choristers at Salisbury and its Influence on other British Anglican Cathedral Choirs' (Ph.D. diss., London Univ., 2020)
Storey, Timothy, 'Forty-one Years in the Fens [Arthur Wills]', *Cathedral Music* (May 2006), 12–15
— 'The Music of St Paul's Cathedral 1872–1972: The Origins and Development of the Modern Cathedral Choir' (M.Mus. diss., Durham Univ., 1998)
Sutcliffe Smith, J., *The Story of Music in Birmingham* (Birmingham, 1945)
Swinson, David, 'The School where Dreams still Happen: A Portrait of the Trinity Boys Choir', *Cathedral Music*, 2018 no. 1, 14–17
Tallis, Thomas, *Motet for 40 Voices*, ed. A.H. Mann (London, [1888])
Tattersall, William, *Improved Psalmody* (London, [1794])
Taylor, Stainton de B., 'Charles Kennedy Scott', *Musical Times*, 92 (1951), 492–6
— *Two Centuries of Music in Liverpool* (Liverpool, 1976)

Temperley, Nicholas, *Jonathan Gray and Church Music in York, 1770–1840* (York, 1977)
— *The Music of the English Parish Church*, 2 vols (Cambridge, 1979)
— (ed.), *The Romantic Age 1800–1914*, The Athlone History of Music in Britain, 5 (London, 1981); reissued as The Blackwell History of Music in Britain, 5 (Oxford, 1988); Bernarr Rainbow, 'Parochial and Nonconformist Church-Music', 144–67; Nicholas Temperley, 'Cathedral Music', 171–213
Terry, Richard Runciman, *Catholic Church Music* (London, 1907)
— *A Forgotten Psalter and Other Essays* (London, 1929); includes 'Why is Church Music so Bad', 105–25
Thompson, Herbert, 'The Leeds Musical Festival', *Musical Times*, 63 (1922), 796
Thoms, William J., 'What it were Good to do for the Choirs, no. II', *Musical World*, 5 (1837), 113–18
Thomson, John Mansfield, *The Oxford History of New Zealand Music* (Auckland, 1991)
Thurmer, John, 'Exeter Cathedral and its Choral Foundation', *The Old Chorister*, 4 (1983), 180–1
The Times, 1785–
Tippett, Michael, *Those Twentieth Century Blues: An Autobiography* (London, 1991)
Todd, R. Larry, *Mendelssohn: A Life in Music* (Oxford, 2003)
Toop, Augustus, *The Organist and his Choir* (London, 1925)
Townhill, Dennis, *The Imp and the Thistle: The Story of a Life of Music Making* ([Edinburgh?], 2000)
Trowell, Brian, 'Faburden and Fauxbourdon', *Musica Disciplina*, 13 (1959), 43–78
Trowles, Tony, 'The Musical Ode in Britain, c.1670–1800' (D.Phil. diss., Oxford Univ., 1992)
[Tuckwell, L.S., as 'A Former Chorister'], *Old Magdalen Days, 1831–1911* (Oxford, 1913)
Turner, Christopher (ed.), *Georgian Psalmody 1: The Gallery Tradition: Papers from the First International Conference Organised by the Colchester Institute* (Corby Glen, 1997); Vic Gammon, 'The Performance Style of West Gallery Music', 43–51; Christopher Turner, 'The Decline of the Gallery Tradition', 71–9
Tyack, Geoffrey, *St John's College, Oxford; A Short History and Guide* (Oxford, 2000)
Tyng, Stephen H., *Recollections of England* (London, 1847)
Vann, Stanley and Brian Ferguson, 'The Golden Opportunity', *Choir & Organ*, 7/5 (Sept.–Oct. 1999), 20–3
Venables, E.M., *Sweet Tones Remembered: Magdalen Choir in the Time of Varley Roberts* (Oxford, 1947)
Vicars, John, *God's Arke Overtopping the Worlds Waves, or the Third Part of the Parliamentary Chronicle* (London, 1646)

Waddell, James, *History of the Edinburgh Choral Union* ([Edinburgh], 1908)

Walker, Christopher, 'Establishing a Musical Tradition at Clifton Cathedral', *Music and Liturgy*, 1/1 (Autumn 1974), 31–5

Ward Jones, Peter, 'Mendelssohn and his English Publishers', in R. Larry Todd (ed.), *Mendelssohn Studies* (Cambridge, 1992), 240–55

Watkin, Aelred, *Dean Cosyn and Wells Cathedral Miscellanies*, Somerset Record Society [Publications], 56 (Frome, 1941 [i.e. 1943])

W[ebb], M.K. and F.A.W. D[ocker], *S. Andrew's Church, Wells Street, S. Marylebone, 1847 to 1897* (London, [1897])

Webster, Donald, 'Parish Past and Present: 275 Years of Leeds Parish Church (Leeds, 1988)

Webster, Peter, *Church and Patronage in 20th Century Britain: Walter Hussey and the Arts* (Basingstoke, 2017)

Welch, C.E., *Two Cathedral Organists: Thomas Weelkes (1601–1623) and Thomas Kelway (1720–1744)* (Chichester, 1957)

Wesley, Samuel Sebastian, *A Few Words on Cathedral Music and the Musical System of the Church with a Plan of Reform* (London, 1849)

Weston, William, *William Weston: the Autobiography of an Elizabethan*, translated from the Latin by Philip Caraman (London, 1955)

Wetenhall, Edward, *Of Gifts and Offices in the Publick Worship of God* (Dublin, 1678)

Whenham, John, *Monteverdi Vespers (1610)* (Cambridge, 1997)

White, Bryan, *Music for St Cecilia's Day: from Purcell to Handel* (Martlesham, 2019)

White, Harry, *The Keeper's Recital: Music and Cultural History in Ireland, 1770–1970* (Cork, 1998)

Whiteside, Alan, 'A Chester Cathedral Chorister 1906–1912', *The Old Chorister*, 4/4 (Apr. 1981), 109–11

Wilkinson, James, *Westminster Abbey: 1000 Years of Music and Pageant* (Leighton Buzzard, 2003)

Williams, C.F. Abdy, *A Short Historical Account of the Degrees in Music at Oxford and Cambridge* (London, 1893)

Williams, E. Lee and A. Herbert Brewer, *Church Music: A Plea for a Simple Service in Village, Town & Cathedral* [2 Papers] (Gloucester, [1918?])

Williams, Gareth, *Valleys of Song: Music and Society in Wales 1840–1914* (Cardiff, 1998)

Williams, Rowan Clare, '"What Sweeter Music": Issues in Choral Church Music c.1960 to 2017, with Special Reference to the Christmas Eve Carol Service at King's College Chapel, Cambridge, and its New Commissions' (M.A. diss., York Univ., 2019)

Williamson, Magnus, *The Eton Choirbook: Facsimile and Introductory Study* (Oxford, 2010)

— 'Liturgical Music in the Late Medieval English Parish: Organs and Voices, Ways and Means', in Clive Burgess and Eamon Duffy (eds), *The Parish in*

Late Medieval England: Proceedings of the 2002 Harlaxton Symposium (Donington, 2006), 177–243
— 'Parish Music in late-medieval England: Local, Regional, National Identities', in Michele C. Ferrari and Beat Kümin (eds), Pfarreien in der Vormoderne: Identität und Kultur im Niederkirchenwesen Europas, Wolfenbütteler Forschungen, 146 (Wiesbaden, 2017), 209–43.
— 'The Role of Religious Guilds in the Cultivation of Ritual Polyphony in England: The Case of Louth, 1450–1550', in Fiona Kisby (ed.), *Music and Musicians in Renaissance Cities and Towns* (Cambridge, 2001), 82–93
Willis, Jonathan, *Church Music and Protestantism in Post-Reformation England: Discourses, Sites and Identities* (Farnham, 2010)
Wilson, R.H., 'Choral Competitions from the Competitors' Point of View', *Musical Times*, 66 (1925), 937–9
Wilson, Ruth M., *Anglican Chant and Chanting in England, Scotland, and America, 1660–1820* (Oxford, 1996)
Wiltshire, Christopher, 'The British Male Voice Choir: A History and Contemporary Assessment' (Ph. D. diss., Goldsmiths College, London Univ., 1993)
— *The Festival Movement: A Portrait of its People* (Macclesfield, 1997)
Wollenberg, Susan, *Music at Oxford in the Eighteenth and Nineteenth Centuries* (Oxford, 2001)
Wood, Henry J., *My Life of Music* (London, 1938)
Woodman, Francis, *The Architectural History of King's College Chapel* (London, 1986)
Woodward, Reg, *Boy on a Hill* (Lincoln, 1984)
The World, 1874–1920
Wridgway, Neville, *The Choristers of St George's Chapel, Windsor Castle* (Slough, 1980)
Wrightson, James, *The Wanley Manuscripts: A Critical Commentary* (New York and London, 1989)
— (ed.), *The Wanley Manuscripts*, Recent Researches in the Music of the Renaissance, 99–101, 3 vols (Madison, Wis., 1995)
Wyn Jones, David (ed.), *Music in Eighteenth-Century Britain* (Aldershot, 2000); Philip Olleson, 'The London Roman Catholic Embassy Chapels and their Music in the Eighteenth and Early Nineteenth Centuries', 101–18; Sally Drage, 'A Reappraisal of Provincial Church Music', 172–90
Yardley, Anne Bagnall, *Performing Piety: Musical Culture in Medieval English Nunneries* (New York, 2006)
Young, Kenneth, *Chapel: The Joyous Days and Prayerful Nights of the Nonconformists in their Heyday, circa 1850–1950* (London, 1972)
Your Herefordshire (htpps://yourherefordhire.co.uk)

Manuscript Sources

Cambridge, Corpus Christi College, MS 473
Eton, Eton College Library, MS 178
London, British Library, Add. MS 25–31
— Add. MS 57950
— Egerton. MS 3512
— Harleian MS 7033
— Harleian MSS 7337–42
Oxford, Bodleian Library, MS Bodl. 775
— MS lat. liturg. d. 20
— MSS Mus. d. 156, 158, 161, 166
— MS Mus. c. 26
— MSS Mus. Sch. E. 420–2
— MSS Mus. Sch. E. 476–81
— MS Tenbury 791
— MS Top. Oxon. a. 76
Oxford, Magdalen College Archives, DD2/X2/2
Salisbury, Cathedral Archives, CO/CH//2/2/1
Worcester Cathedral Library, Add. MS 68

Index

Organizations are generally entered under their locality, except for most London and national ones, which are entered directly under their title. Page references to illustrations are in bold type.

Aberdare Choral Union   160
Aberdeen   95
   Aberdeen Bach Choir   287
   Aberdeen Breviary   326
   musical festivals   162
Aberystwyth, Tabernacle choral society   158
Abinger Choral Society   254
Academy of Ancient Music (founded 1726)   85, 105–6, 126
Academy of Ancient Music (founded 1973)   292
Academy of Vocal Musick *see* Academy of Ancient Music (founded 1726)
'Agincourt carol'   22
Agnus Dei   13, 178
Albert, Prince Consort   12
Alcock, John   73, 98
Aldrich, Henry   74, 105
Alexandra Choir   59
Alexandra Palace Choral and Orchestral Society (later Alexandra Choral and Orchestral Society)   134, 245, 259
Allegri, Gregorio, *Miserere*   264
Allen, Hugh   133, 168, 205, 226, 244, 253
Alleluia   10, 13
Allwood, Ralph   281
almonry schools   19
alto *see* contratenor

Ambrosian Singers   289
Ampleforth School   211
Amsterdams Gemengd Koor   311
Anacreontic Society   107
Andover   116
Andrews, Herbert Kennedy   226–7, 266
Anglican chant   41, 72–3, 89, 172, 174, 176–8, 214
Ante-Communion *see* Holy Communion
anthems   38, 54, 67, 75–6, 88, 90, 92, 94, 95–6, 126, 173, 181, 200, 203, 214 *see also* verse anthems
antiphon   37 *see also* votive antiphon
Apollo Catch and Glee Society   107
Archive of Recorded Church Music   3
Armagh Cathedral   65
Arne, Thomas   104
   Judith   110
Armstrong, Thomas   227
Arnold, Samuel   98, 17, 201
   Redemption   117
Arts Council of Great Britain   261, 296
Ascension Choir   315
Ashley, John   118–19
Association of British Choral Directors   306
Atkins, Ivor   154, 257, 263

Attwood, Thomas   188
    'Teach me, O Lord'   201
    'Turn thy face from my sins'   201
Australia   153, 239, 300, 302
Ave regina caelorum   18
Axminster   116

Bach, Johann Sebastian   21, 230,
    243, 247, 257, 299, 315
  B minor Mass   2, 129, 132, 168,
    169, 241, 245, 246, 247, 250, 251,
    252, 256, 257, 259, 299
  cantatas   245, 251, 256
  Christmas Oratorio   129, 180,
    243, 256, 257, 381
  Ein' feste Burg (cantata)   247
  Magnificat   257, 381
  motets   129, 146, 245, 247
  Singet dem Herrn (*Sing ye to the
    Lord*)   247, 257
  St John Passion   131, 181, 248,
    257, 259, 264, 311
  St Matthew Passion   129, 130–1,
    133, 154, 160, 161, 168, 181, 187,
    196, 202, 243, 248, 251, 254, 257,
    259, 289, 300, 348–9
  Schemelli Gesangbuch   209
Bach Cantata Club   250–1, 289
Bach Choir (London)   132–3, 244–5,
  246, 259, 285–6, 289, 302, 306
Bach Society (London)   129
Baden-Powell, Robert   238
Bairstow, Edward   195, 200, 228
  'Blessed city, heavenly
    Salem'   230
  'Lord, Thou has been our
    Refuge'   79
Balfour, Arthur   133
Bambridge, W.S.   256
Bangor Cathedral   96, 187
Bantock, Granville   147
  part-songs   158
Baptists   111, 213
Bardgett, Herbert   252

Barnard, John   54–5, 74–5, 335
Barnby, Joseph   130–1, 169, 178,
  180–1, 187, 203, 256, 348–9 *see
  also* Mr Joseph Barnby's Choir
Barnsley, choral society   151
Barrow-in-Furness, Methodist
  church choir   240
Bartholomew, William   202
Bartlett, John   46
Bates, James   181
Bates, Joah   114
Bates, Mrs. Joah *see* Harrop, Sarah
Bath   110, 112
  City of Bath Male Choir   302
Batten, Adrian   51, 330
BBC   222, 227–8, 270–1
  BBC National Chorus of
    Wales   287
  BBC Symphony Chorus   288
  'Choir of the Year'   298
  Choral Evensong   194, 224, 227,
    228, 263, 268, 270, 271, 305
  Daily Service   227, 271
  'Let the People Sing'   298
  Wireless Singers (later BBC
    Singers)   227, 249, 309
Beckwith, John   73
Beeston, John   46
Beecham, Thomas   57, 245, 248–9,
  250, 252, 258, 288
Beethoven, Ludwig van   211, 310
  Choral Fantasia   310
  Christus am Ölberge (*The Mount
    of Olives*)   117, 201
  Mass in C major   310
  Missa Solemnis   130, 150, 152, 154,
    169, 245
  Symphony no. 9 ('Choral')   152,
    153, 169 245
Belfast   243
  Belfast Classical Harmonists   165
  Belfast Musical Society   165
  Belfast Philharmonic Society   165
  Catch and Glee Club   165

Methodist College   295, 315
St Anne's Cathedral   219–20, 314, 316
Ulster Hall   165
Benedicamus Domino   22
Benedict, Saint   7, 9
Benedictine monasteries *see under* monasteries
Benedictus (canticle)   41, 42
Benedictus (of Mass Ordinary and Holy Communion)   13, 178, 209
Bennett, George   230
Bennett, William Sterndale   129, 140
  The May Queen   148
Benson, Edward   222
Benton, Alfred   212
Berkeley, Lennox   235
Berlin
  Cathedral   191, 192, 311
  Singakademie   119, 126
Berlioz, Hector
  The Damnation of Faust   153
  Messe des morts   147
Bernstein, Leonard, *Chichester Psalms*   235, 284
Beverley Minster   24, 36
Binchois, Gilles   21, 32
Birmingham   110, 125
  Birmingham Oratorio Choral Society (later Birmingham Festival Choral Society)   122, 140, 146
  Carr's Lane Congregational Church   214
  City of Birmingham Symphony Chorus   288, 302
  General Hospital   112, 122
  musical festival   112–13, 116, 118, 120, 122–5, 146–7, 241, 246, 248
  Oratory   241
  St Chad's Cathedral (Roman Catholic)   210, 211, 277
  St Philip's Church (later Anglican Cathedral)   113, 122
  Town Hall   122
Bizet, Georges, *Carmen*   259
Blackpool, musical festival   157, 254
Blaze, Robin   267
Bliss, Arthur, *Morning Heroes*   243, 258
Blow, John   68, 73, 74, 75, 77, 79, 96, 201
  'God spake sometime in visions'   78
  Venus and Adonis   77
Bloxam, John Rouse   205
Blyth, Benjamin   205
Bognor Bach Choir   257
Book of Common Prayer   37, 38–9, 40, 44, 55, 57, 65, 66, 67, 70, 172, 178, 184, 233, 276
Boorman, Peter   271
Boosey & Co.   140
Borrow, Carlton   234
Boston (UK)
  musical festival   119
  St Botolph's Church   24
Boston (USA), Boston Handel and Haydn Society   301
Bottesford   104
Boughton, Rutland   253
Boulanger, Nadia   258
Boulez, Pierre   285
Boult, Adrian   245, 252, 283
Bowles, William   93
Bowley, Robert   126, 127, 128
Bowman, James   267
boy bishop   17–18
Boyce, William   81, 87, 196, 201
  Cathedral Music   55, **97**, 98, 111, 137, 201, 209
  'I have surely built thee an house'   219
  Solomon   87, 117
boys   57, 59, 107, 113, 142, 167, 307
  in monasteries   31 *see also* oblates

See also charity school children; choristers (boys); Lady Chapel choirs; singing in schools
Brabant Ensemble   293
Bradfield College   256
Bradford
  Bradford Choral Society   142, 146, 148
  Bradford Festival Choral Society   147–8, 154, 250, 252, 257
  musical festival   146, 147
  St George's Hall   147
Brady, Nicholas   87
Brahms, Johannes, *German Requiem*   147, 180, 256
Bramma, Harry   281
Brecon Cathedral   304
Bremner, Robert   95, 340
Brewer, Herbert   154
  services   230
Bridge, Frederick   131, 170, 197, 243–4
Brighton Festival Chorus   267
Bristol
  All Saints Church   25
  Bristol Choral Society   253
  Bristol Madrigal Society (later Bristol Chamber Choir)   167
  Cathedral (Anglican)   35, 36, 86
  Clifton Cathedral (Roman Catholic)   277
  musical festival   156
British Broadcasting Corporation *see* BBC
British Council   260
British Legion *see* Royal British Legion
British Museum Choir   298
Britten, Benjamin   140
  A Ceremony of Carols   265, 272
  Festival Te Deum   274
  The Golden Vanity   294–5
  Jubilate in C   274

Missa brevis   274, 276
'Rejoice in the Lamb'   235
Spring Symphony   288, 294
War Requiem   286, 287–8, 295, 307
Broadcasting *see* BBC
Brooke, Harold *see* Harold Brooke Choir
Brown, Thomas (1662–1704)   74
Brownlee, Colin   3
Bruckner, Anton   315
  Masses   287
Brydges, James, Earl of Carnarvon (later Duke of Chandos)   81
Buccleuch, 5th Duke of   183
Buck, Percy   221
Buck, Zechariah   187, 208, 362
Bullinger, Henry   38
Burgess, Russell   294–5
Burney, Charles   45, 114, 119
Burslem Tonic Sol-fa Choir   157
Burton, Robert Senior   148, 149
Bury St Edmunds Cathedral   271
Butt, John   309
Byng, John (later 5th Viscount Torrington)   101, 103–4
Byrd, William   41, 43 44, 50, 62, 209, 220, 221, 227, 265, 275
  Cantiones sacrae   59
  Gradualia   44, 59
  'Great' service   50
  'Have mercy upon me'   225–6
  Masses   44, 59, 146, 332
  Psalmes, Sonets and Songs of Sadnes and Pietie   51, 58–9
  responses   42
Byzantine Chant Ensemble   315

Calvin, John   39, 56
Cambridge   11, 36, 43, 44, 50, 86, 172, 199, 207, 266
  Addenbrooke's Hospital   86

Cambridge Camden Society (later Ecclesiological Society) 173, 175
Cambridge Choral Society (later Cambridge Philharmonic Society) 168
Cambridge University Musical Society (CUMS) 168, 224, 253
Clare College 267
Gonville and Caius College 28, 267
Great St Mary's (University Church) 207
King's College 23, 36, 49, 152, 169, 196, 207–8, 220, 225, 226, 232, 262, 268, 291, 292, 302, 309, 314
  Carols from King's 313
  Festival of Nine Lessons and Carols 222–5, 275
  under A.H. Mann 208–9, 222–3
  under Boris Ord 223–5
  under David Willcocks 264–5
Pembroke College 305
Peterhouse 54, 168
Queen's College 168, 267
St Catherine's College 305
St John's College 30 207, 208, 209–10, 225–6, 232, 265–6, 274, 302, 312, 314
Trinity College 207, 208 209, 226, 264, 267, 268
Campaign for the Defence of the Traditional Cathedral Choir 273
Canada 153, 225, 235, 239, 265, 302
cantatas 157, 180, 214
Cantate Domino (canticle) 42
Canterbury 239
  Cathedral 6, 28, 36, 39, 52, 53, 61, 63, 72, 75, 102, 198, 232, 262
canticles ,37, 38 41–2, 54, 56, 70, 72–3, 75, 88, 90, 94, 126, 173, 175, 183, 203, 217, 240
Cantores in Ecclesia 263, 289
Cape Town, St George's Cathedral 300
Cappella Nova 309
'Caradog' (Griffith Rhys Jones) 160
Cardiff Bach Choir 287
Cardinall's Musick 293
Carissimi, Giacomo 105, 211
Carl Rosa Opera Company 386
Carlisle Cathedral 35, 36, 236
Carnegie United Kingdom Trust 221, 261
carols 22, 222, 244, 245, 268
Carols for Choirs 275
Carver, Robert 33
Carwood, Andrew 265, 304
cassocks 174
catches 49, 107, 165
Cathedral Choirs' Emergency Fund 314
Cathedral Psalter, The 204–5
cathedrals
  financial problems 39, 41, 190, 217, 262, 270, 277, 303–4, 314, 316
  government and organization 6–8, 35–6
  visiting and voluntary choirs 239, 196, 269, 297
Cavendish, William, 3rd Duke of Devonshire 84
Cecilian movement 212–13
chantry chapels 22, 24, 30–1, 36, 39
Chapel Royal 10, 20–1, 23, 24, 25, 28, 39, 43–4, 45, 50, 52, 53, 57, 59, 61, 63, 66, 67–70, 72, 74, 76–7, 78, 81, 83, 84, 86, 99, 100, 106, 118, 126, 197, 232, 282, 315
Chappell (music publisher) 140
charity school children 88–90, 171, 183
Charles I 45, 53, 64, 65, 66
Charles II 67, 69, 76
Charles III 271, 286, 315

Chelmsford Cathedral 269
Chester
　Cathedral 2, 35, 61, 36, 75, 196, 198, 217–18, 262, 277
　musical festivals 109, 113, 116–17, 125, 156
Chetham, John 94
Chichester Cathedral 47, 50, 101–2, 187, 198, 235, 284, 304, 314
Chilcott, Bob 265
Child, William 54, 75
Child Okeford, church choir **237**
Chirk Castle 56
Chislehurst 236
Choir, The (TV series) 308
Choir of the Earth *see* Self-Isolation Choir
'Choir of the Year' competition *see under* BBC
choir schools 25, 177, 181, 183, 189, 195, 197, 198–9, 205–6, 208, 216, 217–18, 220, 231, 232, 234–5, 262, 269–70, 300, 301, 302, 314
choral conducting training 299, 307
choral scholars 205, 206, 208, 209, 216, 223, 226, 231, 264, 265, 266, 267, 269, 290, 291, 292, 304, 305, 306, 313, 314
choral societies
　early development to 1850 105–6, 108–12, 121, 126–7, 140–5, 163–4
　recovery from Covid-19 pandemic 313
'Chorister for a Day' 273
Chorister Outreach Programme 306
choristers (boys) 8, 9, 26–7, 61–3, 66, 67–8, 69–72, 177, 183, 184, 185–7, 188–9, 190, 191, 192–3, 195, 106, 197, 198, 206, 207, 209, 211–12, 225, 226, 227, 231–2, 233, 234–5, 236–8, 239, 263, 265, 267, 270, 272–3, 276, 279, 282, 300, 302, 312
　accommodation 8, 17, 205, 208
　age of change of voice 61, 218, 332
　behaviour 17, 18, 76, 186, 190
　education 8, 61–2, 189, 192, 195, 198–9, 216–18, 234–5, 267, 269–70
　in early musical societies 106, 120, 121, 122, 142, 144, 167, 168
　in Lady Chapel choirs 19
　in town church choirs 179, 180–1, 233, 234–5, 305
　in village choirs 173, 174, 176
　recruitment 262, 273–4, 277, 303, 314
　See also boy bishop; choir schools
choristers (girls)
　in cathedral and collegiate choirs 271–3, 303, 305–6, 314–15
　in parish choirs 88, 176, 184, 233, 237, 278, 279, 282, 384
Chorus of the Academy of St Martin in the Fields 267
Christchurch (New Zealand), Christ Church Cathedral 300
Christophers, Harry 291
Chudleigh (Devon) 56
Church, Richard (dean of St Paul's) 195
Church Choral Society (later College of Church Music, then Trinity College, London, then Trinity Laban Conservatoire of Music and Dance) 182
Church Langton (Leicestershire) 112
Church Music Society 233, 236
Church of Scotland (Presbyterian) 62–4, 95, 282
Cincinnati 153
Civil War 53, 65–6

Clarence, Thomas, Duke of   21
Clarke-Whitfield, John   201
Cleall, Charles   375
Cleobury, Stephen   265, 275, 276
Clerkes of Oxenford, The   60, 290–1
Clifford, James   76
Clucas, Humfrey, responses   276
Coates, Albert   257
Cocker, Norman   263
Coleridge, Arthur   132
Coleridge-Taylor, Samuel   133
    *Scenes from 'The Song of
        Hiawatha'*   134, 244, 257
    The Death of Minnehaha   156
    Hiawatha's Wedding Feast   256
    A Tale of Old Japan   258
College of St Nicolas   236, 237, 238, 239
College of Organists *see* Royal
    College of Organists
collegiate churches   23–4, 31, 36, 55, 56, 66, 108
Colne Valley Male Voice Choir   285
Cologne   152
Columba, Saint   5
'Come and Sing'   299
community choirs   3, 308
competitive singing   156–8, 166, 169, 215, 253–4, 258, 283, 298–9, 308
Compline   9, 37
Concert of Ancient Music   110, 118
Congregationalists
    (Independents)   213, 214
contratenor (countertenor,
    alto)   29–30, 60, 68, 110, 122, 144, 165–6, 184, 304
Conway, Marmaduke   255
Cook, Melville   219
Cooke, Henry   68, 69
Cooke, Richard   286
Cooper, Janette   280
Cooper, Martin   283
Coram, Thomas   86
Corfe, Arthur   186

Corfe, John   101
Cork
    Ancient Concerts Society   165
    Cork Musical Society   165
    St Fin Barre's Cathedral   65, 8
Cornelius, Peter, 'The three
    kings'   225
cornett   52–3, 54, 64, 68, 69, 71–2
Cornwall Music Service   306
coronations   64, 68, 78, 81–2, 140, 181, 197–8, 282–3, 315
Corporation of the Sons of the
    Clergy   78–9, 99, 129
Cosin, John   53, 54
Costa, Michael   127–8, 130, 144, 146, 147, 381
    Eli   163
countertenor *see* contratenor
country psalmody   91–5, 104, 108, 174, 297
court masques   76
court odes   76–7
Coventry Cathedral   232, 270, 287, 304
Covid-19 pandemic   310–14, 315
Coward, Henry   150–4, 160, 163, 245, 248, 250, 252
Coward, Henry, junior   152
Cranmer, Thomas   36, 37, 38, 39, 50
Credo (Nicene Creed)   13, 42
Croft, William   79, 87, 96, 98, 188, 201
Crompton, John   110, 113
Cromwell, Baron Ralph de   24
Cromwell, Oliver   65, 66
Crouch End Festival Chorus   287
Croydon
    Addinngton Palace   279, 280, 281
    Croydon Philharmonic
        Society   258, 259
    Trinity School, Trinity Boys'
        Choir   295
Curwen, John   140, 135–6, 145
Curwen, John Spenser   185

Cusins, William George,
    Gideon   135
cymanfa canu (hymn-singing
    festivals)   159

Dakers, Lionel   219, 280, 316
Darke, Harold   224, 232, 372
    Communion service in F   230
Darlington, Stephen   266–7
David, Paul   256
Davies, Dan   161
Davies, Henry Walford   133, 180,
    229
    Everyman   258
Davies, Iwan   235
Davies, Meredith   266, 284
Davies, Peter Maxwell   140
Davis, Andrew   265
Davy, Richard   28
Day, John   50, 54, 57
Deane, William   56
Dearnley, Christopher   271
Deighn Layrocks *see* Larks of Dean
Delius, Frederick
    A Mass of Life   157, 248, 258
    Sea Drift   157, 258
Deller, Alfred   289
Deller, Mark   265
Deneke, Margaret   227
Denmark   225
Derby
    Cathedral   270
    Derby Choral Society   142, 151
    musical festival   113, 125
Dering, Richard   66
Dibb, John Edward   204
Dibdin, Charles   110–11
Digby, Suzi   306, 309
diocesan choral festivals   175, 280
*Directory for the Public Worship of
    God*   66
Doddridge, Philip   87
Dorking, Cleveland Lodge   281

Dove, Jonathan, 'See him that
    maketh the seven stars'   274
Dowlais
    Dowlais Harmonic Society   161
    Dowlais Ladies' Choir   161, 167
    Dowlais Philharmonic
        Society   161
Doncaster, St George's Church   110
Downside School   211, 220
D'Oyly Carte Opera Company   386
Drakensberg Boys Choir
    School   301
Dresden, Kreuzkirche   30, 223
Drew, Mr   102
Driscoll, John   212, 241, 276
Dryden, John   77, 83
Dublin   84–5
    Ancient Concerts Society   164
    Charitable Infirmary   84
    Christ Church Cathedral   33, 52,
        64, 75, 84, 200
    Dublin International Exhibition
        of Fine Art and Manufactures
        (1865)   165
    Dublin Musical Society   164
    Grand Musical Festival
        (1831)   164
    Great Industrial Exhibition
        (1853)   165
    Irish Musical Fund Society   163
    Mercer's Hospital   84
    Musick Hall   84
    Royal Choral Institute   164
    St Mary's Pro-Cathedral   213
    St Patrick's Cathedral   64, 65, 84,
        200, 217
    Sons of Handel (choral
        society)   164
    University of Dublin Choral
        Society   164
Dufay, Guillaume   21
Duffy, Philip   277
Duffy, Terence   277
Dundee, choral society   162

428 Index

Dunedin Consort   309
Dunstable, John   21
Durham Cathedral   35, 49, 53–4, 61,
    65, 70, 71, 74, 76, 79, 98, 103, 108,
    187, 190–1, 198, 262, 269
  partbooks   50, 54, 66, 74
Duruflé, Maurice, Requiem   287
Düsseldorf   152
Dvořák, Antonín
  Requiem   147
  St Ludmila   149
  The Spectre's Bride   147
Dykes Bower, John   226, 232, 262
Dyson, George   241
  The Canterbury Pilgrims   258
  services   240

Earle, John   48–9
East, Michael, 'As they
  departed'   330
East, Thomas   57
Ecclesiastical Commissioners Act
  (1840)   189
Ecclesiological Society see
  Cambridge, Cambridge Camden
  Society
Edinburgh   95, 135, 243
  Edinburgh Choral Union (later
    Royal Edinburgh Choral
    Union)   162, 260
  Edinburgh Harmonic
    Association   162
  Edinburgh International
    Festival   283, 286
  Edinburgh Musical Society   113
  George Heriot's Hospital   113
  musical festivals to 1850   113, 162
  St Giles Cathedral (Church of
    Scotland)   282
  St Mary's Cathedral
    (Episcopal)   198, 271
Edington Priory   284
Edward VI   36, 38–9
Edward VII   140, 197

Egerton, Mary   158
Egerton-Warburton, Rowland   183
Elgar, Edward   139, 140, 211, 212, 255,
    257
  The Apostles   147, 156, 157, 161,
    241, 258, 352
  Caractacus   149, 258
  The Dream of Gerontius   129,
    141, 146–7, 151, 152, 153, 155–6,
    157, 161, 162, 228, 241, 243, 248,
    254, 258, 259, 260, 285
  'Give unto 1the Lord'   79
  King Olaf   156, 258
  The Kingdom   147, 156, 157, 241,
    258, 259
  The Music Makers   147, 243
  part-songs   158
Elizabeth I   40, 43, 44, 48, 52, 57,
    209
Elizabeth II   140, 271, 282–3, 315
Elland, Congregational Church   240
Elvey, George   187, 194, 201
Elvey, Stephen   205
Ely
  Cathedral   6, 19, 35, 66, 70, 74,
    96, 194, 204, 263, 386
  choral society   255
Embleton, Henry Cawood   150
Emes, William   56
encores   123, 130
Enfield, Christ Church
  (Congregational)   214
English National Opera, chorus   296
English Singers   251, 292
Erasmus, Desiderius   31
Eton College   23, 44, 131, 256, 325
  Eton Choirbook   27–8, 31, 32, 51,
    60, 267, 291
  Eton Choral Course   281 see also
    Rodolfus Choral Course
Eucharist see Holy Communion
Evans, Harry   161
Evans, Rees   160
Evelyn, John   69

Evensong   10, 36, 37, 40, 41, 44, 67, 174, 180, 193, 203, 216, 219, 270, 275, 279, 282, 300, 302, 303 *see also* BBC, Choral Evensong, Vespers
Ewer & Co.   138
Ex Cathedra   292, 309
Exeter Cathedral   6, 8, 61, 65, 71, 102, 187, 269, 273

faburden   26, 72
Fagiolini, I   292, 309
Fairbairn, Thomas   244, 257
Fanshaw, David, *African Sanctus*   288
Farmer, John   256
Farnham   116
Farrant, John, the elder   46, 62
Farrant, Richard
   'Call to remembrance'   96
   'Lord, for thy tender mercies sake'   173
   Short service   201
Farrow, Miles   196–7
Fauré, Gabriel, Requiem   258, 264, 287, 299
Faversham   25
Fellowes, Edmund Horace   59, 221, 224, 226, 230, 251, 258
female contraltos, entry into choral societies   122, 144
female-voice choirs   166–7, 298
Ferrier, Kathleen   285
Festival of Britain (1951)   285
Festival of Remembrance *see* Royal British Legion
Field, John, *An Admonition to the Parliament*   48
Finzi, Gerald, 'Lo, the full final sacrifice'   235
Fogg, Eric, *The Seasons*   242
foreign choirs, influence of   284, 299–300
Foss, Hubert   250

Fotheringhay, St Mary and All Saints Collegiate Church   36
Foulds, John, *A World Requiem*   258
Frankenhausen   119
Frankfurt am Main   152
Free Church Choir Union *see* Nonconformist Choir Union
Free Presbyterians   64, 214
Friederick William IV, King of Prussia   188
Fry, Stephen   310
Fund for Decayed Musicians (later Royal Society of Musicians)   116

Gabrieli Consort (and Players)   292, 306, 309
Gardiner, John Eliot   291–2
Garner, John   157
Garrett, George   209
Garrett, Leslie   314
Gates, Bernard   99
Gauntlett, Henry   214
George II   81
George III   114, 116, 118
George V   198
German, Edward, *Merrie England*   259, 296
Germany   119, 125, 152, 192, 212, 223
Giardini, Felice, *Ruth*   117
Gibbons, Orlando   224, 265
   'Almighty and everlasting God'   59
   Short service   96, 201
   'This is the record of John'   51, 54
Gilbert, William Schwenck   259, 296, 386
Gilchrist, James   265
Gill, Alan   134, 245
girls *see* choristers (girls)
Giulini, Carlo Maria   285
Glasgow
   Bach Cantata Choir   251, 257
   City Hall   163
   Glasgow Choral Society   162

Glasgow Musical Association (later Glasgow Choral Union)   151, 162, 163
Glasgow Orpheus Choir   163, 260
Glasgow Phoenix Choir   163
musical festivals   157, 162–3, 246, 253
St Andrew's Halls   163
Toynbee House Musical Association   163
glees   2, 107
Gloria (Ordinary of Mass)   13
Gloucester
    Cathedral   17–18, 35, 36, 71, 196, 219, 239, 277
    Three Choirs Festival   79, 109, 123, 131, 138, 154, 155
Glover, John William   164
    St Patrick at Tara   165
Glover, Sarah   135
Glyndebourne Festival Opera, chorus   296
Goehr, Walter   287
Goldschmidt, Otto   132
Goldsmiths Choral Union   246, 259
Goodall, Howard   267, 306
    The Vicar of Dibley   267
Goodall, Reginald   133
Goodman, Roy   264
Goossens, Eugene   244, 249
gospel music   297–8
Goss, John   188, 195, 201
Gostling, John   69
Gothic Voices   293, 309
Goudhurst   25
Gounod, Charles   131, 196, 212, 240, 257
    Faust   259
    Masses   184
    Messe solennelle en l'honneur de Sainte Cécile   178
Gough, Rupert   305
Grace, Harvey   247, 249, 255

Gradual   10, 13
Grainger, Percy   291
Granville, Denis   76
Gravesend, Richard   17
Gray, Alan   209, 226, 238
Great British Home Chorus   311
Greatorex, Thomas   125
Greene, Maurice   81, 86, 87, 96, 98, 99, 196, 201
Greenock, choral society   162
'Gregorians' *see* plainsong
Grey, Lady Jane   39
Grier, Francis   266
Grove, George   169
Guest, George   265–6, 270, 272
Guildford
    Cathedral   270, 273
    Lanesborough School   270

Hackett, Maria   100, 186, 188–9, 194
Haggis, Frederick   246
Hague, Charles   119
Halifax   109, 111
    Halifax Amateur Operatic Society   296, 387
    Halifax Choral Society   142, 144, 146
    Halifax Light Opera Society   387
    musical festival   119
    Musical Society at the Old Cock   111
    Parish Church   109, 206
Hall, Elias   108
Hallé, Charles   145
Halsey, Simon   288
Hamilton, Walter   187, 194
Hampshire Musical Meeting (later Hampshire Musical Festival)   112
Hampton, John   192, 193
Hanbury, William   112
Hancock, Gerre   302
Handel, George Frederic   81–7, 99, 109, 111, 116, 120, 126, 127, 132, 163, 208, 243, 248, 250, 255, 257

Index

Acis and Galatea 83, 84, 110, 117, 251
Alexander's Feast 83, 84, 86, 117
L'Allegro, il Penseroso ed il Moderato 83, 84
Athalia 83
Chandos anthems 81
Chandos Te Deum 81
Coronation anthems 81–2
 'Zadok the priest' 109, 198, 283, 315
Deborah 83
Dettingen Te Deum 78
Dixit Dominus 81, 264
Esther 82, 83
Israel in Egypt 84, 85, 128, 266
Joseph 117
Judas Maccabaeus 86, 110, 113, 117, 128, 139, 240, 257, 259
Messiah 84–6, 96, 109, 110, 113, 114, 115, 116, 117, 123, 127, 128, 136, 139, 148, 149, 153, 154, 156, 158, 160, 162, 164, 169–70, 188, 214, 240, 243, 244, 248, 249, 250, 252, 253, 256, 259, 260, 264, 266, 284, 286, 289–90, 299, 301, 312, 344
Occasional Oratorio 117
Ode for St Cecilia's Day 83
oratorios 82–3, 86, 98, 105, 106, 111, 113, 126, 133, 164, 201
Samson 85, 117, 164, 240
Saul 84, 256
Semele 251
Solomon 248, 257
Utrecht Te Deum and Jubilate 78, 81
Handel Commemorations (1784–91) 114–17, 119, 120, 126, 137–8, 246
Handel Festivals (Crystal Palace) *see under* London, Crystal Palace
Handel Society 133
Hanley

Hanley Glee and Madrigal Society 157
 Victoria Hall 156
Harding, John 186
Hardy, Thomas 93
Harley, Robert, 1st Earl of Oxford and Earl Mortimer 98
Harmonists Society 107
Harold Brooke Choir 251
Harper, John 267, 281
Harris, James 112
Harris, William, 'Faire is the heaven' 226
Harriss, Charles 153
Harrop, Sarah 109
Harrow School 256
Hartley, George 110
Hartland 56
Harty, Hamilton 255
Harvard Glee Club 107–8
Harvey, Jonathan
 'I love the Lord' 274
 'The dove descending' 274
Harwood, Basil 168, 206
Haweis, Hugh Reginald 185
Hawes, William 188
Hawkins, John 45, 106
Haydn, Franz Joseph 89, 104, 106, 117–18, 208, 211, 212, 240
 The Creation 117–18, 119, 120, 125, 127, 136, 139, 153, 164, 201
 Masses 138, 177, 201, 264, 265, 287
 'Nelson' Mass 287, 299
 The Seasons 118, 120
Hayes, William 83, 85, 87, 96–8, 101, 337
'head voice' production 182, 187, 196, 206, 220
Heap, Swinerton 156
Hedgley, John 138, 350
Helmore, Frederick 173
Helmore, Thomas 173, 174, 193
Heltay, László 267

Henrietta Maria, queen of Charles
    I   53, 104
Henry IV   21
Henry V   20, 21
Henry VI   23
Henry VIII   24, 31, 34, 35, 36, 39, 41,
    61
Henry, Prince of Wales (*d.* 1612)   45,
    64
Henry Leslie's Choir   129–30, 132
Hereford
    Cathedral   18, 35, 46, 71, 187, 189,
        193, 198, 199, 200, 219, 314
        Hereford Use   10
    Three Choirs Festival   79, 86, 119,
        241, 259, 283
Higginbottom, Edward   267
Highgate School Choir   295
Hill, David   265, 266, 276, 286
Hill, William   122
Hiller, Johann Adam   347
Hilliard Ensemble   29, 293, 309
Hindemith, Paul, *Mathis der
    Maler*   245
Hogarth, George   111–12
Hogwood, Christopher   266
Holdroyde, Geoffrey   280
Hollingworth, Robert   92
Holst, Gustav   140, 156, 220, 230,
    253, 255, 371
    Choral Symphony   242
    Hymn of Jesus   245, 258, 260
Holy Communion   37, 38, 39, 42,
    174, 177, 178, 180, 181, 195–6,
    233–4, 275, 278, 279, 282
Honegger, Arthur, *King David*   242,
    258
Hook, Walter   176–7
Hooper, Mr   76
Hopkins, Edward John   179–80, 204
Hopkins, John   56, 87
Horne, Robert   40
Horsley, Charles Edward,
    Gideon   162

Hovingham, musical festival   156
How, Martin   280
Howard, Michael   263, 289, 386
Howells, Herbert   220, 232, 241
    'Collegium Regale' service   224
    A Hymn for St Cecilia   274
    Hymnus Paradisi   284
    'Take him, earth for
        cherishing'   274
Howes, Frank   242
Huddersfield
    Huddersfield Choral
        Society   144, 146, 151, 243, 246,
        250, 252, 260, 286, 290
    Town Hall   144
Hughes, Owain Arwel   286
Hull, choral society   151
Hull, Percy   241
Hullah, John   135–6, 137
Humfrey, Pelham   68
Hummel, Johann Nepomuk   208,
    211
    Masses   201, 209
Humperdinck, Engelbert, *Hansel and
    Gretel*   255
Hunt, Donald   285
Hunt, George Henry Bonavia   182
Hurst, Abraham   108
Hussey, Walter   235
Hymns Ancient and Modern   175,
    185, 204

improvisation on plainsong   19, 26
In Tune with Heaven (Archbishops'
    report)   277
Informatur choristarum *see* Master
    of the Choristers
Inglott, William   49
Ipswich
    musical festival   119
    St Mary's College   34
Ireland (including Northern
    Ireland)   33, 64–5, 84–5, 163–5,
    200, 213, 219–20, 295

Ireland, John, 'Greater love hath no man' 230
Irish Musical Fund Society *see* Dublin, Irish Musical Fund Society
Ives, Grayston (Bill) 267

Jackson, Francis 274
Jackson, Frederick 288
Jacob, Gordon 283
Jacques, Reginald 245, 275, 285
James I (and VI of Scotland) 53, 64
James II 69–70, 78
James IV, King of Scotland 33
Janáček, Leoš *Glagolitic Mass* 287
Janes, Robert 204
Japan 302
Jasper, Ronald 268
Jebb, John 177, 193, 204
Jenkins, David 160
Jenkins, Neil 257
Jennens, Charles 83, 85
Jesus Mass 30, 34
John Alldis Choir 289
Jones, Carris 304
Jones, Griffith Rhys *see* 'Caradog'
Josquin des Prez 32
Jubilate (canticle) 42, 94
Junior Philharmonic Choir 245

Kampen Boys Choir 302
Karajan, Herbert von 60
Kay, Brian 265
Keble, John 172
Keenlyside, Simon 265
Kellie, Edward 64, 330
Kendal, musical festivals 157–8, 254
Kent, James 103, 201
Kilkenny Cathedral 65
King, Charles 201
King's Lynn 119
King's Singers 1, 251, 292, 308, 309, 313
Kingston, Thomas 47

Kirby, Alan 258
Kirkcaldy, choral society 162
Knapton, Philip 350
Knaresborough 113
Knight, Gerald 262, 279–80
Knox, John 39, 282
Kodály, Zoltán, *Psalmus Hungaricus* 242, 258
Kyrie 9, 13, 42

La Trobe, John Antes 171
Lady Chapel choirs 7, 18–19, 25, 28, 31, 33, 35
Lady Mass 18, 19, 25, 34, 39 *see also* Mass
Lambert, Constant, *The Rio Grande* 258
Lambeth, Albert 162–3
Lancashire chorus singers 109–10, 113, 114, 122, 143
Lancashire sol-fa 108, 135
Lang, Cosmo 236
Langley 192, 193
Lapwood, Anna 267
Larks of Dean (Deighn Layrocks) 111
Lassus, Orlando de 220
Latin, sung in post-Reformation Anglican services 44, 54, 209, 230, 275
Laud, William 54, 65
Lauds (daily Office) 9, 37
Launceston 56
lay clerks *see* vicars choral
Leamington Spa 239
Leeds 110, 146, 150
  Cathedral Church of St Anne (Roman Catholic) 221, 277
  Leeds Choral Society 148
  Leeds Choral Union 150, 151, 152, 154, 252
  Leeds Festival Chorus 285
  Leeds New Choral Society 252

Leeds Parish Church (later Leeds Minster)   110, 176–7, 199–200, 303
Leeds Philharmonic Society   150
musical festivals   113, 116, 148–50, 242, 250, 251, 283, 285, 287
Town Hall   148, 280
Legge, Walter   288
Leicester   244, 369
Cathedral   270, 271
Leicester Bach Choir   257
Leicester Philharmonic Society   252, 260
musical festival   112
Leighton, Kenneth
Magnificat and Nunc Dimittis (Collegium Magdalenae Oxoniensis)   274
Responses   276
Second service   274
'Solus ad victimam'   274
Leipzig   302
Thomaskirche   39, 192, 223
Leith Hill Musical Festival   254, 259
Leslie, Henry   29–30 see also Mr Henry Leslie's Choir
'Let the People Sing' competition see under BBC
Ley, Henry   227
Lichfield Cathedral   14, 61, 68, 70, 102, 175, 187, 198, 199, 272
Ligeti, György, Nonsense Madrigals   308
Lincoln Cathedral   6, 8, 14, 15, 17, 28, 30, 47, 50, 61, 62, 63, 68, 71, 101, 185–6, 218, 219, 230
Lind, Jenny   132
Lindley, Simon   303
Litany   36, 42, 44, 54, 70, 180, 181, 203, 204, 233
Liverpool   159, 183, 248
Cathedral Church of Christ (Anglican)   219, 270
Festival of Massed Singing   266
Liverpool Choral Society   145
Liverpool Festival Choral Society   145, 164
Liverpool Philharmonic Society   145
chorus   288
Liverpool Welsh Choral Union   161
Metropolitan Cathedral (Roman Catholic)   277
musical festival   109, 113, 123, 125, 145
National Eisteddfod (1900)   160, 161
St Anne's Church, Edge Hill   212, 369
St Francis Xaver Church   212
St George's Church   183
St George's Hall   255
livestreaming   312–13
Llandaff Cathedral   72, 175, 303
Llandudno, National Eisteddfod (1896)   161
Llangollen International Musical Eisteddfod   283, 298
Lloyd, Charles Harford   154, 206
Lloyd Webber, Andrew, Requiem   288
Locke, Matthew   68
'Be thou exalted, Lord'   69
The Tempest   78
London
All Saints, Margaret Street   177–8, 184, 278
All Souls, Langham Place   234
Arundel House   45
Bar Musical Society   166
Bavarian Embassy Chapel   104, 181
British Library   13, 21
Brompton Oratory   211, 241
Buckingham Palace   147, 149
Cardinal Vaughan Memorial School, Schola Cantorum   295

Index 435

Castle Society 105
Cecilian Society 126
Choral Fund (choral society) 126
Choral Harmonists 126
Christ Church, Newgate 55
Christ's Hospital School 55
Church of the Holy
  Sepulchre 236
Church of the Immaculate
  Conception, Farm Street 211–
  12, 241, 276, 281
Civil Service Vocal Union 166
Classical Harmonists 126
Covent Garden Theatre 82, 85,
  110, 118, 295, 296
Crosby Hall 202
Crystal Palace 127, 128, 136, 146,
  156, 160, 215, 238, 240
  Handel Festivals 127–8, 140,
    146, 243
Elgar Festival (1904) 52
Exeter Hall 126, 127, 130, 135
Foundling Hospital 86, 169
Fraternity of St Nicholas 25
Hanover Square Rooms 131
Handelian Society 126
Holy Trinity, Brompton 234
Holy Trinity, Sloane Square 278
Inventions Exhibition (1885) 157
King's College 210, 305
Lincoln's Inn Chapel 179
Madrigal Society 106–7
Magdalen Hospital 90
Margaret Chapel 177
Metropolitan Police Minstrels
  (later Metropolitan Police Male
  Choir, later Metropolitan Police
  Choir) 166
Morley College 253, 260, 287
Noblemen and Gentlemen's Catch
  Club 107
Oratory School 211
Pantheon 113, 114
Portland Chapel Society 126

Portuguese Embassy Chapel 104
Queen Elizabeth Hall 292
Queen's Hall 133, 157, 163, 259
Royal Albert Hall 131, 157, 159,
  169, 235, 238, 244, 246, 257, 259
Royal College of Music 134, 223
Royal Festival Hall 259, 310
Royal Holloway 305
Sacred Heart Church,
  Wimbledon 241, 276
St Andrew's, Kingsbury 270
St Andrew's, Wells Street 178,
  228
St Anne's, Soho 180–1, 185, 243
St Barnabas, Pimlico 192
St Bartholomew-the-Great,
  Smithfield 278
St Bride's, Fleet Street 77
St Dunstan-in-the-East 25
St Dunstan-in-the-West 25, 55
St George's Cathedral,
  Southwark 210, 212
St James's Hall 130, 132, 169
St Luke's, Chelsea 234
St Margaret's, Westminster 25,
  116, 251, 278
St Mark's College, Chelsea 173
St Mary-at-Hill 25, 37
St Michael's, Cornhill 25, 232
St Pancras Church 183
St Paul's Cathedral 21, 63, 67, 70,
  76, 78, 89, 96, 126, 180, 188–9,
  194, 195–8, 202, 209, 216, 217,
  228, 231–2, 262, 270–1, 282, 304,
  314
  behaviour of vicars
    choral 47–8, 74
  choristers' education 99–100,
    188–9, 195, 231
  choristers' engagements at
    concerts 106, 131
St Peter's, Eaton Square 235
St Stephen's, Westminster 21, 23,
  28, 36

Sardinian Embassy Chapel 104
Savoy Chapel 232, 234
Somerset House Chapel 53
Southwark Cathedral Special Choir 259
Stationers' Hall 77
Stock Exchange Orchestral and Choral Society 166
Surrey Chapel Society 26
Temple Church 131, 178–80, 204, 229, 232
Union Chapel, Islington 214
Western Madrigal Society 221
Westminster Abbey 9, 25, 35, 39, 53, 65, 68, 73, 76, 78, 81–2, 96, 99, 100–1, 113–16, 117, 126, 127, 131, 179, 187, 188, 190, 196, 197–8, 199, 216, 217, 218, 219, 225, 227, 232, 236, 239, 262, 266, 270, 277, 282–3, 315
  behaviour of vicars choral 74, 188, 256
  choristers 61, 106, 188, 232
Westminster Cathedral 30, 220–1, 230, 232, 265, 272, 274, 276–7
Westminster Central Hall 240
Westminster Hospital 116
Whitehall Palace 68–9, 76, 116
London Adventist Chorale 297
London Bach Society (formerly South London Bach Society) 289
London Boy Singers 295
London Choir School 181, 232, 234–5
London Choral Society (later London Chorus) 134, 243, 258, 259, 289
London College for Choristers *see* London Training School for Choristers
London Coronation Choir 244
London County Council, Choral Unions 253
London Community Gospel Choir 297
London Gay Men's Chorus 298
London International Gospel Choir 297
London Labour Choral Union 253
London Philharmonic Choir 288
London Symphony Orchestra 241
  see also LSO Chorus
London Training School for Choristers (later London College for Choristers) 181, 229
Lord President of the Welsh Marches 55
Loretto School (Musselburgh) 256
Lough, Ernest 229, 235, 264
Lough, Robin 229
Louth, St James' Church 24, 62
Lowe, Edward 70
Lower Rhine Music Festival 119, 125
LSO Chorus (later London Symphony Chorus) 286, 288
Ludlow 24, 55
Lumsden, Andrew 272
Lumsden, David 266
Luther, Martin 35, 38
Luton Choral Society 249, 252

McCreesh, Paul 292
MacCunn, Hamish 162
Mace, Thomas 4
Macfarren, Walter 188
Mackerras, Charles 285, 292
Mackenzie, Alexander 162
McKie, William 226, 232, 262, 282
MacMillan, James
  'A new song' 274–5
  St John Passion 307
McNaught, William 246, 250, 253
McPhee, George 282
Macpherson, Charles Stewart 169
Macworth, John 15
Madresfield, musical festival 158

madrigal societies 58, 106–7, 106–7, 129, 167–8, 245
madrigals 58, 129, 135–6, 153
Magnificat 27, 37, 41, 42, 51
Mahler-Bruckner Choir 287
Mainzer, Joseph 134–5, 138
Mainzer's Musical Times and Singing Circular see *The National Singing Class Circular*
Malcolm, George 265, 272, 276
male-voice choirs 159–60, 161, 165–6, 298
Malone, Gareth 166, 308, 311
Manchester 109, 125, 135
   Collegiate Church (later Cathedral) 24, 56, 108, 236, 263, 271
   Cooperative Wholesale Society Choir 166
   Manchester Children's Choir 255
   Hallé Concerts Society 260
   Hallé Chorus (later Hallé Choir) 288
   Hargreaves Choral Society 145
   Manchester Boys' Choir 295
   Manchester Choral Society 145
   Manchester Vocal Society 147
   musical festival 113, 125, 145
Mann, Arthur Henry 168, 169, 187, 208–9, 220, 222–3, 224–5, 227
Manning, Henry 211
Manns, August 128
Marbeck, John 38, 41, 178, 234
Maria Theresa of Naples and Sicily, Empress of Austria 118
Market Harborough 119
Markham, George 102
Marlborough College 232, 256
Marlor, Samuel 103
Marsh, John 101–2, 186
Martin, George 182, 195, 196–7
Mary, Princess, daughter of James I 52
Mary Tudor 35, 39–40, 43

Mason, Lowell 188, 191, 196
Mass 9, 13, 17, 26, 30, 31, 32, 33, 36, 37, 41, 42, 44, 59, 61, 220, 240–1, 282; *see also* Jesus Mass; Lady Mass
Master of the Choristers 8, 19, 21, 24, 28, 46, 62, 64, 98, 188
Master of the King's Music 77
Masur, Kurt 302
Matins 9, 10, 31, 36, 37, 41, 42, 54, 57, 67, 174, 178, 193, 205, 227, 233–4, 276, 278
   cathedrals abandon on weekdays 216–17, 262
Maunder, John Henry, *Olivet to Calvary* 203, 270
Mechanics' Institutes 134, 144
Melbourne 244
   St Paul's Cathedral 300
Mendelssohn Bartholdy, Felix 122–5, 126–7, 129, 138, 144, 164, 196, 201, 202
   Elijah 123, **124**, 125, 127, 129, 138, 144, 145, 148, 149, 151, 156, 160, 162, 164, 242, 257, 259, 302
   'Hear my prayer' 164, 202, 203, 206, 229–30, 264, 366
   Hymn of Praise (*Lobgesang*) 123, 138
   Piano Concerto no. 2 123
   St Paul 122–3, 125, 129, 138, 240
   service 201
Merthyr Philharmonic Choir 161
Merton Choirbook, The 268
Methodists 90, 111, 158, 213, 240, 282
metrical psalms 56–7, 63–4, 66, 87–8, 90, 91, 92, 95, 213
Meyerbeer, Giacomo 128
Middleton, Hubert 226
Middleton, Thomas, jr 56
Military Wives Choir 308
Miller, Edward 91, 110
Milner-White, Eric 222, 224

Milsom, John 45
Milton, John 83
Minshall, Ebenezer 215
Missa de angelis 78
monasteries 5–6, 7, 9–10, 19, 31, 35, 211
  Benedictine 6, 13
Monk, Edwin George 194
Monteverdi, Claudio 53
  Vespers 253, 287, 291
Monteverdi Choir 291, 293, 309, 315
Moody, Charles 231
Moody-Manners Opera Company 257
Moore, Dudley 267
Moore, Joseph 122–3
Moore, Philip 274
Moore, Thomas 94
Morecombe, musical festivals 157, 254
Morley, Thomas 26, 44, 46–7, 55, 58, 65
Morris, Wyn 287
Mossman, Sheila 295
motet 12–13, 18, 43, 44
Motett Society 173
Moto proprio (1903) 210, 211–12, 220, 240
Mounsey, Elizabeth 202
Mountain Ash, Three Valleys Festival 250
Mozart, Wolfgang Amadeus 104, 114, 121, 208, 210–11, 240
  arrangement of Handel's *Messiah* 127, 169, 170, 249, 290, 347
  Masses 138, 177, 184, 201, 210–11
  Requiem 118, 120, 121, 256, 299
Mr Joseph Barnby's Choir (later Oratorio Concerts) 130
Mundy, William 39
Munich Bach Choir 299
music publishing 134, 136, 137–40, 300

Musical Times and Singing Class Circular, The (later *The Musical Times*) 138–9
Musical World, The 138
musicals 292, 296

Nares, James 93, 188, 201
National Federation of Music Societies 261
National Plan for Music Education 307
National Singing Class Circular, The (later *Mainzer's Musical Times and Singing Circular*) 138
National Youth Choirs of Great Britain 307
Neath, National Eisteddfod (1934) 243
Nelson, Horatio 99
Netherlands, The 225, 265, 302
Nethsingha, Andrew 265, 266, 315
Neukomm, Sigismond, *David* 122
neumes 11
New London Children's Choir 295
New York, St Thomas Church, Fifth Avenue 301–2
New Zealand 153, 239, 300
Newark-on-Trent, St Mary Magdalene 56, 62
Newcastle-under-Lyne, 7th Duke of 183, 236
Newcastle-on-Tyne
  musical festival 113, 118, 125
  Newcastle Bach Choir 251, 257
  Newcastle and Gateshead Choral Union 151
Newman, John Henry 151, 172
Newport, National Eisteddfod (1897) 161
Nicholas, Benjamin 268
Nicholson, Sydney 225, 230, 236–9, 247, 280, 300
Noble, Thomas Tertius 195, 199, 301–2

Nonconformist Choir Union (later Free Church Choir Union) 215, 240
Nonconformist choirs 111, 185, 213–15, 239–40, 282, 369
Nonconformists in choral societies 126, 158, 240
None (daily Office) 9
Nonsuch Palace 45
Norfolk, Thomas Howard, Duke of 45
Norrington, Roger 289
North, Roger 72, 99, 183–4
North Staffordshire District Choral Society 157
North Staffordshire Festival Choir 156
Northampton
   All Saints Church 24
   St Matthew's Church 235
Northumberland, Henry Percy, 5th Earl of 24
Norwich
   Cathedral 35, 46, 49, 102, 187, 199, 203, 269
   Ladies Choral Society 121
   musical festival 116, 120, 121, 243, 283, 285, 287, 381
   Norwich Choral Society 121, 140, 143
notation 11–12, 13
Nottingham
   choral society 142
   Nottingham Harmonic Society 252
   musical festival 112
Novello, Alfred 138–9, 140
Novello, Clara 212
Novello, Vincent 104, 138, 201, 350
Novello & Co. 130, 134, 138–40, 166, 170, 203, 290
Nunc Dimittis 41–2
nunneries 33–4, 326

Oakeley, Frederick 177
oblates 7
O'Donnell, James 277
Offices, daily 9, 10, 16, 17, 33, 37, 41
Old Hall manuscript 21, 22, 32
Oldham 108
   Hey (or Lees) Chapel 108–9
   Shaw Chapel 108–9
Olivier, Laurence 177
Only Boys Aloud 307
Only Girls Aloud 307
Only Kids Aloud 307
opera choruses, professional 296, 386–7
Opera North, chorus 296
operatic societies 259, 296
ORA Singers 309
oratorio 83–4, 110, 113, 114, 117–18, 126, 149, 155, 160, 214
Oratorio Concerts *see* Mr Joseph Barnby's Choir
Ord, Boris 223–5, 232, 262, 263–4
   'Adam lay ybounden' 225
Orff, Carl, *Carmina Burana* 287
organs 28–9, 49, 50–2, 53, 56, 60, 65, 88, 122, 147, 169, 175, 213
Oriana Madrigal Society 245
Orpington Junior Singers 295
Orr, Robin 225, 232, 265
Oscott, St Mary's College 211
Otley 113
Ottery St Mary, church 36
Oundle School 256
Ouseley, Frederick Gore 60, 192–4, 201
Ouseley Trust 274
Owens, Matthew 314
Oxford 35, 43, 77, 80, 83, 112, 199
   Bodleian Library 11, 13, **33**, 243
   Christ Church (originally Cardinal College) 23, 24, 32, 34, 35, 52, 67, 70, 74, 192, 205, 206, 227, 232, 266–7, 275, 305–6

440 Index

Collegium Musicum Oxoniensis (later Schola Cantorum of Oxford) 267
Exeter College 227
Frideswide Voices 305–6
Hertford College 227
Holywell Music Room 85, 86, 105
Keble College 268
Lady Margaret Hall 227
Magdalen College 23, 28, 65, 83, 194, 195, 196, 197, 205–6, 209, 226, 232, 266, 290–1
Magdalen College School 205
Merton College 268, 305
Music Club (later Oxford Musical Society) 105
musical festivals 110, 243
New College 22–3, 30, 62, 96. 205, 226–7, 232, 266, 267, 309, 312
Oxford Bach Choir 133, 168, 227, 253
Oxford Bach Soloists 311
Oxford Choral Society 142, 145, 168
Oxford Welsh Glee Singers 166
Philharmonic Society 168
Queen's College, The 227, 268
Radcliffe Library 86
St Frideswide's Priory 23
St John's College 54, 206–7, 227
Schola Cantorum of Oxford *see* Collegium Musicum Oxoniensis
Sheldonian Theatre 77, 256
Worcester College 227
Oxford Movement 42, 93, 172–6, 183, 184, 195, 213
Oxford University Press 59, 137, 140, 221, 243
Oxley, Harrison 271

Page, John, *Harmonia sacra* 98, 201

Paisley Abbey 213–14, 282
Palestrina, Giovanni Pierluigi da 173, 209, 211, 212, 220, 221, 275
Pappano, Antonio 315
parallel organum 12
parish choir schools 25, 177, 232
parish church choirs 50, 55–7, 87–9, 90–5, 173–4, 183, 233–4, 278–9, 305, 313
parish clerk 24, 57, 89, 91, 179
parish communion *see* Holy Communion
Parish Psalter, The 238
Parke, Maria 114
Parker, Matthew 40, 57
Parliament Choir 298
Parratt, Walter 206
Parrott, Andrew 29, 30, 60, 292
Parry, Hubert 140, 147, 156, 203, 257
  Blest Pair of Sirens 133
  'I was glad' 197–8, 283, 315
  Judith 133
Parry, Joseph, 'Myfanwy' 160
Parsley, Osbert 49
partbooks 32, 49–50, 54, 56, 59, 74–5, 76, 98, 203
part-songs 107, 129, 153, 158, 163
Patrick, Saint 5
payment-by-results sight-reading in schools 137, 254
Pearsall, Robert Lucas 167–8
  'In dulci jubilo' 224–5
  'Lay a garland' 168
Peebles, David 33
Penrhyn Choral Union 161
Pepusch, John Christopher 106
Pepys, Samuel 67, 68, 71, 76
Perry, George 127
Perth
  choral society 162
  St Ninian's Cathedral 173
Peterborough Cathedral 30, 35, 61, 198, 262–3, 304

Petre family 44
Petrucci, Ottoviano 32
Philharmonia Chorus 288
Philharmonia Voices 310
Philharmonic Choir 245–6, 248, 249, 259, 288
Philharmonic Society (London) (later Royal Philharmonic Society) 130, 162, 244, 257
Phillips, Peter 60, 268, 291, 292
Pickering 244
Pike, Lionel 305
pitch 11, 29, 59–60, 168–9, 291
Pitz, Wilhelm 288
plainsong 8, 10, 13, 19, 26, 33–4, 41, 72, 172–3, 174, 176, 210, 211
Playford, John 74, 88, 91
Pleyel, Ignaz 106
polyphony, medieval 12–14, 19, 25–8, 31, 32, 34
Popchoir (organization) 308
Porter, Samuel 102
Portsmouth 116, 118
    Cathedral 232, 304
Powell, Josiah Wolstancroft 157
Power, Leonel 21, 28
Praetorius, Michael 3
Pratt, John 207
precentor 8, 11, 62, 188, 213
preces and responses 42, 54, 70, 75, 203–4, 276
Preston, choral society 151
Preston, Simon 265, 266, 270
Prime (daily Office) 9, 37
Pro Musica Sacra 289
Proctor, Charles 245, 259
Prout, Ebenezer 149–50, 170, 214, 290
psalm singing 41, 72–3, 90, 102, 179, 180, 204–5, 225, 238, 262–3, 264, 266, 270, 279
psalms 5, 9, 10, 37, 217
Pueri Cantores 282

Purcell, Henry 50, 68, 73, 74, 75, 77–8, 92, 96, 138, 139, 188, 201, 253, 291
    Dido and Aeneas 77
    Dioclesan 78
    The Fairy Queen 78
    Hail, bright Cecilia 77
    King Arthur 78
    'Nymphs and shepherds come away' 255
    'O sing unto the Lord' 69
    'Rejoice in the Lord alway' 69
    Te Deum and Jubilate 77, 78, 79, 81, 109
Pusey, Edward 172

Quinney, Robert 265

Rachmaninoff, Sergei
    The Bells 248, 258
    Vespers 287
Radcliffe, Mary *see* Russell, Mary (née Radcliffe)
Radley College 256
Ramsbothom, Alexander 221
Ramsey, Robert 54
Randall, John 86
Ravenscroft, Thomas 57
recordings 209, 220, 224–7, 228–9, 238, 244, 249, 255, 260, 264–7, 270, 276, 290, 293, 299, 309–10
Red Army Choir 299
Redhead, Richard 177
Redlich, Hans 253, 287
Reeves, Sims 129
Reith, John 227
Regensburg, Domspatzen 30
rehearsals
    before services 223, 269
    lack of time 123, 125, 130, 149, 154–5, 197, 231, 242, 283–4
Reigate, St Mary's Choir School 232
Renaissance Singers 263, 289
responsories 13

Riall, Gertrude 255
Richter, Hans 146–7
Richter, Karl 299
Riley, William 89, 93
Rille, Laurent de, *The Martyrs of the Arena* 159–60
Ripon Minster (later Cathedral) 24, 27, 36, 231
Rippon, Michael 265
Roberton, Hugh 163
   'All in the April Evening' 163
Roberts, John Varley 182, 206
Roberts, Roland 161
Robinson, Christopher 266, 267
Robinson, Francis 164
Robinson, Joseph 164, 165
Rochester Cathedral 35, 199, 232, 314
Rock Choir (organization) 308
Roden Boys Choir 302
Rodolfus Choir 281, 307, 310
Rodolfus Choral Course 281
Rodolfus Foundation 281
Rogers, Benjamin 75
Roman Use 103
Rootham, Cyril 209–10, 225–6, 253
Rose, Barry 270–1
Rose, Bernard 266, 276
Royal Albert Hall Choral Society (later Royal Choral Society) 131, 170, 243–4, 246, 250, 259, 286
Royal British Legion, Festival of Remembrance 235, 258, 308
Royal College of Organists (originally College of Organists) 182, 199
Royal Philharmonic Orchestra and Chorus 249
Royal Philharmonic Society *see* Philharmonic Society (London)
Royal School of Church Music (RSCM, formerly School of English Church Music) 236–9, 279–81, 300, 313
Rubbra, Edmund 235

Ruddlan Castle 158
rulers (*rectores chori*) 9, 11
Russell, Mary (née Radcliffe) 109
Rutter, John
   Communion service 378
   Gloria 288
   Requiem 288

sackbut 52–3, 64, 65, 69, 71
Sacred Harmonic Society 123, 126–7, 129, 130, 143, 144
Sadler's Wells Opera *see* English National Opera
St Andrews
   St Andrews Cathedral Priory 32–3
   University 305
St Cecilia's Day celebrations 77, 78–9, 112
St David's Cathedral 64, 304
St Edmundsbury *see* Bury St Edmunds
Salisbury 77, 80
   Cathedral 6, 8, 16, 17, 28, 35, 46, 62, 102, 112, 119, 125, 186–7, 194, 198, 217, 263, 269, 284, 311
   introduction of girl choristers 271–2
   Sarum Use 20, 32, 39
   musical festival 112, 119, 125
Salem College 281
Salomon, Johann Peter 118
Salonen, Esa-Pekka 310
Salve regina 18, 24
Sanctus 13, 42
Sanders, John 277
Sargent, Malcolm 242, 244, 248, 250, 252, 260, 285, 286
Savage, William 99–100
Schola Polyphonica 289
School of English Church Music (SECM) *see* Royal School of Church Music
school singing *see* singing in schools

Schubert, Franz Peter, Masses 209
Schütz, Heinrich 53
Schütz Choir 289
Schumann, Robert, *Paradise and the Peri* 164
Scotland 6, 32–3, 39, 63–4, 95, 113, 162–3, 213–14, 260, 282, 287, 309
  Scottish Chapel Royal 33, 64, 330
Scott, Charles Kennedy 24, 250–1, 377–8, 288, 289
Scott, John 271, 302
Scottish Chamber Choir 287
Scottish Opera, chorus 296
Seal, Richard 271
Self-Isolation Choir (later Choir of the Earth) 311–12
service settings *see* canticles; verse services
Sext (daily Office) 9
Sharp, Granville 76
Shaw, George Bernard 123, 132, 140
Shaw, Harold Watkins 170, 290
Shaw, Martin, *Anglican Folk Mass* 234
Sheffield 10, 146, 244
  Albert Hall 150
  Cathedral 314
  Fulwood Wesleyan Methodist Church 240
  musical festival 117, 119, 151, **152**, 156, 248, 251, 252
  Queen Street Congregational Chapel 151–2
  St Philip's Church 177
  Sheffield Amateur Musical Society 167
  Sheffield Musical Union *see* Sheffield Tonic Sol-fa Association
  Sheffield Philharmonic Society 252

Sheffield Tonic Sol-fa Association (later Sheffield Musical Union) 151, 152–3, 248, 252
'Sheffield' choir Round the World Tour 153
Shephard, Richard, 'And when the builders' 275
Sheppard, John 43, 39, 291
Shirley-Quirk, John 270
Short, Nigel 309
sight-singing 108, 134–7, 144, 147, 148, 151, 157, 159, 160, 162, 219, 220, 231, 251, 254–5, 256, 294, 316
Simpson, William Sparrow 194, 195
Simpson, W.J. Sparrow 202–3
Sinclair, George 199
Sing for Pleasure 299
'Sing Up' (singing project) 306
singing in schools 137, 254–6, 294–5, 306–7
singing tuition *see* vocal coaching
Sixteen, The 1, 291, 306, 309
Skagit Valley Chorale 311
Skidmore, Jeffrey 292
Skipton 113
Smart, George 118, 121, 123, 125, 127
Smart, Henry 183
Smart, Peter 53–4
Smith, Bernhard ('Father') 178
Smith, John Christopher, senior 82, 83
Smith, Robert Archibald 213
Smith, Samuel 147
Smith, William, of Durham 54
Smyth, Ethel, Mass in D 241, 248
Society for the Promotion of Christian Knowledge 89
Solesmes Abbey 11, 12, 211, 220
Somervell, Arthur 247, 255
song schools, in towns 24, 25, 55, 57, 63
Songs of Praise 238
South Africa 153, 300–1
South Wales Choral Union 160

Southend Boys' Choir   295
Southend Girls' Choir   295
Southern Cathedrals Festival   284
Southampton Musical Society   257
Southwell Minster   24, 46, 66, 103–4, 269, 304
Spark, William   147
Spence, Toby   267
Spencer, Lady Diana, Princess of Wales   271, 286
Spohr, Louis   121, 196, 202, 257
   The Last Judgment (*Die letzte Dinge*)   121
   Calvary (*Des Heilands letzten Stunde*)   121, 131
   Faust   121
   oratorios   201
Squibb, David   295
Statham, Heathcote   285
Stainer, John   129, 136, 168, 184, 194, 195–6, 204, 206
   The Crucifixion   202–3, 240
Stainer & Bell   140
standards in choral societies and festivals   121, 123, 125, 127, 129, 130, 150, 164, 169, 283–4
standards in cathedral and church choirs   46–7, 98–9, 101–4, 171–2, 185–8, 190–1, 194, 205–6, 207–8, 227, 228, 233, 263, 264, 277, 305, 313
Stanford, Charles Villiers   132–3, 134, 136, 140, 147, 150, 156, 165, 168, 200, 203, 209, 220, 226, 230, 302
   Magnificat and Nunc Dimittis in A   79
   motets   209
   service in B flat   209
Stanley, John   87, 117, 178
Stay at Home Choir   311
Steinitz, Paul   289
Sternhold, Thomas   56, 87
Stevens, Denis   289
Stevens, Richard   99–100

Stewart, Charles Hylton   199
Stewart, Haldane Campbell   226
Stile Antico   309, 311
Stockley, William   146, 214
Stokowski, Leopold   153
Stopford, Thomas   109, 110
Stravinsky, Igor
   Mass   266
   Oedipus Rex   285
   Symphony of Psalms   245
Striggio, Alessandro, 'Ecce beatam Lucem'   45
Strutt, John   357
succentor   8, 188, 195, 200
Sullivan, Arthur   140, 149
   The Golden Legend   153, 257
   operettas   259, 296, 386–7
'Sumer is icumen in'   17, 294
Sumsion, Herbert   241, 274
   'They that go down to the sea in ships'   274
Surman, Joseph   127
surplices   174, 177, 182–3, 184
Swansea
   choral society   158
   National Eisteddfod   159
   Swansea Bach Choir   287
Sweden   225
Sydney
   Christ Church St Laurence   300
   St Andrew's Cathedral   300

Tallis, Thomas   25, 39, 43, 44, 57, 220, 291
   Cantiones sacrae   59
   'Dorian' (Short) service   96, 201
   'I call and cry to thee'   96
   'If ye love me'   37
   Litany   70, 204
   responses   42, 204, 276
   'Spem in alium'   1, 44–5, 129, 146, 209, 311
Tallis Scholars, The   60, 291, 282, 309

Index   445

Targett, James   102
Tate, Nahum   87
Tattersall, William   91
Tattershall College   23, 36
Taverner, John   24, 220
    Masses   32, 38
    Missa Gloria tibi Trinitas   32
Taverner Choir (and Consort)   60, 292
Taylor, Edward   107, 121, 167
Taylor, James   205
Taylor, John   199
Taylor, Philip   226
Te Deum   29, 37, 41, 42, 51, 52, 75
Tear, Robert   265, 270
Tenbury Wells, St Michael's College   60, 192–4, 217, 239, 274
Tenebrae (vocal ensemble)   309
tenors, shortage of   246–7
Terce (daily Office)   9
Terfel, Bryn   315
Terry, Richard Runciman   220–1
Thalben-Ball, George   180, 227, 229, 232, 271
'There is no rose of such virtue'   22, 271
Thoms, William   171–2
Thomson, John   118
Three Choirs Festival   79–80, 86, 109, 112, 113, 116, 117, 119, 120, 122, 125, 150, 154–6, 241–2, 246, 259, 264, 283–4, 288
Three Valleys Festival *see* Mountain Ash
Tiffin School Choir   295
Tippett, Michael   140, 253
    A Child of our Time   253, 260
    Magnificat and Nunc Dimittis (Collegium Sancti Johannis Cantabrigiense)   274
Tobin, John   289–90
Tomkins, Giles   330
Tomkins, John   330
Tomkins, Thomas (c1545–1627)   64

Tomkins, Thomas (1572–1656)   50, 60, 64, 266
tonic sol-fa   108, 135–7, 139, 150–1, 156, 159, 164, 176, 214, 243, 254, 255, 256
Toronto
    St Mary Magdalene Church   302
    Toronto Mendelssohn Choir   302
town halls   122, 144, 147, 148, 150, 163, 165
Townhill, Denis   271
Tractarians *see* Oxford Movement
Travers, John   201
Trefusis, Mary   158
Trendell, David   305
Treorchy, Noddfa Chapel   160
Triumph of Peace, The (masque)   76
tropes   9
Trotter, Thomas   265
Truro Cathedral   219, 222, 231, 303, 306, 313, 315
Tudor Church Music (Carnegie United Kingdom Trust)   59, 221
Tudway, Thomas   75, 98, 101
Turle, James   188, 197, 204
Turner, Bruno   289
Twentieth Century Light Music Group   278
Tye, Christopher   41, 221
Tyng, Stephen   190–1, 196
Tysoe, Albert   242

Union of Directors of Music in Secondary Schools (later Music Masters' Association)   256
United States of America   107, 153, 179, 225, 235, 265, 280, 299–300, 301–2, 307
Uppingham School   256, 281

Vann, Stanley   262–3
Vatican II Conference, influence on church music   277, 281–2
Vaughan, Herbert, Cardinal   220

Vaughan Williams, Ralph   133, 140, 156, 230, 241, 244–5, 248, 254, 259
   Dona nobis pacem   252
   Fantasia on Christmas Carols   258
   Five Tudor Portraits   243
   Mass in G minor   220, 275, 371
   'O taste and see'   283
   'Old Hundredth' arrangement   283
   Sea Symphony   149, 258
Verdi, Giuseppe
   Quattro pezzi sacri   155
   Requiem   131, 153, 243, 256, 299
verse anthems   51, 63, 69, 75, 77, 92, 196, 201 *see also* anthems
verse services   51, 75
Vespers   9, 36, 37, 212, 220 *see also* Evensong
vicars choral (lay clerks)   6–7, 8, 10, 13, 14, 18–20, 27, 28, 31, 35, 36, 39, 40–1, 46, 48–9, 52, 62, 63, 66, 75, 98, 100–1, 102, **103**, 105, 112, 194, 195, 200, 206, 207, 208, 209, 216, 218–19, 226, 231, 232, 266, 303, 311
   behaviour   15–17, 46–8, 188, 197, 205, 219
   corporations   15, 191–2, 199, 218
   female lay clerks   304
   number in individual choirs   6, 16, 18, 20, 23–4, 35–6, 64–5, 70, 101, 190, 195, 206–7, 208, 209
   recruitment   41, 262, 269
Vicars, John   65
Vicary, William   46
Victoria, Queen   123, 131, 168, 283
Victoria, Tomás Luis de   220
   Tenebrae responses   276
Vienna Boys Choir   30
Vivaldi, Antonio, Gloria   266, 287
vocal coaching   304
vocal scores, introduction of   139–40, 203
Voces8   306, 309

Voices Foundation   306
Vogt, Augustus Stephen   302
votive antiphon   18, 19, 25, 27, 37, 43

Wagner, Richard, *Parsifal*   131
Wakefield, Mary   157–8, 254
Wales   6, 64, 72, 158–61, 166, 214, 287, 304, 307
   Diocesan choral festivals   175
   National Eisteddfod   147, 159, 160, 243, 376
Walmisley, Thomas Attwood   193, 201, 208, 209
   Evening service in D minor   208
Walond, Willam, junior   102
Walsh, John   83
Walton, William   140, 227
   Belshazzar's Feast   129, 137, 242–3, 250, 258, 259, 260, 284, 285, 302
   Chichester service   235
   Gloria   286
   Orb and Sceptre   283
   Te Deum   283
Wandsworth School Choir   294–5
Wanley partbooks   37–8, 42
Warlock, Peter   255
Warren, Thomas   107
Warwick, St Mary's Church   24, 36, 55, 56, 280
Washington, Henry   289
Waterford Cathedral   65
Watson, Henry   146
Watson, Sydney   226, 266
Watts, Isaac   87, 89, 213
Waynflete, William   23
Webbe, Samuel, the elder   104, 107
Webbe, Samuel, the younger   107
webcasting   312
Weelkes, Thomas   47, 50, 58, 61
Weingartner, Felix   152
Weir, Judith   315
   'Illuminare Jerusalem'   275

Wellesley, Arthur, 1st Duke of
  Wellington   180, 194
Wellington College   256
Wells   116
  Cathedral   8, 9, 14, 15, 16–17, 20, 187, 197, 218, 273
  Wells Cathedral School   269–70
Welsh National Opera, chorus   296
Wesley, Charles   87, 88, 89, 213
Wesley, John   85, 87, 88, 89
Wesley, Samuel   104
Wesley, Samuel Sebastian   131, 154, 177, 183–4, 190, 193, 201
  Service in E   177
  'Thou wilt keep him in perfect peace'   227
  'The Wilderness'   203
West Gallery Music *see* country psalmody
West Gallery Music Association   94, 297
Westmorland Music Festival   381
Wetenhall, Edward   75
Wherwell nunnery   33–4
Whewall, James   157
Whitby, Walter   19
White, Robert   44
Whittaker, William Gillies   251
Whittingham, William   49
Wicks, Allan   263
Wilbye, John   58
Wilcox, Thomas   48
Wilhem, Guillaume   135
Wilkins, Matthew   91
Willan, Healey   302
Willcocks, David   224, 225, 232, 238, 239, 263–5, 275, 284, 285–6, 292, 309
William IV   107
William and Mary (joint sovereigns)   69–70
Williams, Roderick   267, 315
Wilson, Henry   136
Wimborne Minster   56

Winchester
  Cathedral   6, 19, 31, 35, 36, 40, 56, 61, 67, 70, 102, **103**, 177, 187, 190, 198, 219, 269, 272, 284, 313
  musical festival   112, 119
  St Cecilia celebration   77
  Winchester Tropers   11
  Winchester College   23, 44, 47, 205
    Glee Club   256
Windsor, St George's Chapel   21, 23, 34, 41, 68, 71, 75, 131, 187, 194, 197, 206, 219, 225, 229, 262, 282, 314
Wise, Michael   68
Wiseman, Nicholas, Cardinal   210
Wolsey, Thomas, Cardinal   21, 23, 24, 25, 31, 34
Women's Institute   167
women
  in cathedral choirs and choral foundations   72, 190, 196, 200, 304, 314
  in church choirs   171, 178–9, 182, 183–4, 211–12, 233, 237, 238, 300
  in university chapel choirs   267, 293
Wood, Charles   203, 230
Wood, Henry   151, 245, 248, 250, 252, 259, 287
Woodgate, Leslie   288
Worcester
  All Saints Church   366
  Cathedral   6, 19, 35, 50, 52, 61, 68, 75, 103, 191, 196, 198, 202, 241, 262, 263, 366
  St George's Church   211, 212
  Three Choirs Festival   79, 116, 131, 155–6, 241 246, 257, 284
  Worcester Fragments   13, **14**
workplace choirs   166, 298, 308, 357
Wrexham, St Giles' Church   56
Wright, Brian   246
Wulstan, David   60, 290–1

Wykeham, William, Bishop of
    Winchester   22–3

Yale Glee Club   107–8
Yende, Pretty   315
York   142
    Albion Street Methodist
        Chapel   214
    Lendal Congregational
        Chapel   214
    Minster   6, 8, 16, 27, 47, 50, 71,
        102, 108, 185–6, 191, 194–5, 199,
        218, 228, 262, 269
    York Use   10
    musical festival   109, 120, 138
    St Saviour's Church   204
    St Wilfrid's Church   212
    York Choral Society   142
Yorkshire Choral Union   149